TEAS Version 5 Study Guide

Test Prep Secrets for the TEAS V

Printed in the United States of America

Table of Contents

Introduction

Congratulations on your decision to join the field of nursing - few other professions are so rewarding!

By purchasing this book, you've already made the first step towards succeeding in your career; and the second step is to do well on the TEAS exam, which will require you to demonstrate knowledge and competence of those subjects taught at the high school level.

This book will help refresh you on all of those subjects, as well as provide you with some inside-information on how to do well on this test. Even if it's been years since you've graduated high school, studied, or taken a test – don't worry, you'll be ready!

About the Test

The TEAS exam is three-and-a-half hours long, and is divided into the following sections:

1. **Mathematics**
    - 34 Questions: Arithmetic, Basic Geometry, and Data Interpretation.
    - 51-Minute Time Limit.
2. **English and Language Arts**
    - 34 Questions: Grammar and Word Knowledge.
    - 34-Minute Time Limit.
3. **Reading**
    - 48 Questions: Reading Comprehension.
    - 58-Minute Time Limit.
4. **Science**
    - 54 Questions: Biology, Chemistry, Physics, and Ecology.
    - 66-Minute Time Limit

Scoring

You cannot "pass" or "fail" the TEAS exam. Your score is simply indicative of your current level of comprehension. However, each school has their own entrance requirements – some are higher than others. Be sure to check with the requirements of the institutions which you want to attend.

How This Book Works

The subsequent chapters in this book are divided into a review of those topics covered on the exam. This is not intended to "teach" or "re-teach" you these concepts – there is no way to cram all of that material into one book! Instead, we are going to help you recall all of the information which you've already learned. Even more importantly, we'll show you how to apply that knowledge.

Each chapter includes an extensive review, with practice drills at the end to test your knowledge. With time, practice, and determination, you'll be well-prepared for test day.

Chapter 1: Mathematics

This chapter will cover the many subjects included in the math section of the TEAS: basic algebra, geometry, and applied math.

The Most Common Mistakes

People make mistakes all the time – but during a test, those mistakes can make the difference between an excellent score, or one which falls below the requirements. Watch out for these common mistakes that people make on the TEAS:

- Answering with the wrong sign (positive / negative).
- Mixing up the Order of Operations.
- Misplacing a decimal.
- Not reading the question thoroughly (and therefore providing an answer that was not asked for.)
- Circling the wrong letter, or filling in wrong circle choice.

If you're thinking, "Those ideas are just common sense" – exactly! Most of the mistakes made on the TEAS are simple mistakes. Regardless, they still result in a wrong answer and the loss of a potential point.

Strategies for the Mathematics Section

1. **Go Back to the Basics**: First and foremost, practice your basic skills: sign changes, order of operations, simplifying fractions, and equation manipulation. These are the skills used most on the TEAS, though they are applied in different contexts. Remember that when it comes right down to it, all math problems rely on the four basic skills of addition, subtraction, multiplication, and division. All that changes is the order in which they are used to solve a problem.

2. **Don't Rely on Mental Math**: Using mental math is great for eliminating answer choices, but ALWAYS WRITE IT DOWN! This cannot be stressed enough. Use whatever paper is provided; by writing and/or drawing out the problem, you are more likely to catch any mistakes. The act of writing things down forces you to organize your calculations, leading to an improvement in your TEAS score.

3. **The Three-Times Rule**:

    - **Step One – Read the question**: Write out the given information.
    - **Step Two – Read the question**: Set up your equation(s) and solve.
    - **Step Three – Read the question:** Make sure that your answer makes sense (is the amount too large or small; is the answer in the correct unit of measure, etc.).

4. **Make an Educated Guess**: Eliminate those answer choices which you are relatively sure are incorrect, and then guess from the remaining choices. Educated guessing is critical to increasing your score.

Math Concepts Tested on the TEAS

You need to practice in order to score well on the test. To make the most out of your practice, use this guide to determine the areas for which you need more review. Most importantly, practice all areas under testing circumstances (a quiet area, a timed practice test, no looking up facts as you practice, etc.)

When reviewing, take your time and let your brain recall the necessary math. If you are taking the TEAS, then you have already had course instruction in these areas. The examples given will "jog" your memory.

The next few pages will cover various math subjects (starting with the basics, but in no particular order), along with worked examples.

Percentile

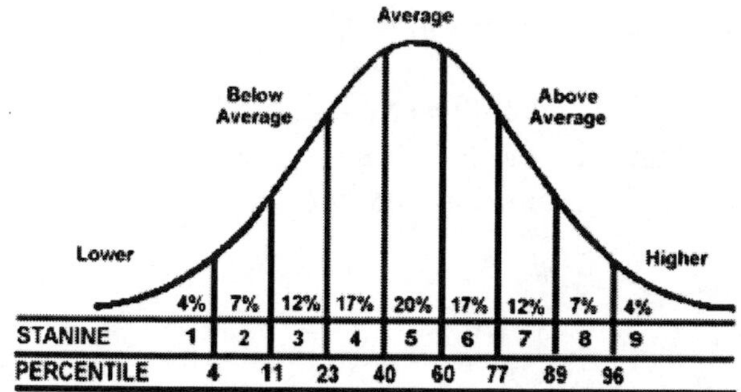

A percentile curve is simply a comparison of results relative to all other results. As you can see, if your score is a stanine of 5, you are right in the middle at the 50th percentile. This means that you did better than half of everyone else, but half did better than you. Approximately 20% of takers will fall into the stanine score range of 5.

Percentile scores do not indicate how many questions answered correctly, only how well you performed against everyone else. For example, if the score range is 90 –100, that means that everyone did very well; but those who scored a 90 are still in the stanine range of 1.

Example: If you and 20% of the rest of your class scored a 95 on a test, using the chart above, would your stanine score be?

5 (50th Percentile).

Positive & Negative Number Rules

(+) + (-) = Subtract the two numbers. Solution gets the sign of the larger number.

(-) + (-) = Negative number.

(-) * (-) = Positive number.

(-) * (+) = Negative number.

(-) / (-) = Positive number.

(-) / (+) = Negative number.

Greatest Common Factor (GCF)

The greatest factor that divides two numbers.

Example: The GCF of 24 and 18 is 6. 6 is the largest number, or greatest factor, that can divide both 24 and 18.

Order of Operations

PEMDAS – **P**arentheses/**E**xponents/**M**ultiply/**D**ivide/**A**dd/**S**ubtract

Perform the operations within parentheses first, and then any exponents. After those steps, perform all multiplication and division. (These are done from left to right, as they appear in the problem) Finally, do all required addition and subtraction, also from left to right as they appear in the problem.

Examples:

1. Solve $(-(2)^2 - (4 + 7))$:
   - $(-4 - 11) =$ **-15**.

2. Solve $((5)^2 \div 5 + 4 * 2)$:
   - $25 \div 5 + 4 * 2$.
   - $5 + 8 =$ **13**.

Probabilities

A probability is found by dividing the number of desired outcomes by the number of possible outcomes. (The piece divided by the whole.)

Example: What is the probability of picking a blue marble if 3 of the 15 marbles are blue?

3/15 = 1/5. The probability is **1 in 5** that a blue marble is picked.

Fractions

Adding and subtracting fractions requires a common denominator.

Find a common denominator for:

$$\frac{2}{3} - \frac{1}{5}.$$

$$\frac{2}{3} - \frac{1}{5} = \frac{2}{3}\left(\frac{5}{5}\right) - \frac{1}{5}\left(\frac{3}{3}\right) = \frac{10}{15} - \frac{3}{15} = \mathbf{\frac{7}{15}}.$$

To add mixed fractions, work first the whole numbers, and then the fractions.

$$2\frac{1}{4} + 1\frac{3}{4} = 3\frac{4}{4} = \mathbf{4}.$$

To subtract mixed fractions, convert to single fractions by multiplying the whole number by the denominator and adding the numerator. Then work as above.

$$2\frac{1}{4} - 1\frac{3}{4} = \frac{9}{4} - \frac{7}{4} = \frac{2}{4} = \mathbf{\frac{1}{2}}.$$

To multiply fractions, convert any mixed fractions into single fractions and multiply across; reduce to lowest terms if needed.

$$2\frac{1}{4} * 1\frac{3}{4} = \frac{9}{4} * \frac{7}{4} = \frac{63}{16} = \mathbf{3\frac{15}{16}}.$$

To divide fractions, convert any mixed fractions into single fractions, flip the second fraction, and then multiply across.

$$2\frac{1}{4} \div 1\frac{3}{4} = \frac{9}{4} \div \frac{7}{4} = \frac{9}{4} * \frac{4}{7} = \frac{36}{28} = 1\frac{8}{28} = \mathbf{1\frac{2}{7}}.$$

Simple Interest

Interest * Principle.

Example: If I deposit $500 into an account with an annual rate of 5%, how much will I have after 2 years?

1st year: 500 + (500*.05) = 525.

2nd year: 525 + (525*.05) = **551.25.**

Prime Factorization

Expand to prime number factors.

Example: 104 = 2 * 2 * 2 * 13.

Absolute Value

The absolute value of a number is its distance from zero, not its value.

So in $|x| = a$, "x" will equal "$-a$" as well as "a."

Likewise, $| 3 | = 3$, and $| -3 | = 3$.

Equations with absolute values will have two answers. Solve each absolute value possibility separately. All solutions must be checked into the original equation.

Example: Solve for x: $|2x - 3| = x + 1$

1. Equation One: $2x - 3 = -(x + 1)$.
    - $2x - 3 = -x - 1$.
    - $3x = 2$.
    - $\mathbf{x = 2/3}$.

2. Equation Two: $2x - 3 = x + 1$.
    - $\mathbf{x = 4}$.

Mean, Median, Mode

Mean is a math term for "average." Total all terms and divide by the number of terms.

Find the mean of 24, 27, and 18.

24 + 27 + 18 = 69 ÷ 3 = **23**.

Median is the middle number of a given set, found after the numbers have all been put in numerical order. In the case of a set of even numbers, the middle two numbers are averaged.

What is the median of 24, 27, and 18?

18, **24**, 27.

What is the median of 24, 27, 18, and 19?

18, 19, 24, 27 (19 + 24 = 43. 43/2 = **21.5**).

Mode is the number which occurs most frequently within a given set.

What is the mode of 2, 5, 4, 4, 3, 2, 8, 9, 2, 7, 2, and 2?

The mode would be **2** because it appears the most within the set.

Arithmetic Sequence

Each term is equal to the previous term plus x.

Example: 2, 5, 8, 11.

- 2 + 3 = 5; 5 + 3 = 8 … etc.
- $x = 3$.

Geometric Sequence

Each term is equal to the previous term multiplied by x.

Example: 2, 4, 8, 16.

- $x = 2$.

Percent, Part, & Whole

Part = Percent * Whole.

Percent = Part / Whole.

Whole = Part / Percent.

Example: Jim spent 30% of his paycheck at the fair. He spent $15 for a hat, $30 for a shirt, and $20 playing games. How much was his check? (Round to nearest dollar.)

Whole = 65 / .30 = **$217.00.**

Percent Change

Percent Change = Amount of Change / Original Amount * 100.

Percent Increase = (New Amount – Original Amount) / Original Amount * 100.

Percent Decrease = (Original Amount – New Amount) / Original Amount * 100.

Amount Increase (or **Decrease**) = Original Price * Percent Markup (or Markdown).

Original Price = New Price / (Whole - Percent Markdown [or Markup]).

Example: A car that was originally priced at $8300 has been reduced to $6995. What percent has it been reduced?

(8300 – 6995) / 8300 * 100 = **15.72%.**

Repeated Percent Change

Increase: Final amount = Original Amount * $(1 + \text{rate})^{\#\text{ of changes}}$.

Decrease: Final Amount = Original Amount * $(1 - \text{rate})^{\#\text{ of changes}}$.

Example: The weight of a tube of toothpaste decreases by 3% each time it is used. If it weighed 76.5 grams when new, what is its weight in grams after 15 uses?

Final amount = $76.5 * (1 - .03)^{15}$.

$76.5 * (.97)^{15}$ = **48.44 grams.**

Combined Average

Weigh each average individual average before determining the sum.

Example: If Cory averaged 3 hits per game during the summer and 2 hits per game during the fall and played 7 games in the summer and 8 games in the fall, what was his hit average overall?

1. Weigh each average.
    - Summer: 3 * 7 = 21.
    - Fall: 2 * 8 = 16.
    - Sum: 21 + 16 = 37.

2. Total number of games: 7 + 8 = 15.

3. Calculate average: 37/15 = ~ **2.46 hits/game**.

You may need to work a combined average problem with a missing term.

Example: Bobbie paid an average of $20 a piece for ten shirts. If five of the shirts averaged $15 each, what was the average cost of the remaining shirts?

1. Calculate sum: 10 * 20 = 200.

2. Calculate sub-sum #1: 5 *15 = 75.

3. Calculate sub-sum #2: 200 – 75 = 125.

4. Calculate average: 125 / 5 = $**25**.

Ratios

To solve a ratio, simply find the equivalent fraction. To distribute a whole across a ratio:

1. Total all parts.

2. Divide the whole by the total number of parts.

3. Multiply quotient by corresponding part of ratio.

Example: There are 90 voters in a room, and they are either Democrat or Republican. The ratio of Democrats to Republicans is 5:4. How many Republicans are there?

1. 5 + 4 = 9.

2. 90 / 9 = 10.

3. 10 * 4 = **40 Republicans**.

Proportions

Direct Proportions: Corresponding ratio parts change in the same direction (increase/decrease).

Indirect Proportions: Corresponding ratio parts change in opposite directions (as one part increases the other decreases).

Example: A train traveling 120 miles takes 3 hours to get to its destination. How long will it take if the train travels 180 miles?

120 mph: 180 mph is to x hours: 3 hours. (Write as fraction and cross multiply.)

- $120/3 = 180/x$.
- $540 = 120x$.
- $x =$ **4.5 hours.**

Roots

Root of a Product: $\sqrt[n]{a \cdot b} = \sqrt[n]{a} \cdot \sqrt[n]{b}$.

Root of a Quotient: $\sqrt[n]{\frac{a}{b}} = \frac{\sqrt[n]{a}}{\sqrt[n]{b}}$.

Fractional Exponent: $\sqrt[n]{a^{m}} = a^{m/n}$.

Fundamental Counting Principle

(The number of possibilities of an event happening) * (the number of possibilities of another event happening) = the total number of possibilities.

Example: If you take a multiple choice test with 5 questions, with 4 answer choices for each question, how many test result possibilities are there?

Solution: Question 1 has 4 choices; question 2 has 4 choices; etc.

4 *4 * 4 * 4 * 4 (one for each question) = **1024 possible test results.**

Literal Equations

Equations with more than one variable. Solve in terms of one variable first.

Example: Solve for y: $4x + 3y = 3x + 2y$.

1. Combine like terms: $3y - 2y = 4x - 2x$.
2. Solve for y. $y =$ **$2x$**.

Linear Systems

A linear system requires the solving of two literal equations simultaneously. There are two different methods (Substitution and Addition) that can be used to solve linear systems.

Substitution Method: Solve for one variable first, and then substitute.

Example: Solve for x and y: $3y - 4 + x = 0$ and $5x + 6y = 11$.

1. Solve for one variable.
   - $3y - 4 + x = 0$.
   - $3y + x = 4$.
   - $x = 4 - 3y$.

2. Substitute into second equation, and solve.
   - $5(4 - 3y) + 6y = 11$.
   - $20 - 15y + 6y = 11$.
   - $20 - 9y = 11$.
   - $-9y = -9$.
   - $y = 1$.

3. Substitute into first equation.
   - $3(1) - 4 + x = 0$.
   - $-1 + x = 0$.
   - $x = 1$.

Addition Method: Manipulate one of the equations so that when added to the other, one variable is eliminated.

Example: Solve $2x + 4y = 8$ and $4x + 2y = 10$.

1. Manipulate one equation to eliminate a variable when added together.
   - $-2(2x + 4y = 8) = (-4x - 8y = -16)$.
   - $(-4x - 8y = -16) + (4x + 2y = 10)$.
   - $-6y = -6$.
   - $y = 1$.

2. Plug into an equation and solve for the other variable.
   - $2x + 4(1) = 8$.
   - $2x + 4 = 8$.
   - $2x = 4$.
   - $x = 2$.

The following is a typical word problem that would use a linear system to solve.

Example: Tommy has a collection of coins worth $5.20. He has 8 more nickels than quarters. How many of each does he have?

1. Set up equations.
   - Let n = nickels and q = quarters.
   - $.05n + .25q = 5.2$.
   - $n = q + 8$.

2. Substitute Equation 2 into Equation 1.
   - $.05(q + 8) + .25q = 5.2$.

3. Solve for q. You can ignore the decimal point and negative sign after this step because you are solving for number of coins.
   - $-.05(q + 8) + .25q = 5.2$.
   - $.05q + .4 + .25q = 5.2$.
   - $q = 16$.

4. Plug into the original equation.
   - $n = q + 8$.
   - **n = 24.**
   - **q = 16.**

Linear Equations

An equation for a straight line. The variable CANNOT have an exponent, square roots, cube roots, etc.

Example: $y = 2x + 1$ is a straight line, with "1" being the y-intercept, and "2" being the positive slope.

Algebraic Equations

When simplifying or solving algebraic equations, you need to be able to utilize all math rules: exponents, roots, negatives, order of operations, etc.

1. Add & Subtract: Only the coefficients of like terms.

   Example: $5xy + 7y + 2yz + 11xy - 5yz = 16xy + 7y - 3yz$.

2. Multiplication: First the coefficients then the variables.

   Example: Monomial * Monomial. (Remember: a variable with no exponent has an implied exponent of 1.)
   - $(3x^4y^2z)(2y^4z^5) = 6x^4y^6z^6$.

   Example: Monomial * Polynomial.
   - $(2y^2)(y^3 + 2xy^2z + 4z) = 2y^5 + 4xy^4z + 8y^2z$

Example: Binomial * Binomial.

- $(5x + 2)(3x + 3)$. Remember: FOIL (First, Outer, Inner, Last).

    First: $5x * 3x = 15x^2$.

    Outer: $5x * 3 = 15x$.

    Inner: $2 * 3x = 6x$.

    Last: $2 * 3 = 6$.

    Combine like terms: $15x^2 + 21x + 6$.

Example: Binomial * Polynomial.

- $(x + 3)(2x^2 - 5x - 2)$.

    First Term: $x(2x^2 - 5x - 2) = 2x^3 - 5x^2 - 2x$.

    Second term: $3(2x^2 - 5x - 2) = 6x^2 - 15x - 6$.

    Added Together: $2x^3 + x^2 - 17x - 6$.

Inequalities

Inequalities are solved like linear and algebraic equations, except the sign must be reversed when dividing by a negative number.

Example: $-7x + 2 < 6 - 5x$.

Step 1 – Combine like terms: $-2x < 4$.

Step 2 – Solve for x. (Reverse the sign): $\boldsymbol{x > -2}$.

Solving compound inequalities will give you two answers.

Example: $-4 \leq 2x - 2 \leq 6$.

Step 1 – Add 2 to each term to isolate x: $-2 \leq 2x \leq 8$.

Step 2: Divide by 2: $-1 \leq x \leq 4$.

Solution set is **[-1, 4]**.

Exponent Rules

Rule	Example
$x^0 = 1$	$5^0 = 1$
$x^1 = x$	$5^1 = 5$
$x^a \cdot x^b = x^{a+b}$	$5^2 * 5^3 = 5^5$
$(xy)^a = x^a y^a$	$(5 * 6)^2 = 5^2 * 6^2 = 25 * 36$
$(x^a)^b = x^{ab}$	$(5^2)^3 = 5^6$
$(x/y)^a = x^a/y^a$	$(10/5)^2 = 10^2/5^2 = 100/25$
$x^a/y^b = x^{a-b}$	$5^4/5^3 = 5^1 = 5$ (remember $x \neq 0$)
$x^{1/a} = \sqrt[a]{x}$	$25^{1/2} = \sqrt[2]{25} = 5$
$x^{-a} = \frac{1}{x^a}$	$5^{-2} = \frac{1}{5^2} = \frac{1}{25}$ (remember $x \neq 0$)
$(-x)^a$ = positive number if "a" is even; negative number if "a" is odd.	

Permutations

The number of ways a set number of items can be arranged. Recognized by the use of a factorial ($n!$), with n being the number of items.

If $n = 3$, then $3! = 3 * 2 * 1 = 6$. If you need to arrange n number of things but x number are alike, then $n!$ is divided by $x!$

Example: How many different ways can the letters in the word **balance** be arranged?

Solution: There are 7 letters, so $n! = 7!$ But 2 letters are the same, so $x! = 2!$ Set up the equation:

$$\frac{7 * 6 * 5 * 4 * 3 * 2 * 1}{2 * 1} = \textbf{2540 ways.}$$

Combinations

To calculate total number of possible combinations, use the formula: $n!/r!\,(n-r)!$
Where n = # of objects; and r = # of objects selected at a time.

Example: If seven people are selected in groups of three, how many different combinations are possible?

Solution:

$$\frac{7 * 6 * 5 * 4 * 3 * 2 * 1}{(3 * 2 * 1)(7-3)} = \textbf{210 possible combinations.}$$

Quadratics

Factoring: converting $ax^2 + bx + c$ to factored form. Find two numbers that are factors of c and whose sum is b.

Example: Factor $2x^2 + 12x + 18 = 0$.

1. If possible, factor out a common monomial: $2(x^2 - 6x + 9)$.
2. Find two numbers that are factors of 9; and also sum to -6: $2(x - \_)(x - \_)$.
3. Fill in the binomials. Be sure to check your answer and signs: $2(x - 3)(x - 3)$.
4. To solve, set each to = 0: $x - 3 = 0$; $\boldsymbol{x = 3}$.

If the equation cannot be factored (there are no two factors of c that sum to = b), the quadratic formula is used.

$$x = \frac{-b \pm \sqrt{b^2 - 4ac}}{2a}$$

Using the same equation from the above example: $a = 2$, $b = 12$, and $c = 18$. Plug into the formula and solve. Remember there will still be two answers due to the (+) and (-) before the radical.

Graphs and Charts

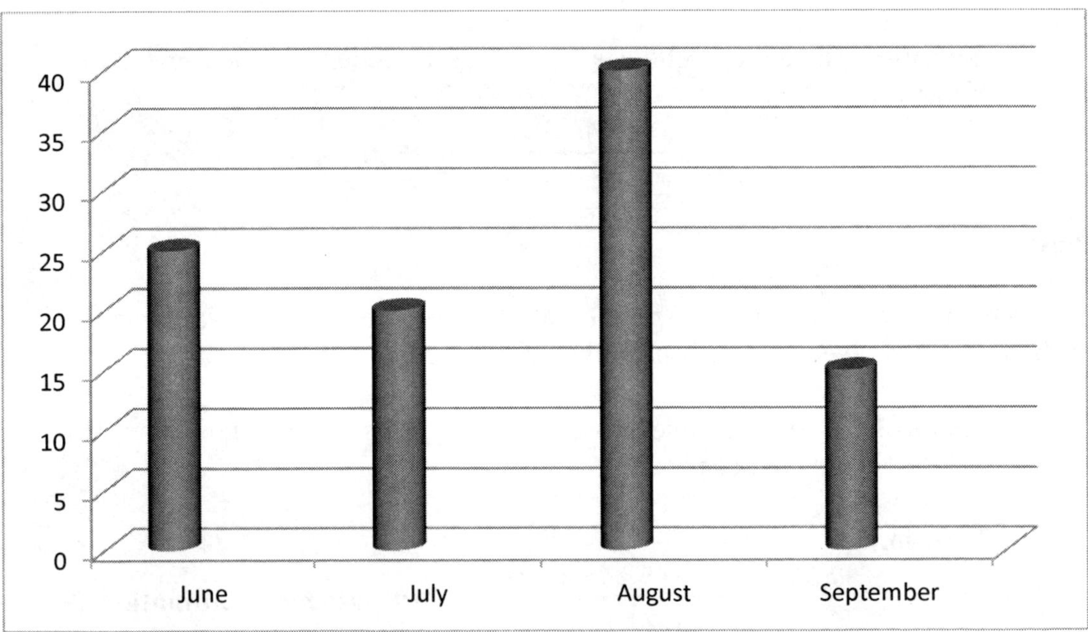

Using the above chart of ice cream sales per month, how many more sales are made in July than September? As you can see, sales in July are 20 and September sales are 15. The correct answer is therefore **5**. If you see any answer choices which are grossly incorrect – such as -10 or 20 – immediately count them out. Don't over-think graphical questions. They are typically straightforward and require only that you pay attention and don't try to answer too quickly.

Geometry

- **Acute Angle**: Measures less than 90°.
- **Acute Triangle**: Each angle measures less than 90°.
- **Obtuse Angle**: Measures greater than 90°.
- **Obtuse Triangle**: One angle measures greater than 90°.
- **Adjacent Angles**: Share a side and a vertex.
- **Complementary Angles**: Adjacent angles that sum to 90°.
- **Supplementary Angles**: Adjacent angles that sum to 180°.
- **Vertical Angles**: Angles that are opposite of each other. They are always congruent (equal in measure).
- **Equilateral Triangle**: All angles are equal.
- **Isosceles Triangle**: Two sides and two angles are equal.
- **Scalene**: No equal angles.
- **Parallel Lines**: Lines that will never intersect. Y **ll** X means line Y is parallel to line X.
- **Perpendicular lines**: Lines that intersect or cross to form 90° angles.
- **Transversal Line**: A line that crosses parallel lines.
- **Bisector**: Any line that cuts a line segment, angle, or polygon exactly in half.
- **Polygon**: Any enclosed plane shape with three or more connecting sides (ex. a triangle).
- **Regular Polygon**: Has all equal sides and equal angles (ex. square).
- **Arc**: A portion of a circle's edge.
- **Chord**: A line segment that connects two different points on a circle.
- **Tangent**: Something that touches a circle at only one point without crossing through it.
- **Sum of Angles**: The sum of angles of a polygon can be calculated using $(n-1)180^{o}$, when n = the number of sides.

Triangles

The angles in a triangle add up to 180°.
Area of a triangle = ½ * b * h, or ½bh.
Pythagoras' Theorem: $a^2 + b^2 = c^2$.

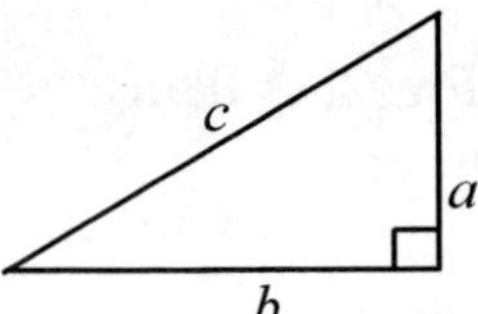

Regular Polygons

Polygon Angle Principle: $S = (n - 2)180$, where S = the sum of interior angles of a polygon with n-sides.

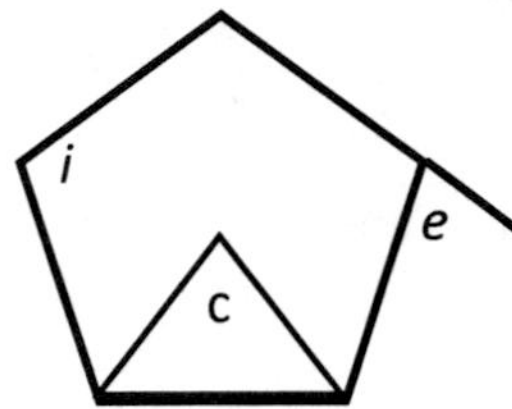

The measure of each central angle (c) is $360^\circ/n$.
The measure of each interior angle (i) is $(n - 2)180^\circ/n$.
The measure of each exterior angle (e) is $360^\circ/n$.
To compare areas of similar polygons: $A_1/A_2 = (\text{side}_1/\text{side}_2)^2$

Trapezoids

Four-sided polygon, in which the bases (and only the bases) are parallel.

Isosceles Trapezoid: Base angles are congruent.

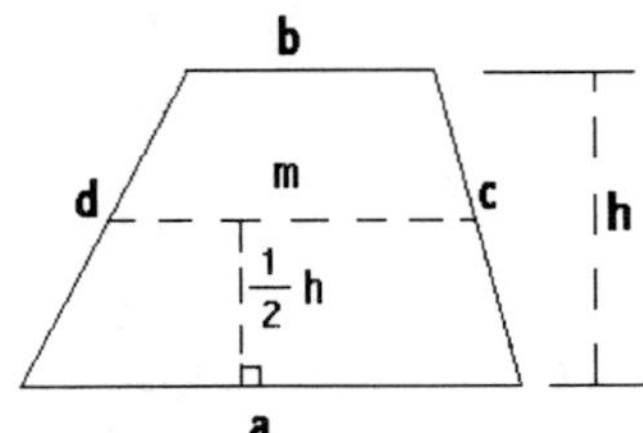

Area and Perimeter of a Trapezoid

$m = \frac{1}{2}(a + b)$

$Area = \frac{1}{2} h * (a + b) = m * h$

$Perimeter = a + b + c + d = 2m + c + d$

If m is the median then: $m \parallel \overline{AB}$ and $m \parallel CD$

Rhombus

Four-sided polygon, in which all four sides are congruent and opposite sides are parallel.

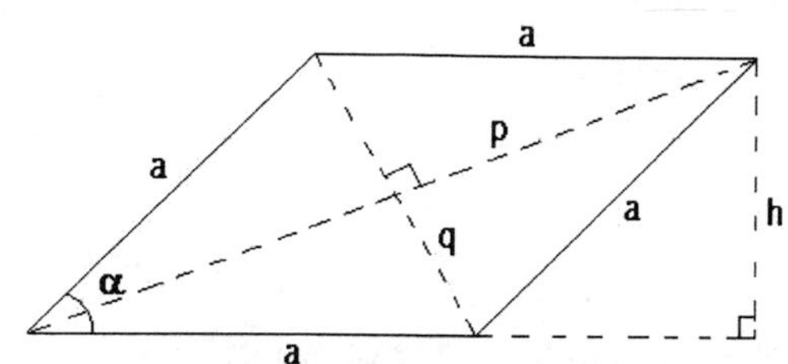

Area and Perimeter of a Rhombus

$$Perimeter = 4a$$

$$Area = a^2 \sin\alpha = a * h = \frac{1}{2}pq$$

$$4a^2 = p^2 + q^2$$

Rectangle

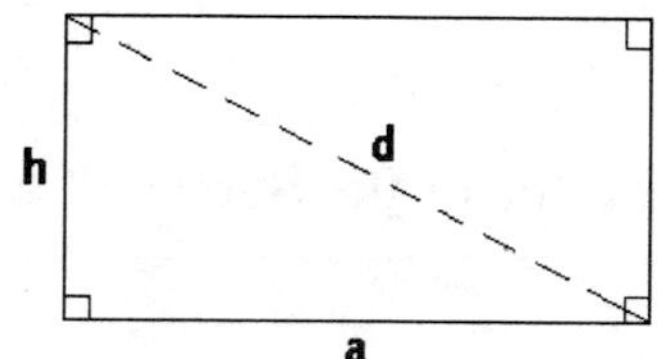

Area and Perimeter of a Rectangle

$$d = \sqrt{a^2 + h^2}$$

$$a = \sqrt{d^2 - h^2}$$

$$h = \sqrt{d^2 - a^2}$$

$$Perimeter = 2a + 2h$$

$$Area = a \cdot h$$

Square

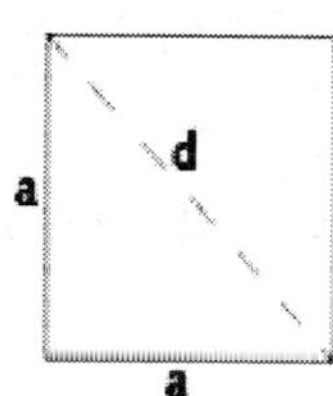

Area and Perimeter of a Square

$$d = a\sqrt{2}$$

$$Perimeter = 4a = 2d\sqrt{2}$$

$$Area = a^2 = \frac{1}{2}d^2$$

Circle

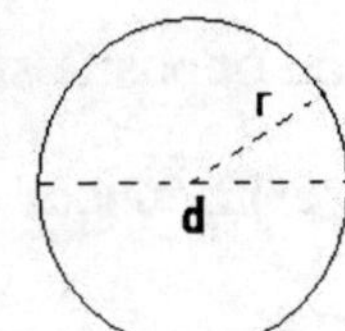

Area and Perimeter of a Circle

$d = 2r$

$Perimeter = 2\pi r = \pi d$

$Area = \pi r^2$

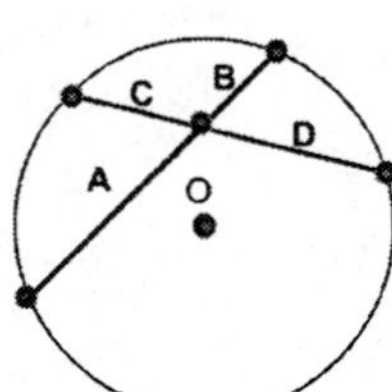

The product length of one chord equals the product length of the other, or:

AB=CD

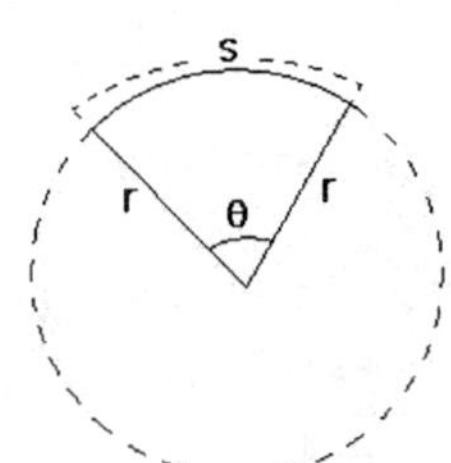

Area and Perimeter of the Sector of a Circle

$\alpha = \frac{\theta\pi}{180}\ (rad)$

$s = r\alpha$

$Perimeter = 2r + s$

$Area = \frac{1}{2}\theta\, r^2\ (radians)\ or\ \frac{n}{360}\pi r^2$

length (l) of an arc $l = \frac{\pi n r}{180}\ or\ \frac{n}{360}2\pi r$

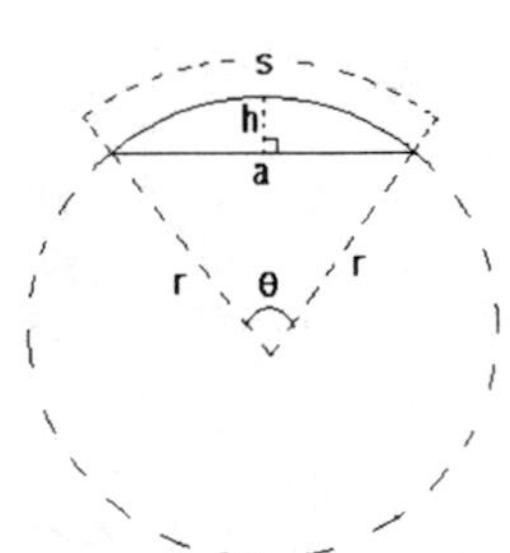

Area and Perimeter of the Segment of a Circle

$\alpha = \frac{\theta\pi}{180}\ (rad)$

$a = 2\sqrt{2hr - h^2}$

$a^2 = 2r^2 - 2r^2 cos\theta$

$s = r\alpha$

$h = r - \frac{1}{2}\sqrt{4r^2 - a^2}$

$Perimeter = a + s$

$Area = \frac{1}{2}[sr - a(r - h)]$

Cube

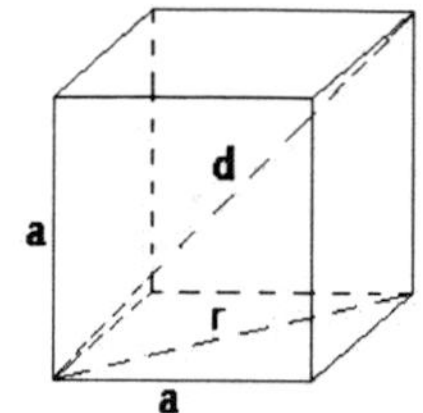

Area and Volume of a Cube

$r = a\sqrt{2}$

$d = a\sqrt{3}$

$Area = 6a^2$

$Volume = a^3$

Cuboid

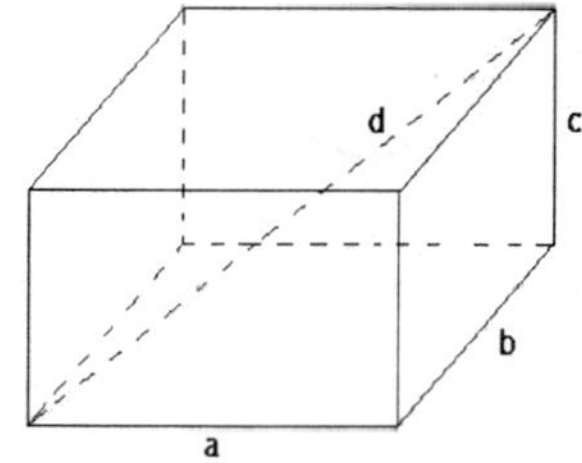

Area and Volume of a Cuboid

$d = \sqrt{a^2 + b^2 + c^2}$

$A = 2(ab + ac + bc)$

$V = abc$

Pyramid

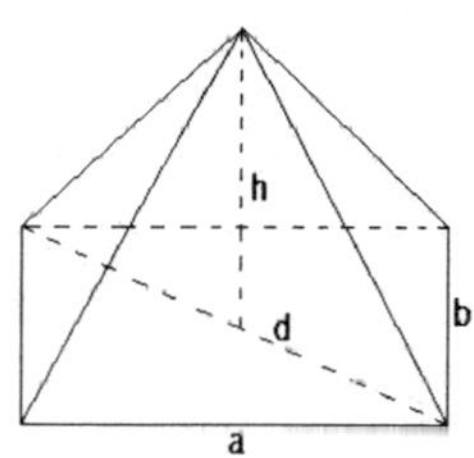

Area and Volume of a Pyramid

$A_{lateral} = a\sqrt{h^2 + \left(\frac{b}{2}\right)^2} + b\sqrt{h^2 + \left(\frac{a}{2}\right)^2}$

$d = \sqrt{a^2 + b^2}$

$A_{base} = ab$

$A_{total} = A_{lateral} + A_{base}$

$V = \frac{1}{3}abh$

Cylinder

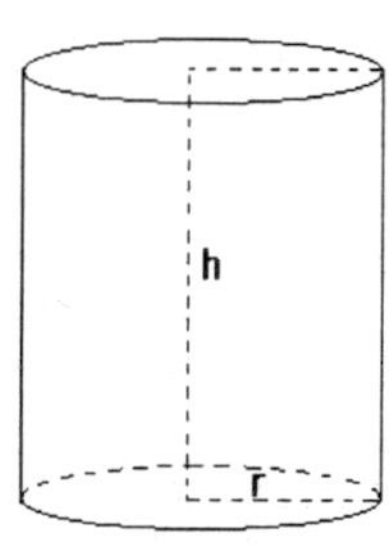

Area and Volume of a Cylinder

$d = 2r$

$A_{surface} = 2\pi rh$

$A_{base} = 2\pi r^2$

$Area = A_{surface} + A_{base}$

$= 2\pi r\,(h + r)$

$Volume = \pi r^2 h$

Cone

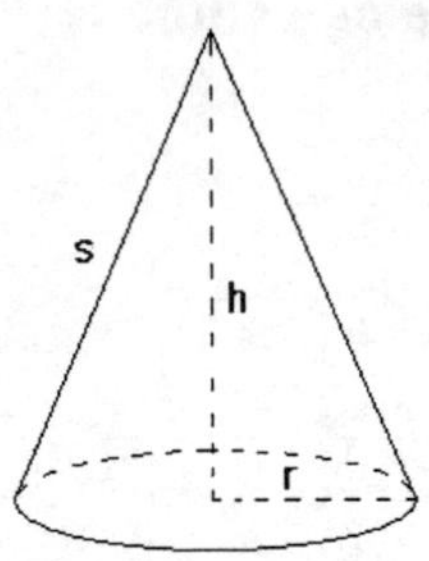

Area and Volume of a Cone

$d = 2r$

$A_{surface} = \pi rs$

$A_{base} = \pi r^2$

$Area = A_{surface} + A_{base}$

$= 2\pi r\,(h + r)$

$Volume = \frac{1}{3}\,\pi r^2 h$

Sphere

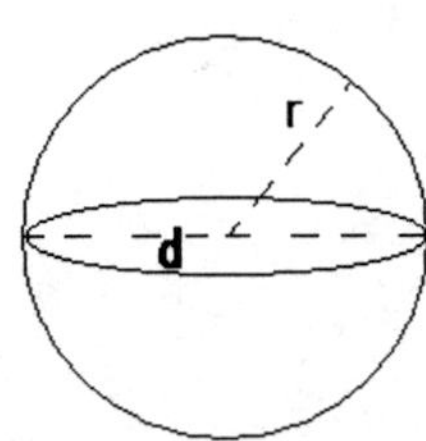

Area and Volume of a Sphere

$d = 2r$

$A_{surface} = 4\pi r^2$

$Volume = \frac{4}{3}\,\pi r^3$

Test Your Knowledge: Mathematics – Question Bank

Test Your Knowledge: Percent/Part/Whole, Percent Change

1. In a class of 42 students, 18 are boys. Two girls get transferred to another school. What percent of students remaining are girls?

a) 14%.
b) 16%.
c) 52.4%.
d) 60%.
e) None of the above.

2. A payroll check is issued for $500.00. If 20% goes to bills, 30% of the remainder goes to pay entertainment expenses, and 10% of what is left is placed in a retirement account, then approximately how much is remaining?

a) $150.
b) $250.
c) $170.
d) $350.
e) $180.

3. A painting by Van Gogh increased in value by 80% from year 1995 to year 2000. If in year 2000, the painting is worth $7200, what was its value in 1995?

a) $1500.
b) $2500.
c) $3000.
d) $4000.
e) $5000.

4. "Dresses and Ties" sells a particular dress for $60 dollars. But, they decide to discount the price of that dress by 25%. How much does the dress cost now?

a) $55.
b) $43.
c) $45.
d) $48.
e) $65.

5. A sweater goes on sale for 30% off. If the original price was $70, what is the discounted price?

a) $48.
b) $49.
c) $51.
d) $65.
e) $52.

6. If the value of a car depreciates by 60% over ten years, and its value in the year 2000 is $2500, what was its value in the year 1990?

a) $6000.
b) $6230.
c) $6250.
d) $6500.
e) $6600.

7. If an account is opened with a starting balance of $500, what is the amount in the account after 3 years if the account pays compound interest of 5%?

a) $560.80.
b) $578.81.
c) $564.50.
d) $655.10.
e) $660.00.

8. A piece of memorabilia depreciates by 1% every year. If the value of the memorabilia is $75000, what will it be 2 years from now? Give the answer as a whole number.

a) $74149.
b) $74150.
c) $73151.
d) $71662.
e) $73507.

9. A dress is marked down by 20% in an effort to boost sales for one week. After that week, the price of the dress is brought back to the original value. What percent did the price of the dress have to be increased from its discounted price?

a) 20%.
b) 25%.
c) 120%.
d) 125%.
e) 15%.

10. A car dealer increases the price of a car by 30%, but then discounts it by 30%. What is the relationship between the final price and the original price?

a) $.91x : x$.
b) $.98x : x$.
c) 1:1.
d) $.88x : x$.
e) $.75x : x$.

Test Your Knowledge: Percent/Part/Whole, Percent - Answers

1. **e)**
The entire class has 42 students, 18 of which are boys, meaning 42 - 18 = 24 is the number of girls. Out of these 24 girls, 2 leave; so 22 girls are left. The total number of students is now 42 - 2 = 40.

   22/40 * 100 = 55%.

   Reminder: If you forget to subtract 2 from the total number of students, you will end up with 60% as the answer. Sometimes you may calculate an answer that has been given as a choice; it can still be incorrect. Always check your answer.

2. **b)**
If out of the entire paycheck, 20% is first taken out, then the remainder is 80%. Of this remainder, if 30% is used for entertainment, then (.8 - .80 * .30) = .560 is left. If 10% is put into a retirement account, then (.56 - .56 * .1) = .504 is remaining. So out of $500, the part that remains is 50%, which is $252.

3. **d)**
In 2005, the value was 1.8 times its value in 1995. So $1.8x = 7200 \rightarrow x = 4000$.

4. **c)**
60 * (100 - 25)/100 → 60 * .75 = 45.

5. **b)**
New price = original price * (1 – discount) → new price = 70(1-.3) = 49.

6. **c)**
Value_{2000} = Original price * (1-.6) → 2500 = .4P = 2500 → P = 6250.

7. **b)**
Amount = $P(1 + r)^t = 500 * 1.05^3$ = $578.81.

8. **e)**
Final value = $75000(1 - .1)^2 = 73507$.

9. **b)**
If the original price of the dress was x, then the discounted price would be $0.8x$. To increase the price from $.8x$ to x, the percent increase would be $(x - .8x)/.8x * 100 = 25\%$.

10. **a)**
Let the original price of the car be x. After the 30% increase, the price is $1.3x$.

    After discounting the increased price by 30%, it now is $.7 * 1.3x = .91x$. Therefore, the ratio of the final price to the original price = $.91x : x$.

Test Your Knowledge: Mean, Median, Mode

1. If test A is taken 5 times with an average result of 21, and test B is taken 13 times with an average result of 23, what is the combined average?
   a) 22.24.
   b) 22.22.
   c) 22.00.
   d) 22.44.
   e) 24.22.

2. A set of data has 12 entries. The average of the first 6 entries is 12, the average of the next two entries is 20, and the average of the remaining entries is 4. What is the average of the entire data set?
   a) 10.
   b) 10.67.
   c) 11.
   d) 12.67.
   e) 10.5.

3. What is the average score of 8 tests where the score for 3 tests is 55, the score for two tests is 35, and the remaining tests have scores of 70?
   a) 50.3.
   b) 52.5.
   c) 55.1.
   d) 56.0.
   e) 55.6.

4. The temperatures over a week are recorded as follows:

Day	High	Low
Monday	80	45
Tuesday	95	34
Wednesday	78	47
Thursday	79	55
Friday	94	35
Saturday	67	46
Sunday	76	54

   What is the approximate average high temperature and average low temperature during the week?
   a) 90, 50.
   b) 80, 40.
   c) 81, 45.
   d) 82, 46.
   e) 81, 47.

5. Twelve teams competed in a mathematics test. The scores recorded for each team are: 29, 30, 28, 27, 35, 43, 45, 50, 46, 37, 44, and 41. What is the median score?

a) 37.
b) 41.
c) 39.
d) 44.
e) 45.

6. A class of 10 students scores 90, 78, 45, 98, 84, 79, 66, 87, 78, and 94. What is the mean score? What is the median score? What is the mode?

a) 69.9, 81.5, 78.
b) 79.9, 80, 78.
c) 79.9, 87, 76.
d) Not enough information given.
e) None of the above.

7. A shop sells 3 kinds of t-shirts: one design sells for $4.50, the second for $13.25, and the third for $15.50. If the shop sold 8 shirts of the first design, 12 shirts of the second design, and 4 shirts of the third design, what was the average selling price of the shirts?

a) $10.71.
b) $10.25.
c) $14.55.
d) $12.55.
e) $5.80.

Test Your Knowledge: Mean, Median, Mode – Answers

1. **d)**
   If test A avg = 21 for 5 tests, then sum of test A results = 21 * 5 = 105.
   If test B avg = 23 for 13 tests, then sum of test B results = 23 * 13 = 299.
   So total result = 299 + 105 = 404.
   Average of all tests = 404/(5 + 13) = 404/18 = 22.44.

2. **b)**
   The average of the first 6 points is 12 → $s_1/6 = 12$ → $s_1 = 72$; s_1 is the sum of the first 6 points.

   The average of the next 2 points is 20 → $s_2/2 = 20$ → $s_2 = 40$; s_2 is the sum of the next 2 points.

   The average of the remaining 4 points is 4 → $s_3/4 = 4$ → $s_3 = 16$; s_3 is the sum of the last 4 points.

   The sum of all the data points = 72 + 40 + 16 = 128.

   The average = 128/12 = 10.67.

3. **e)**
   Average = (3 * 55 + 2 * 35 + 3 * 70)/8 → Average = 55.625.

4. **c)**
   Average of high *s* = (80 + 95 + 78 + 79 + 94 + 67 + 76)/7 = 81.29.

   Average of low *s* = (45 + 34 + 47 + 55 + 35 + 46 + 54)/7 = 45.14.

5. **c)**
   To find the median, we first have to put the list in order:

   27, 28, 29, 30, 35, 37, 41, 43, 44, 45, 46, 50.

   The middle two scores are 37 and 41, and their average is 39.

6. **e) None of the above**
   The mean is just the total score/number of scores → 90 +… + 94)/10 → 79.9.

   The median is the score located in the middle. The middle of the set of the numbers is between 84 and 79. The average of these two scores is 81.5.

   The mode is the number that occurs the most: 78.

7. **a)**
   Multiply each t-shirt price with the number sold; add them together and divide by the total number of shirts sold.

   So Average Price = (4.50 * 8 + 13.25 * 12 + 15.50 * 4)/(8 + 12 + 4) → $10.71.

Test Your Knowledge: Exponents and Roots

1. What is $x^2y^3z^5/y^2z^{-9}$?

a) y^5z^4.
b) yz^4.
c) x^2yz^{14}.
d) $x^2y^5z^4$.
e) xyz.

2. What is k if $(2m^3)^5 = 32m^{k+1}$?

a) 11.
b) 12.
c) 13.
d) 14.
e) 15.

3. What is $x^5y^4z^3/x^{-3}y^2z^{-4}$?

a) $x^6y^4z^7$.
b) x^8yz^7.
c) x^6yz^7.
d) $x^8y^2z^7$.
e) $x^6y^2z^7$.

4. Evaluate $(a^2 * a^{54} + a^{56} + (a^{58}/a^2))/a^4$.

a) a^{56}.
b) $3a^{56}$.
c) $3a^{52}$.
d) $3a^{54}$.
e) a^{54}.

5. $9^m = 3^{-1/n}$. What is mn?

a) .5.
b) 2.
c) -2.
d) -.5.
e) -1.

6. If $2^a*4^a = 32$, what is a?

a) 1/3.
b) 2/3.
c) 1.
d) 4/3.
e) 5/3.

Test Your Knowledge: Exponents and Roots – Answers

1. **c)**
$x^2y^3z^5/y^2z^{-9} = x^2y^3z^5 * y^{-2}z^9$ which gives the answer $x^2y^{(3-2)}z^{(5+9)}$ → x^2yz^{14}.

2. **d)**
Expand $(2m^3)^5$ to give $32m^{15}$.

So$32m^{15} = 32m^{k+1}$ → $k+1 = 15$ → $k = 14$.

3. **d)**
$x^5y^4z^3/x^{-3}y^2z^{-4} = x^5y^4z^3 * x^3y^{-2}z^4 = x^8y^2z^7$.

4. **c)**
$(a^2*a^{54}+a^{56}+ (a^{58}/a^2))/a^4 = (a^{54}+2+a^{56}+a^{58}-2)a^{-4} = 3a^{56}-4 = 3a^{52}$.

5. **d)**
9^m is the same as 3^{2m}.

So $3^{2m} = 3^{-1/n}$ → $2m = -1/n$ → $mn = -.5$.

6. **e)**
$2^a * 4^a$ can be re-written as $2^a * (2^2)^a$.

$32 = 2^5$.

Therefore, $2^{(a+2a)} = 2^5$ → $3a = 5$ → $a = 5/3$.

Test Your Knowledge: Algebraic Equations

1. The number 568*cd* should be divisible by 2, 5, and 7. What are the values of the digits *c* and *d*?
   a) 56835.
   b) 56830.
   c) 56860.
   d) 56840.
   e) 56800.

2. Carla is 3 times older than her sister Megan. Eight years ago, Carla was 18 years older than her sister. What is Megan's age?
   a) 10.
   b) 8.
   c) 9.
   d) 6.
   e) 5.

3. What is the value of $f(x) = (x^2 - 25)/(x + 5)$ when $x = 0$?
   a) -1.
   b) -2.
   c) -3.
   d) -4.
   e) -5.

4. Four years from now, John will be twice as old as Sally will be. If Sally was 10 eight years ago, how old is John?
   a) 35.
   b) 40.
   c) 45.
   d) 50.
   e) 55.

5. I have some marbles. I give 25% to Vic, 20% to Robbie, 10% to Jules. I then give 6/20 of the remaining amount to my brother, and keep the rest for myself. If I end up with 315 marbles, how many did I have to begin with?
   a) 1000.
   b) 1500.
   c) 3500.
   d) 400.
   e) 500.

6. I have some marbles. I give 25% to Vic, 20% of the remainder to Robbie, 10% of that remainder to Jules and myself I then give 6/20 of the remaining amount to my brother, and keep the rest for myself. If I end up with 315 marbles, how many did I have to begin with?
   a) 800.
   b) 833.
   c) 834.
   d) 378.
   e) 500.

7. If $x = 5y + 4$, what is the value of y if $x = 29$?
a) 33/5.
b) 5.5.
c) 5.
d) 0.
e) 29/5.

8. A bag of marbles has 8 marbles. If I buy 2 bags of marbles, how many more bags of marbles would I need to buy to have a total of at least 45 marbles?
a) 3.
b) 4.
c) 5.
d) 6.
e) 29.

9. A factory that produces widgets wants to sell them each for $550. It costs $50 for the raw materials for each widget, and the startup cost for the factory was $10000. How many widgets have to be sold so that the factory can break even?
a) 10.
b) 20.
c) 30.
d) 40.
e) 50.

10. Expand $(3x - 4)(6 - 2x)$.
a) $6x^2 - 6x + 8$.
b) $-6x^2 + 26x - 24$.
c) $6x^2 - 26x + 24$.
d) $-6x^2 + 26x + 24$.
e) $6x^2 + 26x - 24$.

11. If $6n + m$ is divisible by 3 and 5, which of the following numbers when added to $6n + m$ will still give a result that is divisible by 3 and 5?
a) 4.
b) 6.
c) 12.
d) 20.
e) 60.

12. If x is negative, and $x^3/5$ and $x/5$ both give the same result, what could be the value of x?
a) -5.
b) -4.
c) 3.
d) 0.
e) -1.

13. If $m = 3548$, and $n = 235$, then what is the value of $m * n$?

a) 87940.
b) 843499.
c) 87900.
d) 8830.
e) 833780.

14. A ball is thrown at a speed of 30 mph. How far will it travel in 2 minutes and 35 seconds?

a) 1.5 miles.
b) 1.20 miles.
c) 1.29 miles.
d) 1.3 miles.
e) 1.1 miles.

15. Simplify: $30(\sqrt{40} - \sqrt{60})$.

a) $30(\sqrt{5} - \sqrt{15})$.
b) $30(\sqrt{10} + \sqrt{15})$.
c) $60(\sqrt{5} + \sqrt{15})$.
d) $60(\sqrt{10} - \sqrt{15})$.
e) 60.

16. Simplify: $30/(\sqrt{40} - \sqrt{60})$.

a) $3(\sqrt{5} + \sqrt{15})$.
b) $-3(\sqrt{5} - \sqrt{15})$.
c) $-3(\sqrt{10} + \sqrt{15})$.
d) $3(\sqrt{10} + \sqrt{15})$.
e) $3(\sqrt{10} - \sqrt{15})$.

17. What is the least common multiple of 2, 3, 4, and 5?

a) 30.
b) 60.
c) 120.
d) 40.
e) 50.

18. It costs \$6 to make a pen that sells for \$12. How many pens need to be sold to make a profit of \$60?

a) 10.
b) 6.
c) 72.
d) 30.
e) 12.

Test Your Knowledge: Algebraic Equations - Answers

1. **d)**
If the number is divisible by 2, d should be even. If the number is divisible by 5, then b has to equal 0.

Start by making both variables 0 and dividing by the largest factor, 7.

56800/7 = 8114.

2 from 56800 is 56798, a number divisible by 2 and 7.

Next add a multiple of 7 that turns the last number to a 0. 6 * 7 = 42. 56798 + 42 = 56840, which is divisible by 2, 5, and 7.

2. **c)**
Carla's age is c; Megan's age is m. $c = 3m$; $c - 8 = m - 8 + 18$.

Substitute $3m$ for c in equation 2 → $3m - 8 = m + 10$ → $m = 9$.

3. **e)**
We know $(x^2 - 25) = (x + 5)(x - 5)$.

So $(x^2 - 25)/(x + 5) = x - 5$. At $x = 0$, $f(0) = -5$.

4. **b)**
Let j be John's age and s be Sally's age.

$j + 4 = 2(s + 4)$.

$s - 8 = 10$ → $s = 18$.

So $j + 4 = 2(18 + 4)$ → $j = 40$.

5. **a)**
If x is the number of marbles initially, then $.25x$ goes to Vic, $.2x$ goes to Robbie, and $.1x$ goes to Jules.

The number left, x, is $(1 - .25 - .2 - .1) = .45x$.

Of that I give 6/20 to my brother, so $6/20 * .45x$.

I am left with $.45x(1 - (6/20)) = .315x$.

We are also told $.315x = 315$ → $x = 1000$.

6. c)
Always read the question carefully! Questions 5 and 6 are similar, but they are not the same.

Let x be the original number of marbles. After Vic's share is given $.75x$ remains. After Robbie's share $.75x * .80$ remains. After Jules' share, $.75x * .8 * .9$ remains.

After I give my brother his share, $.75x * .8 * .9 * (1 - 6/20)$ remains. The remaining number = $.378x$.

We are told $.378x = 315 \rightarrow x = 833.33$. We need to increase this to the next highest number, 834, because we have part of a marble and to include it we need to have a whole marble.

7. c)
Replace the value of x with its value and solve the equation.

$29 = 5y + 4$.

Solving:

$29 - 4 = 5y + 4 - 4$.

$25 = 5y$ or $5y = 25$.

$5y/5 = 25/5$.

$y = 5$.

8. b)
$2(8) + x > 45$ means $x > 29$, so we need more than 29 marbles. A bag has 8 marbles, so the number of bags needed is 29/8, or 3.625. Since we need 3 bags + part of another bag, we need 4 additional bags to give at least 45 marbles.

9. b)
n is the number of widgets. The cost the factory incurs for making n widgets is $10000 + 50n$. The amount the factory makes by selling n widgets is $550n$.

At the break-even point, the cost incurred is equal to the amount of sales.

$10000 + 50n = 550n \rightarrow n = 20$.

10. b)
Use FOIL:

$(3x - 4)(6 - 2x) = 3x * 6 - 4 * 6 + 3x * (-2x) - 4 * (-2x) = 18x - 24 - 6x^2 + 8x = -6x^2 + 26x - 24$.

11. e)
Since $6n + m$ is divisible by 3 and 5, the new number that we get after adding a value will be divisible by 3 and 5 only if the value that we add is divisible by 3 and 5. The only number that will work from the given choices is 60.

12. e)

We are told $x^3/5 = x/5 \rightarrow x^3 = x$. The possible values are -1, 0, and 1. We are told that x is negative.

So $x = -1$.

13. e)

This problem can be done by elimination. We know that m is in the thousands, which means $x * 10^3$; and n is in the hundreds, which is $y * 10^2$. The answer will be $z * 10^5$, or 6 places in total, so we can eliminate **a)**, **c)**, and **d)**. Also we see that m ends in 8 and n ends in 5, so the answer has to end in 0 (8 * 5 = 40), which eliminates **b)**.

14. c)

The ball has a speed of 30 miles per hour. 30 miles per 60 minutes = .5 mile per minute; 2 minutes and 35 seconds = 2 minutes; and 35/60 minutes = 2.58 minutes.

The ball travels .5 * 2.58 = 1.29 miles.

15. d)

$30(\sqrt{40} - \sqrt{60}) = 30\sqrt{4\,(10 - 15)} = 60(\sqrt{10} - \sqrt{15})$.

16. c)

Multiply the numerator and the denominator by $(\sqrt{40} + \sqrt{60})$.

So $\frac{30}{(\sqrt{40}-\sqrt{60})} * \left[\frac{(\sqrt{40}+\sqrt{60})}{(\sqrt{40}+\sqrt{60})}\right] =$

$30(\sqrt{40} + \sqrt{60})/(\sqrt{40} - \sqrt{60})^2$.

$-3(\sqrt{10} + \sqrt{15})$.

17. b)

Find all the prime numbers that multiply to give the numbers.

For 2, prime factor is 2; for 3, prime factor is 3; for 4, prime factors are 2, 2; and for 5, prime factor is 5. Note the maximum times of occurrence of each prime and multiply these to find the least common multiple.

The LCM is 2 * 2 * 3 * 5 = 60.

18. a)

One pen sells for $12, so on the sale of a pen, the profit is 12 - 6 = 6.

In order to make $60, we need to sell 10 pens.

Test Your Knowledge: Inequalities, Literal Equations, Polynomials, and Binomials

1. If $x < 5$ and $y < 6$, then $x + y$ _?_ 11.

a) $<$
b) $>$
c) $\leq$
d) $\geq$
e) $=$

2. Which of the following is true about the inequality $25x^2 - 40x - 32 < 22$?

a) There are no solutions.
b) There is a set of solutions.
c) There is 1 solution only.
d) There are 2 solutions.
e) There are 3 solutions.

3. If $x - 2y > 6$, what possible values of y always have x as greater than or equal to 2?

a) $y \geq 1$.
b) $y \leq 0$.
c) $y \geq -2$.
d) $y < 2$.
e) $y \leq 6$.

4. Find the point of intersection of the lines $x + 2y = 4$ and $3x - y = 26$.

a) (1, 3).
b) (8, -2).
c) (0, 2).
d) (2, -1).
e) (4, 26).

5. If $a + b = 2$, and $a - b = 4$, what is a?

a) 1.
b) 2.
c) 3.
d) 4.
e) 5.

6. If $\sqrt{a} + \sqrt{b} = 2$, and $\sqrt{a} - \sqrt{b} = 3$, what is $a + b$?

a) 6.5.
b) 6.
c) 5.5.
d) 5.
e) 4.5.

7. If $a = b + 3$, and $3b = 5a + 6$, what is $3a - 2b$?

a) -1.5.
b) 2.5.
c) 3.
d) 4.3.
e) 5.

8. The sum of the roots of a quadratic equation is 8, and the difference is 2. What is the equation?

a) $x^2 - 8x - 15$.
b) $x^2 + 8x + 15$.
c) $x^2 - 8x + 15$.
d) $x^2 + 8x - 15$.
e) $x^2 + 15$.

9. Solve the following system of equations: $3x + 2y = 7$ and $3x + y = 5$.

a) $x = 2, y = 1$.
b) $x = 2, y = 2$.
c) $x = 1, y = 0$.
d) $x = 1, y = 2$.
e) $x = 1, y = 1$.

10. Nine tickets were sold for $41. If the tickets cost $4 and $5, how many $5 tickets were sold?

a) 5.
b) 4.
c) 9.
d) 6.
e) 7.

11. Joe brought a bag of 140 M&Ms to his class of 40 students. Each boy received 2 M&Ms. Each girl received 4. How many boys were in the class?

a) 10.
b) 20.
c) 30.
d) 40.
e) 50.

Test Your Knowledge: Inequalities, Literal Equations, Polynomials, and Binomials – Answers

1. **a)**
   Choice **a)** will always be true, while the other choices can never be true.

2. **b)**
   $25x^2 - 40x + 32 < 22 \rightarrow 25x^2 - 40x + 16 < 6 \rightarrow (5x - 4)^2 < 6 \rightarrow 5x - 4 < 6$.

   $x = 2$, so x has to be all numbers less than 2 for this inequality to work.

3. **c)**
   Rearrange equation $x > 6 + 2y$, so $2 > 6 + 2y$. Solve for y.

   $2 \geq 6 + 2y$.

   $-4 \geq 2y$, so $-2 \leq y$ or $y \geq -2$.

   (When working with inequalities, remember to reverse the sign when dividing by a negative number.)

4. **b)**
   Find the slopes first. If they are not equal, then the lines intersect. The slopes are -1/2 and 3.

   Next, solve by substitution or addition. From the first equation, $x = 4 - 2y$. Plugging this into equation 2, we get $3(4 - 2y) - y = 26 \rightarrow 7y = 12 - 26 \rightarrow y = -2$. Plug this value into either equation to find x.

   With equation 1, we get $x - 4 = 4 \rightarrow x = 8$.

5. **c)**
   Add the equations to eliminate b. $2a = 6 \rightarrow a = 3$.

6. **a)**
   Square both equations.

   Equation 1 becomes $a + 2\sqrt{ab} + b = 4$; and equation 2 becomes $a - 2\sqrt{ab} + b = 9$.

   Add the equations. $2(a + b) = 13 \rightarrow a + b = 13/2$. $13/2 = 6.5$.

7. **a)**
   Solve by substitution.

   If $a = b + 3$, and $3b = 5a + 6$, then $3b = 5(b+3) + 6$.

   If $3b - 5b - 15 = 6$, then $-2b = 21$. Therefore, $b = -10.5$.

   Now use substitution to find a. $a = b + 3$. So $a = -10.5 + 3$. Therefore, $a = -7.5$.

   Solve the equation, $3a - 2b$. $3(-7.5) - 2(-10.5) = -1.5$.

8. c)

If the roots are a and b, then $a + b = 8$ and $a - b = 2$.

Add the equations. $2a = 10 \rightarrow a = 5 \rightarrow b = 3$.

The factors are $(x - 5)(x - 3)$, and the equation is $x^2 - 8x + 15$.

9. d)

From the equation $3x + y = 5$, we get $y = 5 - 3x$. Substitute into the other equation. $3x + 2(5 - 3x) = 7 \rightarrow 3x + 10 - 6x = 7 \rightarrow x = 1$. This value into either of the equations gives us $y = 2$.

10. a)

$4x + 5y = 41$, and $x + y = 9$, where x and y are the number of tickets sold.

From equation 2: $x = 9 - y$.

From equation 1: $4(9 - y) + 5y = 41 \rightarrow 36 + y = 41 \rightarrow y = 5$.

11. a)

b is the number of boys, and g is the number of girls. So $b + g = 40$, and $2b + 4g = 140$.

To do the problem, use the substitution method. Plug $(g = 40 – b)$ into $(2b + 4g = 140)$.

$2b + 4(40 - b) = 140 \rightarrow b = 10$.

Test Your Knowledge: Slope and Distance to Midpoint

1. What is the equation of the line that passes through (3, 5), with intercept $y = 8$?
   a) $y = x + 8$.
   b) $y = x - 8$.
   c) $y = -x - 8$.
   d) $y = -x + 8$.
   e) $y = -x$.

2. What is the value of y in the equation $(3x - 4)^2 = 4y - 15$, if $x = 3$?
   a) 10.
   b) 2.5.
   c) -10.
   d) -2.5.
   e) 5.

3. If $y = 4x + 6y$, what is the range of y if $-10 < x \leq 5$?
   a) $-4 < y \leq 8$.
   b) $-4 < y < 8$.
   c) $8 > y > -4$.
   d) $-4 \leq y < 8$.
   e) $-4 \leq y \leq 8$.

4. If Jennifer gets three times as much allowance as Judy gets, and Judy gets $5/week, how much does Jennifer get every month?
   a) $15.
   b) $20.
   c) $30.
   d) $45.
   e) $60.

5. What is the value of x, if $y = 8$ in the equation $5x + 9y = 3x - 6y + 5$?
   a) 57.5.
   b) 60.
   c) -60.
   d) -57.5.
   e) None of the above.

6.

A (3, 5) B (8, 17)

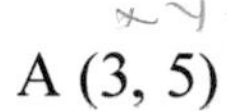

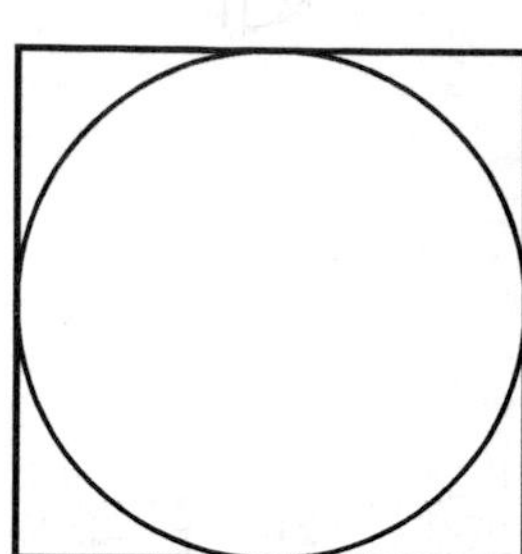

What is the area outside the circle, but within the square whose two corners are A and B?

a) $169(1-\pi)$.
b) $169\ \pi$.
c) $169\ \pi/4$.
d) $169(1-\pi/4)$.
e) 169.

7. A line with a slope of 2 passes through the point (2, 4). What is the set of coordinates where that line passes through the y intercept?

a) (-2, 0).
b) (0, 0).
c) (2, 2).
d) (4, 0).
e) (1, 1).

8.

$$3x + 4y = 7$$
$$9x + 12y = 21$$

Determine where the above two lines intersect:

a) $x = 4$, $y = 3$.
b) $x = 12$, $y = 9$.
c) $x = 1/3$, $y = 1/3$.
d) Not enough information provided.
e) There is no solution; the lines do not intersect.

9.

$$3x + 4y = 7$$
$$8x - 6y = 9$$

Are the above lines parallel or perpendicular?

a) Parallel.
b) Perpendicular.
c) Neither parallel nor perpendicular.
d) Cannot be determined.
e) The angle at the point of intersection is 40.

10. Is the graph of the function $f(x) = -3x^2 + 4$ linear, asymptotical, symmetrical to the x axis, symmetrical to the y axis, or not symmetrical to either axis?

a) Symmetrical to the x axis.
b) Symmetrical to the y axis.
c) Symmetrical to neither axis.
d) Asymptotic.
e) Linear.

11. Two points on a line have coordinates (3, 12) and (9, 20). What is the distance between these two points?

a) 10.
b) 12.
c) 13.
d) 8.
e) 11.

12. In the following graph, what is the equation of line AB if line AB is perpendicular to line PQ? Point coordinates are:

M (-4, 0); O (0, 2); and N (0, -3). The lines intersect at (-2,1).

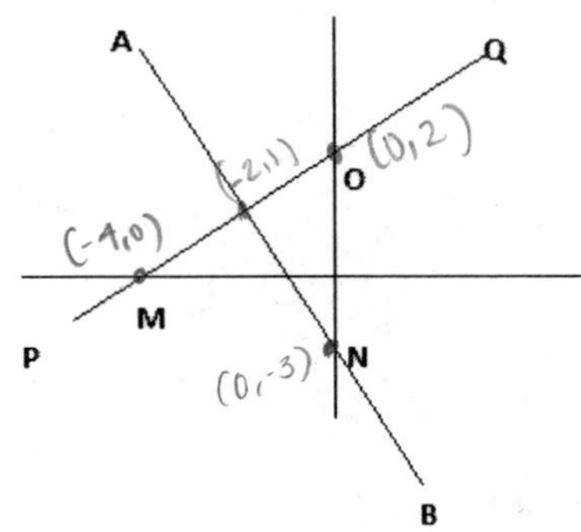

a) $y = 2x + 3$.
b) $y = -2x - 3$.
c) $y = x - 4$.
d) $y = x + 3$.
e) $y = -2x - 3$.

13. What is the equation of a line passing through (1, 2) and (6, 12)?

a) $y = x$.
b) $y = 2x$.
c) $y = x/2$.
d) $y = 2x + 2$.
e) $y = x - 2$.

14. What is the midpoint of the line connecting points (0, 8) and (2, 6)?

a) (-1, 1).
b) (2, 14).
c) (-2, 2).
d) (0, 1).
e) (1, 7).

15. What is the equation of a line passing through (1, 1) and (2, 4)?

a) $3y = x + 2$.
b) $2y = x + 3$.
c) $y = 3x - 2$.
d) $4x = y + 2$.
e) $y = (1/3)x + 2$.

16. Line A passes through (0, 0) and (3, 4). Line B passes through (2, 6) and (3, y). What value of y will make the lines parallel?

a) 20/3.
b) 7.
c) 22/3.
d) 29.
e) 5.

17. Line A passes through (1, 3) and (3, 4). Line B passes through (3, 7) and (5, y). What value of y will make the lines perpendicular?

a) 1.
b) 2.
c) 3.
d) 4.
e) 5.

18. What is the equation of line A that is perpendicular to line B, connecting (8, 1) and (10, 5), that intersects at (x, 14)?

a) $y = 2x - 7$.
b) $y = -2x + 7$.
c) $y = (-1/2)x + 19\frac{1}{4}$.
d) $y = 5x - 7$.
e) $y = 2x - 19\frac{1}{4}$.

Test Your Knowledge: Slope and Distance to Midpoint – Answers

1. **d)**
   The standard form of the line equation is $y = mx + b$. We need to find slope m.

   $m = (y_2 - y_1)/(x_2 - x_1) \rightarrow m = (5 - 8)/(3 - 0) \rightarrow m = -1$.

   Therefore the equation is $y = -x + 8$.

2. **a)**
   At $x = 3$, $((3 * 3) – 4)^2 = 4y – 15$.

   $(9 – 4)^2 = 4y – 15$.

   $25 = 4y – 15$.

   $40 = 4y$.

   $y = 10$.

3. **d)**
   Rearrange the equation and combine like terms. $-5y = 4x$.

   At $x = -10$, $y = 8$. At $x = 5$, $y = -4$. The range of y is therefore $-4 \leq y < 8$.

4. **e)**
   If Judy gets x dollars, then Jennifer gets $3x$ in a week. In a month, Jennifer will then get $4 * 3x$.

   If Judy gets $5 per week, then Jennifer gets $60 in a month.

5. **d)**
   Combine like terms.

   $5x + 9y = 3x - 6y + 5 \rightarrow 2x = -15y + 5 \rightarrow x = -57.5$ when $y = 8$.

6. **d)**
   First we need to find the length of side AB.

   $AB = \sqrt{(17 - 5)^2 + (8 - 3)^2} = 13$.

   If AB = 13, then $A_{square} = 13^2 = 169$.

   AB is also the diameter of the circle. A_{circle} $\pi (d^2/4) = 169 \pi /4$.

   The area outside the circle and within the square is: $A_{square} - A_{circle} = 169(1 - \pi /4)$.

7. b)

The slope of the line is given as $m = (y_2 - y_1)/(x_2 - x_1)$, where (x_1, y_1) and (x_2, y_2) are two points which the line passes through.

The y intercept is the point where the graph intersects the y axis, so $x = 0$ at this point.

Plug in the values of m, etc.; we get $2 = (4 - y)/(2 - 0) \rightarrow y = 0$.

8. e)

While it is tempting to solve this system of simultaneous equations to find the values of x and y, the first thing to do is to see whether the lines intersect. To do this, compare the slopes of the two lines by putting the lines into the standard form, $y = mx + b$, where m is the slope.

By rearranging, equation 1 becomes $y = 7/4 - 3x/4$; and equation 2 becomes $y = 21/12 - 9x/12$.

The slope of line 1 is -3/4, and the slope of line 2 is -9/12, which reduces to -3/4. Since the slopes are equal, the lines are parallel and do not intersect.

9. b)

Find the slopes by rearranging the two equations into the form $y = mx + b$.

Equation 1 becomes $y = -3x/4 + 7/4$ and equation 2 becomes $y = 8x/6 - 9/6$.

So $m_1 = -3/4$ and $m_2 = 8/6 = 4/3$. We see that m_1 is the negative inverse of m_2, so line 1 is perpendicular to line 2.

10. b)

Find the values of the y coordinate for different values of the x coordinate (example, [-3, +3]). We get the following chart:

x	y
-3	-23
-2	-8
-1	1
0	4
1	1
2	-8
3	-23

From these values, we see the graph is symmetrical to the y axis.

11. a)

Distance $s = \sqrt{(x_2 - x_1)^2 + (y_2 - y_1)^2} \rightarrow s = \sqrt{(9 - 3)^2 + (20 - 12)^2} = \sqrt{36 + 64} = 10$.

12. b)

$y = mx + b$; m is the slope and b is the y intercept.

Calculate m for line AB using the given points (0, -3) and (-2, 1). $m = (-3 - 1)/(0-(-2)) = -2$. The y intercept is -3 (from point set given), so $y = -2x - 3$.

13. b)

First, find the slope, $(y_2\text{-}y_1)/(x_2\text{-}x_1)$ → slope = (12 - 2)/(6 - 1) = 2.

Next, use the slope and a point to find the value of *b*.

In the standard line equation, $y = mx + b$, use the point (6, 12) to get 12 = (2 * 6) + *b* → *b* = 0.

The equation of the line is $y = 2x$.

14. e)

The midpoint is at $(x_1 + x_2)/2, (y_1 + y_2)/2 = (1,7)$.

15. c)

Slope = $(y_2 - y_1)/(x_2 - x_1) = 3$. Plug one of the coordinates into $y = mx + b$ to find the value of *b*.

1 = 3(1) + *b* → *b* = - 2.

The equation of the line is $y = 3x - 2$.

16. c)

Calculate the slope of each line. Slope of line A = 4/3; and slope of line B = *y* - 6.

The slopes of the line have to be the same for the lines to be parallel.

4/3 = *y* – 6 → 4 = 3*y* – 18 → *y* = 22/3.

17. c)

The slope of line A = ½; and the slope of line B = (*y* - 7)/2.

The product of the slopes has to equal -1.

(1/2)[(*y* - 7)/2] = -1 → (*y* - 7)/4 = -1 → *y* = 3.

18. c)

Slope_b = (5 - 1)/(10 - 8) = 2. The slope of line A is -1/2.

To find the intercept of line B, use $y = mx + b$.

5 = (2)(10) + *b*, so *b* = -7. Equation of line B is $y = 2x - 7$.

Find intersect *x*, using the given *y* coordinate. 14 = 2*x* – 7; *x* = 10.5.

Find the intercept of line A using the coordinates of intersection.

14 = (-1/2)(10.5)+*b*. $b = 19\frac{1}{4}$.

The equation of line A is $y = -(1/2)x + 19\frac{1}{4}$.

Test Your Knowledge: Absolute Value Equations

1. Factor $x^2 + 2x - 15$.
   a) $(x - 3)(x + 5)$.
   b) $(x + 3)(x - 5)$.
   c) $(x + 3)(x + 5)$.
   d) $(x - 3)(x - 5)$.
   e) $(x - 1)(x + 15)$.

2. Car A starts at 3:15 PM and travels straight to its destination at a constant speed of 50 mph. If it arrives at 4:45 PM, how far did it travel?
   a) 70 miles.
   b) 75 miles.
   c) 65 miles.
   d) 40 miles.
   e) 105 miles.

3. What are the roots of the equation $2x^2 + 14x = 0$?
   a) 0 and 7.
   b) 0 and -7.
   c) 14 and 0.
   d) 2 and 14.
   e) Cannot be determined.

4. If $f(x) = 2x^2 + 3x$, and $g(x) = x + 4$, what is $f[g(x)]$?
   a) $x^2 + 19x + 44$.
   b) $2x^2 + 19x + 44$.
   c) $4x^2 + 35x + 76$.
   d) $x^2 + 8x + 16$.
   e) None of the above.

5. If $|x + 4| = 2$, what are the values of x?
   a) 2 and 6.
   b) -2 and -6.
   c) -2.
   d) -6.
   e) 0.

6. The sale of an item can be written as a function of price: $s = 3p + c$, where s is the amount in sales, p is the price per item, and c is a constant value. If the sales generated are \$20 at a price of \$5 for the item, then what should the price be to generate \$50 in sales?
   a) \$10.
   b) \$15.
   c) \$20.
   d) \$16.
   e) \$14.

7. If $f(n) = 2n + 3\sqrt{n}$, where n is a positive integer, what is $f[g(5)]$ if $g(m) = m - 4$?

a) 1.
b) 2.
c) 3.
d) 4.
e) 5.

8. If $f(x) = (x + 2)^2$, and $-4 \leq x \leq 4$, what is the minimum value of $f(x)$?

a) 0.
b) 1.
c) 2.
d) 3.
e) 4.

9. If $f(x) = (x + 2)^2$, and $0 \leq x \leq 4$, what is the minimum value of $f(x)$?

a) 1.
b) 2.
c) 3.
d) 4.
e) 5.

10. What is $x^2 - 9$ divided by $x - 3$?

a) $x - 3$.
b) $x + 3$.
c) x.
d) $x - 1$.
e) 6.

11. An equation has two roots: 5 and -8. What is a possible equation?

a) $x^2 - 3x + 40$.
b) $x^2 - 3x - 40$.
c) $x^2 + x + 40$.
d) $x^2 + 3x - 40$.
e) $2x^2 - 3x + 40$.

12. In an ant farm, the number of ants grows every week according to the formula $N = 100 + 2^w$, where w is the number of weeks elapsed. How many ants will the colony have after 5 weeks?

a) 115.
b) 125.
c) 135.
d) 132.
e) 233.

13. Find the values of x that validate the following equation: $[(4x + 5)^2 - (40x + 25)]^{1/2} + 3|x| - 14 = 0$.

a) -2, -14.
b) 2, -14.
c) -2, 14.
d) 2, 14.
e) No solution.

14. If $|x| = 4$ and $|y| = 5$, what are the values of $|x + y|$?

a) 1, 9.
b) -1, 9.
c) -1, -9.
d) -1, -9.
e) $1 < |x + y| < 9$.

15. If $y = |x|$, what is the range of y?

a) $y < 0$.
b) $0 < y < \text{x}$.
c) $y > 0$.
d) $y \geq 0$.
e) $y > x$.

Test Your Knowledge: Absolute Value Equations – Answers

1. **a)**
The constant term is -15. The factors should multiply to give -15 and add to give 2. The numbers -3 and 5 satisfy both, $(x - 3)(x + 5)$.

2. **b)**
The time between 3:15 PM and 4:45 PM = 1.5 hours. 1.5 * 50 = 75.

Reminder: half an hour is written as .5 of an hour, not .3 of an hour, even though on a clock a half hour is 30 minutes.

3. **b)**
Rearrange, reduce, and factor.

$2x^2 + 14x + 0 = 0.$

$2(x^2 + 7x + 0) = 0.$

$(x + 7)(x + 0).$

$x = 0$, or -7.

4. **b)**
Substitute $g(x)$ for every x in $f(x)$.

$f[g((x + 4))] = 2(x + 4)^2 + 3(x + 4) = 2x^2 + 16x + 32 + 3x + 12 = 2x^2 + 19x + 44.$

5. **b)**
Two solutions: $(x + 4) = 2$ and $-(x + 4) = 2$.

Or $x + 4 = 2, x = -2$.

And $x + 4 = -2, x = -6$.

6. **b)**
Find the value of the constant by plugging in the given information.

$20 = 3 * 5 + c \rightarrow c = 5.$

Now use the value of c and the new value of s to find p.$50 = 3p + 5 \rightarrow p = 15$.

7. **e)**
$g(5) = 5 - 4 = 1. f[g(5)] = 2 * 1 + 3\sqrt{1} = 5.$

8. **a)**
From the domain of x, the lowest value of x is -4, and the highest value is 4. We are tempted to think that $f(x)$ will have the least value at $x = -4$: $f(-4) = 4$. However, $f(x)$ is equal to a squared value, so the lowest value of $f(x)$ is 0. This happens at $x = -2$.

9. d)

The lowest value of $f(x)$ can be 0, since $f(x)$ is equal to a squared value, but, for $f(x) = 0$, x must equal -2. That is outside the domain of x. The least value of $f(x) = 4$.

10. b)

$x^2 - 9$ can be factored into $(x + 3)$ and $(x - 3)$.

$[(x + 3)(x - 3)]/(x - 3) = x + 3$.

11. d)

If the roots are 5 and -8, then the factors are $(x - 5)(x + 8)$. Multiply the factors to get the equation.

$x^2 + 3x - 40$.

12. d)

After 5 weeks, the number of ants = 100 + 32, or 132.

13. d)

Expand the equation:

$[16x^2 + 40x + 25 - 40x - 25]^{1/2} + 3|x| - 14 = 0$.

$(16x^2)^{1/2} + 3|x| - 14 = 0$.

$4x + 3|x| - 14 = 0$.

$3|x| = 14 - 4x$.

$|x| = \frac{14}{3} - \frac{4x}{3}$ $\qquad x = \frac{14}{3} - \frac{4x}{3} = 2$ $\qquad x = -\frac{14}{3} - \frac{4x}{3} = 14$.

14. a)

$x = 4$ and $y = 5$, $|x + y| = 9$.

$x = -4$ and $y = 5$, $|x + y| = 1$.

$x = 4$ and $y = -5$, $|x + y| = 1$.

$x = -4$ and $y = -5$; $|x + y| = 9$.

15. d)

The absolute value of x can be at least a 0, and is otherwise positive regardless of the value of x.

$y \geq 0$.

Test Your Knowledge: Geometry

1. What is the area, in square feet, of the triangle whose sides have lengths equal to 3, 4, and 5 feet?
   a) 6 square feet.
   b) 7 square feet.
   c) 4 square feet.
   d) 5 square feet.
   e) 8 square feet.

2. In the following figure, where AE bisects line BC, and angles AEC and AEB are both right angles, what is the length of AB?
   a) 1 cm.
   b) 2 cm.
   c) 3 cm.
   d) 4 cm.
   e) 5 cm.

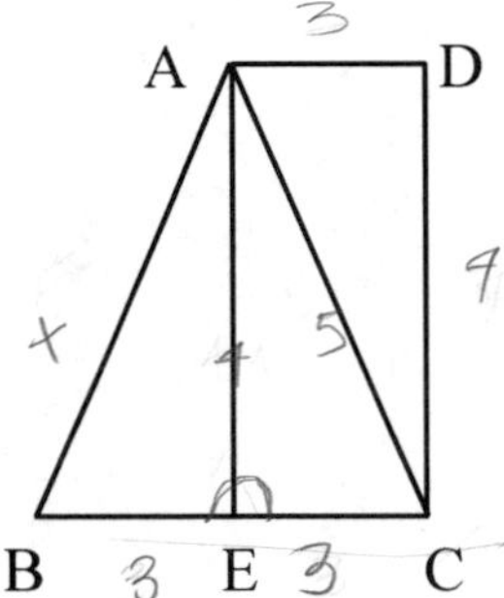

BC = 6 cm
AD = 3 cm
CD = 4 cm

3. In the following triangle, if AB = 6 and BC = 8, what should the length of CA be to make triangle ABC a right triangle?
   a) 10.
   b) 9.
   c) 8.
   d) 4.
   e) 7.

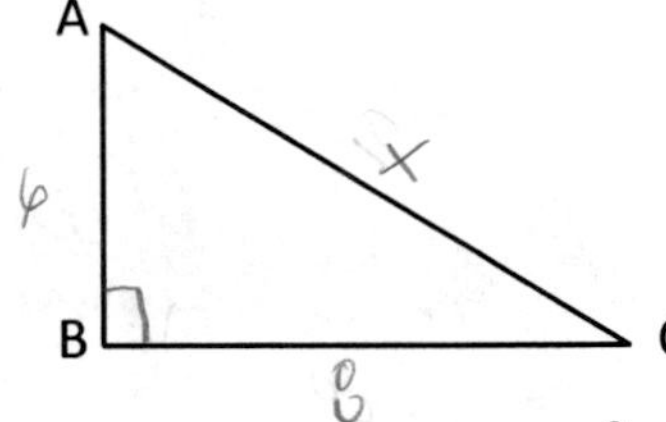

4. In the following circle there is a square with an area of 36 cm^2. What is the area outside the square, but within the circle?
   a) 18π cm^2.
   b) 18π - 30 cm^2.
   c) 18π - 36 cm^2.
   d) 18 cm^2.
   e) -18 cm^2.

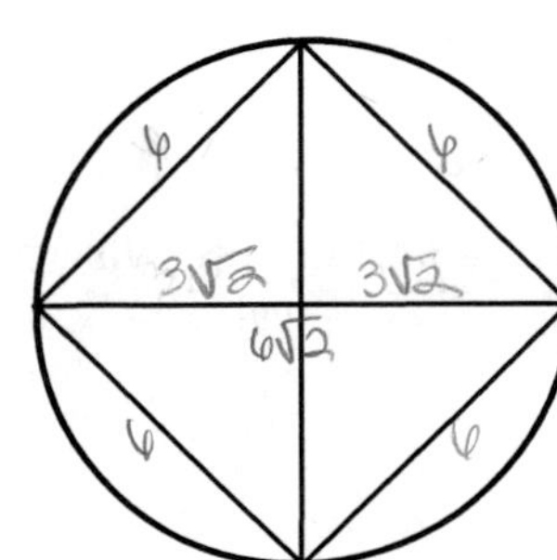

5. The length of a rectangle is 4 times its width. If the width of the rectangle is $5 - x$ inches, and the perimeter of the rectangle is 30 inches, what is x?
   a) 1.
   b) 2.
   c) 3.
   d) 4.
   e) 5.

6. Two sides of a triangle have a ratio AC:BC = 5:4. The length of AB on a similar triangle = 24. What is the actual value of AC for the larger triangle?
   a) 10.
   b) 14.4.
   c) 35.
   d) 40.
   e) 50.

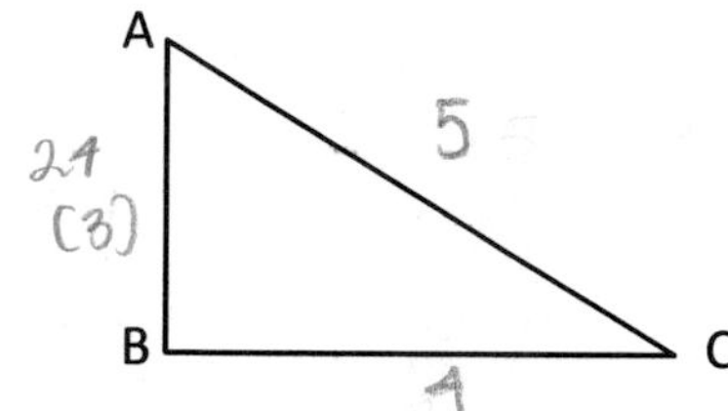

7. If the diameter of a circle is doubled, the area increases by what factor?
   a) 1 time.
   b) 2 times.
   c) 3 times.
   d) 4 times.
   e) 5 times.

8. In the following triangle PQR, what is the measure of angle A?
   a) 145^0.
   b) 140^0.
   c) 70^0.
   d) 50^0.
   e) 40^0.

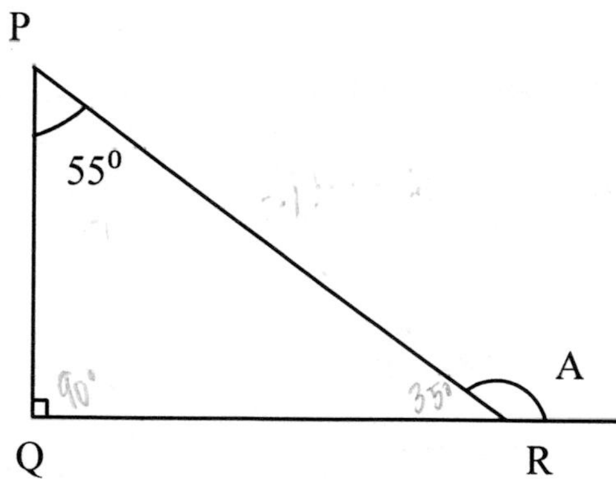

Test Your Knowledge: Geometry – Answers

1. a)
The Pythagorean triple (special right triangle property) means the two shorter sides form a right triangle.

$1/2bh$ = A. So, (1/2)(3)(4) = 6.

2. e)
$AB^2 = AC^2 = AD2 + CD^2 \rightarrow AB^2 = 3^2 + 4^2 \rightarrow AB = 5$.

3. a)
In a right triangle, the square of the hypotenuse = the sum of the squares of the other two sides.

$AB^2 + BC^2 = AC^2 \rightarrow AC^2 = 36 + 64 \rightarrow AC = 10$.

4. c)
If the area of the square is 36 cm^2, then each side is 6 cm. If we look at the triangle made by half the square, that diagonal would be the hypotenuse of the triangle, and its length = $\sqrt{6^2 + 6^2} = 6\sqrt{2}$.

This hypotenuse is also the diameter of the circle, so the radius of the circle is $3\sqrt{2}$.

The area of the circle = A = πr^2= 18π.

The area outside the square, but within the circle is 18π -36.

5. b)
Perimeter of a rectangle = $2(l + w)$. Width = $5 - x$; and length = $4(5 - x)$.

Perimeter = $2(l * w) = 30 \rightarrow 2(20 - 4x + 5 - x) = 30 \rightarrow -10x = -20 \rightarrow x = 2$.

6. d)
Side AC = 5, and side BC = 4. The Pythagorean triple is 3:4:5, so side AB = 3.

Because the other triangle is similar, the ratio of all sides is constant. AB:AB = 3:24. The ratio factor is 8.

AC of the larger triangle = 5 * 8 = 40.

7. d)
The area of a circle = πr^2.

If the diameter is doubled, then the radius is also doubled.

The new area = $\pi * (2r)^2 = 4 * \pi * r^2$. The area increases four times.

8. a)
$\angle P = 55^0$. $\angle Q = 90^0$. $\angle R = 180 - (55 + 90) = 35^0$, and $\angle A = 180 - 35 = 145^0$.

Test Your Knowledge: Fundamental Counting Principle, Permutations, Combinations

1. The wardrobe of a studio contains 4 hats, 3 suits, 5 shirts, 2 pants, and 3 pairs of shoes. How many different ways can these items be put together?
   a) 60.
   b) 300.
   c) 360.
   d) 420.
   e) 500.

2. For lunch, you have a choice between chicken fingers or cheese sticks for an appetizer; turkey, chicken, or veal for the main course; cake or pudding for dessert; and either Coke or Pepsi for a beverage. How many choices of possible meals do you have?
   a) 16.
   b) 24.
   c) 34.
   d) 36.
   e) 8.

3. For an office job, I need to pick 3 candidates out of a pool of 5. How many choices do I have?
   a) 60.
   b) 20.
   c) 10.
   d) 30.
   e) 50.

4. A contractor is supposed to choose 3 tiles out of a stack of 5 tiles to make as many patterns as possible. How many different patterns can he make?
   a) 10.
   b) 20.
   c) 30.
   d) 40.
   e) 60.

5. I have chores to do around the house on a weekend. There are 5 chores I must complete by the end of the day. I can choose to do them in any order, so long as they are all completed. How many choices do I have?
   a) 5.
   b) 25.
   c) 32.
   d) 3125.
   e) 120.

6. Next weekend, I have more chores to do around the house. There are 5 chores I must complete by the end of the day. I can choose to do any 2 of them in any order, and then do any 2 the next day again in any order, and then do the remaining 1 the following day. How many choices do I have?

a) 20.
b) 6.
c) 120.
d) 130.
e) 25.

7. A certain lottery play sheet has 10 numbers from which 5 have to be chosen. How many different ways can I pick the numbers?

a) 150.
b) 250.
c) 252.
d) 143.
e) 278.

8. At a buffet, there are 3 choices for an appetizer, 6 choices for a beverage, and 3 choices for an entrée. How many different ways can I select food from all the food choices?

a) 12.
b) 27.
c) 36.
d) 42.
e) 54.

9. If there is a basket of 10 assorted fruits, and I want to pick out 3 fruits, how many combinations of fruits do I have to choose from?

a) 130.
b) 210.
c) 310.
d) 120.
e) 100.

10. How many ways can I pick 3 numbers from a set of 10 numbers?

a) 720.
b) 120.
c) 180.
d) 150.
e) 880.

Test Your Knowledge: Fundamental Counting Principle, Permutations, Combinations – Answers

1. **c)**
The number of ways = 4 * 3 * 5 * 2 * 3 = 360.

2. **b)**
Multiply the possible number of choices for each item from which you can choose.

2 * 3 * 2 * 2 = 24.

3. **c)**
This is a combination problem. The order of the candidates does not matter.

The number of combinations = 5!/3!(5 - 3)! = 5 * 4/2 * 1 = 10.

4. **e)**
This is a permutation problem. The order in which the tiles are arranged is counted.

The number of patterns = 5!/(5 - 3)! = 5 * 4 * 3 = 60.

5. **e)**
This is a permutation problem. The order in which the chores are completed matters.

$^5P_5$ = 5!/(5 - 5)! = 5! = 5 * 4 * 3 * 2 * 1 = 120.

6. **c)**
$\#Choices_{today}$ = $^5P_2$ = 5!/(5 - 2)! = 5 * 4 = 20.

$\#Choices_{tomorrow}$ = $^3P_2$ = 3!/1! = 6.

$\#Choices_{day3}$ = 1.

The total number of permutations = 20 * 6 * 1 = 120.

7. **c)**
This is a combinations problem. The order of the numbers is not relevant.

$^{10}n_5$ = 10!/5!(10 - 5)! = 10 * 9 * 8 * 7 * 6/5 * 4 * 3 * 2 * 1 = 252.

8. **e)**
There are 3 ways to choose an appetizer, 6 ways to choose a beverage, and 3 ways to choose an entrée. The total number of choices = 3 * 6 * 3 = 54.

9. **d)**
$^{10}C_3$ = 10!/(3!(10 - 3)!) = 10!/(3! * 7!) = 10 * 9 * 8/3 * 2 * 1 = 120.

10. **b)**
$^{10}P_4$ = 10!/3!(10 - 3)! = 10 * 9 * 8/3 * 2 * 1 = 120.

Test Your Knowledge: Ratios, Proportions, Rate of Change

1. A class has 50% more boys than girls. What is the ratio of boys to girls?
   a) 4:3.
   b) 3:2.
   c) 5:4.
   d) 10:7.
   e) 7:5.

2. A car can travel 30 miles on 4 gallons of gas. If the gas tank has a capacity of 16 gallons, how far can it travel if the tank is ¾ full?
   a) 120 miles.
   b) 90 miles.
   c) 60 miles.
   d) 55 miles.
   e) 65 miles.

3. The profits of a company increase by $5000 every year for five years and then decrease by $2000 for the next two years. What is the average rate of change in the company profit for that seven-year period?
   a) $1000/year.
   b) $2000/year.
   c) $3000/year.
   d) $4000/year.
   e) $5000/year.

4. A bag holds 250 marbles. Of those marbles, 40% are red, 30% are blue, 10% are green, and 20% are black. How many marbles of each color are present in the bag?
   a) Red = 90; Blue = 80; Green = 30; Black = 40.
   b) Red = 80; Blue = 60; Green = 30; Black = 80.
   c) Red = 100; Blue = 75; Green = 25; Black = 50.
   d) Red = 100; Blue = 70; Green = 30; Black = 50.
   e) Red = 120; Blue = 100; Green = 10; Black = 20.

5. Two students from a student body of 30 boys and 50 girls will be selected to serve on the school disciplinary committee. What is the probability that first a boy will be chosen, and then a girl?
   a) 1/1500.
   b) 1500/6400.
   c) 1500/6320.
   d) 1.
   e) 30/50.

6. If number n, divided by number m, gives a result of .5, what is the relationship between n and m?
   a) n is twice as big as m.
   b) m is three times as big as n.
   c) n is a negative number.
   d) m is a negative number.
   e) n is ½ of m.

7. In a fruit basket, there are 10 apples, 5 oranges, 5 pears, and 6 figs. If I select two fruits, what is the probability that I will first pick a pear and then an apple?

a) .07.
b) .08.
c) 1/13.
d) 13.
e) 5.

8. In a fruit basket, there are 3 apples, 5 oranges, 2 pears, and 2 figs. If I pick out two fruits, what is the probability that I will pick a fig first and then an apple?
Round to the nearest 100th.

a) .04.
b) .05.
c) .06.
d) .03.
e) .02.

9. If x workers can make p toys in c days, how many toys can y workers make in d days if they work at the same rate?

a) cp/qx.
b) cq/px.
c) cqy/px.
d) pdy/cx.
e) qy/px.

10. If a car travels 35 miles on a gallon of gas, how far will it travel on 13 gallons of gas?

a) 189 miles.
b) 255 miles.
c) 335 miles.
d) 455 miles.
e) 500 miles.

Test Your Knowledge: Ratios, Proportions, Rate of Change – Answers

1. **b)**
   The ratio of boys to girls is 150:100, or 3:2.

2. **b)**
   A full tank has 16 gallons → 3/4 of the tank = 12 gallons. The car can travel 30 miles on 4 gallons, so 12 gallons would take the car 12 * 30/4 = 90 miles.

3. **c)**
   Average Rate of Change = the change in value/change in time = (total profit – initial profit)/change in time. Initial profit = 0; change in time = 7 years.

   Increase = 5000 * 5 = 25000; decrease = 2000 * 2 = 4000; total profit = 25000 - 4000 = 21000.

   (21000 - 0)/7 years = $3000/year.

4. **c)**
   Total number of marbles = 250.

   #red marbles = 250 * 40/100 = 250 * .4 = 100.

   #blue marbles = 250 * .3 = 75.

   #green marbles = 250 * .1 = 25.

   #black marbles = 250 * .2 = 50.

5. **c)**
   The probability of selecting a boy from the entire group = 30:80.

   The probability of selecting a girl from the remaining group = 50:79.

   The probability of selecting a boy and a girl is (30:80) * (50:79) = 1500:6320.

6. **e)**
   If $n/m = .5$, then $n = .5m$, or $n = ½$ of m.

7. **c)**
   The total number of fruit = 26.

   The probability of picking a pear = 5:26.

   The probability of picking an apple = 10:25.

   The probability of picking a pear and an apple = 5:26 * 10:25 = 50:650 = 1:13.

8. b)
The total number of fruit = 12.

The probability of picking a fig = 2:12.

The probability of picking an apple = 3:11.

The probability of picking a fig and an apple = 2:12 * 3:11 = 6:132 = .045.

Round up to .05.

9. d)
The overall rate for x workers = the number of toys/ the number of days, *p/c*. The number of toys one worker makes per day (rate) = *p/cx*. If *q* is the number of toys *y* workers make, and the rates are equal, then the number of toys made = the rate *x*.

The number of days * the number of workers gives us *q* = *p/cx* (*dy*), so:

q = *pdy/cx*.

10. d)
The distance travelled = (35/1)(13) = 455 miles.

Chapter 2: English and Language Arts

The first step in getting ready for this section of the test consists of reviewing the basic techniques used to determine the meanings of words you are not familiar with. The good news is that you have been using various degrees of these techniques since you first began to speak. Sharpening these skills will also help you with the ELA subtest.

Following each section you will find a practice drill. Use your score on these to determine if you need to study that particular subject matter further. At the end of the chapter you will find a review of the concepts and a chapter test. The questions found on the practice drills and chapter test are not given in the two formats found on the ELA subtest; rather they are designed to reinforce the skills needed to score well on the ELA subtest.

VOCABULARY and GRAMMAR

It's time to review those basic techniques used to determine the meanings of words with which you are not familiar. Don't worry though! The good news is that you have been using various degrees of these techniques since you first began to speak.

We have not included a vocabulary list in this book, because reading definitions from a page is the worst way to improve word knowledge. Interaction, and seeing the words used in context, is the best way to learn. We recommend using flashcards to improve your vocabulary knowledge – there are many resources available online. The best we've found is www.vocabulary.com/il; but you should find what suits you specifically!

Below are techniques for improving and utilizing the vocabulary you already have.

Context Clues

The most fundamental vocabulary skill is using the context of a word to determine its meaning. Your ability to observe sentences closely is extremely useful when it comes to understanding new vocabulary words.

Types of Context

There are two different types of context that can help you understand the meaning of unfamiliar words: **sentence context** and **situational context**. Regardless of which context is present, these types of questions are not really testing your knowledge of vocabulary; rather, they test your ability to comprehend the meaning of a word through its usage.

Situational context is context that comes from understanding the situation in which a word or phrase occurs.

Sentence context occurs within the sentence that contains the vocabulary word. To figure out words using sentence context clues, you should first determine the most important words in the sentence.

Example: I had a hard time reading her <u>illegible</u> handwriting.

a) Neat.
b) Unsafe.
c) Sloppy.
d) Educated.

Already, you know that this sentence is discussing something that is hard to read. Look at the word that **illegible** is describing: **handwriting**. Based on context clues, you can tell that illegible means that her handwriting is hard to read.

Next, look at the answer choices. Choice **a) Neat** is obviously a wrong answer because neat handwriting would not be difficult to read. Choice **b) Unsafe** and **d) Educated** don't make sense. Therefore, choice **c) Sloppy** is the best answer choice.

Types of Clues

There are four types of clues that can help you understand context, and therefore the meaning of a word. They are **restatement**, **positive/negative**, **contrast**, and **specific detail**.

Restatement clues occur when the definition of the word is clearly stated in the sentence.

Example: The dog was <u>dauntless</u> in the face of danger, braving the fire to save the girl.

a) Difficult.
b) Fearless.
c) Imaginative.

Demonstrating **bravery** in the face of danger would be **fearless,** choice **b)**. In this case, the context clues tell you exactly what the word means.

Positive/negative clues can tell you whether a word has a positive or negative meaning.

Example: The magazine gave a great review of the fashion show, stating the clothing was **sublime**.

a) Horrible.
b) Exotic.
c) Bland
d) Gorgeous.

The sentence tells us that the author liked the clothing enough to write a **great** review, so you know that the best answer choice is going to be a positive word. Therefore, you can immediately rule out choices **a)** and **c)** because they are negative words. **Exotic** is a neutral word; alone, it doesn't inspire a **great** review. The most positive word is gorgeous, which makes choice **d) Gorgeous** the best answer.

The following sentence uses both restatement and positive/negative clues:

"Janet suddenly found herself destitute, so poor she could barely afford to eat."

The second part of the sentence clearly indicates that destitute is a negative word; it also restates the meaning: very poor.

Contrast clues include the opposite meaning of a word. Words like **but**, **on the other hand**, and **however** are tip-offs that a sentence contains a contrast clue.

Example: Beth did not spend any time preparing for the test, but Tyron kept a rigorous study schedule.

a) Strict.
b) Loose.
c) Boring.
d) Strange.

In this case, the word **but** tells us that Tyron studied in a different way than Beth. If Beth did not study very hard, then Tyron did study hard for the test. The best answer here, therefore, is choice **a) Strict**.

Specific detail clues give a precise detail that can help you understand the meaning of the word.

Example: The box was heavier than he expected and it began to become cumbersome.

a) Impossible.
b) Burdensome.
c) Obligated.
d) Easier.

Start by looking at the specific details of the sentence. Choice **d)** can be eliminated right away because it is doubtful it would become **easier** to carry something that is **heavier**. There are also no clues in the sentence to indicate he was **obligated** to carry the box, so choice **c)** can also be disregarded. The sentence specifics, however, do tell you that the package was cumbersome because it was heavy to carry; something heavy to carry is a burden, which is **burdensome**, choice **b)**.

It is important to remember that more than one of these clues can be present in the same sentence. The more there are, the easier it will be to determine the meaning of the word, so look for them.

Denotation and Connotation

As you know, many English words have more than one meaning. For example, the word **quack** has two distinct definitions: the sound a duck makes; and a person who publicly pretends to have a skill, knowledge, education, or qualification which they do not possess.

The **denotations** of a word are the dictionary definitions.

The **connotations** of a word are the implied meaning(s) or emotion which the word makes you think.

> **Example**: "Sure," Pam said excitedly, "I'd just love to join your club; it sounds so exciting!"
>
> Now, read this sentence:
>
> "Sure," Pam said sarcastically, "I'd just love to join your club; it sounds so exciting!"

Even though the two sentences only differ by one word, they have completely different meanings. The difference, of course, lies in the words "excitedly" and "sarcastically."

Nouns, Pronouns, Verbs, Adjectives, and Adverbs

Nouns

Nouns are people, places, or things. They are typically the subject of a sentence. For example, "The hospital was very clean." The noun is "hospital;" it is the "place."

Pronouns

Pronouns essentially "replace" nouns. This allows a sentence to not sound repetitive. Take the sentence: "Sam stayed home from school because Sam was not feeling well." The word "Sam" appears twice in the same sentence. Instead, you can use a pronoun and say, "Sam stayed at home because *he* did not feel well." Sounds much better, right?

Most Common Pronouns:

- I, me, mine, my.
- You, your, yours.
- He, him, his.
- She, her, hers.
- It, its.
- We, us, our, ours.
- They, them, their, theirs.

Verbs

Remember the old commercial, "Verb: It's what you do"? That sums up verbs in a nutshell! Verbs are the "action" of a sentence; verbs "do" things.

They can, however, be quite tricky. Depending on the subject of a sentence, the tense of the word (past, present, future, etc.), and whether or not they are regular or irregular, verbs have many variations.

Example: "He runs to second base." The verb is "runs." This is a "regular verb."

Example: "I am 7 years old." The verb in this case is "am." This is an "irregular verb."

As mentioned, verbs must use the correct tense – and that tense must remain the same throughout the sentence. "I was baking cookies and eat some dough." That sounded strange, didn't it? That's because the two verbs "baking" and "eat" are presented in different tenses. "Was baking" occurred in the past; "eat," on the other hand, occurs in the present. Instead, it should be "**ate** some dough."

Adjectives

Adjectives are words that describe a noun and give more information. Take the sentence: "The boy hit the ball." If you want to know more about the noun "boy," then you could use an adjective to describe it.

"The **little** boy hit the ball." An adjective simply provides more information about a noun or subject in a sentence.

Adverb
For some reason, many people have a difficult time with adverbs – but don't worry! They are really quite simple. Adverbs are similar to adjectives in that they provide more information; however, they describe verbs, adjectives, and even other adverbs. They do **not** describe nouns – that's an adjective's job.

Take the sentence: "The doctor said she hired a new employee."

It would give more information to say: "The doctor said she **recently** hired a new employee." Now we know more about *how* the action was executed. Adverbs typically describe when or how something has happened, how it looks, how it feels, etc.

Good vs. Well
A very common mistake that people make concerning adverbs is the misuse of the word "good."

"Good" is an adjective – things taste good, look good, and smell good. "Good" can even be a noun – "Superman does good" – when the word is speaking about "good" vs. "evil." HOWEVER, "good" is never an adverb.

People commonly say things like, "I did really good on that test," or, "I'm good." Ugh! This is NOT the correct way to speak! In those sentences, the word "good" is being used to describe an action: how a person **did**, or how a person **is**. Therefore, the adverb "well" should be used. "I did really **well** on that test." "I'm **well**."

The correct use of "well" and "good" can make or break a person's impression of your grammar – make sure to always speak correctly!

The Parts of Words

Although you are not expected to know every word in the English language for your test, you will need to have the ability to use deductive reasoning to find the choice that is the best match for the word in question, which is why we are going to explain how to break a word into its parts of meaning

prefix – root – suffix

One trick in dividing a word into its parts is to first divide the word into its **syllables**. To show how syllables can help you find roots and affixes, we'll use the word **descendant,** which means one who comes from an ancestor. Start by dividing the word into its individual syllables; this word has three: **de-scend-ant**. The next step is to look at the beginning and end of the word, and then determine if these syllables are prefixes, suffixes, or possible roots. You can then use the meanings of each part to guide you in defining the word. When you divide words into their specific parts, they do not always add up to an exact definition, but you will see a relationship between their parts.

Note: This trick won't always work in every situation, because not all prefixes, roots, and suffixes have only one syllable. For example, take the word **monosyllabic** (which ironically means "one syllable"). There are five syllables in that word, but only three parts. The prefix is "mono," meaning "one." The root "syllab" refers to "syllable," while the suffix "ic" means "pertaining to." Therefore, we have one very long word which means "pertaining to one syllable."

The more familiar you become with these fundamental word parts, the easier it will be to define unfamiliar words. Although the words found on the Word Knowledge subtest are considered vocabulary words learned by the tenth grade level of high school, some are still less likely to be found in an individual's everyday vocabulary. The root and affixes list in this chapter uses more common words as examples to help you learn them more easily. Don't forget that you use word roots and affixes every day, without even realizing it. Don't feel intimidated by the long list of roots and affixes (prefixes and suffixes) at the end of this chapter, because you already know and use them every time you communicate with some else, verbally and in writing. If you take the time to read through the list just once a day for two weeks, you will be able to retain most of them and understand a high number of initially unfamiliar words.

Roots, Prefixes, and Suffixes

Roots

Roots are the building blocks of all words. Every word is either a root itself or has a root. Just as a plant cannot grow without roots, neither can vocabulary, because a word must have a root to give it meaning.

Example: The test instructions were **unclear.**

The root is what is left when you strip away all the prefixes and suffixes from a word. In this case, take away the prefix "un-," and you have the root **clear**.

Roots are not always recognizable words, because they generally come from Latin or Greek words, such as **nat**, a Latin root meaning **born**. The word native, which means a person born of a referenced placed, comes from this root, so does the word prenatal, meaning before birth. Yet, if you used the prefix **nat** instead of born, just on its own, no one would know what you were talking about.
Words can also have more than one root. For example, the word **omnipoten**t means all powerful. Omnipotent is a combination of the roots **omni-**, meaning all or every, and **-potent**, meaning power or strength. In this case, **omni** cannot be used on its own as a single word, but **potent** can.

Again, it is important to keep in mind that roots do not always match the exact definitions of words and they can have several different spellings, but breaking a word into its parts is still one of the best ways to determine its meaning.

Prefixes

Prefixes are syllables added to the beginning of a word and suffixes are syllables added to the end of the word. Both carry assigned meanings. The common name for prefixes and suffixes is **affixes**. Affixes do not have to be attached directly to a root and a word can often have more than one prefix and/or suffix. Prefixes and suffixes can be attached to a word to completely change the word's meaning or to enhance the word's original meaning. Although they don't mean much to us on their own, when attached to other words affixes can make a world of difference.

Let's use the word **prefix** itself as an example:

Fix means to place something securely.

Pre means before.

Prefix means to place something before or in front.

Suffixes

Suffixes come after the root of a word.

Example: Feminism

Femin is a root. It means female, woman.

-ism means act, practice or process.

Feminism is the defining and establishing of equal political, economic, and social rights for women.

Unlike prefixes, **suffixes** can be used to change a word's part of speech.

Example: "Randy raced to the finish line." VS "Shana's costume was very racy."

In the first sentence, raced is a verb. In the second sentence, racy is an adjective. By changing the suffix from **-ed** to **-y**, the word race changes from a verb into an adjective, which has an entirely different meaning.

Although you cannot determine the meaning of a word by a prefix or suffix alone, you *can* use your knowledge of what root words mean to eliminate answer choices; indicating if the word is positive or negative can give you a partial meaning of the word.

Study Tips for Improving Vocabulary and Grammar

1. You're probably pretty computer savvy and know the Internet very well. Visit the Online Writing Lab website, which is sponsored by Purdue University, at http://owl.english.purdue.edu. This site provides you with an excellent overview of syntax, writing style, and strategy. It also has helpful and lengthy review sections that include multiple-choice "Test Your Knowledge" quizzes, which provide immediate answers to the questions.

2. It's beneficial to read the entire passage first to determine its intended meaning BEFORE you attempt to answer any questions. Doing so provides you with key insight into a passage's syntax (especially verb tense, subject-verb agreement, modifier placement, writing style, and punctuation).

3. When you answer a question, use the "Process-of-Elimination Method" to determine the best answer. Try each of the four answers and determine which one BEST fits with the meaning of the paragraph. Find the BEST answer. Chances are that the BEST answer is the CORRECT answer.

Test Your Knowledge: Vocabulary and Grammar

1. "The medication must be properly administered to the patient."
Which of the words in the above sentence is an adverb?
a) Medication.
b) Properly.
c) Administered.
d) Patient.

2. "The old man had trouble walking if he did not have his walker and had a long way to go."
What is the subject of the sentence?
a) Walker.
b) His.
c) Trouble.
d) Man.

3. "The boy decided ___ would ride his bike now that the sun was shining."
Which of the following pronouns completes the sentence?
a) His.
b) Him.
c) He.
d) They.

4. "The impatient student hurried through the test and failed as a result."
Which word is an adjective?
a) Hurried.
b) Result.
c) Impatient.
d) Student.

5. Correct the verb: "The nurse decided it were a good time to follow up with a patient about their medication."
a) Was.
b) Is.
c) Has.
d) No error.

Use context clues to determine the meaning of each underlined word.

6. His story didn't seem very <u>realistic</u>; even though it was a documentary.
a) Believable.
b) Humorous.
c) Poetic.
d) Exciting.

7. Listening to music too loudly, especially through headphones, can <u>impair</u> your hearing.
   a) Damage.
   b) Heighten.
   c) Use.
   d) Ensure.

8. Kelly's game happened to <u>coincide</u> with the Sue's recital.
   a) Happen before.
   b) Occur at the same time.
   c) Occur afterward.
   d) Not happen.

9. The weather has been very extreme lately; thankfully, today it's much more <u>temperate</u>.
   a) Troubling.
   b) Beautiful.
   c) Cold.
   d) Moderate.

10. He knew he couldn't win the race after falling off his bike, so he had to <u>concede</u>.
   a) Continue.
   b) Give up.
   c) Challenge.
   d) Be thankful.

11. The editor, preferring a more <u>terse</u> writing style, cut 30% of the words from the article.
   a) Elegant.
   b) Factual.
   c) Descriptive.
   d) Concise.

12. Victor Frankenstein spent the last years of his life chasing his <u>elusive</u> monster, which was always one step ahead.
   a) Unable to be compared.
   b) Unable to be captured.
   c) Unable to be forgotten.
   d) Unable to be avoided.

13. Certain <u>passages</u> were taken from the book for the purpose of illustration.
   a) Excerpts.
   b) Contents.
   c) Paragraphs.
   d) Tables.

14. The investigator searched among the <u>ruins</u> for the cause of the fire.
   a) Terminal.
   b) Foundation.
   c) Rubble.
   d) Establishment.

15. To make her novels more engaging, Cynthia was known to <u>embellish</u> her writing with fictitious details.

a) Add to.
b) Detract.
c) Isolate.
d) Disavow.

16. Robert's well-timed joke served to <u>diffuse</u> the tension in the room and the party continued happily.

a) Refuse.
b) Intensify.
c) Create.
d) Soften.

17. I had a difficult time understanding the book because the author kept <u>digressing</u> to unrelated topics.

a) Deviating, straying.
b) Regressing, reverting.
c) Changing the tone.
d) Expressing concisely.

18. The senator <u>evaded</u> almost every question.

a) Avoided.
b) Answered indirectly.
c) Refused to answer directly.
d) Deceived.

19. Sammie hasn't come out of her room all afternoon, but I would <u>surmise</u> that it is because she is upset about not being able to go to the mall.

a) Confirm.
b) Surprise.
c) Believe.
d) Guess.

20. The details can be worked out later; what's important is that the company follows the <u>crux</u> of the argument, which is that everyone be paid equally.

a) Overall tone.
b) Specific fact.
c) Main point.
d) Logic, reasoning.

Use context clues to choose the best word to complete the sentence.

21. Mr. Collins ______ tomatoes so vehemently that he felt ill just smelling them.

a) Resented
b) Disliked
c) Detested
d) Hated

22. We were rolling on the ground with laughter during the ______ new movie.

a) Comical
b) Humorous
c) Amusing
d) Hilarious

23. Tina's parents made us feel right at home during our visit to their house with their generous ________.

a) Unselfishness
b) Politeness
c) Hospitality
d) Charity

24. Although his mother was not happy that he broke the window, she was pleased that he was ______ about it.

a) Honest
b) Trustworthy
c) Authentic
d) Decent

25. The soldiers ______ to their feet immediately when then officer walked into the room.

a) Stood
b) Leapt
c) Rose
d) Skipped

Try to find the root in each of the underlined words.

26. The bridge was out, so the river was <u>impassable</u>.

a) Im-
b) -pass-
c) -a-
d) –able

27. I am usually on time, but my husband is <u>chronically</u> late.

a) Chron-
b) -chronical-
c) -ally-
d) -ic

28. The only way to succeed is by <u>striving</u> to do your best.

a) Str-
a) Striv-
b) Strive-
c) -ing

29. We drifted along lazily on the tranquil river.

a) Tra-
b) -qui-
c) Tranq-
d) -uil

30. A pediatrician is a doctor who takes care of children.

a) Ped-
b) -ia-
c) -tri-
d) -cian

Choose the word that shares the same root as the given word.

31. Audible:

a) Auditorium.
b) Because.
c) Dribble.
d) Bagel.

32. Nominate:

a) Eaten.
b) Minute.
c) Hated.
d) Synonym.

33. Disappoint:

a) Disappear.
b) Appointment.
c) Interest.
d) Potato.

34. Dilute:

a) Flute.
b) Dictate.
c) Pollute.
d) Hesitate.

35. Sympathy:

a) System.
b) Empathy.
c) Pattern.
d) Rhythm.

36. Science:

a) Conscious.
b) Once.
c) Alien.
d) Parasite.

37. Incline:

a) Recline.
b) Independent.
c) Cluster.
d) Twine.

For each question below, use the Latin root to determine the meaning of the underlined word.

38. An <u>amiable</u> person is:

a) Talkative, loud.
b) Truthful, honest.
c) Highly educated.
d) Friendly, good-natured.

39. A <u>lucid</u> argument:

a) Is very clear and intelligible.
b) Is loosely held together, tenuous.
c) Frequently digresses.
d) Errs repeatedly in its logic.

40. A <u>complacent</u> person:

a) Frequently makes mistakes, but does not accept responsibility.
b) Likes to pick fights.
c) Is contented to a fault, self-satisfied.
d) Is known to tell lies, embellish the truth.

41. To <u>exacerbate</u> a problem means:

a) To solve it.
b) To analyze it.
c) To lessen it.
d) To worsen it.

42. To measure the <u>veracity</u> of something is to measure its:

a) Value or worth.
b) Truthfulness.
c) Weight.
d) Life force.

43. Something that is <u>eloquent</u> is:

a) Dull, trite, hackneyed.
b) Expressed in a powerful and effective manner.
c) Very old, antiquated.
d) Equally divided or apportioned.

44. To <u>indict</u> someone is to:

a) Pick a fight with that person.
b) Stop or block that person from doing something.
c) Charge that person with a crime.
d) Love that person dearly.

45. A <u>quiescent</u> place is:

a) Very isolated.
b) Tumultuous, chaotic.
c) Sacred.
d) Still, at rest.

What are the affixes in each word?

46. Disease:

a) Dis-.
b) -ise-.
c) -eas-.
d) –ase.

47. Uncomfortable:

a) Un-.
b) Un-, -com-.
c) -fort-.
d) Un-, -able.

48. Disrespected:

a) Re-, -spect, -ed.
b) Dis-, -ed.
c) Dis-, re-, -ed.
d) Respect-, -ed.

49. Impressive:

a) Im-, -ive.
b) –ive.
c) Press-, -ive.
d) Impre-, -ive.

50. Predated:

a) Pre-.
b) Pre-, -d.
c) Pre-, -ed.
d) –d.

Using your knowledge of prefixes and root words, try to determine the meaning of the words in the following questions.

51. To take precaution is to:

a) Prepare before doing something.
b) Remember something that happened earlier.
c) Become aware of something for the first time.
d) Try to do something again.

52. To reorder a list is to:

a) Use the same order again.
b) Put the list in a new order.
c) Get rid of the list.
d) Find the list.

53. An antidote to a disease is:

a) Something that is part of the disease.
b) Something that works against the disease.
c) Something that makes the disease worse.
d) Something that has nothing to do with the disease.

54. Someone who is multiethnic:

a) Likes only certain kinds of people.
b) Lives in the land of his or her birth.
c) Is from a different country.
d) Has many different ethnicities.

55. Someone who is misinformed has been:

a) Taught something new.
b) Told the truth.
c) Forgotten.
d) Given incorrect information.

Choose the best answer to each question. (Remember you are looking for the closest meaning.)

56. Exorbitant means:

a) Belonging to a group.
b) To orbit.
c) Beneath conscious awareness.
d) Far beyond what is normal or reasonable.

57. Denunciation means:

a) To denounce or openly condemn.
b) Critical, of or like a condemnation.
c) One who denounces or openly condemns another.
d) The act of denouncing or openly condemning.

58. Metamorphosis means:

a) To transform.
b) One who has changed.
c) A transformation.
d) Tending to change frequently.

59. To reconcile means:

a) To reestablish a close relationship between.
b) To move away from.
c) To undermine.
d) To surpass or outdo.

60. Didactic means:

a) A teacher or instructor.
b) Intended to instruct, moralizing.
c) To preach or moralize.
d) The process of instructing.

61. Unilateral means:

a) To multiply.
b) Understated.
c) Literal.
d) One-sided.

62. Subordinate means:

a) Under someone else's authority or control.
b) Organized according to rank; hierarchical.
c) Something ordinary or average, without distinction.
d) Repeated frequently to aid memorization.

63. Incisive means:

a) Insight.
b) Worthy of consideration.
c) Penetrating.
d) To act forcefully.

64. Intermittent means:

a) Badly handled.
b) Occurring at intervals
c) Greatly varied.
d) A number between one and ten.

65. Miscreant means:

a) Someone who is unconventional.
b) Someone who lacks creativity.
c) A very naive person.
d) An evil person or villain.

Test Your Knowledge: Vocabulary and Grammar – Answers

1. **b)**
   "Properly" is the adverb which describes the verb "administered."

2. **d)**
   Although there are other nouns in the sentence, the "man" is the subject.

3. **c)**
   "He" is the correct answer; the other pronouns are possessive or otherwise in the wrong tense.

4. **c)**
   "Impatient" describes the noun "student."

5. **a)**
   "Was" is the correct answer; the other choices are in the wrong tense.

6. a) **Believable**.
   Realistic means accurate, truthful, and believable.

7. a) **Damage.**
   This is the only logical choice.

8. b) **Occur at the same time**.
   According to information in the sentence, the game was scheduled at the same time as the recital.

9. d) **Moderate**.
   The context says that the weather has been "extreme." It does not say if the weather has been extremely hot or cold; therefore, choices **b) Beautiful** and **c) Cold** can be ruled out. The sentence also indicates a change from negative to positive making moderate the best choice.

10. b) **Give up**.
    The speaker of the sentence knows they cannot win, so choice **b)** is the best choice.

11. d) **Concise.**
    Terse means concise, using no unnecessary words. The main clue is that the editor cut words from the article, reducing its wordiness.

12. b) **Unable to be captured.**
    Elusive means evasive, difficult to capture.

13. a) **Excerpt.**
    An excerpt is a passage or quote from a book, article, or other publication

14. c) **Rubble** is synonymous with ruin.

15. a) Add to.
To embellish is to add details to a story to make it more appealing.

16. d) Soften.
The clues *tension* and *continue happily* tell you that **d)** is the best choice

17. a) To deviate, stray.
To digress means to deviate; to stray from the main subject in writing or speaking.

18. a) To avoid.
To evade means to avoid by cleverness. The senator avoids answering the question by changing the subject.

19. d) Guess.
The speaker is guessing why Samantha is upset based on circumstances; she has not actually given a reason.

20. c) Main point.
Crux means the central or main point, especially of a problem. The main context clue is that the speaker isn't concerned with the details but is focused on getting agreement on the main point.

21. c) Detested.
The knowledge that Mr. Collins feels ill just smelling tomatoes suggests that his hatred for tomatoes is intense; therefore, the best choice will be the most negative. To **dislike** tomatoes – choice **b)** – is the most neutral word, so this choice can be ruled out. **Resented** is a word that generally applies to people or their actions, ruling out choice **a).** Given the choice between **c)** and **d),** the most negative is **c) Detested.**

22. d) Hilarious.
The movie must be extremely funny for the audience to have this sort of reaction, and, while all of the answer choices are synonyms for funny, the only one that means extremely funny is choice **d) Hilarious.**

23. c) Hospitality.
Although all four choices describe different types of kindness, **unselfishness** – choice **a)** – can be ruled out because it has the same basic meaning as the adjective, generous. Choice **d) Charity** is a kindness usually associated with those less fortunate; since nothing in the context indicates this type of relationship, this choice can also be eliminated.

Left with choices **b) Politeness** and **c) Hospitality**, hospitality best describes the kindness of welcoming someone into your home.

24. a) Honest.
Again we have a case in which all of the word choices are synonyms for the word honest. In this case, the most neutral word is the best choice. Choice **b) Trustworthy**, **c) Authentic**, and **d) Decent** do not make as much sense as the most basic synonym, **honest.**

25. b) Leapt. The word immediately is the main clue. **a) Stood** and **c) Rose** are neutral words that do not convey a sense of urgency. Choice **b) Leapt** is the only word that implies the immediacy demanded by the sentence context.

26. b) –pass- .

27. a) Chron-.

28. c) Strive-.

29. b) –qui-.
Quies is a Latin root meaning rest or quiet.

30. a) Ped-.
Ped is a Latin root meaning child or education. You might recognize that the suffix **-cian** refers to what someone does, such as physician or beautician. The suffix **-iatr** relates to doctors, as you can see in the words psychiatry and podiatry. Both suffixes support the root of the word.

31. a) Auditorium.
From the Latin root **aud**, meaning hearing or listening.

32. d) Synonym.
The words nominate and synonym share the root, **nom**, meaning name. Remember, roots are not necessarily going to be in the same position in other words.

33. b) Appointment.
Greek root **poie**, meaning to make.

34. c) Pollute.
Both dilute and pollute come from the root **lut**, meaning to wash.

35. b) Empathy.
The words sympathy and empathy come from the Greek root **path,** meaning feeling, suffering, or disease.

36. a) Conscious.
Science and conscious share the Latin root **sci,** which means to know.

37. a) Recline.
The words incline and recline both share the Greek root ***clin*****,** meaning to lean toward or bend.

38. d)
The root **am** means love. Amiable means friendly and agreeable or good natured, likeable, or pleasing.

39. a)
The root **luc/lum/lus** means light. Lucid means very clear, easy to understand, intelligible.

40. c)
The root **plac** means to please. Complacent means contented to a fault; self-satisfied (pleased with oneself).

41. d) The root **ac** means sharp, bitter. To exacerbate means to make worse or to increase the severity, violence, or bitterness of.

42. b)
The root **ver** means truth. Veracity means truth or truthfulness.

43. b)
The root **loc/log/loqu** means word or speech. Eloquent means expressed in a powerful, fluent, and persuasive manner.

44. c)
The root **dic/dict/dit** means to say, tell, or use words. To indict means to formally accuse of or charge with a crime.

45. d)
The root **qui** means quiet. Quiescent means inactive, quiet, or at rest.

46. a) Dis-.
The prefix **dis-** means away from, deprive of, reversal, or not. If someone has a **disease** they are not well.

47. d) Un-, **-able**.
The prefix **un-** means not. The suffix **-able** means ability or worthy of. **Uncomfortable** means not able to be in a state of comfort.

48. c) Dis-, **re-**, **-ed**.
The prefix **dis-** means away from, reversal, or not. The prefix **re-** means back or again. The suffix **-ed** indicates that the word is in the past tense. **Disrespected** means showed a lack of respect towards.

49. a) Im-, **-ive**.
The prefix **im-** means in, into, or within. The suffix **-ive** means having the nature of. **Impressive** means having the ability inspire an internal feeling of awe.

50. c) Pre-, **-ed**.
The prefix **pre-** means before. The suffix **-ed** indicates that the word is in the past tense. **Predated** means came before the date.

51. a) Prepare before doing something.
Pre- means before; to take **caution** is to be careful or take heed.

52. b) Put the list in a new order.
Re- means again. In this case, order means organize. Reorder then means to organize the list again or to put the list into a different order.

53. b) Something that works against the disease.
The prefix **anti-** means against. An **antidote** is something that works against a disease or a poison.

54. d) Has many different ethnicities.
The prefix **multi-** means many. Someone who is **multiethnic** has relatives from many different ethnic groups.

55. d) Given incorrect information.
Mis- means opposite, and to be **informed** is to have the correct information.

56. d) Far beyond what is normal or reasonable.
The prefix **ex-** means out, out of, away from.

57. a) The act of denouncing or openly condemning.
The prefix **de-** means against, the root **nounc** means to state or declare, and the noun suffix **-tion** means the act or state of.

58. c) A transformation.
The prefix **meta-** means change, while the root **morph** means shape or form, and the **noun** suffix **-sis** means the process of. **Metamorphosis** means a marked change of form or a transformation.

59. a) Means to reestablish a relationship.
The prefix **re-** means back or again and, the root **con** means with. Together they mean back together again or reestablishing a relationship.

60. b) Intended to instruct or moralize.
The adjective suffix **-ic** means pertaining or relating to, having the quality of. Only choices **b)** and **d)** define a quality, and choice **d)** would require an additional suffix.

61. d) One-sided.
The prefix **uni-** means one.

62. a) Under someone else's authority or control.
The prefix **sub-** means under, beneath or below.

63. c) Penetrating.
The adjective suffix **-ive** means having the nature of.

64. b) Occurring at intervals.
The prefix **inter-** means between or among.

65. d) An evil person or villain.
The prefix **mis-** means bad, evil, or wrong. The suffix **–ant** means an agent or something that performs the action.

Chapter 3: Reading

There are three types of questions that you can encounter in the Reading Comprehension section of the TEAS:

1. **About the Author**: The question will ask about the author's attitude, thoughts, opinions, etc. When encountering a question asking specifically about the author, pay attention to context clues in the article. The answer may not be explicitly stated, but instead conveyed in the overall message.

2. **Passage Facts**: You must distinguish between facts and opinions presented in the passage. Remember, a fact is something verifiable or proven, whereas an opinion is simply a belief that cannot be proven for sure. For example: "The sky is blue" is a fact that cannot be argued; "the sky is a prettier blue today than it was yesterday" is an opinion, since there is no scientific basis for what makes the sky "prettier" to a person.

3. **Additional Information**: These questions will have you look at what kind of information could be added to or was missing from the passage. They may also ask in what direction the passage was going. Questions may ask what statement could be added to strengthen the author's statement, or weaken it; they may also provide a fill-in-the-blank option to include a statement that is missing from, but fits with the rest of, the passage. When looking over answer choices, read them with the passage to see if they sound correct in context.

Strategies

Despite the different types of questions you will face, there are some strategies for Reading Comprehension which apply across the board:

- **Read the Answer Choices First**, then read the passage. This will save you time, as you will know what to look out for as you read.

- **Use the Process of Elimination**. Some answer choices are obviously incorrect, and are relatively easy to detect. After reading the passage, eliminate those blatantly-incorrect answer choices; this increases your chance of finding the correct answer much more quickly.

- **Avoid "Negatives."** Generally, test-makers will not make negatives statements about anyone or anything. Statements will be either neutral or positive; so if it seems like an answer choice is making a negative connotation, it is very likely that the answer is intentionally false.

Here are some examples of the kinds of questions you may encounter in the Reading Section. Each passage will have at least one of the above listed question types – try to answer them for yourself before reading the solution. If you run into trouble, don't worry. We'll provide more practice drills later in the book, as well.

Sample One:

Exercise is a critical aspect for healthy development in children. Today, there is an epidemic of unhealthy children in the United States who will face health problems in adulthood due to poor diet and lack of exercise as children. This is a problem for all Americans, especially with the rising cost of health care.

It is vital that school systems and parents encourage their children to engage in a minimum of 30 minutes of cardiovascular exercise each day, meaning their heart rate is mildly increased for sustained period. This is proven to decrease the likelihood of development diabetes, becoming obese, and a multitude of other health problems. Also, children need a proper diet rich in fruits and vegetables so that they can grow and development physically, as well as learn healthy eating habits early on.

1. Which of the following describes the author's use of the word "vital"?

a) Debatable.
b) Very important.
c) Somewhat important.
d) Not important.
e) Indicator.

Answer: This is an example of an "About the Author" question. You can tell, from both the tone and the intention of the article, that the author feels very strongly about the health of children and that action should be taken. Therefore, answer **b)** is the correct choice.

2. Which of the following is a fact in the passage, not an opinion?

a) Fruits and vegetables are the best-tasting foods.
b) Children today are lazier than they were in previous generations.
c) The risk of diabetes in children is reduced by physical activity.
d) Health care costs too much.
e) Soccer is a better physical activity than tennis.

Answer: A fact is typically presented as a direct statement, not a comparison, which makes answer choice **c)** the correct answer. Notice that many of the incorrect answers contain words that can hint at it being an opinion such as "best," "better," "too much," or other comparisons. Also keep an eye out for answer choices that may be facts, but which are not stated in the passage.

3. What other information might the author have provided to strengthen the argument?

a) Example of fruits and vegetables children should eat.
b) How much health insurance costs today vs. 10 years ago.
c) How many people live in the United States today.
d) The rules of baseball and soccer.
e) How many calories the average person burns by running 1 mile.

Answer: All of the choices would provide additional information, but only one pertains specifically to the improvement of health in children: choice **a)**.

Sample Two:

My "office" measures a whopping 5 feet by 7 feet. A large desk is squeezed into one corner, leaving just enough room for a rickety chair between the desk and the wall. Yellow paint is peeling off the walls in dirty chunks. The ceiling is barely six feet tall; it's like a hat that I wear all day long. The window, a single 2 x 2 pane, looks out onto a solid brick wall just two feet away.

1. What is the main idea implied by this paragraph?

a) This office is small but comfortable.
b) This office is in need of repair.
c) This office is old and claustrophobic.
d) This office is large and luxurious.
e) None of the above.

Answer: Notice that all of the sentences in the passage relate to the office feeling small and cramped. The correct answer is choice **c)**. While choice **b)** is tempting, since one would think the office could use some repair, it is not the main point of the passage.

2. Which of the following describes the structure of the passage?

a) The passage asks a question, then explains the answer using supporting arguments.
b) The passage presents a statement, then follows with more detailed information.
c) The passage makes an argument, then provides three examples to support it.
d) The passage introduces a hypothesis, then explores more questions about the hypothesis.
e) The passage starts with an argument, which is countered with a different argument leaving the reader to make their own conclusion.

Answer: No questions, arguments, or hypothesis were provided anywhere in the passage. Simply a statement of the size of the office and then additional details were given afterward. The correct answer is choice **b)**.

3. What is the author's meaning of the use of the word "hat" in the passage?

a) An expression of a style of clothing the author prefers.
b) To illustrate how very close the ceiling is to the author's head.
c) The author does not like to wear hats, especially all day.
d) The author enjoys wearing hats.
e) None of the above.

Answer: The author uses the word "hat" to describe how low the ceiling sits in the office: that it feels as though it envelopes their head, much like a hat. While it can be inferred that the author does not like their office, there is no indication of whether the author likes or dislikes hats. The correct answer is choice **b)**.

Sample Three

1. Using the below Index, on which page would you find information on Organic Chemistry?

Science

Geology: 110-124
Astronomy: 126-137
Physics: 140-159
Chemistry: 161-170
Biology: 171-179

Math

Geometry: 201-209
Calculus: 210-222
Graphing: 225-251

a) 210-222
b) 225-251
c) 126-137
d) 161-170
e) None of the above

Answer: The correct answer is choice **d)**. Pretty simple, huh? These types of questions are the easiest that you will find on the TEAS. Simply look for key-words (in this case "Chemistry" is the only matching word), and then eliminate everything else that doesn't relate.

REVIEW: READING

This section will measure your ability to understand, analyze, and evaluate written passages. The passages will contain material from a variety of sources, and will cover a number of different topics.

The Main Idea

Finding and understanding the main idea of a text is an essential reading skill. When you look past the facts and information and get to the heart of what the writer is trying to say, that's the **main idea**.

Imagine that you're at a friend's home for the evening:

> "Here," he says, "Let's watch this movie."
>
> "Sure," you reply. "What's it about?"

You'd like to know a little about what you'll be watching, but your question may not get you a satisfactory answer, because you've only asked about the subject of the film. The subject—what the movie is about—is only half the story. Think, for example, about all the alien invasion films ever been made. While these films may share the same general subject, what they have to say about the aliens or about humanity's theoretical response to invasion may be very different. Each film has different ideas it wants to convey about a subject, just as writers write because they have something they want to say about a particular subject. When you look beyond the facts and information to what the writer really wants to say about his or her subject, you're looking for the main idea.

One of the most common questions on reading comprehension exams is, "What is the main idea of this passage?" How would you answer this question for the paragraph below?

> "Wilma Rudolph, the crippled child who became an Olympic running champion, is an inspiration for us all. Born prematurely in 1940, Wilma spent her childhood battling illness, including measles, scarlet fever, chicken pox, pneumonia, and polio, a crippling disease which at that time had no cure. At the age of four, she was told she would never walk again. But Wilma and her family refused to give up. After years of special treatment and physical therapy, 12-year-old Wilma was able to walk normally again. But walking wasn't enough for Wilma, who was determined to be an athlete. Before long, her talent earned her a spot in the 1956 Olympics, where she earned a bronze medal. In the 1960 Olympics, the height of her career, she won three gold medals."

What is the main idea of this paragraph? You might be tempted to answer, "Wilma Rudolph" or "Wilma Rudolph's life." Yes, Wilma Rudolph's life is the **subject** of the passage—who or what the passage is about—but the subject is not necessarily the main idea. The **main idea** is what the writer wants to say about this subject. What is the main thing the writer says about Wilma's life?

Which of the following statements is the main idea of the paragraph?

a) Wilma Rudolph was very sick as a child.
b) Wilma Rudolph was an Olympic champion.
c) Wilma Rudolph is someone to admire.

Main idea: The overall fact, feeling, or thought a writer wants to convey about his or her subject.

The best answer is **c)**: Wilma Rudolph is someone to admire. This is the idea the paragraph adds up to; it's what holds all of the information in the paragraph together. This example also shows two important characteristics of a main idea:

1. It is **general** enough to encompass all of the ideas in the passage.

2. It is an **assertion.** An assertion is a statement made by the writer.

The main idea of a passage must be general enough to encompass all of the ideas in the passage. It should be broad enough for all of the other sentences in that passage to fit underneath it, like people under an umbrella. Notice that the first two options, "Wilma Rudolph was very sick as a child" and "Wilma Rudolph was an Olympic champion", are too specific to be the main idea. They aren't broad enough to cover all of the ideas in the passage, because the passage talks about both her illnesses and her Olympic achievements. Only the third answer is general enough to be the main idea of the paragraph.

A main idea is also some kind of **assertion** about the subject. An assertion is a claim that something is true. Assertions can be facts or opinions, but in either case, an assertion should be supported by specific ideas, facts, and details. In other words, the main idea makes a general assertion that tells readers that something is true.

The supporting sentences, on the other hand, show readers that this assertion is true by providing specific facts and details. For example, in the Wilma Rudolph paragraph, the writer makes a general assertion: "Wilma Rudolph, the crippled child who became an Olympic running champion, is an inspiration for us all." The other sentences offer specific facts and details that prove why Wilma Rudolph is an inspirational person.

Writers often state their main ideas in one or two sentences so that readers can have a very clear understanding about the main point of the passage. A sentence that expresses the main idea of a paragraph is called a **topic sentence.**

Notice, for example, how the first sentence in the Wilma Rudolph paragraph states the main idea:

> "Wilma Rudolph, the crippled child who became an Olympic running champion, is an inspiration for us all."

This sentence is therefore the topic sentence for the paragraph. Topic sentences are often found at the beginning of paragraphs. Sometimes, though, writers begin with specific supporting ideas and lead up to the main idea, and in this case the topic sentence is often found at the end of the paragraph. Sometimes the topic sentence is even found somewhere in the middle, and other times there isn't a clear topic sentence at all—but that doesn't mean there isn't a main idea; the author has just chosen not to express it in a clear topic sentence. In this last case, you'll have to look carefully at the paragraph for clues about the main idea.

Main Ideas vs. Supporting Ideas

If you're not sure whether something is a main idea or a supporting idea, ask yourself the following question: is the sentence making a **general statement,** or is it providing **specific information?** In the Wilma Rudolph paragraph above, for example, all of the sentences except the first make specific statements. They are not general enough to serve as an umbrella or net for the whole paragraph.

Writers often provide clues that can help you distinguish between main ideas and their supporting ideas. Here are some of the most common words and phrases used to introduce specific examples:

1. **For example...**
2. **Specifically...**
3. **In addition...**
4. **Furthermore...**
5. **For instance...**
6. **Others...**
7. **In particular...**
8. **Some...**

These signal words tell you that a supporting fact or idea will follow. If you're having trouble finding the main idea of a paragraph, try eliminating sentences that begin with these phrases, because they will most likely be too specific to be a main ideas.

Implied Main Idea

When the main idea is **implied**, there's no topic sentence, which means that finding the main idea requires some detective work. But don't worry! You already know the importance of structure, word choice, style, and tone. Plus, you know how to read carefully to find clues, and you know that these clues will help you figure out the main idea.

For Example:

"One of my summer reading books was *The Windows of Time.* Though it's more than 100 pages long, I read it in one afternoon. I couldn't wait to see what happened to Evelyn, the main character. But by the time I got to the end, I wondered if I should have spent my afternoon doing something else. The ending was so awful that I completely forgot that I'd enjoyed most of the book."

There's no topic sentence here, but you should still be able to find the main idea. Look carefully at what the writer says and how she says it. What is she suggesting?

a) *The Windows of Time* is a terrific novel.
b) *The Windows of Time* is disappointing.
c) *The Windows of Time* is full of suspense.
d) *The Windows of Time* is a lousy novel.

The correct answer is **b)** – the novel is disappointing. How can you tell that this is the main idea? First, we can eliminate choice **c)**, because it's too specific to be a main idea. It deals only with one specific aspect of the novel (its suspense).

Sentences **a)**, **b)**, and **d)**, on the other hand, all express a larger idea – a general assertion about the quality of the novel. But only one of these statements can actually serve as a "net" for the whole paragraph. Notice that while the first few sentences praise the novel, the last two criticize it. Clearly, this is a mixed review.

Therefore, the best answer is **b)**. Sentence **a)** is too positive and doesn't account for the "awful" ending. Sentence **d)**, on the other hand, is too negative and doesn't account for the reader's sense of suspense and interest in the main character. But sentence **b)** allows for both positive and negative aspects – when a good thing turns bad, we often feel disappointed.

Now let's look at another example. Here, the word choice will be more important, so read carefully.

"Fortunately, none of Toby's friends had ever seen the apartment where Toby lived with his mother and sister. Sandwiched between two burnt-out buildings, his two-story apartment building was by far the ugliest one on the block. It was a real eyesore: peeling orange paint (orange!), broken windows, crooked steps, crooked everything. He could just imagine what his friends would say if they ever saw this poor excuse for a building."

Which of the following expresses the main idea of this paragraph?

a) Toby wishes he could move to a nicer building.
b) Toby wishes his dad still lived with them.
c) Toby is glad none of his friends know where he lives.
d) Toby is sad because he doesn't have any friends.

From the description, we can safely assume that Toby doesn't like his apartment building and wishes he could move to a nicer building **a)**. But that idea isn't general enough to cover the whole paragraph, because it's about his building.

Because the first sentence states that Toby has friends, the answer cannot be **d)**. We know that Toby lives only with his mother and little sister, so we might assume that he wishes his dad still lived with them, **b)**, but there's nothing in the paragraph to support that assumption, and this idea doesn't include the two main topics of the paragraph—Toby's building and Toby's friends.

What the paragraph adds up to is that Toby is terribly embarrassed about his building, and he's glad that none of his friends have seen it **c)**. This is the main idea. The paragraph opens with the word "fortunately," so we know that he thinks it's a good thing none of his friends have been to his house. Plus, notice how the building is described: "by far the ugliest on the block," which says a lot since it's stuck "between two burnt-out buildings." The writer calls it an "eyesore," and repeats "orange" with an exclamation point to emphasize how ugly the color is. Everything is "crooked" in this "poor excuse for a building." Toby is clearly ashamed of where he lives and worries about what his friends would think if they saw it.

Cause and Effect

Understanding cause and effect is important for reading success. Every event has at least one cause (what made it happen) and at least one effect (the result of what happened). Some events have more than one cause, and some have more than one effect. An event is also often part of a chain of causes and effects. Causes and effects are usually signaled by important transitional words and phrases.

Words Indicating Cause:

1. **Because (of)**

2. **Created (by)**

3. **Caused (by)**

4. **Since**

Words Indicating Effect:

1. **As a result**
2. **Since**
3. **Consequently**
4. **So**
5. **Hence**
6. **Therefore**

Sometimes, a writer will offer his or her opinion about why an event happened when the facts of the cause(s) aren't clear. Or a writer may predict what he or she thinks will happen because of a certain event (its effects). If this is the case, you need to consider how reasonable those opinions are. Are the writer's ideas logical? Does the writer offer support for the conclusions he or she offers?

Reading Between the Lines

Paying attention to word choice is particularly important when the main idea of a passage isn't clear. A writer's word choice doesn't just affect meaning; it also creates it. For example, look at the following description from a teacher's evaluation of a student applying to a special foreign language summer camp. There's no topic sentence, but if you use your powers of observation, you should be able to tell how the writer feels about her subject.

> "As a student, Jane usually completes her work on time and checks it carefully. She speaks French well and is learning to speak with less of an American accent. She has often been a big help to other students who are just beginning to learn the language."

What message does this passage send about Jane? Is she the best French student the writer has ever had? Is she one of the worst, or is she just average? To answer these questions, you have to make an inference, and you must support your inference with specific observations. What makes you come to the conclusion that you come to?

The **diction** of the paragraph above reveals that this is a positive evaluation, but not a glowing recommendation.

Here are some of the specific observations you might have made to support this conclusion:

- The writer uses the word "usually" in the first sentence. This means that Jane is good about meeting deadlines for work, but not great; she doesn't always hand in her work on time.
- The first sentence also says that Jane checks her work carefully. While Jane may sometimes hand in work late, at least she always makes sure it's quality work. She's not sloppy.

- The second sentence tells us she's "learning to speak with less of an American accent." This suggests that she has a strong accent and needs to improve in this area. It also suggests, though, that she is already making progress.

- The third sentence tells us that she "often" helps "students who are just beginning to learn the language." From this we can conclude that Jane has indeed mastered the basics. Otherwise, how could she be a big help to students who are just starting to learn? By looking at the passage carefully, then, you can see how the writer feels about her subject.

Test Your Knowledge: Reading

Remember to read the questions first, make sure that you read ALL answer choices ALL THE WAY THROUGH, and use process of elimination to make your job of selecting the correct answer easier. If you can answer a majority of these questions correctly, you are likely ready for the Reading Section of the TEAS.

Read each of the following paragraphs carefully and answer the questions that follow.

My "office" measures a whopping 5 x 7 feet. A large desk is squeezed into one corner, leaving just enough room for a rickety chair between the desk and the wall. Yellow paint is peeling off the walls in dirty chunks. The ceiling is barely six feet tall; it's like a hat that I wear all day long. The window, a single 2 x 2 pane, looks out onto a solid brick wall just two feet away.

1. What is the main idea implied by this paragraph?
   a) This office is small but comfortable.
   b) This office is in need of repair.
   c) This office is old and claustrophobic.
   d) None of the above.

There are many things you can do to make tax time easier. The single most important strategy is to keep accurate records. Keep all of your pay stubs, receipts, bank statements, and other relevant financial information in a neat, organized folder so that when you're ready to prepare your form, all of your paperwork is in one place. The second thing you can do is start early. Get your tax forms from the post office as soon as they are available and start calculating. This way, if you run into any problems, you have plenty of time to straighten them out. You can also save time by reading the directions carefully. This will prevent time-consuming errors. Finally, if your taxes are relatively simple (you don't have itemized deductions or special investments), use the shorter tax form. It's only one page, so if your records are in order, it can be completed in less than an hour.

2. How many suggestions for tax time does this passage offer?
   a) One.
   b) Two.
   c) Three.
   d) Four.

3. The sentence "It's only one page, so if your records are in order, it can be completed in less than an hour" is:
   a) The main idea of the passage.
   b) A major supporting idea.
   c) A minor supporting idea.
   d) A transitional sentence.

4. A good summary of this passage would be:
   a) Simple strategies can make tax time less taxing.
   b) Don't procrastinate at tax time.
   c) Always keep good records.
   d) Get a tax attorney.

5. According to the passage, who should use the shorter tax form?
   a) Everybody.
   b) People who do not have complicated finances.
   c) People who do have complicated finances.
   d) People who wait until the last minute to file taxes.

6. The sentence, "The single most important strategy is to keep accurate records," is a(n):
   a) Fact.
   b) Opinion.
   c) Both of the above.
   d) Neither of the above.

Being a secretary is a lot like being a parent. After a while, your boss becomes dependent upon you, just as a child is dependent upon his or her parents. Like a child who must ask permission before going out, you'll find your boss coming to you for permission, too. "Can I have a meeting on Tuesday at 3:30?" you might be asked, because you're the one who keeps track of your boss's schedule. You will also find yourself cleaning up after your boss a lot, tidying up papers and files the same way a parent tucks away a child's toys and clothes. And, like a parent protects his or her children from outside dangers, you will find yourself protecting your boss from certain "dangers"—unwanted callers, angry clients, and upset subordinates.

7. The main idea of this passage is:
   a) Secretaries are treated like children.
   b) Bosses treat their secretaries like children.
   c) Secretaries and parents have similar roles.
   d) Bosses depend too much upon their secretaries.

8. Which of the following is the topic sentence of the paragraph?
   a) Being a secretary is a lot like being a parent.
   b) After a while, your boss becomes dependent upon you, just as a child is dependent upon his or her parents.
   c) You will also find yourself cleaning up after your boss a lot, tidying up papers and files the same way a parent tucks away a child's toys and clothes.
   d) None of the above.

9. According to the passage, secretaries are like parents in which of the following ways?
   a) They make their bosses' lives possible.
   b) They keep their bosses from things that might harm or bother them.
   c) They're always cleaning and scrubbing things.
   d) They don't get enough respect.

10. This passage uses which point of view?
   a) First person.
   b) Second person.
   c) Third person.
   d) First and second person.

11. The tone of this passage suggests that:

a) The writer is angry about how secretaries are treated.
b) The writer thinks secretaries do too much work.
c) The writer is slightly amused by how similar the roles of secretaries and parents are.
d) The writer is both a secretary and a parent.

12. The sentence, "'Can't I have a meeting on Tuesday at 3:30?' you might be asked, because you're the one who keeps track of your boss's schedule," is a:

a) Main idea.
b) Major supporting idea.
c) Minor supporting idea
d) None of the above.

13. "Being a secretary is a lot like being a parent" is:

a) A fact.
b) An opinion.
c) Neither of the above.
d) Both of the above.

14. The word "subordinates" probably means:

a) Employees.
b) Parents.
c) Clients.
d) Secretaries.

Day after day, Johnny chooses to sit at his computer instead of going outside with his friends. A few months ago, he'd get half a dozen phone calls from his friends every night. Now, he might get one or two a week. It used to be that his friends would come over two or three days a week after school. Now, he spends his afternoons alone with his computer.

15. The main idea is:

a) Johnny and his friends are all spending time with their computers instead of one another.
b) Johnny's friends aren't very good friends.
c) Johnny has alienated his friends by spending so much time on the computer.
d) Johnny and his friends prefer to communicate by computer.

We've had Ginger since I was two years old. Every morning, she wakes me up by licking my cheek. That's her way of telling me she's hungry. When she wants attention, she'll weave in and out of my legs and meow until I pick her up and hold her. And I can always tell when Ginger wants to play. She'll bring me her toys and will keep dropping them (usually right on my homework!) until I stop what I'm doing and play with her for a while.

16. A good topic sentence for this paragraph would be:

a) I take excellent care of Ginger.
b) Ginger is a demanding pet.
c) Ginger and I have grown up together.
d) Ginger is good at telling me what she wants.

Test Your Knowledge: The Reading Section – Answers

1. **c)**
2. **d)**
3. **c)**
4. **a)**
5. **b)**
6. **b)**
7. **c)**
8. **a)**
9. **b)**
10. **b)**
11. **c)**
12. **c)**
13. **b)**
14. **a)**
15. **c)**
16. **d)**

Chapter 4: Science

The TEAS will measure your knowledge of the life sciences and physical sciences: Chemistry, Biology, and Physics. Although we can't cover 12 years of schooling – not without a much larger book, anyway! – this section will refresh your memory on the necessary fundamental science principles. Take particular note to the bold faced words. These are the terms most commonly seen on the test.

Here's a breakdown of areas covered:

1. **Biology**
    - Basics of Life
    - Cellular Respiration
    - Classification of Organisms
    - Microorganisms
    - Animals
    - Plants
    - Ecology
    - Cells, Tissues, and Organs
    - Reproduction
    - Heredity
    - The Systems of the Body: Circulatory; Respiratory; Skeletal; Nervous; Muscular; Digestive; Renal

2. **Chemistry**
    - Elements, Compounds, and Mixtures
    - States of Matter
    - The Periodic Table and Chemical Bonds
    - Acids and Bases

3. **Physics**
    - Motion
    - Thermal Physics
    - Heat Transfer
    - Wave Motion (Sound) and Magnetism

Biology

BASICS OF LIFE

We began learning the difference between living (**animate**) beings and nonliving (**inanimate**) objects from an early age. Living organisms and inanimate objects are all composed of **atoms** from elements. Those atoms are arranged into groups called **molecules**, which serve as the building blocks of everything in existence (as we know it). Molecular interactions are what determine whether something is classified as animate or inanimate. The following is a list of the most commonly-found elements found in the molecules of animate beings:

- Oxygen
- Carbon
- Sodium
- Magnesium
- Iodine
- Sulfur
- Potassium
- Chlorine
- Nitrogen
- Calcium
- Phosphorous
- Iron
- Hydrogen

Another way to describe living and nonliving things is through the terms **organic** and **inorganic.**

- **Organic molecules** are from living organisms. Organic molecules contain **carbon-hydrogen bonds.**

- **Inorganic molecules** come from non-living resources. They do not contain carbon-hydrogen bonds.

There are four major classes of organic molecules:

1. **Carbohydrates**

2. **Lipids**

3. **Proteins**

4. **Nucleic acids.**

Carbohydrates

Carbohydrates consist of only hydrogen, oxygen, and carbon atoms. They are the most abundant single class of organic substances found in nature. Carbohydrate molecules provide many basic necessities such as: fiber, vitamins, and minerals; structural components for organisms, especially plants; and, perhaps most importantly, energy. Our bodies break down carbohydrates to make **glucose**: a sugar used to produce that energy which our bodies need in order to operate. Brain cells are exclusively dependent upon a constant source of glucose molecules.

There are two kinds of carbohydrates: simple and complex.

Simple carbohydrates can be absorbed directly through the cell, and therefore enter the blood stream very quickly. We consume simple carbohydrates in dairy products, fruits, and other sugary foods.

Complex carbohydrates consist of a chain of simple sugars which, over time, our bodies break down into simple sugars (which are also referred to as stored energy.) **Glycogen** is the storage form of glucose in human and animal cells. Complex carbohydrates come from starches like cereal, bread, beans, potatoes, and starchy vegetables.

Lipids

Lipids, commonly known as fats, are molecules with two functions:

1. They are stored as an energy reserve.

2. They provide a protective cushion for vital organs.

In addition to those two functions, lipids also combine with other molecules to form essential compounds, such as **phospholipids,** which form the membranes around cells. Lipids also combine with other molecules to create naturally-occurring **steroid** hormones, like the hormones estrogen and testosterone.

Proteins

Proteins are large molecules which our bodies' cells need in order to function properly. Consisting of **amino acids,** proteins aid in maintaining and creating many aspects of our cells: cellular structure, function, and regulation, to name a few. Proteins also work as neurotransmitters and carriers of oxygen in the blood (hemoglobin).

Without protein, our tissues and organs could not exist. Our muscles bones, skin, and many other parts of the body contain significant amounts of protein. **Enzymes**, hormones, and antibodies are proteins.

Enzymes

When heat is applied, chemical reactions are typically sped up. However, the amount of heat required to speed up reactions could be potentially harmful (even fatal) to living organisms. Instead, our bodies use molecules called enzymes to bring reactants closer together, causing them to form a new compound. Thus, the whole reaction rate is increased without heat. Even better – the enzymes are not consumed during the reaction process, and can therefore be used reused. This makes them an important biochemical part of both photosynthesis and respiration.

Nucleic Acid

Nucleic acids are large molecules made up of smaller molecules called **nucleotides. DNA** (deoxyribonucleic acid) transports and transmits genetic information. As you can tell from the name, DNA is a nucleic acid. Since nucleotides make up nucleic acids, they are considered the basis of reproduction and progression.

Test Your Knowledge: Basics of Life

1. Life depends upon:
   a) The bond energy in molecules.
   b) The energy of protons.
   c) The energy of electrons.
   d) The energy of neutrons.

2. Which of the following elements is **NOT** found in carbohydrates?
   a) Carbon.
   b) Hydrogen.
   c) Oxygen.
   d) Sulfur.

3. Which of the following is a carbohydrate molecule?
   a) Amino acid.
   b) Glycogen.
   c) Sugar.
   d) Lipid.

4. Lipids are commonly known as:
   a) Fat.
   b) Sugar.
   c) Enzymes.
   d) Protein.

5. Proteins are composed of:
   a) Nucleic acids.
   b) Amino acids.
   c) Hormones.
   d) Lipids.

Test Your Knowledge: Basics of Life – Answers

1. a)
2. d)
3. c)
4. a)
5. b)

CELLULAR RESPIRATION

As you can imagine, there are a great deal of processes which require energy: breathing, blood circulation, body temperature control, muscle usage, digestion, brain and nerve functioning are all only a few examples. You can refer to all of the body's physical and chemical processes which convert or use energy as **metabolism**.

All living things in the world, including plants, require energy in order to maintain their metabolisms. Initially, that energy is consumed through food. That energy is processed in plants and animals through **photosynthesis** (for plants) and **respiration** (for animals). **Cellular respiration** produces the actual energy molecules known as **ATP** (Adenosine Tri-Phosphate) molecules.

Plants use ATP during **photosynthesis** for producing glucose, which is then broken down during cellular respiration. This cycle continuously repeats itself throughout the life of the plant.

Photosynthesis: Plants, as well as some Protists and Monerans, can use light energy to bind together small molecules from the environment. These newly-bound molecules are then used as fuel to make more energy. This process is called photosynthesis, and one of its byproducts is none other than oxygen. Most organisms, including plants, require oxygen to fuel the biochemical reactions of metabolism.

You can see in the following equation that plants use the energy taken from light to turn carbon dioxide and water – the small molecules from their environment – into glucose and oxygen.

The photosynthesis equation:

$$\underset{\text{Carbon Dioxide}}{CO_2} + \underset{\text{Water}}{H_2O} \xrightarrow{\text{Light}} \underset{\text{Glucose (sugar)}}{C_6H_{12}O_6} + \underset{\text{Oxygen}}{O_2}$$

Chlorophyll

In order for photosynthesis to occur, however, plants require a specific molecule to capture sunlight. This molecule is called **chlorophyll**. When chlorophyll absorbs sunlight, one of its electrons is stimulated into a higher energy state. This higher-energy electron then passes that energy onto other electrons in other molecules, creating a chain that eventually results in glucose. Chlorophyll absorbs red and blue light, but not green; green light is reflected off of plants, which is why plants appear green to us. It's important to note that chlorophyll is absolutely necessary to the photosynthesis process in plants –if it photosynthesizes, it will have chlorophyll.

The really fascinating aspect of photosynthesis is that raw sunlight energy is a very nonliving thing; however, it is still absorbed by plants to form the chemical bonds between simple inanimate compounds. This produces organic sugar, which is the chemical basis for the formation of all living compounds. Isn't it amazing? Something nonliving is essential to the creation of all living things!

Respiration

Respiration is the metabolic opposite of photosynthesis. There are two types of respiration: **aerobic** (which uses oxygen) and **anaerobic** (which occurs without the use of oxygen).

You may be confused at thinking of the word "respiration" in this way, since many people use respiration to refer to the process of breathing. However, in biology, breathing is thought of as **inspiration** (inhaling) and **expiration** (exhalation); whereas **respiration** is the metabolic, chemical reaction supporting these processes. Both plants and animals produce carbon dioxide through respiration. **Aerobic respiration** is the reaction which uses enzymes to combine oxygen with organic matter (food). This yields carbon dioxide, water, and energy.

The respiration equation looks like this:

$$C6H12O6 + 6O2 \xrightarrow{\textbf{Enzymes}} 7\ 6CO2 + 6H2O + \text{energy}$$

If you look back the equation for photosynthesis, you will see that respiration is almost the same equation, only it goes in the opposite direction. (Photosynthesis uses carbon dioxide and water, with the help of energy, to create oxygen and glucose. Respiration uses oxygen and glucose, with the help of enzymes, to create carbon dioxide, water, and energy.)

Anaerobic respiration is respiration that occurs WITHOUT the use of oxygen. It produces less energy than aerobic respiration produces, yielding only two molecules of ATP per glucose molecule Aerobic respiration produces 38 ATP per glucose molecule.

So, plants convert energy into matter and release oxygen gas – animals then absorb this oxygen gas in order to run their own metabolic reaction and, in the process, release carbon dioxide. That carbon dioxide is then absorbed by plants in the photosynthetic conversion of energy into matter. Everything comes full circle! This is called a **metabolic cycle.**

Test Your Knowledge: Cellular Respiration

1. Which of the following is **NOT** true of enzymes?

a) Enzymes are lipid molecules.
b) Enzymes are not consumed in a biochemical reaction.
c) Enzymes are important in photosynthesis and respiration.
d) Enzymes speed up reactions and make them more efficient.

2. Plants appear green because chlorophyll:

a) Absorbs green light.
b) Reflects red light.
c) Absorbs blue light.
d) Reflects green light.

3. Photosynthesis is the opposite of:

a) Enzymatic hydrolysis.
b) Protein synthesis.
c) Respiration.
d) Reproduction.

4. The compound that absorbs light energy during photosynthesis is:

a) Chloroform.
b) Chlorofluorocarbon.
c) Chlorinated biphenyls.
d) Chlorophyll.

5. What is the name of the sugar molecule produced during photosynthesis?

a) Chlorophyll.
b) Glycogen.
c) Glucose.
d) Fructose.

Test Your Knowledge: Cellular Respiration – Answers

1. **a)**
2. **d)**
3. **c)**
4. **d)**
5. **c)**

CLASSIFICATION OF ORGANISMS

All of Earth's organisms have characteristics which distinguish them from one another. Scientists have developed systems to organize and classify all of Earth's organisms based on those characteristics.

Kingdoms

Through the process of evolution, organisms on Earth have developed into many diverse forms, which have complex relationships. Scientists have organized life into five large groups called **kingdoms**. Each kingdom contains those organisms that share significant characteristics distinguishing them from organisms in other kingdoms. These five kingdoms are named as follows:

1. **Animalia**
2. **Plantae**
3. **Fungi**
4. **Protista**
5. **Monera** (bacteria)

Kingdom Animalia

This kingdom contains multicellular organisms multicellular, or those known as complex organisms. These organisms are generically called **heterotrophs,** which means that they must eat preexisting organic matter (either plants or other animals) in order to sustain themselves.

Those heterotrophs which eat only plants are called **herbivores** (from "herbo," meaning "herb" or "plant"); those that kill and eat other animals for food are called **carnivores** (from "carno," meaning "flesh" or "meat"); and still other animals eat both plants *and* other animals – they are called **omnivores** (from "omnis," which means "all").

Those organisms in the Animal Kingdom have nervous tissue which has developed into nervous systems and brains; they are also able to move from place to place using muscular systems. The Animal Kingdom is divided into two groups: **vertebrates** (with backbones) and **invertebrates** (without backbones).

Kingdom Plantae

As you can guess from its name, the Plant Kingdom contains all plant-based life. Plants are multicellular organisms that use chlorophyll, which is held in specialized cellular structures called **chloroplasts,** to capture sunlight energy. Remember: photosynthesis! They then convert that sunlight energy into organic matter: their food. Because of this, most plants are referred to as **autotrophs** (self-feeders). There are a few organisms included in the Plant Kingdom which are not multicellular – certain types of algae which, while not multicellular, have cells with a nucleus. These algae also contain chlorophyll.

Except for algae, most plants are divided into one of two groups: **vascular plants** (most crops, trees, and flowering plants) and **nonvascular plants** (mosses). Vascular plants have specialized tissue that allows them to transport water and nutrients from their roots, to their leaves, and back again – even when the plant is several hundred feet tall. Nonvascular plants cannot do this, and therefore remain very small in size. Vascular plants are able to grow in both wet and dry environments; whereas nonvascular plants, since they are unable to transport water, are usually found only in wet, marshy areas.

Kingdom Fungi

The Fungi Kingdom contains organisms that share some similarities with plants, but also have other characteristics that make them more animal-like. For example, they resemble animals in that they lack chlorophyll – so they can't perform photosynthesis. This means that they don't produce their own food and are therefore heterotrophs.

However, they resemble plants in that they reproduce by spores; they also resemble plants in appearance. The bodies of fungi are made of filaments called **hyphae**, which in turn create the tissue **mycelium.** The most well-known examples of organisms in this Kingdom are mushrooms, yeasts, and molds. Fungi are very common and benefit other organisms, including humans.

Kingdom Protista

This kingdom includes single-celled organisms that contain a nucleus as part of their structure. They are considered a simple cell, but still contain multiple structures and accomplish many functions. This Kingdom includes organisms such as paramecium, amoeba, and slime molds. They often move around using hair-like structures called *cilia* or *flagellums.*

Kingdom Monera

This kingdom contains only bacteria. All of these organisms are single-celled and do not have a nucleus. They have only one chromosome, which is used to transfer genetic information. Sometimes they can also transmit genetic information using small structures called **plasmids.** Like organisms in the Protista Kingdom, they use flagella to move. Bacteria usually reproduce asexually.

There are more forms of bacteria than any other organism on Earth. Some bacteria are beneficial to us, like the ones found in yogurt; others can cause us to get sick such as the bacteria *E. coli.*

KINGDOM	DESCRIPTION	EXAMPLES
Animalia	Multi-celled; parasites; prey; consumers; can be herbivorous, carnivorous, or omnivorous	Sponges, worms, insects, fish, mammals, reptiles, birds, humans
Plantae	Multi-celled; autotrophs; mostly producers	Ferns, angiosperms, gymnosperms, mosses
Fungi	Can be single or multi-celled; decomposers; parasites; absorb food; asexual; consumers	Mushrooms, mildew, molds, yeast
Protista	Single or multi-celled; absorb food; both producers and consumers	Plankton, algae, amoeba, protozoans
Monera	Single-celled or a colony of single-cells; decomposers and parasites; move in water; are both producers and consumers	Bacteria, blue-green algae

Levels of Classification

Kingdom groupings are not very specific. They contain organisms defined by broad characteristics, and which may not seem similar at all. For example, worms belong in Kingdom Animalia – but then, so do birds. These two organisms are very different, despite sharing the necessary traits to make it into the animal kingdom. Therefore, to further distinguish different organisms, we have multiple levels of classification, which gradually become more specific until we finally reach the actual organism.

We generally start out by grouping organisms into the appropriate kingdom. Within each kingdom, we have other subdivisions: **Phylum, Class, Order, Family, Genus, and Species.** (In some cases, "Species" can be further narrowed down into "Sub-Species.")

As we move down the chain, characteristics become more specific, and the number of organisms in each group decreases. For an example, let's try to classify a grizzly bear. The chart would go as follows:

Kingdom - insect, fish, bird, pig, dog, bear

Phylum - fish, bird, pig, dog, bear

Class - pig, dog, bear

Order - dog, bear

Family -panda,brown,grizzly

Genus -
brown, grizzly

Species -
grizzly

Here is an easy way to remember the order of terms used in this classification scheme:

Kings **P**lay **C**ards **O**n **F**riday, **G**enerally **S**peaking.

Kingdom, **P**hylum, **C**lass, **O**rder, **F**amily, **G**enus, **S**pecies

Binomial Nomenclature

Organisms can be positively identified by two Latin words. Therefore, the organism naming system is referred to as a binomial nomenclature ("binomial" referring to the number two, and "nomenclature" referring to a title or name). Previously-used words help illustrate where the organism fits into the whole scheme, but it is only the last two, the genus and species, that specifically name an organism. Both are written in italics. The genus is always capitalized, but the species name is written lowercase.

Grizzly bears fall underneath the genus *Ursus*, species *arctos*, and sub-species *horribilis*. Therefore, the scientific name of the grizzly bear would be *Ursus arctos horribilis. Canis familiaris* is the scientific name for a common dog, *Felis domesticus* is a common cat, and humans are *Homo sapiens*.

Test Your Knowledge: Classification of Organisms

1. Which feature distinguishes those organisms in Kingdom Monera from those in other kingdoms? Organisms in Kingdom Monera:

a) Contain specialized organelles.
b) Contain a nucleus.
c) Contain chloroplasts.
d) Lack a nucleus.

2. Which of the following has the classification levels in the correct order, from most general to most specific?

a) Kingdom, Phylum, Class, Order, Family, Genus, Species.
b) Order, Family, Genus, Species, Class, Phylum, Kingdom.
c) Species, Genus, Family, Order, Class, Phylum, Kingdom.
d) Kingdom, Phylum, Class, Species, Genus, Family, Order.

3. The ____________contains organisms with both plant-and-animal-like characteristics?

a) Animal Kingdom.
b) Plant Kingdom.
c) Fungi Kingdom.
d) Monera Kingdom.

4. Which of the following statements is true about the binomial nomenclature system of classification?

a) The genus and species names describe a specific organism.
b) The category of kingdom is very specific.
c) The category of species is very broad.
d) Three names are needed to correctly specify a particular organism.

5. Which of the following kingdom's members are multicellular AND autotrophic?

a) Fungi.
b) Animalia.
c) Protista.
d) Plantae.

6. Which of the following kingdom's members have tissue called hyphae?

a) Fungi.
b) Animalia.
c) Protista.
d) Plantae.

Test Your Knowledge: Classification of Organisms – Answers

1. **d)**

2. **a)**

3. **c)**

4. **a)**

5. **d)**

6. **a)**

MICROORGANISMS

Microorganisms (microbes) are extremely small and cannot be seen with the naked eye. They can be detected using either a microscope or through various chemical tests. These organisms are everywhere, even in such extreme environments as very hot areas, very cold areas, dry areas, and deep in the ocean under tremendous pressure. Some of these organisms cause diseases in animals, plants, and humans. However, most are helpful to us and the Earth's ecosystems. In fact, we are totally dependent upon microbes for our quality of life. There are three types of microorganisms: **bacteria, protists, and fungi.**

Bacteria

Bacteria are microorganisms that do not have a true nucleus; their genetic material simply floats around in the cell. They are very small, simple, one-celled organisms. Bacteria are normally found in three variations: **bacilli** (rod-shaped), **cocci** (sphere-shaped), and **spirilla** (spiral-shaped). Bacteria are widespread in all environments and are important participants within all ecosystems. They are **decomposers**, because they break down dead organic matter into basic molecules.

Bacteria are also an important part of the food-chain, because they are eaten by other organisms. Still, bacteria remain the most numerous organisms on Earth. This is due to the fact that they are small, can live practically anywhere, and have great metabolic flexibility. But most importantly, bacteria have the ability to rapidly reproduce. In the right environment, any bacteria can reproduce every 20 or 30 minutes, each one doubling after each reproduction.

Benefits of Bacteria – Some bacteria are found in our intestinal tracts, where they help to digest our food and make vitamins.

To demonstrate the significance of bacteria, let's look at the cycle of nitrogen, which is used by organisms to make proteins. The cycle starts with dead plants being decomposed by bacteria. The nitrogen from the plant tissue is released into the atmosphere, where nitrifying bacteria convert that nitrogen into ammonia-type compounds. Other bacteria act upon these compounds to form nitrates for plants to absorb. When these new plants die, we are brought back again to the decomposing bacteria releasing the plant's nitrogen into the atmosphere.

Bacterial Diseases - Microorganisms, including bacteria, enter our bodies in a variety of ways: through the air we breathe, ingestion by mouth, or through the skin via a cut or injury. We can eliminate much of this threat by disinfecting utensils and thoroughly washing our hands. This destroys bacteria and other microorganisms which may cause disease.

Protists

Protists are very diversified and include organisms that range greatly in size – from single cells to considerably complex structures, some longer than 100 meters. Protists have a wide variety of reproductive and nutritional strategies, and their genetic material is enclosed within a nucleus. Even though protists are more simplistic than other organisms with cellular nuclei, they are not as primitive as bacteria.

Some are autotrophic and contain chlorophyll; others are heterotrophic and consume other organisms to survive. Because protists obtain food in both of these ways, it is generally believed that early protists were both animal- and plant-like. Protists are important to food chains and ecosystems, although some protists do cause disease.

Fungi

Fungi are heterotrophic and can be either single-celled or multi-celled. They play an important decomposition role in an ecosystem, because they consume dead organic matter. This returns nutrients to the soil for eventual uptake by plants.

There are three types of fungi which obtain food: saprophytic, parasitic, and mycorrhizal-associated.

Saprophytic fungi consume dead organic matter; **parasitic** fungi attack living plants and animals; and **mycorrhizal-associated** fungi form close relationships (**symbiosis**) with trees, shrubs, and other plants, where each partner in the relationship mutually benefits. An organism called **lichen** is an example of a symbiotic union between a fungus and algae.

Fungi produce **spores** (reproductive structures) that are highly resistant to extreme temperatures and moisture levels. This gives them the ability to survive for a long time, even in aggressive environments. When their environments become more favorable, the spores **germinate** (sprout) and grow. Spores are able to travel to new areas, which spreads the organism. Fungi absorb food through **hyphae**. A large mass of joined, branched hyphae is called the **mycelium**, which constitutes the main body of the multicellular fungi. However, the mycelium is not usually seen, because it is hidden throughout the food source which is being consumed. The largest organism in the world is believed to be a soil fungus whose mycelium tissue extends for many acres!

What we do usually see of a fungus is the fungal fruiting body. A mushroom is a fruiting body filled with spores. The main body of the mushroom (the **mycelium**) is under the soil surface.

Test Your Knowledge: Microorganisms

1. Fungi are decomposers, which is important for______________.
   a) Making nutrients available for recycling back into the soil.
   b) Producing oxygen by photosynthesizing.
   c) Producing oxygen by respiration.
   d) Living in mostly aquatic environments.

2. Which is the most numerous organism on Earth?
   a) Paramecium from the Protist Kingdom.
   b) Yeast from the Fungi Kingdom.
   c) Euglena from the Protist Kingdom.
   d) Bacteria from the Moneran Kingdom.

3. Which kingdom contains organisms that are able to convert atmospheric nitrogen to nitrate?
   a) Animalia.
   b) Plantae.
   c) Monera.
   d) Protista.

4. Why are spores produced?
   a) They are part of resistance.
   b) To reproduce.
   c) To photosynthesize.
   d) They are part of the support system.

5. Members of the Kingdom Monera are found in our digestive tracts and perform which of the following functions?
   a) Produce carbohydrates.
   b) Produce vitamins.
   c) Produce lipids.
   d) Produce proteins.

Test Your Knowledge: Microorganisms – Answers

1. **a)**
2. **d)**
3. **c)**
4. **b)**
5. **b)**

ANIMALS

Animals are multi-celled and unable to produce their own food internally, just like plants. As mentioned previously, the Animal Kingdom is divided into two large groupings: the **invertebrates** and **vertebrates.**

Invertebrates are multicellular, have no back bone or cell walls, reproduce sexually, and are heterotrophic. They make up approximately 97% of the animal population.

Vertebrates, on the other hand, have well-developed internal skeletons, highly developed brains, an advanced nervous system, and an outer covering of protective cellular skin. They make up the remaining 3% of the animals.

What Is an Animal?

All animals, from sponges to human beings, share some fundamental characteristics. One such characteristic is cellular division. At the beginning of reproduction, an egg is fertilized and then undergoes several cell divisions (cleavages); this process quickly produces a cluster of cells. Cell division continues through many distinct stages before finally resulting in an embryo. The full, multi-celled organism then develops tissues and organ systems, eventually developing into its adult form.

All multicellular animals must come up with solutions to several basic problems:

- **Surface-area-to-volume issues:** Nutrients, air, and water must be able to enter an animal's body in order to sustain life; therefore, the surface area of an animal's body must be large enough to allow a sufficient amount of these elements to be consumed by the organism. In single-celled organisms, the cell size is limited to the amount of nutrients able to pass through the cell membrane to support the cell. In multi-celled organisms, specialized tissues and organ systems with very large surface areas bring in the necessary elements and then carry them to the cells. Those specialized tissues are found in the respiratory system, urinary system, excretory system, and the digestive system. These tissues and organs, along with the circulatory system, are able to support a large-sized body.

- **Body support and protection:** All animals have some form of support and protection in the form of their internal or external skeletal systems. These skeletal systems provide support for the animal's body and protect the internal organs from damage.

- **Mobility:** Animals are heterotrophs and must acquire food; this need, along with the need to mate and reproduce, requires the animal to move. Although plants move, they are considered stationary because they are rooted. Animals, on the other hand, move from place to place; this is called **locomotion.** Locomotion requires a muscular system. Muscles are found only in animals; they are not present in plants, fungi, or single-celled microorganisms.

- **Sensory integration**: Animals have many specialized sensory organs: eyes, ears, noses, etc. These organs make animals aware of the environment and give them the ability to respond to environmental stimuli. The integration and coordination of sense organs with other bodily functions requires an organized collection of specialized nervous tissue, known as a **central nervous system** (CNS).

A Few Animal Phyla

Phylum Porifera: Sponges.
Collections of individual cells with no tissues or organs, and no nervous system or skeleton.

Phylum Coelenterata: Jellyfish, sea anemones, and coral.
Bodies symmetrical in a circular fashion with rudimentary organs and systems, but no skeleton.

Phylum Echinodermata: Sea stars and sea urchins.
Bodies have circular symmetry with five body parts arranged around a central axis. They have calcium spines or plates just under the skin.

Phylum Mollusca: Snails, clams, and octopi.
These have a well-developed circulatory system, nervous system, and digestive system; octopuses have particularly well-developed brains.

Phylum Arthropoda: Crustaceans, spiders, and insects.
This phylum has more species than the other phyla. They have exoskeletons, and most undergo **metamorphosis** (a physical transformation that is a part of the growth process). They often have specialized body parts (antennae, pinchers, etc.), and they are well adapted to many environments.

Phylum Chordata: Amphibians, reptiles, fish, birds, and mammals (including humans).
All share four characteristics: a notochord that develops into the vertebral column in vertebrates, a nerve cord that runs along the spinal column, gill slits at some point in our development, and a tail or at least a vestigial tail (humans have the tailbone or coccyx).

Test Your Knowledge: Animals

1. Multicellular animals have developed respiratory and excretory systems to overcome which of the following issues?
   a) Weight versus mass.
   b) Surface-area-to-volume.
   c) Height to weight.
   d) Mass to volume.

2. The two categories of animals are:
   a) Single-celled and multi-celled.
   b) Autotrophic and heterotrophic.
   c) Those that live in water and those that live on land.
   d) Vertebrate and invertebrate.

3. Jellyfish and coral are related to:
   a) Octopi.
   b) Sea anemones.
   c) Sea urchins.
   d) Sponges.

4. The Phylum Arthropoda contains which of the following animals?
   a) Spiders.
   b) Sea stars.
   c) Sponges.
   d) Seals.

5. Humans are classified under which of the following Phyla?
   a) Echinodermata.
   b) Chordata.
   c) Mollusca.
   d) Platyhelminthes.

Test Your Knowledge: Animals – Answers

1. **b)**
2. **d)**
3. **b)**
4. **a)**
5. **b)**

PLANTS

Organisms within Kingdom Plantae are very diverse, but they usually share certain characteristics which make them recognizable as plants. Chlorophyll ensures that some, if not all, of a plants body will have a green color, and their root systems render plants incapable of locomotion. Remember photosynthesis? Plants are autotrophs; they create their own food through photosynthesis, which turns carbon dioxide and water into sugars and oxygen gas. This process takes place using chlorophyll in structures called **chloroplasts**. Plants also have hard cell walls made of the carbohydrate **cellulose**.

Diverse Environments and Plants

Plants are found in nearly every place on Earth. Since plants need light to photosynthesize, their ability to survive in different environments depends upon their access to sources of light. Water is also an important part of a plant's growth and development, partly because the water contained within a plant cells (by the cell wall) provide a plant with structure and support.

Land plants evolved from algae into two large groups: **bryophytes** (nonvascular plants) and **tracheophytes** (vascular plants).

Bryophytes

Quite different from tracheophytes, bryophytes lack roots, leaves, and stems. Instead, structures called **rhizoids** (root-like hairs) absorb water and nutrients. Since they do not have a tubular system with which to move water throughout their bodies, bryophytes rely on diffusion to distribute water and nutrients. This process is slow, and not efficient enough to support large bodies, so bryophytes cannot grow very large. The largest types of bryophytes are liverworts and mosses.

Tracheophytes

These plants have tubes (vessels) which provide both support and a means of transporting water and nutrients throughout their bodies. This support enables them to grow much larger than bryophytes.

The tracheophyte group is further broken down into two types: **seedless** and **seeded** vascular plants.

Seedless vascular plants require moist environments, because they need water to reproduce. Millions of years ago, seedless plants dominated the Earth; you can see many of them still today, such as club mosses, horsetails, and ferns.

Seeded vascular plants have become dominant today because they have developed a reproductive system that includes pollen and seeds. In response to harsh and dangerous conditions, plants have developed **pollen** as a structure to protect sperm cells until they can safely reach the female part of a flower. Another structure which protects plants against the environment is a seed. **Seeds** contain and protect an immature plant in a state of dormancy until conditions are favorable. They then germinate and form a new plant.

Since plants cannot transport themselves (remember: no locomotion), they depend on dispersal systems to establish themselves in new areas. Many systems help distribute seeds, including wind, water, and animals.

Seeded vascular plants are divided into two groups: **gymnosperms** and **angiosperms**.

Gymnosperms are seeded vascular plants that do not flower. They include plants such as pines, spruce, and cypresses. Gymnosperms are adapted to cold dry areas. They have very thin, small leaves covered with a waterproof layer that keeps them from drying out; additionally, a biological antifreeze in their sap keeps them from freezing. Gymnosperms retain green leaves year-round and produce seeds in cones.

Angiosperms are seeded vascular plants that *do* form flowers. These plants have thrived. They dominate the Earth and are highly diverse, largely because they have developed flowers, fruits, and broad leaves.

Broad leaves capture more sunlight, and therefore produce more food than the narrow, thin leaves of the gymnosperms are able to produce.

Flowers are the place in plants where sperm and egg cells are produced – they contain both the male and female sexual parts. A flower is designed to attract animals, which is why their structures are so colorful and fragrant. Animals assist in the pollination process by carrying pollen and other seeds to diverse locations; the animal often receives a "reward" from the plant in the form of nectar or pollen. Bees, for example, receive nectar and pollen for food from flowering plants.

Fruits contain the fully developed seed of flowering seed plants. Animals are attracted to the plant, eat the fruit, and then disperse the seeds.

Test Your Knowledge: Plants

1. Which of the following characteristics is NOT a characteristic of plants?
    a) They are able to engage in locomotion by moving from place to place.
    b) They use chlorophyll contained in chloroplasts.
    c) They produce sugars and oxygen.
    d) They use carbon dioxide and water in photosynthesis.

2. Which of the following is a bryophyte?
    a) Horsetail.
    b) Fern.
    c) Liverwort.
    d) Spruce tree.

3. Which plant group currently dominates the Earth in terms of quantity over other plant groups?
    a) Gymnosperms.
    b) Bryophytes.
    c) Seedless vascular plants.
    d) Angiosperms.

4. "Tracheophytes" is another name for:
    a) Nonvascular plants.
    b) Angiosperm plants.
    c) Gymnosperm plants.
    d) Vascular plants.

5. Which of the following strategies does an angiosperm plant NOT use to attract animals?
    a) It produces pollen.
    b) It produces nectar.
    c) It produces chloroplasts.
    d) It produces fruit.

6. Rhizoids are similar to ______________ in vascular plants?
    a) Leaves
    b) Chloroplasts
    c) Roots
    d) Stems

Test Your Knowledge: Plants – Answers

1. a)
2. c)
3. d)
4. d)
5. c)
6. c)

ECOLOGY

Biosphere and Biome

Life is possible due to the presence of air (**atmosphere**), water (**hydrosphere**), and soil (**lithosphere**). These factors interact with each other and the life on Earth to create an environment called a **biosphere**. The biosphere contains all of Earth's living organisms. Smaller living systems called **biomes** exist in large areas, both on land and in water; they are defined by the physical characteristics of the environment which they encompass, and by the organisms living within it.

Ecosystem

An ecosystem is a community of living and non-living things that work together. Ecosystems have no particular size; from large lakes and deserts, to small trees or puddles. Everything in the natural world – water, water temperature, plants, animals, air, light, soil, etc. – all form ecosystems.

The physical environment of an ecosystem includes soils, weather, climate, the topography (or shape) of the land, and many other factors. If there isn't enough light or water within an ecosystem, or if the soil doesn't have the right nutrients, plants will die. If plants die, the animals which depend on them will die. If the animals depending upon the plants die, any other animals depending upon those animals will also die. Regardless of the type of ecosystem they are in, all organisms – even microscopic ones – are affected by each other and their physical surroundings.

There are two components of an ecosystem. The **biotic** (biological) component includes the living organisms; nonliving factors – such as water, minerals, and sunlight – are collectively known as the **abiotic** (non-biological) component. While all ecosystems have different organisms and/or abiotic factors, they all have two primary features:

1. **Energy flows in one direction**. Beginning in the form of chemical bonds from photosynthetic organisms, like green plants or algae, energy flows first to the animals that eat the plants, then to other animals.

2. **Inorganic materials are recycled.** When taken up from the environment through living organisms, inorganic minerals are returned to the environment – mainly via decomposers such as bacteria and fungi. Other organisms called **detritivores** (such as pill bugs, sow bugs, millipedes, and earthworms), help break down large pieces of organic matter into smaller pieces that are handled then by the decomposers.

But since that's a lot of information to take in at once, here's a simple and complete definition of an ecosystem: a combination of biotic and abiotic components, through which energy flows and inorganic material is recycled.

An Organism's Niche

The area in which an organism lives – and therefore acquires the many things needed to sustain their lives – is called a **habitat.** An organism's role within its community, how it affects its habitat and how it is affected by its habitat, are the factors that define the organism's **niche**. A niche is like an organism's "location" and "occupation" within a community. For example, birds and squirrels both live in a tree habitat; however, they eat different foods, have different living arrangements, and have different food-gathering abilities. Therefore, the do not occupy the same niche.

THE ECOLOGICALORDER OF LIFE

Biosphere - All ecosystems on the planet make up the biosphere.

Ecosystem – Large community of numerous communities, and the physical non-living environment.

Community - A group of populations in a given area.

Population - A group of organisms of the same species in a given area.

Organism - A living thing.

Organ Systems - A group of organs that perform certain functions to form an organism.

Organs - A group of tissues that perform a certain function to form organ systems.

Tissues - A group of cells that perform certain functions to form an organ.

Cells - The building blocks of life which form tissues.

Organelles - Small parts of cells that have specific functions.

Atoms and Molecules - the building blocks of everything in the universe as we know it

One of the most important relationships among organisms exists between predators and their prey. You may have heard of this relationship described through **food chains** and **food webs**.

Food Chains represent the flow of energy obtained from the chemical breakdown of food molecules. When one animal (the predator) consumes another (the prey), the chemical bonds making up the tissues of the prey's body are broken down by the predator's digestive system. This digestive process releases energy and smaller chemical molecules that the predator's body uses to make more tissue. Prior to being the consumed, the prey obtains energy from foods for its own life processes.

Here's a basic example of a food chain:

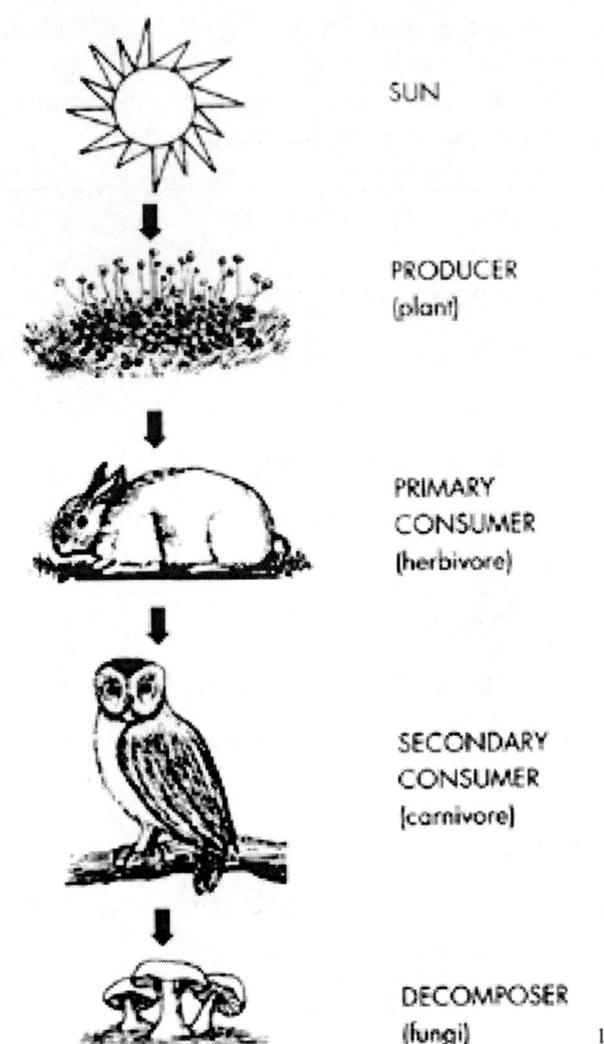

[1]

Food chains are a part of **food webs**, which offer a more complex view of energy transfer. They include more organisms, taking into account more than one predator-prey relationship. Each step along a food chain, or within a food web, is called a **trophic** (or feeding) level. Organisms at that first trophic level are known as **primary producers**, and are always photosynthetic organisms, whether on land or in water.

At the second trophic level, herbivores (referred to as **primary consumers**) eat plants to produce the energy needed for their metabolism. Much of the energy that transfers from the first trophic level to the second level is not turned into tissue. Instead, it is used for the digestive process, locomotion, and is lost as heat. As you move from one trophic level to another, it is estimated that only 10% of the available energy gets turned into body tissue at the next level up.

[1] Graphic from: http://www.king.portlandschools.org

The following is an example of a food web:

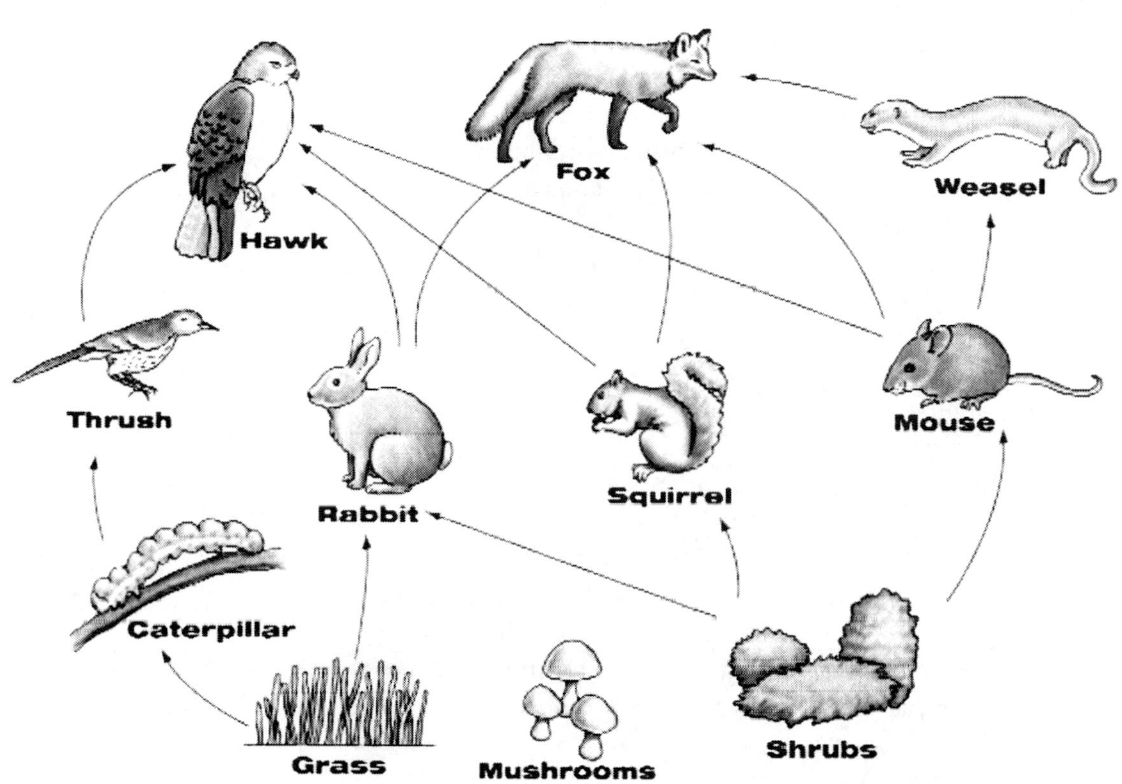

[2]

[2] Graphic from: http://www.education.com

Test Your Knowledge: Ecology

1. Ecology is the study of organisms interacting with:
   a) The physical environment only.
   b) The internal environment only.
   c) The physical environment and each other.
   d) Each other and the internal environment.

2. In terms of energy, an ecosystem is defined as:
   a) Moving energy back and forth between organisms.
   b) Moving energy in one direction from plants to animals.
   c) Not utilizing energy.
   d) Moving energy in one direction from animals to plants.

3. Decomposers are important because they:
   a) Recycle nutrients.
   b) Produce sugars.
   c) Produce oxygen.
   d) Engage in asexual reproduction.

4. Which of the following best describes the concept of an organism's niche?
   a) It is the organism's function, or "occupation", within an ecosystem.
   b) It is the organism's location, or "address", within an ecosystem.
   c) It is both an organism's function and location in an ecosystem.
   d) It is the binomial classification of an organism in an ecosystem.

5. Pillbugs are also known as:
   a) Decomposers.
   b) Detritivores.
   c) Producers.
   d) Autotrophs.

6. The steps in a food chain or food web are called ______ and represent the _______of an organism.
   a) biome levels; energy level
   b) trophic levels; energy level
   c) trophic levels; feeding level
   d) energy levels; feeding level

7. Another term for herbivores is:
   a) Plants.
   b) Secondary consumers.
   c) Primary consumers
   d) Third trophic-level organisms.

8. Several interacting food chains form a:
   a) Food pyramid.
   b) Food web.
   c) Food column.
   d) Food triangle.

9. Herbivores are at the second trophic level, so they are:

a) Primary producers.
b) Primary consumers.
c) Secondary consumers.
d) Secondary producers.

Test Your Knowledge: Ecology – Answers

1. **c)**
2. **b)**
3. **a)**
4. **c)**
5. **b)**
6. **c)**
7. **c)**
8. **b)**
9. **b)**

CELLS, TISSUES, AND ORGANS

All organisms are composed of microscopic cells, although the type and number of cells may vary. A cell is the minimum amount of organized living matter that is complex enough to carry out the functions of life. This section will briefly review both animal and plant cells, noting their basic similarities and differences.

Cell Structure

Around the cell is the **cell membrane**, which separates the living cell from the rest of the environment and regulates the comings and goings of molecules within the cell. Because the cell membrane allows some molecules to pass through while blocking others, it is considered **semipermeable.** Each cell's membrane communicates and interacts with the membranes of other cells. In additional to a cell membrane, *plants* also have a **cell wall** which is necessary for structural support and protection. Animal cells do not contain a cell wall.

Organelle

Cells are filled with a gelatin-like substance called **protoplasm** which contains various structures called **organelles**; called so because they act like small versions of organs. The diagram on the next page illustrates the basic organelles of both a plant and an animal cell. Pay attention to the differences and similarities between the two.

PLANT CELL (A)

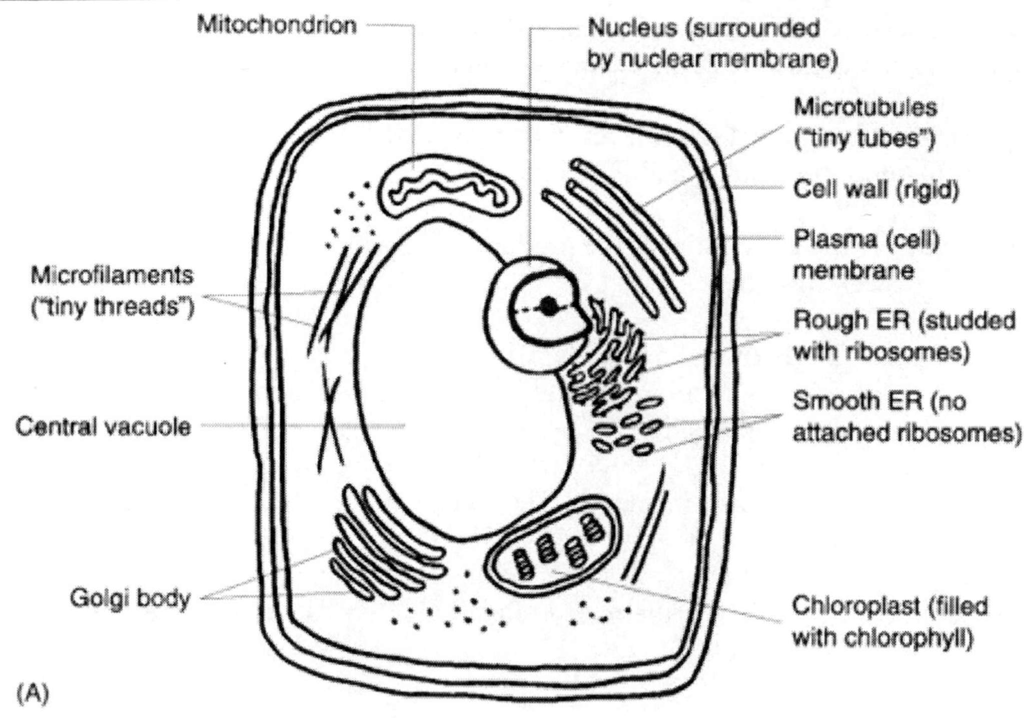

ANIMAL CELL (B) [3]

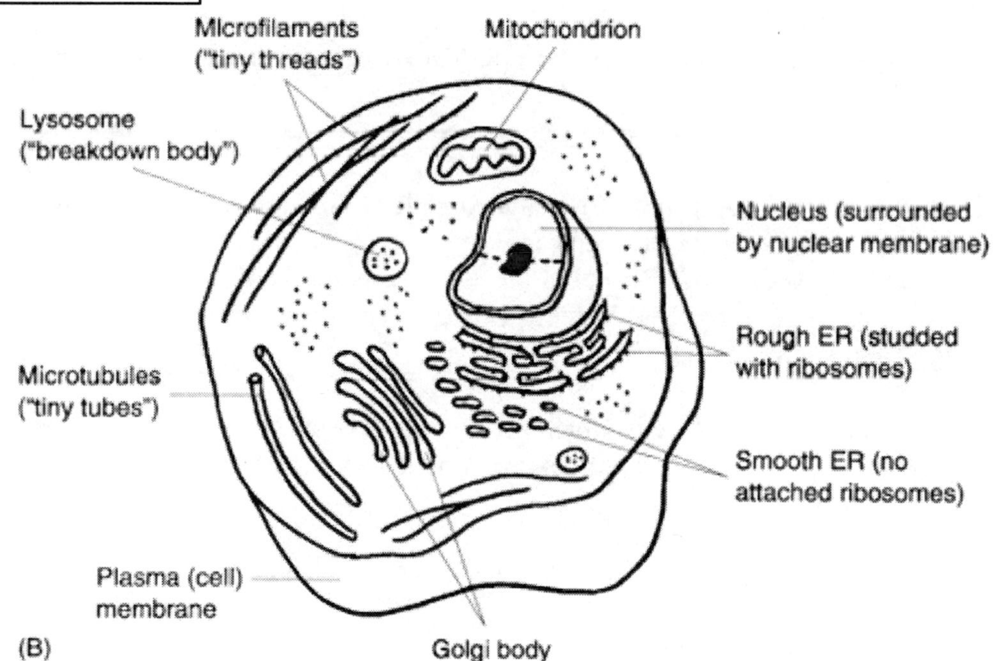

[3] Graphics from: http://www.education.com

Organelles (Defined)

Mitochondria are spherical or rod-shaped organelles which carry out the reactions of aerobic respiration. They are the power generators of both plant and animal cells, because they convert oxygen and nutrients into ATP, the chemical energy that powers the cell's metabolic activities.

Ribosomes are extremely tiny spheres that make proteins. These proteins are used either as enzymes or as support for other cell functions.

The **Golgi Apparatus** is essential to the production of polysaccharides (carbohydrates), and made up of a layered stack of flattened sacs.

The **Endoplasmic Reticulum** is important in the synthesis and packaging of proteins. It is a complex system of internal membranes, and is called either rough (when ribosomes are attached), or smooth (no ribosomes attached).

Chloroplasts are only found in plants. They contain the chlorophyll molecule necessary for photosynthesis.

The **Nucleus** controls all of the cell's functions, and contains the all-important genetic information, or DNA, of a cell.

Cellular Differentiation

Single-celled organisms have only one cell to carry out all of their required biochemical and structural functions. On the other hand, multi-celled organisms – except for very primitive ones (i.e. sponges) – have various groups of cells called **tissues** that each perform specific functions (**differentiation**).

There are four main types of tissues: **epithelial**, **connective, muscular,** and **nervous**.

Epithelial tissue is made up groups of flattened cells which are grouped tightly together to form a solid surface. Those cells are arranged in one or many layer(s) to form an external or internal covering of the body or organs. Epithelial tissue protects the body from injury and allows for the exchange of gases in the lungs and bronchial tubes. There's even a form of epithelial tissue that produces eggs and sperm, an organism's sex cells.

Connective tissue is made of cells which are surrounded by non-cellular material. For example, bones contain some cells, but they are also surrounded by a considerable amount of non-cellular, extracellular material.

Muscular tissue has the ability to contract. There are three types:

1. **Cardiac** tissue, found in the heart.
2. **Smooth** tissue, located in the walls of hollow internal structures such as blood vessels, the stomach, intestines, and urinary bladder.
3. **Skeletal** (or striated) tissue, found in the muscles.

Nervous tissue consists of cells called **neurons.** Neurons specialize in making many connections with and transmitting electrical impulses to each other. The brain, spinal cord, and peripheral nerves are all made of nervous tissue.

Organs and Organ Systems

As living organisms go through their life cycle, they grow and/or develop. Single-celled organisms grow and develop very rapidly; whereas complex, multi-celled organisms take much longer to progress. All organisms go through changes as they age. These changes involve the development of more complex functions, which in turn require groups of tissues to form larger units called **organs.** Here are some examples of organs:

1. **The heart** - Made of cardiac muscle and conjunctive tissue (conjunctive tissue makes up the valves), the heart pumps blood first to the lungs in order to pick up oxygen, then through the rest of the body to deliver the oxygen, and finally back to the lungs to start again.

2. **Roots** - A tree's are covered by an epidermis which is in turn made up of a protective tissue. They are also *composed* of tissue, which allows them to grow. The root organ also contains **conductive tissue** to absorb and transport water and nutrients to the rest of the plant.

Generally, in complex organisms like plants and animals, many organs are grouped together into **systems.** For example, many combinations of tissues make up the many organs which create the digestive system in animals. The organs in the digestive system consist of the mouth, the esophagus, the stomach, small and large intestines, the liver, the pancreas, and the gall bladder.

Test Your Knowledge: Cells, Tissues, and Organs

1. Which statement is true about Earth's organisms?
   a) All organisms are based on the cell as the basic unit of life.
   b) Protists are an exception to the cell theory and are not based on cells.
   c) Only single-celled organisms are based on cells.
   d) All organisms are based on tissues as the basic unit of life.

2. What organelle produces the cell's energy source?
   a) Chloroplast.
   b) Nucleus.
   c) Mitochondrion.
   d) Endoplasmic reticulum.

3. The formation of tissue depends upon:
   a) Cell differentiation.
   b) Cell membranes.
   c) Cell death.
   d) Cell organelles.

4. Cardiac muscle is an example of what tissue?
   a) Smooth muscle.
   b) Nervous.
   c) Contractile.
   d) Connective.

5. Which organelle has two forms: rough and smooth?
   a) Mitochondrion.
   b) Golgi apparatus.
   c) Nucleus.
   d) Endoplasmic reticulum.

6. Which organelle is important in the production of polysaccharides (carbohydrates)?
   a) Mitochondrion.
   b) Golgi apparatus.
   c) Nucleus
   d) Endoplasmic reticulum.

Test Your Knowledge: Cells, Tissues, and Organs – Answers

1. a)
2. c)
3. a)
4. c)
5. d)
6. b)

REPRODUCTION

Individual organisms have limited life spans; however, life continues due to reproduction. There are two types of reproduction. One requires the exchange of genetic material between two organisms (**sexual reproduction**), and the other does not (**asexual reproduction**).

Asexual Reproduction

All kingdoms have organisms that engage in asexual reproduction. Asexual reproduction very quickly produces large numbers of genetically identical (or **cloned**) offspring. Some organisms that engage in asexual reproduction can also engage in sexual reproduction at least part of the time.

Comparison Chart

	Asexual Reproduction	**Sexual Reproduction**
Number of organisms involved:	One	Two
Cell division:	Mitosis	Meiosis
Variation in offspring:	No	Yes
Advantages:	Quick. No need to search for mate	Variation
Disadvantages:	No variation	Requires two organisms

In single-celled organisms such as bacteria and protists, asexual reproduction occurs through a process known as **binary fission** (or **bipartition**). The cell first duplicates parts of itself before splitting into two separate, but identical, cells. Some organisms reproduce asexually using the process of **budding**, wherein an offshoot of their body grows into a complete organism.

Many multi-cellular invertebrates can also reproduce asexually by a process called **fragmentation**, where a portion of the organism's body is separated and then grows into a whole organism. This is similar to budding, except that the original body repairs itself as well, leaving behind two complete organisms.

Plants can reproduce asexually by budding or fragmentation, when they form tubers, rhizomes, bulbs, and other extensions of their bodies. Plants also have a major sexual phase of their life cycle, which is part of a process called **alternation of generations.**

Alternation of Generations

Although asexual reproduction allows plants to reproduce quickly, most plants engage in sexual reproduction, at least part of the time. Sexually reproducing plants cycle between two distinctly different body types. The first is called the **sporophyte**, and the second is called the **gametophyte.**

An adult sporophyte (the part of the plant we see) produces spores. The spores are transported to new areas by animals, wind, water, etc. If the conditions are suitable, those spores will sprout into a **gametophyte** form of the plant, which is not usually seen. This gametophyte produces the eggs and sperm that will join to form a new sporophyte. This change from sporophyte to gametophyte represents an alternation of generations. The gametophyte generation is small and dependent upon the sporophyte generation. An oak tree, for example, is really the sporophyte generation of the plant; the gametophyte generation is contained within its flowers.

Sexual Reproduction

Sexual reproduction is when genetic material from one parent is combined with the genetic material from another, producing offspring that are not identical to either parent. Each parent produces a specialized cell called a **gamete** that contains half of his or her genetic information.

Male animals produce the smaller, more mobile gamete known as a **sperm cell**. Females produce the larger, more sedentary gamete known as an **egg cell**. When these two gametes come into contact, they fuse and combine their genetic information in a process known as **fertilization**. This can happen either externally or internally.

An example of **external fertilization** would be **spawning,** where eggs and sperm are both released into water and must find each other. **Spawning** is dependent upon each gender's reproductive cycle matching the other.

Internal fertilization is dependent upon **copulation**: the process wherein a male deposits sperm cells directly into the reproductive tract of a female. Because a medium like water cannot be used to transport gametes on land, internal fertilization is critical to land-based organisms.

Test Your Knowledge: Reproduction

1. The formation of tubers is an example of what kind of asexual reproduction?
   a) Budding.
   b) Binary fission.
   c) Bipartition.
   d) Root zone development.

2. Which of the following best describes alternation of generation?
   a) The sporophyte produces eggs and sperm that join and lead to the development of a gametophyte.
   b) The gametophyte produces eggs and sperm that join and lead to the development of a sporophyte.
   c) The gametophyte produces eggs and the sporophyte produces sperm that join to form a new plant.
   d) The sporophyte produces eggs and the gametophyte produces sperm that join to form a new plant.

3. In sexually reproducing organisms, gametes come from which parent?
   a) Only the male.
   b) Only the female.
   c) Both the male and female.
   d) Neither.

4. What is the main difference between asexual and sexual reproduction?
   a) Asexual reproduction is only for aquatic organisms.
   b) Asexual reproduction is practiced only by plants.
   c) Humans are the only organisms that utilize sexual reproduction.
   d) Asexual reproduction does not require a mate.

5. Which of the following is **NOT** a form of asexual reproduction?
   a) Fertilization.
   b) Cloning.
   c) Budding.
   d) Fragmentation.

Test Your Knowledge: Reproduction – Answers

1. a)
2. b)
3. c)
4. d)
5. a)

HEREDITY

A duck's webbed feet, a tree whose leaves change color in the fall, and humans having backbones are all characteristics inherited from parent organisms. These inheritable characteristics are transmitted through **genes** and **chromosomes**. In sexual reproduction, each parent contributes half of his or her genes to the offspring.

Genes

Genes influence both what we look like on the outside and how we work on the inside. They contain the information that our bodies need to make the proteins in our bodies. Genes are made of DNA: a double helix (spiral) molecule that consists of two long, twisted strands of nucleic acids. Each of these strands are made of sugar and phosphate molecules, and are connected by pairs of chemicals called **nitrogenous bases** (just bases, for short). There are four types of bases:

1. **Adenine (A)**
2. **Thymine (T)**
3. **Guanine (G)**
4. **Cytosine (C)**

These bases link in a very specific way: **A** always pairs with **T**, and **C** always pairs with **G**.

A gene is a piece of DNA that codes for a specific protein. Each gene contains the information necessary to produce a single trait in an organism, and each gene is different from any other. For example, one gene will code for the protein insulin, and another will code for hair. For any trait, we inherit one gene from our father and one from our mother. Human beings have 20,000 to 25,000 genes, yet those genes only account for about 3% of our DNA.

Alternate forms of the same gene are called **alleles**. When the alleles are identical, the individual is **homozygous** for that trait. When the alleles are different, the individual is **heterozygou**s for that trait.

For example, a child may have red hair because she inherited two identical red color genes from each parent; that would make her homozygous for red hair. However, a second child may have brown hair because he inherited different hair color genes from each parent; this would make him heterozygous for brown hair. When genes exist in a heterozygous pairing, usually one is expressed over the other. The gene which is expressed is **dominant**. The unexpressed gene is called **recessive**.

If you took the DNA from all the cells in your body and lined it up, end to end, it would form a (very thin!) strand 6000 million miles long! DNA molecules, and their important genetic material, are tightly packed around proteins called **histones** to make structures called **chromosomes**. Human beings have 23 pairs of chromosomes in every cell, for 46 chromosomes in total. The sex chromosomes determine whether you are a boy (XY) or a girl (XX). The other chromosomes are called autosomes.

Patterns of Inheritance

Biologists refer to the genetic makeup of an organism as its **genotype**. However, the collection of physical characteristics that result from the action of genes is called an organism's **phenotype.** You can remember this differentiation by looking at the beginning of each word: *geno*type is *gen*etic, and *pheno*type is *phy*sical. Patterns of inheritance can produce surprising results, because the genotype determines the phenotype.

Test Your Knowledge: Heredity

1. On paired chromosomes, two identical alleles are called:
   a) Heterozygous.
   b) Homozygous.
   c) Tetrad.
   d) Binomial.

2. The physical characteristics of an organism are known as its:
   a) Chromosomes.
   b) Genotype.
   c) DNA.
   d) Phenotype.

3. Which of the following is **NOT** a nucleotide found in DNA?
   a) Uracil.
   b) Guanine.
   c) Cytosine.
   d) Thymine.

4. The genotype describes an organism's:
   a) Appearance.
   b) Genetic code.
   c) Type of DNA.
   d) Eye color only.

5. The shape of the DNA molecule is a:
   a) Single spiral.
   b) Double spiral.
   c) Straight chain.
   d) Bent chain.

Test Your Knowledge: Heredity – Answers

1. **b)**
2. **d)**
3. **a)**
4. **b)**
5. **b)**

THE CIRCULATORY SYSTEM (CARDIOVASCULAR SYSTEM)

The cells in living organisms need to receive nutrients and have their waste products removed. Single-celled organisms are able to pass these substances to and from their environment directly through the cell membrane. However, in multi-celled organisms, these substances are transported by way of the circulatory system.

The cardiovascular system has three main parts: the heart (which is the pump in the system), the blood vessels providing a route for fluids in the system, and the blood which transports nutrients and oxygen and contains waste products.

Heart

The human heart has four chambers – right atrium, right ventricle, left atrium, and left ventricle – which separate fresh blood from the blood that is full of cellular waste.

When leaving the heart, blood travels through **arteries**. To remember this, imagine that the "a" in "arteries" stands for "away". *A*rteries carry blood *a*way from the heart. On its way to the heart, blood travels through **veins.**

The **superior vena cava** is the vein which brings blood from the body into the top right chamber of the heart. This top right chamber is called the **right atrium**. The right atrium is separated from the chamber below it by a valve, and separated from the chamber next to it by a wall of muscle tissue. The heart relaxes after each beat, which allows blood to flow from the right atrium, through the valve, and into the chamber below called the **right ventricle.**

The right ventricle sends blood through the **pulmonary arteries** to the lungs. Blood picks up oxygen in the lungs and then is moved through the **pulmonary veins** back to the upper part of the heart. But this time, it enters on the left side into the **left atrium.** Use that first-letter rule again to remember this: blood from the *l*ungs enters the *l*eft atrium.

The left atrium – like the right – is separated from the left ventricle below it by a valve. When this valve opens during the relaxed phase of the heart, blood flows into the left ventricle. This chamber has the largest and strongest muscular wall so that it can force blood into the **aorta**, which is the body's largest artery, pulling blood away from the heart to the rest of the body.

The Heart:

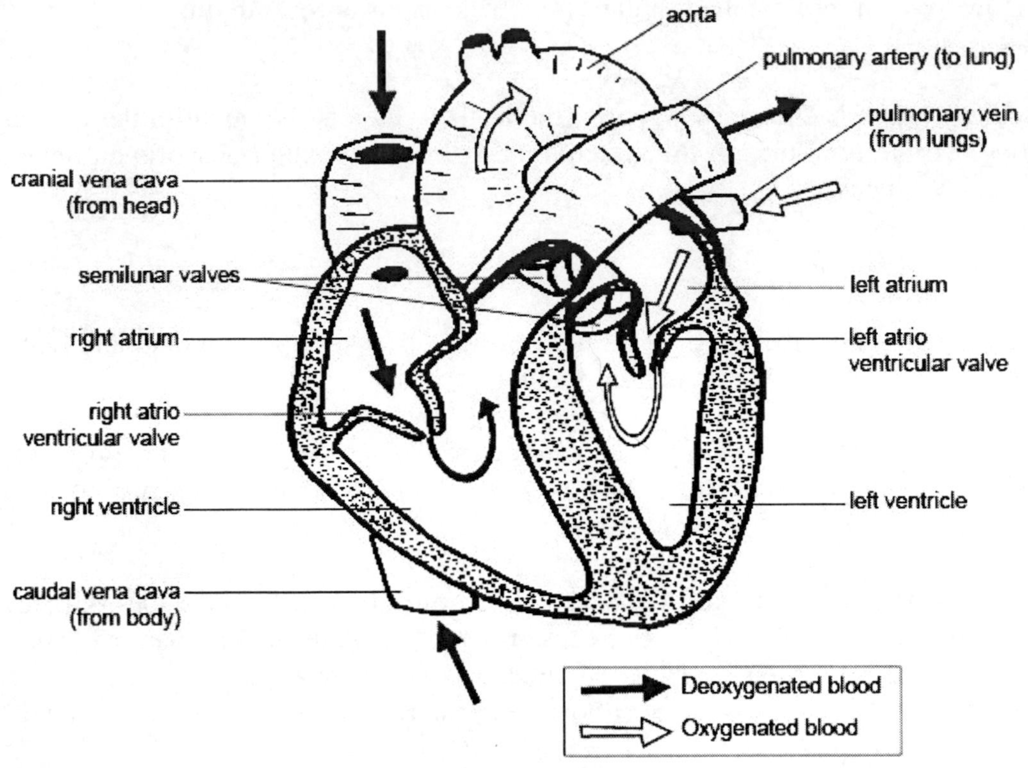

[4]

Arteries branch off from the aorta and travel to all parts of the body, continuing to branch and get smaller until they become **arterioles.** Arterioles lead to very small beds of tiny blood vessels called **capillaries.** Capillary beds are the site where the exchange of nutrients, gases, and wastes occurs. Blood that now contains wastes leaves the capillary beds, and enters small vessels called **venules**. These travel back through the body to the heart, becoming larger veins on the way, ending with the **large vena cava vein** that empties into the heart. This begins the cycle all over again!

Things the Circulatory System Carries:

- Oxygen from the lungs to the body's cells.
- Carbon dioxide from the body's cells to the lungs.
- Nutrients from the digestive system to the cells.
- Waste products, other than carbon dioxide, to the liver and kidneys.
- Hormones and other messenger chemicals, from the glands and organs of their production to the body's cells.

[4] Graphic from: http://www.en.wikibooks.org

Blood

Blood helps regulate our internal environment and keeps us in a generally constant state known as **homeostasis**. Blood transports and mixes elements up, making it possible for all the organs to contribute to maintaining homeostasis.

Blood is not a liquid; it is a **suspension** (fluids containing particles suspended inside them). Blood has two components: **plasma**, the liquid part, and the solid **blood cells** suspended throughout. There are three major types of cells: **red blood cells**, **white blood cells**, and cellular fragments called **platelets.**

Plasma

Plasma is mostly water, in which some substances such as proteins, hormones, and nutrients (glucose sugar, vitamins, amino acids, and fats) are dissolved. Gases (carbon dioxide and oxygen), salts (of calcium, chloride, and potassium), and wastes other than carbon dioxide are also dissolved in blood.

Red Blood Cells

Red blood cells contain a protein molecule called **hemoglobin**, which holds an atom of iron. The hemoglobin molecule binds with oxygen and carbon dioxide, thus providing the mechanism by which the red blood cells can carry these gases around the body.

White Blood Cells

White blood cells come in many specialized forms and are used in the immune system to fight off invading organisms and keep us from getting diseases.

Platelets

Platelets release substances at the site of a wound that start the blood-clotting reaction.

Circulation within Plants

In plants, the transport system is based on the special properties of water.

The cells that make up the vascular tissue of plants form a continuous system of tubes running from the roots, through the stems, and to the leaves. Water and nutrients flow to the leaves through a vascular tissue called **xylem**, where they are used in the process of photosynthesis. Following that process, the products of photosynthesis then flow through a vascular tissue called **phloem** back down to the roots.

Test Your Knowledge: The Circulatory System

1. Which of the following is NOT one of the chambers in the four-chambered vertebrate heart?
  a) Right atrium.
  b) Right ventricle.
  c) Left alveolar.
  d) Left ventricle.

2. Which of the following is true about blood flow in the four-chambered vertebrate heart circulatory system?
  a) Blood in the pulmonary vein is oxygenated.
  b) Blood in the pulmonary artery is oxygenated.
  c) Blood in the aorta is not oxygenated.
  d) Blood in the vena cava is oxygenated.

3. Which of the following are the major components of blood?
  a) Proteins and lipids.
  b) Plasma and cells.
  c) Proteins and platelets.
  d) Dells and lipids.

4. Platelets perform which of the following functions?
  a) Blood clotting.
  b) Carrying oxygen.
  c) Carrying carbon dioxide.
  d) Disease protection.

5. Capillary beds occur between:
  a) Arteries and veins.
  b) Aortas and vena cavas.
  c) Arterioles and venules.
  d) Atria and ventricles.

6. Red blood cells perform which of the following functions?
  a) Blood clotting.
  b) Carrying oxygen and carbon dioxide.
  c) Disease protection.
  d) Wound healing.

7. Xylem and phloem are plant tissues that:
  a) Produce sugar molecules and oxygen.
  b) Transport water and nutrients throughout the plant.
  c) Contain chloroplasts.
  d) Produce seeds.

8. The products of photosynthesis in the leaves flow to the roots through vascular tissue called:
   a) Phloem.
   b) Xylem.
   c) Meristem.
   d) Angiosperm.

Test Your Knowledge: The Circulatory System – Answers

1. **c)**

2. **a)**

3. **b)**

4. **a)**

5. **c)**

6. **b)**

7. **b)**

8. **a)**

THE RESPIRATORY SYSTEM

The human respiratory system is made up of a series of organs responsible for taking in oxygen and expelling carbon dioxide, and can be divided into two parts: **air conduction** and **gas exchange.** (We'll cover those in more detail soon.)

The respiratory system's primary organs are the lungs, which take in oxygen and expel carbon dioxide when we breathe. Breathing involves **inhalation** (the taking in of air) and **exhalation** (the releasing of air). Blood gathers oxygen from the lungs and transports it to cells throughout the body, where it exchanges the oxygen for carbon dioxide. The carbon dioxide is then transported back to the lungs, where it is exhaled.

Air Conduction

The **diaphragm**, a dome-shaped muscle located at the bottom of the lungs, controls breathing. When a breath is taken, the diaphragm flattens and pulls forward, making more space for the lungs. During exhalation, the diaphragm expands upwards to force air out.

Humans breathe through their noses or mouths, which causes air to enter the **pharynx (**upper part of the throat). The air then passes the **larynx** (the Adam's apple on the inside of the throat). The larynx is also known as the voice box because it changes shape to form sounds. Inhaled air passes into a tube in the center of the chest known as the **trachea**, (the windpipe) which filters the air.

The trachea branches into two **bronchi**, two tubes which carry air into the lungs. Once inside the lungs, each bronchus branches into smaller tubes called **bronchioles**. Bronchioles then lead to sac-like structures called **alveoli**, where the second function of the respiratory system – gas exchange – occurs.

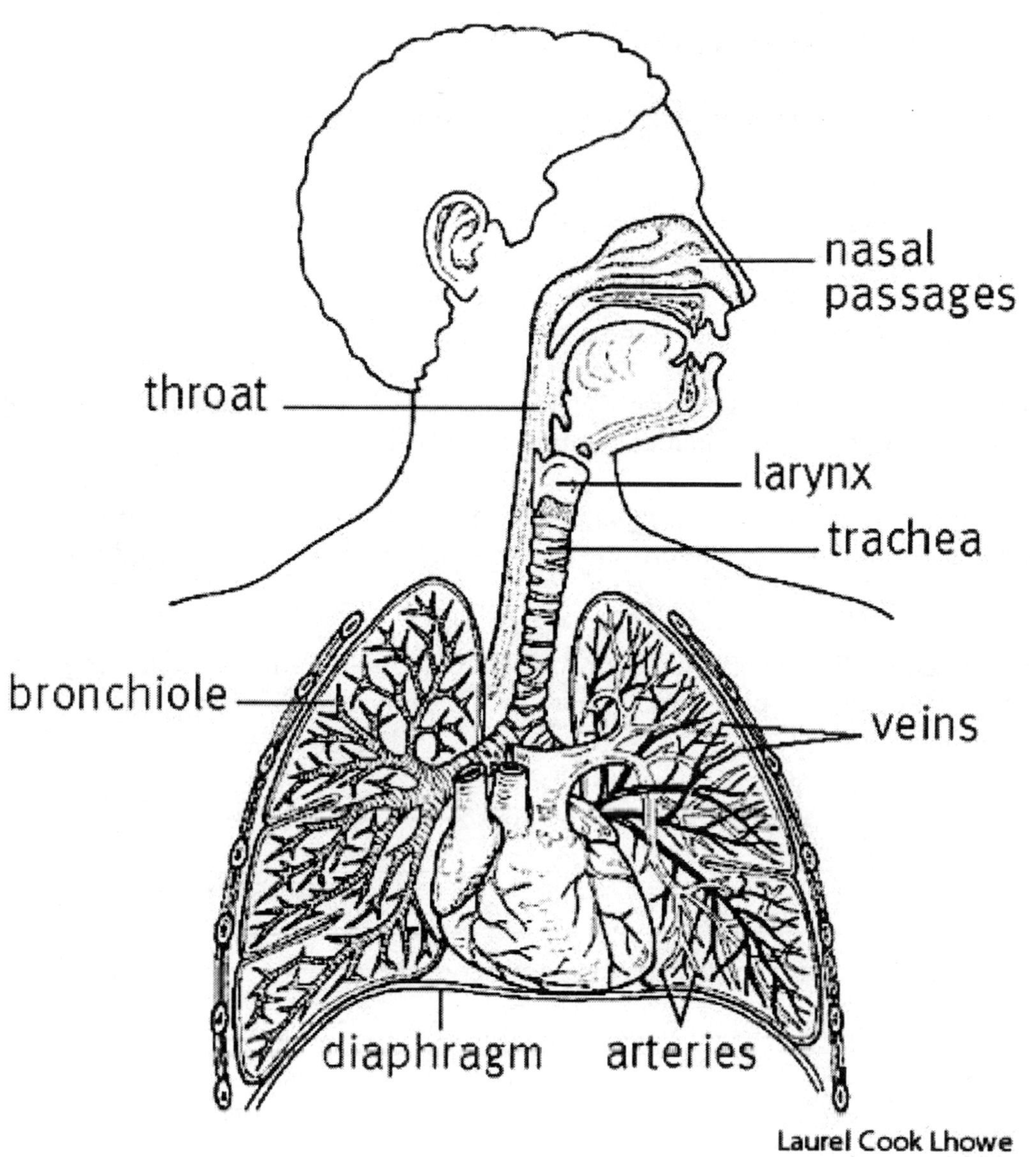

5

[5] The American Heritage® Science Dictionary Copyright © 2010 by Houghton Mifflin Harcourt Publishing Company. Published by Houghton Mifflin Harcourt Publishing Company.

Gas Exchange

Each lung contains over two million alveoli, which creates a large surface area for gas exchange: approximately 800 square feet!

The alveoli and the surrounding blood vessels have very thin walls, which allows for the diffusion of gases in either direction – specifically oxygen and carbon dioxide. Air entering the lungs from the atmosphere is high in oxygen and low in carbon dioxide. This means that the alveoli have a high concentration of oxygen and a low concentration of carbon dioxide.

The opposite is true for the blood within the alveoli's blood vessels. Blood entering the lungs is *low* in oxygen and *high* in carbon dioxide because of cellular respiration (metabolism).

Because the alveoli have a high concentration of oxygen and a low concentration of carbon dioxide, while their blood vessels have the opposite condition, the two gases flow in opposite directions (gas exchange).

Plants exchange gas as well. Single-celled plants, like their animal counterparts, simply exchange gases through the cell membranes. Multicellular plants use pores on the leaf surface, called **stomata**, to exchange gases with the atmosphere.

Test Your Knowledge: The Respiratory System

1. The conduction of air through the respiratory system follows which of the following paths?
   a) Pharynx, larynx, alveoli, trachea, bronchus, bronchioles.
   b) Alveoli, bronchioles, bronchus, trachea, larynx, pharynx.
   c) Pharynx, larynx, trachea, bronchus, bronchioles, alveoli.
   d) Bronchus, bronchioles, alveoli, pharynx, larynx, trachea.

2. Each alveolus in the lungs is covered by tiny blood vessels to perform which of these functions?
   a) Excretion of fluids.
   b) Gas exchange.
   c) Blood production.
   d) Air intake.

3. The pores on a plant leaf that allow for gas exchange are called:
   a) Alveoli.
   b) Cell pores.
   c) Membrane gaps.
   d) Stomata.

4. Which of the following occurs during gas exchange in a cell?
   a) Oxygen is flowing from a low concentration inside the cell to a high concentration outside the cell.
   b) Oxygen is flowing from a high concentration in the red blood cells to a low concentration inside the body cell.
   c) Carbon dioxide is moving from the red blood cells into the body cells, while oxygen is moving from the body cells into the red blood cells.
   d) Carbon dioxide is flowing from a low concentration outside the cells to a high concentration inside the cells.

5. The lungs are very efficient at gas exchange because they have a:
   a) High mass.
   b) Low volume.
   c) High surface-area-to-volume ratio.
   d) Low surface-area-to-volume ratio.

Test Your Knowledge: The Respiratory System – Answers

1. c)
2. b)
3. d)
4. b)
5. c)

THE SKELETAL SYSTEM

Skeletal systems provide structure, support, form, protection, and movement. Of course, muscles do the actual *moving* of an organism, but bones – a major component of the skeletal system –create the framework through which muscles and organs connect. The bone marrow in animal skeletal systems performs **hematopoiesis** (the manufacturing of both red blood cells and white blood cells).

Skeletal systems come in many different forms - those inside of the body are called **endoskeletons**, while those skeletal structures formed outside of the body are known as **exoskeletons**. Crabs and insects have hard shells made of **chitin** to protect their entire bodies. Some organisms, such as starfish, have skeletons made up of tubes filled with fluids running through their bodies. These fluid skeletal systems are called **hydrostatic**.

Joints are where two bones come together. **Connective tissues** at the joint prevent the bones from damaging each other. Joints can be freely movable (elbow or knee), slightly movable (vertebrae in the back), or immovable (skull).

Plants also have a need for support, shape, and protection. While nonvascular do not have a great need for support (remember, they don't grow very tall), vascular plants require a great deal of support. Remember cell walls (a semi-permeable, rigid structure that surrounds each cell outside the cell membrane)? The support and structure of plant cells are primarily derived from the cell wall. Additional support and structure is provided by the tubes used to move water and nutrients through the plant.

Test Your Knowledge: The Skeletal System – Answers

1. Which of the following is NOT a function of the skeletal system in animals?
    a) Transport fluids.
    b) Produce oil.
    c) Placement of internal organs.
    d) Production of blood cells.

2. Which of the following is true of bones?
    a) They contain nerves.
    b) Some are unbreakable.
    c) They are present in vertebrates.
    d) They directly touch each other at a joint.

3. Which of the following animals does **NOT** have an exoskeleton?
    a) Insects.
    b) Crabs.
    c) Lobsters.
    d) Earthworms.

4. What type of tissue is found at joints and protects bones from rubbing against each other and becoming damaged?
    a) Contractile.
    b) Connective.
    c) Conductive.
    d) Catabolic.

5. Fluid skeletal systems are ________________.
    a) Hydrostatic.
    b) Hydrolic.
    c) Hydrophobic.
    d) Hydroskeleton.

Test Your Knowledge: The Skeletal System – Answers

1. b)
2. c)
3. d)
4. b)
5. a)

THE NERVOUS SYSTEM

Irritability is a term used to describe an organism's response to changes, or **stimuli**, in its surroundings. All living organisms respond to environmental stimulus, usually by taking some sort of action: movement of a muscle, gland secretion, activating entire systems like digestion, etc.

Plants have cellular receptors that use chemical messengers to detect and respond to aspects of their environment such as light, gravity, and touch. For example, the orientation of a plant toward or away from light, called **phototropism** is mediated by hormones.

In multi-celled animals, a nervous system controls these responses.

The functioning unit of the nervous system is the **neuron**, a cell with structures capable of transmitting electrical impulses. A neuron must be able to first receive information from internal or external sources, before integrating the signal and sending it to another neuron, gland, or muscle. In multi-celled vertebrates, each neuron has four regions.

At one end of the neuron, there are branch-like extensions called **dendrites**, which receive signals from other neurons.

The **cell body** of the neuron is where the cellular functions take place and where signals are integrated.

The **axon** is an extension from the cell body which the nerve impulses travel along. Axons can be several feet in length, carrying signals from one end of the body to the other.

At the very end of the axon is the **synaptic terminal**, an area that contains chemical substances called **neurotransmitters.**

When an electrical nerve signal reaches the synaptic terminal, it causes neurotransmitters to be released. Neurotransmitters then move across the small space between the neuron and the next neuron (or gland or muscle). This small space is called the **synapse.** Once across the synapse, the neurotransmitter is received by the dendrites of another neuron (or the receptors on a gland or muscle) and then turned back into an electrical signal to be passed on.

The nervous system is divided into two main systems, the **central nervous system** (**CNS**) and the **peripheral nervous system** (**PNS**).

CNS

The central nervous system consists of the brain and spinal cord (contained within the vertebral column or backbone). The brain integrates all the signals in the nervous system, and therefore is responsible for controlling every aspect of the body.

PNS

The peripheral nervous system consists of the nerves outside of the brain and spinal cord. The main function of the PNS is to connect the CNS to the limbs, organs, and **senses**. Unlike the CNS, the PNS is not protected by the bone of spine and skull. This leaves the PNS exposed to toxins and mechanical injuries. The peripheral nervous system is divided into the **somatic nervous system** and the **autonomic nervous system**.

The **somatic nervous system** deals with motor functions. Its nerves connect with skeletal muscle and control movement of all kinds, from fine motor skills to walking and running.

The **autonomic nervous system** works mostly without our conscious control. It is often responsible for critical life functions such as breathing and heart rate. The autonomic nervous system has two divisions.

The **sympathetic division** is responsible for the fight-or-flight response; it prepares the body for high-energy, stressful situations.

The **parasympathetic division** is responsible for rest and digestion functions, so it tends to slow down the body.

Nerves from each of these divisions usually make contact with the same organs, but they often have opposite effects.

The Endocrine System

Another important system in our body is the endocrine, or glandular, system. It controls growth rate, feelings of hunger, body temperature, and more. Many organs run the endocrine system: the **pituitary gland**, the **pancreas**, the **ovaries** (only in females) and **testes** (only in males), the **thyroid** gland, the **parathyroid** gland, the **adrenal** glands, etc.

Of all these, the pituitary gland is the most important endocrine gland in your body. About the size of a pea, the pituitary gland hangs down from the base of your brain and produces the hormone which controls growth.

Fun Fact: Humans grow faster at night because more hormones are released into your blood when you are sleeping.

Test Your Knowledge: The Nervous System

1. __________ is the functional unit of the nervous system.
   a) The nephron
   b) The nucleus
   c) The neuron
   d) The neutrophil

2. Which of the following is a part of the CNS?
   a) Autonomic nerves.
   b) Sympathetic nerves.
   c) Peripheral nerves.
   d) Spinal cord nerves.

3. What is the chemical substance that carries a message from one cell to another?
   a) Axon fluid.
   b) Dendrite fluid.
   c) Neurotransmitter.
   d) Hormone.

4. Dendrites receive information from:
   a) The axon of other neurons.
   b) The dendrites of other neurons.
   c) The cell body of other neurons.
   d) The nucleus of other neurons.

5. __________ release neurotransmitters.
   a) Axons.
   b) Dendrites.
   c) Cell bodies.
   d) The nucleus.

6. Which of the following is NOT true about irritability?
   a) Plants do not experience irritability.
   b) Activates neurons in the brain.
   c) Requires axons in animals.
   d) Neurons act upon muscles.

7. The most important gland in the human body is:
   a) The pancreas.
   b) The pituitary.
   c) The ovaries.
   d) The thyroid.

Test Your Knowledge: The Nervous System – Answers

1. **c)**
2. **d)**
3. **c)**
4. **a)**
5. **a)**
6. **a)**
7. **b)**

THE MUSCULAR SYSTEM

Muscles are often viewed as the "machines" of the body. They help move food from one organ to another, and carry out physical movement. There are three types of muscles in our body: cardiac, smooth, and skeletal. The nervous system controls all three types of muscle tissue, both consciously (controlled) and unconsciously (automatic).

Skeletal (or **striated**) muscle tissue is consciously controlled. The muscle is attached to bones, and when it contracts, the bones move. Skeletal tissue also forms visible muscles, as well as much of the body mass.

Smooth muscle is under automatic control and is generally found in the internal organs, especially in the intestinal tract and in the walls of blood vessels.

Cardiac muscle is found only in the heart. This type of muscle tissue is so automated that it will continue to contract even without stimulation from the nervous system. Isolated heart cells in a dish will continue to contract on their own until oxygen or nutrient sources are used up.

Muscle contraction begins when a nerve impulse causes the release of a chemical called a **neurotransmitter**. Muscle contraction is explained as the interaction between two necessary muscle proteins: thick bands of **myosin** and thin bands of a**ctin**. The thick myosin filaments have small knob-like projections that grab onto the thin actin filaments. As these knobs move slightly, they pull the actin filaments, which slide alongside the myosin filaments. This has the effect of shortening the muscle and thus causing a contraction.

Connective tissues known as **tendons** form a link between muscles and bones (whereas **ligaments** form a link between two bones). The contraction of a muscle causes an exertion of force upon the tendon, which then pulls its attached bone. This movement is synchronized by the central nervous system and results in movement.

Uni-cellular organisms, such as protists and sperm cells, have the ability to move as well. This kind of movement can be accomplished in three different ways. In the case of amoebas, which are one-celled formless blobs of protoplasm, movement is accomplished by extending a portion of the cell itself and then flowing into that portion. Other organisms use **cilia,** which are tiny hair-like projections from the cell membrane, or **flagellum**, which is a tail-like projection that whips around or spins to move.

Test Your Knowledge: The Muscular System

1. What are the three types of muscle cells?
   a) Cardiac, synaptic, and skeletal.
   b) Cardiac, autonomic, and smooth.
   c) Skeletal, cardiac, and smooth.
   d) Smooth, cardiac, and spinal.

2. Which of the following is true about skeletal muscles?
   a) They all contract unconsciously.
   b) All muscle movement is consciously controlled.
   c) They connect directly to one another.
   d) They are also known as striated muscles.

3. What two protein molecules are needed for muscles to contract?
   a) Pepsin and insulin.
   b) Myosin and pepsin.
   c) Hemoglobin and insulin.
   d) Myosin and actin.

4. Flagellum and cilia:
   a) Work with an organism's muscles for movement.
   b) Are parts of all cells and are required for movement.
   c) Are used by organisms without muscular systems.
   d) None of the above.

5. Peristalsis is a process performed by which type of muscle tissue?
   a) Catabolic.
   b) Cardiac.
   c) Smooth.
   d) Skeletal.

Test Your Knowledge: The Muscular System – Answers

1. **c)**
2. **d)**
3. **d)**
4. **c)**
5. **c)**

THE DIGESTIVE SYSTEM

Digestion involves mixing food with digestive juices, moving it through the digestive tract, and breaking down large molecules of food into smaller molecules. The digestive system is made up of the **digestive tract**: a series of hollow organs joined in a long, twisting tube that leads from the mouth to the anus. Several other organs that help the body break down and absorb food are a part of the digestive system as well.

The organs that make up the digestive tract are the **mouth, esophagus, stomach, small intestine, large intestine (colon), rectum,** and **anus**. These organs are covered with a lining called the **mucosa**. In the mouth, stomach, and small intestine, the mucosa contains tiny glands which produce juices to help break down food.

Two "solid" digestive organs, the **liver** and the **pancreas**, produce digestive juices that travel to the intestine through small tubes called **ducts**. The **gallbladder** stores the liver's digestive juices until they are needed in the intestine. The circulatory and nervous systems are also important to the digestive system.

Digestive pathway

The large, hollow organs of the digestive tract contain a layer of muscle that enables their walls to move. This movement propels food and liquid through the system and assists in mixing the contents within each organ. The movement of food molecules from one organ to the next, through *muscle action*, is called **peristalsis**.

The first major muscle movement occurs when food or liquid is swallowed. Although you are able to start swallowing by choice, once the swallow begins, it becomes involuntary (controlled by nerves).

Swallowed food is pushed into the esophagus, which connects the throat with the stomach. At the junction of the esophagus and stomach, there is a ring-like muscle (**lower esophageal sphincter**) that controls the passage between the two organs. As food approaches the closed sphincter, it relaxes and allows the food to pass through to the stomach.

The stomach has three mechanical tasks:

1. It stores the swallowed food and liquid.

2. It mixes the stored food and liquid with digestive juices produced by the stomach.

3. It empties its contents slowly into the small intestine.

Once in the stomach, the food is churned and bathed in a very strong acid (**gastric acid**). When food in the stomach is partly digested and mixed with stomach acids, it is called **chyme**. Several factors affect how long food molecules remain in the stomach, including the type of food, the degree of muscle action of the emptying stomach, and the breakdown of food occurring in the small intestine. Carbohydrates spend the least amount of time in the stomach, followed by proteins; fats remain in the stomach for the longest amount of time.

From the stomach food molecules enter the first part of the small intestine called the **duodenum**. They then enter the **jejunum**, and then the **ileum** (the final part of the small intestine). In the small intestine, **bile** (produced in the liver and stored in the gall bladder), pancreatic enzymes, and other digestive enzymes produced in the small intestine help break down the food even further. Many accessory organs such as the liver, pancreas, and gall bladder contribute enzymes and buffering fluids to the mix inside of the small intestine; this also aids in the chemical break down of food molecules.

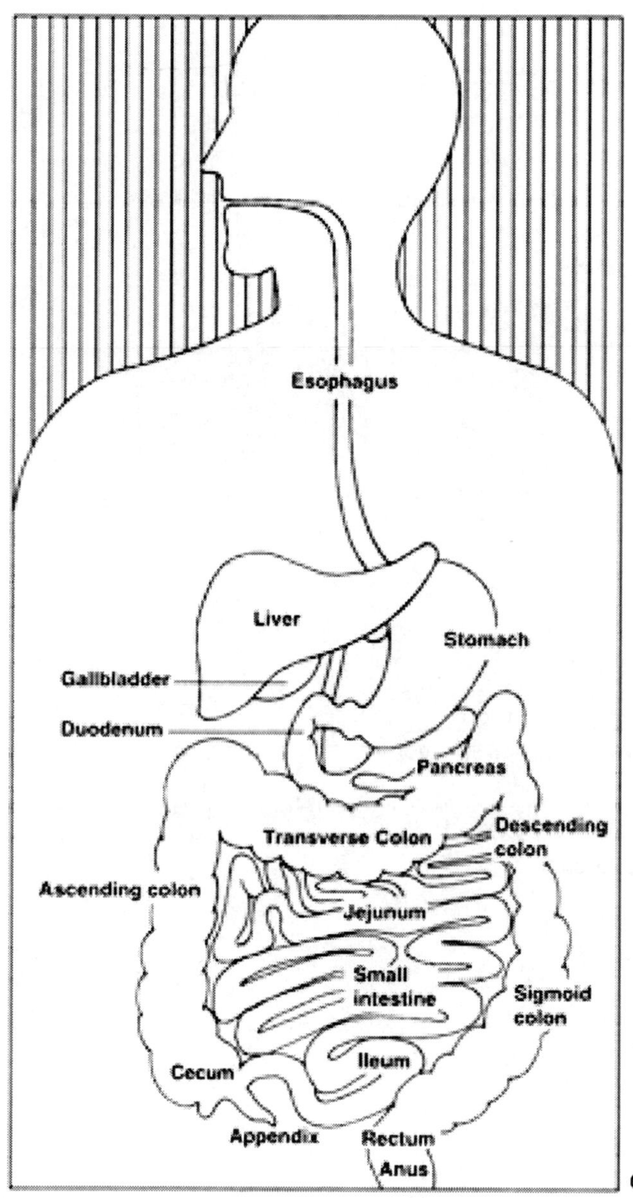

[6]

Food then passes into the large intestine, also known as the colon. The main function of the colon is to absorb water, which reduces the undigested matter into a solid waste called feces. Microbes in the large intestine help in the final digestion process. The first part of the large intestine is called the cecum (the appendix is connected to the cecum). Food then travels upward in the ascending colon. The food travels across the abdomen in the transverse colon, goes back down the other side of the body in the descending colon, and then through the sigmoid colon. Solid waste is then stored in the rectum until it is excreted.

[6] Graphic from: http://digestive.niddk.nih

Test Your Knowledge: The Digestive System

1. Food begins the digestive process in the:
    a) Esophagus.
    b) Stomach.
    c) Intestines.
    d) Mouth.

2. Chyme is:
    a) Water and completely broken down food molecules.
    b) Acids and completely broken down food molecules.
    c) Acids and partially broken down some food molecules.
    d) Water and partially broken down some food molecules.

3. Where is bile stored?
    a) In the pancreas.
    b) In the gallbladder.
    c) In the liver.
    d) In the small intestines.

4. Which of the following is NOT an accessory organ of the digestive system?
    a) Liver.
    b) Pancreas.
    c) Gall bladder.
    d) Urinary bladder.

5. The chief function of the colon is to:
    a) Absorb water from undigested waste.
    b) Produce sugars.
    c) Absorb protein from undigested waste.
    d) Produce carbohydrates.

Test Your Knowledge: The Digestive System – Answers

1. **d)**
2. **c)**
3. **b)**
4. **d)**
5. **a)**

THE RENAL SYSTEM (FILTRATION/EXCRETION SYSTEM)

Single-celled organisms excrete toxic substances either by diffusion through their cell membranes, or through specialized organelles called **vacuoles.** When metabolic chemical reactions occur within the cells of organisms, wastes are produced that could cause harm to the body. Those wastes therefore must be excreted. Multicellular organisms require special organ systems – humans specifically utilize the circulatory and excretory systems – to eliminate wastes.

Organisms need to be able to respond to changes in their external environment, all the while still maintaining a relatively constant internal environment. They must maintain a balance of water, temperature, and salt concentration, to name just a few. The physical and chemical processes that work to maintain an internal balance are called **homeostasis.** You may recognize this term from the previous discussion on blood and the circulatory system. Homeostasis is maintained by the cooperation of both the circulatory and the renal systems.

We have discussed digestions: food is broken down, absorbed as very small molecules, and carried to the cells by blood. Cells need these broken-down molecules to perform the life-sustaining biochemical reactions of metabolism, which produce wastes.

1. Aerobic respiration produces water and **carbon dioxide**.

2. Anaerobic respiration produces **lactic acid** and carbon dioxide.

3. Dehydration synthesis produces water.

4. Protein metabolism produces **nitrogenous wastes**, (i.e. **ammonia**).

5. Other metabolic processes can produce salts, oils, etc.

Non-toxic wastes can be retained, released, or recycled through other reactions. **Toxic** wastes however, are disposed of according to their molecular make-up. For example, blood carries gaseous wastes like carbon dioxide to the lungs for exhalation. Other wastes need to be filtered out of the blood and then excreted. Nitrogenous wastes are the result of excess amino acids broken down during cellular respiration. The toxicity (harmfulness) of those nitrogenous wastes varies from:

Extremely Toxic - **Ammonia**
Less Toxic - **Urea**
Non-toxic – **Uric Acid**

The Kidneys

Toxic wastes are carried by blood to the liver, where they are converted into **urea.** The blood then carries the urea to the **kidneys** (bean-shaped, fist-sized organs), where it will be converted from urea into **urine**. Urine is able to mix with water and be excreted from the body; the amount of water that is used in this process is regulated by the kidneys in order to prevent body dehydration.

The kidneys are complex filtering systems which maintain the proper levels of various life-supporting substances, including sodium; potassium; chloride; calcium; glucose sugar; and amino acids. These life-supporting substances are absorbed by the kidneys from urine before it I expelled. The kidneys also help maintain blood pressure and the acidity (pH) level of the blood.

Each kidney contains at least a million individual units called **nephrons.** Nephrons perform similar functions as the alveoli do in the lungs; but whereas the alveoli function as areas of gas exchange, the kidney nephrons are structured to function as areas of *fluid* interchange. Each nephron contains a bed of capillaries. Those capillaries which are bringing in blood are surrounded by a **Bowman's capsule**.

A Bowman's capsule is an important part of the filtration system in the kidneys. The capsule separates the blood into two components: a cleaned blood product, and a filtrate which is moved through the nephron. As the filtrate travels through the nephron, more impurities are removed. The filtrate is concentrated into **urine**, which is then processed for elimination. The collected urine flows into the **ureters**, which take it to the **urinary bladder**. Urine will collect in the urinary bladder until the pressure causes an urge to expel it from the body through the **urethra**.

Each nephron in the kidneys is attached to its own Bowman's capsule, and there are hundreds of thousands of nephrons. Functioning kidneys can process the blood in the body about 20 times each day, illustrating just how important these structures are. The kidneys are truly a feat of natural engineering. In fact, despite the medical community's best efforts, it has so far been impossible to build a fully artificial kidney.

Kidneys also regulate the amount of water circulating in the bloodstream. If the brain detects depleted levels of water in the blood, it increases the release of the **antidiuretic hormone (ADH)**. ADH causes the kidneys to reabsorb water into the bloodstream, which in turn concentrates the urine and preserves water for the body. The reason why you urinate more frequently when drinking alcohol is because alcohol inhibits the ADH signal from the brain.

Test Your Knowledge: The Renal System

1. The kidneys filter which of the following from blood?
   a) Undigested food.
   b) Metabolic wastes.
   c) Blood cells.
   d) Platelets.

2. Which of the following is **NOT** a function of the kidneys?
   a) Regulating pH (acidity) of blood.
   b) Regulating blood pressure.
   c) Assisting in the maintenance of homeostasis.
   d) Regulating hormone release.

3. The nephron is where ____________ is produced.
   a) Urine.
   b) Ammonia.
   c) Nucleic acid.
   d) Amino acid.

4. Waste concentrated in the Bowman's capsule is called:
   a) Urine.
   b) Salts.
   c) Nucleic acids.
   d) Amino acids.

5. Alcohol consumption increases urination because it:
   a) Increases the amount of water in the body.
   b) Increases the action of antidiuretic hormone.
   c) Decreases the action of antidiuretic hormone.
   d) Stops water reabsorption.

Test Your Knowledge: The Renal System – Answers

1. **b)**
2. **d)**
3. **a)**
4. **a)**
5. **c)**

Chemistry

ELEMENTS, COMPOUNDS, AND MIXTURES

Matter

Matter is commonly defined as anything that takes up space and has mass. **Mass** is the quantity of matter something possesses, and usually has a unit of weight associated with it.

Matter can undergo two types of change: chemical and physical.

> A **chemical change** occurs when an original substance is transformed into a new substance with different properties. An example would be the burning of wood, which produces ash and smoke.
>
> Transformations that do not produce new substances, such as stretching a rubber band or melting ice, are called **physical changes**.

The fundamental properties which we use to measure matter are mass, weight, volume, density and specific gravity.

Extrinsic properties are directly related to the amount of material being measured, such as weight and volume.

Intrinsic properties are those which are independent of the quantity of matter present, such as density and specific gravity.

Atom
An atom is the ultimate particle of matter; it is the smallest particle of an element that still is a part of that element. All atoms of the same element have the same mass. Atomic chemical changes involve the transfer of whole atoms from one substance to another; but atoms are not created or destroyed in ordinary chemical changes.

An atom is made up of several parts. The center is called the **nucleus**, and is made up of two particles: a positively-charged particle, called a **proton,** and a particle that does not have a charge, called a **neutron**. The masses of a proton and neutron are about the same.

The nucleus of the atom is surrounded by negatively-charged particles called **electrons**, which move in orbits around the nucleus. The nucleus is only a small portion of the total amount of space an atom takes up, even though most of an atom's mass is contained in the nucleus.

Molecular Weight

A **mole** is the amount of substance that contains 6.02×10^{23} basic particles. This is referred to as **Avogadro's number** and is based on the number of atoms in C_{12} (Carbon 12). For example, a mole of copper is the amount of copper that contains exactly 6.02×10^{23} atoms, and one mole of water contains 6.02×10^{23} H_2O molecules. The weight of one mole of an element is called its **atomic weight**. The atomic weight of an element with isotopes, which are explained further on the next page, is the average of the isotopes' individual atomic weights.

The negatively-charged electrons are very light in mass. An atom is described as neutral if it has an equal number of protons and electrons, or if the number of electrons is the same as the atomic number of the atom. You may have already assumed –correctly! – from that information that the atomic number of an atom equals the number of protons in that atom. The **atomic weight** or **mass** of the atom is the total number of protons and neutrons in the atom's nucleus.

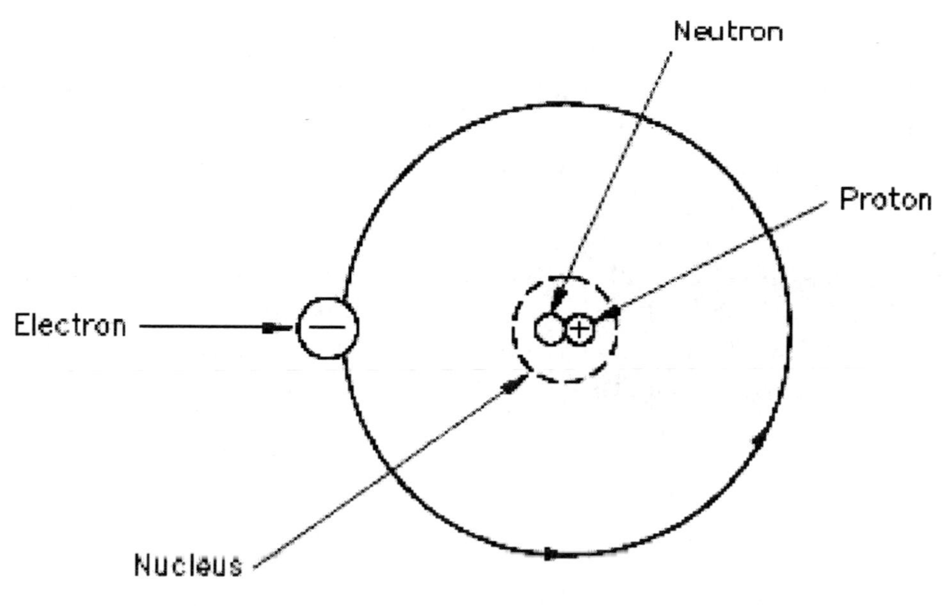

[7]

Elements

An element is a substance which cannot be broken down by chemical means; they are composed of atoms that have the same **atomic number** and are defined by the number of protons and neutrons they have. Some elements have more than one form, such as carbon; these alternate forms are called **isotopes.** There are approximately 109 known elements. Eighty-eight of these occur naturally on earth, while the others are **synthesized** (manufactured).

Hydrogen is the most abundant element in the Universe. It is found in 75% of all matter known to exist. **Helium** is the second most abundant element, found in approximately 25% of all known matter. The Earth is composed mostly of iron, oxygen, silicon, and magnesium, though these elements are not evenly distributed. 90% of the human body's mass consists of oxygen, carbon, hydrogen, nitrogen, calcium, and phosphorus. 75% of elements are metals, and eleven are gases in their natural state. We'll cover this more in-depth when we view the periodic table.

Molecules

A molecule is the smallest part of a substance that isn't chemically bonded to another atom. **Chemical formulas** are used to represent the atomic composition of a molecule. For example, one molecule of water contains 2 atoms of Hydrogen and 1 atom of Oxygen; its chemical formula is $\mathbf{2H + O = H_2O}$.

---

[7] Graphic from: http://www.circuitlab.org

Compounds and Mixtures

Substances that contain more than one type of element are called **compounds.** Compounds that are made up of molecules which are all identical are called **pure substances**. A **mixture** consists of two or more substances that are not chemically bonded. Mixtures are generally placed in one of two categories:

> **Homogeneous mixture** – Components that make up the mixture are uniformly distributed; examples are water and air.

> **Heterogeneous mixture** - Components of the mixture are not uniform; they sometimes have localized regions with different properties. For example: the different components of soup make it a heterogeneous mixture. Rocks, as well, are not uniform and have localized regions with different properties.

A uniform, or homogenous, mixture of different molecules is called a **solution**. If the solution is a liquid, the material being dissolved is the **solute** and the liquid it is being dissolved in is called the **solvent.** Both solids and gases can dissolve in liquids. A **saturated** has reached a point of maximum concentration; in it, no more solute will dissolve.

Test Your Knowledge: Elements, Compounds, and Mixtures

1. Which statement best describes the density of an atom's nucleus?
   a) The nucleus occupies most of the atom's volume, but contains little of its mass.
   b) The nucleus occupies very little of the atom's volume, and contains little of its mass.
   c) The nucleus occupies most of the atom's volume, and contains most of its mass.
   d) The nucleus occupies very little of the atom's volume, but contains most of its mass.

2. Which of the following is not a physical change?
   a) Melting of aspirin.
   b) Lighting a match.
   c) Putting sugar in tea.
   d) Boiling of antifreeze.

3. A solid melts gradually between 85°C and 95°C to give a milky, oily liquid. When a laser beam shines through the liquid, the path of the beam is clearly visible. The milky liquid is likely to be:
   a) A heterogeneous mixture.
   b) An element.
   c) A compound.
   d) A solution.

4. The identity of an element is determined by:
   a) The number of its protons and neutrons.
   b) The number of its neutrons.
   c) The number of its electrons.
   d) Its atomic mass.

5. True or False? When a match burns, some matter is destroyed.
   a) True.
   b) False.

6. What is the reason for your answer to question **5**?
   a) This chemical reaction destroys matter.
   b) Matter is consumed by the flame.
   c) The mass of ash is less than the match it came from.
   d) The atoms are not destroyed, they are only rearranged.
   e) The match weighs less after burning.

7. An unsaturated solution:
   a) Hasn't dissolved as much solute as is theoretically possible.
   b) Has dissolved exactly as much solute as is theoretically possible.
   c) Is unstable because it has dissolved more solute than would be expected.
   d) None of the above.

Test Your Knowledge: Elements, Compounds, and Mixtures – Answers

1. **d)**
2. **b)**
3. **c)**
4. **a)**
5. **b)**
6. **d)**
7. **a)**

STATES OF MATTER

The physical states of matter are generally grouped into three main categories:

1. **Solids:** Rigid; they maintain their shape and have strong intermolecular forces.

2. **Liquids:** Cannot maintain their own shape, conform to their containers, and contain forces strong enough to keep molecules from dispersing into spaces.

3. **Gases:** Have indefinite shape; disperse rapidly through space due to random movement and are able to occupy any volume. They are held together by weak forces.

Two specific states of matter are **liquid crystals**, which can maintain their shape as well as be made to flow, and **plasmas**, gases in which electrons are stripped from their nuclei.

There are four physical properties of gases that are related to each other. If any one of these changes, a change will occur in at least one of the remaining three.

1. Volume of the gas.

2. Pressure of the gas.

3. Temperature of the gas.

4. The number of gas molecules.

The laws that relate these properties to each other are:

Boyle's Law: The volume of a given amount of gas at a constant temperature is inversely proportional to pressure. In other words; if the initial volume decreases by half, the pressure will double and vice versa. The representative equation is: $P_1V_1 = P_2V_2$.

Charles's Law: The volume of a given amount of gas at a constant pressure is directly proportional to absolute (Kelvin) temperature. If the temperature of the gas increases, the volume of the gas also increases and vice versa. The representative equation is: $V_1/T_1 = V_2/T_2$.

Avogadro's Law: Equal volumes of all gases under identical conditions of pressure and temperature contain the same number of molecules. The molar volume of all ideal gases at 0° C and a pressure of 1 atm. is 22.4 liters.

The **kinetic theory of gases** assumes that gas molecules are very small compared to the distance between the molecules. Gas molecules are in constant, random motion; they frequently collide with each other and with the walls of whatever container they are in.

Test Your Knowledge: States of Matter

1. Under the same conditions of pressure and temperature, a liquid differs from a gas because the molecules of the liquid:
   a) Have no regular arrangement.
   b) Are in constant motion.
   c) Have stronger forces of attraction between them.
   d) Take the shape of the container they are in.

2. Methane (CH4) gas diffuses through air because the molecules are:
   a) Moving randomly.
   b) Dissolving quickly.
   c) Traveling slowly.
   d) Expanding steadily.

3. Which of the following would not change if the number of gas molecules changed?
   a) Volume of the gas.
   b) Type of gas.
   c) Pressure of the gas.
   d) Temperature of gas.

4. When the pressure is increased on a can filled with gas, its volume ___________.
   a) Stays the same.
   b) Increases.
   c) Decreases.
   d) Turns to liquid.

5. Equal volumes of all gases at the same temperature and pressure contain the same number of molecules. This statement is known as:
   a) Kinetic theory of gases.
   b) Charles's Law.
   c) Boyle's Law.
   d) Avogadro's Law.

Test Your Knowledge: States of Matter – Answers

1. **c)**
2. **a)**
3. **b)**
4. **c)**
5. **d)**

THE PERIODIC TABLE AND CHEMICAL BONDS

The Periodic table

The Periodic Table is a chart which arranges the chemical elements in a useful, logical manner. Elements are listed in order of increasing atomic number, lined up so that elements which exhibit similar properties are arranged in the same row or column as each other.

12 <- Atomic number
Mg <- Chemical symbol
24.31 <- Atomic weight

1a	IIa	IIIb	IVb	Vb	VIb	VIII	VIII	VIII	Ib	IIb	IIIb	IVa	Va	VIa	VIIa	0
1 H 1.008																2 He 4.00
3 Li 6.94	4 Be 9.01										5 B 10.81	6 C 12.01	7 N 14.00	8 O 15.99	9 F 18.99	10 Ne 20.18
11 Na 22.99	12 Mg 24.31										13 Al 26.98	14 Si 28.09	15 P 30.97	16 S 32.06	17 Cl 35.45	18 Ar 39.95
19 K 39.10	20 Ca 40.08	21 Sc 44.6	22 Ti 47.90	23 V 50.94	24 Cr 51.99	25 Mn 54.94	26 Fe 55.85	27 Co 58.93	28 Ni 58.71	29 Cu 63.54	30 Zn 65.37	31 Ga 69.72	32 Ge 72.59	33 As 74.92	34 Se 78.96	35 Br 79.91	36 Kr 83.80
37 Rb 85.47	38 Sr 87.62	39 Y 88.91	40 Zr 91.22	41 Nb 92.91	42 Mo 95.94	43 Tc 99	44 Ru 101.97	45 Rh 102.91	46 Pd 106.4	47 Ag 107.87	48 Cd 112.40	49 In 114.82	50 Sn 118.69	51 Sb 121.75	52 Te 127.60	53 I 126.90	54 Xe 131.30
55 Cs 132.91	56 Ba 137.34	57-71 see below	72 Hf 178.49	73 Ta 180.95	74 W 183.85	75 Re 186.2	76 Os 190.2	77 Ir 192.2	78 Pt 195.09	79 Au 196.97	80 Hg 200.59	81 Tl 204.37	82 Pb 207.19	83 Bi 208.98	84 Po 210	85 At 210	86 Rn 222
87 Fr 223	88 Ra 226	89-103 see below	104 Rf 261	105 Ha 260	106 Sg 263												

57 La 138.91	58 Ce 140.12	59 Pr 140.91	60 Nd 144.24	61 Pm 147	62 Sm 150.35	63 Eu 151.96	64 Gd 157.24	65 Tb 158.92	66 Dy 162.50	67 Ho 164.93	68 Er 167.26	69 Tm 168.93	70 Yb 173.04	71 Lu 174.97
89 Ac 227	90 Th 232.04	91 Pa 231	92 U 238.03	93 Np 237	94 Pu 242	95 Am 243	96 Cm 247	97 Bk 247	98 Cf 251	99 Es 254	100 Fm 253	101 Md 256	102 No 254	103 Lw 257

[8]

- Each box contains the symbol of the element, its atomic number, and its atomic weight.
- The elements appear in increasing order according to their atomic numbers, except for the 2 separate rows.
- The vertical columns are called **groups**. Elements within a group share several common properties and often have the same outer electron arrangement. There are two categories: the main group and the transition elements.
    - The number of the main group corresponds to the number of valence electrons.
    - Most of the transition elements contain 2 electrons in their valence shells.
- The horizontal rows are called **periods** and correspond to the number of occupied electron shells of the atom.
- The elements set below the main table are the **lanthanoids** (upper row) and **actinoids**. They also usually have 2 electrons in their outer shells.
- Most of the elements on the periodic table are metals. The alkali metals, alkaline earths, basic metals, transition metals, lanthanides, and actinides are all groups of metals.

[8] Graphic from: http://volcano.oregonstatevolcano.oregonstate.edu.edu

- In general, the elements increase in mass from left to right and from top to bottom.
- The main difference between the modern periodic table and the one Mendeleev (the periodic table's creator) came up with is that Mendeleev's original table arranged the elements in order of increasing atomic weight, while the modern table orders the elements by increasing atomic number.

Electronic Structure of Atoms

The electrons of an atom have fixed energy levels. Electrons in the principle energy levels are said to be in **electron shells**. Those shells which correspond to the highest energy levels include the electrons usually involved in chemical bonding. Those shells are called **valence shells.** Chemical formulas of simple compounds can often be predicted from valences. The valence electrons increase in number as you go across the periodic table.

The electrons in the outer orbit can combine with other atoms by giving up electrons or taking on electrons. Atoms that give up electrons (**cations**) change from being neutral to having a *positive* charge. Atoms that gain electrons (**ions**) change from being neutral to having a *negative* charge. The **octet rule** is a chemical rule which states that atoms of a low atomic number will share, gain, or lose electrons in order to fill outer electron shells with eight electrons. This is achieved through different types of bonding.

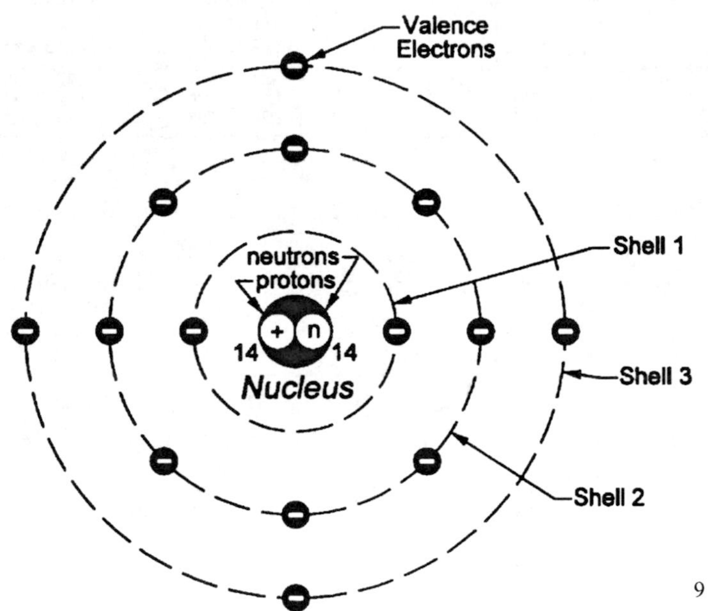

[9]

Chemical Bonds

Electromagnetism is a force that is involved in all chemical behavior, including the chemical bonds which hold atoms together in order to form molecules, as well as those that hold molecules together to form all substances. **Electronegativity** is a measure of the tendency of an atom to attract a bonding pair

[9] Graphic from: http://www.circuitlab.org

of electrons. Electronegativity is affected by both the atomic number and the distance between the valence electrons and the charged nucleus. The higher the assigned electronegativity number, the more an element or compound attracts electrons.

The two main types of bonds formed between atoms are **ionic bonds** and **covalent bonds.** As a result of being negatively and positively charged, anions and cations usually form bonds known as ionic bonds and exist because of the attraction of opposite charges.

A covalent bond forms when atoms share valence electrons. Atoms do not always share the electrons equally, which results in a **polar covalent bond**. When electrons are shared by two metallic atoms, a **metallic bond** can form. The electrons which participate in metallic bonds may be shared between any of the metal atoms in the region.

If the electronegativity values of two atoms are similar, then:

- Metallic bonds form between two metal atoms.
- Covalent bonds form between two non-metal atoms.
- Non-polar covalent bonds form when the electronegativity values are very similar.
- Polar covalent bonds form when the electronegativity values are a little further apart.

If the electronegativity values of two atoms are different, then ionic bonds are formed.

Most metals have less than 4 valence electrons, which allows them to either gain a few electrons or lose a few; they generally tend to lose electrons, which causes them to become more positive. (This means that metals tend to form cations.)

A **hydrogen bond** is not considered a chemical bond. Instead, in a hydrogen bond, the attractive force between hydrogen is attached to an electronegative atom of one molecule and an electronegative atom of a different molecule. Usually the electronegative atom is oxygen, nitrogen, or fluorine, which have partial negative charges. The hydrogen has the partial positive charge. Hydrogen bonds are much weaker than both ionic and covalent bonds.

Test Your Knowledge: The Periodic Table and Chemical Bonds

1. When cations and anions join, they form what kind of chemical bond?
   a) Ionic.
   b) Hydrogen.
   c) Metallic.
   d) Covalent.

2. Generally, how do atomic masses vary throughout the periodic table of the elements?
   a) They decrease from left to right and increase from top to bottom.
   b) They increase from left to right and increase bottom to top.
   c) They increase from left to right and increase top to bottom.
   d) They increase from right to left and decrease bottom to top.

3. The force involved in all chemical behavior is:
   a) Electronegativity.
   b) Covalent bonds.
   c) Electromagnetism.
   d) Ionic bonds.

4. Which one of the following is not a form of chemical bonding?
   a) Covalent bonding.
   b) Hydrogen bonding.
   c) Ionic bonding.
   d) Metallic bonding.

5. Two atoms which do not share electrons equally will form what type of bond?
   a) Metallic bonds.
   b) Polar covalent.
   c) Ionic bonds.
   d) They cannot form bonds.

6. Chemical bonding:
   a) Uses electrons that are closest to the nucleus of the atoms bonding.
   b) Always uses electrons from only one of the atoms involved.
   c) Uses all the electrons in all atoms involved.
   d) Uses the valence electrons of all the atoms involved.

Test Your Knowledge: The Periodic Table and Chemical Bonds

1. a)
2. c)
3. c)
4. b)
5. b)
6. d)

ACIDS AND BASES

pH Scale

0 — 0.0 Hydrochloric acid (1M)

2.0 Stomach acid

3.0 Lemon juice

acids

5.0 Urine

6.5 Saliva

7 — **7.0 Pure water**

7.4 Blood 8.0 Pancreatic juice

bases

11.0 Ammonia cleansers

13.5 Oven cleaner

14 — 14.0 Sodium hydroxide (1 M) [10]

Acids

Naturally-occurring **acid solutions**, in which the solvent is always water, have several characteristic properties in common. They:

- Have a sour taste.
- Speed up the corrosion, or rusting, of metals.
- Conduct electricity.
- Introduce H^+ cations into aqueous solutions.

These characteristic properties can be changed by the addition of a base.

---

[10] Graphic from: http://bioserv.fiu.edu

Bases (Alkalis)

Bases don't occur in as many common materials as do acids. A few examples of bases are: lime, lye, and soap. Basic solutions:

- Have a bitter taste.
- Conduct electricity, when their solvent is water.
- Introduce OH^- ions into an aqueous solution.

The characteristic properties can be changed by the addition of an acid.

The acidity or basicity of a solution is expressed by **pH values**. A neutral solution is defined by the following: it has equal concentrations of H^+ cations and OH^- ions, and a pH of 7. Neutrality is based on the pH of pure water. The more acidic a solution, the lower the pH is below 7. The more basic the solution, the higher the pH is above 7. The pH scale is based on logarithms of base 10. (If one solution has a pH of 8 and another has a pH of 10, then there is a 10^2 or 100 fold difference between the two.)

Buffers

A **buffer** is used to make a solution which exhibits very little change in its pH when small amounts of an acid or base are added to it.

An acidic buffer solution is simply one which has a pH less than 7. Acidic buffer solutions are commonly made from a weak acid and one of its salts - often a sodium salt. A strong basic solution can be weakened by adding an acidic buffer.

An alkaline buffer solution has a pH greater than 7. Alkaline buffer solutions are commonly made from a weak base and one of its salts. A strong acid can be made weaker by adding an alkaline buffer.

The human body contains many enzymes that only function at a specific pH. Once outside of this range, the enzymes are either unable to catalyze reactions or, in some cases, will break down. Our bodies produce a buffer solution that is a mixture of carbonic acid and bicarbonate, in order to keep the pH of blood at 7.4.

Test Your Knowledge: Acids and Bases

1. One of the characteristic properties of an acid is that they introduce:
   a) Hydrogen ions.
   b) Hydroxyl ions.
   c) Hydride ions.
   d) Oxide ions.

2. A solution with a pH of 12 is:
   a) Very acidic.
   b) Neutral.
   c) Very basic.
   d) You can't have a solution with a pH of 12.

3. Buffers keep the pH of a solution from changing by:
   a) Converting strong acids to weak ones.
   b) Converting weak acids to strong ones.
   c) Converting weak bases to strong ones.
   d) More than one of the above answers is correct.

4. Proper blood pH level for humans is:
   a) 7.0.
   b) 7.2.
   c) 7.6.
   d) 7.4.

5. All of the following are properties of alkalis except:
   a) Bitter taste.
   b) Basic solutions are high conductors of electricity.
   c) Introduce OH^- ions into an aqueous solution.
   d) The characteristic properties can be changed by the addition of an acid.

Test Your Knowledge: Acids and Bases – Answers

1. a)

2. c)

3. a)

4. d)

5. b)

Physics

MOTION

Speed is a scalar quantity and is defined as distance divided by time. (Ex: miles per hour.)

Velocity is a vector quantity that describes speed and the direction of travel.

Magnitude of Acceleration is defined as the change in velocity divided by the time interval.

A **scalar quantity** is described only by its magnitude, whereas a **vector quantity** is described by magnitude and direction.

Acceleration is change in velocity divided by time; an object accelerates not only when it speeds up, but also when slowing down or turning. The **acceleration due to gravity** of a falling object near the Earth is a constant $9.8 m/s^2$; therefore an object's magnitude increases as it falls and decreases as it rises.

Newton's Three Laws of Motion

1. An object at rest will remain at rest unless acted on by an unbalanced force. An object in motion continues in motion with the same speed and in the same direction unless acted upon by an unbalanced force. This law is often called "**The Law of Inertia**."

2. Acceleration is produced when a force acts on a mass. The greater the mass (of the object being accelerated) the greater the amount of force needed (to accelerate the object). Think of it like this: it takes a greater amount of force to push a boulder, than it does to push a feather.

3. Every action requires an equal and opposite reaction. This means that for every force, there is a reacting force both equal in size and opposite in direction. (I.e. whenever an object pushes another object, it gets pushed back in the opposite direction with equal force.)

An object's **density** is its mass divided by its volume. **Frictional forces** arise when one object tries move over or around another; the frictional forces act in the opposite direction to oppose such a motion. **Pressure** is the force per unit area which acts upon a surface.

There are **Three Important Conservation Laws** which are embodied within Newton's Laws. They offer a different and sometimes more powerful way to consider motion:

1. **Conservation of Momentum** – Embodied in Newton's first law (Law of Inertia), this reiterates that the momentum of a system is constant if no external forces act upon the system.

2. **Conservation of Energy** - Energy is neither created nor destroyed; it can be converted from one form to another (i.e. potential energy converted to kinetic energy), but the total amount of energy within the domain remains fixed.

3. **Conservation of Angular Momentum** – If the system is subjected to no external force, then the total angular momentum of a system has constant magnitude and direction. This is the common physics behind figure-skating and planetary orbits.

Energy and Forces

The energy stored within an object is called its **potential energy** – it has the potential to do work. But where does that energy come from? When gravity pulls down on an object (**gravitational energy**) the object receives potential energy. **Kinetic energy**, the energy of motion, is the energy possessed because of an object's motion.

The sum of an object's kinetic and potential energies is called the total **mechanical energy** (or, **internal energy**).

Frictional forces convert kinetic energy and gravitational potential energy into **thermal energy**. **Power** is the energy converted from one form to another, divided by the time needed to make the conversion. A **simple machine** is a device that alters the magnitude or direction of an applied force. Example: an inclined plane or lever.

Objects that move in a curved path have acceleration towards the center of that path. That acceleration is called a **centripetal acceleration. Centripetal force** is the inward force causing that object to move in the curved path. If the centripetal force is the action, the (opposite) reaction is an outwardly-directed **centrifugal force**.

THERMAL PHYSICS

Temperature and Heat

Heat and temperature are two different things. **Heat** is a measure of the work required to change the speeds in a collection of atoms or molecules. **Temperature** is a measure of the average kinetic energy of the atoms or molecules of a substance.

A **calorie** is the amount of heat required to raise the temperature of 1 gram of water by 1 degree Celsius. The **specific heat** of a substance is the ratio of the amount of heat added to a substance, divided by the mass and the temperature change of the substance.

The change of a substance from solid to liquid, or liquid to gas, etc., is called a **phase change**.

Heat of Fusion: The amount of heat required to change a unit mass of a substance from solid to liquid at the *melting point*.

Heat of Vaporization: The amount of heat needed to change a unit mass of a substance from liquid to vapor at the *boiling point*.

HEAT TRANSFER

Temperature Scales

There are three common temperature scales: **Celsius**, **Fahrenheit**, and **Kelvin**. Because it is based upon what we believe to be **absolute zero** (the lowest theoretical temperature possible before life ceases), the Kelvin scale is also known as the **absolute scale**.

Temperature Scale	Point at Which Water Freezes
Celsius	0° C
Fahrenheit	32° F
Kelvin	273K

The Two Mechanisms of Heat Transfer

Conduction: Heat transfer via conduction can occur in a substance of any phase (solid, liquid, or gas), but is mostly seen in solids.

Convection: Convection heat transfer occurs only in fluids (liquids and gases).

Both types of heat transfer are caused by molecular movement in the substance of interest.

WAVE MOTION (SOUND) AND MAGNETISM

Waves

Waves can be placed in one of two categories: **longitudinal** or **transverse**.

In a **transverse wave**, the motion of the medium is perpendicular to the motion of the wave; for example, waves on water. In a **longitudinal wave**, the motion of the medium is parallel to the motion of the wave. Sound waves are transverse waves.

A wave's **wavelength** is the distance between successive high points (**crests**) and low points (**troughs**). The **speed of a wave** is the rate at which it moves. **Frequency** – measured in **Hertz** (Hz) – is the number of repetitions, or cycles, occurring per second. The **amplitude** is the intensity (or strength) of the wave.

Sound

When vibrations disturb the air, they create sound waves. The **speed of a sound wave** is approximately 331m/s at 0° C. Human ears are capable of hearing frequencies between 20 to 16,000 Hz. The **decibel** (dB) scale is used to measure the loudness (amount of energy) of a sound wave. The scale starts at zero, which is the softest audio, and increases tenfold in intensity for every 10dB.

Magnetism is a force which either pulls magnetic materials together or pushes them apart. Iron and nickel are the most common magnetic materials. All magnetic materials are made up of tiny groups of atoms called domains. Each domain is like a mini-magnet with north and south poles. When material is magnetized, millions of domains line up.

Around every magnet there is a region in which its effects are felt, called its **magnetic field**. The magnetic field around a planet or a star is called the **magnetosphere**. Most of the planets in the Solar System, including Earth, have a magnetic field. Planets have magnetic fields because of the liquid iron in their cores. As the planets rotate, so does the iron swirl, generating electric currents which create a magnetic field. The strength of a magnet is measured in **teslas**. The Earth's magnetic field is 0.00005 teslas.

An electric current creates its own magnetic field. **Electromagnetism** (the force created together by magnetism and electricity) is one of the four fundamental forces in the Universe; the other three are gravity and the two basic forces of the atomic nucleus.

A magnet has two poles: a north pole and a south pole. Like (similar) poles (e.g. two north poles) repel each other; unlike poles attract each other. The Earth has a magnetic field that is created by electric currents within its iron core. The magnetic north pole is close to the geographic North Pole. If left to swivel freely, a magnet will turn so that its north pole points to the Earth's magnetic north pole.

Test Your Knowledge: Physics

1. The temperature at which all molecular motion stops is:
   a) −460 °C.
   b) −273 K.
   c) 0 K.
   d) 0C.

2. _____________is the amount of heat required to raise the temperature of 1 gram of water by 1 degree Celsius.
   a) Specific heat
   b) Heat of fusion
   c) calorie
   d) Heat of vaporization

3. An object that has kinetic energy must be:
   a) Moving.
   b) Falling.
   c) At an elevated position.
   d) At rest.

4. The amount of heat required to melt an ice cube is called:
   a) Conduction.
   b) Specific Heat.
   c) A calorie.
   d) Heat of fusion.

5. A moving object has
   a) Velocity.
   b) Momentum.
   c) Energy.
   d) All of these.

6. Heat transferred between a pot of boiling water and the air above it is an example of:
   a) Conduction.
   b) Convection.
   c) Heat of vaporization.
   d) Phase change.

7. ______________ increases, decreases, or changes the direction of a force is:
   a) A simple machine.
   b) Energy.
   c) Momentum.
   d) Inertia.

8. _______ is a measure of the average kinetic energy of the atoms or molecules of a substance.

a) Specific Heat
b) Temperature
c) Heat
d) Force

9. Average speed is:

a) A measure of how fast something is moving.
b) The distance covered per unit of time.
c) Always measured in terms of a unit of distance divided by a unit of time.
d) All of the above.

10. Which of the following controls can change a car's velocity?

a) The steering wheel.
b) The brake pedal.
c) Both A and B.
d) None of the above.

11. The distance between two corresponding parts of a wave.

a) Wavelength.
b) Crest.
c) Energy.
d) Equidistance.

12. The high part of a transverse wave.

a) Height.
b) Period.
c) Crest.
d) Wavelength.

13. The magnetic field around a planet or a star is called a(an):

a) Electromagnetic field.
b) Magnetosphere.
c) Magnetic field.
d) Magnetic energy field.

14. The number of waves that pass a given point in one second.

a) Trough.
b) Energy.
c) Crest.
d) Frequency.

Test Your Knowledge: Physics – Answers

1. **c)**
2. **c)**
3. **a)**
4. **d)**
5. **d)**
6. **b)**
7. **a)**
8. **b)**
9. **d)**
10. **c)**
11. **a)**
12. **c)**
13. **b)**
14. **d)**

Final Thoughts

In the end, we know that you will be successful in taking the TEAS. Although the road ahead may at times be challenging, if you continue your hard work and dedication (just like you are doing to prepare right now!), you will find that your efforts will pay off.

If you are struggling after reading this book and following our guidelines, we sincerely hope that you will take note of our advice and seek additional help. Start by asking friends about the resources that they are using. If you are still not reaching the score you want, consider getting the help of a tutor.

If you are on a budget and cannot afford a private tutoring service, there are plenty of independent tutors, including college students who are proficient in TEAS subjects. You don't have to spend thousands of dollars to afford a good tutor or review course.

We wish you the best of luck and happy studying. Most importantly, we hope you enjoy your coming years – after all, you put a lot of work into getting there in the first place.

Sincerely,
The Trivium Team

CPSIA information can be obtained at www.ICGtesting.com
Printed in the USA
LVOW09s1659140414
381646LV00015B/496/P

MKSAP® 16

Medical Knowledge Self-Assessment Program®

Hematology and Oncology

Welcome to the Hematology and Oncology section of MKSAP 16!

Inside, we address hematopoietic stem cells and their disorders, approach to anemia, multiple myeloma, transfusion disorders, bleeding disorders, and platelets, thrombotic disorders, and hematologic issues in pregnancy. We also cover breast, ovarian, cervical, lung, head and neck cancer, as well as other clinical challenges. All of these topics are uniquely focused on the needs of generalists and subspecialists *outside* of hematology and oncology.

The publication of the 16th edition of Medical Knowledge Self-Assessment Program heralds a significant event, culminating 2 years of effort by dozens of leading subspecialists across the United States. Our authoring committees have strived to help internists succeed in Maintenance of Certification, right up to preparing for the MOC examination, and to get residents ready for the certifying examination. MKSAP 16 also helps you update your medical knowledge and elevates standards of self-learning by allowing you to assess your knowledge with 1,200 all-new multiple-choice questions, including 144 in Hematology and Oncology.

MKSAP began more than 40 years ago. The American Board of Internal Medicine's examination blueprint and gaps between actual and preferred practices inform creation of the content. The questions, refined through rigorous face-to-face meetings, are among the best in medicine. A psychometric analysis of the items sharpens our educational focus on weaknesses in practice. To meet diverse learning styles, we offer MKSAP 16 online and in downloadable apps for tablets, laptops, and phones. We are also introducing the following:

High-Value Care Recommendations: The Hematology and Oncology section starts with several recommendations based on the important concept of health care value (balancing clinical benefit with costs and harms) to address the needs of trainees, practicing physicians, and patients. These recommendations are part of a major initiative that has been undertaken by the American College of Physicians, in collaboration with other organizations.

Content for Hospitalists: This material, highlighted in blue and labeled with the familiar hospital icon (H), directly addresses the learning needs of the increasing number of physicians who work in the hospital setting. MKSAP 16 Digital will allow you to customize quizzes based on hospitalist-only questions to help you prepare for the Hospital Medicine Maintenance of Certification Examination.

We hope you enjoy and benefit from MKSAP 16. Please feel free to send us any comments to mksap_editors@acponline.org or visit us at the MKSAP Resource Site (mksap.acponline.org) to find out how we can help you study, earn CME, accumulate MOC points, and stay up to date. I know I speak on behalf of ACP staff members and our authoring committees when I say we are honored to have attracted your interest and participation.

Sincerely,

Patrick Alguire

Patrick Alguire, MD, FACP
Editor-in-Chief
Senior Vice President
Medical Education Division
American College of Physicians

Hematology and Oncology

Associate Editor

Richard S. Eisenstaedt, MD, FACP[1]
Professor of Medicine
Temple University School of Medicine
Chair, Department of Medicine
Abington Memorial Hospital
Abington, Pennsylvania

HEMATOLOGY COMMITTEE

Marc J. Kahn, MD, MBA, FACP, Editor[1]
Peterman-Prosser Professor of Medicine
Hematology/Medical Oncology
Senior Associate Dean for Admissions and Student Affairs
Tulane University School of Medicine
New Orleans, Louisiana

Alice Ma, MD[2]
Associate Professor of Medicine
Division of Hematology/Oncology
University of North Carolina
Chapel Hill, North Carolina

Michael B. Streiff, MD, FACP[2]
Associate Professor of Medicine
Medical Director, Johns Hopkins Anticoagulation Management Service and Outpatient Clinics
Medical Director, Johns Hopkins Special Coagulation Laboratory
Johns Hopkins Medical Institutions
Baltimore, Maryland

Peter M. Voorhees, MD[2]
Assistant Professor of Medicine
Division of Hematology/Oncology
University of North Carolina
Chapel Hill, North Carolina

Marc S. Zumberg, MD, FACP[2]
Associate Professor of Medicine
Department of Medicine
Division of Hematology and Oncology
University of Florida
Gainesville, Florida

ONCOLOGY COMMITTEE

Michael D. Spiritos, MD, Editor[2]
Chief, Medical Oncology
Duke Raleigh Hospital
Raleigh, North Carolina

John M. Feigert, MD[2]
Clinical Assistant Professor
Georgetown University Medical Center
Arlington, Virginia

Andrew L. Pecora, MD, CPE, FACP[2]
Vice President of Cancer Services
Chief Innovations Officer
John Theurer Cancer Center at Hackensack University Medical Center
Professor of Medicine, UMDNJ
Northern New Jersey Cancer Associates
Hackensack, New Jersey

Leonard Saltz, MD[2]
Chief, Gastrointestinal Oncology Service
Department of Medicine
Memorial Sloan Kettering Cancer Center
Professor of Medicine
Weill Cornell Medical College
New York, New York

Editor-in-Chief

Patrick C. Alguire, MD, FACP[1]
Senior Vice President, Medical Education
American College of Physicians
Philadelphia, Pennsylvania

Deputy Editor-in-Chief

Philip A. Masters, MD, FACP[1]
Senior Medical Associate for Content Development
American College of Physicians
Philadelphia, Pennsylvania

Senior Medical Associate for Content Development

Cynthia D. Smith, MD, FACP[2]
American College of Physicians
Philadelphia, Pennsylvania

Hematology and Oncology Clinical Editor

Richard S. Eisenstaedt, MD, FACP[1]

Hematology Reviewers

Lee R. Berkowitz, MD, FACP[1]
Stephanie L. Elkins, MD[2]
Richard A. Fatica, MD[1]
Jose A. Joglar, MD[2]
Dan L. Longo, MD, MACP[1]
Robert T. Means, MD, FACP[2]
Jerry L. Spivak, MD[2]

Hematology Reviewers Representing the American Society for Clinical Pharmacology & Therapeutics

Raymond J. Hohl, MD, FACP[1]
Qing Alan Ma, MD[1]

Oncology Reviewers

Raymond F. Bianchi, MD, FACP[1]
Bernard A. Mason, MD, FACP[1]
Medha Munshi, MD[2]
Mark Pasanen, MD, FACP[1]
Michael W. Peterson, MD, FACP[1]
Steven Reichert, MD, FACP[1]

Oncology Reviewers Representing the American Society for Clinical Pharmacology & Therapeutics

Shariq Asad Syed, MD[2]

Hematology and Oncology ACP Editorial Staff

Margaret Wells[1], Managing Editor
Sean McKinney[1], Director, Self-Assessment Programs
John Haefele[1], Assistant Editor

ACP Principal Staff

Patrick C. Alguire, MD, FACP[1]
Senior Vice President, Medical Education

D. Theresa Kanya, MBA[1]
Vice President, Medical Education

Sean McKinney[1]
Director, Self-Assessment Programs

Margaret Wells[1]
Managing Editor

Valerie Dangovetsky[1]
Program Administrator

Becky Krumm[1]
Senior Staff Editor

Ellen McDonald, PhD[1]
Senior Staff Editor

Katie Idell[1]
Senior Staff Editor

Randy Hendrickson[1]
Production Administrator/Editor

Megan Zborowski[1]
Staff Editor

Linnea Donnarumma[1]
Assistant Editor

John Haefele[1]
Assistant Editor

Developed by the American College of Physicians

---

1. Has no relationships with any entity producing, marketing, re-selling, or distributing health care goods or services consumed by, or used on, patients.

2. Has disclosed relationships with entities producing, marketing, re-selling, or distributing health care goods or services consumed by, or used on, patients. See below.

Conflicts of Interest

The following committee members, reviewers, and ACP staff members have disclosed relationships with commercial companies:

Stephanie L. Elkins, MD
Speakers Bureau
Celgene, Cephalon Oncology, GlaxoSmithKline

John M. Feigert, MD
Consultantship
Alexion Pharmaceuticals

Jose A. Joglar, MD
Research Grants/Contracts
Medtronic, St. Jude Corporation
Honoraria
Astellas Pharmaceutical, St. Jude Corporation

Alice Ma, MD
Other
CSL Behring, NovoNordisk, Bayer
Speakers Bureau
NovoNordisk

Robert T. Means, MD, FACP
Consultantship
Beckman Coulter

Medha Munshi, MD
Consultantship
Novartis (spouse), Celgene (spouse), Millenium (spouse)

Andrew L. Pecora, MD, CPE, FACP
Stock Options/Holdings
NeoStem, Amorcyte, TetraLogics
Board Member
Cancer Genetics

Leonard Saltz, MD
Consultantship
Roche, Genentech, Bristol-Myers Squibb, Imclone, Merck, Amgen, Pfizer, Novartis, Genzyme, Genomic Health
Honoraria
Johnson and Johnson

Cynthia D. Smith, MD, FACP
Stock Options/Holdings
Merck and Company

Michael D. Spiritos, MD
Speakers Bureau
Sanofi-Aventis

Jerry L. Spivak, MD
Consultantship
Teva, Akebia, Fibrogen, Celgene

Michael B. Streiff, MD
Honoraria
Sanofi-Aventis, GlaxoSmithKline, Eisai, Inc., Educational Concepts Group, Inc., Medical Communications Media, Inc., OrthoBiotech
Research Grants/Contracts
Bristol-Myers Squibb, Sanofi-Aventis
Consultantship
Sanofi-Aventis, Daiichi-Sankyo, Johnson and Johnson, Eisai, Inc.

Shariq Asad Syed, MD
Employment
Bristol-Myers Squibb

Peter M. Voorhees, MD
Speakers Bureau
Millennium Pharmaceuticals, Celgene
Consultantship
MedImmune
Research Grants/Contracts
Merck, Centocor OrthoBiotech, Pfizer

Marc S. Zumberg, MD, FACP
Honoraria
GlaxoSmithKline, Amgen, Johnson and Johnson

Acknowledgments

The American College of Physicians (ACP) gratefully acknowledges the special contributions to the development and production of the 16th edition of the Medical Knowledge Self-Assessment Program® (MKSAP® 16) made by the following people:

Graphic Services: Michael Ripca (Technical Administrator/Graphic Designer) and Willie-Fetchko Graphic Design (Graphic Designer).

Production/Systems: Dan Hoffmann (Director, Web Services & Systems Development), Neil Kohl (Senior Architect), and Scott Hurd (Senior Systems Analyst/Developer).

MKSAP 16 Digital: Under the direction of Steven Spadt, Vice President, ACP Digital Products & Services, the digital version of MKSAP 16 was developed within the ACP's Digital Product Development Department, led by Brian Sweigard (Director). Other members of the team included Sean O'Donnell (Senior Architect), Dan Barron (Senior Systems Analyst/Developer), Chris Forrest (Senior Software Developer/Design Lead), Jon Laing (Senior Web Application Developer), Brad Lord (Senior Web Developer), John McKnight (Senior Web Developer), and Nate Pershall (Senior Web Developer).

The College also wishes to acknowledge that many other persons, too numerous to mention, have contributed to the production of this program. Without their dedicated efforts, this program would not have been possible.

Introducing the MKSAP Resource Site (mksap.acponline.org)

The MKSAP Resource Site (mksap.acponline.org) is a continually updated site that provides links to MKSAP 16 online answer sheets for print subscribers; access to MKSAP 16 Digital, Board Basics® 3, and MKSAP 16 Updates; the latest details on Continuing Medical Education (CME) and Maintenance of Certification (MOC) in the United States, Canada, and Australia; errata; and other new information.

ABIM Maintenance of Certification

Check the MKSAP Resource Site (mksap.acponline.org) for the latest information on how MKSAP tests can be used to apply to the American Board of Internal Medicine for Maintenance of Certification (MOC) points.

RCPSC Maintenance of Certification

In Canada, MKSAP 16 is an Accredited Self-Assessment Program (Section 3) as defined by the Maintenance of Certification Program of The Royal College of Physicians and Surgeons of Canada (RCPSC) and approved by the Canadian Society of Internal Medicine on December 9, 2011. Approval of this and other Part A sections of MKSAP 16 extends from July 31, 2012, until July 31, 2015. Approval of Part B sections of MKSAP 16 extends from December 31, 2012, to December 31, 2015. Fellows of the Royal College may earn three credits per hour for participating in MKSAP 16 under Section 3. MKSAP 16 will enable Fellows to earn up to 75% of their required 400 credits during the 5-year MOC cycle. A Fellow can achieve this 75% level by earning 100 of the maximum of 174 *AMA PRA Category 1 Credits*™ available in MKSAP 16. MKSAP 16 also meets multiple CanMEDS Roles for RCPSC MOC, including that of Medical Expert, Communicator, Collaborator, Manager, Health Advocate, Scholar, and Professional. For information on how to apply MKSAP 16 CME credits to RCPSC MOC, visit the MKSAP Resource Site at mksap.acponline.org.

The Royal Australasian College of Physicians CPD Program

In Australia, MKSAP 16 is a Category 3 program that may be used by Fellows of The Royal Australasian College of Physicians (RACP) to meet mandatory CPD points. Two CPD credits are awarded for each of the 174 *AMA PRA Category 1 Credits*™ available in MKSAP 16. More information about using MKSAP 16 for this purpose is available at the MKSAP Resource Site at mksap.acponline.org and at www.racp.edu.au. CPD credits earned through MKSAP 16 should be reported at the MyCPD site at www.racp.edu.au/mycpd.

Continuing Medical Education

The American College of Physicians is accredited by the Accreditation Council for Continuing Medical Education (ACCME) to provide continuing medical education for physicians.

The American College of Physicians designates this enduring material, MKSAP 16, for a maximum of 174 *AMA PRA Category 1 Credits*™. Physicians should claim only the credit commensurate with the extent of their participation in the activity.

Up to 20 *AMA PRA Category 1 Credits*™ are available from July 31, 2012, to July 31, 2015, for the MKSAP 16 Hematology and Oncology section.

Learning Objectives

The learning objectives of MKSAP 16 are to:

- Close gaps between actual care in your practice and preferred standards of care, based on best evidence
- Diagnose disease states that are less common and sometimes overlooked and confusing
- Improve management of comorbid conditions that can complicate patient care
- Determine when to refer patients for surgery or care by subspecialists
- Pass the ABIM Certification Examination
- Pass the ABIM Maintenance of Certification Examination

Target Audience

- General internists and primary care physicians
- Subspecialists who need to remain up-to-date in internal medicine
- Residents preparing for the certifying examination in internal medicine
- Physicians preparing for maintenance of certification in internal medicine (recertification)

Earn "Same-Day" CME Credits Online

For the first time, print subscribers can enter their answers online to earn CME credits in 24 hours or less. You can submit your answers using online answer sheets that are provided at mksap.acponline.org, where a record of your MKSAP 16 credits will be available. To earn CME credits, you need to answer all of the questions in a test and earn a score of at least 50% correct (number of correct answers divided by the total number of questions). Take any of the following approaches:

1. Use the printed answer sheet at the back of this book to record your answers. Go to mksap.acponline.org, access the appropriate online answer sheet, transcribe your answers, and submit your test for same-day CME credits. There is no additional fee for this service.

2. Go to mksap.acponline.org, access the appropriate online answer sheet, directly enter your answers, and submit your test for same-day CME credits. There is no additional fee for this service.

3. Pay a $10 processing fee per answer sheet and submit the printed answer sheet at the back of this book by mail or fax, as instructed on the answer sheet. Make sure you calculate your score and fax the answer sheet to 215-351-2799 or mail the answer sheet to Member and Customer Service, American College of Physicians, 190 N. Independence Mall West, Philadelphia, PA 19106-1572, using the courtesy envelope provided in your MKSAP 16 slipcase. You will need your 10-digit order number and 8-digit ACP ID number, which are printed on your packing slip. Please allow 4 to 6 weeks for your score report to be emailed back to you. Be sure to include your email address for a response.

If you do not have a 10-digit order number and 8-digit ACP ID number or if you need help creating a username and password to access the MKSAP 16 online answer sheets, go to mksap.acponline.org or email custserv@acponline.org.

Disclosure Policy

It is the policy of the American College of Physicians (ACP) to ensure balance, independence, objectivity, and scientific rigor in all of its educational activities. To this end, and consistent with the policies of the ACP and the Accreditation Council for Continuing Medical Education (ACCME), contributors to all ACP continuing medical education activities are required to disclose all relevant financial relationships with any entity producing, marketing, re-selling, or distributing health care goods or services consumed by, or used on, patients. Contributors are required to use generic names in the discussion of therapeutic options and are required to identify any unapproved, off-label, or investigative use of commercial products or devices. Where a trade name is used, all available trade names for the same product type are also included. If trade-name products manufactured by companies with whom contributors have relationships are discussed, contributors are asked to provide evidence-based citations in support of the discussion. The information is reviewed by the committee responsible for producing this text. If necessary, adjustments to topics or contributors' roles in content development are made to balance the discussion. Further, all readers of this text are asked to evaluate the content for evidence of commercial bias and send any relevant comments to mksap_editors@acponline.org so that future decisions about content and contributors can be made in light of this information.

Resolution of Conflicts

To resolve all conflicts of interest and influences of vested interests, the ACP precluded members of the content-creation committee from deciding on any content issues that involved generic or trade-name products associated with proprietary entities with which these committee members had relationships. In addition, content was based on best evidence and updated clinical care guidelines, when such evidence and guidelines were available. Contributors' disclosure information can be found with the list of contributors' names and those of ACP principal staff listed in the beginning of this book.

Hospital-Based Medicine

For the convenience of subscribers who provide care in hospital settings, content that is specific to the hospital setting has been highlighted in blue. Hospital icons (H) highlight where the hospital-only content begins, continues over more than one-page, and ends.

Educational Disclaimer

The editors and publisher of MKSAP 16 recognize that the development of new material offers many opportunities for error. Despite our best efforts, some errors may persist in print. Drug dosage schedules are, we believe, accurate and in accordance with current standards. Readers are advised, however, to ensure that the recommended dosages in MKSAP 16 concur with the information provided in the product information material. This is especially important in cases of new, infrequently used, or highly toxic drugs. Application of the information in MKSAP 16 remains the professional responsibility of the practitioner.

The primary purpose of MKSAP 16 is educational. Information presented, as well as publications, technologies, products, and/or services discussed, is intended to inform subscribers about the knowledge, techniques, and experiences of the contributors. A diversity of professional opinion exists, and the views of the contributors are their own and not those of the ACP. Inclusion of any material in the program does not constitute endorsement or recommendation by the ACP. The ACP does not warrant the safety, reliability, accuracy, completeness, or usefulness of and disclaims any and all liability for damages and claims that may result from the use of information, publications, technologies, products, and/or services discussed in this program.

Publisher's Information

Unauthorized Use of This Book Is Against the Law

MKSAP 16 ISBN: 978-1-938245-00-8
(Hematology and Oncology) ISBN: 978-1-938245-04-6

Printed in the United States of America.

For order information in the U.S. or Canada call 800-523-1546, extension 2600. All other countries call 215-351-2600. Fax inquiries to 215-351-2799 or email to custserv@acponline.org.

Errata and Norm Tables

Errata for MKSAP 16 will be available through the MKSAP Resource Site at mksap.acponline.org as new information becomes known to the editors.

MKSAP 16 Performance Interpretation Guidelines with Norm Tables, available July 31, 2013, will reflect the knowledge of physicians who have completed the self-assessment tests before the program was published. These physicians took the tests without being able to refer to the syllabus, answers, and critiques. For your convenience, the tables are available in a printable PDF file through the MKSAP Resource Site at mksap.acponline.org.

Table of Contents

Hematology and Oncology High-Value Care Recommendations

The American College of Physicians, in collaboration with multiple other organizations, is embarking on a national initiative to promote awareness about the importance of stewardship of health care resources. The goals are to improve health care outcomes by providing care of proven benefit and reducing costs by avoiding unnecessary and even harmful interventions. The initiative comprises several programs that integrate the important concept of health care value (balancing clinical benefit with costs and harms) for a given intervention into various educational materials to address the needs of trainees, practicing physicians, and patients.

To integrate discussion of high-value, cost-conscious care into MKSAP 16, we have created recommendations based on the medical knowledge content that we feel meet the below definition of high-value care and bring us closer to our goal of improving patient outcomes while conserving finite resources.

High-Value Care Recommendation: A recommendation to choose diagnostic and management strategies for patients in specific clinical situations that balances clinical benefit with cost and harms with the goal of improving patient outcomes.

Below are the High-Value Care Recommendations for the Hematology and Oncology section of MKSAP 16.

- Do not institute therapy in patients with asymptomatic multiple myeloma.
- Perform an abdominal fat pad aspirate or bone marrow biopsy as a less invasive method for diagnosing AL amyloidosis (see Item 40).
- Do not treat asymptomatic paroxysmal nocturnal hemoglobinuria in the absence of hemolysis.
- Use ferrous sulfate, 325 mg three times daily, as the least expensive preparation for treating iron deficiency (see Item 61).
- Do not add ascorbic acid to facilitate absorption of oral iron salts in the treatment of iron deficiency.
- Do not perform intrinsic factor antibody testing in diagnosing pernicious anemia.
- Treat cobalamin deficiency with oral cobalamin, 1000 to 2000 µg/d orally, instead of parenteral therapy (see Item 28).
- To establish a diagnosis of folate deficiency, institute a therapeutic trial of folate after cobalamin deficiency is excluded.
- Do not initiate iron replacement therapy in patients with inflammatory anemia (see Item 26).
- Do not screen for hereditary hemochromatosis in the general population.
- Most patients with immune thrombocytopenic purpura do not require a bone marrow biopsy to establish the diagnosis; reserve bone marrow biopsy for patients with atypical findings including anemia or leukopenia (see Item 23).
- In adults with immune thrombocytopenic purpura, reserve therapy for patients with platelet counts lower than 30,000 to 40,000/µL ($30\text{-}40 \times 10^9/L$) or with bleeding (see Item 23).
- The likelihood of heparin-induced thrombocytopenia should be calculated using the "4T score" prior to diagnostic testing or treatment.
- Do not routinely perform thrombophilia testing in patients with venous thromboembolism; in most instances, the results will not influence treatment duration.
- Use pretest probability models to determine the diagnostic likelihood of deep venous thrombosis and pulmonary embolism in outpatients; patients with low pretest probability scores and a normal D-dimer assay do not require imaging studies.
- Low-molecular-weight heparin (LMWH) rather than unfractionated heparin should be used whenever possible for the initial inpatient treatment of deep venous thrombosis; unfractionated heparin or LMWH is appropriate for the initial treatment of pulmonary embolism (see Item 29).
- Outpatient treatment of deep venous thrombosis, and possibly pulmonary embolism, with low-molecular-weight heparin is safe and cost-effective for carefully selected patients and should be considered if the required support services are in place.
- Preoperative coagulation screening is recommended only in patients with a personal or family history of mucocutaneous or postsurgical bleeding; there is no indication for routine coagulation screening of most surgical patients.
- Hematologic evaluation for anemia in pregnant women is necessary only in patients with marked anemia, additional cytopenias, abnormal reticulocyte counts, or abnormal cellular indices.
- In pregnant women with microcytic anemia and no obvious blood loss, empiric oral iron supplementation is appropriate, and additional evaluation is not necessary.

- There is no benefit to routine erythrocyte transfusion during pregnancy in patients with sickle cell anemia.
- No data support superiority of cesarean or vaginal delivery in pregnant patients with sickle cell anemia.
- Do not use screening blood tests (including tumor markers) and imaging (except for mammography) in the routine follow-up of otherwise asymptomatic patients with a history of treated breast cancer and no specific findings on clinical examination (see Item 123).
- Perform *BRCA1/BRCA2* testing only in high-risk patients and only when the results will be likely to change management of the patient or family members (see Item 83).
- Manage patients with low-risk prostate cancer and a life expectancy of less than 10 years with observation and palliation if necessary (see Item 84).
- Do not routinely use transrectal ultrasonography to diagnose prostate cancer in a patient with an abnormal prostate-specific antigen value or an abnormal digital rectal examination, because it is associated with a high-false negative rate, and patients with a normal ultrasound will still require a biopsy.
- Testicular cancer staging should include a CT scan of the abdomen and pelvis, chest CT (if pulmonary symptoms or with abnormal chest radiograph), and serum tumor markers (α-fetoprotein, β-human chorionic gonadotropin, and lactate dehydrogenase levels); PET scanning is associated with frequent false-negative results and is not recommended.
- Do not use PET scanning in routine postoperative colorectal cancer surveillance (see Item 143).
- Follow-up imaging is not necessary in low-risk individuals (never-smokers, no history of a first-degree relative with lung cancer or significant radon or asbestos exposure) with incidentally found pulmonary nodules (see Item 81).
- Young, otherwise asymptomatic patients with lymphadenopathy and benign clinical features (small mobile lymph nodes, present for a short duration, in the cervical and inguinal regions) only need reassurance and clinical follow up, not additional laboratory or imaging studies.
- To attempt induction of remission of gastric mucosa-associated lymphoid tissue lymphoma, use antimicrobial agents and proton pump inhibitors as initial treatment instead of surgery or chemotherapy (see Item 80).
- Do not treat asymptomatic patients with chronic lymphocytic leukemia and good-risk prognostic findings, regardless of the leukocyte count.
- The presence of tumor markers in patients with cancer of unknown primary (CUP) site is rarely diagnostic, and an undirected initial screening for carcinoembryonic antigen, CA-19-9, CA-15-3, CA-125, and other markers is unwarranted.
- PET scanning has not been shown to improve outcomes in patients with cancer of unknown primary site and is not recommended as part of the standard evaluation.
- Patients with cancer of unknown primary site and disseminated adenocarcinoma have an unfavorable prognosis, regardless of the degree of differentiation, and should not receive aggressive platinum-based chemotherapy regimens.
- Observation alone is an acceptable standard management option for asymptomatic patients with resected melanoma versus routine surveillance imaging studies (CT, MRI, and PET), which have low yield and a fairly high false-positive rate (see Item 102).

Hematology and Oncology

Hematopoietic Stem Cells and Their Disorders

Overview

Hematopoiesis refers to the orderly formation and differentiation of circulating blood cells. Hematopoietic stem cells are the earliest cellular precursors, have the unique capacity for self-renewal and differentiation, and can develop into cells of other lineages such as brain cells. Stem cells are recognized by their unique surface markers such as CD34. The development of mature blood cells follows an orderly progression from committed progenitor cells (**Figure 1**) to the well-recognized cellular elements of the peripheral blood. The bone marrow microenvironment, stroma, and growth factors are essential to the production of mature blood cells. Failure of the stem cell itself or any of its developmental regulators may lead to bone marrow failure or abnormal maturation.

Bone Marrow Failure Syndromes

Aplastic Anemia

Aplastic anemia refers to conditions in which the bone marrow fails to produce blood cells, resulting in a hypocellular bone marrow and pancytopenia. The disease can be acquired or congenital and may be classified as moderate, severe, or very severe (**Table 1**). Most cases are idiopathic, but drugs, infection, toxins, and radiation exposure must first be excluded as

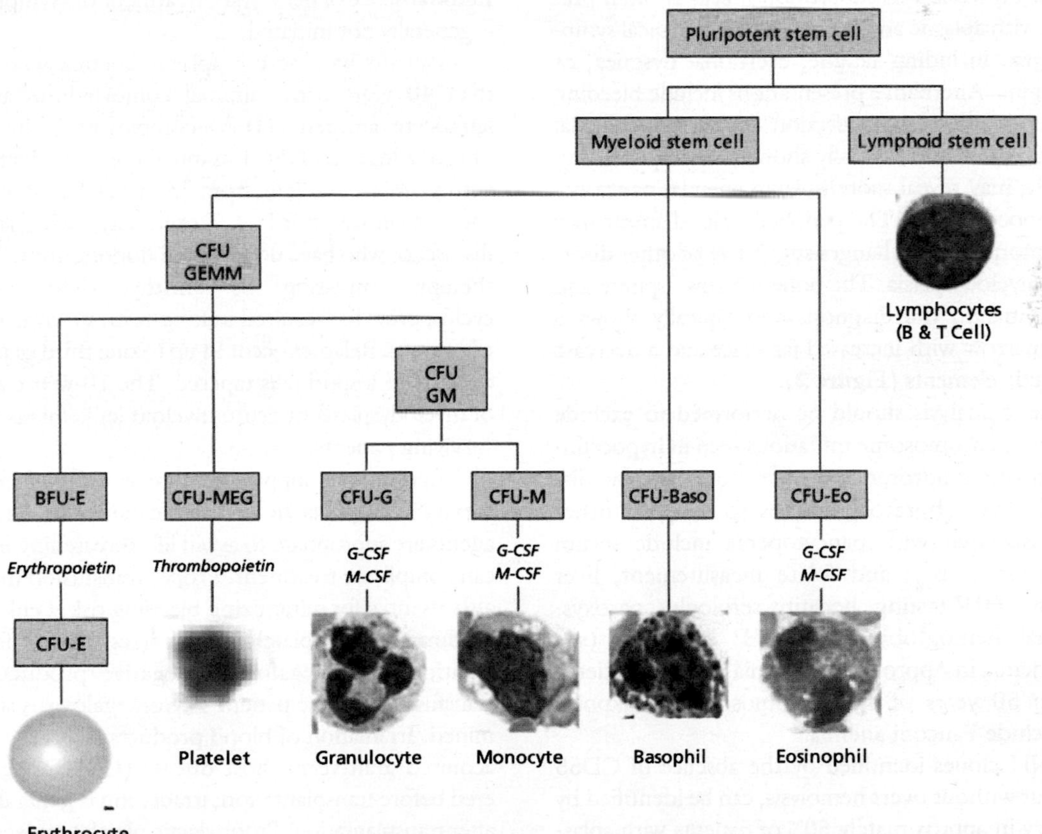

FIGURE 1. Regulation of hematopoiesis. The process of hematopoiesis is regulated by lineage-specific cytokines. These cytokines stimulate the proliferation and/or differentiation of pluripotent stem cells to committed mature peripheral blood cells.

CFU GEMM = colony-forming unit–granulocyte, erythrocyte, megakaryocyte, monocyte; CFU GM = colony-forming unit–granulocyte, monocyte; BFU-E = burst-forming unit–erythrocyte; CFU MEG = colony-forming unit–megakaryocyte; CFU-G = colony-forming unit–granulocyte; CFU-M = colony-forming unit–monocyte; CFU-Baso = colony-forming unit–basophil; CFU-Eo = colony-forming unit–eosinophil; G-CSF = granulocyte colony-stimulating factor; M-CSF = macrophage colony-stimulating factor; CFU-E = colony-forming unit–erythrocyte.

TABLE 1. Classification of Aplastic Anemia	
Classification	**Characteristics**
Very severe aplastic anemia	ANC <200/μL (0.2×10^9/L)
Severe aplastic anemia	Two or more of the following: ANC 200-500/μL (0.2-0.5 $\times 10^9$/L) Platelet count <20,000/μL (20 $\times 10^9$/L) Absolute reticulocyte count <40,000/μL (40 $\times 10^9$/L)
Moderate aplastic anemia	ANC 500-1000/μL (0.5-1.0 $\times 10^9$/L)

ANC = absolute neutrophil count.

potential causes. Aplastic anemia is inherited in approximately 15% to 20% of patients.

The most common form of congenital aplastic anemia, Fanconi anemia, is an autosomal recessive, or X-linked, disorder, often accompanied by skin defects, short stature, hypogonadism, microcephaly, and urogenital abnormalities.

In most patients with acquired aplastic anemia, immune dysfunction is thought to be central to the pathophysiology, and abnormal expression of suppressor T cells is often present. Patients with aplastic anemia may have the typical symptoms of anemia, including fatigue, exertional dyspnea, or worsening angina. Alternative presentations include bleeding due to thrombocytopenia or infection due to neutropenia. The complete blood count usually shows pancytopenia but, less commonly, may reveal more isolated anemia, neutropenia, or thrombocytopenia. The peripheral blood smear may demonstrate morphologic changes suggestive of other disorders, such as myelodysplasia. The bone marrow aspirate and biopsy is essential to the diagnosis and typically shows a hypocellular marrow with increased fat space and a decrease in hematopoietic elements (**Figure 2**).

Cytogenetic analysis should be performed to exclude the characteristic chromosome mutations seen in hypocellular myelodysplastic syndrome and other bone marrow disorders. Additional laboratory studies to evaluate other conditions associated with pancytopenia include serum cobalamin (vitamin B_{12}) and folate measurement, liver chemistry tests, HIV testing, hepatitis serologies, paroxysmal nocturnal hemoglobinuria (PNH) screening (see Hemolytic Anemia in Approach to Anemia), and, in patients younger than 50 years of age, chromosomal breakpoint analysis to exclude Fanconi anemia.

Small PNH clones identified by the absence of CD55 and CD59, but without overt hemolysis, can be identified by flow cytometry in approximately 50% of patients with aplastic anemia, whereas patients with classic PNH may later develop aplastic anemia. In patients with aplastic anemia who have not undergone hematopoietic stem cell transplantation (HSCT), annual screening for a PNH clone is recommended because an increase may predate a more classic hemolytic

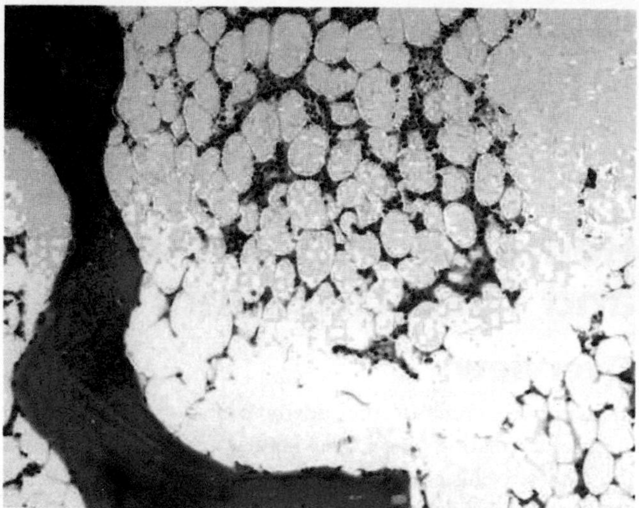

FIGURE 2. Aplastic anemia. Hypocellular bone marrow with increased fat content in a patient with pancytopenia. Almost no identifiable hematopoiesis can be seen.

presentation or an evolving bone marrow failure syndrome. In the absence of hemolysis, treatment of asymptomatic PNH is generally not initiated.

Patients with severe aplastic anemia who are younger than 40 years with minimal comorbidities and a human leukocyte antigen (HLA)–compatible sibling should be offered allogeneic HSCT as initial therapy, which is associated with a cure rate ranging from 75% to 90% in some studies. For patients who are not HSCT candidates, who have less severe disease, or who have no matched donors, immunosuppressive therapy consisting of antithymocyte globulin and cyclosporine has resulted in long-term survival in 60% to 85% of patients. Relapses occur in up to one third of patients, especially as cyclosporine is tapered. The 10-year cumulative rate of myelodysplasia or acute myeloid leukemia is 5% to 10% in surviving patients.

Appropriate supportive care is essential for long-term survival. Prophylactic antibiotic, antiviral, and antifungal agents are appropriate to avoid life-threatening infections that can complicate treatment. Proper transfusion management is also essential for minimizing bleeding risk. Leukodepletion of erythrocytes and platelets minimizes the risk for alloimmunization. Cytomegalovirus–negative products should be transfused until the patient's cytomegalovirus status is determined. Irradiation of blood products to prevent transfusion-acquired graft-versus-host disease (GVHD) can be considered before transplantation; irradiation is generally performed after transplantation. Prophylactic platelet transfusions may be appropriate in patients at high risk or in those with a platelet count of less than 10,000/μL (10×10^9/L). The use of growth factors such as granulocyte colony-stimulating factor (G-CSF) has been shown to be ineffective as primary therapy and is a controversial adjunctive treatment. H

KEY POINTS

- The bone marrow aspirate and biopsy is essential in the diagnosis of aplastic anemia, typically showing a hypocellular marrow with increased fat space and a decrease in hematopoietic elements.
- Patients with severe aplastic anemia who are younger than 40 years with minimal comorbidities and a human leukocyte antigen–compatible sibling should be offered hematopoietic stem cell transplantation as initial therapy.

Pure Red Cell Aplasia

Pure red cell aplasia (PRCA) is an acquired syndrome characterized by severe anemia, lack of reticulocytosis, and absence of erythroid precursors in the bone marrow. In contrast to aplastic anemia, leukocyte and platelet production are not affected. PRCA is typically classified as idiopathic or secondary (**Table 2**).

Patients usually present with symptoms of anemia. The complete blood count is normal except for isolated normocytic anemia. The bone marrow typically shows a lack of erythroblasts and an excess of precursor pronormoblasts but is otherwise unremarkable.

Assessment for potential underlying causes of PRCA includes identification of any new drugs or the presence of toxins, CT to exclude thymoma, peripheral blood or bone marrow flow cytometry, testing for parvovirus B19 and HIV infection, and serologic evaluation for autoimmune disorders. Evaluation for parvovirus B19 infection is particularly important in patients with underlying hemolytic anemia if they develop acute severe hypoproliferative anemia. Large granular lymphocytosis, a common cause of secondary PRCA, is a lymphoproliferative syndrome characterized by large numbers of granular lymphocytes with abundant cytoplasm and azurophilic granules that are noted on the peripheral blood smear (**Figure 3**) and infiltrate the bone marrow.

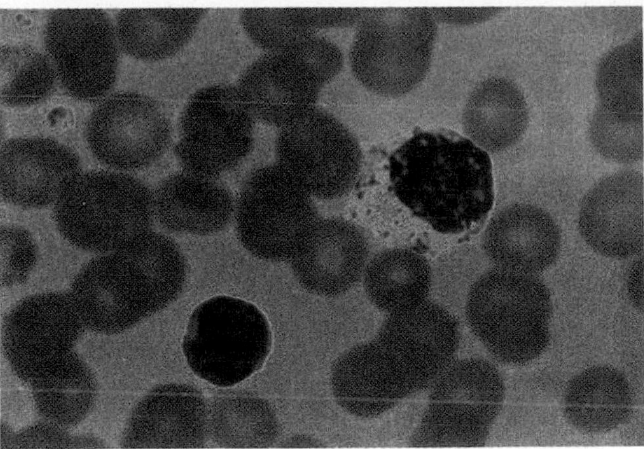

FIGURE 3. Large granular lymphocyte. This large granular lymphocyte has a nucleus characteristic of a mature lymphoid cell but also contains prominent azurophilic granules in the cytoplasm.

TABLE 2. Secondary Causes of Acquired Pure Red Cell Aplasia

Parvovirus B19 infection
Thymoma
Collagen vascular or autoimmune diseases
Lymphoproliferative disorders
Other bone marrow disorders
Solid tumors
Anti-EPO antibodies after treatment with exogenous EPO
Other drugs (for example, phenytoin, chloramphenicol, isoniazid)
Pregnancy
ABO-incompatible stem cell transplant

EPO = erythropoietin.

Flow cytometry revealing CD57-positive T cells and clonality on T-cell receptor gene rearrangement studies are diagnostic. Patients often have splenomegaly, and approximately one third have a rheumatic syndrome suggesting rheumatoid arthritis.

In addition to erythrocyte transfusion for patients with symptomatic anemia, initial management of PRCA includes the removal of offending drugs and treatment of any underlying disease, including appropriate chemotherapy for lymphoproliferative disorders. In patients with chronic primary PRCA and secondary PRCA that does not respond to the initial management, treatment is often immune based. Prednisone, antithymocyte globulin, cyclosporine A, and cyclophosphamide have become standard first-line agents, with most patients responding within 3 to 12 weeks.

Intravenous immune globulin can be used in patients with parvovirus B19 infection–related PRCA, although patients with normal immune function may recover spontaneously. Surgical resection for patients in whom a thymoma is identified may be considered, although only a few patients respond to this approach. Approximately 10% of idiopathic cases of PRCA resolve without therapy.

KEY POINTS

- Patients with pure red cell aplasia may have symptoms of anemia, a normal complete blood count except for isolated normocytic anemia, and bone marrow abnormalities confined to the erythroid cell line.
- Assessment for potential underlying causes of pure red cell aplasia is indicated, particularly for parvovirus B19, in patients with underlying hemolytic anemia who develop severe hypoproliferative anemia.

Neutropenia

Because neutrophils figure significantly in the defense against bacteria, patients with neutropenia may experience life-threatening bacterial, and to a lesser extent, fungal infections. Infectious risk increases greatly when the absolute neutrophil count (ANC) is less than 500/µL (0.5×10^9/L) and is greatest when the ANC is less than 200/µL (0.2×10^9/L). Mild congenital asymptomatic neutropenia in patients with ANCs between 1000/µL (1.0×10^9/L) and 1500/µL (1.5×10^9/L) is common in certain ethnic populations, including blacks, Yemenite Jews, and Jordanian Arabs; is not associated with increased infections; and requires no therapy.

More severe neutropenia can be congenital or acquired as a result of drugs, vitamin deficiencies, autoimmune disorders, viral syndromes, and malignant conditions such as large granular lymphocytosis. Severe congenital neutropenia represents a heterogeneous group of disorders with varied inheritance and pathogenesis characterized by onset early in life and life-threatening infections.

Autoimmune neutropenia is an acquired abnormality that may be associated with underlying disorders of immune regulation such as systemic lupus erythematosus, or it may exist in a more isolated form. In general, the degree of neutropenia is not severe enough to be linked with frequent infections, and spontaneous remissions may occur in patients with the primary form. Antineutrophil antibodies may be detected, although these tests, which differ from the antineutrophil cytoplasmic antibody (ANCA) tests used to evaluate vasculitis, may not be widely available and have variable sensitivity and specificity. In patients who are negative for antineutrophil antibodies, the diagnosis is established by excluding other causes.

Various drugs can cause neutropenia as an expected side effect or as an idiosyncratic reaction. Chemotherapeutic agents, especially alkylating agents and antimetabolites, are expected to produce neutropenia (see MKSAP 16 Oncology). Many different antibiotics, such as cephalosporins and trimethoprim-sulfamethoxazole, may produce severe neutropenia in a very few patients. Chloramphenicol is rarely used today because it may cause agranulocytosis. Anticonvulsants such as carbamazepine and phenytoin; antiarrhythmic agents such as amiodarone and procainamide; NSAIDs such as naproxen; the thionamide agent propylthiouracil; and gold salts can also cause neutropenia. In most patients, drug-induced neutropenia is self-limited and resolves with discontinuation of the drug; however, neutropenia may rarely be prolonged after drug withdrawal.

Many viral infections, including HIV, cytomegalovirus, and Epstein-Barr virus, may lead to neutropenia. Patients with rickettsial infection or overwhelming infection and sepsis syndrome from *Streptococcus pneumoniae* or *Neisseria meningitidis* may have neutropenia.

Cyclic neutropenia is caused by a disorder in stem cell regulation leading to recurrent neutropenia and infectious risk at defined intervals, typically, every 2 to 4 weeks. Nonimmune chronic idiopathic neutropenia is a diagnosis of exclusion and rarely requires treatment.

Felty syndrome is characterized by rheumatoid arthritis, splenomegaly, and neutropenia and may present similarly to large granular lymphocytosis. Other bone marrow syndromes, such as myelodysplasia, may be characterized by isolated neutropenia. Deficiencies of serum cobalamin (vitamin B_{12}) or folate may also cause isolated neutropenia, although, as with myelodysplastic syndromes, they are more likely to cause anemia as well or pancytopenia. Bone marrow evaluation in patients with neutropenia may be useful in identifying dysplastic cell maturation or cytogenetic abnormalities supporting an underlying stem cell disorder.

The therapeutic approach typically consists of treating the underlying cause of neutropenia and includes drug withdrawal and management of any concomitant vitamin deficiencies, autoimmune disorders, and viral syndromes. The management of neutropenic infections, including the use of G-CSF, is discussed in Oncologic Urgencies and Emergencies (see MKSAP 16 Oncology).

G-CSF therapy in patients with severe congenital neutropenia has been effective in increasing neutrophil counts and decreasing infectious risks; however, patients remain at high risk for myelodysplasia and acute myeloid leukemia. G-CSF administration may also be effective in patients with cyclic neutropenia at the time of the nadir neutrophil count to avoid infection.

KEY POINTS

- Mild congenital neutropenia is not uncommon among some Middle Eastern, African, and black populations; is not associated with increased infection risk; and does not progress to a more serious stem cell disorder.
- The therapeutic approach to patients with neutropenia typically consists of treating the underlying cause and includes drug withdrawal and management of any concomitant vitamin deficiencies, autoimmune disorders, and viral syndromes.

Thrombocytopenia

Most cases of isolated thrombocytopenia are acquired and are not due to a bone marrow failure syndrome. Although patients with vitamin B_{12} or folate deficiency usually present with anemia or pancytopenia, isolated thrombocytopenia may be seen.

KEY POINT

- Isolated thrombocytopenia in most patients does not arise from an underlying bone marrow or stem cell disorder.

The Myelodysplastic Syndromes

The myelodysplastic syndromes (MDS) are clonal hematopoietic stem cell disorders characterized by ineffective hematopoiesis and a variable rate of transformation to acute myeloid leukemia (AML). The incidence of MDS increases with age. Risk factors include DNA damage from previous chemotherapy (alkylating agents, topoisomerase II inhibitors) or radiation, inherited defects in DNA repair (Fanconi anemia), and Down syndrome.

Symptoms include fatigue and easy bleeding. Infections due to neutropenia are a common cause of death. Laboratory studies reveal normocytic or macrocytic anemia. Dysplastic changes on the peripheral blood smear may include nucleated erythrocytes and hypolobated, hypogranular neutrophils (**Figure 4**). Platelet and neutrophil counts are variably affected. The bone marrow is usually hypercellular, and dysplasia is identified in affected hematopoietic lineages.

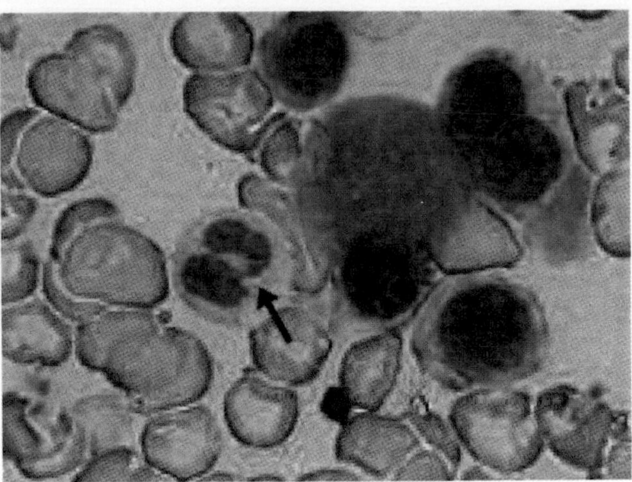

FIGURE 4. Hypogranular neutrophil with pseudo-Pelger-Huët morphology, characterized by a bi-lobed nucleus connected by a thin strand.

Other entities associated with cytopenias and dysplastic changes must be excluded, including vitamin B_{12} and folate deficiencies, medication effects (mycophenolate mofetil), recent cytotoxic chemotherapy or radiation therapy, and HIV infection. Other causes of sideroblastic anemia, including congenital sideroblastic anemias, drug toxicity (chloramphenicol, isoniazid), alcoholism, copper deficiency, and zinc excess, must be considered in the presence of dysplasia with excess ringed sideroblasts.

The World Health Organization recognizes seven variants of MDS (**Table 3**). The International Prognostic Scoring System (IPSS) is based on the number of cytopenias present, burden of blasts in the bone marrow, and cytogenetic characteristics and is predictive of outcome. Age adds additional prognostic value (**Table 4**).

Asymptomatic patients with low-risk disease can be observed closely, with blood counts checked periodically and patients counseled about anemia, bleeding, and infection symptoms. Infections are managed with appropriate antibiotics, whereas bleeding related to thrombocytopenia is managed with platelet transfusions. Erythrocyte transfusions are required for those with symptomatic anemia, but secondary iron overload may occur. Although iron overload is associated with a worse prognosis, prospective survival data on the use of iron chelation therapy in patients with MDS are not available. Iron chelation therapy may be considered in those with a serum ferritin level of 1000 ng/mL (1000 µg/L) or more and disease associated with longer survival.

The erythrocyte-stimulating agents (ESAs), epoetin and darbepoetin alfa, may improve hemoglobin levels in patients with symptomatic anemia and lower-risk MDS. The addition of G-CSF may increase erythroid responses further. Lower

TABLE 3. World Health Organization Classification of Myelodysplastic Syndromes

Category	Features	Median Overall Survival (months)
Refractory cytopenias with unilineage dysplasia	Unilineage (i.e., single cell line) dysplasia, <5% marrow blasts	69
Refractory anemia with ringed sideroblasts	Erythroid dysplasia, ≥15% ringed sideroblasts, <5% marrow blasts	69
MDS associated with isolated 5q deletion	<5% marrow blasts, increased megakaryocytes with hypolobated nuclei	116
Refractory cytopenia with multilineage dysplasia	<5% marrow blasts, dysplasia in ≥2 lineages, +/- ringed sideroblasts	33
Refractory anemia with excess blasts-1	5%-9% marrow blasts, unilineage or multilineage dysplasia, no Auer rods	18
Refractory anemia with excess blasts-2	10%-19% blasts, unilineage or multilineage dysplasia	10
MDS, unclassified	<5% marrow blasts, does not fit other categories	Currently not known

MDS = myelodysplastic syndrome.

TABLE 4. The International Prognostic Scoring System (IPSS) for MDS

IPSS score[a]	Median Overall Survival (years)		Death Associated with Leukemia
	≤60 years old	>60 years old	
0	11.8	4.8	19%
0.5-1.0	5.2	2.7	30%
1.5-2.0	1.8	1.1	33%
≥2.5	0.3	0.5	45%

IPSS Calculation

Risk factor	Score			
	0	0.5	1.0	1.5
Bone marrow blasts	<5%	5%-10%	—	11%-20%
Cytogenetics[b]	Good	Intermediate	Poor	—
Cytopenias[c]	0 or 1	2 or 3	—	—

MDS = myelodysplastic syndrome; ANC = absolute neutrophil count.

[a]IPSS score is based on the IPSS calculation above.

[b]Good karyotype: normal, -Y, del(5q), del(20q); poor karyotype: ≥3 unrelated abnormalities, chromosome 7 abnormalities; intermediate: all others.

[c]ANC <1800/µL (1.8 × 10^9/L), hemoglobin <10 g/dL (100 g/L), platelet count <100,000/µL (100 × 10^9/L).

baseline erythropoietin levels (<100-200 mU/mL [100-200 units/L]) and less severe transfusion requirements are predictors of response. ESAs with or without G-CSF do not appear to increase the risk of progression to AML.

Azacitidine is a pyrimidine nucleoside analogue that, compared with standard care, produced better complete response rates, decreased the risk of transformation to AML, and improved median overall survival in patients with higher-risk MDS. Decitabine is a related agent that has produced similar results. For patients with transfusion-dependent, lower-risk MDS associated with deletion of chromosome 5q, treatment with lenalidomide led to transfusion independence in 67% of patients. Some patients may have an immune-mediated component to their marrow failure and respond to antithymocyte globulin and cyclosporine. HLA-DR15 positivity and younger age predict response to immunosuppressive therapy. Allogeneic HSCT is potentially curative but is associated with a high rate of transplant-related mortality and morbidity and reserved for younger patients with higher-risk disease.

Chronic myelomonocytic leukemia (CMML) is another clonal hematopoietic stem cell disorder with features of an MDS and myeloproliferative disorder. Constitutional symptoms of weight loss and sweats and hepatosplenomegaly are more prominent in CMML than in MDS. Leukocytosis is common, and an absolute monocyte count of greater than 1000/µL (1.0 × 10^9/L) (normal range: male, 300/µL to 820/µL [0.30 to 0.82 × 10^9/L]; female, 240/µL to 860/µL [0.24 - 0.86 × 10^9/L]) is required for diagnosis. Variable levels of anemia and thrombocytopenia may be present. Treatment is largely supportive. Hydroxyurea can be used to palliate constitutional symptoms and hepatosplenomegaly. Azacitidine and decitabine appear promising, but experience with these agents is limited. Younger patients are considered for allogeneic HSCT, which is potentially curative.

KEY POINTS

- Risk factors for myelodysplastic syndromes include DNA damage from previous chemotherapy or radiation, inherited defects in DNA repair, and Down syndrome.
- Asymptomatic patients with myelodysplastic syndrome and low-risk disease can be observed closely.
- The erythropoiesis-stimulating agents epoetin and darbepoetin alfa may improve hemoglobin levels in patients with symptomatic anemia and lower-risk myelodysplastic syndrome.

Myeloproliferative Disorders

Polycythemia Vera

Polycythemia vera (PV) is a neoplastic disorder that originates from a pluripotent hematopoietic stem cell. It has an estimated annual incidence of 10 new cases per million persons. Although PV occurs most commonly in patients aged 50 to 75 years, 5% of patients are younger than 40 years.

In healthy adults, hematopoietic cells derive from a multitude of hematopoietic stem cells. In patients with PV, many, if not all, of the circulating erythrocytes, leukocytes, and platelets are derived from a single neoplastic stem cell. The erythroid progenitor cells of patients with PV, unlike those of healthy persons, are capable of growing and dividing in the absence of erythropoietin.

PV has a latent, proliferative, and spent phase. The diagnosis of PV is established in most patients when they are relatively asymptomatic, during the latent phase. In the proliferative phase, hyperviscosity or hypermetabolic symptoms or thrombosis may develop. Approximately 20% of patients with PV enter the spent phase, during which fibrosis occurs in the bone marrow, driving hematopoietic activity into the liver and spleen and leading to progressive hepatosplenomegaly. During this phase, cytopenias can become prominent, blood transfusions may be necessary, and constitutional symptoms are common.

The symptoms of PV are the same as those of erythrocytosis from any cause and include confusion, transient ischemic attack–like symptoms, tinnitus, blurred vision, and headache, the last of which occurs in 50% of patients. Symptoms more specific for PV and other myeloproliferative diseases include generalized pruritus that often worsens after bathing, erythromelalgia (a burning sensation in the palms and soles possibly caused by platelet activation), and hypermetabolic symptoms such as fever, weight loss, and sweating. On physical examination, patients may have plethora and hepatosplenomegaly. Thrombotic and bleeding symptoms are common in PV. Twenty percent of patients experience arterial or venous thrombosis as their initial symptom. PV predisposes to the development of the Budd-Chiari syndrome and should be suspected in patients who have this syndrome. Gastrointestinal symptoms, including bleeding, are prominent. The bleeding may be chronic and occult and may result in autophlebotomy with the development of iron deficiency without anemia. The presence of an elevated hematocrit with microcytosis is virtually pathognomonic of PV.

Previously, diagnosis of PV relied on detection of an increased red blood cell mass in the absence of other causes of secondary erythrocytosis. Assessment of red blood cell mass is no longer available at most laboratories, and this criterion is no longer needed. Although patients may present with less dramatic erythrocytosis, consistent findings of a hemoglobin level greater than 18.5 g/dL (185 g/L) in men or greater than 16.5 g/dL (165 g/L) in women invariably indicate an elevated red blood cell mass. Concomitant leukocytosis (often with basophilia) and thrombocytosis (suggesting trilineage myeloproliferation) and hepatosplenomegaly further support the diagnosis. Elevated serum vitamin B_{12} levels and hyperuricemia are common, albeit nonspecific, findings. Other causes of erythrocytosis, such as ectopic erythropoietin production from a kidney tumor, or hypoxia from chronic lung or cyanotic heart disease, can be excluded by the finding of a low or undetectable serum erythropoietin level and normal oxygen saturation. In addition, more than 97% of patients with PV have an activating mutation in the signaling protein JAK2 (*JAK2 V617F*).

If results of *JAK2 V617F* mutation testing are negative and the erythropoietin level is normal or high, then PV is excluded, and causes of secondary erythrocytosis should be investigated. These include sleep apnea, emphysema, carbon monoxide poisoning, cigarette smoking, renal artery stenosis, congenital heart disease with right to left shunting, shunts within the lungs from arteriovenous malformations, and intrinsic lung disease with hypoxemia.

Low-dose aspirin has been shown to decrease the risk of thrombosis and should be given to all patients in the absence of contraindications.

Phlebotomy results in the best overall survival and should be performed once or twice weekly until a target hematocrit of less than 45% is achieved, followed by intermittent phlebotomy to maintain the hematocrit between 40% and 45%. Iron deficiency will eventually develop as a result of phlebotomy, limiting further hematopoiesis and decreasing the need for additional phlebotomies. Phlebotomy has no effect on the development of myelofibrosis, and phlebotomy alone may be insufficient to control thrombocytosis and hepatosplenomegaly.

The addition of the myelosuppressive agent hydroxyurea to phlebotomy decreases thrombotic events. Patients with PV and an increased risk for thrombosis, defined as age older than 60 years or history of a previous thrombotic event, should be treated with hydroxyurea. Other myelosuppressive agents, such as chlorambucil or busulfan, are leukemogenic and should not be used.

A single dose of ^{32}P may control the hemoglobin level and platelet count for 1 year or more. Although it confers an increased risk for leukemia (up to 11%), ^{32}P may be beneficial for patients who are intolerant of or nonadherent to hydroxyurea or who have short expected survival. Interferon alfa is also used to treat PV and can control the hemoglobin level and platelet count and reduce splenomegaly with no increased risk for thrombosis or leukemogenesis. Additionally, interferon alfa is safe in pregnancy. However, this agent must be given by injection, and side effects, including fever, malaise, myalgia, and flu-like symptoms, render it intolerable to many patients, with 20% discontinuing therapy.

KEY POINTS

- Laboratory findings in polycythemia vera include leukocytosis, thrombocytosis, basophilia, elevated serum uric acid and vitamin B_{12} levels, low erythropoietin levels, normal oxygen saturation, and the presence of the *JAK2 V617F* gene mutation.
- Low-dose aspirin and phlebotomy are the most appropriate initial treatments for most patients with polycythemia vera.
- Patients with polycythemia vera who are older than 60 years or who have had a previous thrombotic event should receive hydroxyurea with phlebotomy to decrease the risk of subsequent thrombosis.

Essential Thrombocythemia

Essential thrombocythemia is characterized by an elevated platelet count in the absence of conditions known to cause secondary thrombocytosis. In essential thrombocythemia, increased megakaryocyte production of platelets with normal platelet survival occurs, but the mechanism responsible for the increased platelet production is unclear. Thrombopoietin levels are not low and may even be high in individuals with essential thrombocythemia.

Because many patients are asymptomatic on presentation, essential thrombocythemia is often identified incidentally on the routine complete blood count. Symptoms can include microvascular thrombi manifesting as digital ischemia. Vasomotor symptoms such as erythromelalgia may also occur and respond to antiplatelet agents. Hemorrhagic symptoms, sometimes due to inherent platelet function, develop in 40% of patients.

Diagnosis requires the presence of a platelet count of greater than 600,000/µL (600×10^9/L) on two separate occasions, at least 1 month apart. Secondary causes of thrombocytosis (iron deficiency, especially with chronic bleeding; cancer; inflammation; infection; and the post-splenectomy setting) should be excluded. Extreme thrombocytosis characterized by platelet counts greater than 1 million/µL (1000×10^9/L) strongly suggests essential thrombocythemia. The absence of the Philadelphia chromosome excludes chronic myeloid leukemia, which can be characterized by isolated thrombocytosis. Splenomegaly and basophilia may be present.

Unlike PV, essential thrombocythemia rarely progresses to acute myeloid leukemia (<1% of patients). Arterial or venous thrombosis is the major complication of essential thrombocythemia, occurring in 20% to 30% of patients. When the platelet count increases to more than 1.5 million/µL (1500×10^9/L), patients can develop a qualitative functional defect analogous to type 2 von Willebrand disease. If the platelet count is very high, laboratory findings may show pseudohyperkalemia and pseudohypoglycemia as the metabolically active platelets use glucose and release potassium. Platelet morphology can be very bizarre, demonstrating giant and oddly shaped platelets (some larger than erythrocytes). Bone marrow examination shows clusters of abnormal megakaryocytes and may demonstrate increased reticulin fibrosis. The activating *JAK2* mutation (*JAK2 V617F*) is found in only 50% of patients and may portend a more aggressive course. Treatment of essential thrombocythemia requires reduction of the platelet count; however, when and whom to treat remain controversial. Although the exact level of platelet count does not determine the risk for thrombosis, lowering the platelet count in patients at risk for thrombosis will decrease this risk, and, possibly, the risk for myelofibrosis. Additionally, it now appears that leukocytosis may be a better predictor of thrombosis risk than the platelet count.

Platelet-lowering agents should be used in patients with thrombocythemia who have had a thrombotic event or have risk factors for thrombosis and who are older than 65 years of age. Anagrelide, initially developed as an antihypertensive agent that was found to decrease platelet counts, is effective in patients who can tolerate it. Anagrelide interferes with megakaryocyte maturation into platelets without causing depression of other cell lines and confers no increased risk for leukemogenesis. Side effects may include hypotension, palpitations and arrhythmias, severe headaches, fluid retention, heart failure, and bloating and diarrhea in lactose-intolerant patients. Because of anagrelide's potential for cardiac toxicity, its use has been reserved for nonelderly patients without heart disease.

Hydroxyurea has supplanted anagrelide as a first-line agent since findings of the PT-1 study showed a reduced risk for arterial thrombosis and bleeding (regardless of the platelet count achieved) in patients with essential thrombocythemia treated with hydroxyurea plus low-dose aspirin compared with those treated with anagrelide plus low-dose aspirin. Complete blood counts should be monitored frequently because leukocyte counts can decrease in patients receiving hydroxyurea. Patients whose leukocyte counts cannot support the hydroxyurea dose needed to control the platelet count may require alternative therapy. As with PV, alternative therapies may include interferon alfa in pregnant patients or ^{32}P in older patients who are unable to tolerate the side effects of the more commonly used drugs.

KEY POINTS

- Diagnosis of essential thrombocythemia requires a platelet count of greater than 600,000/µL (600×10^9/L) on two separate occasions, at least 1 month apart; exclusion of secondary causes of thrombocytosis; and the absence of the Philadelphia chromosome.
- Platelet-lowering agents should be used in patients with thrombocythemia who have had a thrombotic event or have risk factors for thrombosis and who are older than 65 years of age.
- In patients with essential thrombocythemia, hydroxyurea plus low-dose aspirin results in a reduced risk for arterial thrombosis and bleeding, regardless of the platelet count achieved, compared with anagrelide plus low-dose aspirin.

Chronic Myeloid Leukemia

Chronic myeloid leukemia (CML) is a clonal hematopoietic stem cell disorder characterized by myeloid proliferation. CML consists of a chronic, accelerated, and blast phase. In the blast phase, the disease can manifest as AML (80%) or acute lymphoblastic leukemia (ALL) (20%). All cases of CML harbor the Philadelphia chromosome, the (9;22) translocation that gives rise to expression of the constitutively active tyrosine kinase, *BCR-ABL*.

Diagnosis may be established incidentally, or patients may present with symptoms including fatigue, night sweats, weight loss, abdominal discomfort, early satiety, and bleeding. On physical examination, splenomegaly is the most common finding. In chronic-phase CML, the leukocyte count is high, the hemoglobin level low or normal, and the platelet count normal or high. The peripheral blood smear reveals neutrophilia and left-shifted granulopoiesis. Basophilia is common. An increasing proportion of blasts are seen as the disease progresses to more advanced phases. The serum lactate dehydrogenase and uric acid levels are elevated, whereas the leukocyte alkaline phosphatase score is low. The bone marrow is hypercellular with myeloid hyperplasia.

CML must be distinguished from leukemoid reactions and other myeloproliferative disorders. Detection of the (9;22) translocation by routine cytogenetics or fluorescence in situ hybridization or of the *BCR-ABL* fusion transcript by reverse transcriptase-polymerase chain reaction is diagnostic. Cytogenetic testing and morphologic evaluation of the marrow help to determine the phase of disease.

A diagnosis of CML mandates treatment, even in asymptomatic patients. In chronic-phase CML, the *BCR-ABL* inhibitor imatinib produced unprecedented response rates, an overall survival of 89% at 5 years, and a low risk of progression to advanced-phase disease. The more potent *BCR-ABL* inhibitors, nilotinib and dasatinib, are used in patients who are intolerant of or have disease resistant to imatinib. Early phase III results with nilotinib and dasatinib as front-line therapy are highly encouraging. Because of the success of *BCR-ABL* inhibitors, allogeneic HSCT is typically reserved for eligible patients with accelerated- or blast-phase disease or for those with disease resistant to *BCR-ABL* inhibitors, regardless of phase.

KEY POINTS

- Chronic myeloid leukemia may be asymptomatic or characterized by fatigue, night sweats, weight loss, abdominal discomfort, early satiety, and bleeding; splenomegaly is the most common physical examination finding.
- Detection of the (9;22) translocation by routine cyto genetics or fluorescence in situ hybridization or the *BCR-ABL* fusion transcript by reverse transcriptase-polymerase chain reaction is diagnostic of chronic myeloid leukemia.
- A diagnosis of chronic myeloid leukemia mandates treatment, even in asymptomatic patients.

Primary Myelofibrosis

Primary myelofibrosis is a clonal hematopoietic stem cell disorder characterized by abnormal myeloid and megakaryocyte proliferation. The megakaryocytes produce fibroblast growth factors that stimulate collagen production, bone marrow fibrosis, impaired marrow function, and extramedullary hematopoiesis.

Most patients are symptomatic at diagnosis, with varying degrees of fatigue, night sweats, weight loss, abdominal pain, and early satiety. On physical examination, hepatosplenomegaly is prominent. Other sites of extramedullary hematopoiesis may include the vertebral column, lymph nodes, or other locations. Gout, bone pain, arterial or venous thrombosis, and pulmonary hypertension can also occur. Most patients are anemic, but the leukocyte and platelet counts may be normal, increased, or decreased. The peripheral blood smear reveals a leukoerythroblastic picture characterized by left-shifted granulopoiesis and nucleated and teardrop-shaped erythrocytes (**Figure 5**).

The serum lactate dehydrogenase, uric acid, and alkaline phosphatase levels are commonly elevated. The bone marrow is often difficult to aspirate, and the diagnosis is made by bone marrow biopsy. The *JAK2* mutation is present in 50% of patients.

Primary myelofibrosis must be distinguished from secondary causes of myelofibrosis, including metastatic cancer, MDS, and other myeloproliferative disorders. Prognosis is dictated by increasing age, the presence of constitutional symptoms, anemia, leukocytosis, and increased circulating blasts.

Treatment of primary myelofibrosis is palliative. Asymptomatic patients with low-risk disease should be followed expectantly. Symptomatic anemia is managed with transfusions. Androgen therapy, including danazol, will improve anemia in 30% of patients. Hydroxyurea is used to treat constitutional symptoms, symptomatic hepatosplenomegaly, and thrombocytosis. Splenectomy is performed in select patients but is associated with significant perioperative morbidity (bleeding, thrombosis, infection, worsening hepatomegaly) and mortality. Radiation has been used to treat splenomegaly and other sites of symptomatic extramedullary hematopoiesis, but responses are short-lived. Allogeneic HSCT may be a curative option but is associated

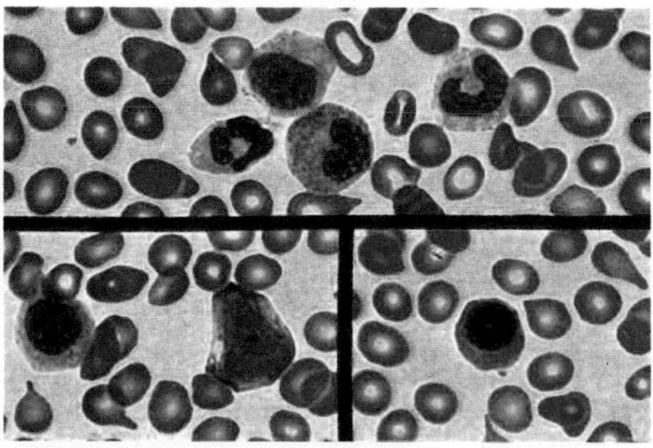

FIGURE 5. Left-shifted granulopoiesis and nucleated and teardrop-shaped erythrocytes in a patient with primary myelofibrosis.

with significant morbidity and mortality in older patients. Treatment with ruxolitinib, a *JAK* inhibitor that is FDA approved for the treatment of intermediate-risk to high-risk myelofibrosis, can lead to improvement in constitutional symptoms, pruritus, and splenomegaly.

KEY POINTS

- Abnormal megakaryocyte proliferation in primary myelofibrosis leads to excess fibroblast growth factors that stimulate collagen production and cause marrow fibrosis and extramedullary hematopoiesis.
- Watchful waiting is appropriate management of patients with primary myelofibrosis who are asymptomatic; symptomatic patients should receive palliative treatment.

Acute Myeloid Leukemia

AML is a malignancy of myeloid progenitor cells. The median age at diagnosis is 67 years, although patients of many ages are affected. Risk factors include DNA damage from previous chemotherapy or radiation, an antecedent MDS or myeloproliferative disorder, inherited defects in DNA repair (Fanconi anemia), Down syndrome, and bone marrow failure syndromes, including aplastic anemia and paroxysmal nocturnal hemoglobinuria.

Clinical manifestations of marrow failure develop over days to months and include fatigue, dyspnea, and easy bleeding. Fever is commonly caused by infection. Extramedullary spread may manifest with gingival hypertrophy or violaceous, nontender cutaneous plaques (leukemia cutis). Extramedullary tumors (myeloid sarcomas) can occur at any site, including skin, soft tissue, and bone. An acute neutrophilic dermatosis (Sweet syndrome) may also occur. Central nervous system involvement can be seen but is uncommon.

The leukocyte count can be low, normal, or high, but circulating myeloblasts are present in most cases. Auer rods are sometimes seen and suggest a diagnosis of AML rather than ALL (**Figure 6**). Severe cytopenias are common. Disseminated intravascular coagulation (DIC) may be seen, especially in patients with acute promyelocytic leukemia (APL). Metabolic abnormalities associated with tumor lysis syndrome or hypokalemia due to lysozyme-mediated renal wasting may occur. The bone marrow is hypercellular with a monotonous population of blasts or promyelocytes.

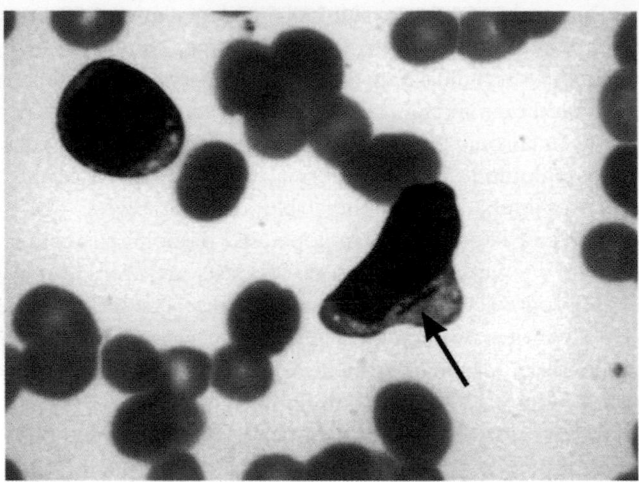

FIGURE 6. An Auer rod in the blast of a patient with acute myeloid leukemia.

Diagnosis requires 20% or more blasts in the blood or bone marrow. Cytochemical stains (myeloperoxidase) and flow cytometry distinguish myeloblasts from the lymphoblasts seen in ALL. The World Health Organization uses a combination of biologic and clinical features to classify AML (**Table 5**). Adverse prognostic features include advanced age, an antecedent history of MDS or myeloproliferative disorder, treatment-related disease, and high-risk cytogenetics (**Table 6**).

TABLE 6. Five-year Overall Survival in Acute Myeloid Leukemia by Age and Cytogenetics

Cytogenetic Category	Age ≤55 y	Age >55 y
Favorable		
t(8;21), t(15;17), inv(16)	65%	34%
Intermediate		
All others	41%	13%
High		
Complex (≥5 unrelated abnormalities), -5, del(5q), -7, 3q abnormalities	14%	2%

TABLE 5. World Health Organization Classification of Acute Myeloid Leukemia

Category	Examples
AML with recurrent genetic abnormalities	t(15;17), t(8;21), inv(16), 11q23 translocations, normal cytogenetics but mutated *Flt3* or *NPM1*
AML with myelodysplasia-related changes	With or without antecedent MDS
Therapy-related AML and MDS	Exposure to alkylating agents, ionizing radiation, topoisomerase II inhibitors
AML, not otherwise specified	AML with or without maturation, AML with minimal differentiation, acute myelomonocytic leukemia, acute monoblastic or monocytic leukemia, acute erythroid leukemia, acute megakaryoblastic leukemia

AML = acute myeloid leukemia; MDS = myelodysplastic syndrome.

Supportive treatment of AML consists of transfusions and management of neutropenic infection. Intravenous fluid hydration and allopurinol with or without rasburicase are used to treat and prevent tumor lysis syndrome. Symptomatic hyperleukocytosis can occur when the leukocyte count is 50,000/µL (50×10^9/L) or more. Central nervous system and respiratory manifestations predominate and include headaches, visual and mental status changes, hypoxia, and diffuse infiltrates on chest radiograph. Erythrocyte transfusions and diuresis may exacerbate symptoms. Treatment with leukapheresis or hydroxyurea should be considered in this setting pending confirmation of a diagnosis of AML. DIC is managed with appropriate transfusion support. Early institution of all-*trans*-retinoic acid (ATRA) in cases of suspected APL will lead to faster resolution of DIC.

In adults, cure rates for AML reach 30% to 40% with standard chemotherapy. Induction chemotherapy consists of a 7-day cytarabine infusion and a concomitant 3-day infusion of an anthracycline ("7 and 3"), with the goal of achieving complete remission. Consolidation therapy is used to eradicate minimal residual disease. For those who are younger and have favorable-risk disease, consolidation includes three to four courses of high-dose cytarabine, whereas those with high-risk disease and a suitable match undergo allogeneic HSCT. Optimal consolidation therapy for younger intermediate-risk patients is unsettled. Older adult patients with favorable- to intermediate-risk disease who are otherwise healthy are treated with standard induction chemotherapy followed by consolidation with an abbreviated 5-day course of the original therapy ("5 and 2") or intermediate-dose cytarabine-based therapy. High-dose cytarabine is not used in older adults because of cerebellar toxicity and increased mortality. Older patients with high-risk disease or comorbidities precluding the use of intensive therapy may be best treated with supportive care and low-dose, outpatient chemotherapy to control leukocytosis (cytarabine or hydroxyurea) or participation in a clinical trial.

APL is a clinically and biologically distinct variant of AML characterized by the presence of a (15;17) gene translocation, which gives rise to the promyelocytic leukemia–retinoic acid receptor-α fusion transcript and arrest of leukemic cells at the promyelocyte stage. The addition of ATRA to standard induction and consolidation chemotherapy releases the block in promyelocyte maturation and produces cure in up to 80% of patients. Like ATRA, arsenic trioxide can induce differentiation of APL cells, produces high complete remission rates in relapsed disease, and improves outcomes when incorporated into initial consolidation therapy. QT-interval prolongation can be a serious complication of arsenic trioxide treatment. ATRA and arsenic trioxide may produce a differentiation syndrome with fever, dyspnea with or without pulmonary infiltrates, edema, and hypotension. Treatment of this syndrome consists of institution of dexamethasone therapy and temporary discontinuation of the offending agent in severe cases.

KEY POINTS

- Acute myeloid leukemia–related marrow failure may be characterized by the onset of fatigue, dyspnea, and easy bleeding; gingival hypertrophy or violaceous, nontender cutaneous plaques (leukemia cutis); and extramedullary tumors at any site developing over several weeks to months.
- Twenty percent or more blasts in the blood or bone marrow is diagnostic of acute myeloid leukemia.
- Older patients with high-risk acute myeloid leukemia or comorbidities precluding the use of intensive therapy are given supportive care and low-dose, outpatient chemotherapy.

Acute Lymphoblastic Leukemia

ALL is a malignancy of B or T lymphoblasts. The leukemic variant of Burkitt lymphoma, Burkitt leukemia, is managed identically to Burkitt lymphoma and will not be discussed here.

Symptoms of marrow failure emerge over days to weeks and include fatigue, dyspnea, bleeding, and infection-related fever. On physical examination, lymphadenopathy and hepatosplenomegaly are common. Patients with T-cell ALL may present with a large anterior mediastinal mass, pleural effusions, and superior vena cava syndrome. Central nervous system involvement is more common in ALL than AML and may be characterized by headaches, lethargy, nausea/vomiting, nuchal rigidity, cranial nerve palsy, or radiculopathy. The leukocyte count can be low, normal, or elevated, but most patients have circulating lymphoblasts. Severe cytopenias and metabolic derangements related to tumor lysis syndrome are common.

Diagnosis requires the presence of 25% or more lymphoblasts on bone marrow examination. Cytochemical stains and flow cytometry can help distinguish ALL from AML and B-cell from T-cell ALL. ALL is typically positive for terminal deoxynucleotidyl transferase and negative for myeloperoxidase, whereas AML is negative for terminal deoxynucleotidyl transferase and often positive for myeloperoxidase. Predictors of a poor prognosis include advanced age, adverse cytogenetics, B-cell disease, and a high circulating leukocyte count at diagnosis (30,000/µL [30×10^9/L] or more in B-cell disease). Favorable-risk cytogenetic characteristics include hyperdiploidy and the (12;21) gene translocation. High-risk cytogenetics include hypodiploidy and translocations involving the *MLL* gene and the Philadelphia chromosome, t(9;22).

Tumor lysis syndrome is common at diagnosis or shortly after institution of chemotherapy; consequently, all patients should receive intravenous fluid hydration and allopurinol. Rasburicase converts uric acid to allantoin and can be used to rapidly lower uric acid levels to prevent or treat tumor lysis syndrome. Prior to treatment, patients should be tested for glucose-6-phosphate dehydrogenase deficiency because rasburicase may induce hemolysis in this setting from the generation of hydrogen peroxide. Methemoglobinemia has also been reported after rasburicase treatment.

In adults, cure rates for ALL approach 30% to 40% with standard chemotherapy. For younger adults, induction therapy commonly consists of an anthracycline, vincristine, L-asparaginase, and a corticosteroid. Patients who achieve complete remission receive further intensive chemotherapy with multiple chemotherapeutic agents for several months followed by 2 to 3 years of maintenance chemotherapy. Given the risk for central nervous system involvement in ALL, intrathecal chemoprophylaxis is routinely administered with or without cranial irradiation. Patients with high-risk disease who are otherwise healthy and have a suitable donor are considered for allogeneic HSCT in first remission. For patients with Philadelphia chromosome–positive ALL, the *BCR-ABL* inhibitors are routinely used as adjuncts to cytotoxic chemotherapy.

KEY POINTS

- Twenty-five percent or more lymphoblasts on bone marrow examination are diagnostic of acute lymphoblastic leukemia.
- In adults, chemotherapy for acute lymphoblastic leukemia is associated with cure rates of 30% to 40%.
- Intrathecal chemoprophylaxis is routinely administered with or without cranial irradiation because of the risk for central nervous system involvement in acute lymphoblastic leukemia.

Hematopoietic Growth Factors

The ESAs are hematopoietic growth factors that stimulate erythrocyte production and relieve anemia-related symptoms but should be used very cautiously. ESAs increase hemoglobin levels in patients with cancer-related anemia but may have deleterious effects on survival in patients undergoing curative chemotherapy and patients with cancer-related anemia who are not undergoing chemotherapy. The inferior survival in these situations may be due to a higher rate of venous thromboembolism or inferior tumor control. ESA use in patients with cancer is restricted to those with symptomatic chemotherapy-related anemia (hemoglobin ≤10 g/dL [100 g/L]) for whom treatment is not curative. ESAs are also used for management of anemia (hemoglobin ≤10 g/dL [100 g/L]) related to dialysis-independent and dialysis-dependent kidney failure. Initiation of ESAs in kidney failure can be considered when the hemoglobin drops below 10 g/dL (100 g/L), using the lowest dose necessary to reduce the need for erythrocyte transfusions. Targeting hemoglobin levels greater than 11 g/dL (110 g/L) should be avoided because of an associated higher rate of all-cause mortality, serious cardiovascular events, and stroke documented in controlled trials. Iron stores should be checked before and during treatment. A pretreatment serum iron saturation of 20% or greater and a ferritin level of 100 to 200 ng/mL (100-200 µg/L) or greater are acceptable.

G-CSF and granulocyte-macrophage colony-stimulating factor (GM-CSF) stimulate production of neutrophils and are used as primary prophylaxis for those undergoing myelosuppressive chemotherapy associated with a high risk of febrile neutropenia and in those with infectious complications of neutropenia associated with nonmalignant diseases such as autoimmune neutropenia. The use of the thrombopoietin mimetics remains restricted to management of patients with relapsed/refractory idiopathic thrombocytopenic purpura.

KEY POINTS

- Erythropoiesis-stimulating agent use in patients with cancer is restricted to those with symptomatic chemotherapy-related anemia (hemoglobin ≤10 g/dL [100 g/L]) for whom treatment is not curative.
- In patients in whom erythropoiesis-stimulating agents are used, targeting hemoglobin levels greater than 11 g/dL (110 g/L) should be avoided because of an associated higher rate of all-cause mortality, serious cardiovascular events, and stroke.

Hematopoietic Stem Cell Transplantation

HSCT is used for the treatment of hematologic malignancies, congenital and acquired bone marrow failure syndromes, and other inherited disorders. The patient serves as the source of stem cells in autologous HSCT, whereas stem cells are acquired from an HLA-matched donor in allogeneic HSCT. Advances in HLA typing have decreased complications associated with matched, unrelated donor HSCT, producing outcomes approaching that of sibling-matched HSCT. Stem cell mobilization is achieved with high doses of G-CSF, which leads to increased numbers of CD34-positive stem cells in the circulation.

Before stem cell infusion, patients undergo conditioning therapy to allow successful engraftment of stem cells and eradicate residual disease for those with hematologic malignancies. Conditioning consists of the administration of myeloablative doses of cytotoxic chemotherapy with or without total body irradiation. The toxicities of conditioning may be substantial and are regimen specific. Diffuse alveolar hemorrhage and hepatic venoocclusive disease may occur, especially when total body irradiation is used. The use of reduced-intensity conditioning regimens in allogeneic HSCT has reduced early treatment-related toxicity and mortality, thus allowing older patients to undergo the procedure. Immunosuppressive therapy is required to facilitate engraftment and reduces the risk of graft-versus-host disease (GVHD) in allogeneic HSCT.

Opportunistic infections are a common complication of HSCT and may include bacterial infections, *Pneumocystis jirovecii* pneumonia, invasive fungal infections (aspergillosis),

and viral infections (respiratory viruses, herpes simplex virus, varicella zoster virus, and cytomegalovirus) (see MKSAP 16 Infectious Disease). The risk for fungal and viral infections occurring 3 months or more after transplantation is significantly greater after allogeneic HSCT than autologous transplantation. Lymphocytes derived from the donor can mount an immune response to the recipient's organs, leading to GVHD, which may affect the skin, gastrointestinal tract, liver, ocular adnexae, lungs, bone marrow, and soft tissues. GVHD is frequently complicated by infection-related morbidity and mortality. H

KEY POINTS

- The use of reduced-intensity conditioning regimens in allogeneic hematopoietic stem cell transplantation has reduced early treatment-related toxicity and mortality, allowing older patients to undergo the procedure.
- Immunosuppressive therapy is required to facilitate engraftment and reduce the risk of graft-versus-host disease in allogeneic hematopoietic stem cell transplantation.

Multiple Myeloma and Related Disorders

Overview

Proliferation of monoclonal plasma cells may lead to various clinical syndromes, ranging from monoclonal gammopathy of undetermined significance (MGUS), an asymptomatic condition manifested only by a laboratory abnormality; to AL amyloidosis, in which precipitated proteins cause end-organ dysfunction; to plasma cell and lymphoplasmacytic malignancies, such as multiple myeloma and Waldenström macroglobulinemia.

Multiple Myeloma

Multiple myeloma is a malignancy of plasma cells involving bone and bone marrow. The median age at diagnosis is 70 years, and blacks are more commonly affected than whites. Most myelomas produce a monoclonal (M) protein consisting of an intact immunoglobulin composed of a heavy chain (IgG, IgA, or IgD) and a K or λ light chain, but they may secrete free light chains alone (16% of cases), or, rarely, no immunoglobulin. Symptomatic myeloma must be distinguished from smoldering, or asymptomatic, myeloma because the prognosis and management differ significantly.

Clinical Manifestations and Findings

Fifty-eight percent of patients with newly diagnosed symptomatic myeloma have bone pain due to lytic bone lesions. Patients may have motor weakness, bowel or bladder dysfunction, or other neurologic symptoms from spinal cord compression, a medical emergency that may occur because of retropulsed bone fragments from vertebral-body compression fractures or plasmacytomas. Sinopulmonary infections are common. Peripheral neuropathy is rare but may occur in myeloma complicated by coexisting AL amyloidosis or osteosclerotic myeloma (POEMS syndrome: Polyneuropathy, Organomegaly, Endocrinopathies, Monoclonal protein, Skin changes). Hyperviscosity is more common in Waldenström macroglobulinemia because of the pentameric structure of IgM but can also be seen in IgA and other myelomas.

Anemia occurs in 73% of patients, and rouleaux formation may be seen. Leukopenia and thrombocytopenia are present in 20% and 5% of patients, respectively. Hypercalcemia occurs in 28% of patients, and the serum creatinine level is elevated in 48% of patients. The most common cause of kidney dysfunction is cast nephropathy in which filtered monoclonal free light chains cause obstruction from intratubular precipitation. Hypercalcemia; nephrotoxic agents such as CT contrast dye, loop diuretics, and NSAIDs; and AL amyloidosis are other causes of renal impairment. A urinalysis will not detect monoclonal immunoglobulins but may reveal albuminuria in cases of myeloma complicated by AL amyloidosis. Protein electrophoresis and immunofixation of serum and a 24-hour urine collection will identify an M protein in 97% of patients, and these studies can be used to monitor treatment response. The remaining 3% of patients have nonsecretory disease that may be detectable using serum free light-chain testing.

A myeloma bone survey consists of plain radiographs of the skeleton and may reveal lytic bone lesions or diffuse osteopenia (**Figure** 7). A bone scan, which may detect increased osteoblastic activity characteristic of most bone metastases, is not sensitive for detecting myeloma bone lesions because they are more purely osteolytic. An MRI may be

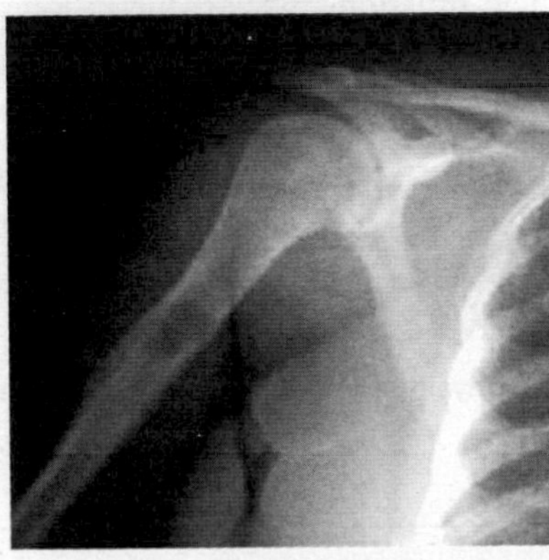

FIGURE 7. Lytic bone lesions in the right humerus of a patient with multiple myeloma.

required for patients with suspected myeloma who have back, neck, or other bone pain and unrevealing plain films.

KEY POINTS

- Spinal cord compression is a medical emergency that may occur in patients with multiple myeloma because of retropulsed bone fragments from vertebral-body compression fractures or plasmacytomas.
- Protein electrophoresis and immunofixation of serum and a 24-hour urine collection will identify an M protein in 97% of patients with multiple myeloma and can be used to monitor treatment response.

Diagnosis and Prognosis

Symptomatic myeloma is diagnosed by the presence of 10% or more clonal plasma cells on bone marrow biopsy, the presence of an M protein, and evidence of myeloma-related end-organ damage (**Table 7**). Asymptomatic myeloma is characterized by an M protein level of 3 g/dL or more, regardless of isotype, or 10% or more of clonal plasma cells on bone marrow examination and the absence of myeloma-related end-organ damage. Prognostic factors in symptomatic myeloma include international stage, which consists of serum β_2 microglobulin and albumin (**Table 8**), and cytogenetics.

The risk of asymptomatic myeloma progressing to symptomatic myeloma or AL amyloidosis is 73% at 15 years, with a median time to progression of 4.8 years. Plasma cell burden and M protein level can be used to predict risk of progression (**Table 9**). The presence of an abnormal serum free K to λ light chain ratio, a measure of excess free light-chain production by the myeloma or decreased production of nonclonal light chains, is also predictive of disease progression.

TABLE 7. International Myeloma Working Group Diagnostic Criteria for Plasma Cell Dyscrasias

Diagnosis	M Protein (g/dL)	Bone Marrow Plasma Cells	Myeloma-related Organ Dysfunction[a]
MGUS	<3 g/dL	<10%	No
Asymptomatic myeloma	≥3 g/dL[b]	≥10%[b]	No
Symptomatic myeloma	Present	≥10%	Yes

MGUS = monoclonal gammopathy of undetermined significance.

[a]The CRAB criteria for myeloma-related organ dysfunction are defined as (1) hypercalcemia (serum calcium >10.5 mg/dL [2.6 mmol/L]); (2) renal failure (serum creatinine >2 mg/dL [176.8 µmol/L]); (3) anemia (hemoglobin <10 g/dL [100 g/L] or 2 g/dL [20 g/L] below the lower limit of normal); (4) bone disease (lytic bone lesions or osteoporosis); and/or (5) other (hyperviscosity, recurrent bacterial infections, AL amyloidosis).

[b]Patients with asymptomatic myeloma may have ≥3 g/dL M protein AND/OR ≥10% bone marrow plasma cells.

TABLE 8 The International Staging System for Multiple Myeloma

Stage	Definition	Median Survival (months)[a]
I	Serum β_2-microglobulin <3.5 mg/L, serum albumin ≥3.5 g/dL (35 g/L)	62
II	Not stage I or III	44
III	Serum β_2-microglobulin >5.5 mg/L	29

[a]Survival data obtained from patients treated before widespread use of bortezomib and lenalidomide.

TABLE 9 Risk of Progression to Clinically Symptomatic Plasma Cell Dyscrasia

Diagnosis	Risk Factors (RFs)	Progression[a]
MGUS	M protein ≥1.5 g/dL	3 RFs: 58%
	Non-IgG M protein	2 RFs: 37%
	Abnormal serum FLC ratio	1 RF: 21%
		0 RFs: 5%
Asymptomatic myeloma	M protein ≥3 g/dL	M protein ≥3 g/dL, PCs ≥10%: 87%
	Bone marrow plasma cells (PCs) ≥10%	M protein <3 g/dL, PCs ≥10%: 70%
		M protein ≥3 g/dL, PCs <10%: 39%

MGUS = monoclonal gammopathy of undetermined significance; FLC = free light-chain ratio.

[a]Risk of progression at 20 years for MGUS, at 15 years for asymptomatic myeloma.

KEY POINTS

- Symptomatic myeloma is diagnosed by the presence of 10% or more clonal plasma cells on bone marrow biopsy, the presence of an M protein, and evidence of myeloma-related end-organ damage.
- Asymptomatic myeloma is characterized by an M protein level of 3 g/dL or more or by 10% or more plasma cells on bone marrow examination and the absence of myeloma-related end-organ damage.

Treatment

Advances in chemotherapy have improved overall survival in patients with myeloma. The core therapeutics include the immunomodulatory drugs thalidomide and lenalidomide, the proteasome inhibitor bortezomib, and the alkylating agent melphalan. Thalidomide and lenalidomide are teratogenic agents and are associated with an increased risk for venous thrombosis. The risk of venous thrombosis is further increased by concomitant use of anthracyclines or high-dose corticosteroids or the presence of other risk factors, including immobilization and hyperviscosity. Somnolence, constipation, and peripheral neuropathy are common with thalidomide, whereas myelosuppression occurs more often with lenalidomide. Bortezomib may cause thrombocytopenia and peripheral neuropathy. Melphalan is well tolerated at low doses but can cause myelosuppression and stem cell toxicity, precluding its use as induction therapy in autologous hematopoietic stem cell transplantation (HSCT) candidates.

H The choice of initial chemotherapy is dictated by the patient's candidacy for autologous HSCT. For older patients and those with comorbidities precluding HSCT, treatment may consist of low-dose melphalan and prednisone with the addition of thalidomide or bortezomib. For all others, autologous HSCT remains an important component of treatment. Transplant candidates are treated initially with bortezomib and dexamethasone with or without thalidomide or lenalidomide. Autologous HSCT with high-dose melphalan is used as consolidation after initial induction therapy and improves disease-free and overall survival compared with continued chemotherapy. Maintenance thalidomide, used with or without corticosteroids, improves disease-free survival after HSCT but causes cumulative toxicities and has inconsistent effects on overall survival. Relapsed disease is typically treated with a lenalidomide- or bortezomib-based regimen.

Lytic bone disease is a major cause of morbidity in myeloma. Pathologic or impending fractures may require surgical stabilization. Kyphoplasty can improve pain from vertebral-body compression fractures, and radiation therapy can palliate symptomatic bone disease. The bisphosphonates pamidronate and zoledronic acid help prevent pathologic fractures. Nephrotoxicity is uncommon, but focal segmental glomerulosclerosis and acute tubular necrosis can occur with pamidronate and zoledronic acid, respectively. Monitoring for changes in serum calcium and creatinine and proteinuria is important. Bisphosphonate-associated osteonecrosis of the jaw can occur and is commonly characterized by pain. On physical examination, exposed bone can be seen in the maxilla or mandible. Risk factors include recent dental extraction, poor dentition, and periodontal disease. Dental evaluation should be performed before institution of therapy.

Management of myeloma-related kidney failure consists of treatment of hypercalcemia, if present, including intravenous fluids to achieve euvolemia, and bisphosphonate therapy. Kidney failure can be precipitated by intravenous CT contrast dye, loop diuretics, and NSAIDs, and exposure to these and other nephrotoxic agents should be avoided. Although results on the efficacy of plasmapheresis are conflicting, this therapy should be considered in those with probable or biopsy-proven cast nephropathy to reduce the concentration of serum free light chains by at least 50%. Prompt institution of chemotherapy to reduce light-chain burden in patients with cast nephropathy is crucial.

Transfusions are used to treat anemia, and erythropoiesis-stimulating agents may be used for symptomatic, chemotherapy-related anemia. Vaccinations for pneumococcus and influenza virus should be provided. H

Early institution of therapy does not improve overall survival in patients with asymptomatic myeloma. These patients should be monitored every 3 to 6 months and offered treatment when disease progresses.

KEY POINTS

- Risk factors for bisphosphonate-associated osteonecrosis of the jaw include recent dental extraction, poor dentition, and periodontal disease, and dental evaluation should be performed before institution of therapy.
- Kidney failure in multiple myeloma can be precipitated by intravenous CT contrast dye, loop diuretics, and NSAIDs, and exposure to these and other nephrotoxic agents should be avoided.
- For older patients with multiple myeloma and those with comorbidities precluding hematopoietic stem cell transplantation, treatment consists of melphalan and prednisone with thalidomide or bortezomib.

Monoclonal Gammopathy of Undetermined Significance

MGUS is found incidentally on protein electrophoresis and is defined as the presence of an M protein of less than 3 g/dL, fewer than 10% plasma cells on bone marrow examination, and no evidence of anemia, kidney failure, bone disease, or other myeloma-related end-organ damage.

The prevalence of MGUS increases with age, with 7.5% of those 85 years or older affected. MGUS is more common in men and blacks. Although MGUS precedes most cases of multiple myeloma, most patients with MGUS do not develop a plasma cell dyscrasia requiring therapy. Therefore, screening for monoclonal gammopathies should not be done, but testing should be considered for patients with incidentally discovered hyperproteinemia, unexplained anemia or kidney dysfunction, hypercalcemia, peripheral neuropathy, or lytic bone lesions. M protein testing using serum protein electrophoresis, immunofixation, and free light-chain testing will identify most plasma cell dyscrasias, but a 24-hour urine protein electrophoresis and immunofixation assay may be necessary if these results are normal and the suspicion of a plasma cell dyscrasia persists. Current recommendations for the initial evaluation of patients with an established M protein, if not already performed as part of the original workup, include a complete blood count; serum calcium, albumin, and creatinine measurement; urinalysis; protein electrophoresis and immunofixation performed on serum and a 24-hour urine collection; quantitative immunoglobulin measurement (IgG, IgM, IgA); serum free light-chain testing; and a skeletal survey. CT scans to assess lymphadenopathy in the thorax and abdomen may be indicated for patients with an IgM MGUS because this finding is more likely associated with Waldenström macroglobulinemia or other B-cell non-Hodgkin lymphoma than myeloma. Bone marrow examination should be performed in patients with findings suspicious for a plasma cell dyscrasia requiring treatment, a non-IgG M protein, an M protein level of 1.5 g/dL or more, or an abnormal serum free light-chain ratio. Follow-up testing for patients with MGUS vary depending on the individual circumstances but may include a complete blood count, serum calcium and creatinine measurement, protein electrophoresis and immunofixation of serum and urine, and serum free light-chain testing.

The risk for progression of MGUS to a clinically relevant plasma cell dyscrasia is approximately 1% per year. A risk model for progression has been developed using the level of the M protein, M-protein isotype, and serum free light-chain ratio (see Table 9). IgG, IgA, or light-chain MGUS may progress to multiple myeloma, AL amyloidosis, or other plasma cell dyscrasia, whereas IgM MGUS can progress to a B-cell non-Hodgkin lymphoma such as Waldenström macroglobulinemia or AL amyloidosis. Patients with MGUS are monitored every 6 to 12 months for signs and symptoms of progression. Bone mineral density testing should be considered at baseline because MGUS is associated with osteoporosis.

KEY POINTS

- Monoclonal gammopathy of undetermined significance is found incidentally on protein electrophoresis and is defined as the presence of an M protein of less than 3 g/dL, fewer than 10% plasma cells on bone marrow examination, and no evidence of myeloma-related end-organ damage.
- Patients with monoclonal gammopathy of undetermined significance (MGUS) are monitored every 6 to 12 months for signs and symptoms of progression and may benefit from bone mineral density testing for MGUS-associated osteoporosis.

Immunoglobulin Light-Chain Amyloidosis

The amyloidoses are characterized by tissue deposition of protein fibrils of a β-pleated sheet configuration and subsequent end-organ damage. AL amyloidosis is the most common amyloidosis and is caused by the deposition of monoclonal light chains, more often λ than K. Overt myeloma is present in only 10% of patients.

Clinical manifestations include nephrotic-range proteinuria with worsening kidney function, restrictive cardiomyopathy, and hepatomegaly. Neurologic findings include a symmetric, distal sensorimotor neuropathy, carpal tunnel syndrome, and autonomic neuropathy with orthostatic hypotension. Periorbital purpura (**Figure 8**) and macroglossia (**Figure 9**) are characteristic of AL amyloidosis. Other sites of amyloid deposition include, but are not limited to, the gastrointestinal tract (malabsorption, dysmotility), muscles, skin, and joints. Bleeding caused by acquired factor X deficiency may also occur.

A diagnosis of AL amyloidosis requires characteristic findings on tissue biopsy, the presence of a monoclonal plasma cell disorder, and evidence that the amyloid deposits are composed of clonal light chains. Amyloid deposits consist of amorphous eosinophilic material that demonstrates apple-green birefringence when stained with Congo red and viewed under polarized light. An abdominal fat pad aspirate or bone marrow biopsy may be positive in up to 80% of patients. If results of the abdominal fat pad aspirate or marrow biopsy are negative, a more invasive biopsy of a clinically affected tissue is required. Immunofluorescence, immunohistochemistry, or

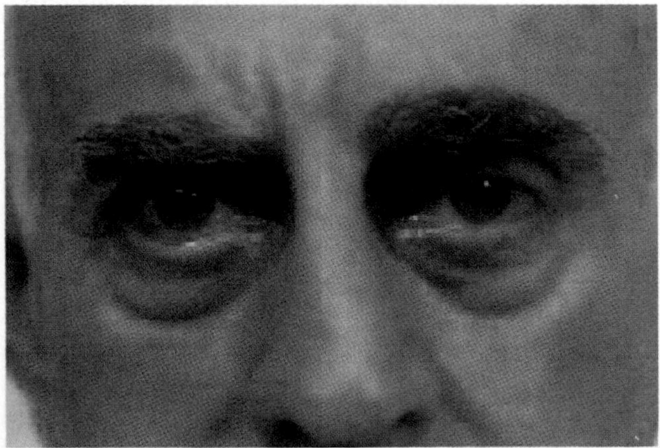

FIGURE 8. Periorbital ecchymoses demonstrated as "raccoon eyes" in a patient with AL amyloidosis.

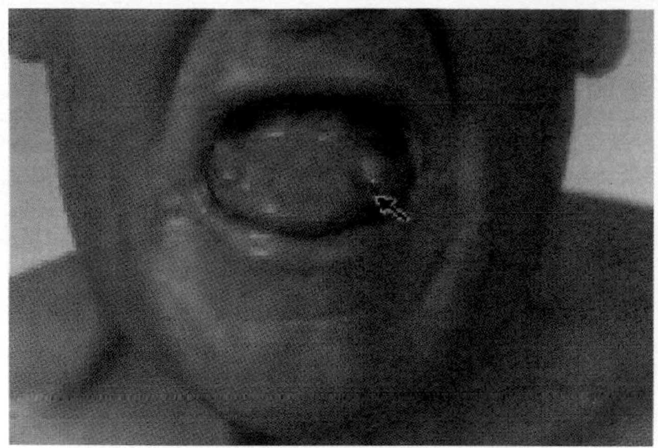

FIGURE 9. Macroglossia, a hallmark feature of AL amyloidosis.

direct protein sequencing can confirm that the deposits are composed of clonal light chains. Protein electrophoresis and immunofixation of serum and urine, serum free light-chain testing, and a bone marrow biopsy are required to establish the presence of a clonal plasma cell process. After a diagnosis is established, a cardiac assessment is critical, including electrocardiography and transthoracic echocardiography, which may show interventricular septal hypertrophy, restrictive physiology, and occasional "sparkling" changes in the myocardium (see MKSAP 16 Cardiovascular Medicine).

Treatment consists of melphalan and dexamethasone chemotherapy to eradicate the clonal plasma cells responsible for producing the pathogenic light chain. Autologous HSCT should be considered in younger patients without significant comorbidities, but transplant-related morbidity and mortality are higher than that in patients with myeloma. Studies evaluating the use of newer myeloma agents are ongoing.

Cardiac involvement is associated with a worse outcome, and the serologic markers N-terminal pro–B-type natriuretic peptide and troponin T can be used to predict prognosis. Elevation of none, one, or both of these markers is associated with median overall survivals of 26.4, 10.5, and 3.5 months, respectively. Hematologic response to treatment significantly affects outcomes, with those in complete remission (no detectable M protein after therapy) experiencing longer survival than those who have a partial or no remission.

KEY POINTS

- A diagnosis of AL amyloidosis requires characteristic findings on tissue biopsy, the presence of a monoclonal plasma cell disorder, and evidence that the amyloid deposits are composed of clonal light chains.
- Treatment of AL amyloidosis consists of chemotherapy to eradicate the clonal plasma cells responsible for producing the pathogenic light chain and, possibly, autologous hematopoietic stem cell transplantation in younger patients without significant comorbidities.

Waldenström Macroglobulinemia

Waldenström macroglobulinemia is a lymphoplasmacytic lymphoma characterized by production of monoclonal IgM antibodies. The median age at diagnosis is 64 years, and men and whites are most commonly affected.

Constitutional symptoms, lymphadenopathy, and hepatosplenomegaly may be present. Hyperviscosity syndrome–related symptoms, which may occur in up to 30% of patients, include variable headaches, blurred vision, dizziness, tinnitus, deafness, and mental status changes. Funduscopic changes of hyperviscosity include dilated, tortuous retinal veins and retinal hemorrhage. Serum viscosity is typically elevated in patients with compatible symptoms.

A peripheral sensorimotor neuropathy involving antimyelin-associated glycoprotein antibodies may develop. Mucosal bleeding from platelet dysfunction is common. Dysfibrinogenemia, glomerulonephritis, cryoglobulinemia, and cold agglutinin disease are rare manifestations of Waldenström macroglobulinemia. Anemia with rouleaux formation is common.

Diagnosis requires demonstration of lymphoplasmacytic lymphoma comprising 10% or more of the bone marrow cellularity and the presence of an IgM M protein. As in multiple myeloma, symptomatic Waldenström macroglobulinemia must be distinguished from smoldering Waldenström macroglobulinemia (≥10% marrow involvement or M protein level ≥3 g/dL and no signs or symptoms) and IgM MGUS (<10% marrow involvement and M protein level <3 g/dL and no signs or symptoms).

Asymptomatic patients do not benefit from early institution of therapy and are watched closely. Hyperviscosity syndrome requires emergent treatment with plasmapheresis. Chemotherapy may consist of the monoclonal anti-CD20 antibody rituximab with or without cytotoxic chemotherapy including an alkylating agent–based (chlorambucil, cyclophosphamide) or nucleoside analog–based (fludarabine, cladribine) regimen.

KEY POINTS

- Waldenström macroglobulinemia may be characterized by constitutional symptoms, lymphadenopathy, and hepatosplenomegaly as well as hyperviscosity syndrome–related symptoms.
- Diagnosis of Waldenström macroglobulinemia requires demonstration of lymphoplasmacytic lymphoma comprising 10% or more of the bone marrow cellularity and the presence of an IgM M protein.
- Treatment of Waldenström macroglobulinemia consists of chemotherapy (rituximab with or without cytotoxic chemotherapy) and emergent plasmapheresis for patients with hyperviscosity syndrome.

Approach to Anemia

Introduction

Anemia is a pathologic state resulting from insufficient erythrocytes to carry oxygen to peripheral tissues. Anemia can be categorized into three pathophysiologic states: (1) blood loss, (2) underproduction of erythrocytes, and (3) destruction of erythrocytes (hemolysis). Patients with anemia may be asymptomatic or have signs and symptoms, including tachycardia, dyspnea on exertion, pallor of nails and conjunctivae, fatigue, and decreased exercise tolerance. Signs and symptoms generally relate to the degree of anemia and the amount of time over which the red blood cell mass has decreased.

The complete blood count (CBC) identifies the percentage of blood volume composed of erythrocytes (hematocrit), the concentration of hemoglobin, the erythrocyte count, and the red blood cell indices indicative of erythrocyte size (mean corpuscular volume of erythrocytes [MCV]), shape, and size distribution (red blood cell distribution width). The normal hemoglobin level in men ranges from 14 to 17 g/dL (140-170 g/L), whereas the normal hemoglobin level in women is lower (12-16 g/dL [120-160 g/L]). The higher level in men is due to the erythropoietic effects of androgens. In elderly patients, lower hemoglobin values may be found, although this is the subject of debate. Erythrocyte production is controlled by erythropoietin that is synthesized by the kidneys in response to hypoxia. Hypoxia sensing by the kidney induces the formation of hypoxia induction factors (HIF1α) that act as transcription factors to increase transcription and translation of the erythropoietin gene. Erythropoietin stimulates proliferation and maturation of erythroid cells through ligand binding to the erythropoietin receptor. In addition to erythropoietin, erythrocyte production requires iron, cobalamin, folate, and a suitable marrow microenvironment.

Reviewing the red blood cell indices, including mean corpuscular hemoglobin and MCV, to determine whether the anemia is microcytic, normocytic, or macrocytic, and examining the morphology demonstrated on the peripheral blood smear, are the first steps in evaluating patients with anemia. Wright-Giemsa staining enables interpretation of erythrocyte morphology under light microscopy. The peripheral blood smear also allows for the review of other cellular blood elements, which can be useful in diagnosis. **Table 10** lists common erythrocyte abnormalities found on blood films and their interpretations.

In addition to review of the peripheral blood smear, obtaining a reticulocyte count provides an indication of erythrocyte production. Patients with normal bone marrow who have lost blood or undergone hemolysis have increased reticulocyte counts, whereas patients with underproduction anemia have low reticulocyte counts for their degree of anemia.

The reticulocyte count is often reported as a percentage of normal erythrocytes. Because patients with anemia have a reduced total number of erythrocytes, and because bone marrow stress results in increased erythropoietin production that leads to a doubling of the half-life of circulating reticulocytes, the reticulocyte count is often corrected as the reticulocyte index, which is represented by:

TABLE 10. Common Erythrocyte Findings on Peripheral Blood Smears

Peripheral Blood Smear Finding	Interpretation
Microcytosis, anisocytosis	Iron deficiency
Spherocytes	Hereditary spherocytosis, warm autoimmune hemolytic anemia
Macrocytes or macroovalocytes	Cobalamin or folate deficiency; myelodysplasia, use of antimetabolites
Target cells (codocytes)	Hemoglobinopathy, liver disease, splenectomy
Schistocytes	Microangiopathy (TTP, HUS, DIC)
Nucleated erythrocytes	Marrow stress (hemolysis, hypoxia)
Teardrop cells (dacryocytes)	Fibrosis, marrow granuloma, marrow infiltration
Bite cells	G6PD deficiency
Rouleaux	Paraproteinemia (myeloma)
Burr cells (echinocytes)	Kidney disease
Spur cells (acanthocytes)	Severe liver disease
Elliptocytes	Hereditary elliptocytosis
Sickle cells (drepanocytes)	Sickle cell anemia
Stomatocytes	Hereditary stomatocytosis, artifact

DIC = disseminated intravascular coagulation; G6PD = glucose-6-phosphate dehydrogenase; HUS = hemolytic uremic syndrome; TTP = thrombotic thrombocytopenic purpura.

Reticulocyte index = percentage of reticulocytes × patient's hematocrit ÷ 45 × 0.5

More commonly, laboratories report an absolute number of reticulocytes using flow cytometry. Normal values for the absolute number of reticulocytes range from 23,000 to 90,000/µL (23 to 90 × 10^9/L). Values higher than 110,000/µL (110 × 10^9/L) suggest a normal marrow response to anemia. The flow cytometric reticulocyte count is preferred over the reticulocyte count, corrected reticulocyte count, or reticulocyte index because it is less awkward to interpret.

An algorithm for the basic workup of anemia is found in **Figure 10**. Examination of the bone marrow may be helpful in discerning between the various causes of a hypoproliferative anemia. Additionally, Prussian blue staining of the bone marrow can be useful in determining iron stores when iron deficiency is not readily apparent.

KEY POINTS

- Symptoms and signs of anemia include tachycardia, dyspnea on exertion, pallor of nails and conjunctivae, fatigue, and decreased exercise tolerance.
- Reviewing the red blood cell indices, including mean corpuscular hemoglobin and mean corpuscular volume, and examining the morphology demonstrated on the peripheral blood smear are the first steps in evaluating patients with anemia.

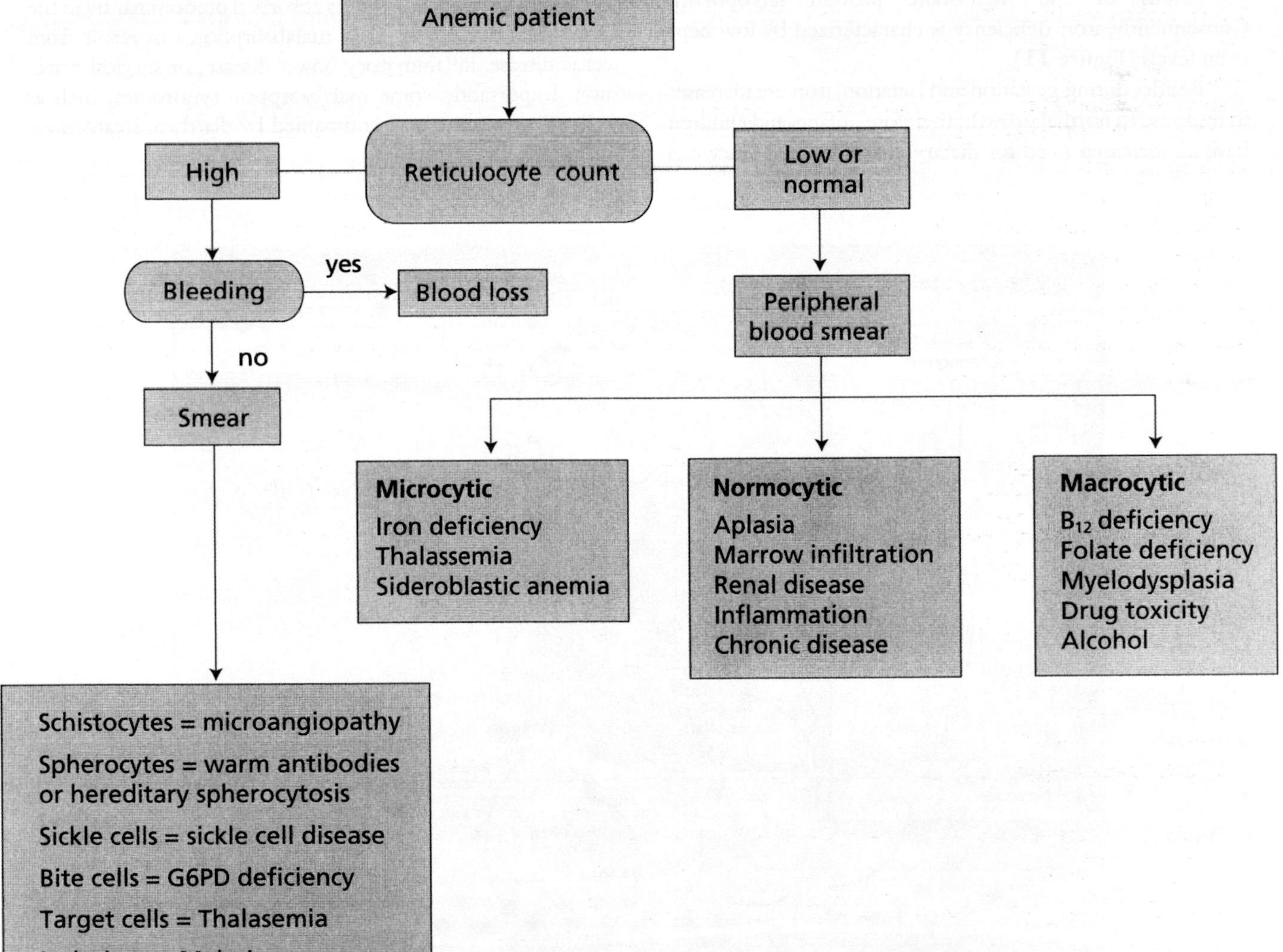

FIGURE 10. Diagnostic workup of the patient with anemia.

G6PD = glucose-6-phosphate dehydrogenase.

Anemia Due to Erythrocyte Underproduction or Maturation Defects

Iron Deficiency

Iron is necessary for erythrocyte production and maturation. Because of the precarious balance between iron intake and use, iron deficiency is a worldwide problem exacerbated by states of increased iron utilization such as pregnancy and lactation. Iron is necessary for DNA synthesis, cellular respiration, and oxygen transport. Most of all total body iron is found in the erythrocyte mass. Each milliliter of packed red blood cells contains about 1 mg of elemental iron. Iron absorption is negatively regulated by the small peptide hepcidin, which is synthesized in the liver. Hepcidin causes decreased iron absorption from enterocytes and decreased iron release by macrophages through internalization and proteolysis of the membrane protein ferroportin. Consequently, iron deficiency is characterized by low hepcidin levels (**Figure 11**).

Besides during gestation and lactation, iron use increases in response to normal growth; therefore, infants and children have an increased need for dietary iron. Iron deficiency can result from blood loss or malabsorption in addition to increased iron use. Women of reproductive age may lose enough iron through normal menstrual blood loss to become iron deficient in the absence of uterine or gastrointestinal disease. In men and nonmenstruating women, gastrointestinal blood loss is always the presumed cause of iron deficiency unless proven otherwise and may develop secondary to an undiagnosed colonic neoplasm.

The typical adult consumes about 5 mg of iron for every 1000 calories. Dietary iron in the form of heme iron is found in red meat, fish, and poultry. Nonheme iron is found in vegetables including lentils, beans, leafy vegetables, tofu, chickpeas, and black-eyed peas. Vegetable iron is often chelated by phytates and oxalates that may limit iron availability and uptake.

Because humans have a limited ability to rid the body of iron, iron absorption is tightly regulated such that the amount of iron absorbed daily is approximately equal to the amount lost in the gastrointestinal tract (about 1 mg/d for men and 1.5 mg/d for women). Iron is absorbed predominantly in the proximal small bowel. Iron malabsorption can result from celiac disease, inflammatory bowel disease, or surgical resection. Importantly, some malabsorption syndromes, such as celiac disease, are not accompanied by diarrhea, steatorrhea, or weight loss.

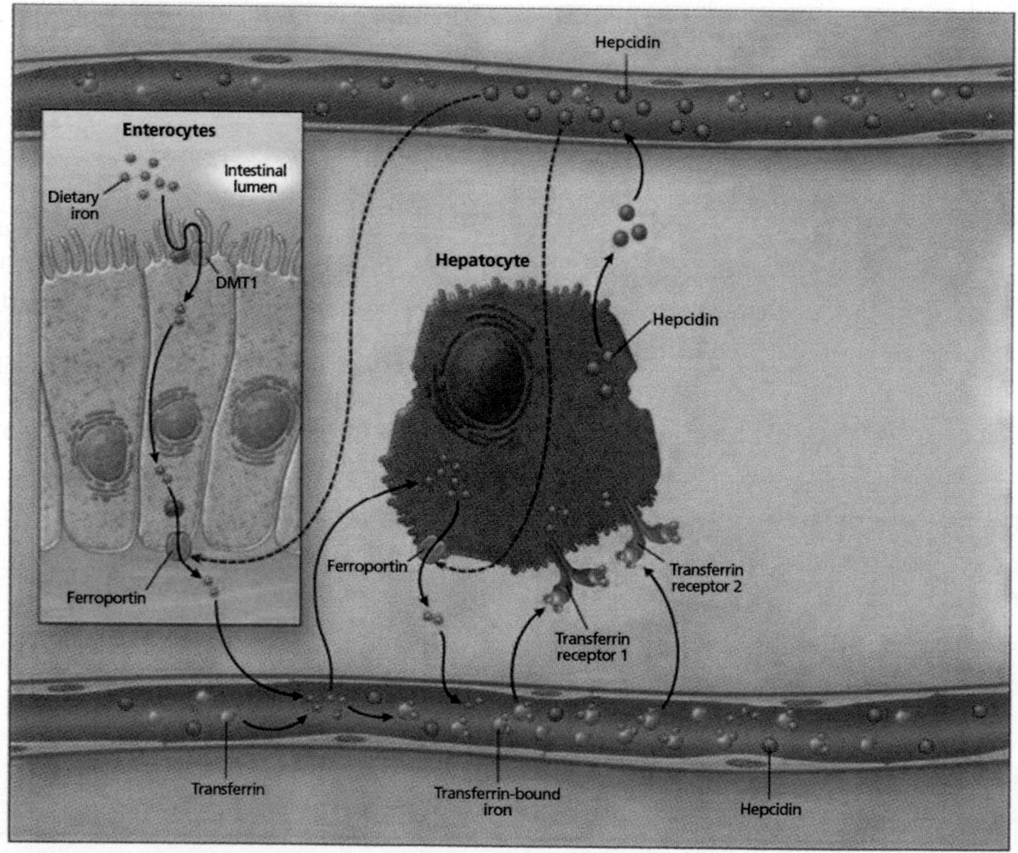

FIGURE 11. Regulation of iron absorption.

Patients with mild iron deficiency may note fatigue, lack of sense of well-being, irritability, decreased exercise tolerance, and headaches before symptoms of overt anemia occur. Occasionally, patients with advanced iron deficiency exhibit the tendency to eat ice, clay, starch, paper, and crunchy materials (pica). The physiology of pica is largely unknown.

Although the physical examination findings are typically normal in patients with iron deficiency, abnormal findings include facial pallor, glossitis, stomatitis, and, in particular, conjunctival pallor. Severe iron deficiency can result in spooning of the nails (koilonychia).

In addition to peripheral blood smear findings of microcytosis and anisopoikilocytosis (abnormalities in erythrocyte size and shape) (**Figure 12**), patients with iron deficiency have reduced serum iron and ferritin levels, increased total iron-binding capacity, and reduced transferrin saturation (iron/total iron-binding capacity). Because ferritin is an acute phase reactant, ferritin levels may be normal or slightly elevated in iron deficiency accompanied by inflammation. However, ferritin levels greater than 100 ng/mL (100 µg/L) seldom occur in patients with iron deficiency, and ferritin values less than 15 ng/mL (15 µg/L) are virtually diagnostic of iron deficiency. Although elevations in soluble transferrin receptor and zinc protoporphyrin have been used to diagnose iron deficiency, overlap is considerable between levels found in patients with and without iron deficiency, therefore diminishing the value of these tests. Thrombocytosis also occurs in iron deficiency because of blood loss. Although a bone marrow biopsy stained with Prussian blue can detect iron stores, bone marrow biopsy is seldom necessary in the diagnosis of iron deficiency.

Iron deficiency is most easily treated with oral iron salts. Oral ferrous sulfate, 325 mg three times daily, is the least expensive preparation. Each 325-mg tablet of ferrous sulfate contains 66 mg of iron, 1% to 2% of which is absorbed. Although ascorbic acid can facilitate iron absorption, no convincing data suggest the addition of this agent is worth the increase in cost or gastrointestinal toxicity. Although other oral iron salts, such as ferrous gluconate or ferrous fumarate, are available, none of these have proven superior to ferrous sulfate in tolerability or efficacy. Additionally, delayed-release and slow-release preparations are perhaps better tolerated, but these preparations may result in markedly reduced iron absorption because they bypass many of the intestinal sites in which iron absorption occurs. Iron absorption is inhibited by antacids, antibiotics, and many foods, including cereals and dietary fiber; consequently, iron should not be taken with meals. Oral iron is generally well tolerated. The principal side effects are nausea, mild abdominal pain, and constipation. For symptomatic patients receiving oral iron replacement, lower doses of iron can be used initially, with increased dosing as symptoms warrant. Iron replacement typically results in reticulocytosis after 7 to 12 days. Noticeable increases in hemoglobin levels typically occur within several weeks. When the hemoglobin level returns to normal, supplemental oral iron is generally continued for an additional 3 to 6 months to replenish iron stores.

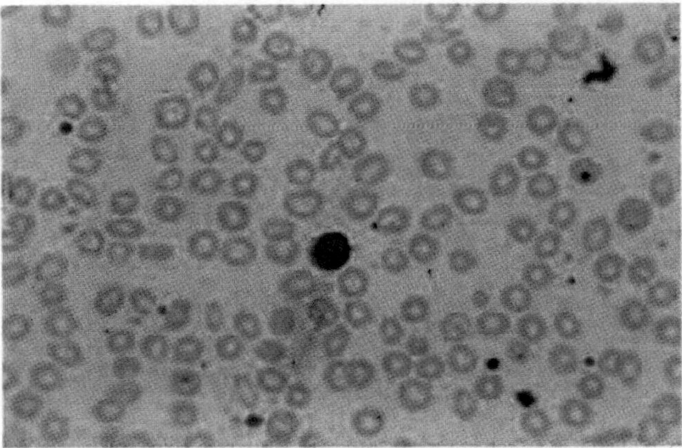

FIGURE 12. Hypochromia and microcytosis with anisopoikilocytosis in a patient with iron deficiency.

For those patients unable to absorb oral iron or for patients receiving dialysis who are taking erythropoiesis-stimulating agents (ESAs), parenteral iron preparations are available. Although iron dextran has been used previously, newer parenteral iron preparations, including iron sucrose, ferric gluconate, and ferumoxytol, appear to have fewer safety concerns, including reduced risk for anaphylactic reactions.

KEY POINTS

- Iron deficiency is characterized by low hepcidin levels.
- Patients with mild iron deficiency may note fatigue, lack of sense of well-being, irritability, decreased exercise tolerance, and headaches before symptoms of overt anemia occur; pica may also sometimes occur.
- Physical examination findings of iron deficiency include facial pallor, glossitis, and stomatitis, and, in particular, conjunctival pallor.
- Oral ferrous sulfate, 325 mg three times daily, is the least expensive preparation to treat iron deficiency.

Cobalamin (Vitamin B_{12}) Deficiency

Dietary cobalamin (vitamin B_{12}) is necessary for DNA synthesis because humans cannot synthesize cobalamin. Cobalamin is found in calf's liver, sardines, shrimp, scallops, and other animal meats. On ingestion, cobalamin is released from food by gastric peptidases. In the acidic environment of the stomach, cobalamin is bound to R-binders contained in saliva and gastric secretions. In the alkaline small bowel, cobalamin is transferred from R-binders to intrinsic factor that is necessary for cobalamin absorption in the ileum. Cobalamin is then bound to transcobalamin and stored in the reticuloendothelial system. Because of the efficient enterohepatic reuptake of cobalamin, and because of the large hepatic reservoir of cobalamin, cobalamin deficiency from decreased oral intake develops over many years. Cobalamin deficiency is almost always due to malabsorption, which may result from antibody-directed destruction of gastric parietal cells that synthesize intrinsic factor (pernicious anemia), or, more commonly, from malabsorption caused by aging and accompanying achlorhydria, inflammatory bowel disease, celiac disease, pancreatic insufficiency, or bacterial overgrowth. Some medications, such as metformin or proton pump inhibitors, have rarely been associated with cobalamin deficiency that is possibly caused by inhibition of calcium-mediated cobalamin absorption in the terminal ileum.

Physical examination findings in patients with cobalamin deficiency include glossitis, weight loss, and pale yellow skin caused by the combination of anemia and hemolysis resulting from ineffective erythropoiesis. Cobalamin deficiency can cause neurologic manifestations, including loss of position or vibratory sense that can progress to spastic ataxia. Additionally, psychiatric findings may occur, including hallucinations, dementia, and psychosis, or so-called megaloblastic mania.

The peripheral blood smear of patients with cobalamin deficiency is identical to that of patients with folate deficiency or other megaloblastic processes and is characterized by oval macrocytes (**Figure 13**), and sometimes, basophilic stippling. Additionally, hypersegmented neutrophils with more than five lobes can be found. Patients may also have thrombocytopenia and leukopenia due to ineffective hematopoiesis.

In addition to measurement of serum cobalamin and folate levels, laboratory evaluation should include homocysteine and methylmalonic acid measurement when cobalamin levels are in the low-normal range. Both of these analytes increase with cobalamin deficiency and reflect tissue cobalamin levels (**Figure 14**). An elevated serum methylmalonic acid level is more sensitive and specific for diagnosing cobalamin deficiency than low serum cobalamin levels, especially in patients with low-normal serum cobalamin levels (200-400 pg/mL [148-295 pmol/L]). Because cobalamin deficiency results in ineffective erythropoiesis, patients with cobalamin deficiency may have laboratory features of hemolysis, including

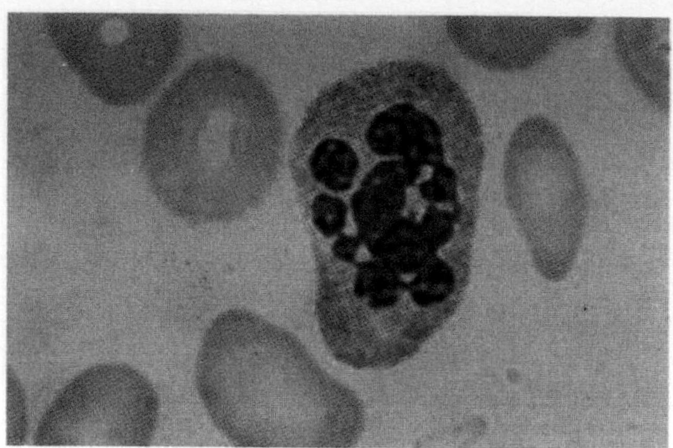

FIGURE 13. Hypersegmented polymorphonuclear cell in a patient with pernicious anemia.

decreased haptoglobin and elevated serum lactate dehydrogenase and unconjugated bilirubin levels, although the intramedullary nature of the hemolysis in cobalamin deficiency is associated with a low reticulocyte count.

Pernicious anemia is a specific cause of cobalamin deficiency caused by antibodies directed against hydrogen potassium adenosine triphosphatase in the parietal cell membrane. These antibodies, which cause parietal cell atrophy and reduce intrinsic factor levels, are found in 90% of patients with pernicious anemia compared with 5% of the general population. Additionally, antibodies to intrinsic factor are found in 70% of patients with pernicious anemia. Although antibody testing is sometimes used in the diagnosis of pernicious anemia, the relatively poor sensitivity and specificity of these tests limit their utility. Even in the setting of low cobalamin levels and macrocytosis, anti–intrinsic factor testing is reported to have a broad range of sensitivity ranging from 50% to 84%. Previously, the Schilling test was used to diagnose pernicious anemia and distinguish it from other causes of vitamin B_{12} deficiency, but this test is seldom performed currently because of the unavailability

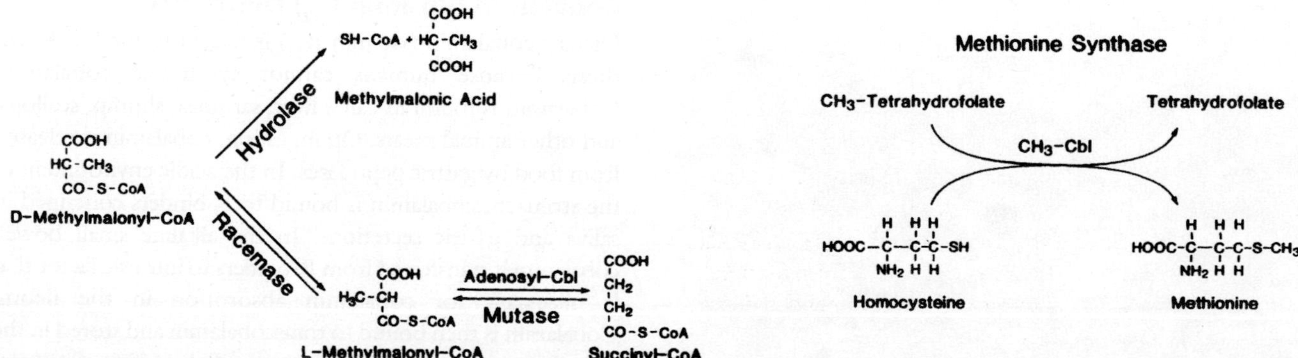

FIGURE 14. The two vitamin B_{12}-dependent enzymes, L-methylmalonyl-CoA mutase (left) and methionine synthase (right).

Reprinted with permission from Sumner AE, Chin MM, Abrahm JL, et al. Elevated methylmalonic acid and total homocysteine levels show high prevalence of vitamin B_{12} deficiency after gastric cancer. Ann Intern Med. 1996;124:469-476. Copyright 1996 American College of Physicians.

of radioactive cobalamin. Currently, making a precise diagnosis of PA is probably unnecessary as the treatment for cobalamin deficiency does not depend on cause.

Anemia resulting from cobalamin deficiency can be corrected by the administration of supplemental folate. However, neuropsychiatric symptoms may worsen in such patients despite the correction of anemia. Therefore, it is important to exclude cobalamin deficiency in patients with presumed folate deficiency. A major distinction between folate and cobalamin deficiency is that serum methylmalonic acid and homocysteine levels are increased in cobalamin deficiency, whereas only homocysteine levels are increased in folate deficiency.

Cobalamin deficiency used to be treated with parenteral cobalamin, 1000 μg/month intramuscularly. However, oral replacement of cobalamin, 1000 to 2000 μg/d orally, has been shown to be as effective as and less expensive and cumbersome than parenteral therapy. Intranasal, tablet, and gel formulations of cobalamin are available. Bilirubin and lactate dehydrogenase levels typically decrease within days in patients undergoing cobalamin replacement. Within 12 hours, megaloblastic marrow changes improve, and within 3 to 5 days, reticulocytosis occurs. Hemoglobin levels take several months to normalize, and if normalization does not occur after several months, an alternative diagnosis, such as myelodysplasia, must be considered. The neuropsychiatric findings in patients with cobalamin deficiency may take longer to resolve, if they resolve at all, following cobalamin replacement.

KEY POINTS

- An elevated serum methylmalonic acid level is more sensitive and specific for diagnosing cobalamin deficiency than low serum cobalamin levels, especially in patients with low-normal serum cobalamin levels.
- Oral replacement of cobalamin has been shown to be as effective as and less expensive and cumbersome than parenteral therapy in patients with cobalamin deficiency.
- Excluding cobalamin deficiency in patients presumed to have folate deficiency is important because although folate can correct anemia found in cobalamin-deficient patients, it does not reverse the neuropsychiatric symptoms.

Folate Deficiency

Dietary folate is contained in green leafy vegetables and fruits such as melons, lemons, and bananas. Additionally, grains in the United States are fortified with folate. Dietary folate is conjugated with glutamic acid residues. Absorption of folate requires deglutination to the monoglutamate form for uptake by cells as methyltetrahydrofolate. The recommended dietary allowance of folate is 400 μg/d.

Folate deficiency caused by decreased folate consumption occurs infrequently because normal diets are replete with folate. However, patients with folate-deficient diets, especially those with generalized malnutrition or poor nutrition associated with alcohol dependence, can become folate deficient in weeks to months because of relatively limited stores of folate in the body. Pregnant women require additional dietary or supplemental folate (see Hematologic Issues in Pregnancy). Other less common causes of folate deficiency include conditions such as hemolytic anemia (for example, sickle cell disease), desquamating skin disorders (for example, psoriasis), and other conditions associated with increased cellular turnover.

Drugs such as triamterene or phenytoin can accelerate folate metabolism, and alcohol inhibits the enzyme responsible for folate deglutination, which can impair folate absorption. Folate absorption can also be inhibited by small bowel disorders such as celiac disease, inflammatory bowel disease, or amyloidosis.

The peripheral blood smear in patients with folate deficiency is identical to that of patients with cobalamin deficiency and other megaloblastic conditions. Measuring serum folate levels is typically unreliable in the diagnosis of folate deficiency because folate levels increase rapidly after a single folate-containing meal. Erythrocyte folate may be a better indication of long-term folate balance, but erythrocyte folate is also increased in cobalamin deficiency. Serum homocysteine levels increase in folate deficiency, whereas homocysteine and methylmalonic acid levels are increased in cobalamin deficiency. Elevated homocysteine has a sensitivity and specificity of greater than 90% in the diagnosis of folate deficiency, making homocysteine measurement a reasonable test when the disorder is suspected but the serum folate level is normal.

Before initiating treatment in patients with folate deficiency, it is necessary to exclude cobalamin deficiency because folate therapy can improve cobalamin deficiency–associated anemia but will not hinder the progression of neurologic complications. After cobalamin deficiency is excluded, a therapeutic trial of folate in patients with presumed folate deficiency may be the most cost-effective way of establishing the diagnosis of folate deficiency. Patients with folate deficiency or hemolytic anemia and those who are pregnant are treated with folate, 1 to 5 mg/d orally.

KEY POINTS

- The serum folate level may be normal after a single folate-containing meal in patients with longstanding folate deficiency, therefore making measurement of erythrocyte folate a better indicator of long-term folate balance.
- Elevated homocysteine has a sensitivity and specificity of greater than 90% in the diagnosis of folate deficiency, making homocysteine measurement a reasonable test when the disorder is suspected but the serum folate level is normal.
- After cobalamin deficiency is excluded, a therapeutic trial of folate in patients with presumed folate deficiency may be the most cost-effective way of establishing the diagnosis of folate deficiency.

Inflammatory Anemia

Chronic infections such as tuberculosis or osteomyelitis, malignancies, and collagen vascular diseases are associated with anemia. Because these conditions are chronic diseases, inflammatory anemia was previously called "anemia of chronic disease." In response to inflammatory states, erythropoietin production is inhibited and the erythroid precursor response to erythropoietin is blunted. Inflammation leads to increased levels of inflammatory cytokines, including tumor necrosis factor α, interleukin (IL)-6, IL-1, and interferon, which lead to altered erythropoietin responsiveness. In particular, IL-6 causes hepatic synthesis of the small peptide hepcidin, which is pivotal in regulating iron absorption. Hepcidin causes decreased iron absorption from the gastrointestinal tract and decreased iron release by macrophages by inducing internalization and proteolysis of the transporter protein ferroportin. No laboratory test is currently commercially available for measuring hepcidin levels. The peripheral blood smear may be normal in patients with inflammatory anemia, or, over time, may show microcytic hypochromatic erythrocytes such as in iron deficiency. Typically, inflammatory anemia is characterized by a hemoglobin level greater than 8 g/dL (80 g/L). Because of erythrocyte underproduction, the reticulocyte count is typically low for the degree of anemia. The serum iron level is initially normal but decreases over time, and the total iron-binding capacity is low and the ferritin level is typically elevated. Although bone marrow evaluation is seldom necessary, ample stainable iron will be present. **Table 11** lists the laboratory features of inflammatory anemia, iron deficiency, and iron deficiency with inflammation.

Inflammatory cytokine levels may also increase with chronic heart failure and diabetes mellitus, causing the typical features of inflammatory anemia. Some patients with findings consistent with inflammatory anemia do not have an identifiable inflammatory condition and do not need evaluation for infection or malignancy in the absence of symptoms.

Inflammatory anemia does not usually require treatment. Iron replacement is not necessary and will not improve anemia developing secondary to inflammation. When absolutely necessary, an erythrocyte-stimulating agent (ESA) can be given to improve inflammatory anemia but must be used with extreme caution because it confers an increased risk for hypertension or thrombosis.

KEY POINTS

- Inflammatory anemia is typically characterized by a hemoglobin level greater than 8 g/dL (80 g/L), a generally low reticulocyte count for the degree of anemia, a low serum iron level, a low total iron-binding capacity, and an elevated ferritin level.
- Inflammatory anemia does not usually require treatment.

Anemia of Kidney Disease

The decreased renal cortical mass and resultant decreased erythropoietin levels in patients with kidney disease cause anemia that is typically normochromic and normocytic, with a reduced reticulocyte count. The peripheral blood smear may also show burr cells (echinocytes) (**Figure 15**).

Microcytosis in patients with kidney disease often suggests gastrointestinal blood loss caused by peptic ulcer disease or angiodysplasia. Because minor elevations in creatinine levels can be associated with low erythropoietin levels, measurement of the erythropoietin level can help in evaluating anemia in patients with mild kidney impairment.

Guidelines recommend the use of an ESA to achieve target hemoglobin values of 11 to 12 g/dL (110-120 g/L) for patients receiving dialysis. Increased complications occur when hemoglobin values are greater than 12 g/dL (120 g/L).

TABLE 11. Laboratory Characteristics of Inflammatory Anemia, Iron Deficiency Anemia (IDA), and IDA with Inflammation

	Type of Anemia		
Finding	**Inflammatory Anemia**	**IDA**	**IDA with Inflammation**
MCV	72-100 fL	<85 fL	<100 fL
MCHC	<36 g/dL (360 g/L)	<32 g/dL (320 g/L)	<32 g/dL (320 g/L)
Serum iron	<60 µg/dL (10.7 µmol/L)	<60 µg/dL (10.7 µmol/L)	<60 µg/dL (10.6 µmol/L)
TIBC	<250 µg/dL (44.8 µmol/L)	>400 µg/dL (71.6 µmol/L)	<400 µg/dL (71.6 µmol/L)
TIBC saturation	2%-20%	<15% (usually <10%)	<15%
Ferritin	>35 ng/mL (35 µg/L)	<15 ng/mL (15 µg/L)	<100 ng/mL (100 µg/L)
Serum soluble transferrin receptor concentration	Normal	Increased	Increased
Stainable iron in bone marrow	Present	Absent	Absent

MCV = mean corpuscular volume; MCHC = mean corpuscular hemoglobin concentration; TIBC = total iron-binding capacity.

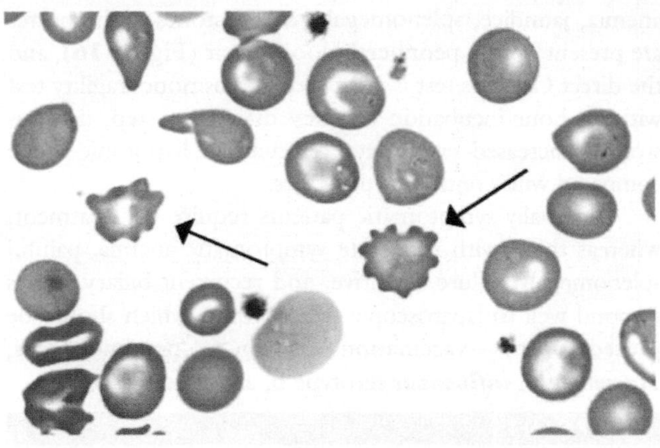

FIGURE 15. Echinocytes are erythrocytes with a relatively small number of spicules of uniform size and distribution that project from the cell surface.

ESAs are generally well tolerated but can cause hypertension and thrombosis. Cardiovascular events including myocardial infarction and stroke have occurred in patients whose hemoglobin levels increase by more than 1 g/dL (10 g/L) in a 1-week period. For maximum efficacy, iron stores must be adequate when supplemental erythropoietin is administered. Current recommendations suggest maintaining serum ferritin at a level higher than 100 ng/mL (100 µg/L), with an iron saturation of at least 20%, in patients receiving erythropoietin.

Patients receiving dialysis have increased iron requirements because of blood loss and the need for freely available iron to maintain adequate responses to erythropoietin. Most patients receiving dialysis require intravenous iron to achieve these target values. Newer iron preparations such as ferric gluconate, iron sucrose, and ferumoxytol are preferred to iron dextran because of their better side-effect profiles. Although more than 95% of patients with kidney failure respond to ESAs, patients may respond insufficiently to these agents because of folate deficiency, aluminum toxicity, inflammation, or ongoing blood loss.

KEY POINTS

- Current guidelines recommend the use of supplemental erythropoiesis-stimulating agents to achieve target hemoglobin values of 11 to 12 g/dL (110-120 g/L) in patients receiving dialysis.
- Maintaining serum ferritin at a level higher than 100 ng/mL (100 µg/L), with an iron saturation of at least 20%, is recommended in patients receiving erythropoiesis-stimulating agents.

Hemolytic Anemias

Overview

The hemolytic anemias represent a diverse group of diseases that share accelerated erythrocyte destruction in common. The origin of erythrocyte destruction can be inherited (as in hereditary spherocytosis) or acquired (as in thrombotic thrombocytopenic purpura [TTP]). The congenital hemolytic anemias are further grouped based on whether the defect involves the erythrocyte membrane, erythrocyte metabolic enzymes, or hemoglobin structure or function (**Table 12**).

Patients with congenital hemolytic anemia may be asymptomatic, especially if the rate of hemolysis is mild and well compensated, but these patients may develop symptoms if their bone marrow becomes unable to compensate. Patients with acquired hemolysis typically present with features of anemia (for example, tachycardia, dyspnea on exertion, pallor of nails and conjunctivae, fatigue, and decreased exercise tolerance) that vary depending on the rate of hemolysis and degree of bone marrow compensation. Jaundice, scleral icterus, gallstones, and splenomegaly are other common findings. A detailed family history is essential in the evaluation of hemolytic anemia and may reveal additional family members with anemia or pigmented gallstones.

Assuming normal bone marrow function and erythropoietin production, the typical response to hemolysis is

TABLE 12. Examples of Congenital and Acquired Causes of Hemolytic Anemia

Congenital hemolytic anemias	**Examples**
Defects in the erythrocyte membrane	Hereditary spherocytosis
Deficiencies in erythrocyte metabolic enzymes	G6PD deficiency
Defects in hemoglobin structure or synthesis	Sickle cell disease, α- and β-thalassemia
Acquired hemolytic anemias	**Examples**
Autoimmune hemolytic anemia	WAIHA, cold agglutinin disease
Microangiopathic hemolytic anemias	TTP, DIC
Paroxysmal nocturnal hemoglobinuria	
Infectious, chemical, and physical agents	Malaria, arsine gas, venoms and toxins

DIC = disseminated intravascular coagulation; G6PD = glucose-6-phosphate dehydrogenase; TTP = thrombotic thrombocytopenic purpura; WAIHA = warm autoimmune hemolytic anemia.

increased erythrocyte production, resulting in an increased reticulocyte count. The absence of such a reticulocytosis in patients whose bone marrow is unable to respond does not preclude the possibility of severe hemolysis and will likely lead to a severe anemia. Because of accelerated erythrocyte destruction, the hemolytic anemias are commonly characterized by an increase in the indirect bilirubin level and an elevated lactate dehydrogenase level. With accelerated, chronic, or intravascular hemolysis, a decreased haptoglobin level and hemoglobinuria may be detected. Review of the peripheral blood smear is essential because many hemolytic anemias demonstrate morphologic changes in erythrocytes that aid in diagnosis (see Table 10). If a diagnosis is not readily apparent, the direct Coombs test (also known as the direct antiglobulin test), which is used in the evaluation of immune-mediated hemolysis, is often the initial diagnostic test.

Treatment is based on the underlying disorder, but all patients with chronic hemolysis require supplementation with folic acid, 1 mg/d. If the bone marrow's ability to compensate for hemolysis becomes impaired as it does in parvovirus B19 infection (aplastic crisis), the anemia may become more severe. Anemia may also acutely worsen with accelerated hemolysis as occurs in infection (hyperhemolytic crisis), or rarely because of folate deficiency (megaloblastic crisis).

KEY POINTS

- An increased reticulocyte count, increased indirect bilirubin and increased lactate dehydrogenase levels, and a decreased haptoglobin level as well as morphologic changes in erythrocytes may aid in the diagnosis of hemolytic anemia.
- Treatment of hemolytic anemia is based on the underlying disorder, but all patients with chronic hemolysis require supplementation with folic acid, 1 mg/d.

Congenital Hemolytic Anemias

Hereditary Spherocytosis

Hereditary spherocytosis is the most common disorder of the erythrocyte membrane, occurring in 1 of 2000 individuals of Northern European descent. Inheritance is most commonly autosomal dominant but may occasionally be sporadic. Penetrance is variable, and the incidence of clinically recognized disease is much lower than the genotypic incidence. Mutations in ankyrin and other erythrocyte-anchoring proteins lead to spectrin deficiency and subsequent loss of erythrocyte surface area. These changes destabilize the erythrocyte, leading to a spherocytic shape, reduced deformability, trapping, and subsequent destruction in the spleen.

The clinical manifestations of hereditary spherocytosis range from severe neonatal jaundice or severe parvovirus B19 infection–related aplastic crisis to only minimal symptoms with diagnosis in adulthood. Hereditary spherocytosis should be suspected in patients with a personal or family history of anemia, jaundice, splenomegaly, or gallstones. Spherocytes are present on the peripheral blood smear (**Figure 16**), and the direct Coombs test is negative. The osmotic fragility test with 24-hour incubation is a key diagnostic step, demonstrating increased erythrocyte fragility in hypotonic saline compared with control erythrocytes.

Minimally symptomatic patients require no treatment, whereas those with moderate symptomatic anemia, painful splenomegaly, failure to thrive, and recurrent biliary stones respond well to laparoscopic splenectomy, which should be preceded by vaccinations against pneumococcus, *Haemophilus influenzae* serotype b, and meningococcus.

KEY POINTS

- A personal or family history of anemia, jaundice, splenomegaly, or gallstones may be suggestive of hereditary spherocytosis.
- Minimally symptomatic patients with hereditary spherocytosis require no treatment, whereas those with moderate symptomatic anemia, painful splenomegaly, and recurrent biliary stones should receive laparoscopic splenectomy.

Glucose-6-Phosphate Dehydrogenase Deficiency

G6PD deficiency is the most common erythrocyte enzyme defect, affecting more than 200 million people worldwide. G6PD deficiency is caused by various mutations on the X chromosome and occurs more commonly in males, often of African American descent. Heterozygous deficiency in patients with G6PD deficiency is thought to protect against *Plasmodium falciparum* malaria.

Because of the inability of the erythrocyte to generate nicotinamide adenine dinucleotide phosphate (NADPH) and maintain glutathione in a reduced state, the more common African

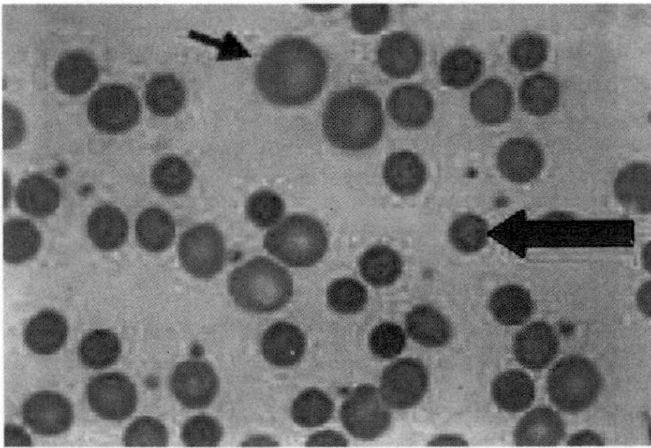

FIGURE 16. Spherocytes are characterized by erythrocytes with a spherical shape and lack of central pallor (red arrow). Spherocytes may be seen in hereditary spherocytosis and warm autoimmune hemolytic anemia. The larger and lighter pinks cells are reticulocytes (blue arrow).

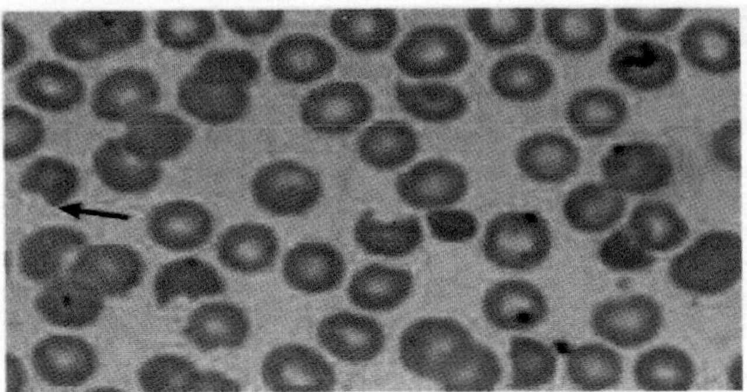

FIGURE 17. G6PD deficiency is characterized by erythrocytes with the appearance of a "bite" removed from the surface membrane (arrow). These cells may be confused with schistocytes.

American variant typically leads to episodic hemolysis in response to oxidant stressors (for example, infection or drugs such as dapsone, trimethoprim-sulfamethoxazole, and nitrofurantoin). The less common Mediterranean variant typically leads to chronic hemolysis and is associated with favism, a potentially fatal hemolytic anemia that develops after ingestion of the fava bean.

During an acute hemolytic episode, bite cells may be seen on the peripheral blood smear (**Figure 17**), and a brilliant cresyl blue stain may reveal Heinz bodies (denatured oxidized hemoglobin). In the more common African American variant, elevated levels of G6PD are found in young reticulocytes, and G6PD levels may therefore be falsely normal during a hemolytic episode. Consequently, G6PD levels should only be checked a few months after the occurrence of an acute event.

Treatment during an acute crisis is usually supportive and includes avoidance and withdrawal of the responsible drug and treatment of any underlying infection. Because of increased G6PD levels in young reticulocytes in the African American variant, anemia may improve even if the offending drug is continued. If the offending drug is essential and prescribed only for a finite period, continued therapy remains a secondary option.

Published lists of safe and unsafe drugs are available and should be reviewed before prescribing medications in patients with known G6PD deficiency (for example, go to www.g6pd.org/favism/english/index.mvc?pgid=safe).

KEY POINTS

- Bite cells may be seen on the peripheral blood smear of patients with glucose-6-phosphate dehydrogenase deficiency during an acute hemolytic episode, and a brilliant cresyl blue stain may reveal Heinz bodies.
- In patients with the African American variant of glucose-6-phosphate dehydrogenase deficiency (G6PD) deficiency, G6PD levels should only be checked a few months after the occurrence of an acute event.
- Treatment of glucose-6-phosphate dehydrogenase deficiency during an acute crisis is usually supportive, including avoidance and withdrawal of the responsible drug and treatment of any underlying infection.

Thalassemia

Adult hemoglobin is composed of two α-globin chains and two β-globin chains linked to heme (iron and protoporphyrin) to form the tetrameric structure necessary for oxygen delivery. The common thalassemic syndromes result from various genetic defects, leading to decreased or absent synthesis of normal α or β chains. An imbalance in production of α or β chains leads to ineffective erythropoiesis, intravascular hemolysis caused by precipitation of the excess insoluble globin chain, and decreased hemoglobin production. α-Thalassemia mutations result in decreased production of α chains, whereas β-thalassemia is caused by genetic mutations leading to decreased production of β chains. Microcytic hypochromic erythrocytes and target forms may be seen on the peripheral blood smear in both α- and β-thalassemia (**Figure 18**). Iron overload may develop because of increased iron absorption, even in the absence of transfusion. Prenatal screening programs are available to reduce births of neonates with homozygous thalassemia in high-prevalence populations.

α-Thalassemia is common in individuals of African, Mediterranean, Southeast Asian, and Middle Eastern descent. Because of the presence of duplicate copies of the α chain on each copy of chromosome 16, four different genotypes are possible (**Table 13**).

A single gene deletion (–α/αα) results in a silent carrier state that is normal clinically and hematologically. α-Thalassemia trait (or α-Thalassemia minor) (–α/–α or – –/αα) is associated with mild anemia, microcytosis, hypochromia, target cells on the peripheral blood smear, and, in adults, normal hemoglobin electrophoresis results. The (–α/–α) variant is found in 2% to 3% of all blacks and is often mistaken for iron deficiency. The red cell distribution width (RDW) may be useful in distinguishing between these two diagnoses because the RDW is often elevated in iron deficiency but normal in thalassemia. Gene deletion studies are only available from reference laboratories, and the diagnosis

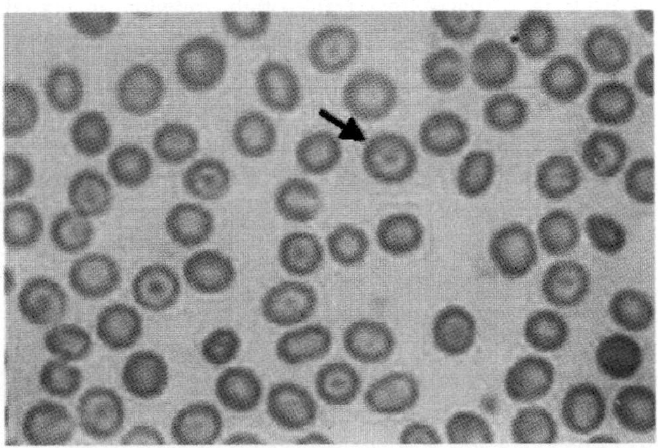

FIGURE 18. Target cells are seen in α- and β-thalassemia (arrow).

TABLE 13. α- and β-Thalassemia Genotype/Phenotype Correlation

Variant/Genotype	Clinical Scenario	Treatment
α-Thalassemia minor (–α/–α) or (––/αα)	Asymptomatic, mild microcytic anemia	None
Hemoglobin H (––/–α)	Moderate to severe anemia, splenomegaly	Intermittent transfusion
Hemoglobin Barts (––/––)	Usually lethal in utero	In utero transfusion
β-Thalassemia trait (β^+)	Asymptomatic, mild microcytic anemia	None
β-Thalassemia intermedia	Moderate to severe anemia, iron overload	Intermittent transfusion, iron chelation
β-Thalassemia major (β^o)	Severe anemia, poor growth, skeletal abnormalities, iron overload	Transfusion, iron chelation, consider splenectomy and HSCT

HSCT = hematopoietic stem cell transplantation.

of α-thalassemia trait is often made after exclusion of other causes of microcytic anemia; long-standing anemia and a family history are also supportive. No treatment is necessary for α-thalassemia trait.

The deletion of three α genes (––/–α) leads to hemoglobin H (γ_4) disease, which may be associated with severe anemia and clinical sequelae, including heart failure and hypoxia, and is identifiable on hemoglobin electrophoresis. Hydrops fetalis results from homozygous inheritance of a double gene deletion (––/––) and is typically associated with in utero fetal demise if no intervention is taken.

β-Thalassemia is most prevalent in the Mediterranean region, Southeast Asia, India, and Pakistan. The clinical syndromes of β-thalassemia depend on the degree of expression of the single β-globin gene on each copy of chromosome 11. Patients with mildly decreased expression of a single β gene have β-thalassemia trait (β^+) and present similarly to those with α-thalassemia trait, with mild anemia, microcytosis, hypochromia, and target cells. The Mentzer index is a ratio of the mean corpuscular volume (MCV) in fL divided by the erythrocyte count. Values less than 13 are associated with β-thalassemia.

Hemoglobin electrophoresis serves as a useful diagnostic tool in β-thalassemia trait, often showing increased hemoglobin A_2 ($\alpha_2\delta2$) and hemoglobin F ($\alpha_2\gamma2$). When both β-chains are affected, the phenotype is more severe and dependent on the degree of β-chain suppression. β-Thalassemia major (Cooley anemia) is caused by the almost completely absent synthesis of β globin (β^o) and is associated with severe anemia, growth retardation, skeletal complications, and iron overload. Blood transfusion is required throughout life as is iron chelation therapy. Allogeneic hematologic stem cell transplantation may be curative, whereas splenectomy may be helpful in decreasing transfusion requirements. Thalassemia intermedia is most often caused by decreased, but not absent, synthesis of both β genes and leads to a phenotype intermediate between β-thalassemia trait and β-thalassemia major.

KEY POINTS

- A single α gene deletion (–α/αα) results in a silent carrier state that is normal clinically and hematologically.
- Hydrops fetalis results from homozygous inheritance of a double α gene deletion (––/––) and is typically associated with in utero fetal demise if no intervention is taken.
- Patients with β-thalassemia trait (β^+) have mild anemia, microcytosis, hypochromia, target cells, and increased hemoglobin A_2 ($\alpha_2\delta2$) and, at times, hemoglobin F ($\alpha_2\gamma2$) on electrophoresis.
- β-thalassemia major (Cooley anemia) requires lifelong blood transfusion and iron chelation therapy; allogeneic hematologic stem cell transplantation may be curative, whereas splenectomy decreases transfusion requirements.

Sickle Cell Syndromes

Hemoglobin S (Hb S) results from a point mutation leading to a single amino acid substitution at the sixth position of the β-globin chain. Eight to 9% of blacks are heterozygous for Hb S and are considered to have sickle cell trait (Hb AS). Sickle cell trait is generally considered a benign condition, although hematuria, renal medullary carcinoma, risk of splenic rupture at high altitudes, venous thromboembolism, and sudden death during extreme conditions have been reported. In 2010, the National Collegiate Athletic Association (NCAA) recommended screening of all incoming student athletes for sickle cell trait before participation in athletic activities. It is uniformly recommended that individuals with sickle cell trait should remain well hydrated during strenuous activity, but how screening results will otherwise impact participation and eligibility remains very controversial. In a 2012 policy statement, The American Society of Hematology (ASH) indicated that it does not support testing or disclosure of sickle cell trait status as a prerequisite for participation in athletic activities. In addition, ASH notes that the NCAA policy can cause potential harms to student athletes and the larger community of patients with sickle cell trait. The ASH policy statement also recommends universal interventions to reduce exertion-related injuries and deaths because this approach can be effective for all athletes irrespective of their sickle cell status. The policy statement also cites the need for further research into the relationship between sickle cell trait and exertion-related illness.

Sickle cell disease encompasses those genotypes associated with hemolysis and vasoocclusive crisis; examples include homozygous sickle cell anemia (Hb SS), sickle-β° thalassemia (Hb Sβ°), sickle-β⁺ thalassemia (Hb Sβ⁺), and hemoglobin SC disease (Hb SC). Phenotypic differences exist among and within these genotypes.

Hb SS is associated with reduced life expectancy, moderate to severe anemia, and, often, frequent pain crises, and may be closely mimicked clinically by Hb Sβ° thalassemia. Patients with Hb SC and Hb Sβ⁺ often have less severe anemia and a lower frequency of vasoocclusive crisis, but the spectrum of potential complications is identical to that of Hb SS. A higher frequency of ocular complications and bony infarcts has been noted in Hb SC disease because of increased blood viscosity. Genetic polymorphisms and environmental and psychosocial factors account for the phenotypic diversity within a given genotype, such as Hb SS. Differentiating among the sickle cell syndromes can be accomplished by considering the degree of anemia, mean corpuscular volume, and erythrocyte morphology in conjunction with hemoglobin electrophoresis results (**Table 14**, **Figure 19**).

Management of Sickle Cell Disease Complications

Sickle cell disease is a systemic, multiorgan disease (**Table 15**) that requires lifelong routine medical care, including regular updating of vaccinations, annual ophthalmologic examinations, and screening for hypertension, proteinuria, and pulmonary hypertension. Genetic counseling should be offered to families before pregnancy.

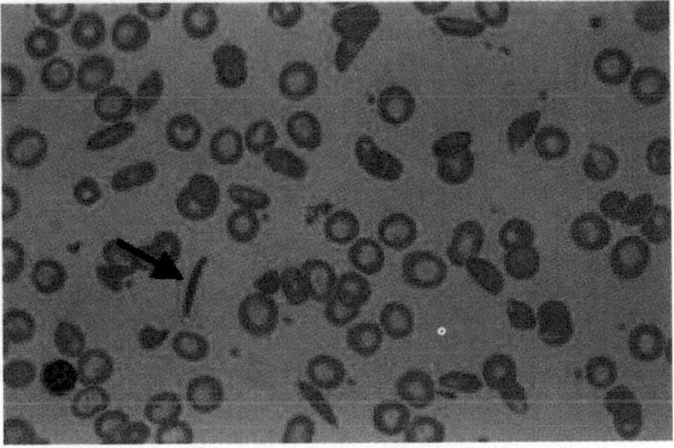

FIGURE 19. Sickle cells are thin, elongated, irregularly shaped erythrocytes (arrow).

Hydroxyurea therapy has resulted in decreased mortality in Hb SS and is indicated in patients with recurrent painful episodes, acute chest syndrome, and symptomatic anemia. Because of the potential teratogenicity of hydroxyurea, proper contraception before initiation should be discussed.

Pain

Pain is the most common complication of sickle cell disease and may be the initial presenting symptom in patients who subsequently develop more severe complications, such as acute chest syndrome or multiorgan failure.

Patients commonly have musculoskeletal symptoms, but vasoocclusion can occur in any organ system. No reliable physical or laboratory findings serve as useful surrogate

TABLE 14. Characteristics of Adult Sickle Cell Syndromes

Disease Type	Hb	MCV	Hb S (%)	Hb A (%)	Hb A_2 (%)	Peripheral Blood Smear Findings	Clinical Severity[b] 0 to +++
Sickle trait (AS)	NL	NL	40	60	<3.5	NL	0
Hb SS	6-8	NL	>90	0	<3.5	Sickle cells	+++
Sβ⁺-Thalassemia	9-12	70-75	>60	10-30	>3.5	Rare sickle cells Target cells	+ to ++
Sβ⁰-Thalassemia	7-9	65-70	>80	0	>3.5	Sickle cells Target cells	+++
SC	10-15	75-NL	50	0	Hb A_2 = 0 Hb C = 50[a]	Fat sickle cells Target cells	+ to ++

Hb = hemoglobin; Hb SS = homozygous sickle cell anemia; MCV = mean corpuscular volume; NL = normal; Sβ⁺ = sickle β⁺; Sβ⁰ = sickle β⁰; SC = sickle cell disease.

[a]Clinical severity is variable within each genotype.

[b]Note that Hb C co-migrates with Hb A_2 on standard alkaline cellulose acetate electrophoresis but will separate on citrate agar electrophoresis.

Note: Hb percentages may not total 100% because Hb F is not included in this table.

TABLE 15. Common Complications and Treatments in Adult Sickle Cell Disease

Complication	Treatment
Vasoocclusive pain episodes	**Acute:** narcotic analgesia, NSAIDS, IV fluids **Recurring:** HU, nonnarcotic and narcotic analgesia
Acute chest syndrome	**Acute:** oxygenation, incentive spirometry, analgesics, empiric antibiotics, IV fluids, simple or erythrocyte exchange transfusion **Prevention:** HU, incentive spirometry
Ischemic stroke	**Acute:** erythrocyte exchange transfusion, aspirin[a] **Prevention:** chronic erythrocyte transfusion to target Hb S <30%-50%
Multiorgan failure/hepatopathy	Erythrocyte exchange transfusion
Pulmonary hypertension	Similar to patients with primary pulmonary hypertension, erythrocyte exchange transfusion,[a] HU[a]
Priapism	**Acute:** IV fluids, narcotic analgesia, oxygenation, erythrocyte transfusion[a]; if no relief by 2 hours, local decompression, irrigation, and shunting **Prevention:** pseudoephedrine, terbutaline
Gallstones	Cholecystectomy with preoperative transfusion to Hb 10 g/dL (100 g/L) if symptomatic; otherwise, no treatment
Symptomatic chronic anemia	HU, erythrocyte exchange transfusion if severe; treat non-sickle cell causes
Aplastic crisis	Supportive care, erythrocyte exchange transfusion based on symptoms and severity
Chronic kidney insufficiency	ACE inhibitor, blood pressure control
Infection	**Acute:** broad-spectrum antibiotics to cover encapsulated bacteria, gram-negative bacteria, and atypical organisms **Prevention:** vaccinations against meningococcus, pneumococcus, *Haemophilus influenzae*, hepatitis B
Retinopathy	Annual ophthalmologic examination, laser phototherapy as needed
Peripheral skin ulceration	Bed rest, topical therapy, erythrocyte exchange transfusion[a]
Osteonecrosis	Bed rest, analgesics, joint replacement
Delayed hemolytic transfusion reaction	Supportive care, transfusion with antigen-matched erythrocytes depending on symptoms and severity

Hb = hemoglobin; HU = hydroxyurea; IV = intravenous.

[a]Although often used in treatment, efficacy remains unproven.

CONT.

markers for excluding vasoocclusion; therefore, treatment of sickle cell disease is based on symptoms.

Management of an uncomplicated painful sickle cell episode includes hydration, nonopioid and opioid analgesia, and incentive spirometry to avoid acute chest syndrome. Morphine and hydromorphone are the opioid analgesics of choice.

During hospitalization, opioid analgesia is most effectively delivered through patient controlled analgesia (PCA) pumps that include a basal rate and a demand option. Meperidine is generally avoided because of its short half-life and low seizure threshold. Chronic severe pain is typically managed with daily nonopioid or oral opioid analgesia. Hydroxyurea has been shown to decrease the frequency of painful episodes and hospitalizations. Adherence to hydroxyurea therapy may be inferred by identification of an increased mean corpuscular volume (MCV). Erythrocyte transfusion is not indicated for uncomplicated painful episodes.

Stroke

Patients with sickle cell disease have an increased risk for subclinical and overt stroke. Acute treatment of stroke consists of erythrocyte exchange transfusion to reduce the Hb S concentration to less than 30%. Chronic transfusion can decrease the risk for stroke recurrence but may be associated with iron overload, vascular access difficulties, and alloimmunization. Vasculopathy and neovascularization can lead to collateral vascular formation (moyamoya syndrome) and subsequent risk for hemorrhagic events.

Acute Chest Syndrome

Patients with acute chest syndrome present with dyspnea, fever, hypoxia, and a new infiltrate usually involving an entire segment on chest radiography. This syndrome has various causes, including infection, bone marrow fat emboli, and pulmonary infarction. Management includes empiric broad-spectrum antibiotics, supplemental oxygen, pain medication

CONT.

to diminish chest splinting, and avoidance of overhydration. Incentive spirometry may reduce atelectasis. Bronchodilators may be helpful in patients with concomitant reactive airways disease. Erythrocyte transfusion is indicated if hypoxia persists despite supplemental oxygen. Erythrocyte exchange transfusion may be preferred when hypoxia is severe or progressive. Hydroxyurea for outpatients and incentive spirometry during hospitalization have been shown to decrease the incidence of acute chest syndrome.

Pulmonary Hypertension

Pulmonary hypertension is an increasingly recognized complication of sickle cell disease. Chronic intravascular hemolysis leads to reduction in the vasodilator nitric oxide and subsequent pulmonary arterial vasoconstriction. Patients may have signs or symptoms of right heart failure. Current therapy is supportive and similar to that used to treat primary pulmonary hypertension. The role of chronic erythrocyte transfusion is unclear. Hydroxyurea has not proven an effective treatment.

Priapism

Acute priapism is another complication of sickle cell disease. Prolonged and recurrent priapism can lead to impotence and requires prompt treatment. Immediate therapy includes intravenous fluid administration, adequate oxygenation, and pain control. Urgent urologic consultation should be obtained for consideration of local aspiration and irrigation for priapism lasting longer than 2 hours. The use of pseudoephedrine, α-blockers, hormonal manipulation, and erythrocyte transfusion may decrease recurrence but has not been studied in clinical trials.

Infection

Patients with sickle cell disease are at increased risk for life-threatening infections. Vaccinations against infection with pneumococcus, meningococcus, *Haemophilus influenzae* type b, and hepatitis B virus are recommended as is annual vaccination against influenza virus. Prompt administration of broad-spectrum antibiotics to cover encapsulated bacteria, gram-negative organisms, and atypical community-acquired organisms is appropriate when infection is suspected.

Anemia

Severe acute anemia may develop secondary to bone marrow suppression from parvovirus B19 infection–associated aplastic crisis. Alternative diagnoses include splenic sequestration in Hb SC or Hb Sβ^+, hepatic sequestration, or superimposed G6PD deficiency, which also occurs commonly in blacks. Chronic worsening of anemia may be due to reduced erythropoietin levels from kidney insufficiency, folate deficiency, or anemia of chronic inflammation.

Erythrocyte Transfusion in Sickle Cell Disease

Erythrocyte transfusion in sickle cell disease is appropriate only for specific indications. Acute indications include stroke, symptomatic anemia, acute chest syndrome, and surgical interventions. Chronic indications include secondary prevention of stroke or acute chest syndrome, and, possibly, prevention of priapism, pulmonary hypertension, and nonhealing ulcers. Transfusion is not indicated for uncomplicated pregnancy, routine painful episodes, minor surgery not requiring anesthesia, and asymptomatic anemia. Erythrocyte exchange transfusion is indicated for acute ischemic stroke, acute chest syndrome with significant hypoxia, and multiorgan failure/hepatopathy, as well as in individuals in whom simple transfusion would raise the hemoglobin level to greater than 10 g/dL (100 g/L). Chronic transfusion can lead to iron overload, alloimmunization, and an increased risk for a delayed hemolytic transfusion reaction. Erythrocytes used in transfusion should be leukoreduced, HbS negative, and phenotypically matched for the E, C, and Kell antigens as well as for any known alloantibodies. Hemoglobin targets should remain less than 10 g/dL (100 g/L) to avoid hyperviscosity. H

Other Hemoglobinopathies

Hemoglobin E variants have become more prevalent in the United States because of increased emigration of persons from Southeast Asia. Patients heterozygous for hemoglobin E (AE) have microcytosis but no anemia. Homozygous individuals have mild anemia and more severe microcytosis. Doubly heterozygous Hb E/β-thalassemia is associated with a wide spectrum of clinical presentations ranging from moderate to more severe thalassemic phenotypes.

Heterozygous hemoglobin C (AC) is found in up to 3% of blacks. Affected individuals have normal hemoglobin but may have target cells on the peripheral blood smear. Homozygous individuals have mild microcytic anemia and more prominent target cells but no sickling.

Hemoglobin D has a prevalence of 3% in the Northwest Punjab region of India. Neither heterozygous (AD) nor homozygous (DD) hemoglobin D leads to hemolysis. However, coinheritance with hemoglobin D and Hb S may result in a sickling syndrome.

KEY POINTS

- Hydroxyurea therapy has resulted in decreased mortality in patients with sickle cell disease and is indicated for recurrent painful episodes, acute chest syndrome, and symptomatic anemia.
- Management of an uncomplicated painful sickle cell episode includes hydration, nonopioid and opioid analgesia, and incentive spirometry to avoid acute chest syndrome.
- Acute treatment of stroke in patients with sickle cell disease consists of erythrocyte exchange transfusion to reduce the Hb S concentration to less than 30%.

- Management of acute chest syndrome in patients with sickle cell disease includes empiric broad-spectrum antibiotics, supplemental oxygen, pain medication to diminish chest splinting, avoidance of overhydration, and, possibly, bronchodilators and erythrocyte transfusion.
- Prolonged and recurrent priapism, which is a complication of sickle cell disease, can lead to impotence and requires prompt treatment.

Acquired Hemolytic Anemias

A thorough review of personal and family history can be helpful in differentiating between the congenital and the acquired hemolytic anemias. Patients with an acquired hemolytic anemia typically do not have a personal history or strong family history of anemia, gallstones, or splenomegaly. A history of previously normal hemoglobin values also favors an acquired cause of anemia but may also be characteristic of some episodic congenital hemolytic disorders such as G6PD deficiency.

Autoimmune Hemolytic Anemia

Autoimmune hemolytic anemia (AIHA) may be idiopathic or associated with other autoimmune, lymphoproliferative, malignant, infectious, or drug-related processes. The most common antibodies involved are of the IgG (80%) or IgM (20%) subclass. AIHA is commonly classified by the temperature at which the autoantibodies optimally bind to erythrocytes.

Warm Autoimmune Hemolytic Anemia

Warm autoimmune hemolytic anemia (WAIHA) is caused by IgG antibodies that optimally bind to erythrocyte Rh antigens at 37.0 °C (99.0 °F). Hemolysis is typically caused by clearance of antibody-coated erythrocytes through binding to the Fc receptor on splenic macrophages. Partial phagocytosis of the erythrocyte membrane leads to the formation of spherocytes (see Figure 16), which become entrapped and removed by the spleen. Complement fixation by warm IgG antibodies is usually absent or weak.

Patients with WAIHA may present with rapid or more insidious symptoms of anemia or jaundice; mild splenomegaly is often present. Spherocytes are seen on the peripheral blood smear. The direct Coombs (antiglobulin) test is used to diagnose WAIHA and is typically positive for IgG and negative or only weakly positive for complement (C3) (**Table 16**). In less than 10% of patients, the Coombs test may be normal, in which case more sensitive diagnostic testing through a reference laboratory or blood center is required.

First-line therapy for WAIHA consists of corticosteroids, which interfere with antibody production and macrophage-mediated clearance. Prednisone is typically prescribed at a dose of 1 mg/kg/d followed by a prolonged taper, and approximately two thirds of patients respond to this therapy. Splenectomy is considered for nonresponders, patients who relapse, and those requiring chronic corticosteroids. Rituximab has been shown to be beneficial in recent nonrandomized trials for those refractory or intolerant to corticosteroids. In patients with more refractory disease, danazol and other immunosuppressive medications such as cyclophosphamide, cyclosporine, and azathioprine have shown variable efficacy.

KEY POINTS

- Warm autoimmune hemolytic anemia is characterized by rapid or more insidious symptoms of anemia or jaundice and mild splenomegaly.
- The direct Coombs (antiglobulin) test is used to diagnose autoimmune hemolytic anemia and is typically positive for IgG and negative or only weakly positive for complement (C3) in warm autoimmune hemolytic anemia, whereas it is positive for only complement (C3) in cold agglutinin disease.
- First-line therapy for warm autoimmune hemolytic anemia is corticosteroids.

Cold Agglutinin Disease

Cold agglutinin disease (CAD) is caused by the binding of IgM antibodies to erythrocyte antigens, typically I or i, at temperatures below 37.0 °C (99.0 °F), with maximal activity around 4.0 °C (39.0 °F). IgM antibodies efficiently fix complement to the erythrocyte membrane, leading to erythrocyte clearance by direct intravascular lysis or through binding to macrophages in the liver. Anemia is typically mild to moderate, chronic, and worsened at cold temperatures. CAD occasionally develops a few weeks after infection with mycoplasma or Epstein-Barr virus, often after typical clinical symptoms have resolved. The peripheral blood smear in CAD may show clumping or agglutination of erythrocytes, which leads to a falsely elevated mean corpuscular volume (**Figure 20**).

TABLE 16. Direct Coombs (Antiglobulin) Test and Peripheral Blood Smear Findings in Autoimmune Hemolytic Anemia

Type	IgG	C3	Erythrocyte Morphology
Warm autoimmune hemolytic anemia	Positive	Negative or weakly positive	Spherocytes
Cold agglutinin disease	Negative	Positive	Agglutination
Drug dependent	Variable and dependent on implicated drug	Variable and dependent on implicated drug	Variable and dependent on implicated drug

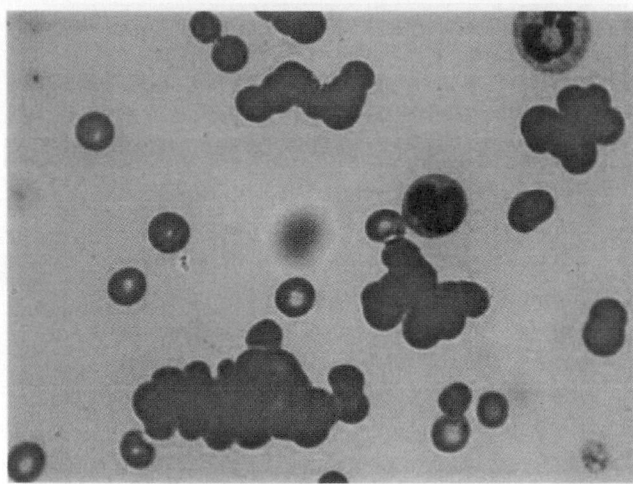

FIGURE 20. In cold agglutinin disease, the erythrocytes are clumped together, often leading to a falsely elevated mean corpuscular volume.

Erythrocyte agglutination often reverses with warming of the specimen. In patients with CAD, the direct Coombs test is typically negative for IgG and strongly positive for complement (see Table 16). In most patients, evidence of a small B-cell clone can be elucidated by serum protein electrophoresis or peripheral blood flow cytometry. The thermal amplitude refers to the highest temperature at which the antibody titer remains significant. When the thermal amplitude approaches temperatures of approximately 32.0 °C (90.0 °F) or higher, the antibody titer becomes more clinically significant.

Avoidance of cold temperatures is the typical initial treatment of CAD. Patients often need to wear gloves, hats, and thick socks to protect those areas most vulnerable to the cold. When further treatment becomes necessary, chemotherapeutic agents such as chlorambucil, cyclophosphamide, and, more recently, rituximab, have shown benefit. Corticosteroids and splenectomy are typically ineffective. In acute settings, plasmapheresis may provide transient benefit because of the larger and primarily intravascular nature of IgM.

Owing to potential difficulties with cross-matching, blood transfusion should be used sparingly in patients with AIHA, although it should not be withheld in patients with emergent cardiac or central nervous system symptoms. Alloantibodies may be masked during blood bank evaluation, increasing the risk for an acute or delayed hemolytic transfusion reaction. This risk is quite low in men or nulliparous women who have not previously been transfused. Close communication with the blood bank is essential to minimize this risk. Transfusion through a blood warmer is recommended in patients with CAD.

KEY POINT

- Avoiding cold is the usual initial treatment of cold agglutinin disease.

Drug-induced Autoimmune Hemolytic Anemia

Drug-induced autoimmune hemolytic anemia may be caused by a drug, a drug metabolite, or an interaction between a drug and the erythrocyte membrane. The anemia typically occurs several days to weeks after drug initiation. Identifying the causative agent is often difficult because patients often take several drugs. Although many drugs and drug classes can cause immune-mediated hemolysis, the second- and third-generation cephalosporins are currently the most commonly implicated agents.

Testing for drug-induced antibodies remains suboptimal. Depending on the cause, the direct Coombs test may be positive for IgG, C3, both, or neither; however, a positive Coombs test result can occur in up to 1% to 2% of hospitalized patients and does not itself indicate hemolysis; therefore, causation is often difficult to prove. Hemolysis typically resolves with drug removal but may be prolonged with certain drugs such as fludarabine.

KEY POINT

- In patients with drug-induced hemolytic anemia, hemolysis typically resolves with drug removal but may be prolonged with certain drugs such as fludarabine.

Microangiopathic Hemolytic Anemia

Microangiopathic hemolytic anemia refers to the disruption, fragmentation, and subsequent lysis of erythrocytes during travel through the vascular system. Erythrocyte fragmentation leads to the classic peripheral blood smear finding of schistocytes or helmet cells (**Figure 21**). Laboratory findings typically reflect intravascular hemolysis with low haptoglobin levels, hemoglobinuria, and often, a markedly elevated serum lactate dehydrogenase level.

Macrovascular causes of microangiopathic hemolytic anemia include localized lesions that expose the erythrocyte

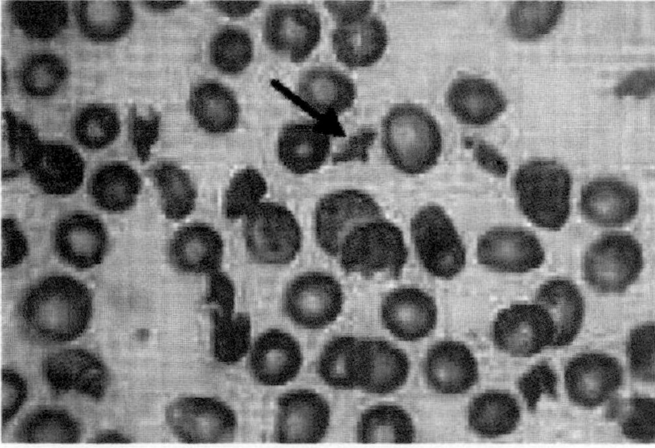

FIGURE 21. Microangiopathic hemolytic anemia. Schistocytes (arrow) represent fragmented erythrocytes and can be seen in various conditions, including thrombotic thrombocytopenic purpura.

to high shear stress. Turbulent flow around an aged or damaged mechanical heart valve is a classic example and should be evaluated by echocardiography. Intra-aortic balloon pumps, intraventricular assist devices, and localized aneurysms are additional examples.

Thrombotic thrombocytopenic purpura (TTP) and the hemolytic uremic syndrome are two classic examples of microvascular causes of microangiopathic diseases (see Quantitative Platelet Disorders). Because of the high mortality of TTP in untreated patients, this diagnosis should be considered whenever schistocytes are seen on a peripheral blood smear. Disseminated intravascular coagulation (DIC) (see Hemostasis) should also be considered, especially when coagulopathy is present. Drugs that can cause a syndrome mimicking TTP include cyclosporine, tacrolimus, antiplatelet agents such as ticlopidine and clopidogrel, and the chemotherapeutic drugs mitomycin C and gemcitabine. Several other diseases may cause microangiopathic hemolytic anemia and should be considered in the differential diagnosis (**Table 17**).

H

Treatment of microangiopathic hemolytic anemia is based on the underlying diagnosis. Plasma exchange therapy may be lifesaving in patients with TTP, and possibly, hemolytic uremic syndrome. Prompt treatment of infection, obstetric emergencies, and other conditions is essential in DIC. Drug withdrawal is mandatory if an inciting agent is identified. Early delivery of the fetus may be necessary in patients with the HELLP syndrome (*h*emolysis with a microangiopathic blood smear, *e*levated *l*iver enzymes, and a *l*ow *p*latelet count). Blood pressure control is usually curative in patients with malignant hypertension. Successful treatment of vasculitis and organ rejection following transplantation may lead to resolution of microangiopathic changes. When intravascular hemolysis is chronic, iron deficiency may develop, further damaging the erythrocytes and worsening hemolysis. Iron replacement, and occasionally, an erythropoietin-stimulating agent, may be helpful in improving the anemia when the underlying cause cannot be corrected. H

TABLE 17. Differential Diagnosis of Microangiopathic Hemolytic Anemia

Thrombotic thrombocytopenic purpura
Hemolytic uremic syndrome
Disseminated intravascular coagulation
Intravascular foreign devices
HELLP syndrome
Preeclampsia
Malignant hypertension
Severe vasculitis
Scleroderma renal crisis
Catastrophic antibody syndrome
Malignancy
Drugs
Bone marrow and solid organ transplantation

HELLP = hemolysis with a microangiopathic blood smear, elevated liver enzymes, and a low platelet count.

KEY POINTS

- Erythrocyte fragmentation leads to the classic peripheral blood smear finding of schistocytes or helmet cells in microangiopathic hemolytic anemia.
- Thrombotic thrombocytopenic purpura, the hemolytic uremic syndrome, and disseminated intravascular coagulation should be considered whenever schistocytes are seen on a peripheral blood smear.
- Plasma exchange therapy may be lifesaving in patients with thrombotic thrombocytopenic purpura, and possibly, the hemolytic uremic syndrome.

Paroxysmal Nocturnal Hemoglobinuria

Paroxysmal nocturnal hemoglobinuria (PNH) is an acquired clonal stem cell disorder that should be considered in patients presenting with hemolytic anemia, pancytopenia, or unprovoked atypical thrombosis. Mutations in the *PIG-A* gene lead to the reduction or absence of glycosylphosphatidylinositol, an important erythrocyte-anchoring protein. Hemolysis is caused by the absence of decay-accelerating factor (CD55) and the membrane inhibitor of reactive lysis (CD59), which are glycosylphosphatidylinositol-dependent complement regulatory proteins. Diagnosis of PNH is based on flow cytometry results, which can detect CD55 and CD59 deficiency on the surface of peripheral erythrocytes or leukocytes.

Thrombotic complications of PNH may occur in atypical locations, such as the mesenteric or cerebral circulation, and develop more frequently in patients with large PNH clones. Aggressive anticoagulation is indicated in patients with acute thrombotic events, whereas prophylaxis may be considered if more than 50% of cells are CD55- or CD59-deficient, even in the absence of thrombosis. Pancytopenia is common, even in patients without an identified bone marrow syndrome.

Recently, randomized controlled trials of eculizumab, a humanized monoclonal antibody against the C5 terminal complement component, have shown decreased transfusion requirements, improved quality of life, and potentially decreased thrombosis in transfusion-dependent patients with PNH. Because of an increased susceptibility to neisserial infection, vaccination against meningococcus is mandatory before eculizumab administration. In patients with marked bone marrow failure or severe, unresponsive hemolysis, treatment is similar to that of aplastic anemia and may consist of immunosuppressive therapy or allogeneic bone marrow transplantation. Corticosteroids to reduce complement activation and iron and erythropoietin levels have occasionally led to the improvement of anemia. Median survival of patients with

PNH is 10 to 15 years, with death often resulting from thrombosis or progressive pancytopenia.

KEY POINTS

- Paroxysmal nocturnal hemoglobinuria should be considered in patients presenting with hemolytic anemia, pancytopenia, or unprovoked atypical thrombosis.
- Aggressive anticoagulation is indicated in patients with paroxysmal nocturnal hemoglobinuria and acute thrombotic events, whereas prophylaxis may be considered if more than 50% of cells are CD55- or CD59-deficient.
- Eculizumab has resulted in decreased transfusion requirements, improved quality of life, and potentially decreased thrombosis in transfusion-dependent patients with paroxysmal nocturnal hemoglobinuria.

Other Causes of Hemolysis

Many different infectious organisms, physical and chemical agents, and toxins and venoms may lead to hemolysis. Malaria is the most common infectious cause of hemolytic anemia, resulting from splenic removal of infected erythrocytes. Babesiosis may also lead to severe hemolytic anemia in patients with previous splenectomy or functional asplenia and should be suspected in patients with hemolysis after recent travel to high-incidence areas, such as Nantucket Island, Cape Cod, and northern California. Clostridial sepsis can cause hemolysis through production of its α-toxin, which disrupts the erythrocyte membrane. Other gram-positive and gram-negative organisms cause hemolysis through various mechanisms, including direct invasion, toxins, or antibody formation. Bartonellosis (Oroya fever), found most commonly in South America, may occur after a patient is bitten by an infected sand fly and can cause severe, rapid, and life-threatening hemolysis.

Arsine gas exposure occurring during various industrial operations may lead to a chemical-related hemolysis. Copper toxicity, which occurs in Wilson disease, can disrupt normal erythrocyte metabolic function. The brown recluse or hobo spider bite is occasionally associated with hemolysis. Venom from snake bites and massive bee and wasp stings may rarely cause hemolysis. Severe burns, radiation, and hypophosphatemia are less common causes of hemolysis.

KEY POINTS

- Malaria is the most common infectious cause of hemolytic anemia, resulting from both intravascular hemolysis and splenic removal of infected erythrocytes.
- Babesiosis may lead to severe hemolytic anemia and should be suspected in patients with hemolysis after recent travel to high-incidence areas such as Nantucket Island, Cape Cod, and northern California.

Iron Overload Syndromes

Hemochromatosis

Hemochromatosis is an autosomal recessive disorder characterized by increased absorption of iron from the gut and occurs in 1 of 200 people of Northern European ancestry. Although the genetic defect is relatively common, the full expression of disease is much less prevalent and also requires long-term iron ingestion and the absence of bleeding.

Iron absorption is closely regulated in humans because they have a limited ability to eliminate excess iron. Iron loss is achieved mostly through the gastrointestinal tract in men and postmenopausal women and amounts to a loss of about 1 mg/d. In addition to losses through the gastrointestinal tract, premenopausal women lose approximately 30 mg of iron monthly.

The principal molecule regulating iron homeostasis is the small hepatically synthesized peptide hepcidin. Hepcidin production is increased in inflammatory conditions through IL-6. Hepcidin works by decreasing iron absorption from the gut and inhibiting iron release from macrophages by causing internalization and proteolysis of the iron transporter ferroportin.

In addition to genetic abnormalities of hepcidin or ferroportin, hemochromatosis can result from abnormalities in any one of several iron regulatory proteins, including human hemochromatosis protein (HFE), hemojuvelin, transferrin receptor 2, or TMPRSS6, and is always associated with low hepcidin levels. The most common abnormality found in patients with hemochromatosis involves the *HFE* gene, the gene product of which interacts with the transferrin receptor, bone morphogenic protein, and SMAD proteins to regulate hepcidin production. A G→A mutation in *HFE* that leads to a substitution of tyrosine for cysteine at residue 282 (C282Y) and a G→C mutation at nucleotide 187 that leads to a substitution of aspartic acid for histidine at residue 63 (H63D) are the two most common mutations leading to hemochromatosis. Ninety percent of patients with clinical hemochromatosis are homozygous for C282Y. Mild iron overload also develops in patients homozygous for H63D or who are compound heterozygotes for C282Y and H63D. Conversely, iron overload seldom develops in heterozygotes for C282Y.

Clinical manifestations of hemochromatosis include heart involvement characterized by cardiomyopathy and arrhythmias and liver involvement characterized by cirrhosis and cancer. Other complications and findings include diabetes mellitus, arthropathy, and endocrinopathy. Skin bronzing also commonly occurs.

Evaluation for hemochromatosis is warranted in patients with unexplained increases in serum aminotransferase levels and a family history of cirrhosis because early detection may prompt treatment that can prevent subsequent cirrhosis or hepatocellular cancer. Additionally, patients with hemochromatosis can develop life-threatening heart failure.

The initial step in evaluating patients with suspected hemochromatosis is serum transferrin saturation measurement, which is the most sensitive test in diagnosing this condition. Transferrin saturations greater than 60% in men and 50% in women suggest hemochromatosis. Serum ferritin is often used as a surrogate for iron stores, and values greater than 1000 ng/mL (1000 µg/L) in the absence of an inflammatory state or hepatitis-induced liver necrosis suggest hemochromatosis. A liver biopsy specimen stained for iron provides a definitive diagnosis. Noninvasive technologies, including MRI and superconductive quantitative interference device measurements, are used in some centers for diagnosis of hepatic iron stores. Genetic testing for *HFE* mutations can confirm the diagnosis. Mutations in other iron proteins including hemojuvelin, hepcidin, and transferrin receptor 2, although rare, can also lead to hemochromatosis. Because of a varied penetrance of disease in persons harboring *HFE* mutations, there are currently no consensus guidelines for population-based hemochromatosis screening.

Phlebotomy remains the mainstay of treatment for hemochromatosis, with the goal of maintaining serum ferritin levels at values less than 50 ng/mL (50 µg/L). If instituted early enough, this therapy can prevent serious liver disease or cardiomyopathy. Following several courses of phlebotomy, serum aminotransferase levels typically improve, arthralgia and myalgia may also improve, and hyperpigmentation may resolve; however, cirrhosis, heart failure, and diabetes, if present at the time phlebotomy is initiated, typically do not regress.

KEY POINTS

- Patients with unexplained increases in serum aminotransferase levels or a family history of hemochromatosis or cirrhosis should be evaluated for hemochromatosis.
- Transferrin saturations greater than 60% in men and 50% in women suggest hemochromatosis.
- Phlebotomy remains the mainstay of treatment for hemochromatosis, with the goal of maintaining serum ferritin levels at values less than 50 ng/mL (50 µg/L).

Secondary Iron Overload

Secondary iron overload can occur in patients who have received extensive transfusions, especially in those with hemolytic disorders such as thalassemia. Iron overload can also occur in patients with myelodysplastic disorders, many of whom are anemic; consequently, management of these patients involves iron chelation rather than phlebotomy. Previously, parenteral deferoxamine was used as an iron chelator; however, deferasirox, an oral iron chelator, is most often used currently. Deferasirox is generally well tolerated, but it can cause rare, serious side effects, including agranulocytosis and kidney failure.

KEY POINT

- Patients with secondary iron overload are treated with deferasirox, an oral iron chelator.

Transfusion

Cellular Products

Erythrocytes

ABO/Rh System and Compatibility Testing

The ABO system is a group of carbohydrate antigens that governs the transfusion of erythrocytes. Depending on their terminal saccharide component, erythrocytes are referred to as group A or B. If both carbohydrate moieties are present, the blood group is AB; if neither is present, the blood group is O (**Table 18**). Persons develop antibodies against the ABO antigens that are not present on their erythrocytes. The Rh system consists of different blood group antigens, but the D antigen is the most immunogenic, such that Rh positive and Rh negative refer to the D antigen only. Rh(D)-negative individuals should ideally only receive blood from Rh(D)-negative donors, whereas Rh(D)-positive individuals can receive erythrocytes from either Rh(D)-negative or -positive donors. Blood group O-negative individuals are considered universal erythrocyte donors, whereas AB-positive individuals are universal erythrocyte recipients. Women of childbearing age who are Rh-negative should not receive Rh-positive blood products to avoid the

TABLE 18. ABO Compatibility Between Donor and Recipient Erythrocytes and Fresh Frozen Plasma

	Blood Type of Recipient			
	A	**B**	**AB**	**O**
Erythrocyte antigen	A	B	A and B	None
Isohemagglutinins	Anti-B	Anti-A	None	Anti-A, anti-B
Compatible donor erythrocytes	A, O	B, O	Any	O
Compatible donor fresh frozen plasma	A, AB	B, AB	AB	Any

Note: Rh-negative patients should receive Rh-negative erythrocytes. Rh-positive patients can receive Rh-negative or Rh-positive erythrocytes.

risk of anti-Rh(D) antibody production and neonatal hemolysis with subsequent pregnancy. Type O-negative blood should be given when emergent transfusion is indicated, and the recipient's blood type is unknown or unavailable.

Before transfusion, typing and antibody screening are performed to determine the ABO and Rh phenotype (for example, AB-negative) and identify preformed alloantibodies that become increasingly frequent in multiply transfused patients. Cross-matching of erythrocyte units must also be performed before transfusion to ensure compatibility between the patient and the prospective donor.

Alloantibodies are typically directed against non-ABO blood group antigens and formed after exposure to mismatched antigens during a previous blood transfusion or pregnancy. The presence of alloantibodies may lead to a delay in finding compatible blood for a patient. Screening for alloantibodies consists of mixing a patient's serum against panels of test erythrocytes for which the blood group antigens are known. Based on the pattern of reactivity, the presence and specificity of alloantibodies can be determined.

Clinical Transfusion Issues

The volume of one unit of transfused packed red blood cells is typically 250 to 300 mL with an expected increase in the hemoglobin of 1 g/dL (10 g/L) in a nonbleeding adult. The only true indication for erythrocyte transfusion is to improve the oxygen-carrying capacity of blood. Humans display many compensatory responses to maintain oxygen delivery, and no single hemoglobin trigger exists for erythrocyte transfusion. The decision to transfuse erythrocytes should be based on hemodynamic parameters, the acuity of anemia, coexisting medical problems, and ongoing blood loss. Randomized studies have suggested that critically ill patients who are not actively bleeding and without cardiac compromise do equally well with a hemoglobin transfusion threshold of 7 g/dL (70 g/L) as with 10 g/dL (100 g/L).

See **Table 19** for indications for transfusion. In patients with coronary artery disease, the hemoglobin is often maintained at a level near 10 g/dL (100 g/L), but data supporting this practice remain controversial.

Preparation

Pretransfusion leukoreduction of erythrocytes (removal of leukocytes) is performed at many centers in the United States. Randomized studies have shown that this practice can decrease HLA alloimmunization, febrile nonhemolytic reactions, and cytomegalovirus transmission. Other indications

TABLE 19. Transfusion Indications[a]

Erythrocytes
Acute blood loss, surgical or nonsurgical
Anemia with hemodynamic compromise
Critically ill patients with hemoglobin <7 g/dL (70 g/L)
Critically ill patients with cardiopulmonary disease with hemoglobin <7-10 g/dL (70-100 g/L)[b]
Platelets (Treatment)
Active bleeding with platelet count <50,000-100,000/µL (50-100 × 10^9/L)
Active bleeding with dysfunctional platelets
Platelets (Prophylaxis)
Platelet count <10,000/µL (10 × 10^9/L) in patients with leukemia with no other bleeding risk factors
Platelet count <50,000/µL (50 × 10^9/L) and planned surgery
Platelet count <100,000/µL (100 × 10^9/L) and planned intracranial surgery
FFP
Multiple clotting deficiencies with active bleeding (e.g., DIC, liver disease)
Thrombotic thrombocytopenic purpura
Reversal of warfarin in patients with intracranial bleeding
Factor replacement when specific factor concentrates not available
Massive transfusion of packed red blood cells to avoid dilutional coagulopathy
Cryoprecipitate
Hypofibrinogenemia or dysfibrinogenemia
Factor XIII deficiency
Hemophilia A or von Willebrand disease if factor concentrate not available

DIC = disseminated intravascular coagulation; FFP = fresh frozen plasma.

[a]This list is not all inclusive. Although this list should serve as a guideline, transfusion decisions need to be made on a case-by-case basis.

[b]The proper transfusion threshold remains controversial in patients with cardiopulmonary disease.

for specialized pretransfusion manipulations are summarized in Table 20.

Strategies to Minimize Allogeneic Blood Transfusion

The use of recombinant human erythropoietin (rhEPO) has reduced the number of erythrocyte transfusions in patients with kidney insufficiency and malignancy-associated anemia. Because of an increased risk for venous thromboembolism, rhEPO should not be used to increase the hemoglobin level above 10 to 12 g/dL (100-120 g/L). Additionally, the use of rhEPO in cancer is becoming increasingly controversial because of its unclear benefit and the potential for thrombosis, tumor progression, and increased mortality. Preoperative autologous donation decreases allogeneic blood exposure but does not decrease the risk for clerical error, volume overload, and bacterial contamination. Intraoperative hemodilution and cell-saver techniques can also decrease the volume of blood transfused. With the use of rhEPO, iron replacement, and pharmacologic interventions to minimize bleeding, many Jehovah's witnesses, who decline blood transfusions based on religious beliefs, have been able to undergo complex medical and surgical procedures. Techniques to develop blood substitutes, such as hemoglobin solutions and perfluorochemical solutions, have been ineffective to date.

Platelets

ABO/Rh System, Human Leukocyte Antigen System, and Compatibility Testing

ABO and Rh matching are generally not required for platelet transfusion as they are in erythrocyte transfusion. Alloimmunization to human leukocyte antigens (HLA) leads to refractoriness to future platelet transfusions. Only HLA class I antigens have been shown to be significant in this process, and matching for HLA antigens is important in immunized patients.

Clinical Transfusion Issues

Platelets may be provided as pooled random donor units from several donors or from a single donor collected through apheresis. A single-donor unit is equal to approximately six random donor units and should raise the platelet count by at least 20,000 to 30,000/µL (20-30 × 10^9/L). Whether transfusion of single-donor platelets leads to a decreased incidence of alloimmunization and transfusion reactions is uncertain.

Platelets are stored at room temperature for a maximum of 5 days after collection; the warmer storage conditions allow for proliferation of any contaminating bacteria that may occur during phlebotomy. Consequently, the risk for bacterial infection and sepsis is increased in patients receiving platelet transfusions compared with other blood products. *Staphylococcus aureus* from donor skin contamination is the most common isolated pathogen.

The prophylactic and therapeutic transfusion of platelets has greatly reduced hemorrhagic risk and facilitated organ and bone marrow transplantation, leukemia induction, and complex cardiovascular surgeries. Randomized studies in nonbleeding patients who have leukemia without other risk factors have shown that the platelet transfusion trigger could be decreased to a threshold of 10,000/µL (10 × 10^9/L) without an increased bleeding incidence (see Table 19). For most surgical procedures or in patients with active bleeding, the targeted platelet count is 50,000 to 100,000/µL (50-100 × 10^9/L). For central nervous system bleeding or planned central nervous system surgery, the platelet target is typically increased above 100,000/µL (100 × 10^9/L).

Transfused platelets typically survive 7 to 9 days, but this period may be much shorter in patients with acute illness or active bleeding. Checking the posttransfusion platelet count within 1 hour of transfusion is essential to properly evaluate for refractoriness.

TABLE 20. Prevention and Treatment of Nonhemolytic Transfusion Complications

Transfusion Complication	Preventive/Treatment Measures
Febrile reaction	Prevention: antipyretics, leukoreduction Treatment: stop the transfusion and rule out an acute hemolytic transfusion reaction, antipyretics, consider antibiotics
Allergic reaction	Prevention: antihistamine, washing of cellular blood products Treatment: antihistamine, epinephrine if severe
Anaphylaxis	Prevention: washing cellular blood products, IgA-deficient donor Treatment: stop the transfusion, IV fluids, epinephrine, supportive care
Transfusion-related acute lung injury	Prevention: eliminate multiparous women as blood donors Treatment: supportive care, supplemental oxygenation
Graft-versus-host disease	Prevention: γ-irradiation Treatment: supportive care
Cytomegalovirus transmission	Prevention: leukoreduction, cytomegalovirus-negative donor Treatment: antivirals including ganciclovir or foscarnet

H CONT.

Platelet Transfusion Refractoriness

Platelet refractoriness, an inappropriately low increment in the platelet count following a transfusion, occurs in 5% to 15% of chronic platelet recipients. A commonly used definition for platelet transfusion refractoriness is a posttransfusion platelet count increment of less than 10,000/µL (10×10^9/L). Nonimmune causes of platelet transfusion refractoriness are most common and should first be considered, including fever, disseminated intravascular coagulation (DIC), and drugs such as amphotericin B. Alloimmunization to HLA platelet antigens accounts for about one third of platelet refractoriness in multiply transfused patients and should be considered after other possible causes are excluded.

After platelet transfusion refractoriness has been identified, the freshest single-donor, ABO-matched platelets are transfused. If the transfusion is unsuccessful and HLA antibodies are identified, HLA-matched platelets or cross-matched compatible platelets should be administered. H

KEY POINTS

- Critically ill patients without cardiac compromise do equally well with a hemoglobin transfusion threshold of 7 g/dL (70 g/L) as with 10 g/dL (100 g/L).
- Because of an increased risk for venous thromboembolism, recombinant human erythropoietin should not be used to increase the hemoglobin level above 10 to 12 g/dL (100-120 g/L).
- The risk for bacterial infection and sepsis is increased in patients receiving platelet transfusions compared with other blood products.
- For most surgical (but not neurosurgical) procedures, or in patients with active bleeding, the targeted platelet count is 50,000 to 100,000/µL ($50\text{-}100 \times 10^9$/L).

Plasma Products

Fresh Frozen Plasma

Fresh frozen plasma (FFP) contains all the blood clotting factors and is indicated for warfarin reversal in actively bleeding patients (either alone or concomitantly with a three-factor [II, IX, and X] prothrombin complex concentrate [PCC]; see Thrombosis), treatment of thrombotic thrombocytopenic purpura, dilutional coagulopathy during massive transfusion, and in bleeding patients with several factor deficiencies such as in DIC or liver disease (see Table 19). The prophylactic use of FFP in nonbleeding, nonsurgical patients remains unproven.

A typical unit of FFP has a volume of 200 to 300 mL. Although one to two units of FFP are often prescribed, this dose is unlikely to be effective in adult patients. The typical effective dose of FFP is 10 to 15 mL/kg. Although the risk of transmitting intracellular viruses such as cytomegalovirus may be somewhat lower, the risk of most transfusion-transmitted infections from FFP is analogous to that associated with erythrocyte transfusion. Other risks include volume overload, transfusion-related acute lung injury (TRALI), and febrile, allergic, and anaphylactic reactions.

Cryoprecipitate

Cryoprecipitate is the precipitated fraction of material remaining when FFP is thawed at 4.0 °C (39.2 °F). Cryoprecipitate contains a concentrated source of factor VIII, von Willebrand factor, factor XIII, fibronectin, and fibrinogen and is the treatment of choice in bleeding patients with hypofibrinogenemia from liver disease, thrombolytic therapy, or DIC (see Table 19). The recommended dose is typically one to two units per 10 kg.

Other Plasma-derived Transfusion Products

Although often unrecognized, many other transfused products are derived from plasma. Examples include immunoglobulin preparations such as intravenous immune globulin, monoclonal factor VIII, PCCs (containing factors II, IX and X), α_1-antitrypsin, protein C, and antithrombin III concentrates. Although specific isolation and viral inactivation techniques are used in the preparation of plasma-derived products, a small risk of infectious disease transmission remains. PCCs with intravenous vitamin K are also used for warfarin reversal (see Thrombosis).

KEY POINTS

- Fresh frozen plasma is indicated for warfarin reversal in actively bleeding patients (either alone or concomitantly with a three-factor [II, IX, and X] prothrombin complex concentrate [PCC]), thrombotic thrombocytopenic purpura treatment, dilutional coagulopathy during massive transfusion, and in bleeding patients with multiple factor deficiencies.
- Cryoprecipitate is the treatment of choice in bleeding patients with hypofibrinogenemia from liver disease, thrombolytic therapy, or disseminated intravascular coagulation.

Transfusion Complications

Hemolytic Reactions

Acute Hemolytic Transfusion Reaction

The acute hemolytic transfusion reaction (AHTR) is the most feared complication of transfusion and is almost always caused by ABO incompatibility between donor and recipient. Most cases result from a clerical error such as the mislabeling of a pretransfusion specimen. Affected patients may experience hypotension, fever, kidney failure, pain at the infusion site, and DIC. When AHTR is suspected, the transfusion must be stopped immediately and a specimen sent to the blood bank to check for incompatibility and hemolysis. Treatment is supportive, consisting of fluid resuscitation, vasopressor support, and mannitol.

CONT.

Delayed Hemolytic Transfusion Reaction

The delayed hemolytic transfusion reaction (DHTR) is caused by an amnestic response of a preformed erythrocyte alloantibody after reexposure to an erythrocyte antigen outside the ABO system. Following a transfusion, there is a 1% to 1.6% chance of developing these alloantibodies. DHTR may then occur after reexposure with subsequent transfusion. Clinical symptoms, which typically develop approximately 5 to 10 days after erythrocyte transfusion, include anemia, jaundice, and fever, although many patients will be asymptomatic. Patients with sickle cell disease may present with a worsening pain crisis. Hemolysis is typically extravascular, and life-threatening complications are rare. A repeat type and screen will identify the presence of a new alloantibody. Treatment is supportive. Subsequent transfusions should be minimized but not withheld when indicated.

Nonhemolytic Reactions

See **Table 20** for methods of preventing nonhemolytic transfusion reactions.

Transfusion-associated Circulatory Overload

Transfusion-associated circulatory overload (TACO) is a frequent, serious, yet under-recognized complication of transfusion. TACO most commonly affects those with limited cardiopulmonary reserve, including the very young and the elderly. Presenting symptoms include dyspnea, cough, tachycardia, cyanosis, edema, and chest tightness during or within 1 to 2 hours of a transfusion. Physical examination will typically reveal classic signs of fluid overload. Treatment consists of supplemental oxygenation and intravenous diuretics.

Transfusion-related Acute Lung Injury

Transfusion-related acute lung injury (TRALI) occurs in 1 of 5000 transfusions. It is the most common cause of transfusion-related death, with a mortality rate of 5%. TRALI results from antibodies in donor plasma directed against recipient neutrophil antigens. Upon binding, leukocyte sequestration occurs in the lung, and capillary leak ensues. Patients typically present with hypoxia and dyspnea resembling noncardiac pulmonary edema during or within 6 hours of a transfusion. Fever and hypotension may also occur, and bilateral infiltrates with pulmonary edema are shown on chest radiograph. Intubation may be required. The implicated donor should be excluded from future transfusions. The clinical and radiographic differential diagnosis includes TACO, acute respiratory distress syndrome, and heart failure. Unlike patients with acute respiratory distress syndrome, patients with TRALI typically improve within days. As such, treatment of TRALI is primarily supportive.

Febrile Nonhemolytic Transfusion Reaction

Fever occurs relatively commonly during transfusion. Recipient-derived leukoreactive antibodies and donor-derived cytokines are thought to represent the most common causes. When fever develops, the transfusion should be stopped immediately until an AHTR can be excluded and causes of fever unrelated to the transfusion considered. After AHTR has been excluded, the transfusion can continue with close monitoring. Pretransfusion antipyretics or leukoreduction of cellular blood products may prevent recurrence.

Allergic Reactions and Anaphylaxis

Mild allergic reactions consisting of urticaria occur commonly, especially in multiply transfused patients. Most reactions are caused by donor plasma proteins and may not recur with subsequent transfusion. Pretreatment with antihistamines or washing of cellular blood products to remove plasma proteins is often effective in preventing recurrence.

Severe anaphylactic reactions, which are rare, typically occur in patients who are IgA deficient and have anti-IgA antibodies. These antibodies react to IgA contained in the transfused blood. IgA deficiency may first come to medical attention after an anaphylactic reaction to a blood transfusion. All subsequent cellular products should be washed thoroughly to remove plasma proteins. Plasma products for transfusion of patients identified as IgA deficient must be obtained from IgA-deficient donors.

Transfusion-associated Graft-Versus-Host Disease

Transfusion-associated graft-versus-host disease (T-GVHD) is a rare, but often fatal, transfusion complication. The pathophysiology is thought to involve engraftment of donor lymphocytes, which contaminate a transfused product, into an immunocompromised recipient. Hematopoietic stem cell transplant recipients, recipients of blood transfusion from first-degree relatives, and patients with immunosuppression associated with hematologic malignancies such as Hodgkin lymphoma are at risk for T-GVHD. Affected patients experience severe pancytopenia, and, to a variable degree, diarrhea, skin rash, and liver chemistry test abnormalities. No treatment has proved effective. γ-Irradiation of cellular products virtually eliminates the risk for T-GVHD and should be performed before transfusion for all at-risk patients.

Infectious Complications

Given improved donor screening and pretransfusion testing, blood is currently safer than at any time previously. For example, the risk of HIV is less than 1 in 1,900,000 units; hepatitis C, less than 1 in 1,000,000 units; and hepatitis B, less than 1 in 37,000 units. However, infectious risk, including the transmission of West Nile virus, prions causing Creutzfeldt-Jakob disease, Chagas disease, and babesiosis, still remain, and new bloodborne pathogens will continue to emerge. Because platelets are stored at room temperature, bacterial contamination occurs more commonly with platelet transfusions, at an estimated frequency of 1 in 3000 platelet units. *Yersinia enterocolitica* may survive refrigeration of erythrocyte units and can lead to fatal sepsis. H

KEY POINTS

- Acute hemolytic transfusion reaction is characterized by hypotension, fever, kidney failure, pain at the infusion site, and disseminated intravascular coagulation following transfusion and requires immediate transfusion cessation and analysis of the specimen for incompatibility and hemolysis.
- Symptoms of delayed hemolytic transfusion reaction typically develop approximately 5 to 10 days after erythrocyte transfusion, and symptomatic patients may have anemia, jaundice, and fever.
- Patients with transfusion-related acute lung injury typically experience hypoxia and dyspnea resembling noncardiac pulmonary edema during or within 6 hours of a transfusion, possibly with fever and hypotension, and bilateral infiltrates with pulmonary edema on chest radiograph.
- When transfusion-related fever develops, the transfusion should be stopped immediately until an acute hemolytic transfusion reaction can be excluded and causes of fever unrelated to the transfusion considered.
- Severe anaphylactic transfusion reactions typically occur in patients who are IgA deficient and have anti-IgA antibodies, requiring thorough washing of all subsequent cellular products to remove plasma proteins and subsequent transfusion with plasma products from IgA-deficient donors.
- Hematopoietic stem cell transplant recipients, recipients of blood transfusion from first-degree relatives, and patients with various hematologic malignancies are at risk for transfusion-related graft-versus-host disease and require γ-irradiation of cellular products before transfusion.

H Therapeutic Apheresis

Therapeutic apheresis refers to the separation of whole blood into its components, treatment or removal of the affected component, and return of the remaining blood products. Erythrocytapheresis is typically performed in patients with sickle cell disease presenting with acute chest syndrome, stroke, or multiorgan failure. The goal is to decrease the hemoglobin S fractionation to improve oxygen-carrying capacity. Erythrocytapheresis is also occasionally performed for malaria and *Babesia* infections associated with significant parasitemia.

Plasmapheresis involves the removal of patient plasma with replacement of donor plasma (plasma exchange) or an albumin/saline mixture. Plasmapheresis is indicated for diverse hematologic, rheumatologic, kidney, and neurologic diseases. Evidence supporting the use of plasmapheresis is variable and depends on the disease process. Diseases with the highest levels of supporting evidence (categories I and II) for the use of apheresis and the most common applications are listed in **Table 21**.

TABLE 21. Sample of Common Category I and Category II Indications for Therapeutic Apheresis

Disease	Modality
Category Ia	
Cryoglobulinemia	PE
Thrombotic thrombocytopenic purpura	PE
Acute inflammatory demyelinating polyneuropathy	PE
Chronic inflammatory demyelinating polyneuropathy	PE
Myasthenia gravis	PE
Goodpasture syndrome	PE
Granulomatosis with polyangiitis (also known as Wegener granulomatosis)-related RPGN	PE
Renal transplant antibody-mediated rejection	PE
IgM-related polyneuropathy	PE
Sickle cell disease with end-organ complications	Erythrocytapheresis
Leukostasis with acute leukemia	Leukocytapheresis
Familial homozygous hypercholesterolemia	Selective LDL cholesterol removal
Category IIb	
Disease	**Modality**
Malaria (severe)	Erythrocytapheresis
Lambert-Eaton syndrome	PE
Multiple sclerosis, acute CNS	PE
Myeloma cast nephropathy	PE
IgM-related polyneuropathy	PE
Cardiac allograft rejection (treatment)	Extracorporeal photopheresis
Thrombocytosis- symptomatic	Thrombocytapheresis
Familial heterozygous hypercholesterolemia	Selective LDL cholesterol removal

PE = plasma exchange/plasmapheresis; CNS = central nervous system; RPGN = rapidly progressive glomerulonephritis.

Note: List is not all inclusive.

[a]Diseases for which therapeutic apheresis is standard and acceptable primary or first-line adjuvant therapy.

[b]Diseases for which therapeutic apheresis is generally accepted but considered supportive adjuvant therapy.

Data from Szczepiorkowski ZM, Winters JL, Bandarenko N, et al; Apheresis Applications Committee of the American Society for Apheresis. Guidelines on the use of therapeutic apheresis in clinical practice—evidence-based approach from the Apheresis Applications Committee of the American Society for Apheresis. J Clin Apher. 2010;25(3):83-177. [PMID: 20568098]

CONT.

Mild adverse reactions such as hypocalcemia due to citrate anticoagulant, mild hypotension, and allergic reactions can affect up to one third of patients. Severe life-threatening infections occur much less commonly. Cardiovascular and neurologic instability may develop with severe hypocalcemia. Daily monitoring for coagulopathy when albumin/saline is used as replacement fluid is warranted. Ionized calcium levels should be closely monitored and calcium replaced when low. Because of an increased risk for hypotension, withholding ACE inhibitors 24 hours before elective apheresis, especially if albumin is used as the replacement fluid, is indicated. H

KEY POINTS

- Mild adverse reactions such as hypocalcemia due to citrate anticoagulant, mild hypotension, and allergic reactions can affect up to one third of patients undergoing plasmapheresis.
- Because of an increased risk for hypotension, withholding ACE inhibitors 24 hours before elective apheresis procedures is indicated.

Bleeding Disorders

Overview of Normal Hemostasis

The hemostatic system is a tightly regulated network of cells and proteins that facilitates bleeding cessation and wound healing at sites of vascular injury. Coagulation begins with primary hemostasis, in which the injured blood vessel constricts and platelets adhere to tissue-factor–bearing cells through interactions between glycoprotein Ib/IX/V and von Willebrand factor (vWF). After activation by agonists, platelets secrete their granular contents, potentiating further activation. Glycoprotein IIb/IIIa undergoes a conformational change, allowing it to bind fibrinogen, which then cross-links platelets. The surface of activated platelets serves as a phospholipid scaffold to support the biochemical reactions of secondary hemostasis, which eventuates in a burst of thrombin and generation of an insoluble fibrin meshwork. This liquid phase of coagulation begins as factors III and VIIa generate factor IXa, as well as a small amount of thrombin sufficient to generate factor VIIIa, to activate platelets. On the surface of an activated platelet, factor VIIIa and factor IXa serve as the "tenase" complex, generating factor Xa. Factor Xa, along with factor Va, acts as the prothrombinase complex, activating prothrombin to thrombin, which then converts soluble fibrinogen to insoluble fibrin (**Figure 22**). Factor XIII is also activated by thrombin, and factor XIIIa will cross-link the fibrin monomers, leaving behind a strong fibrin meshwork.

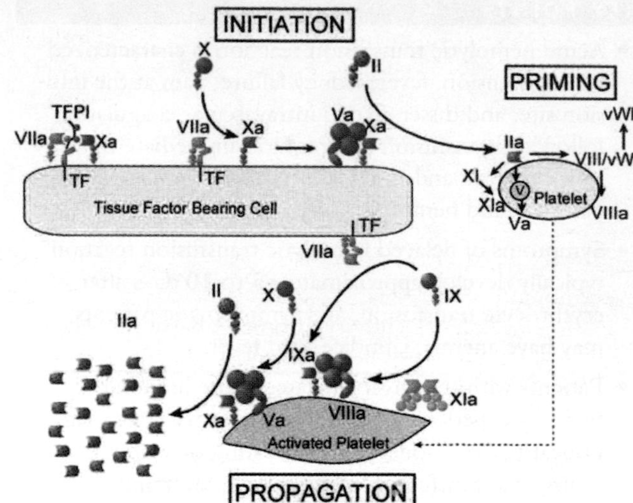

FIGURE 22. Cell-based model of secondary hemostasis. The initiation of coagulation occurs on the surface of a tissue-factor–bearing cell, such as a macrophage, tumor cell, or an activated endothelial cell. Tissue factor and a small amount of factor VIIa generate factor Xa, which joins with factor Va to form a small amount of thrombin. In the priming step, this small amount of thrombin activates platelets and factor VIII, which joins with factor IX to generate factor Xa. On the platelet surface, the prothrombinase complex can generate a large thrombin burst in the propagation step, allowing for cleavage of fibrinogen into fibrin.

(Figure courtesy of D. Monroe)

Evaluation of Patients with Suspected Bleeding Disorders

History and Physical Examination

The history of patients with a suspected bleeding disorder should include an orderly description of bleeding during infancy and childhood, including umbilical stump bleeding, bleeding with circumcision or loss of deciduous teeth, and bleeding with trauma and surgeries, including dental procedures. Other bleeding episodes occurring later in life, whether spontaneous or provoked, should also be discussed. For surgery-related bleeding, the physician should ask about the timing of bleeding (immediate versus delayed) and the need for transfusion.

A history of bleeding into muscles and joints is characteristic of disorders of humoral clotting factors, whereas mucosal bleeding occurs more commonly in disorders of primary hemostasis, thrombocytopenia, or qualitative platelet disorders. A history of gynecologic bleeding, including duration and severity of menstrual flow, is significant because an underlying bleeding disorder is found in 10% to 30% of women with menorrhagia. Determining whether a family history of bleeding exists is appropriate; however, a negative family history does not exclude a congenital bleeding disorder. Certain medications or herbal and dietary supplements increase the risk of bleeding and may precipitate a hemorrhage in those with milder bleeding disorders. Easy bruisability is neither sensitive nor specific in predicting an underlying hemorrhagic diathesis.

Skin examination may disclose petechiae indicative of thrombocytopenia or the characteristic ecchymoses and lax skin found in senile purpura. Patients with scurvy have characteristic perifollicular hemorrhages and "corkscrew hairs." Telangiectasias around the lips or on the fingertips may represent hereditary hemorrhagic telangiectasia. An enlarged tongue, carpal tunnel syndrome, and periorbital purpura may indicate amyloidosis, which is associated with an acquired deficiency of many clotting proteins, especially factor X. Joint hypermobility and skin hyperelasticity may be found in patients with Ehlers-Danlos syndrome. A harsh systolic murmur may indicate severe aortic stenosis, which can cause an acquired type 2 von Willebrand disease (vWD). Splenomegaly can be associated with thrombocytopenia and may indicate underlying cirrhosis. Other stigmata of liver disease may also suggest liver coagulopathy.

Laboratory Evaluation

The assays described below are used in the evaluation of patients with abnormal bleeding or with a family history of abnormal bleeding. Sometimes, they are used to assess the potential for bleeding associated with an upcoming invasive procedure (see MKSAP 16 General Internal Medicine). It is said that the prothrombin time (PT)/activated partial thromboplastin time (aPTT) assays add nothing to the preoperative evaluation of a patient with no history of abnormal bleeding. Nonetheless, frequently, the internist is called on to interpret abnormal results, and an understanding of these assays is important to perform that function.

The Prothrombin Time and the Activated Partial Thromboplastin Time

The PT and the aPTT are assays performed on citrated plasma that require enzymatic generation of thrombin on a phospholipid surface. Because the volume of citrate is carefully titrated to the expected volume of plasma, underfilled tubes may produce falsely elevated results. Prolongation of the PT and the aPTT may occur in individuals with deficiencies of or inhibitors to humoral clotting factors, although not all patients with PT or aPTT prolongations have bleeding diatheses. The pattern of prolongation provides clues about the causes of bleeding or prolongation (**Table 22**). In general, a prolonged PT is most commonly due to an acquired deficiency of factor VII, from vitamin K deficiency, liver disease, DIC, or warfarin use. An isolated prolonged aPTT is most commonly due to a lupus inhibitor, but hemophilia is also a concern.

The Thrombin Clotting Time

The thrombin clotting time (TCT) measures the time needed for clot formation after thrombin is added to citrated plasma. This test may be indicated when both the PT and aPTT are prolonged or when heparin contamination is suspected. The TCT is prolonged in the presence of any thrombin inhibitor, such as heparin, lepirudin, or argatroban. Fibrinogen, which is present in low levels or is structurally abnormal in disorders such as dysfibrinogenemia, also leads to TCT prolongation.

Mixing Studies

Mixing studies are used to evaluate prolongations of the aPTT (less commonly the PT or the TCT) and are useful in distinguishing between the presence of an inhibitor and a clotting-factor deficiency. Following a prolonged aPTT, the patient's plasma is mixed in a 1:1 ratio with normal plasma, and the abnormal assay is repeated. Full and complete correction of the clotting test into the normal range signifies a factor deficiency because the normal plasma will supply the deficient factor. Incomplete correction of the clotting test after mixing suggests the presence of an inhibitor. Notably, the clotting time may partially correct, but this should not be taken as full correction. A mixing study that remains outside of the normal range should be interpreted as signifying the presence of an inhibitor.

Other Assays

Other assays helpful in the evaluation of a bleeding patient include measurement of activity levels of the individual clotting factors such as factors VIII and IX. D-dimer measurement is helpful in detecting breakdown products of fibrin. The Bethesda assay measures the strength of inhibitors directed against factor VIII or, much less commonly, factor IX.

KEY POINTS

- A history of bleeding into muscles and joints is characteristic of disorders of humoral clotting factors, whereas mucosal bleeding occurs more commonly in disorders of primary hemostasis, thrombocytopenia, and qualitative platelet defects.
- Prolongation of the prothrombin time and the activated partial thromboplastin time may occur in individuals with deficiencies of or inhibitors to humoral clotting factors.
- The thrombin clotting time is prolonged in the presence of any thrombin inhibitor, such as heparin, lepirudin, or argatroban.
- Correction of the clotting test after an abnormal mixing study signifies a factor deficiency, whereas incomplete correction of the clotting test after mixing suggests the presence of an inhibitor.

Congenital Bleeding Disorders

Hemophilia A and B

Factor VIII and factor IX deficiencies produce hemophilia A and B, respectively, which are X-linked recessive disorders. Mild, moderate, and severe forms of hemophilia are determined by activity levels of the deficient factor. The clinical manifestations of hemophilia A and B are practically indistinguishable. Severe hemophilia A and B are characterized by

TABLE 22. Classification of Congenital and Acquired Disorders Leading to Abnormalities in Coagulation Parameters

Patients with Bleeding			
Coagulation Test Result	**Inherited or Acquired**	**Underlying Cause/Disorder**	**Treatment**
↑PT, normal aPTT	Congenital	Factor VII deficiency	FFP, recombinant factor VIIa
	Acquired	DIC	Treat underlying cause, supportive transfusions (FFP, cryoprecipitate, platelets)
	Acquired	Liver disease	FFP
	Acquired	Vitamin K deficiency	Vitamin K
	Acquired	Vitamin K antagonists	Vitamin K, FFP, PCCs
	Acquired	Certain paraproteins	No specific treatment for hemostasis. Treatment for paraproteinemia as otherwise indicated
	Acquired	Certain dysfibrinogenemias	Cryoprecipitate
Normal PT, ↑aPTT	Congenital	Hemophilia A (factor VIII deficiency)	Factor VIII concentrates, desmopressin for mild cases
	Congenital	Hemophilia B (factor IX deficiency)	Factor IX concentrates
	Congenital	Factor XI deficiency	FFP
	Congenital	vWD	Desmopressin or vWF-containing factor VIII concentrates
	Acquired	Acquired hemophilia	Bypassing agents to treat bleeding Immunosuppressants to eradicate inhibitor
	Acquired	Acquired vWD	—
	Acquired	Heparin	Protamine sulfate
	Acquired	Direct thrombin inhibitors	No antidote available
↑PT, ↑aPTT	Congenital	Factor V deficiency	FFP
	Congenital	Factor X, factor II deficiency	PCCs
	Congenital	Hypofibrinogenemia or afibrinogenemia	Cryoprecipitate or fibrinogen concentrates
	Congenital	Combined deficiency of factor V and factor VIII	Factor VIII concentrates and FFP
	Congenital	Combined deficiency of factors II, VII, IX, and X	High-dose vitamin K, FFP, PCCs
	Acquired	Fibrinolysis (tPA, urokinase, etc.)	Cryoprecipitate
	Acquired	Factor V inhibitors	FFP, platelets, immunosuppression
	Acquired	Lupus inhibitor–associated hypoprothrombinemia	FFP, PCCs
	Acquired	Factor X deficiency from amyloidosis	PCCs, FFP
	Acquired	Vitamin K deficiency	Vitamin K
	Acquired	Vitamin K antagonists	Vitamin K, FFP, PCCs
	Acquired	Heparin	Protamine sulfate
	Acquired	Direct thrombin inhibitors	No antidote available
	Acquired	DIC	Treat underlying cause, supportive transfusions (FFP, cryoprecipitate, platelets)
	Acquired	Liver disease	Supportive transfusions (FFP, cryoprecipitate)
Normal PT and aPTT	Congenital	vWD	Desmopressin or vWF-containing factor VIII concentrates

(continued on next page)

TABLE 22. Classification of Congenital and Acquired Disorders Leading to Abnormalities in Coagulation Parameters *(continued)*

Patients with Bleeding			
Coagulation Test Result	**Inherited or Acquired**	**Underlying Cause/Disorder**	**Treatment**
Normal PT and aPTT	Congenital	Factor XIII deficiency	Cryoprecipitate
	Congenital	Platelet deficiency or dysfunction	Platelets
	Congenital	Deficiencies of fibrinolytic inhibitors (PAI-1 or α_2-antiplasmin)	ε-Aminocaproic acid
	Congenital	Hereditary hemorrhagic telangiectasia (Osler-Weber-Rendu syndrome)	ε-Aminocaproic acid
	Congenital	Ehlers-Danlos syndrome	—
	Acquired	Low-molecular-weight heparin and fondaparinux	No antidote. Protamine reverses ≤50% of enoxaparin activity at most
	Acquired	Drugs and herbs causing platelet dysfunction	Desmopressin, platelet transfusion
	Acquired	Uremia	Desmopressin, cryoprecipitate
	Acquired	Scurvy	Vitamin C
	Acquired	Myeloproliferative disorders	—
	Acquired	Factor XIII inhibitors	—
Patients without Bleeding			
Coagulation Test Result	**Inherited or Acquired**	**Disorder**	**Treatment**
Normal PT, ↑aPTT	Congenital	Deficiency of contact factors (HMWK, PK, factor XII)	—
	Acquired	Lupus inhibitor	—

aPTT = activated partial thromboplastin time; DIC = disseminated intravascular coagulation; FFP = fresh frozen plasma; HMWK = high-molecular-weight kininogen; PAI-1 = plasminogen activator inhibitor-1; PCC = prothrombin complex concentrate; PK = prekallikrein; PT = prothrombin time; tPA = tissue-type plasminogen activator; vWD = von Willebrand disease; vWF = von Willebrand factor.

recurrent hemarthroses that result in chronic, crippling degenerative joint disease unless treated prophylactically with factor replacement. Central nervous system hemorrhage is especially hazardous, remaining one of the leading causes of death. Mild hemophilia may present in adulthood and is characterized by posttraumatic or surgical bleeding. Plasma-derived and recombinant factor VIII and factor IX concentrates are used to treat hemophilia A and B, and patients and families can undergo training in intravenous administration for home use. Desmopressin can sometimes be helpful for treating mild hemophilia A. Aspirin and NSAID use is contraindicated in patients with hemophilia A and B.

KEY POINTS

- Severe hemophilia A and B are characterized by recurrent hemarthroses that result in chronic, crippling degenerative joint disease and central nervous system hemorrhage.
- Plasma-derived and recombinant factor VIII and factor IX concentrates are used to treat hemophilia.

von Willebrand Disease

vWD is the most common inherited bleeding disorder, with low levels of vWF found in 1% of the population. It is an autosomal disorder, with mild disease being codominant and more severe disease being recessive. vWF protects factor VIII from degradation, and factor VIII levels can be low enough in vWD to cause slight prolongation of the aPTT, although the hemorrhagic manifestations are characterized by mucocutaneous bleeding, not hemarthroses as in hemophilia. Many women with vWD have significant menorrhagia, endometriosis, and postpartum hemorrhage. Mild vWD may not be detected by the bleeding time and the Platelet Function Analyzer (PFA-100®) assay, necessitating measurement of vWF antigen and activity levels for diagnosis. Additionally, levels of vWF fluctuate in response to estrogens, stress, exercise, inflammation, and bleeding, and repeated assays may be required to make the diagnosis. Desmopressin can be used to treat mild type 1 vWD, but more severe bleeding and bleeding in types 2 and 3 vWD typically require infusion of vWF-containing factor VIII concentrates.

KEY POINTS

- Many women with von Willebrand disease have significant menorrhagia, endometriosis, and postpartum hemorrhage.
- Mild von Willebrand disease may not be detected by the bleeding time and the Platelet Function Analyzer (PFA-100®) necessitating measurement of von Willebrand factor antigen and activity levels for diagnosis.

Acquired Bleeding Disorders

Acquired Hemophilia

Acquired hemophilia causes bleeding with an isolated aPTT prolongation. It is associated with the postpartum state, malignancy, or autoimmune conditions, but 50% of cases are idiopathic. Patients have no history of bleeding, but bleeding on presentation can be severe. Unlike congenital hemophilia, bleeding in acquired hemophilia tends to be mucocutaneous and multifocal, and hemarthroses are rare. Factor VIII levels are reduced, and mixing study results show unsuccessful correction, consistent with an inhibitor. Test results for the lupus inhibitor are negative.

Patients with low titers of inhibitor (measured in Bethesda units) may be treated with factor VIII concentrates. Patients with high inhibitor titers (>5 Bethesda units) require treatment with recombinant human factor VIIa concentrate or prothrombin complex designed to activate factor X and secure hemostasis independent of factor VIII and the intrinsic pathway. Patients may require immunosuppression for inhibitor eradication.

KEY POINTS

- Treatment for acute bleeding episodes in acquired hemophilia requires factor VIII concentrate if the titer of inhibitor is low.
- Prothrombin complex or recombinant human factor VIIa may be required to secure hemostasis by activating factor X independent of the intrinsic pathway in patients with acquired hemophilia who have a high titer of inhibitor.

Coagulopathy of Liver Disease

The liver synthesizes most coagulation factors, and liver failure is usually a hemorrhagic condition. Coagulopathy of liver disease is characterized by a prolonged PT and aPTT. The TCT can also be prolonged, not only from the low levels of fibrinogen in affected patients, but also because abnormal glycosylation of the fibrinogen renders the fibrinogen functionally abnormal. Splenomegaly leads to thrombocytopenia, which may be refractory to transfused platelets. Clearance of D-dimers is impaired, fibrinolysis may be accelerated, and platelet consumption is accelerated, independent of hypersplenism, analogous to the hemostatic defects in disseminated intravascular coagulation (DIC). Despite having prolonged INR values, patients with liver disease are not "autoanticoagulated," and patients with cirrhosis may experience venous thromboembolism.

Anticoagulation in patients with liver disease should be undertaken with caution because of the risk for bleeding. Full correction of the INR is difficult to achieve using fresh frozen plasma alone because of the short half-life of factor VII (see Transfusion). If fresh frozen plasma is needed to treat patients with liver disease and coagulopathy, vitamin K should be given as well.

KEY POINTS

- Hemostatic defects in patients with liver disease include coagulopathy, hypofibrinogenemia and dysfibrinogenemia, and thrombocytopenia.
- Fresh frozen plasma may be used to correct the coagulopathy of liver disease, but the short half-life of factor VII limits the duration of efficacy.
- If fresh frozen plasma is needed to treat patients with liver disease and coagulopathy, vitamin K also should be given.

Disseminated Intravascular Coagulation

DIC begins with abnormal thrombin generation, rapid consumption of clotting factors and platelets, and accelerated fibrinolysis. Although hemorrhage may result from low levels of clotting factors and platelets, histopathologic examination of affected tissues shows a fibrin clot in the microvasculature. A thrombotic microangiopathy may ensue, and schistocytes develop in 30% of patients. A list of conditions leading to DIC is found in **Table 23**. Low platelet levels, a prolonged PT (the aPTT is prolonged in severe DIC), a low or decreasing fibrinogen level, and an elevated D-dimer level are diagnostic. Treatment of the underlying cause is the mainstay of DIC therapy, but supportive transfusions with plasma, cryoprecipitate, and platelets may be necessary in bleeding patients.

KEY POINT

- Low platelet levels, a prolonged prothrombin time, a low or decreasing fibrinogen level, and an elevated D-dimer level are diagnostic of disseminated intravascular coagulation.

Vitamin K Deficiency

Vitamin K is required for generation of the active forms of factors II, VII, IX, and X. Sources of vitamin K are gastrointestinal flora and green leafy vegetables consumed in the diet. Deficiency is most common in malnourished patients who take systemic antibiotics and patients with fat malabsorption because vitamin K is fat soluble. Oral

TABLE 23. DIC-associated Disorders
Obstetric complications
Eclampsia
Retained products
Fetal demise
Amniotic fluid embolus
Placental abruption
Infection
Gram-negative bacteria
Gram-positive bacteria
Rickettsial organisms
Fungi
Viruses (hemorrhagic fevers such as dengue, Ebola, in particular)
Tissue injury
Crush injuries
Severe burns
Brain injury
Tumors
Solid tumors
Acute leukemias (especially acute promyelocytic leukemia)
Envenomations
Snake bites
Brown recluse spider bites

DIC = disseminated intravascular coagulation.

supplementation with vitamin K, 5 to 10 mg/d, is sufficient to replace stores (see Approach to Anemia). Anticoagulation with warfarin may be difficult in patients with underlying vitamin K deficiency, with small amounts of warfarin potentially producing alarmingly high INR values after only 1 or 2 days of therapy. Partial repletion with vitamin K may be warranted in such patients.

KEY POINT

- Anticoagulation with warfarin may be difficult in patients with underlying vitamin K deficiency, with small amounts of warfarin potentially producing alarmingly high INR values after only 1 or 2 days of therapy, and potentially requiring vitamin K repletion.

Platelets

Normal Platelet Physiology

Platelets are normally made in the bone marrow from megakaryocytes through stimulus of several cytokines and growth factors, the most important of which is thrombopoietin. The lifespan of a normal platelet is 7 to 10 days, and one tenth of the total platelet population is replaced daily. A normal platelet count in most laboratories ranges from 150,000 to 350,000/µL (150-350 × 10^9/L). Platelets are required for hemostatic plug formation, and they serve as the phospholipid scaffold on which the reactions of secondary hemostasis occur. Platelet deficiency or dysfunction produces mucocutaneous bleeding.

Approach to the Patient with Thrombocytopenia

Thrombocytopenia is defined as a platelet count of less than 150,000/µL (150 × 10^9/L), and it can be caused by underproduction, peripheral destruction, or splenic sequestration of platelets (**Table 24**).

Thrombocytopenia may be associated with no symptoms and detected incidentally on a routine complete blood count or may be characterized by bleeding symptoms. Bleeding symptoms are more likely to develop if the thrombocytopenia is severe, rapidly occurring, or accompanied by other defects in hemostasis, such as coagulopathy. Platelet counts between 100,000/µL and 150,000/µL (100-150 × 10^9/L) do not confer an increased risk for hemorrhage, those between 50,000/µL and 100,000/µL (50-100 × 10^9/L) are usually associated with no symptoms, those between 20,000 and 50,000/µL (20-50 × 10^9/L) are associated with symptoms of mucocutaneous bleeding, and those below 10,000/µL (10 × 10^9/L) confer an increased risk for spontaneous intracranial hemorrhage.

Establishing the underlying cause is an important part of the evaluation and management of patients with thrombocytopenia. A history of previous platelet counts and family history of thrombocytopenia may provide clues regarding the diagnosis. Determining whether there is a history of ingestion of medications and herbal preparations that could affect platelet function or lead to immune destruction as well as recent infections, such as HIV, Epstein-Barr virus, hepatitis, cytomegalovirus, and rickettsia, which are associated with thrombocytopenia, is appropriate.

Symptoms and signs of liver disease may be associated with portal hypertension, splenomegaly, and platelet sequestration, and autoimmune thyroid and rheumatologic disease may predispose to autoimmune thrombocytopenia. A pregnant patient with thrombocytopenia requires special consideration (see Hematologic Issues in Pregnancy).

Notable physical examination findings include lymphadenopathy or hepatosplenomegaly. Skin examination may disclose stigmata of mucocutaneous bleeding, including petechiae and ecchymoses. Wet purpura (petechiae within the oral mucosa) may signify an increased risk for spontaneous intracranial hemorrhage.

Laboratory evaluation should include the complete blood count with differential to identify perturbations in

TABLE 24. Causes of Thrombocytopenia
Underproduction
Congenital
Wiskott-Aldrich syndrome
Thrombocytopenia with absent radii
Fanconi anemia
May-Hegglin anomaly
Bernard-Soulier syndrome
Nutritional deficiencies
Vitamin B_{12}
Folate (rarely iron)
Infectious
Viral
HIV
Parvovirus B19
Hepatitis C virus
EBV
Rubella
Mumps
Varicella
Mycobacterial
Tuberculosis
Autoimmune
Aplastic anemia
Amegakaryocytic thrombocytopenia
Neoplastic medications
Alcohol
Chemotherapy
Radiation
Portal hypertension
Malignancy
CLL
CML
Hodgkin lymphoma
NHL
Hairy cell leukemia
Myelofibrosis
Chronic hemolysis
Thalassemia major
Hemoglobin C disease
Hereditary spherocytosis
Infection
Malaria
Leishmaniasis
Granulomatous disease
Sarcoidosis
Peripheral destruction
Immune-mediated
ITP
Posttransfusion purpura
Drug-related (heparin, quinine, quinidine, β-lactam antibiotics, sulfa-containing drugs, valproic acid)
Antiphospholipid syndrome
Nonimmune mediated
DIC
TTP/HUS
HELLP syndrome
Gestational thrombocytopenia
Mechanical destruction by cardiopulmonary bypass or LVADs
Localized intravascular coagulopathy: giant cavernous hemangioma, aortic dissection
Splenic sequestration: any cause of splenomegaly

CLL = chronic lymphocytic leukemia; CML = chronic myeloid leukemia; EBV = Epstein-Barr virus; NHL = non-Hodgkin lymphoma; ITP = immune thrombocytopenic purpura; DIC = disseminated intravascular coagulation; TTP/HUS = thrombotic thrombocytopenic purpura-hemolytic uremic syndrome; HELLP = hemolysis, elevated liver enzymes, and low platelet count; LVADs = left ventricular assist devices.

other cell lines as well as a peripheral blood smear, which is essential to diagnosis. Anemia and leukopenia may suggest bone marrow failure, whereas leukocytosis may herald an acute or chronic leukemic process. Platelet clumping signifies pseudothrombocytopenia, which is caused in vitro by inadequate anticoagulation of the sample or by the presence of ethylenediaminetetraacetic acid (EDTA) agglutinins, naturally occurring in approximately 0.1% of the population. The automated platelet counter does not recognize the clumping as a mass of platelets, and the platelet count is, therefore, spuriously low. Drawing a complete blood sample into a citrated or heparinized tube may abrogate the clumping.

Erythrocyte morphology is also important in the evaluation of thrombocytopenia. Schistocytes may suggest a microangiopathic process, whereas spherocytes may indicate autoimmune hemolysis.

Assessment of kidney, liver, and thyroid function, as well as measurement of serum electrolytes and vitamin B_{12} and folate levels, is appropriate. The prothrombin time and activated partial thromboplastin time should be calculated and fibrinogen and D-dimer levels measured in patients in whom intravascular coagulation is a possibility. Bone marrow examination is typically reserved for evaluation of patients with perturbations in multiple cell lines, in whom myelodysplasia is a consideration, or in whom therapy (typically for immune thrombocytopenic purpura) is unsuccessful.

KEY POINTS

- Establishing the underlying cause is an important part of the evaluation and management of patients with thrombocytopenia.
- Bleeding from mucous membranes (wet purpura) confers an increased risk for spontaneous intracranial hemorrhage.
- Diagnostic evaluation of patients with thrombocytopenia includes a complete blood count with differential, a peripheral blood smear, liver chemistry tests, thyroid function tests, and measurement of serum electrolytes, creatinine, vitamin B_{12}, and folate.
- Bone marrow examination is typically reserved for evaluation of patients with perturbations in multiple cell lines, in whom myelodysplasia is a consideration, or in whom therapy (typically for immune thrombocytopenic purpura) is unsuccessful.

Immune (Idiopathic) Thrombocytopenic Purpura

Immune (also termed "idiopathic") thrombocytopenic purpura (ITP) is an acquired autoimmune condition in which autoantibodies are directed against platelet surface proteins, leading to platelet destruction that may be only partially counteracted by increased bone marrow platelet production. ITP is a common disorder, occurring more often in children than adults, but the course is frequently self-limited in children and not in adults.

Clinical findings may include signs or symptoms of mild to severe bleeding or hemorrhage. Although ITP is a diagnosis of exclusion, supportive clinical findings include an otherwise normal blood count or concomitant anemia from bleeding and the absence of additional organ dysfunction. Variants of ITP may be drug induced or part of a broader illness of abnormal immune regulation, as with systemic lupus erythematosus, HIV infection, or lymphoproliferative malignancies.

Platelets, when present, may be large because typically, they would have been recently released from the marrow, and the enhanced hemostatic function of these young platelets may account for less severe bleeding symptoms than those associated with other diseases with a similar platelet count.

Not all patients with ITP require therapy, and monitoring for signs of bleeding or further declines in platelet counts may be appropriate. Asymptomatic patients without evidence of bleeding and platelet counts above 30,000 to 40,000/µL (30-40 × 10^9/L) have less than a 15% chance of developing more severe thrombocytopenia requiring treatment. In such patients, the most appropriate course of action is to provide counseling on potential bleeding symptoms and repeat the complete blood count at a designated interval, generally 1 to 2 weeks.

In adults, therapy may be required for patients with platelet counts lower than 30,000 to 40,000/µL (30-40 × 10^9/L) or with bleeding. Initial therapy consists of prednisone or methylprednisolone (1-2 mg/kg/d). Some health care providers advocate initial therapy with dexamethasone (40 mg/d for 4 days) owing to a higher response and lower relapse rate. Initial responses to corticosteroid therapy, without relapse, occur in 25% of patients, but treatment failures occur in 75%. Patients who do not respond to corticosteroid therapy and who continue to bleed should be treated with an additional agent such as intravenous immune globulin or anti-D immune globulin or with newer options, such as rituximab or mycophenolate mofetil. Splenectomy can also be considered, but awareness of postsplenectomy complications and the availability of more immunosuppressant options have decreased its use. Splenectomy leads to a sustained remission in 75% of patients. Adjunctive therapy, including intravenous immune globulin or anti-D immune globulin, with corticosteroids is appropriate for the initial therapy of patients in whom a rapid rise in platelets is desirable because of bleeding or a platelet count lower than 10,000/µL (10 × 10/L). Two new agents that stimulate the thrombopoietin receptor and induce platelet production, romiplostim and eltrombopag, have been approved for use in refractory ITP. The risk of bleeding from continued thrombocytopenia must be weighed against the toxicity of additional treatment when the need for alternative immunosuppressive therapy is considered in patients who are refractory to initial corticosteroid therapy. Some patients with chronic ITP can tolerate thrombocytopenia for long periods without symptomatic bleeding.

β-Lactam antibiotics, cephalosporins, sulfa-containing drugs, vancomycin, quinine and its derivatives, and glycoprotein IIb/IIIa inhibitors can cause ITP. Discontinuation of the offending drug should result in platelet recovery.

KEY POINTS

- In adults with immune thrombocytopenic purpura, therapy may be required for patients with platelet counts lower than 30,000 to 40,000/µL (30-40 × 10^9/L) or with bleeding.
- Initial therapy for immune thrombocytopenic purpura consists of prednisone or methylprednisolone.
- Patients with immune thrombocytopenic purpura who do not respond to corticosteroids should receive intravenous immune globulin, anti-D immune globulin, rituximab, or mycophenolate mofetil; splenectomy can also be considered in patients with refractory disease.
- In patients with immune thrombocytopenic purpura refractory to initial corticosteroid therapy, the risk of bleeding from continued thrombocytopenia must be weighed against the toxicity of additional treatment.

- In patients with drug-induced immune thrombocytopenic purpura, discontinuation of the offending drug should result in platelet recovery.

Heparin-induced Thrombocytopenia

Heparin-induced thrombocytopenia (HIT) occurs in 1% to 3% of patients treated with standard unfractionated heparin and in a much smaller proportion of patients treated with low-molecular-weight heparin. Patients who receive heparin in the setting of cardiothoracic surgery or after orthopedic surgery are more likely to develop HIT than are medical patients who receive heparin for dialysis or for deep venous thrombosis prophylaxis. HIT develops 5 to 10 days after exposure to heparin, with a decrease in platelet counts of 50% or more and, in a subset of patients, paradoxical arterial or venous thrombotic events despite the presence of thrombocytopenia. In these patients, the platelet count nadir is usually not low enough to cause bleeding symptoms and may be missed unless screening and platelet counts are routinely done. The onset of HIT is typically 5 to 10 days after heparin exposure. It is therefore critical to monitor the platelet count around this time frame in high-risk patients when heparin is being used.

The likelihood of HIT is based on the timing of thrombocytopenia (5 to 10 days after heparin exposure), degree of decrease in platelets (more than 50%), presence or absence of thrombosis, and exclusion of other reasons for thrombocytopenia. The "4T score" has been devised to help clinicians decide the pretest probability for diagnosing HIT and is based on the criteria just discussed (**Table 25**). The 4T score has been tested and prospectively validated.

Diagnostic testing for HIT is based on enzyme-linked immunosorbent assay measurement of an antibody directed against the heparin–platelet factor 4 complex. This method is more readily available than the functional platelet activation assays but lacks specificity and may be too sensitive because many patients with these platelet-activating antibodies do not develop clinical HIT. Consequently, use of the 4T score to calculate the pretest probability for HIT is essential before diagnostic testing is initiated. The heparin-induced platelet aggregation assay and, in particular, the 14C-serotonin release assay, are more specific diagnostic tests. Given the grave clinical consequences of HIT, it is worth mentioning several atypical presentations of this disorder. First, thrombocytopenia may occur earlier than 5 to 10 days after heparin exposure in patients who have had prior heparin treatment. Second, in delayed HIT, a thrombotic episode can occur even after heparin has been discontinued. Additionally, patients

TABLE 25. The "4T Score" for Diagnosis of Heparin-Induced Thrombocytopenia

Thrombocytopenia
1. Platelet count fall >50% and nadir >20,000/µL (20×10^9/L): 2 points
2. Platelet count fall 30% to 50% or nadir 10,000 to 19,000/µL (10-19 $\times 10^9$/L): 1 points
3. Platelet count fall <30 percent or nadir <10,000/µL (10×10^9/L): 0 points
Timing of platelet count fall
Clear onset between days 5 and 10 or platelet count decrease at ≤1 day if prior heparin exposure within the last 30 days: 2 points
Consistent with platelet count decrease at 5 to 10 days but not documented (e.g., missing platelet counts) or onset after day 10 or fall ≤1 day with prior heparin exposure within the last 30 to 100 days: 1 point
Platelet count fall at <4 days without recent exposure: 0 points
Thrombosis or other sequelae
Confirmed new thrombosis, skin necrosis, or acute systemic reaction after intravenous unfractionated heparin bolus: 2 points
Progressive or recurrent thrombosis, nonnecrotizing (erythematous) skin lesions, or suspected thrombosis that has not been proven: 1 point
No thrombosis or sequelae: 0 points
Other causes for thrombocytopenia present
None apparent: 2 points
Possible: 1 point
Definite: 0 points
Test interpretation
A score is determined for each of the four categories, resulting in a total score from 0 to 8. Pretest probabilities for HIT are, as follows:
0 to 3: Low probability
4 to 5: Intermediate probability
6 to 8: High probability

HIT = heparin-induced thrombocytopenia.

H CONT.

may have skin necrosis similar to that produced by warfarin. In such patients, the decrease in platelet count may be minimal, and the heparin exposure may be accompanied by allergic symptoms such as hives and angioedema.

Heparin cessation and treatment with a non-heparin alternative anticoagulant are mandatory when there is a high pretest probability for disease and a positive enzyme-linked immunosorbent assay because 30% to 50% of patients experience thromboses when treated with heparin withdrawal alone, and results of the serotonin release assay may not be available for several days. Anticoagulants approved for the treatment of HIT include lepirudin, argatroban, or danaparoid. Bivalirudin is indicated for use only in patients with HIT or who are at risk for HIT and are undergoing acute cardiac interventions if they are unable to be delayed. Lepirudin is cleared through the kidneys and should be used with caution in patients with kidney impairment. Argatroban is cleared through the liver, and dose adjustments are necessary in patients with elevated liver chemistry test values, including bilirubin level. H

KEY POINTS

- Heparin-induced thrombocytopenia usually develops 5 to 10 days after heparin exposure, with a decrease in platelet counts of 50% or more and, in a subset of patients, paradoxical arterial or venous thrombotic events despite the presence of thrombocytopenia.
- The risk of heparin-induced thrombocytopenia is sevenfold higher with unfractionated heparin than with low-molecular-weight heparin.
- The 4T score is a prospectively validated tool to help calculate the clinical pretest probability for HIT before a diagnostic workup or empiric treatment is begun.
- Heparin-induced thrombocytopenia treatment consists of heparin cessation and anticoagulation with lepirudin, argatroban, or danaparoid; bivalirudin is indicated for those undergoing acute cardiac interventions.

H Thrombotic Thrombocytopenic Purpura–Hemolytic Uremic Syndrome

Thrombotic thrombocytopenic purpura (TTP) is a process characterized by abnormal activation of platelets and endothelial cells, deposition of fibrin in the microvasculature, and peripheral destruction of erythrocytes and platelets. TTP is thought to have an immune cause. Most patients with the typical sporadic form of TTP have developed autoantibodies directed against the protease that cleaves the high-molecular-weight multimers of von Willebrand factor (vWF). The function of this protease, now known as ADAMTS13, is neutralized by these autoantibodies. High-molecular-weight vWF multimers therefore accumulate, leading to abnormal platelet adhesion and activation. TTP can also be triggered by drugs, especially quinine ticlopidine, mitomycin C, cyclosporine, or gemcitabine because of endothelial cell damage rather than formation of antibodies against ADAMTS13. TTP incidence increases during pregnancy and in patients with HIV/AIDS infection or bone marrow and solid organ transplants.

TTP should be suspected in patients who have the presence of (1) microangiopathic hemolytic anemia, characterized by schistocytes on the peripheral blood smear and increased serum lactate dehydrogenase levels; and (2) thrombocytopenia. A peripheral blood smear is essential to determine whether the anemia is caused by a microangiopathic hemolytic process as indicated by the presence of schistocytes. Patients may also have fever; renal manifestations such as hematuria, elevated creatinine, and proteinuria; and fluctuating neurologic manifestations, such as headache, confusion, sleepiness, coma, seizures, and stroke, but the absence of these symptoms does not exclude the diagnosis. Other clinical features may include nausea, vomiting, and abdominal pain with or without elevations of serum amylase and lipase levels. Assays for ADAMTS13 activity and inhibitor titer are available but are best used for prognosis rather than to guide therapy because this life-threatening disease requires immediate treatment that cannot be delayed until results of laboratory testing are available. The presence of low activity levels and a positive inhibitor titer confers a higher risk for relapse.

TTP is treated with plasma exchange, which was shown to be superior to simple plasma transfusions in a randomized clinical trial. Plasma exchange should be instituted emergently at diagnosis because 10% of patients die of this disease despite therapy, usually within the first 24 hours. In patients in whom neurologic symptoms or other signs of clinical decline develop prior to initiation of plasma exchange, immediate infusion of fresh frozen plasma is indicated. Plasma exchange should continue daily until the platelet count is greater than 150,000/µL (150×10^9/L) for 2 days. Because abnormal platelet activation is a hallmark of pathogenesis, transfusion of fresh platelets can lead to more microvascular occlusion and is, therefore, relatively contraindicated. Corticosteroids have been used to treat TTP, but there are no prospective data validating their use.

TTP can overlap with hemolytic uremic syndrome (HUS), which usually occurs in children. HUS is characterized by more renal manifestations and fewer neurologic sequelae than TTP. HUS may be precipitated by an infectious diarrheal illness, especially *Escherichia coli* subtype O157:H7 or *Shigella* species. These bacteria elaborate a toxin that resembles antigens on renal endothelial cells and bind and cause renal cell death. HUS can also occur in patients with abnormalities in the complement protein system. In adults, HUS is also treated with plasma exchange. It

CONT.

is not clinically helpful to attempt to distinguish between TTP and HUS, because many patients with HUS also respond to plasma exchange.

Other conditions that may be confused with TTP include malignant hypertension, HELLP (*h*emolysis, *e*levated *l*iver enzymes, and *l*ow *p*latelet count) syndrome/preeclampsia, antiphospholipid syndrome, and scleroderma renal crisis. These entities may be difficult to distinguish with precision, but if TTP is possible, a trial of plasma exchange should generally be undertaken. **H**

KEY POINTS

- Findings of microangiopathic hemolytic anemia, schistocytes on the peripheral blood smear, increased lactate dehydrogenase, and thrombocytopenia are suspicious for thrombotic thrombocytopenic purpura.
- Plasma exchange should be instituted emergently in patients with a high clinical suspicion for thrombotic thrombocytopenic purpura.
- Hemolytic uremic syndrome is characterized by more kidney manifestations and fewer neurologic sequelae than thrombotic thrombocytopenic purpura and may be precipitated by an infectious diarrheal illness.

Other Thrombocytopenias Due to Underproduction

The hallmark of thrombocytopenias caused by underproduction is inadequate megakaryocyte numbers in the bone marrow. Bone marrow failure syndromes include aplastic anemia, myelodysplasia, vitamin B_{12}/folate deficiency, and Fanconi anemia. The marrow may be invaded by leukemias, tumors, granulomatous diseases, or fibrosis or may be injured by ionizing radiation, infections, and drugs (especially alcohol and chemotherapeutic agents). Platelet transfusions are usually effective for prevention of bleeding.

Qualitative Platelet Disorders

Platelet Function Testing

Screening tests for disorders of primary hemostasis include the bleeding time and the Platelet Function Analyzer-100 (PFA-100®). In many hospital laboratories, bleeding time is no longer available, having been replaced by the PFA-100®. Screening for a defect in primary hemostasis is recommended in patients with a personal or family history of mucocutaneous or postsurgical bleeding There is no indication for routine coagulation screening of all patients preoperatively.

The bleeding time test is performed by making a nick of standard size and depth on the forearm and inflating a sphygmomanometer to 40 mm Hg on the upper arm. Blood is blotted away at standard intervals with a filter paper, and the time until bleeding cessation is measured. By blotting away excess blood, primary hemostasis, rather than fibrin formation, is tested. The bleeding time is prolonged in cases of platelet dysfunction, von Willebrand disease (vWD), thrombocytopenia and anemia, and disorders of vascular contractility. Test results can be affected by operator experience, cold exposure, vigorous exercise, anxiety, direction of the incision, and excessive skin wiping. Additionally, mild disorders of primary hemostasis may not produce an abnormal bleeding time, diminishing its usefulness as a screening test.

The PFA-100® assay is performed on whole citrated blood, which is aspirated through an aperture in a cartridge where it contacts a membrane coated with a mixture of collagen and epinephrine or collagen and adenosine diphosphate. Contact with these agonists leads to platelet adhesion, aggregation, and activation, culminating in occlusion of the aperture and cessation of blood flow. The time for aperture closure is known as the closure time, and it is prolonged in patients with anemia and thrombocytopenia. The closure times are reliably prolonged in cases of severe platelet dysfunction and vWD but may not be prolonged in milder cases. More detailed information on platelet function can be obtained by platelet aggregation testing, which is available only at tertiary centers.

KEY POINTS

- Bleeding time tests are not reliable, rarely indicated, and no longer performed at many hospitals and have been replaced by the Platelet Function Analyzer (PFA-100®) assay.
- Screening for a defect in primary hemostasis is recommended in patients with a personal or family history of mucocutaneous or postsurgical bleeding, but routine coagulation screening of all patients preoperatively is not indicated.

Acquired Platelet Dysfunction

Uremia leads to platelet dysfunction, which can be abrogated by desmopressin. Dialysis improves platelet function and decreases bleeding. Conjugated estrogens can improve mucosal bleeding. Patients with myeloproliferative and myelodysplastic syndromes may produce dysfunctional platelets because of their bone marrow disorders, and platelet transfusions may help treat those with clinical bleeding.

Many drugs and herbs influence platelet function. Aspirin irreversibly acetylates and inhibits cyclooxygenase in platelets, rendering them hypofunctional for the life of the platelets. NSAIDs also affect platelet function, but reversibly. The thienopyridine adenosine diphosphate antagonists also block platelet function irreversibly. Foods such as garlic, Chinese black tree fungus, and ginseng have also been linked to moderate degrees of platelet dysfunction. Most drugs that affect platelet function cause mild defects that alone do not cause bleeding symptoms.

KEY POINTS

- Desmopressin is the first-line treatment for patients with uremia and acute bleeding.
- Dialysis improves platelet function and decreases bleeding in patients with uremia, and conjugated estrogens can improve mucosal bleeding if desmopressin and dialysis are not effective.
- The functional effects of aspirin on platelets are irreversible for the life of the platelets, whereas the effects of NSAIDS are reversible.

Thrombotic Disorders

Pathophysiology of Thrombosis and Thrombophilia

Thrombosis occurs when the delicate balance between prothrombotic and antithrombotic forces in the blood is disturbed. The three global conditions that contribute to thrombogenesis, often termed "Virchow triad," are stasis, vessel-wall integrity, and hypercoagulability. Stasis facilitates the accumulation of activated coagulation proteins. Vascular damage exposes procoagulant tissue factor and collagen and reduces local concentrations of antithrombotic proteins, including thrombomodulin, prostacyclin, and tissue factor pathway inhibitor. Inherited or acquired hypercoagulability synergizes with stasis and vascular damage to tip the hemostatic balance toward thrombosis.

Inherited Thrombophilic Conditions

The most potent inherited thrombophilic states are antithrombin, protein C, and protein S deficiencies. Factor V Leiden (FVL) and the prothrombin G20210A gene mutation (PGM) are less potent, but much more common, thrombophilic states. Consequently, they are more likely to be identified in patients with venous thromboembolism (VTE).

Factor V Leiden

FVL is the most common inherited thrombophilic disorder. It occurs in 5% of whites, 2% of Latinos, 1% of African Americans and American Indians, and 0.5% of Asian Americans. The FVL mutation disrupts the first of three activated protein C (APC) cleavage sites, slowing the degradation of activated factor V (factor Va) and, ultimately, factor VIIIa. FVL heterozygosity and homozygosity increase the risk of VTE by 5- and 50-fold, respectively. In FVL heterozygotes, the absolute annual risk of VTE is small (0.49%) compared with 1.8% in patients with FVL homozygosity or antithrombin deficiency. Acquired risk factors such as oral contraceptives (fivefold) and travel (two- to threefold) synergize with FVL to further increase the thrombosis risk. FVL does not predispose to arterial thromboembolism. The diagnosis of FVL relies on the APC resistance assay and confirmatory DNA testing

Prothrombin G20210A Gene Mutation

The prothrombin G20210A gene mutation (PGM) occurs in 1% to 2% of non-Hispanic whites and Mexican Americans and in 0.3% of blacks. PGM stabilizes prothrombin mRNA, increasing prothrombin protein levels by 30% and 70% in heterozygotes and homozygotes, respectively. Heterozygous PGM increases the risk for VTE 2.5-fold. Double heterozygosity for factor V Leiden and the PGM confers a sevenfold increased risk for initial and fivefold increased risk for recurrent VTE. The diagnosis of PGM relies on DNA testing.

Antithrombin Deficiency

Antithrombin is an endogenous antithrombotic protein that inhibits serine proteases such as thrombin and factor Xa. Heparin accelerates antithrombin activity several thousandfold, an interaction exploited therapeutically with unfractionated heparin (UFH), low-molecular-weight heparin (LMWH), and fondaparinux.

Antithrombin deficiency (ATD) is characterized by a high risk for initial (1.8% per year) and recurrent thromboembolism (55% at 10 years), with onset early in life (peak age of onset, 15-35 years). ATD can rarely result in heparin resistance. Thrombotic events are typically venous, and most are unprovoked. This risk varies by ATD subtype.

Type I ATD is caused by mutations that impair protein synthesis and is associated with a high risk for thromboembolism. Type II ATD results from mutations affecting the thrombin (type IIa) or heparin (type IIb) binding sites. Type IIb ATD is associated with a lower risk for thromboembolism. Antithrombin activity assays that detect all three types of ATD should be used for diagnosis. Most symptomatic patients have antithrombin levels of 40% to 60%.

Protein C Deficiency

Protein C is a serine protease that inactivates factors Va and VIIIa. Protein C deficiency is associated with a high risk for initial (1.5% per year) and recurrent (6.2% per year) VTE. Type I protein C deficiency is caused by mutations affecting protein synthesis such that protein C activity and antigen levels are equally reduced. Type II protein C deficiency results from mutations affecting protein function, such that protein C activity is disproportionately reduced relative to protein C antigen levels. Most symptomatic patients present between 10 and 50 years of age and have protein C activity of 35% to 65%.

Protein S Deficiency

Protein S is a cofactor for protein C. Protein S deficiency impairs degradation of factors Va and VIIIa by protein C.

Protein S also facilitates the inactivation of factor Xa by tissue factor pathway inhibitor. Protein S circulates in a more active free form (40% of total protein S) and a less active form bound to C4b binding protein. Type I (quantitative), type II (qualitative), and type III (inherited or acquired increase in C4b-bound fraction of protein S) protein S deficiency states exist. About half of the thromboembolic events associated with protein S deficiency are unprovoked. Fifty percent of patients with protein S deficiency are symptomatic before age 55 years.

Dysfibrinogenemia

Dysfibrinogenemia is a rare thrombophilic state caused by mutations in the Aα, Bβ, or γ fibrinogen genes. These mutations can cause thrombosis or bleeding or both. The diagnosis is confirmed by disproportionate reductions in fibrinogen activity compared with antigen levels.

KEY POINTS

- Factor V Leiden is the most common, but least potent, genetic risk factor associated with venous thromboembolism, and diagnosis relies on the activated protein C resistance assay and confirmatory DNA testing.
- Antithrombin, protein C, and protein S deficiency are less common genetic risk factors, characterized by a high risk for initial and recurrent thromboembolism, with onset early in life and higher risk for unprovoked venous thromboembolism.

H Acquired Thrombophilic Conditions

Acquired thrombophilia is much more common and often associated with greater thrombotic risks than inherited thrombophilia. VTE incidence increases with age. VTE is extremely uncommon in children. In adults, the risk of VTE rises sharply after age 55 years, perhaps because of the increased prevalence of acquired VTE risk factors such as surgery and cancer in this population.

Surgery

Major inpatient surgery increases the risk for VTE 70-fold; ambulatory surgery is associated with a 10-fold increase. VTE risk persists for up to 1 year after surgery, with the risk greatest during the first 3 months after surgery. Hip and knee arthroplasty, trauma, and cancer surgery are associated with especially high risk. VTE prophylaxis reduces VTE by 60% in surgical patients.

Trauma

In the absence of prophylaxis, 58% of trauma patients develop venographic evidence of deep venous thrombosis (DVT), and up to 4% experience symptomatic pulmonary embolism. Older age, lower extremity or pelvic fractures, spinal cord injury, femoral venous line insertion, major venous repairs, prolonged immobility, and delayed institution of VTE prophylaxis increase VTE risk.

Cancer

Cancer increases the risk of VTE by 4- to 20-fold. Cancers express tissue factor on their surface and induce tissue factor expression by endothelial cells and monocytes, contributing to a prothrombotic state. Thrombotic risk varies by cancer type and stage; risk is highest with pancreatic and brain tumors, intermediate with lung cancer and lymphoma, and lower in breast and prostate cancer. Metastatic disease increases thrombotic risk twofold. Cancer treatments including surgery, chemotherapy, indwelling venous catheters, and growth factors such as erythropoietin increase risk. Patients with cancer with VTE should receive anticoagulation for at least 3 to 6 months or as long as evidence of active disease or cancer treatment persists, whichever is longer.

Antiphospholipid Syndrome

The antiphospholipid syndrome (APS) is an acquired autoimmune disorder associated with venous or arterial thromboembolism, pregnancy loss, thrombocytopenia, renal insufficiency, vasculitis, and cardiac valvular abnormalities. APS can occur in a primary form or in association with other autoimmune diseases such as systemic lupus erythematosus. APS is characterized by the presence of antibodies against phospholipids (for example, cardiolipin) or phospholipid binding proteins (for example, β_2 glycoprotein I) that can be detected with enzyme immunoassays or phospholipid-dependent coagulation tests such as the activated partial thromboplastin time (aPTT) and the dilute Russell viper venom time. Although the biology of APS remains incompletely understood, APS can cause thrombosis by inducing tissue factor expression, disrupting protein C and antithrombin function, or activating platelets and the complement cascade. Because APS antibodies can be detected transiently in 1% to 5% of asymptomatic adults, both clinical and laboratory criteria are required for diagnosis (**Table 26**). APS is associated with a high risk for thromboembolism.

VTE is the most common thrombotic manifestation of APS (59%); arterial thromboembolism (28%) and VTE and arterial thromboembolism (13%) occur less commonly. In patients with APS and a prolonged aPTT, anti-Xa assays should be used for monitoring of UFH therapy, or LMWH should be used. Long-term anticoagulation (target INR, 2-3) is necessary to treat thromboembolism because these patients are at high risk for recurrence. A higher INR target range (3 to 4) or LMWH or fondaparinux should be considered in occasional patients who develop recurrent thromboembolism despite therapeutic warfarin.

TABLE 26. Diagnostic Criteria for Antiphospholipid Syndrome

Clinical Criteria	Definitions
Vascular events	One or more objectively confirmed, symptomatic episodes of arterial, venous, or microvascular thrombosis. Histopathologic specimens must demonstrate thrombosis in the absence of vessel-wall inflammation to qualify
Pregnancy morbidity	One or more unexplained fetal deaths at or beyond the 10th week of gestation, with normal fetal morphology; or One or more premature births of a morphologically normal neonate before the 34th week of gestation because of eclampsia, severe preeclampsia, or placental insufficiency; or Three or more unexplained, consecutive, spontaneous abortions before the 10th week of gestation in the absence of maternal anatomic, chromosomal, or hormonal abnormalities or paternal chromosomal abnormalities
Laboratory Criteria	**Definitions**
Lupus anticoagulant	Positive result for a lupus anticoagulant using a phospholipid-dependent clotting assay (aPTT, dilute Russell viper venom assay, kaolin clotting time, dilute PT) with evidence of phospholipid dependence present on two or more occasions at least 12 weeks apart; or
Anticardiolipin antibody	Medium- or high-titer IgG or IgM anticardiolipin antibody measured using a standardized ELISA on two or more occasions at least 12 weeks apart; or
β_2 Glycoprotein I antibody	High-titer anti-β_2 glycoprotein I IgG or IgM antibody measured using a standardized ELISA on two or more occasions at least 12 weeks apart

aPTT = activated partial thromboplastin time; ELISA = enzyme-linked immunosorbent assay; PT = prothrombin time.

Data from Miyakis S, Lockshin MD, Atsumi T, et al. International consensus statement on an update of the classification criteria for definite antiphospholipid syndrome (APS). J Thromb Haemost. 2006;4(2):295-306. [PMID: 16420554]; and Devreese K, Hoylaerts MF. Laboratory diagnosis of the antiphospholipid syndrome: a plethora of obstacles to overcome. Eur J Haematol. 2009;83(1):1-16. [PMID: 19226362]

CONT.

In patients in whom APS antibodies artifactually prolong the PT/INR, warfarin should be monitored by measurement of chromogenic factor X levels. The risk for APS-induced miscarriage can be reduced with prophylactic-dose UFH or LMWH plus aspirin.

Catastrophic Antiphospholipid Syndrome

Catastrophic antiphospholipid syndrome is a rare, life-threatening manifestation of APS that results in disseminated microvascular thrombosis and multiorgan failure. Catastrophic antiphospholipid syndrome is often precipitated by infections, surgery, or discontinuation of immunosuppression or anticoagulation. Anticoagulation and high-dose corticosteroids are recommended. Intravenous immune globulin and plasma exchange are indicated in critically ill patients. Despite multimodality therapy, mortality remains as high as 48%. H

Other Acquired Thrombophilic Disorders

Some primarily inherited thrombophilic disorders can also be acquired in certain circumstances. Acquired antithrombin, protein C, and protein S deficiency can occur with acute thrombosis, liver disease, and anticoagulant therapy. Antithrombin deficiency is also associated with nephrotic syndrome. Protein S deficiency is associated with pregnancy, inflammation, and estrogen therapy, which increase C4b binding protein levels. Acquired protein C and protein S deficiency occur with vitamin K deficiency, whereas dysfibrinogenemia can result from cirrhosis, liver cancer, and renal cell carcinoma.

KEY POINTS

- Acquired thrombophilia is much more common and often associated with greater thrombotic risk than inherited thrombophilia.
- Venous thromboembolism risk persists for up to 1 year after surgery, with the highest risk in the first 3 months.
- Hip and knee arthroplasty, trauma, and cancer surgery are associated with particularly high risks of venous thromboembolism.
- Cancer increases the risk of venous thromboembolism by 4- to 20-fold.
- The antiphospholipid syndrome is associated with venous or arterial thromboembolism, pregnancy loss, thrombocytopenia, kidney insufficiency, vasculitis, and cardiac valvular abnormalities.
- Long-term anticoagulation (target INR, 2-3) is the most effective prophylaxis against recurrent thromboembolism in patients with the antiphospholipid syndrome.

Management and Prevention

Thrombophilia Testing

Currently, there is debate as to the value of thrombophilia testing in patients with VTE. Generally, the clinical setting of a thrombotic event (unprovoked versus provoked) provides greater prognostic information as to recurrence risk than the results of thrombophilia testing. Common thrombophilic defects such as FVL heterozygosity modestly increase recurrence risks (1.5 fold). In contrast, more potent thrombophilic states such as antithrombin deficiency that are associated with significant recurrence risks are rarely identified. Therefore, in most instances, the results of thrombophilia testing will not influence treatment duration. If thrombophilia testing is planned, targeted testing of higher-risk groups may increase the diagnostic yield (**Table 27**). Randomized trials of thrombophilia testing are needed to establish its value.

Screening for FVL and the prothrombin G20210A gene mutation can be done at any time, but antithrombin, protein C, protein S, and dysfibrinogenemia testing may be altered during acute thrombotic events and their treatment. Therefore, these levels are most accurately assessed after the acute thrombotic event has resolved and anticoagulants have been discontinued for at least 2-4 weeks.

KEY POINTS

- The clinical setting of a thrombotic event (unprovoked versus provoked) provides greater prognostic information as to recurrence risk than the results of thrombophilia testing.
- The results of thrombophilia testing generally will not influence treatment duration; when testing is done, targeted testing of higher-risk groups may increase diagnostic yield.

H

Diagnosis

The symptoms and signs of DVT and pulmonary embolism are notoriously insensitive and nonspecific. Duplex ultrasound imaging and CT or magnetic resonance angiography have emerged as the diagnostic studies of choice, although the contrast associated with CT imaging may be relatively or absolutely contraindicated in patients with acute kidney failure or serious contrast reactions. To reduce the need for diagnostic imaging, pretest probability models, such as the Wells model, have been developed to determine the diagnostic likelihood of DVT (**Table 28**) and pulmonary embolism in outpatients (see MKSAP 16 Pulmonary and Critical Care Medicine).

In patients at low risk for a first DVT (Wells score ≤0), the initial use of a moderately to highly sensitive D-dimer assay is appropriate. If the D-dimer test is negative, no further testing is indicated. If positive, an objective imaging study, such as duplex ultrasonography of the proximal vein system, should be performed. In patients at intermediate risk (Wells score 1 or 2), several clinical guidelines consider initial testing with a highly sensitive D-dimer assay to be a preferred initial study, although venous imaging is also considered a reasonable first test. For high-risk patients (Wells score ≥3), proximal duplex ultrasonography, or possibly venography, is indicated as an initial study; D-dimer testing is not recommended as a standalone study for these patients. H

KEY POINT

- In conjunction with D-dimer assays, the Wells criteria have been used to exclude venous thromboembolism without the need for radiographic testing.

H

Use of Anticoagulants

The principal anticoagulants used in venous thromboembolism therapy are UFH, LMWH, fondaparinux, and the oral vitamin K antagonist, warfarin (see Venous Thromboembolism Treatment). The direct thrombin inhibitors lepirudin, argatroban, and bivalirudin are reserved for the treatment

TABLE 27. Criteria for Thrombophilia Testing

Higher Yield	Lower Yield
Young patients (age ≤40 years)	Older patients (age >40 years)
Patients with positive family history (first-degree relative with VTE)	Patients in situations in which artifactual test results may occur (pregnancy, warfarin therapy)
Patients with idiopathic thromboembolism[a]	Patients with cancer
Patients with thromboembolism in unusual sites[b]	Patients with strong transient risk factors (major trauma, surgery)
Patients with recurrent thromboembolism[a]	Patients in whom testing will not influence therapy
Patients with warfarin skin necrosis	Patients with arterial thromboembolism should not be tested for venous thrombophilic states
Pediatric patients with purpura fulminans	
Patients planning future pregnancies	

VTE = venous thromboembolism.

[a]Warrants consideration of long-term therapy regardless of the results of thrombophilia testing.

[b]The impact of thrombophilia on therapy remains unclear.

TABLE 28. Wells Clinical Deep Venous Thrombosis Model

Clinical Characteristic	Score
Active cancer (patient receiving treatment for cancer within 6 months or currently receiving palliative treatment)	1
Paralysis, paresis, or recent plaster cast immobilization of the lower extremities	1
Recently bedridden for 3 days or more, or major surgery within the previous 12 weeks requiring general or regional anesthesia	1
Localized tenderness along the distribution of the deep venous system	1
Entire leg swollen	1
Calf swelling at least 3 cm larger than the asymptomatic side (measured 10 cm below the tibial tuberosity)	1
Pitting edema confined to the symptomatic leg	1
Collateral superficial veins (nonvaricose)	1
Previously documented deep venous thrombosis	1
Alternative diagnosis at least as likely as deep venous thrombosis	-2

A score of less than 2 indicates that a deep venous thrombosis is unlikely. A score of 2 points or higher indicates that a deep venous thrombosis is likely.

Reprinted with permission from Wells PS, Anderson DR, Rodger M, et al. Evaluation of D-dimer in the diagnosis of suspected deep-vein thrombosis. N Engl J Med. 2003;349(13):1227-1235. [PMID: 14507948]

H CONT.

of heparin-induced thrombocytopenia (HIT) (see Platelets). Dabigatran, an oral direct thrombin inhibitor, and rivaroxaban, an oral factor Xa inhibitor, have been recently approved for thromboprophylaxis in nonvalvular atrial fibrillation (see MKSAP 16 Cardiovascular Medicine). Published clinical trials indicate dabigatran and rivaroxaban have equivalent efficacy to warfarin in patients with VTE.

Unfractionated Heparin

UFH is a heterogeneous mixture of glycosaminoglycans (average weight, 15,000 Da; range, 3000-30,000 Da) that bind to antithrombin and accelerate its inhibition of activated serine proteases such as factor Xa and thrombin. UFH bioavailability varies greatly because of avid protein binding. Therefore, laboratory monitoring, usually using the aPTT, is essential. UFH is principally degraded by endothelial cells and macrophages. Renal elimination plays a secondary role. UFH's half-life is approximately 60 minutes. Because body weight roughly approximates blood volume, initial UFH doses should be calculated using a weight-based nomogram (**Table 29**).

Low-Molecular-Weight Heparin

LMWH is derived from UFH by enzymatic or chemical degradation. Its mean molecular weight is 4500 Da (range, 2000-9000 Da). Consequently, LMWH exhibits less protein binding and more predictable pharmacokinetics, allowing administration of weight-based doses without laboratory monitoring. LMWH undergoes renal elimination and has a mean half-life of 3 to 6 hours. LMWH should be used cautiously and in reduced doses in patients with severe kidney insufficiency (creatinine clearance <30 mL/min). Obese patients should receive doses based on actual body weight (for example, weight 200 kg = enoxaparin 200 mg every 12 h).

TABLE 29. Heparin Dosing Nomogram

Heparin Dosing and Monitoring Activities	
Check baseline aPTT, INR, CBC/platelet count	
Give heparin bolus, 80 units/kg, IV	
Begin IV heparin infusion, 18 units/kg/h	
Target aPTT for institution-specific therapeutic range[a]	
aPTT-based Dosing Adjustments	
aPTT	**Dosing Adjustment**
<35 sec[a]	80 units/kg bolus; increase drip by 4 units/kg/h
35–50 sec[a]	40 units/kg bolus; increase drip by 2 units/kg/h
51–70 sec[a]	No change
71–90 sec[a]	Reduce drip by 2 units/kg/h
>90 sec[a]	Hold heparin for 1 h; reduce drip by 3 units/kg/h

aPTT = activated partial thromboplastin time; IV = intravenous; CBC = complete blood count; INR = International Normalized Ratio.

[a]Each laboratory must perform its own in vitro heparin titration curve to establish the therapeutic range for the specific aPTT reagent in use, which is equivalent to a heparin concentration of 0.3-0.7 anti Xa units/mL (by anti Xa assay) or 0.2-0.4 units/mL (by protamine titration assay). The therapeutic range varies depending on the aPTT reagent in use.

Adapted with permission from Raschke RA, Reilly BM, Guidry JR, et al. The weight-based heparin dosing nomogram compared with a standard care nomogram. Ann Intern Med. 1993;119(9):874-881. [PMID: 8214998] Copyright 1993, American College of Physicians.

Fondaparinux

Fondaparinux is a synthetic anticoagulant composed of the five sugar residues found in UFH and LMWH that bind to antithrombin. Because of its short chain length, fondaparinux exclusively catalyzes antithrombin inhibition of factor Xa. Fondaparinux has a half-life of 17 to 21 hours and undergoes renal elimination. It should be used cautiously in patients with

CONT.

a creatinine clearance of 30 to 50 mL/min and avoided in patients with more severe kidney dysfunction.

Warfarin

Vitamin K antagonists such as warfarin inhibit vitamin K oxide reductase, the hepatic enzyme that recycles vitamin K into a reduced form that is essential to the synthesis of factors II, VII, IX, and X and proteins C and S. Consequently, warfarin results in a gradual onset of anticoagulation and must be administered initially with a rapidly acting parenteral anticoagulant. Warfarin has a long half-life (mean, 32-40 h; range, 20-60 h). Therefore, the full impact of a dose change is not manifested for 7 to 10 days. Individual warfarin dose requirements vary by as much as 50- to 100-fold (0.5-50 mg/d) depending on patients' genetics, diet, medications, and comorbidities. Rapid genotyping may allow more accurate individualized dosing in the future, although improved clinical outcomes and the value of genetic testing in this setting have not been established; consequently, genetic testing is currently not recommended for routine use in patients in whom treatment is being initiated. Warfarin metabolism is influenced by many medications that affect the cytochrome P-450 microsomal enzyme system, and attention must be paid to potential drug interactions when medications are prescribed to patients taking warfarin (**Table 30**). Preemptive dose adjustments or close INR monitoring is warranted when co-administration cannot be avoided. Dietary vitamin K content can also strongly influence warfarin therapy. Patients should be instructed to maintain consistent consumption of vitamin K content rather than to avoid vitamin K–containing foods. In fact, low-dose vitamin K supplementation (100-150 µg/d) has been demonstrated to improve INR control in patients with highly variable INRs. Nevertheless, the routine use of vitamin K supplementation in patients on warfarin therapy is not recommended.

Bleeding or thrombosis can occur with warfarin mismanagement; the risk increases exponentially as the INR deviates from the therapeutic range. Consequently, careful INR monitoring is essential. During initial therapy with warfarin and a parenteral anticoagulant, monitoring of the INR several times weekly is indicated. After an INR of 2 is achieved for at least 24 hours, parenteral therapy can be discontinued and the frequency of INR monitoring can be gradually decreased from weekly to monthly in the absence of dose changes; once patients achieve consistently stable INR levels on an established dose, testing frequency may be extended to every 12 weeks. In patients with stable therapeutic INRs with a single out-of-range INR of less than or equal to 0.5 above or below the desired therapeutic range, the current dose should be maintained with repeat testing in 1-2 weeks. Nomograms are particularly useful in helping health care providers make dose adjustments of warfarin in the ambulatory setting based on the patient's INR. Anticoagulant therapy should be reversed in patients with serious bleeding. Warfarin reversal in patients with urgent, life-threatening bleeding requires cessation of warfarin plus intravenous vitamin K (10 mg over 1 hour) ; fresh frozen plasma (FFP) has traditionally been given to replace the vitamin K–dependent coagulation factors, although use of prothrombin complex concentrates (PCCs) is increasingly recommended for this purpose. Only three-factor PCCs (containing factors II, IX, and X) are currently available in the United States and are indicated for treatment of factor IX deficiency; although they may be used to reverse warfarin anticoagulation, the addition of some FFP or recombinant factor VII is usually required for normalization of the INR. Four-factor PCCs, containing all of the vitamin K–dependent factors, are available for warfarin reversal in Canada and Europe and are undergoing clinical trials in the United States. Anticoagulation reversal strategies are listed in **Table 31**. H

TABLE 30. Medications that Influence Warfarin Metabolism

Significant Increase in the INR	Significant Decrease in the INR
Alcohol	Aprepitant
Amiodarone	Barbiturates
Cimetidine	Carbamazepine
Ciprofloxacin	Cholestyramine
Citalopram	Griseofulvin
Clofibrate	Mercaptopurine
Diltiazem	Mesalamine
Erythromycin	Methimazole
Fenofibrate	Nafcillin
Fluconazole	Rifabutin
Isoniazid	Rifampin
Metronidazole	
Miconazole	
NSAIDs/COX-2 inhibitors	
Omeprazole	
Propafenone	
Propranolol	
Quinidine	
Sulfinpyrazone	
Sulfisoxazole	
Tamoxifen	
Trimethoprim-sulfamethoxazole	
Voriconazole	

COX-2 = cyclooxygenase 2.

KEY POINTS

- Dabigatran, an oral antithrombin agent that does not require laboratory monitoring, is approved for thromboprophylaxis in patients with nonvalvular atrial fibrillation.

- In patients receiving unfractionated heparin, laboratory monitoring, usually using the aPTT, is essential.
- Because of warfarin's long half-life, the full impact of a dose change is not manifested for 7 to 10 days.

Prevention

Evidence-based prophylaxis reduces the incidence of VTE by 50% to 60%. Nevertheless, only 50% of hospitalized patients currently receive adequate VTE prophylaxis. All hospitalized patients should be assessed for their risk of VTE and contraindications to anticoagulant prophylaxis on admission and receive risk-appropriate prophylaxis. VTE risk increases as the number of risk factors increases (**Table 32**). In patients in whom the potential benefit of prophylaxis outweighs the risk of bleeding, UFH given twice or thrice daily and LMWH are equally effective in preventing VTE in medical inpatients, whereas LMWH is associated with fewer clinical VTEs in surgical inpatients, patients following stroke, and patients with cancer. Dose-adjusted warfarin (INR 2-3), LMWH, and fondaparinux are recommended for orthopedic surgery, whereas LMWH is preferred for trauma surgery. In patients with significant kidney dysfunction (creatinine clearance <30 mL/min), UFH is preferred over LMWH and fondaparinux because of the potential for accumulation with the latter agents. Morbidly obese patients should probably receive increased doses of LMWH and UFH, but evidence-based guidelines are lacking.

The utility of any form of mechanical prophylaxis is poorly studied in medical patients; therefore, the risks and benefits of this form of prophylaxis should be carefully weighed on a case by case basis, particularly regarding graduated compression stockings because of unproven efficacy and the risk of lower extremity skin damage. Pharmacologic prophylaxis therefore is preferred over mechanical prophylaxis. Medical patients eligible for prophylaxis but with contraindications to pharmacologic therapy should receive mechanical prophylaxis with intermittent pneumatic compression devices until the increased thromboembolic risk is

TABLE 31. Anticoagulation Reversal

Anticoagulant	Reversal	Additional Considerations
Unfractionated heparin (half-life 60 min)	Protamine, 1 mg/100 units unfractionated heparin, infuse slowly (<5 mg/min)	Maximum dose: 100 mg in 2 h, risk of anaphylaxis
Low-molecular-weight heparin (half-life 3.5-7 h)	Within 8 hours: protamine, 1 mg/1 mg enoxaparin or 1 mg/100 IU dalteparin/tinzaparin	Maximum dose: 100 mg in 2 h, risk of anaphylaxis
	More than 8 hours: protamine, 0.5 mg/1 mg enoxaparin or 100 IU dalteparin	Reverses 60% of enoxaparin and 80% of dalteparin
Fondaparinux (half-life 17-21 h)[a]	Protamine ineffective Recombinant human factor VIIa, 90 µg/kg IV may be beneficial	Recombinant human factor VIIa has been associated with thromboembolic events
Warfarin (effective half-life 20-60 h)[b]	Vitamin K, 10 mg IV over 1 hour, PLUS Prothrombin complex concentrate, 25-50 units/kg IV plus FFP 2 units; or FFP, 15-20 mL/kg IV, or Recombinant human factor VIIa, 25-90 µg/kg IV	Rapid administration of vitamin K is associated with an increased risk of anaphylaxis Prothrombin complex concentrate and recombinant human factor VIIa are preferred over FFP, although they may be associated with risk of thromboembolism
Direct thrombin inhibitors (25-80 min)[c]	Activated prothrombin complex concentrates, 50-100 units/kg IV Hemofiltration with a polysulfone membrane (for lepirudin, bivalirudin) Hemodialysis (for dabigatran) Oral activated charcoal (within 2 hours of dabigatran dose)	Activated prothrombin complex concentrates have been associated with a risk of thromboembolism

FFP = fresh frozen plasma; IV = intravenous.

[a]No true antidote exists for fondaparinux. Beneficial effects on hemostatic tests have been noted in normal volunteers on fondaparinux who were treated with recombinant human factor VIIa.

[b]Prothrombin complex concentrates preferred rapid reversal strategy for life-threatening bleeding in conjunction with intravenous vitamin K. FFP requires greater preparation and administration time, whereas recombinant human factor VIIa only provides one of four vitamin K–dependent factors and is therefore suboptimal for warfarin reversal. A recent review recommended against rhFVIIa use for warfarin reversal.

[c]No true antidote for intravenous or oral direct thrombin inhibitors. Lepirudin, bivalirudin, and dabigatran can be removed with hemodialysis/hemofiltration. In life-threatening bleeding, activated prothrombin complex concentrates reduced the bleeding time in animal models of direct thrombin inhibitor therapy.

Adapted from Crowther MA, Warkentin TE. Bleeding risk and the management of bleeding complications in patients undergoing anticoagulant therapy: focus on new anticoagulant agents. Blood. 2008;111(10):4871-4879. [PMID: 18309033]

TABLE 32. VTE Risk Factors and Prophylaxis

VTE Risk Factors	Prophylaxis Options	Contraindications to Pharmacologic Prophylaxis
NYHA class III/IV HF Acute respiratory failure Active cancer Stroke with paresis History of VTE Acute infectious illness Age >60 years Thrombophilia Acute rheumatic disease Inflammatory bowel disease Immobility	Unfractionated heparin, 5000 units SC every 8-12 hours Enoxaparin, 40 mg SC every 24 h Dalteparin, 5000 units SC every 24 h Fondaparinux, 2.5 mg SC every 24 h Or Intermittent pneumatic compression devices if pharmacologic prophylaxis is contraindicated	Active or high risk for bleeding Coagulopathy (abnormal aPTT or PT not due to lupus anticoagulant) Thrombocytopenia (platelets <50,000/µL [50×10^9/L])

Note: In patients with stroke, active cancer, and surgery, low-molecular-weight heparin is superior to unfractionated heparin.

aPTT = activated partial thromboplastin time; PT = prothrombin time; HF = heart failure; NYHA = New York Heart Association; SC = subcutaneous; VTE = venous thromboembolism.

TABLE 33. Pre- and Postoperative Bridging Guidelines for Patients Receiving Warfarin

Guideline	Grade of Recommendation[a]
Stop warfarin therapy ~5 days preoperatively	1C
Resume warfarin therapy ~12-24 h postoperatively if hemostasis is secure	2C
For patients with MHV, AF, or VTE at high risk of TE, bridging with full-dose SC LMWH or IV UFH is recommended	2C
For patients with MHV, AF, or VTE at low risk of TE, no bridging is recommended	2C
Administer last dose of full-dose SC LMWH 24 h preoperatively	2C
If receiving IV UFH, stop infusion 4-6 h preoperatively	2C
Resume full-dose SC LMWH following high bleeding-risk procedures ~48–72 h postoperatively if hemostasis is secured	2C

MHV = mechanical heart valve; AF = atrial fibrillation; VTE = venous thromboembolism; TE = thromboembolism; SC LMWH = subcutaneous low-molecular-weight heparin; IV UFH = intravenous unfractionated heparin; INR = International Normalized Ratio.

[a]Grade 1 recommendations are considered strong and indicate that the benefits do (or do not) outweigh risks, burdens, and costs, whereas grade 2 recommendations are referred to as suggestions and imply that individual patient values may lead to different management choices.

Adapted with permission from Douketis JD, Spyropoulos AC, Spencer FA, et al. Perioperative management of antithrombotic therapy: antithrombotic therapy and prevention of thrombosis, 9th ed: American College of Chest Physicians evidence-based clinical practice guidelines. Chest. 2012;141(2)(suppl):e326S-e350S.

CONT.

no longer present based on demonstrated efficacy in a surgical patient population, although the benefit of intermittent pneumatic compression devices in medical patients has not yet been studied. Graduated compression stockings have also not shown to be of benefit in stroke patients and were associated with increased skin complications. Therefore, they should not be used in this population until data supporting their utility are published. For most patients, VTE prophylaxis should continue for the duration of the hospitalization. Patients undergoing elective hip arthroplasty and hip fracture surgery should receive prophylaxis for up to 35 days after surgery. Continuation of prophylaxis is suggested for 4 weeks following surgery in patients undergoing abdominal/pelvic cancer surgery and knee arthroplasty. Patients who have experienced major trauma should continue prophylaxis throughout inpatient rehabilitation. For more information on perioperative venous thromboembolism prophylaxis, including bridging guidelines, see MKSAP 16 General Internal Medicine and **Table 33**.

See MKSAP 16 Cardiovascular Medicine for discussion of thromboprophylaxis in patients with atrial fibrillation. H

KEY POINTS

- All hospitalized patients with venous thromboembolism risk factors and no significant contraindications should receive risk-appropriate venous thromboembolism prophylaxis to decrease their risk of venous thromboembolism by approximately 50%.

- Fondaparinux is approved for prophylaxis in hip and knee replacement, abdominal surgery, and treatment of venous thromboembolism.

H

Treatment

In recent years, LMWH and fondaparinux have largely replaced UFH in the treatment of acute VTE because they have more reliable pharmacokinetics and facilitate outpatient management. Stable patients with uncomplicated DVT can be treated as outpatients, whereas patients at high risk for adverse outcomes, such as most patients with pulmonary embolism, require inpatient management (see MKSAP 16 Pulmonary and Critical Care Medicine).

Warfarin remains the mainstay of chronic VTE therapy. Warfarin therapy may be initiated on the first or second day of heparin therapy. Because factor II and X levels require at least 5 days to decline, parenteral anticoagulation should overlap with warfarin for at least 5 days and until an INR of 2 or more is achieved. The initial warfarin dose may be based on a patient's predicted maintenance dose using available calculators, although there is some evidence that an initial dose of 10 mg/d for the first 2 days of treatment is reasonable. Higher initial doses should be avoided because they can lead to supratherapeutic INR values and premature discontinuation of parenteral therapy. Patients should be followed closely with frequent INR studies at the initiation of therapy to achieve values consistently within the desired range. Once patients achieve consistently stable INR levels on an established dose, their INR monitoring may eventually be extended to every 12 weeks for the duration of treatment. In patients with stable therapeutic INRs with a single out-of-range INR of less than or equal to 0.5 above or below the desired therapeutic range, the current dose should be maintained with repeat testing in 1-2 weeks. The decision to treat with parenteral anticoagulation for subtherapeutic INR values below this value depends on the indication for anticoagulation and the risk for further thrombosis. The duration of warfarin therapy is determined by the type of thrombotic event and the presence or absence of situational triggers (provoked vs. unprovoked), thrombophilic states, active cancer, and a history of thrombotic events. See **Table 34** for duration of VTE therapy.

Patients with idiopathic (unprovoked) VTE are at high risk for recurrence, with approximately 50% experiencing a recurrence within 10 years; therefore, these patients often require longer-term anticoagulation. Elevated D-dimer levels on or after discontinuation of therapy and the presence of persistent thrombosis on duplex ultrasound imaging have been associated with a higher risk of recurrent VTE after discontinuation of anticoagulation. Risk assessment models to identify patients with idiopathic VTE at low risk for recurrence are currently being studied. Conversely, patients with strong situational triggers for thrombosis such as major surgery or trauma (provoked) can receive limited-duration therapy (3-6 months) and experience a low risk of recurrence (0.7% per year). Because the risk of major bleeding with warfarin is at least 1% to 2% per year, the risk-to-benefit ratio of continued therapy in low-risk patients is unfavorable. Patients with distal DVT, such as in the calf vein, should receive anticoagulation for 3 months.

In patients with advanced cancer, LMWH is associated with a 50% lower incidence of recurrent thromboembolism than warfarin and may be the preferred VTE therapy, especially for patients who are expected to have significant longevity.

Catheter-directed pharmacomechanical thrombolysis or surgical thrombectomy are options for patients with massive extremity thrombosis. See MKSAP 16 Pulmonary and Critical Care Medicine for discussion of pulmonary embolism.

Placement of a vena cava filter is appropriate treatment for acute DVT with or without pulmonary embolism in patients with contraindications to anticoagulation. A retrievable filter is indicated unless the patient will never be a candidate for anticoagulation. When therapeutic anticoagulation can be safely resumed, removal of the retrievable filter is

TABLE 34. Duration of Therapy for Venous Thromboembolism

Type of Thrombotic Event	Duration of Therapy
Triggered DVT (for example, associated with surgery, trauma)	3 months
Triggered PE (for example, associated with surgery, trauma)	3 months
Idiopathic DVT	At least 3 months, with consideration of extended therapy based on potential risks and benefits
Idiopathic PE	At least 3 months, with consideration of extended therapy based on potential risks and benefits
Cancer-associated VTE	Indefinite or as long as cancer is active or being treated
Recurrent VTE	Indefinite
Distal DVT (e.g., calf)	3 months

DVT = deep venous thrombosis; PE = pulmonary embolism; VTE = venous thromboembolism.

Adapted from Kearon C, Akl EA, Comerota AJ, et al. Antithrombotic therapy for VTE disease: antithrombotic therapy and prevention of thrombosis, 9th ed: American College of Chest Physicians evidence-based clinical practice guidelines. Chest. 2012;141(2)(suppl):e419S-e494S.

CONT.

necessary to avoid filter-related complications such as filter-component migration or inferior vena cava thrombosis.

Superficial vein thrombophlebitis has traditionally been treated with compression stockings and NSAIDs. However, because DVT (6% to 44%) or symptomatic pulmonary embolism (2% to 13%) develops in some patients, the use of anticoagulant therapy should be considered, particularly in those with superficial thrombi in the proximal greater saphenous vein or superficial thrombosis of 5 cm or more in length. Objective imaging should be considered to document the extent of thrombosis and determine whether there is evidence of proximal, extensive, or progressive superficial vein thrombophlebitis that would benefit from anticoagulation. H

KEY POINTS

- Low-molecular-weight heparin allows for administration of weight-based doses without laboratory monitoring and can be used as an alternative to unfractionated heparin for many indications.
- In patients with advanced cancer, low-molecular-weight heparin is associated with a 50% lower incidence of recurrent thromboembolism.
- Placement of a vena cava filter is appropriate treatment of acute deep venous thrombosis or pulmonary embolism in patients with contraindications to anticoagulation.

Hematologic Issues in Pregnancy

Gestational Anemia

Normal gestation is associated with mild maternal anemia despite an increase in erythropoietin production and red cell mass. Anemia in pregnancy predominantly results from a dramatic increase in plasma volume that is proportionally larger than the increase in erythrocyte production. The resulting physiologic state in pregnancy is characterized by increased capacity for oxygen delivery to the developing fetus, with decreased blood viscosity to ensure oxygen delivery.

Anemia is typically apparent by week 8 of gestation and continues throughout most of the third trimester. Several weeks before delivery, anemia stabilizes and then rapidly improves before delivery. Gestational anemia typically results in hemoglobin levels greater than 11.0 g/dL (110 g/L) in the first and third trimesters and greater than 10.5 g/dL (105 g/L) in the second trimester. Healthy pregnant women have normochromic and normocytic indices. Hematologic evaluation is necessary in pregnant women with marked anemia, additional types of cytopenia, abnormal reticulocyte counts, or abnormal cellular indices. Severe anemia or anemia accompanied by other types of cytopenia always requires further evaluation.

Iron Deficiency

Iron deficiency is a major issue in pregnancy, with a worldwide incidence as high as 40%. Because the developing fetus selectively uses iron from the maternal circulation and because of the increased red cell mass accompanying pregnancy, iron requirements typically exceed iron intake in pregnant women. As in nonpregnant patients, pregnant patients with iron deficiency have a microcytic, hypochromic anemia with low serum iron and ferritin levels and an elevated total iron-binding capacity. In pregnant women without obvious blood loss with red cell indices suggestive of iron deficiency, oral iron supplementation is appropriate, but additional evaluation is not necessary.

Although iron deficiency leads to preterm delivery and low birth weight in neonates, routine iron supplementation for pregnant patients who are not iron deficient is not supported by randomized trials. However, despite the absence of data, most pregnant women in the United States receive iron supplementation as a matter of routine. Oral iron salts are typically used and are effective for pregnant patients with iron deficiency. Parenteral iron is necessary only in patients with malabsorption. Iron dextran is a pregnancy class C drug (safety uncertain) because it confers a risk for anaphylaxis and other side effects. Newer parenteral preparations, including iron sucrose and ferric gluconate, are better tolerated and do not appear to cause anaphylaxis. As such, they are pregnancy class B drugs (presumed safe); however, larger clinical trials are needed to firmly establish the safety and efficacy of these preparations in the treatment of iron deficiency in pregnant patients.

Folate Deficiency

Because of folate needs in the developing fetus, the requirement for folate in pregnant patients is nearly double the normal requirement. Additionally, folate supplementation has been shown to decrease the risk for neural tube defects. Consequently, folate is routinely added to prenatal vitamin preparations in the United States. Folate deficiency occurs rarely in pregnant patients in the United States because of adequate prenatal care and folate supplementation of grains and cereals.

KEY POINTS

- Gestational anemia typically results in hemoglobin levels greater than 11.0 g/dL (110 g/L) in the first and third trimesters and greater than 10.5 g/dL (105 g/L) in the second trimester.
- In pregnant women without obvious blood loss with red cell indices suggestive of iron deficiency, oral iron supplementation is appropriate, but additional evaluation is not necessary.
- The folate requirement in pregnant patients is nearly double the normal requirement, and folate supplementation decreases the risk for neural tube defects.

H Sickle Cell Disease

Patients with homozygous sickle cell (SS) anemia have later menarche, later first pregnancies, and increased complications in pregnancy, including fetal loss and low-birth-weight neonates. The pregnancy-related mortality in patients with SS anemia is significantly higher than that in the general population and is estimated to range from 0.5% to 2%. Because of the inherent complications in achieving full-term gestation for pregnant patients who are homozygous for SS anemia, a team-based approach to management, including collaboration among obstetricians, pediatricians, hematologists, and internists, is necessary. Patients with SS anemia who are of childbearing age should consult their physicians before planning a pregnancy.

Eclampsia and hypertension, initially thought to be more common in pregnant patients with SS anemia, appear to occur with the same frequency as in patients with normal hemoglobin. Women with sickle cell trait are not anemic and do not have increased obstetric complications. Conversely, women who are compound heterozygotes for hemoglobin S and have β-thalassemia or hemoglobin C experience obstetric complications at a rate that is intermediate between healthy patients and patients homozygous for SS anemia.

Randomized trials have not found a clinical benefit to routine erythrocyte transfusion during pregnancy in patients with SS anemia. However, transfusions may be appropriate for severely anemic patients with signs and symptoms of heart failure. Similarly, no data support superiority of cesarean or vaginal delivery in pregnant patients with SS anemia.

The incidence of pain crises in patients with SS anemia is increased in pregnancy, and opiate analgesics can be used. One exception is the use of meperidine, which can lower the seizure threshold owing to accumulation of the toxic metabolite normeperidine. Because of potential teratogenicity, hydroxyurea is contraindicated in pregnancy and should be stopped at least 3 months before conception. H

KEY POINTS

- Patients with homozygous sickle cell (SS) anemia have increased complications during pregnancy and a resulting higher pregnancy-related mortality compared with the general population.
- Although routine erythrocyte transfusions have not been found to be beneficial in pregnant patients with SS anemia, transfusions may be appropriate for those who are severely anemic with signs and symptoms of heart failure.
- Opiate analgesics, except for meperidine, can be used to treat pain crises in pregnant patients with SS anemia; hydroxyurea is also contraindicated in pregnancy and should be stopped at least 3 months before conception.

Thrombocytopenia in Pregnancy

Gestational Thrombocytopenia

Thrombocytopenia occurs in approximately 5% of pregnant women, usually in the last trimester of pregnancy. Causes include a combination of hemodilution and accelerated platelet clearance. Gestational thrombocytopenia should not cause maternal or fetal complications such as fetal thrombocytopenia.

A platelet count lower than 50,000/µL (50×10^9/L) developing in the third trimester is not characteristic of gestational thrombocytopenia and may indicate other diagnoses. Repeating the complete blood count in 1 to 2 weeks is appropriate in affected patients.

Immune Thrombocytopenic Purpura

Adult women of childbearing age may have chronic immune thrombocytopenic purpura (ITP), which occurs in 1 to 5 of every 10,000 pregnancies. ITP may present initially during pregnancy as an incidental finding on a routine complete blood count during prenatal screening. Additionally, women with known ITP may have a flare during pregnancy, and severe ITP-associated bleeding may first occur during pregnancy. As with nonpregnant patients, ITP is a diagnosis of exclusion and should be distinguished from thrombocytopenia occurring in other pregnancy-associated conditions, such as preeclampsia, the HELLP (*h*emolysis, *el*evated *l*iver enzymes, and *l*ow *p*latelet counts) syndrome, thrombotic thrombocytopenic purpura, and disseminated intravascular coagulation. Thrombocytopenia developing in the first two trimesters of pregnancy or a platelet count lower than 50,000/µL (50×10^9/L) distinguishes ITP from gestational thrombocytopenia. Treatment is determined by maternal platelet counts. No therapy may be necessary for asymptomatic patients with platelet counts higher than 50,000/µL (50×10^9/L). The goal platelet count should be higher than 30,000 to 40,000/µL ($30\text{-}40 \times 10^9$/L) until the end of the third trimester, when an increased platelet count is necessary to allow for neuraxial anesthesia and a safe delivery. Cesarean delivery usually requires a platelet count higher than 50,000/µL (50×10^9/L), whereas neuraxial anesthesia requires a platelet count higher than 80,000/µL (80×10^9/L). Corticosteroids and intravenous immune globulin may be used for therapy. Splenectomy and other immunosuppressive therapy for ITP is usually not required.

Thrombocytopenia develops in 9% to 15% of neonates because of antiplatelet antibodies crossing the placenta, with intracranial hemorrhage occurring in 1.5% of neonates. However, fetal platelet counts cannot be reliably predicted by maternal platelet counts. Fetal scalp sampling is usually erroneous, and percutaneous umbilical cord blood sampling confers a 1% risk for miscarriage. Cesarean delivery should not be performed routinely in pregnant patients with ITP but should be reserved for those in whom standard obstetrical indications exist.

H Microangiopathy of Pregnancy

Several disorders are characterized by microangiopathic hemolytic anemia (MAHA) and thrombocytopenia during pregnancy, and each has its own diagnostic features requiring specific treatment. Preeclampsia, the HELLP syndrome, thrombotic thrombocytopenic purpura (TTP)–hemolytic uremic syndrome (HUS), and acute fatty liver of pregnancy (AFLP) have different clinical features but with significant overlap (**Table 35**).

Preeclampsia typically presents with hypertension, peripheral edema, and proteinuria, most commonly in the third trimester of pregnancy. TTP-HUS is characterized by MAHA and thrombocytopenia developing in the first or second trimesters. Additionally, neurologic findings and fever are more common in TTP-HUS than in the other syndromes. ADAMTS13 deficiency may be found, but diagnosis and therapy should not be delayed pending these results. The HELLP syndrome is characterized by right upper quadrant pain and elevated liver enzymes. Disseminated intravascular coagulation parameters may be found in patients with preeclampsia and the HELLP syndrome but should be absent in those with TTP-HUS. Patients with AFLP have cholestatic findings on liver chemistry tests, hypoglycemia, and a markedly increased prothrombin time and activated partial thromboplastin time. Liver biopsy may show steatosis, necrosis, and hemorrhage in patients with the HELLP syndrome and AFLP.

Generally, if preeclampsia or the HELLP syndrome is suspected in the third or late second trimester, the treatment of choice is delivery of the fetus. If MAHA and thrombocytopenia worsen after delivery, or if they are present in the first or early second trimester, then TTP-HUS should be suspected and plasma exchange begun. H

TABLE 35. Features of Preeclampsia, the HELLP Syndrome, TTP-HUS, and Acute Fatty Liver of Pregnancy

Diagnosis	Clinical Features
Preeclampsia	Hypertension
	Peripheral edema
	Proteinuria
	44% of cases occur postpartum
	4%-12% of patients develop HELLP syndrome
HELLP syndrome	MAHA (elevated LDH, schistocytes on peripheral blood smear)
	Thrombocytopenia
	Right upper quadrant pain
	Elevated aminotransferases
	Normal PT and aPTT
	Liver biopsy shows necrosis, fibrosis, steatosis, hemorrhage
	50% of patients are normotensive
	6% of patients have no proteinuria
TTP-HUS	MAHA
	Thrombocytopenia
	Fever
	Kidney dysfunction
	Neurologic manifestations
Acute fatty liver of pregnancy	Cholestatic picture of liver chemistry testing abnormalities
	Increased PT and aPTT
	Hypoglycemia
	Severe DIC
	Liver biopsy shows necrosis, fibrosis, steatosis, hemorrhage

aPTT = activated partial thromboplastin time; DIC = disseminated intravascular coagulation; HELLP = hemolysis, elevated liver enzymes, low platelet count; HUS = hemolytic uremic syndrome; LDH = lactate dehydrogenase; MAHA = microangiopathic hemolytic anemia; PT = prothrombin time; TTP = thrombotic thrombocytopenic purpura.

KEY POINTS

- Thrombocytopenia occurs in the last trimester of pregnancy and is generally not characterized by platelet counts lower than 50,000/µL (50×10^9/L).
- The goal platelet count in pregnant patients with immune thrombocytopenic purpura should be higher than 30,000 to 40,000/µL ($30\text{-}40 \times 10^9$/L) until the end of the third trimester, when an increased platelet count is necessary to allow for neuraxial anesthesia and a safe delivery.
- Preeclampsia typically presents with hypertension, peripheral edema, and proteinuria, most commonly in the third trimester of pregnancy.
- The HELLP (hemolysis, elevated liver enzymes, and low platelet counts) syndrome is characterized by right upper quadrant pain and elevated liver enzymes.

Thrombophilia and Venous Thromboembolism in Pregnancy

Epidemiology, Pathophysiology, and Risk Factors

Pregnancy is associated with a fourfold to fivefold increased risk for venous thromboembolism (VTE) that increases throughout pregnancy and peaks after delivery, returning to baseline 6 to 12 weeks postpartum (**Figure 23**). Risk factors for pregnancy-associated VTE are listed in **Table 36**.

Pregnancy is associated with decreases in protein S activity and protein S antigen level, normal total protein S levels, and increases in factor VIII, von Willebrand factor, and plasminogen activator inhibitor 1 and 2 levels, producing a procoagulant phenotype. These alterations synergize with congenital thrombophilia such as factor V Leiden to produce even greater prothrombotic tendencies. In addition, the gravid uterus reduces mobility and compresses the left iliac venous system, resulting in stasis and venous distention, further increasing the risk for clot formation. Deep venous thrombosis (DVT) (80% of venous thromboembolic events) predominantly affects the proximal left leg.

Pharmacologic VTE prophylaxis should be considered after delivery in hospitalized women with multiple VTE risk

TABLE 36. Risk Factors for Pregnancy-associated Venous Thromboembolism

Medical Condition/Risk Factor	Odds Ratio (95% CI)
Previous VTE	24.8 (17.1-36)
SLE	8.7 (5.8-13)
Heart disease	7.1 (6.2-8.3)
Sickle cell anemia	6.7 (4.4-10.1)
Obesity	4.4 (3.4-5.7)
Anemia	2.6 (2.2-2.9)
Age >35 years	2.1 (2.0-2.3)
Diabetes	2.0 (1.4-2.7)
Hypertension	1.8 (1.4-2.3)
Smoking	1.7 (1.4-2.1)
Black race	1.4 (1.2-1.7)

SLE = systemic lupus erythematosus. VTE = venous thromboembolism.

Adapted from James AH, Jamison MG, Brancazio LR, Myers ER. Venous thromboembolism during pregnancy and the postpartum period: incidence, risk factors, and mortality. Am J Obstet Gynecol. 2006;194(5):1311-1315. [PMID: 16647915] and Chunilal SD, Bates SM. Venous thromboembolism in pregnancy: diagnosis, management and prevention. Thromb Haemost. 2009;101(3):428-438. [PMID: 19277402]

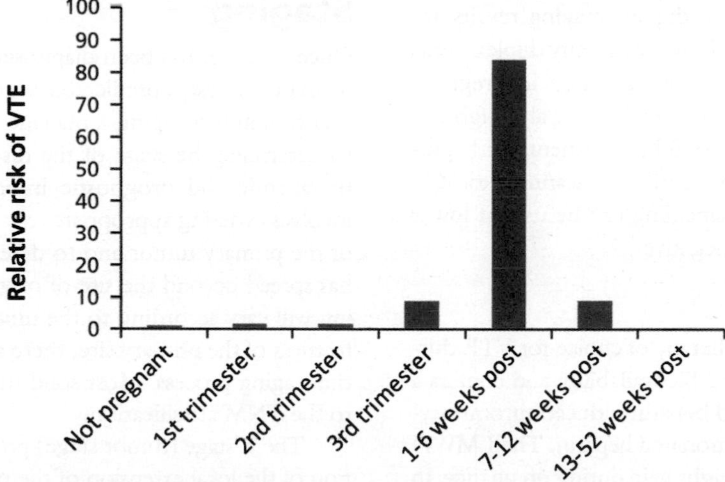

FIGURE 23. Relative risk of venous thromboembolism during pregnancy and the postpartum period.

Reprinted with permission from Pomp ER, Lenselink AM, Rosendaal FR, Doggen CJ. Pregnancy, the postpartum period and prothrombotic defects: risk of venous thrombosis in the MEGA study. J Thromb Haemost. 2008;6(4):632-637.

factors (age >35 years, cesarean delivery, immobility). Mechanical prophylaxis (for example, intermittent pneumatic compression devices) is appropriate for women at lower risk. Previous VTE increases the risk of pregnancy-associated VTE by 3.5-fold. Because the risk of recurrent VTE is highest in the postpartum period, all patients with previous VTE are prescribed postpartum anticoagulant prophylaxis for at least 6 weeks. Women at high risk for recurrent VTE during pregnancy (previous idiopathic, pregnancy-, or estrogen-associated VTE or concomitant thrombophilia) are prescribed antepartum and postpartum prophylactic anticoagulation. Prophylactic-dose anticoagulation (for example, enoxaparin, 40 mg/d) is used for low-risk patients, whereas intermediate-dose (for example, enoxaparin, 40 mg twice daily) or therapeutic-dose anticoagulation (for example, enoxaparin, 1 mg/kg twice daily) is reserved for high-risk patients. Patients with thrombophilia in the absence of previous thrombosis are treated with postpartum prophylactic-dose anticoagulation except for patients with antithrombin deficiency, who receive antepartum and postpartum intermediate-dose anticoagulant prophylaxis. More detailed recommendations are not available owing to the limited number of studies in pregnant women.

Diagnosis

In pregnant patients with suspected lower extremity DVT, proximal duplex compression ultrasonography is the diagnostic study of choice instead of initial evaluation with D-dimer testing. If this initial study is negative, then subsequent serial ultrasound studies at days 3 and 7 after presentation are indicated to exclude DVT. Another option is to obtain a sensitive D-dimer assay following the initial negative ultrasound study; if negative, no further evaluation is suggested, and if positive, serial ultrasound studies are indicated. MRI venography is useful for less assessable central vessels, such as the inferior vena cava, if ultrasound duplex imaging results are negative and suspicion is high. Lower extremity duplex ultrasonography is also a reasonable initial study in pregnant patients with suspected pulmonary embolism, although the study may be normal in at least 50% of patients with pulmonary embolism. Ventilation perfusion scanning or CT angiography with abdominal shielding can be used if lower extremity imaging results are negative.

Management

Weight-based LMWH is the therapy of choice for VTE during pregnancy. It has improved bioavailability and confers a lower risk for osteoporosis and heparin-induced thrombocytopenia compared with unfractionated heparin. The LMWH dose should be adjusted for weight gain during pregnancy. In the last month of pregnancy, use of weight-based unfractionated heparin is a consideration because of its shorter half-life and more complete protamine reversibility.

Induced deliveries facilitate safe late-term anticoagulation management. In the event of VTE occurring within 1 month prior to delivery, placement of vena cava filter is a consideration. Continuing anticoagulation for at least 6 to 12 weeks postpartum and for a minimum of 3 to 6 months during the pregnancy plus postpartum period is appropriate. Warfarin may be used by nursing mothers postpartum because it is not excreted into breast milk in any appreciable quantities.

KEY POINTS

- Pregnancy is associated with a four- to fivefold increased risk of venous thromboembolism that increases during pregnancy and peaks after delivery, returning to baseline 6 to 12 weeks postpartum.
- Duplex ultrasonography is the diagnostic study of choice for pregnant patients with suspected lower extremity venous thromboembolism.
- Weight-based, low-molecular-weight heparin is the therapy of choice for venous thromboembolism during pregnancy.
- The duration of anticoagulation for venous thromboembolism in a pregnant patient is at least 6 months and should extend 6 weeks beyond parturition.

Issues in Oncology

The field of oncology is changing rapidly as a result of scientific advancements that support the care of patients. Many of these advancements devoted to specific tumor types will be described in later chapters of this book. However, basic concepts of staging and treatment can be applied to the approach and management of all patients with cancer.

Staging

Once a patient has been diagnosed with cancer and referred to an oncologist, a predictable sequence of events occurs that is critical in developing a management plan. The first step is to determine the stage of the disease, which provides both therapeutic and prognostic information. Staging typically involves ordering appropriate tests to identify the local extent of the primary tumor and to determine whether the disease has spread beyond the site of origin. Although specific staging will vary according to the unique anatomic and biologic features of the primary site, there are many common steps to the staging process. Most solid tumors are staged according to the TNM classification.

The T stage (tumor stage) provides a pathologic description of the local extension of the primary tumor. If surgery is the primary therapy, the pathologist measures the tumor size and determines the T stage using a microscopic description of the tumor's level of tissue penetration. If the pathologist stages the disease, the letter "p" precedes the T stage (for example, pT3). If radiation therapy or chemotherapy is used preoperatively, which potentially results in tumor shrinkage before surgical resection, the letters "yp" precede the pathologic T stage. If chemotherapy or radiation therapy is the definitive treatment, only the radiographic assessment of tumor size is used (that is, preceding letters are not added to indicate clinical staging). Tumor stages are typically listed as T0 to T4, with 0 indicating no evidence of tumor and increasing numbers reflecting larger tumor size or greater local tissue invasion.

The N stage (node stage) refers to the presence or absence of lymph node involvement by the cancer. For certain cancer types, removing a minimum number of lymph nodes is necessary for accurate staging and prognostic assessment. In breast cancer and malignant melanoma, a procedure to identify a sentinel lymph node is performed. The sentinel node is presumed to be the first lymph node that lies in the drainage path of the primary tumor. If the cancer does not involve the sentinel node, involvement of other regional lymph nodes is unlikely, and these nodes do not need to be removed. Cancerous involvement of the sentinel lymph node requires a more extensive dissection to identify and remove any other potential nodal metastases. Lymph node staging is typically classified as N0 to N3, with 0 indicating no regional lymph node involvement and higher numbers reflecting increasing numbers of involved nodes or spread to more distant lymph nodes.

The M stage (metastasis stage) indicates whether or not there is systemic spread of the cancer beyond the local lymph nodes. Cancer staging reflects either the absence (M0) or presence (M1) of metastases. However, for most tumors, the extent of metastatic spread does not change the M stage.

Tumor staging classifications are frequently updated to incorporate recent data that affect the diagnostic evaluation, treatment, and prognosis of a patient with cancer. Such staging systems are often complex but critical to the oncologist in developing an appropriate treatment plan and defining prognosis. Generally, the degree of lymph node involvement has a greater negative impact on prognosis than does a higher T stage, and the presence of metastatic disease beyond lymph node involvement has the worst prognosis.

KEY POINTS

- Staging of newly diagnosed cancer typically involves ordering appropriate tests to identify the local extent of the primary tumor and to determine whether the disease has spread beyond the site of origin.
- Most solid tumors are staged according to the TNM classification.

Treatment

Surgical Resection

Surgical resection is the primary treatment modality for almost all malignancies. The preoperative staging evaluation is performed to determine whether the extent of the cancer is confined to the primary organ site and regional lymph nodes and, if so, whether both can be safely resected. Methods for identifying resectability may include radiographic studies, endoscopic procedures, and biopsies. For nearly all solid tumors, the potential for cure is usually related to whether or not the tumor and its local extensions can be completely removed at surgery.

Surgical resection allows determination of the pathologic stage of the tumor, which, in turn, determines the prognosis. The percentage of likelihood of cure for resected tumors decreases with advancing T and N stages. Knowing the natural history and initial cancer stage allows oncologists to identify the statistical risk for a future local recurrence or development of distant disease. Potential local recurrences are minimized with radiation therapy, which is sometimes recommended before surgical resection. Cancers that are not cured by surgery often recur as a result of microscopic spread of the cancer before resection.

Adjuvant Therapy

Adjuvant therapy, typically chemotherapy, is given in the absence of any objective evidence of remaining cancer and has been demonstrated to increase the statistical chances of cure for many cancers, theoretically by eradicating any micrometastases. For many years, only patients with breast and colon cancer had manifest benefits from this type of treatment. More recently, adjuvant therapy in most tumor types, including brain, lung, esophageal, gastric, and pancreatic, has proven beneficial. A reality that needs to be addressed when adjuvant therapy is recommended is that some patients will have been cured through surgical resection alone or may have disease recurrence despite the addition of chemotherapy. As such, providing therapy to these patients would not present any additional benefit and would expose them to unnecessary toxicity. Nonetheless, all patients medically fit enough to tolerate chemotherapy are considered for adjuvant treatment with the understanding that many will not benefit. Tools are needed to identify specific patients who are more or less likely to benefit from adjuvant therapy. In breast cancer, the Onco*type* DX® assay analyzes 23 genes within an individual's tumor. This test has been demonstrated to identify women with little likelihood of benefit from adjuvant chemotherapy, and in these patients, no treatment is typically recommended.

Defining Treatment Goals

Defining goals of oncologic interventions is important in patients' decision-making process and requires support from internists. If there is any reasonable likelihood that a tumor is curable, oncologists will encourage patients to follow the recommended treatment algorithm strictly and will provide the necessary support to minimize the attendant toxic effects of therapy. However, if goals are not curative because of tumor or patient characteristics, a palliative approach is indicated to prolong life, with a focus on quality of life.

Studies reporting therapeutic outcomes can often be misleading to patients and internists. Understanding the terms used when clinical trials present data is helpful in assessing the true value of the reported oncologic interventions. The term "cure" is not used frequently because it describes the state of being cancer-free indefinitely, and study timelines, by definition, are of limited duration. The term "disease-free survival" encompasses both being alive and being cancer free. When patients die of other illnesses without a demonstrated cancer recurrence, they are not identified as disease-free survivors. Cure is often equivalent to prolonged disease-free survival. In palliative care settings, when cure is not feasible, the outcomes reported from clinical trials can also be confusing. "Response rates" are defined as the percentage of patients who fulfill a standard analysis of tumor shrinkage. Response rates are further classified as "partial responses," often defined as a greater than 50% reduction in tumor size, and "complete responses," defined as resolution of all visible tumor. More recently, therapeutic benefit has been ascribed when disease is stabilized by the treatment, even without measurable tumor shrinkage. This is defined as the "clinical benefit rate." Finally, "overall survival rate" is a term used to define how long people in a study are alive, with or without having active disease. Improving overall survival is the ultimate goal of clinical trials involving both adjuvant and advanced disease.

In therapeutic trials involving palliative treatment goals for patients with advanced cancer, reports of prolonged survival of a few weeks or months may be statistically significant. Such studies may have great importance in the validation of a scientific concept even though the therapeutic benefits may be modest. Such "advances" need to be interpreted for patients, internists, and the lay press. Certainly, any prolongation of survival with reasonable quality of life is a valid goal, especially if confirmation of the scientific question can lead to further advances. However, many of these new therapies are potentially toxic or expensive. In light of rising health care costs, researchers analyze many of these treatments to assess the financial costs associated with the use of such therapies to prolong life. When benefits are truly modest, oncologists must explain these gains honestly to patients and family members so that they can make appropriate, personalized care decisions.

KEY POINTS

- Surgical resection is the primary treatment modality for almost all malignancies.
- For nearly all solid tumors, the potential for cure is usually related to whether or not the tumor and its local extensions can be completely removed at surgery.
- If cure of a tumor is unlikely, a palliative approach is indicated to prolong life with a focus on quality of life.

Era of Personalized Cancer Treatment

Medical oncology is benefiting from scientific advances in genomics, proteomics, and tumor microenvironments on which new treatment strategies are being developed. Cancers are traditionally described by disease site and cancer stage, and these findings lead to treatment algorithms. Implicit in this standard approach, for example, is that all stage III adenocarcinomas of the lung are treated similarly. However, because of advances in understanding tumor and host biology, treatment of patients with similar tumors and stages is beginning to be individualized, based on individual tumor or host variables, rather than treatment of all patients with the same approach.

An individualized approach to cancer treatment involves identifying unique characteristics of the malignant cells and developing therapies that target these characteristics. This approach has been standard for decades in treating patients with breast cancer, in whom tumors are assayed for the presence of estrogen and progesterone receptors. If these receptors are expressed on the cancer cells, antiestrogen therapy is recommended because of a high likelihood of benefit. If hormone receptors are absent, hormonal therapy is not helpful and is therefore not recommended. The estrogen receptor is both a prognostic and predictive factor. Its presence indicates a better outcome (prognosis) and a better response to therapy (predictor).

More recently, the *HER2/neu* protein was found to be overexpressed in 20% to 25% of breast cancers. Its presence is a strong negative prognostic factor, suggesting aggressive tumor biology. Cancer cells with this molecular characteristic are dependent on the growth pathway controlled by this receptor. The development of trastuzumab, a humanized monoclonal antibody to this protein, has been shown to greatly increase the curability of early-stage *HER2*-positive disease and to increase response rates in advanced disease.

This individualized approach is evolving in the treatment of other tumor types. A small percentage of patients with adenocarcinoma of the lung have a mutation in the epidermal growth factor receptor (EGFR). Typically, these are women who have never smoked. In this subset of patients, erlotinib, a drug targeting the EGFR, is associated with a 70% to 80% response rate, which is higher and often more durable than the response rate associated with standard chemotherapy regimens.

Further evolution of an individualized approach to cancer therapy will likely rely less and less on standard chemotherapeutic agents, defined as medications that affect all cells by inhibiting cell growth by interruption of DNA/RNA replication. These agents do not target a cancer cell specifically. Instead, they inhibit replication of cancer cells to a greater extent than replication of normal cells. However, development of drugs that disrupt aspects of a network of signaling pathways upon which the cancer cells are uniquely dependent, termed "targeted therapies," will be the focus of drug development in the years ahead. These newer agents differ from standard chemotherapeutic agents in several ways that have clinical relevance to internists. In addition to their unique mechanism of action, these drugs have a different toxicity profile than typical chemotherapeutic agents. Management of these side effects involves both the oncologist and the internist (**Table 37**). These new targeted agents include the EGFR pathway inhibitors just mentioned, vascular endothelial growth factor (VEGF) pathway inhibitors, and aromatase inhibitors. VEGF pathway inhibitors are commonly used in the treatment of kidney, colon, lung, breast, and ovarian cancers. This class of agents includes bevacizumab (a humanized monoclonal antibody to the extracellular component of the VEGF receptor) and several tyrosine kinase inhibitors. Tyrosine kinase inhibitors inhibit the pathway by blocking "downstream" protein activation once the surface receptor has been bound by its ligand. The most common toxic effect of the VEGF inhibitors is hypertension, which is often controlled with calcium channel blockers or ACE inhibitors. These medications can also disrupt major blood vessels in a minority of patients, causing catastrophic thrombotic or bleeding complications as well as abdominal perforations. Another toxic effect of VEGF tyrosine kinase inhibitors is a potentially painful rash on the hands or feet, called the hand-foot syndrome. Management includes emollients for mild symptoms and dose reduction or discontinuation of the drug for more severe symptoms. An uncommon complication of bevacizumab is the nephrotic syndrome.

EGFR pathway inhibitors also include both monoclonal antibodies and tyrosine kinase inhibitors. These agents are used in the treatment of colon, pancreatic, lung, and head and neck cancers as well as gastrointestinal stromal tumors and chronic myeloid leukemia. A common toxic effect of nearly all of these agents is an acne-like eruption on the face, scalp, and trunk that can be pruritic or painful. Current recommendations for management are maintenance of clean skin, application of emollients, and intermittent use of a tetracycline antibiotic. More severe rashes may require dose reductions or drug discontinuation. Some EGFR tyrosine kinase inhibitors may also cause periorbital and ankle edema.

Aromatase inhibitors are used for patients with hormone-dependent breast cancer and are given to postmenopausal women who are receiving adjuvant therapy as well as patients who are being treated for advanced disease. In addition to hot flushes, common side effects include joint stiffness and discomfort that do not improve with anti-inflammatory agents and may sometimes require drug discontinuation. Because these agents are antiestrogens, they may cause bone loss that may require bisphosphonate therapy. Bisphosphonates can rarely be associated with osteonecrosis of the jaw, which typically occurs after a dental procedure.

KEY POINTS

- Treatment of patients with similar tumors and stages is beginning to be individualized rather than standardized for all of these patients.
- New targeted agents for treatment of cancer include vascular endothelial growth factor pathway inhibitors, epidermal growth factor receptor pathway inhibitors, and aromatase inhibitors.

Breast Cancer

Introduction

Excluding skin cancer, breast cancer is the most common malignancy among women in the United States and was expected to affect 207,090 women in 2010. It is the second leading cause of cancer-related mortality among women (after lung cancer) and was expected to cause 39,840 deaths in 2010.

Epidemiology and Risk Factors

Breast cancer rates are higher among white women than black women. This may be owing to earlier detection because of

TABLE 37. Newer Cancer Treatment Options, Mechanisms of Actions, and Associated Toxicities

Agent	Mechanism of Action	Applicable Diseases	Toxicities
Bevacizumab	VEGF monoclonal antibody	Colon, lung, brain, ovary, breast	Hypertension, nephrotic syndrome, bleeding/thrombosis, abdominal perforations
Sunitinib, sorafenib	Tyrosine kinase inhibitor, blocks VEGF as well as *raf*, PDGFR	Renal, GIST, hepatocellular	Hypertension, rash, thromboses, cardiotoxicity, hypothyroidism
Cetuximab, panitumumab	EGFR monoclonal antibodies	Colon, head and neck, lung	Rash, fatigue, hypersensitivity, hypomagnesemia
Imatinib, gefitinib	EGFR tyrosine kinase inhibitors	CML, lung, GIST, pancreas	Rash, edema, fatigue, diarrhea, cytopenias

CML = chronic myeloid leukemia; EGFR: epidermal growth factor receptor; GIST = gastrointestinal stromal tumor; PDGFR = platelet-derived growth factor receptor; VEGF: vascular endothelial growth factor.

more frequent mammography screenings, later age at birth of a first child, and greater use of menopausal hormone replacement therapy among white women.

Risk factors for breast cancer include nulliparity, first childbirth after age 30 years, early menarche, late menopause, older age, postmenopausal obesity, alcohol use, lack of physical activity, and a maternal and paternal family history of breast cancer. Atypical ductal hyperplasia, lobular carcinoma in situ, and ductal carcinoma in situ also increase a woman's risk for invasive breast cancer. Early exposure to ionizing radiation is another risk factor, especially for survivors of Hodgkin lymphoma who received mantle radiation therapy and who subsequently have a 25% increased lifetime risk for developing breast cancer.

Approximately 5% to 10% of all women with breast cancer have a germline mutation of *BRCA1*, *BRCA2*, *p53*, or other mutations. *BRCA1/BRCA2* gene mutations are responsible for 90% of hereditary breast cancers and are associated with a significantly increased risk of breast and ovarian cancer. Ashkenazi Jewish women have an increased risk of carrying these mutations. Testing for *BRCA1/BRCA2* gene mutations should be performed in patients with a history suggestive of a breast and ovarian cancer syndrome. A complete family history, including maternal and paternal first- and second-degree relatives, should be documented. Testing should be performed only when the results will be likely to change patient management or management of family members. Guidelines vary concerning which women should be tested, but the consensus is that an extensive discussion regarding implications of testing and results is needed before and after testing, coordinated by health care professionals with expertise in such genetic counseling. The U.S. Preventive Services Task Force has published guidelines for testing non–Ashkenazi Jewish women for *BRCA1/BRCA2* gene mutations (**Table 38**). Testing is indicated for women of Ashkenazi Jewish descent who have a family history of breast or ovarian cancer in any first-degree relative or in two second-degree relatives on the same side of the family.

Although no data yet support early-onset radiographic screening in high-risk subgroups, an expert panel convened by the American Cancer Society recommended that patients who received mantle radiation as well as those who are *BRCA1* or *BRCA2* carriers should undergo yearly mammography and breast MRI.

KEY POINTS

- Risk factors for breast cancer include nulliparity, first childbirth after age 30 years, early menarche, late menopause, older age, postmenopausal obesity, lack of physical activity, alcohol, and a maternal and paternal family history of breast cancer.
- Testing for *BRCA1/BRCA2* gene mutations should be performed in patients with a history suggestive of a breast and ovarian cancer syndrome.

Chemoprevention and Other Risk Reduction Strategies

The National Surgical Adjuvant Breast and Bowel Project–Protocol P-1(NSABP P-1) trial randomized both pre- and postmenopausal women with an increased lifetime risk of breast cancer to receive tamoxifen, 20 mg/d for 5 years, or placebo. Risk was determined by calculating the Gail Model score (minimum absolute risk of 1.67% over 5 years). A 49% reduction in invasive breast cancer was noted in the women who took tamoxifen, which is a selective estrogen receptor modulator (SERM). Side effects experienced by women in the tamoxifen arm included increased thromboembolic events, endometrial cancer, hot flushes, and cataracts. This decrease in the incidence of invasive breast cancer has not yet translated into a survival advantage. The NSABP P-2 trial, also known as the Study of Tamoxifen and Raloxifene (STAR) trial, compared use of tamoxifen and raloxifene, another SERM, in postmenopausal women with an increased risk of breast cancer by the Gail Model or with a history of lobular carcinoma in situ. This study demonstrated that raloxifene was equivalent to tamoxifen in preventing invasive breast cancer. However, the incidence of noninvasive breast cancer was slightly lower in the group that received

TABLE 38. USPSTF-Recommended *BRCA1/BRCA2* Gene Mutation Testing Criteria in Women of Non-Ashkenazi Jewish Descent
Two first-degree relatives with breast cancer, one at age 50 years or younger
A combination of three or more first- or second-degree relatives with breast cancer
A combination of both breast and ovarian cancer among first- or second-degree relatives
A first-degree relative with bilateral breast cancer
A combination of two or more first- or second-degree relatives with ovarian cancer
A first- or second-degree relative with both breast and ovarian cancer
A male relative with breast cancer

USPSTF = United States Preventive Services Task Force.

tamoxifen. Compared with tamoxifen, raloxifene is associated with fewer endometrial cancers, vaginal side effects, thromboembolic events, and cataracts. Both tamoxifen and raloxifene are approved by the FDA for breast cancer prevention and also to help prevent bone loss in postmenopausal women. There are no safety or efficacy data regarding the use of raloxifene in premenopausal women. Physicians are encouraged to use the Gail Model calculator tool to advise their female patients regarding risk reduction strategies.

Because the benefits of SERMs are not well defined in carriers of *BRCA1/BRCA2* mutations, carriers should undergo increased screening, including bilateral mammography and MRI annually. Prophylactic bilateral mastectomy in these high-risk patients decreases the risk of invasive breast cancer by greater than 90%. Prophylactic salpingo-oophorectomy decreases the risk of primary ovarian cancer by greater than 95% and, in premenopausal women, decreases the risk of invasive breast cancer by 50%. The decision regarding use of prophylactic surgery to reduce breast cancer risk should be made only after extensive discussion with women considering this procedure.

KEY POINTS

- Both tamoxifen and raloxifene reduce the incidence of hormone receptor–positive invasive breast cancer by approximately 50%, but raloxifene is less effective than tamoxifen in reducing the incidence of noninvasive breast cancer, and these treatments do not translate into a survival advantage.
- Prophylactic bilateral mastectomy decreases the risk for invasive breast cancer by greater than 90%.

Primary Breast Cancer Therapy

Ductal Carcinoma in Situ

More than 50,000 cases of noninvasive, stage 0 ductal carcinoma in situ (DCIS) were estimated to be diagnosed in the United States in 2010. These lesions are identified mostly through mammography, but some can present as palpable masses. Local therapy for patients with DCIS consists of breast-conserving treatment (lumpectomy plus radiation therapy) or mastectomy. Lymph node evaluation is not typically recommended. After adequate local therapy for hormone receptor–positive DCIS, the standard of care is to discuss the use of tamoxifen for 5 years to reduce both the risk of recurrence and the development of a new primary tumor in the ipsilateral or contralateral breast. There are no data on the use of aromatase inhibitors in patients with DCIS. There is also currently no role for adjuvant chemotherapy, trastuzumab, or raloxifene as standard therapy for DCIS.

H

Invasive Breast Cancer

Once a diagnosis of invasive breast cancer has been established, the primary treatment of early-stage breast cancer is surgical excision. Staging with a CT scan and bone scan to detect advanced disease is typically indicated only for patients with large tumors, palpable lymph nodes, and obvious locally advanced or inflammatory breast cancer.

Historically, modified radical mastectomy (removing all breast tissue and ipsilateral axillary lymph node tissue) was the standard treatment. However, the current standard of care is mastectomy and sentinel lymph node evaluation; or lumpectomy and sentinel lymph node evaluation followed by whole-breast radiation therapy. Studies evaluating newer radiation techniques that reduce the amount of breast tissue being irradiated (partial breast radiation) or the length of therapy (hypofractionation) are ongoing. Breast-conserving therapy is less suitable for most women with tumors greater than 5 cm (or for smaller tumors if the breast is small), tumors involving the nipple and areola complex, and multicentric tumors. It is also not recommended for women with scleroderma or systemic lupus erythematosus and for women with a history of previous irradiation to the field that will undergo breast cancer treatment. Sentinel lymph node examination has replaced axillary lymph node dissection as the standard of care. If the first draining (sentinel) lymph node is negative for malignancy, there is only a 5% to10% chance that other axillary lymph nodes are involved. Lymphedema and other morbidity from a more extensive axillary lymph node dissection can therefore be avoided. Lymph node dissection of the ipsilateral axilla is typically performed if the sentinel lymph node evaluation is positive.

Most patients undergoing mastectomy do not require radiation therapy to complete local therapy. However, radiation therapy to the chest wall and surrounding lymph nodes may be indicated after mastectomy for patients with positive surgical margins despite mastectomy, inflammatory breast cancer, large tumors (>5 cm), or four or more positive axillary lymph nodes. Postmastectomy radiation not only improves local control but may also improve survival in these high-risk patients. Postmastectomy radiation therapy for patients with one to three positive lymph nodes is controversial. H

KEY POINTS

- Treatment of ductal carcinoma in situ involves local breast-conserving therapy or mastectomy with consideration of tamoxifen in estrogen receptor–positive cases.
- The standard of care for patients with invasive breast cancer is mastectomy and sentinel lymph node evaluation or lumpectomy and sentinel lymph node evaluation followed by whole-breast radiation therapy.
- In patients with invasive breast cancer, if the sentinel lymph node is negative for malignancy, there is only a 5% to 10% chance of involvement of other axillary lymph nodes.

Adjuvant Systemic Therapy for Early-Stage Breast Cancer

Adjuvant systemic therapy is indicated to improve survival through eradication of occult microscopic metastatic disease when the benefits of preventing a recurrence, or at least delaying its development, outweigh treatment risks. The risks of treatment are partly inherent to the specific drugs used but may also vary depending on the patient's age and comorbidities. Benefits of adjuvant therapy have been shown to be proportional to the likelihood of disease recurrence. A computer program based on the Surveillance, Epidemiology, and End Results (SEER) database of the National Cancer Institute (www.adjuvantonline.com) can be used to estimate the risk of cancer recurrence as well as the benefits of adjuvant chemotherapy or hormonal therapy for individual patients.

Because prognostic variables determine the risk of distant cancer recurrence, it is paramount to establish the lymph node status; tumor grade and size; estrogen, progesterone, and *HER2/neu* expression; and presence or absence of lymphovascular invasion for each patient. Favorable prognostic variables include expression of estrogen or progesterone receptors, small tumor size, and low pathologic grade. Poor prognostic variables include large tumor size, lymph node involvement, overexpression of *HER2/neu*, and hormone receptor negativity. Some of these characteristics influence the type of therapy and the prognosis. With the use of genomic technology, tumors may be analyzed for the simultaneous expression of multiple genes, a process termed "gene array analysis." Such analysis provides valuable prognostic information that influences treatment of early-stage (axillary lymph node–negative), hormone receptor–positive breast cancer.

Stage I disease is characterized by tumors less than 2 cm in diameter and negative lymph nodes. Stage II disease includes patients with tumors smaller than 2 cm who also have one to three positive lymph nodes, patients with tumors between 2 and 5 cm with zero to three positive lymph nodes, or patients with tumors greater than 5 cm and negative lymph nodes. Patients with stage III cancer have four or more positive axillary lymph nodes, tumors greater than 5 cm with one to three positive lymph nodes, or tumors that extend into the chest wall or skin. Patients with stage IV disease have distant metastatic disease.

Patients with stage I, II, and III disease generally have 5-year relative survival rates of 100%, 86%, and 57%, respectively. Both adjuvant endocrine therapy and adjuvant chemotherapy are used to treat early-stage breast cancer.

Adjuvant Endocrine Therapy

The presence of hormone receptors on a breast cancer cell suggests that this cell is dependent on estrogen for growth, and antiestrogen therapy can be lethal to such cells. Endocrine therapy can reduce the relative risk of cancer recurrence by approximately 50% and is indicated for almost all patients with estrogen or progesterone-positive tumors. The magnitude of benefit to hormonal therapy is proportionate to the degree of receptor expression.

In premenopausal women, estrogen is predominantly produced in the ovaries. Tamoxifen will not inhibit its production but instead blocks its effect on cellular receptors. In postmenopausal women, estrogen is no longer made in the ovaries but rather in other tissues such as fat and muscle through the aromatase enzymes. Use of aromatase inhibitors therefore is an effective strategy in postmenopausal women only.

In premenopausal women, a 5-year course of tamoxifen is the standard adjuvant endocrine therapeutic regimen. In patients in whom tamoxifen is contraindicated, ovarian ablation is the treatment of choice. Aromatase inhibitors currently are contraindicated in premenopausal women because they are ineffective in inhibiting ovarian production of estrogen. However, many randomized clinical trials are under way to evaluate the role of ovarian ablation with gonadotropin-releasing hormone agonists plus either tamoxifen or an aromatase inhibitor in premenopausal women to improve on the benefits of standard tamoxifen therapy. Tamoxifen is the typical choice of adjuvant treatment for men with breast cancer. Raloxifene currently has no role as adjuvant therapy for any patient.

Postmenopausal women with hormone receptor–positive breast cancer should take an aromatase inhibitor as primary therapy for 5 years, after 2 to 3 years of initial tamoxifen therapy, or for 5 additional years after completion of 5 years of adjuvant tamoxifen. These recommendations are based on results from several large clinical trials demonstrating that aromatase inhibitors provide a small statistical benefit in reducing recurrences compared with tamoxifen. As such, aromatase inhibitors should be the endocrine treatment of choice in most postmenopausal patients with newly diagnosed, hormone receptor–positive breast cancer. As with any treatment, individualized risk-to-benefit analyses should guide treatment.

The maximum recommended duration of aromatase inhibitor therapy is currently 5 years, although women continue to have an ongoing risk of recurrence of 1% to 2% per year. Ongoing studies will determine whether extending antiestrogen therapy will decrease this risk. Compared with tamoxifen, aromatase inhibitors provide modest improvement in disease-free survival, which is defined as lack of development of contralateral breast cancer and distant or locoregional recurrence. Aromatase inhibitors and tamoxifen have different toxicity profiles. Side effects of tamoxifen include increased thromboembolic events, endometrial cancer, hot flushes, and cataracts. Aromatase inhibitors do not increase the risk for thromboembolic disease or endometrial cancer; however, they are associated with greater loss of bone mineral density and more fractures. Administration of bisphosphonates may reduce bone density loss. Aromatase inhibitors may also cause the musculoskeletal/arthralgia syndrome, which is characterized by symmetric pain and joint stiffness. Discontinuation of therapy usually results in symptom resolution.

Adjuvant Chemotherapy

Use of adjuvant chemotherapy was historically considered for patients with the most significant risk of recurrence as defined by the presence of a large tumor or known involvement of axillary lymph nodes and those with hormone-independent tumors. More recently, subsets of patients with historically lower-risk profiles have been reported to benefit from the addition of adjuvant chemotherapy. Gene profiling of the patient's tumor may help identify those candidates. The decision to begin chemotherapy is largely individualized after extensive discussion with the patient regarding the risk-benefit ratio. Patients with triple-negative tumors (estrogen receptor negative, progesterone receptor negative, *HER2*-negative) or those with *HER2/neu* overexpression have a poorer prognosis and seem to derive significant benefit from adjuvant chemotherapy, including in the latter case, trastuzumab, a monoclonal antibody targeting the *HER2* receptor. Women younger than 50 years of age with lymph node–positive disease also benefit significantly from chemotherapy. However, advanced age alone should not be a contraindication to chemotherapy. Adjuvant chemotherapy generally consists of 3 to 6 months of treatment with two or three agents, administered concurrently or sequentially. The specific regimen chosen should be based on the patient's disease stage and tumor characteristics as well as baseline comorbid findings and functional status. However, frequently, there is no true standard of care. Commonly used agents include cyclophosphamide, anthracyclines (doxorubicin or epirubicin), methotrexate, 5-fluorouracil, and one of the taxanes (docetaxel or paclitaxel). Side effects of chemotherapy include nausea, vomiting, alopecia, and, with taxanes, peripheral neuropathy, fluid retention, allergic reactions, bone marrow suppression, neutropenic fever, and transient or permanent amenorrhea. Much less common, but important, risks of chemotherapy include leukemia, myelodysplastic syndrome, and anthracycline-induced cardiotoxicity (see Oncologic Urgencies and Emergencies).

Trastuzumab is a humanized monoclonal antibody that targets the *HER2* receptor and is used to treat patients with tumors that overexpress *HER2/neu*. Historically, these patients have had a poor prognosis with a high risk for systemic recurrence. Four large randomized trials have demonstrated that adjuvant trastuzumab, given for 1 year, either sequentially or concurrently with chemotherapy, significantly reduced breast cancer recurrence by approximately 50% and improved overall survival. Trastuzumab can impair systolic ventricular function and cause heart failure. Risk factors for trastuzumab-induced cardiotoxicity include age older than 50 years, hypertension, and previous or concurrent use of anthracyclines. In contrast to anthracycline-induced cardiotoxicity, trastuzumab-induced cardiotoxicity is usually reversible when this agent is discontinued. Patients who will receive adjuvant trastuzumab for 1 year require evaluation of the left ventricular ejection fraction at baseline and every 3 months during treatment.

KEY POINTS

- Adjuvant endocrine therapy can reduce the relative risk of breast cancer recurrence by approximately 50% and is indicated for almost all patients with estrogen receptor–positive or progesterone receptor–positive tumors.
- Tamoxifen is the standard endocrine therapy for premenopausal women with early-stage breast cancer, whereas postmenopausal women with hormone receptor–positive breast cancer are treated with aromatase inhibitors.
- Adjuvant trastuzumab, given for 1 year sequentially or concurrently with chemotherapy, can significantly reduce breast cancer recurrence and improve overall survival in patients with tumors that overexpress *HER2/neu*.

Locally Advanced and Inflammatory Breast Cancer Therapy

Patients with two subtypes of breast cancer, locally advanced and inflammatory cancer, are treated with systemic therapy before local therapy is begun. Patients with locally advanced breast cancer generally have large, potentially inoperable, tumors with skin or chest wall involvement (T4), or extensive lymph node involvement and are typically offered preoperative chemotherapy. The goals of preoperative therapy are to reduce the size of the breast mass to facilitate later mastectomy and improve local control. Preoperative systemic therapy has been shown to be equivalent to standard adjuvant therapy in providing systemic control. Patients with locally advanced, but operable, T3 lesions are often offered preoperative hormonal or chemotherapy to increase rates of breast conservation and to add systemic benefit.

A unique subtype of breast cancer is inflammatory breast cancer, which is a clinical diagnosis characterized by erythema, skin thickening, and a peau d'orange (dimpling of the skin typically due to obstruction of dermal lymphatics) appearance of the breast. No distinct mass may be apparent. The diagnosis is established by the presence of invasive breast cancer and consistent physical examination findings. Skin biopsy may or may not reveal dermal lymphatic invasion but is not required for a definitive diagnosis. The prognosis is poor, although 30% of patients may be cured through optimal multimodality treatment with systemic chemotherapy, mastectomy, and radiation therapy.

KEY POINTS

- Both locally advanced breast cancer and inflammatory breast cancer are treated with systemic therapy before local therapy is begun.
- Optimal management of patients with inflammatory breast cancer requires multimodality treatment with systemic therapy, surgery, and radiation therapy.

Breast Cancer Follow-up and Survivorship

Survivors of early-stage breast cancer should have a clinical evaluation (detailed history and physical examination) every 6 months for at least 5 years and annually thereafter. Breast self-examinations are recommended monthly, and annual mammography is recommended for the preserved and contralateral breast. The role of breast MRI in this population is evolving but is currently not recommended for survivors of breast cancer. Routine radiologic studies, other than mammography, and routine laboratory studies, including tumor marker measurement, are not recommended based on the American Society of Clinical Oncology guidelines because no subsequent treatment benefit has been associated with performing such screening in asymptomatic patients.

Breast cancer survivors have many ongoing side effects secondary to chemotherapy and endocrine therapy. A multimodality approach is required to manage vasomotor symptoms, sexual side effects, cognitive dysfunction, weight gain, and osteopenia/osteoporosis. Healthy lifestyle modifications, including increased physical activity, a well-balanced diet, and adequate calcium and vitamin D supplementation, are important. Systemic hormone replacement therapy should not be used to manage side effects of therapy. Topical estrogen therapy for vaginal atrophy or dyspareunia is not believed to increase the risk of recurrent breast cancer. Antidepressants, such as venlafaxine, are often given to counteract vasomotor symptoms. However, potent inhibitors of CYP2D6 enzymes, such as bupropion, fluoxetine, and paroxetine, are contraindicated in women taking tamoxifen because metabolism of tamoxifen requires adequate CYP2D6 enzyme activity.

Chemotherapy-induced amenorrhea may result in early menopause, and loss of fertility may be of concern to younger patients. Women who are interested in childbearing should consult a fertility specialist before systemic chemotherapy is begun. Because treatment-related amenorrhea is not always associated with lack of ovarian function, breast cancer survivors should be told of the need for contraception. However, oral contraceptive agents are contraindicated, and an alternative form of contraception should be used.

KEY POINTS

- Follow-up for survivors of early-stage breast cancer includes a detailed history and physical examination every 6 months for at least 5 years, monthly breast self-examination, and annual mammography.
- Antidepressants that are potent inhibitors of the CYP2D6 enzyme, such as bupropion, fluoxetine, and paroxetine, are contraindicated in women taking tamoxifen.

Metastatic Breast Cancer

Metastatic breast cancer is generally an incurable disease with a median survival of 2 years. However, survival rates for patients with metastatic breast cancer are improving compared with historical controls, which is likely because of availability of better systemic and supportive therapies. Goals of therapy for patients with metastatic breast cancer are to improve clinical outcome while minimizing toxicity and preserving quality of life. Establishing treatment goals and discussing advanced directives are also important. Clinical trials are imperative in this patient population to facilitate development of novel therapeutic agents and broaden therapeutic options.

Typically, women with metastatic breast cancer do not receive surgical or radiation treatment for their primary tumor unless they have local symptoms requiring specific palliation. In contrast to resection of metastases in colon cancer, surgical resection of metastatic breast cancer lesions provides no survival benefit.

Systemic therapy is the cornerstone of treatment. Treatment decisions are based on the biologic profile of the tumor. Lesions due to first recurrences, including to bone, usually require biopsy because the hormone receptor and *HER2/neu* status of the new lesion may differ from that of the original tumor, or the new lesion may represent another malignancy.

Patients with hormone receptor–positive tumors without critical visceral burden and with normal organ function should receive serial endocrine therapy, beginning with tamoxifen in premenopausal women or an aromatase inhibitor in postmenopausal women. Ovarian ablation should be considered in premenopausal patients. Once the metastatic disease progresses despite initial hormonal therapy, second-line agents such as exemestane or fulvestrant are used.

Patients with tumors that overexpress *HER2/neu* are treated with trastuzumab and chemotherapy. Trastuzumab has also been shown to be effective when used as a single agent or in combination with endocrine therapy such as aromatase inhibitors. Patients whose disease progresses while receiving trastuzumab-containing therapy may also be given lapatinib, which is an oral *HER1/HER2* tyrosine kinase inhibitor. Toxic effects include dermatitis and diarrhea, and rarely, liver disease and cardiotoxicity. Patients whose tumors are triple-negative or are refractory to endocrine treatment generally receive sequential single-agent chemotherapy. Although combination chemotherapy may increase the response rate, it is associated with more toxicity and does not prolong survival.

For patients with metastatic bone disease, monthly administration of an intravenous bisphosphonate, either pamidronate or zoledronic acid (or a receptor activator of nuclear factor kappa B (RANK)-ligand inhibitor), reduces skeletal-related events, including fractures, bone pain, and the need for radiation therapy. The most common toxic effects of these drugs are musculoskeletal symptoms and low-grade fever. The dosage must be adjusted in patients with renal failure. Prolonged treatment with bisphosphonates may result in osteonecrosis of the jaw. Dental evaluation before and during treatment is therefore required. Bisphosphonate therapy is usually not resumed in patients who develop osteonecrosis of the jaw.

KEY POINTS

- Metastatic breast cancer is generally an incurable disease with a median survival of 2 years.
- Systemic therapy is the cornerstone of treatment for patients with metastatic breast cancer, and local therapy such as surgery or radiation therapy is used for symptom palliation and treatment of spinal cord compression.
- For patients with metastatic bone disease, monthly administration of an intravenous bisphosphonate reduces new bone metastases and fractures.

Ovarian and Cervical Cancer

Ovarian Cancer

Ovarian cancer accounts for approximately 21,500 cases and 15,500 deaths annually in the United States and is the fifth most common cause of cancer-related death in women. Because 90% of primary ovarian tumors are derived from epithelial cells, only epithelial cell cancer will be reviewed in this chapter.

Epidemiology and Risk Factors

Ovarian cancer is predominantly a disease of postmenopausal women. It is rarely diagnosed in women younger than 40 years of age unless they have a genetic predisposition for the disease. The incidence of ovarian cancer is higher in white women than in black women.

The most significant risk factor for developing ovarian cancer is the presence of *BRCA1/BRCA2* gene mutations. These mutations account for 5% to 10% of all cases of ovarian cancer with increased risk especially in younger patients. Women with hereditary nonpolyposis colorectal cancer syndrome are also at significantly increased risk. Other risk factors include a high-fat diet, nulliparity, and delayed menopause.

Use of oral contraceptive agents decreases the risk of ovarian cancer by as much as 50%, with the protective effect lasting up to 20 years after discontinuation of oral contraception. Multiparity, breast feeding, and tubal ligation are also thought to reduce the risk of developing ovarian cancer.

KEY POINTS

- The most significant risk factor for ovarian cancer, especially in premenopausal women, is the presence of *BRCA1/BRCA2* gene mutations; hereditary nonpolyposis colorectal cancer syndrome also confers a significantly increased risk.
- Use of oral contraceptive agents decreases the risk of ovarian cancer by as much as 50% with the protective effect lasting up to 20 years after oral contraception cessation.

Screening and Risk Reduction Strategies

Screening for ovarian cancer is not recommended for average-risk women because no screening test to date has been shown to be sensitive or specific enough to establish the diagnosis. There are also no data to demonstrate a survival advantage with any screening modality.

However, patients at high risk for developing ovarian cancer because of the presence of the hereditary nonpolyposis colorectal cancer syndrome or *BRCA1/BRCA2* gene mutations should be advised to undergo prophylactic bilateral salpingo-oophorectomy, after childbearing is complete, and, ideally, before age 40 years. This procedure has been shown to reduce the risk of developing ovarian cancer by 95%. The finding that a small percentage of women who undergo prophylactic surgery still develop peritoneal carcinoma suggests that the entire peritoneal surface may be affected by the genetic defect. Based on National Comprehensive Cancer Network guidelines, women who decline prophylactic surgery should have intensive surveillance with pelvic examinations, measurement of serum CA-125 levels, and pelvic and abdominal ultrasonography every 6 months starting at age 35 years or 10 years earlier than development of cancer in any family member. Although oral contraceptive agents are associated with a decreased risk for ovarian cancer, their use in mutation carriers in preventing ovarian cancer is controversial because they confer an increased risk for breast cancer. *BRCA1/BRCA2* gene mutations are also associated with a significantly increased risk of breast cancer. Prophylactic salpingo-oophorectomy decreases the risk of invasive breast cancer by 50% in premenopausal women. Prophylactic bilateral mastectomy decreases the risk of invasive breast cancer by greater than 90%.

KEY POINTS

- Screening for ovarian cancer is not recommended for average-risk women.
- In women at high risk for developing ovarian cancer, prophylactic bilateral salpingo-oophorectomy before age 40 years reduces the risk of developing cancer by 95%.

Diagnosis

The symptoms of early-stage ovarian cancer are vague and nonspecific. However, this diagnosis should be considered in any woman with the recent onset of abdominal or pelvic symptoms, especially in postmenopausal woman with symptoms that are persistent or more severe than expected. Most patients with ovarian cancer have advanced disease at initial evaluation and present with signs and symptoms of abdominal distention, pain, nausea, bloating, and anorexia, all of which are due to ascites and bulk tumor effects.

Abdominal examination often shows signs of ascites with distention and a fluid wave. The presence of a pelvic or adnexal mass in a postmenopausal woman is suspicious for ovarian cancer. A similar mass in a premenopausal woman has a much lower predictive value for the presence of cancer.

Findings on ultrasonography suggestive of ovarian cancer include a solid mass, a cyst with thick septations, and ascites. A CT scan of the abdomen and pelvis is recommended to define the extent of disease. However, results of these imaging techniques are not sensitive enough to outweigh findings based on the history and physical examination when establishing the diagnosis. PET scanning and MRI are not usually recommended.

Serum CA-125 values greater than 65 units/mL (normal <35 units/mL) are found in more than 80% of patients with ovarian cancer. However, elevated CA-125 values are not specific for ovarian cancer. Increased levels also occur in patients with endometrial cancer, fallopian tube cancer, cervical cancer, and nonmalignant gynecologic disorders such as endometriosis, functional ovarian cysts, leiomyomata, and pelvic inflammatory disease, as well as in pregnant women. Patients with liver disease, colitis, diverticulitis, peritonitis, sarcoid, and chronic heart failure may also have false-positive CA-125 findings.

The diagnosis of advanced ovarian cancer is usually made by CT- or ultrasound-guided biopsy of a suspicious mass or cytologic examination of ascitic fluid. If the imaging is strongly suggestive of ovarian cancer, the diagnosis may be made at the time of a surgical debulking procedure.

KEY POINTS

- Most patients with ovarian cancer have advanced disease at initial evaluation.
- Findings on ultrasonography suggestive of ovarian cancer include a solid mass, a cyst with thick septations, and ascites.
- The diagnosis of advanced ovarian cancer is usually made by CT or ultrasound-guided biopsy of a suspicious mass or cytologic examination of ascitic fluid.

Treatment

Surgery

Surgery is needed for the diagnosis, staging, and treatment of ovarian cancer. Tumor debulking (surgical cytoreduction) is performed along with total abdominal hysterectomy, bilateral salpingo-oophorectomy, omentectomy, selective lymphadenectomy, and appendectomy. Following this procedure, approximately 25% of patients with suspected stage I or II ovarian cancer based on clinical findings are actually found to have stage III disease. High-grade cancers increase the risk of finding more advanced disease at surgery. The extent of cancer found at surgery defines the stage and guides further treatment decisions (**Table 39**). H

TABLE 39. Staging, Treatment, and Prognosis of Ovarian Cancer

Stage	Histologic Description	Typical Therapy	5-Year Survival Rate (%)
I	Limited to the ovaries	Low risk[a] – surgery only	>90
		High risk[b] – surgery followed by chemotherapy[c]	75-80
II	Pelvic extension	Surgery followed by chemotherapy[c]	60-70
III	Peritoneal implants outside the pelvis and/or retroperitoneal or inguinal lymph nodes, or superficial liver metastases	Surgery followed by chemotherapy[c,d]	25-40
IV	Distant metastases	Surgery (dependent on distribution and resectability of disease) and chemotherapy[c]	10-15

[a]Low risk: grade 1.

[b]High risk: grade 3 or clear cell histology and/or stage IC or II.

[c]Chemotherapy usually consists of some form of a platinum/taxane doublet.

[d]Chemotherapy can be given either intravenously or intraperitoneally in patients who have been optimally debulked (no residual disease greater than 1 cm).

Many studies have reported that optimal tumor debulking (no residual tumor mass >1 cm) is associated with increased survival. Optimal debulking is achieved in more than 80% of patients when surgery is performed by gynecologic oncologists and occurs at a much lower rate when performed by physicians without training in this subspecialty. Some patients who are not candidates for initial surgery are first treated with neoadjuvant chemotherapy. This sequence usually permits eventual surgical assessment.

Chemotherapy

Patients with low-grade, well-differentiated stage I ovarian cancer do not benefit from adjuvant chemotherapy. Chemotherapy is indicated for patients with high-risk, early-stage disease and those with advanced disease. Patients with high-grade cancer, positive cytology in ascites or pelvic washings, or pelvic extension have a 30% to 40% relapse rate following surgery alone and should receive three to six cycles of adjuvant chemotherapy. Two European trials demonstrated an increase in 5-year overall survival from 74% to 82% when patients in this high-risk, early-stage subgroup were treated with surgery and adjuvant chemotherapy rather than with surgery and observation alone. The management of patients with intermediate or high-grade stage I disease is controversial. The National Comprehensive Cancer Network guidelines recommend surgery followed by either observation or chemotherapy for these patients.

Patients with advanced ovarian cancer (stages II, III, and IV) are currently treated with adjuvant chemotherapy regimens consisting of a taxane with cisplatin or carboplatin. Ovarian cancer is unique in that its spread is mostly confined to the peritoneal cavity. Based on this observation and on findings from older trials demonstrating the efficacy of intraperitoneal chemotherapy, the Gynecologic Oncology Group 172 trial compared the use of intraperitoneal chemotherapy plus intravenous taxane/platinum-based agents versus intravenous taxane/platinum-based agents alone. The overall survival in the intraperitoneal-plus-intravenous–chemotherapy arm was 66 months compared with 50 months for the intravenous arm alone. However, this survival advantage was associated with substantially increased toxicity. Intraperitoneal chemotherapy regimens are therefore usually offered only to vigorous and highly motivated patients.

Second-Look Surgery

Surgical re-exploration to assess the pathologic response after completion of chemotherapy is no longer recommended because this procedure has not been shown to improve survival.

Management of Recurrent Ovarian Cancer

Surgery

Surgical resection is appropriate for patients with a solitary recurrent tumor or with limited relapse of cancer at sites favorable for surgical removal, especially if the patient has good functional status and has had a long treatment-free interval.

Chemotherapy

Chemotherapy is not curative once a relapse has occurred. The goals of chemotherapy in this setting are therefore to control the cancer, extend survival, and maintain a better quality of life.

Multiple chemotherapeutic agents are active in this setting. Ovarian cancer often remains sensitive to platinum-based agents, especially if the platinum-free interval (the time from completion of platinum-based therapy to recurrence of disease) is greater than 6 months. Patients with platinum-resistant disease can be given any of the multiple active single agents that are available. The choice is based on which drugs have already been used, their relative toxic effects, and their convenience to the patient. Response to multiple subsequent chemotherapy regimens does occur, and survival is often prolonged for years. Bevacizumab, a humanized monoclonal antibody directed against vascular endothelial growth factor, is a promising new agent undergoing investigation for treatment of recurrent ovarian cancer. Hormonal therapies using agents that are active in the treatment of breast cancer also have a role in the palliative care of patients with advanced ovarian cancer.

Monitoring and Follow-Up

After completing initial treatment, patients should be monitored frequently for recurrence. Clinical evaluation, including a history, physical examination, and measurement of serum CA-125 levels, should be performed every 2 to 4 months for the first 2 years, then every 3 to 6 months for 3 years, and then annually. National Comprehensive Cancer Network guidelines recommend performing CT scans only if clinically indicated, as regularly scheduled scans have not been associated with improved survival.

Supportive Care

Use of hematopoietic growth factors to maintain adequate blood counts has helped improve the quality of life and decrease complication rates in patients receiving chemotherapy. Some patients require frequent paracentesis procedures to drain symptomatic ascitic fluid. Bowel obstruction often develops late in the course of ovarian cancer. A surgical bypass procedure should be considered if the obstruction is localized and there are options for additional chemotherapy. Draining gastrostomy tubes are sometimes needed to relieve chronic nausea and vomiting associated with obstruction. Difficult decisions may need to be made regarding the use of total parenteral nutrition because such treatment has not been shown to prolong survival in these patients.

KEY POINTS

- Optimal tumor debulking (no residual tumor mass >1 cm) is associated with increased survival in patients with ovarian cancer.
- Adjuvant chemotherapy is indicated for patients with high-risk, early-stage ovarian cancer and those with advanced disease.
- Surgical resection is appropriate for patients with a recurrent solitary ovarian tumor or with limited relapse of cancer at sites favorable for surgical removal.
- Patients who have completed initial treatment for ovarian cancer require routine follow-up clinical evaluations, including history, physical examination, and serum CA-125 measurement.
- Use of hematopoietic growth factors to maintain adequate blood counts has helped improve the quality of life and decrease complication rates in patients with ovarian cancer who are receiving chemotherapy.

Cervical Cancer

In 2009, approximately 11,270 new cases of cervical cancer were diagnosed in the United States, and there were 4070 cervical cancer–related deaths.

Epidemiology and Risk Factors

The incidence of cervical cancer is highest among minority populations in the United States. The rate among Hispanic women is twice that of non-Hispanic white women, and the rate in black women is 30% higher than in white women. Incidence and mortality rates from cervical cancer have decreased by 75% in developed countries over the past 50 years as a result of widespread screening and prevention programs (see MKSAP 16 General Internal Medicine). Decreased rates have not occurred in developing countries, however.

The mean age at diagnosis is 47 years. The most important risk factor for the development of cervical cancer is persistent human papillomavirus infection. Other risk factors include early-onset sexual activity, multiple sexual partners, sexually transmitted diseases, smoking, multiparity, prolonged use of oral contraceptive agents, and immunosuppression. Squamous cell carcinoma accounts for 70% to 80% of all cervical cancers, adenocarcinoma for 20%, and adenosquamous cell carcinoma for 3% to 5%. Adenosquamous cell carcinoma has the poorest prognosis.

Diagnosis and Staging

The most common signs of cervical cancer are vaginal bleeding between menstrual periods or after menopause, postcoital vaginal bleeding, and abnormal vaginal discharge. Pelvic or low back pain may be a symptom of more advanced disease.

Direct examination usually shows an abnormal cervix, although a tumor in the cervical canal may be difficult to see. The diagnosis is usually established by punch biopsy of obvious lesions or by colposcopy with directed biopsy. Cone biopsy is needed if colposcopy is not diagnostic.

Careful pelvic examination and routine laboratory studies are performed in the initial assessment of clinical stage. Stage I cervical cancer is confined to the uterus and is further classified as stage IA (limited to microscopic lesions) or stage IB (presence of macroscopic disease). Stage II cancer extends beyond the uterus but does not invade the pelvic side wall or lower third of the vagina. Extension to the side wall or lower vagina or the presence of urethral obstruction is classified as stage III disease. Stage IV cancer invades the bladder or rectum, extends beyond the pelvis, or has distant metastases. Final pathologic staging after surgery is often different but does not change the clinical stage.

Radiographic imaging (chest radiography, abdominal/pelvic CT or MRI, and, sometimes, PET) is recommended for patients with more advanced local disease but does not change the clinical stage.

Treatment

Several treatment options are available for patients with the International Federation of Gynecology and Obstetrics stage IA, IB, and nonbulky stage II cervical cancer. Observation may be considered for patients with very-early-stage IA disease who are not candidates for surgery or who wish to preserve fertility after an excisional cone biopsy. Radiation therapy or surgery with radical hysterectomy or a more limited surgical procedure is commonly recommended for patients with small stage I or II tumors. Patients with higher-risk, early-stage disease may also be treated with surgery or radiation therapy plus concurrent cisplatin-based chemotherapy. If high-risk factors are identified at surgery (large primary tumor, deep stromal invasion, lymphovascular invasion, positive lymph nodes, or positive surgical margins), postoperative radiation therapy with concurrent chemotherapy is recommended.

Radiation therapy and concurrent chemotherapy are recommended for patients with large stage IB cancers through stage IV disease, as large randomized clinical trials have confirmed a survival advantage with this combined approach.

Prognosis

The clinical disease stage is the best predictor of survival, followed by lymph node status identified at the time of surgery. The 5-year overall survival rate is 90% to 95% for patients with early-stage clinical disease and negative pelvic lymph nodes identified at surgery. Patients with positive pelvic lymph nodes have a 5-year overall survival rate of approximately 70%. Para-aortic lymph node involvement is associated with a poorer prognosis.

Surveillance

Patients who have completed therapy should have a pelvic examination and Pap smear every 3 to 6 months for 2 years, then every 6 months for the next 3 years, and then annually. Radiographic imaging is optional based on clinical indications.

Patients who develop a local recurrence of cervical cancer after surgery should be evaluated for salvage radiation therapy and chemotherapy. Pelvic exenteration is an option for patients who develop a relapse after radiation therapy. Palliative chemotherapy or best supportive care is offered to patients with distant or unresectable recurrent cancer.

KEY POINTS

- The most important cervical cancer risk factor is the presence of persistent human papillomavirus infection.
- The most common signs of cervical cancer are vaginal bleeding between menstrual periods or after menopause, postcoital vaginal bleeding, and abnormal vaginal discharge.
- The diagnosis of cervical cancer is usually established by punch biopsy of obvious lesions or by colposcopy with directed biopsy.
- Observation may be appropriate for patients with very-early-stage IA cervical cancer who are not candidates for surgery or who wish to preserve fertility.
- Routine follow-up for patients who have completed therapy for cervical cancer involves a pelvic examination and Pap smear every 3 to 6 months for 2 years, then every 6 months for the next 3 years, and then annually.

Gastrointestinal Malignancies

Colorectal Cancer

Colorectal cancer is the fourth most common cause of cancer in the United States and the second leading cause of cancer-related deaths. No specific signs or symptoms indicate whether a patient has colorectal cancer or a benign process, and many cancers remain asymptomatic until reaching an advanced stage. Bleeding per rectum, melena, cramping, bloating, change in the frequency or the caliber of bowel movements, and other nonspecific signs and symptoms may indicate the presence of a benign polyp, another nonmalignant process, or cancer. Healthy individuals should therefore be screened for colorectal cancer. Current recommendations indicate colorectal cancer screening (stool-based test, flexible sigmoidoscopy, or optical colonoscopy) for all men and women at average risk, beginning no later than age 50 years or optical colonoscopy for patients at high risk (patients 40 years of age with a family history of colorectal cancer, adenomatous polyps, or symptoms of concern or 10 years younger than the age at which the youngest affected relative was diagnosed with colorectal cancer). See MKSAP 16 Gastroenterology and Hepatology for discussion of colorectal cancer screening.

The large intestine includes the colon, which is the largest segment, and rectum, which is limited to the most distal 12 to 15 cm. Most of the colon lies in the abdomen, whereas the rectum is in the pelvis. The peritoneal reflection is the anatomic landmark that separates these two structures. When metastatic disease is present, cancers of the colon and rectum appear to be essentially the same entity and are referred to as colorectal cancer. However, management strategy for localized disease tends to differ based on whether the primary tumor is in the rectum or the colon.

Staging

Staging is the most accurate predictor of outcome in patients with colorectal cancer. At surgery, all tumors are staged on a scale of I to IV using the American Joint Committee on Cancer TNM staging system *(**Table 40**)*. The Dukes classification is no longer used. Preoperative staging includes a complete colonoscopy (if technically feasible) and contrast-enhanced CT of the chest, abdomen, and pelvis. PET scanning has not been validated for use in preoperative staging.

KEY POINTS

- All men and women, beginning at age 50 years, should undergo screening colonoscopy.
- Preoperative colorectal cancer staging includes a complete colonoscopy (if technically feasible) and contrast-enhanced CT scans of the chest, abdomen, and pelvis.

TABLE 40. Staging of Colorectal Cancer

Stage	Description	Approximate 5-year Disease-Free Survival Rate
I	Tumor does not invade the full thickness of bowel wall (T1, T2); lymph nodes not involved (N0)	90%-95%
II	Tumor invades full thickness of bowel wall and may invade into pericolonic or perirectal fat (T3, T4); lymph nodes not involved (N0)	70%-85%
III	One or more lymph nodes involved with cancer (N1, N2); any T stage	25%-70%
IV	Metastatic tumor spread to distant site (M1); any T stage, any N stage	0%-10%

H Treatment

Most patients diagnosed with colorectal cancer fear having a permanent colostomy postoperatively. However, colorectal cancer surgery almost never results in the need for a permanent colostomy. A permanent colostomy is typically needed only if a rectal tumor is too distal or too low to permit an adequate margin of resection without resecting the anal sphincter muscles.

Treatment of Colon Cancer

Patients with local or locoregional colon cancer should undergo surgical resection of the primary tumor. This procedure also allows for definitive staging. Adjuvant chemotherapy is used to eradicate any residual micrometastatic disease that may still be present after surgery. The need for postoperative adjuvant chemotherapy is determined by the cancer stage. All patients with stage III colon cancer, regardless of age, should receive adjuvant chemotherapy unless contraindicated because of medical or psychiatric disorders. Randomized controlled trials have demonstrated that adjuvant chemotherapy regimens incorporating the cytotoxic agent 5-fluorouracil (5-FU) can reduce the risk of death in these patients. 5-FU, which was patented in 1957, remains the single most active chemotherapeutic agent in the treatment of colorectal cancer. No drug developed since has been more effective, and the newer drugs are typically used in combination with 5-FU or with each other. FOLFOX chemotherapy (folinic acid [leucovorin], 5-FU, and oxaliplatin) is modestly, but statistically significantly superior, to leucovorin and 5-FU alone in treating stage III colon cancer. Therefore, FOLFOX chemotherapy for approximately 6 months is the current standard adjuvant treatment of patients with stage III disease.

The role of adjuvant chemotherapy for patients with stage II colon cancer is more complicated. High-risk patients with stage II colon cancer appear to have a prognosis similar to that of patients with stage III disease and are also treated with FOLFOX adjuvant chemotherapy. High-risk factors include T4 tumor stage, inadequate lymph node sampling (less than 12 lymph nodes examined), lymphovascular invasion, poorly differentiated histology, and clinical perforation or obstruction. Most studies do not find a survival advantage for use of adjuvant chemotherapy for patients with stage II colon cancer without high-risk factors, and surgery without adjuvant chemotherapy is acceptable standard practice for these patients. However, some patients with stage II disease without high-risk factors may be treated with 5-FU and leucovorin (without oxaliplatin). Although there are no current definitive standards regarding adjuvant chemotherapy for patients with stage II colon cancer, a consensus statement from the American Society of Clinical Oncology recommends that all such patients consult with a medical oncologist regarding the advantages and disadvantages of adjuvant therapy.

Treatment of Rectal Cancer

Because it is located in the pelvis, the rectum is technically difficult to remove. The accepted technique for rectal cancer surgery is total mesorectal excision, and only surgeons who are trained and experienced in this technique should perform this procedure. In addition to the workup required for colon cancer, additional staging with endorectal ultrasonography or pelvic MRI is also required to assess the depth of tumor penetration (T stage).

Patients with rectal tumors that are not full-thickness lesions and do not have obvious lymph node involvement (T1-2, N0) based on pretreatment evaluation typically undergo primary surgical resection. Patients with full-thickness tumors (T3 or T4) or clearly enlarged lymph nodes should receive preoperative combined radiation therapy and chemotherapy. A large randomized clinical trial showed that although survival was the same with preoperative or postoperative combined therapy, preoperative therapy was associated with a lower local cancer recurrence rate and less toxicity. Therefore, patients with stage II or III rectal tumors, based on preoperative staging, require radiation therapy and chemotherapy before surgery and chemotherapy alone after surgery. Patients with stage I rectal tumors determined preoperatively who are found to have local lymph node metastases or full-thickness tumor penetration at surgery require postoperative radiation therapy and chemotherapy. If the tumor is confirmed to be stage I at surgery, no postoperative treatment is indicated. The chemotherapeutic agent used with concurrent radiation therapy is typically 5-FU, which is most often given by protracted intravenous infusion. An oral 5-FU prodrug, capecitabine, is available and widely used, although definitive randomized studies of effectiveness are pending. The FOLFOX regimen is typically used after preoperative radiation/chemotherapy and surgery to complete a total of approximately 6 months of chemotherapy.

Treatment of Metastatic Colorectal Cancer

Unresectable metastatic colorectal cancer is almost always incurable, and the goal of treatment is to extend survival and palliate symptoms. Resection for cure may be an option for those patients who have metastatic disease confined to a single organ, usually the liver or lung. Patients with unifocal or oligometastatic disease confined to a single organ should therefore be referred for surgical evaluation. 5-FU is usually given intravenously with leucovorin, which has no intrinsic antitumor activity of its own but causes 5-FU to bind more tightly to its target enzyme in preclinical models. The oral prodrug capecitabine is an acceptable alternative to 5-FU in a reliable, motivated patient who is able to comply with the complex oral medication schedule required. Irinotecan and oxaliplatin also have modest activity against colorectal cancer. Bevacizumab, a monoclonal antibody against vascular endothelial growth factor (VEGF), modestly improves outcome when added to chemotherapy regimens. Cetuximab

CONT.

and panitumumab are monoclonal antibodies that block the ligand-binding site of the epidermal growth factor receptor (EGFR). Recent studies indicate that the antitumor activity of these agents is limited to those tumors that do not have mutations in the K-*ras* gene. Therefore, K-*ras* genotyping is now a routine part of the management of patients with stage IV colorectal cancer.

The major side effect of the EGFR inhibitors is an acneiform rash, which can be uncomfortable and socially debilitating. Development of the rash and antitumor activity of EGFR inhibitors are apparently correlated, and patients in whom a significant rash does not develop are extremely unlikely to benefit from these agents. Two large randomized trials have demonstrated an unexpected deleterious effect of concurrent use of anti-VEGF and anti-EGFR monoclonal antibodies associated with a decrease in overall survival; therefore, these agents should not be used together. Although irinotecan, bevacizumab, and cetuximab have activity in treating patients with metastatic colorectal cancer, randomized trials have shown that they have no benefit as adjuvant chemotherapy for patients with nonmetastatic colorectal tumors and are associated with added toxicity and expense in this setting. H

Postoperative Colorectal Cancer Surveillance

Studies have not shown that early treatment of asymptomatic patients with surgically incurable recurrent colorectal cancer is better than later treatment. The role of monitoring patients after initial resection is therefore to detect recurrent, surgically curable tumors, such as oligometastatic liver or lung metastases, and monitor for the development of new primary cancer. Monitoring typically includes a physical examination and measurement of serum carcinoembryonic antigen (CEA) levels every 3 to 6 months for the first 3 years and every 6 months during years 4 and 5. CT scans of the chest, abdomen, and pelvis are recommended annually for at least the first 3 years postoperatively. PET scanning should not be used for routine surveillance. Colonoscopy is recommended 1 year after resection, then in 3 years, and then every 5 years unless abnormalities are found. Colonoscopy is primarily performed to detect new polyps that could become second primary tumors and, to a much lesser extent, to identify recurrent disease.

KEY POINTS

- Colorectal cancer surgery almost never results in the need for a permanent colostomy.
- All patients with stage III colon cancer, regardless of age, should receive postoperative adjuvant chemotherapy unless contraindicated because of medical or psychiatric disorders.
- Patients with rectal cancers that are not full-thickness lesions and do not have obvious lymph node involvement typically are managed with primary surgical resection.

Anal Cancer

Anal cancer is an epidermoid or squamous cell tumor that is almost always associated with human papillomavirus infection. Patients with HIV infection are also at increased risk. Unlike rectal cancer, anal cancer is treated initially with combined radiation therapy and chemotherapy with curative intent; surgery is not indicated. Patients with anal cancer that grows locally despite combination therapy can often be treated with surgical resection. However, such surgery invariably involves an abdominal-perineal resection with permanent colostomy.

Mitomycin plus 5-FU is the standard chemotherapy regimen used in conjunction with radiation therapy. Studies comparing cisplatin and mitomycin found cisplatin to be more toxic and no more effective than mitomycin in treating anal cancer.

KEY POINTS

- Anal cancer is treated initially with combined radiation therapy and chemotherapy.
- Mitomycin plus 5-fluorouracil is the standard chemotherapy regimen used in conjunction with radiation therapy in the treatment of anal cancer.

Pancreatic Cancer

Although the incidence of pancreatic cancer is substantially lower than that of colorectal cancer, the 1-year mortality rate for patients with this disease is very high. Pancreatic cancer is the fourth leading cause of cancer-related death in the United States, with more than 38,000 deaths estimated to occur annually. Patients with metastatic pancreatic cancer have a dismal prognosis. Median survival ranges from 4 to 6 months. Patients with locally unresectable disease have a slightly better prognosis, with a median survival of about 1 year.

Few risk factors have been clearly identified. Chronic pancreatitis predisposes to the development of pancreatic cancer, and tobacco use appears to increase risk. Obesity, diabetes mellitus, a diet high in red meat, and heavy alcohol use are implicated as risk factors in some studies but not in others. Although most pancreatic cancer appears to be sporadic, approximately 5% to 10% of patients have a strong family history of this cancer or an identifiable gene mutation that confers increased risk. Patients with a *BRCA2* gene mutation are at increased risk for development of pancreatic cancer.

Signs and symptoms are nonspecific. Patients may present with unexplained weight loss, painless jaundice, abdominal pain, fever of unexplained origin, or evidence of gastric outlet obstruction. The Trousseau syndrome (hypercoagulability in the setting of malignancy) may be the presenting finding in some patients.

CT of the chest and abdomen is the preferred imaging study for the initial evaluation of possible pancreatic malignancy. MRI is an acceptable alternative but is not superior to CT. PET scanning is not part of standard evaluation algorithms. Endoscopic ultrasonography is appropriate for a more detailed, but more invasive, examination of the pancreas and may be used to obtain a needle aspirate for diagnosis. Needle aspiration biopsy is not necessary for patients with potentially resectable cancer because an isolated, technically resectable pancreatic mass should be removed. In addition, malignancy is not excluded by a negative needle aspiration biopsy.

H Surgery is the only potentially curative intervention for patients with a technically resectable pancreatic tumor without evidence of metastases. However, the cure rate is low even in patients who undergo total resection. In patients with locally unresectable disease because of tumor involvement of critical vessels such as the superior mesenteric artery or the celiac trunk, combined chemotherapy and radiation therapy is often used as definitive therapy or to attempt to convert the tumor to a resectable lesion. Postoperative treatment of patients with fully resected pancreatic cancer is controversial. Older data that supported the benefit of adjuvant chemotherapy and radiation treatment had significant methodologic flaws, and these data have not been confirmed. A more recent trial of postoperative gemcitabine compared with observation alone showed a modest benefit for patients in the gemcitabine arm. Postoperative treatment of patients with fully resected pancreatic cancer should therefore be individualized because current data are insufficient to establish a definitive standard of care.

Single-agent gemcitabine is standard therapy for most patients with metastatic pancreatic cancer. Combining gemcitabine with cisplatin or oxaliplatin increases the response rate. However, toxic effects are also increased, and a survival benefit has not been demonstrated. A randomized trial of gemcitabine plus the oral EGFR inhibitor erlotinib showed an increased median survival of less than 2 weeks compared with gemcitabine alone. Although this difference was statistically significant, the clinical significance of such a modest benefit can be debated. More recently, a randomized trial comparing 5-FU, leucovorin, irinotecan, and oxaliplatin (FOLFIRINOX) with single-agent gemcitabine showed a survival benefit (10.5 months versus 6.9 months) for patients in the FOLFIRINOX arm, although these patients experienced substantially greater toxicity. The trial was limited to extremely fit patients with excellent performance status, and FOLFIRINOX chemotherapy is a reasonable consideration for such patients. Both cetuximab and bevacizumab have been investigated in large phase III trials in pancreatic cancer and both failed to improve survival. These drugs should not be used in this disease. H

KEY POINTS

- Patients with metastatic pancreatic cancer have a median survival ranging from 4 to 6 months; those with locally unresectable disease have a median survival of about 1 year.
- Surgery is the only potentially curative intervention for patients with pancreatic cancer who have an apparent technically resectable tumor without evidence of metastases.

Esophageal Cancer

About 16,500 new cases of esophageal cancer are expected in the United States annually, resulting in 14,500 deaths. The incidence is increasing. Most esophageal cancers diagnosed in the United States in the 1960s were squamous cell carcinomas, which are associated with tobacco and alcohol use and lower socioeconomic status. Currently, adenocarcinoma is the predominant histologic type, although epidermoid and squamous cell esophageal carcinomas remain common in Asia and Africa.

Gastroesophageal reflux disease (GERD) and obesity are risk factors associated with adenocarcinoma of the esophagus, which most often develops in the lower third of the esophagus and the gastroesophageal junction. The development of Barrett esophagus as a result of GERD is a particularly concerning risk factor, warranting surveillance. Presenting signs and symptoms of esophageal cancer may include dysphagia, odynophagia, dyspepsia, weight loss, nausea, and vomiting. The diagnosis is typically established by upper endoscopy and biopsy. Endoscopic ultrasonography is commonly used for staging and is especially accurate for establishing the tumor stage (T stage). CT of the chest and abdomen is the standard imaging study to determine the extent of disease. Combined PET/CT scanning is gaining acceptance as part of standard preoperative staging in patients with apparently resectable tumors.

Local and locoregional esophageal cancers (American Joint Committee on Cancer stages I, II, and III) are usually H treated surgically. Although older trials suggested no benefit from perioperative chemotherapy or radiation therapy, more recent trials suggest that preoperative chemotherapy, alone or combined with radiation therapy, may improve the chance for cure. Treatment of metastatic esophageal cancer remains unsatisfactory, with combination regimens currently being evaluated because of the insufficient activity of any single agent. H

KEY POINTS

- Gastroesophageal reflux disease, Barrett esophagus, and obesity are risk factors for esophageal cancer.
- The diagnosis of esophageal cancer is established by upper endoscopy and biopsy.

- Local and locoregional esophageal cancers are usually treated surgically; perioperative treatment with chemotherapy or chemotherapy plus radiation therapy may improve survival.

Gastric Cancer

Gastric cancer is relatively uncommon in the United States, with an estimated 21,000 cases annually, but it is extremely common in Asia, parts of Africa, and South America. *Helicobacter pylori* infection is a major risk factor. Tobacco use and a family history of gastric cancer are other risk factors. Staging techniques are similar to those used for esophageal cancer. Curative treatment requires a complete surgical resection; metastatic disease is treated palliatively with chemotherapy. The MAGIC trial demonstrated the superiority of preoperative and postoperative chemotherapy (epirubicin, cisplatin, and 5-FU) compared with surgery alone for treatment of gastric and esophageal/gastroesophageal junction adenocarcinomas. In patients who undergo surgery as initial therapy, postoperative 5-FU and leucovorin plus radiation therapy have been shown to confer a survival benefit compared with postoperative observation alone.

Management of metastatic gastric cancer is also similar to that of esophageal adenocarcinoma. The newer targeted agents have been disappointing in treating gastric cancer. A phase III trial of chemotherapy with or without bevacizumab failed to show a survival benefit, and the anti-EGFR agents cetuximab and panitumumab have thus far been ineffective. Recently, however, a trial of 594 patients with gastric and gastroesophageal junction adenocarcinomas expressing *HER2* found that the median survival was statistically significantly improved by adding trastuzumab to cisplatin plus 5-FU or capecitabine (13.5 months versus 11.1 months).

KEY POINTS

- *Helicobacter pylori* infection is a major risk factor for development of gastric cancer.
- In patients who undergo surgery as initial therapy for gastric cancer, postoperative 5-fluorouracil and leucovorin plus radiation therapy have been shown to confer a survival benefit compared with postoperative observation alone.
- Patients with gastric and gastroesophageal junction adenocarcinoma whose tumors expressed *HER2* experienced statistically significantly improved median survival when trastuzumab was added to cisplatin plus 5-fluorouracil or capecitabine.

Gastrointestinal Neuroendocrine Tumors

Neuroendocrine tumors (NETs) that are derived from neuroendocrine tissue of the aerodigestive tract are called carcinoid tumors, and those derived from the endocrine cells of the pancreas are called pancreatic NETs or islet cell tumors (derived from the islets of Langerhans). Typically, gastrointestinal NETs are moderately to well differentiated and have an indolent growth pattern. Less commonly, these tumors may be poorly differentiated and have an aggressive growth pattern. Most NETs are hormonally nonfunctioning, but about 25% secrete a functional hormone. In carcinoid tumors, this hormone is typically serotonin, which can cause the classic carcinoid syndrome of diarrhea and facial flushing. Pancreatic NETs, when hormonally active, may secrete insulin, gastrin, glucagon, somatostatin, or vasoactive intestinal peptide, and the resulting hormonal syndromes are based on the type of hormone secreted (see MKSAP 16 Endocrinology & Metabolism).

Although patients with hormonally functional tumors may seek medical care because of symptoms, those with hormonally nonfunctional tumors may be asymptomatic and may have metastatic disease for many years before the tumor is diagnosed. The liver is the most common site of metastasis, and diagnosis is often made after an incidental finding of hepatomegaly.

H

The most common site of carcinoid tumor is the appendix. Well-differentiated carcinoids of the appendix measuring less than 1 cm are cured by simple appendectomy, whereas tumors larger than 2 cm, or those with high-grade features, are typically treated with right hemicolectomy to remove the lymph nodes in the right mesocolon that drain the appendix. H

Because well-differentiated NETs are so indolent, patients with metastatic disease can often be managed with expectant observation and serial imaging studies. Triple-phase contrast-enhanced CT and gadolinium-enhanced MRI are the preferred imaging modalities. Indium-111 pentetreotide scanning can be used to establish the presence of somatostatin receptors, which are commonly expressed on these tumors. NETs that have somatostatin receptors and are causing hormone-induced symptoms or are showing definite growth while the patient is being monitored may be treated with octreotide, a synthetic somatostatin analogue. Hepatic artery embolization may be used to reduce tumor bulk in the liver and decrease hormone production. Chemotherapy is only minimally active in treating these tumors, although pancreatic NETs are somewhat more sensitive to chemotherapeutic agents than are carcinoid tumors. Agents targeting VEGF, such as sunitinib and bevacizumab, and agents targeting mammalian target of rapamycin (mTOR) are showing evidence of antitumor activity; however, such approaches remain investigational for carcinoid tumors at the time of this writing. Sunitinib and everolimus have recently received regulatory approval for treatment of pancreatic NETs and are reasonable considerations once these tumors show clear signs of progression or become symptomatic.

KEY POINTS

- Because well-differentiated gastrointestinal neuroendocrine tumors have an indolent growth pattern, patients can often be managed with expectant observation and serial imaging studies for considerable time before intervention is needed.
- Chemotherapy is only minimally active in treating gastrointestinal neuroendocrine tumors (NETs), although pancreatic NETs are slightly more sensitive to chemotherapeutic agents than are carcinoid tumors.

Lung Cancer

Epidemiology

Lung cancer is the leading cause of cancer-related death in the United States. The two major histologic types are small cell lung cancer (SCLC) and non–small cell lung cancer (NSCLC). Approximately 220,000 cases of lung cancer occurred in the United States in 2009 (85% of which were NSCLC), and 160,000 cancer-related deaths were reported. Most patients with SCLC or NSCLC have a history of cigarette smoking. The risk of lung cancer increases with the number of pack-years of cigarette exposure. In persons who stop smoking, the risk decreases proportionate to the number of years of abstinence but never returns to that of a person who has never smoked. Approximately 15% of patients with NSCLC are never smokers or have a minimal exposure (defined as less than a 10-pack-year smoking history). This subgroup will be discussed in detail later. Second-hand smoke is the likely cause of NSCLC in approximately 25% of patients who have never smoked.

Other risk factors for developing lung cancer include environmental exposures such as asbestos, radon, and heavy metals (arsenic, cadmium, nickel). Radiation therapy for malignancies such as breast cancer or Hodgkin lymphoma is also a risk factor. There is a small genetic risk as well, although the specific genes that confer susceptibility have not yet been identified.

KEY POINTS

- Lung cancer is the leading cause of cancer-related mortality in the United States.
- Although most patients with lung cancer have a history of cigarette smoking, approximately 15% of patients with non–small cell lung cancer are never smokers or have a minimal smoking history.

Screening

An effective cancer screening program demonstrates a benefit in reducing mortality. Prior studies evaluating chest radiographs and sputum cytology in cigarette smokers were not able to demonstrate improvements in lung cancer mortality. However, a recent study evaluating low-dose spiral CT scans has shown such a benefit, leading to advocacy to begin lung cancer screening in appropriate populations. The National Lung Screening Trial evaluated low-dose CT scans or chest radiographs in current or prior smokers with a minimum 30-pack-year smoking history. Participants were screened yearly for 3 years and followed for an additional 5 years. More than 53,000 men and women participated in this study, which showed a statistically significant 20% reduction in lung cancer mortality with screening by spiral CT. Recommendations for screening with low-dose spiral CT are pending based on these new data, including the appropriate populations and intervals for screening.

Routine CT screening also identifies many patients with small nodules that are of indeterminate significance. These nodules require periodic follow-up or biopsy to determine whether they represent early-stage lung cancer. The recent National Lung Screening Trial study evaluated noncalcified nodules greater than 4 mm in size but did not comment on an approach to smaller nodules.

The Fleischner Society for Thoracic Imaging and Diagnosis has published recommendations on the need for and frequency of follow-up for incidentally discovered nodules of various sizes. In low-risk individuals (never smokers, no history of a first-degree relative with lung cancer or significant radon or asbestos exposure), follow-up imaging is not required in patients with nodules less than or equal to 4 mm. In high-risk individuals (smoking history, environmental exposure), nodules less than 4 mm require follow-up imaging in 12 months (see MKSAP 16 Pulmonary and Critical Care Medicine).

KEY POINTS

- Screening for lung cancer in high-risk individuals with low-dose spiral CT scans has recently been found to reduce lung cancer mortality; new guidelines on this recent finding are pending.
- In low-risk individuals, follow-up imaging of incidentally found pulmonary nodules of less than or equal to 4 mm is not required.

Diagnosis

One reason for advocating lung cancer screening is that any lesions found are frequently early-stage, asymptomatic tumors. Otherwise, patients typically present with a cough, occasionally associated with hemoptysis, as a result of disease within the bronchus. Other symptoms include shortness of breath, which is due to mass effect of the primary tumor or development of a pleural effusion, and chest pain or hoarseness, the latter of which is caused by recurrent laryngeal nerve involvement. Patients with tumors of the lung apex have

Pancoast tumors and often present with pain due to invasion of the chest wall or brachial plexus or with Horner syndrome (miosis, ptosis, and ipsilateral anhidrosis). Overall, approximately 25% of all patients with lung cancer have advanced-stage disease at initial evaluation and present with weight loss, bone pain, or neurologic symptoms.

Patients with lung cancer may have an associated paraneoplastic syndrome, which is a constellation of abnormal clinical or laboratory findings that are not directly related to local effects of tumor masses but instead result from an immune response to the tumor or to substances secreted by tumor cells. Hypercalcemia is more common in patients with NSCLC and is likely due to bone metastases rather than to the production of a parathyroid hormone–related protein. The syndrome of inappropriate antidiuretic hormone secretion occurs more often in patients with SCLC and may cause profound hyponatremia. The primary therapy is treatment of the lung cancer, with implementation of water restriction, vasopressin receptor antagonists, and potentially, hypertonic saline, if resistant. Hypertrophic osteoarthropathy can occur, more often in patients with adenocarcinoma, resulting in clubbing of the digits (**Figure 24**), periostitis, and joint swelling.

Cushing disease due to overproduction of adrenocorticotropic hormone may also develop. Neurologic disorders are often the result of secretion of specific autoantibodies, resulting in the Lambert-Eaton myasthenic syndrome, cerebellar ataxia, or limbic encephalitis (see MKSAP 16 Neurology). Lambert-Eaton myasthenic syndrome is characterized by proximal weakness that typically improves with activity as well as diminished reflexes and a dry mouth.

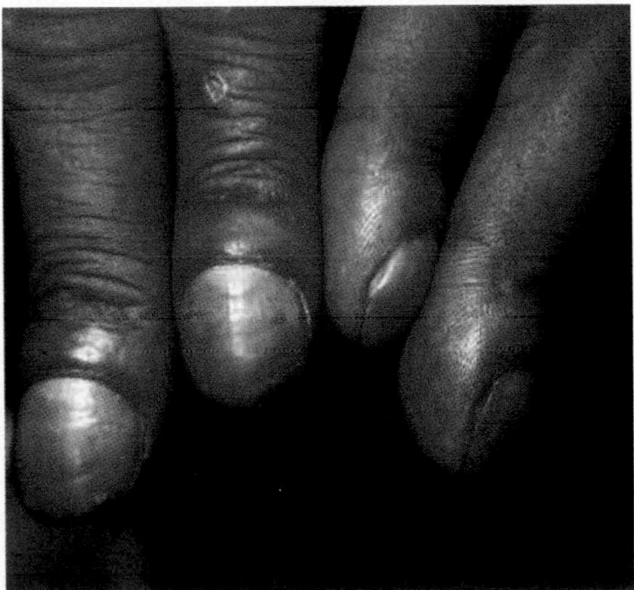

FIGURE 24. Flattening of the normal angle between the base of the nail and the cuticle, as well as possible swelling of the distal digit, is called clubbing. Although seen in patients with lung cancer, it can also occur in other pulmonary, cardiac, and gastrointestinal conditions.

Diagnostic evaluation of a lung mass depends on its size and location as well as the presence or absence of enlarged mediastinal lymph nodes or radiographic evidence of metastatic disease. Centrally located lesions can be assessed by sputum cytology or bronchoscopy. Peripheral masses often require CT-guided needle biopsy for diagnosis. CT- or ultrasound-guided needle biopsy is also indicated to evaluate suspected sites of metastatic involvement. If a lung mass appears to be resectable and there is no overt mediastinal lymph node enlargement, a surgeon may choose to obtain diagnostic tissue during surgical resection rather than preoperatively.

Distinguishing between SCLC and NSCLC is important because each has different treatment options. SCLC tends to disseminate systemically before diagnosis, which precludes surgical resection even if the cancer is apparently confined to one lung. NSCLC accounts for most lung cancers and is potentially curable with surgical resection if limited-stage disease is found at diagnosis. NSCLC is further classified histologically as adenocarcinoma, squamous cell carcinoma, and large cell carcinoma. Adenocarcinomas and large cell carcinomas are often located peripherally in the lung, and squamous cell carcinomas tend to be centrally located. Bronchioalveolar carcinomas are a subtype of adenocarcinoma and present as an infiltrate rather than a mass lesion. Although these subtypes of NSCLC are staged and treated similarly, they have important biologic, therapeutic, and prognostic differences.

KEY POINTS

- Cough, occasionally accompanied by hemoptysis, is the most frequent symptom of lung cancer, followed by shortness of breath, chest pain, and hoarseness.
- Approximately 25% of patients who have advanced-stage lung cancer at initial evaluation present with weight loss, bone pain, or neurologic symptoms.
- Histologic differentiation of small cell lung cancer and non–small cell lung cancer is important because only the latter is potentially curable by surgical resection.

Non–Small Cell Lung Cancer

Staging

The histologic subtypes of NSCLC are all staged similarly. A solitary tumor without regional (peribronchial or hilar) or mediastinal lymph node involvement is classified as stage I. Tumors measuring less than 3 cm are classified as stage IA and greater than 3 cm as stage IB. Stage II tumors are characterized by regional lymph node involvement or the presence of primary tumors that invade local structures such as the pleura or chest wall or are located near the carina. Stage III disease is defined mainly by mediastinal lymph node involvement.

Metastatic disease, as well as an ipsilateral malignant pleural effusion, is classified as stage IV.

Treatment

After NSCLC is diagnosed based on biopsy findings of a suspicious lung mass, staging studies are obtained to develop an appropriate treatment plan. Because the cancer may spread systemically, studies are also done to detect common sites of involvement, typically liver, bone, adrenal glands, or brain. Imaging studies include CT of the chest and abdomen plus a bone scan or PET/CT plus contrast-enhanced MRI of the brain.

Once advanced-stage IV disease is excluded, a thoracic surgeon should decide whether complete surgical resection is feasible, which is based on the presence or absence of mediastinal lymph node involvement. If positive lymph nodes are found by mediastinoscopy or bronchoscopic ultrasonography, surgery is not usually indicated for definitive therapy (see later discussion of stage III disease).

If the mediastinum and distant sites are disease-free, surgical resection is considered feasible. The next steps are determining the extent of the surgical procedure to remove all known disease and deciding whether postoperative residual lung function will be adequate. Because most patients with lung cancer have damage to the lungs from tobacco use, collaboration between surgeons and pulmonologists is important. Lung function studies should be obtained to evaluate total lung capacity, forced expiratory volumes, and diffusing capacity for carbon monoxide. Values below a certain level may preclude surgery. If a pneumonectomy is required, ventilation scans should be performed to identify the contribution of the diseased lung to overall lung function.

Treatment of Stage I, II, and III Non–Small Cell Lung Cancer

Surgery is the primary therapy for patients with stage I and II NSCLC, which accounts for approximately 30% of all cases. A classic procedure involving a thoracotomy incision or a minimally invasive procedure such as video-assisted thoracoscopic surgery (VATS) can be used. The thoracoscopic procedure is associated with less discomfort because of the smaller incision and shorter hospitalizations. Patients with stage I NSCLC have the most favorable prognosis, but only 60% of these patients are cured following surgery. Cure rates for patients with stage II disease are approximately 30%.

Although stage III NSCLC is the most common stage at presentation, management of patients with this stage of cancer is controversial. Historically, patients underwent surgical resection, but cure rates were typically less than 10%. Patients who have a single lymph node involved with microscopic disease that is usually found incidentally at surgery have a somewhat better prognosis. However, most patients with stage N2 disease (involvement of ipsilateral mediastinal or subcarinal lymph nodes) have multiple lymph nodes involved with bulky disease. These patients are usually treated with combined radiation therapy and chemotherapy rather than with surgery. Chemotherapy is given to increase the rate of local control achieved by regional radiation therapy and is associated with a 5-year disease-free survival rate of approximately 5% to 20%. Despite the use of combined radiation therapy and chemotherapy, local treatment failure and the development of metastatic disease are common. Studies are currently underway to determine which patients with stage N2 disease may benefit from surgery following induction radiation therapy and chemotherapy.

One problem of treating NSCLC with surgery or radiation therapy for the primary tumor is the possibility that the patient already had micrometastatic disease at presentation, which leads to eventual relapse of systemic disease. Many trials have investigated whether administering systemic chemotherapy after surgical resection improves overall survival. Five recent international studies have reported that adding cisplatin-based chemotherapy following attempted curative surgical resection improves 5-year survival rates for patients with stage II and III NSCLC by approximately 10%. Most patients who are appropriate candidates should therefore be considered for adjuvant chemotherapy after surgical resection.

Treatment of Stage IV Non–Small Cell Lung Cancer

Stage IV (metastatic) NSCLC is incurable. Goals of therapy are symptom palliation and possible prolongation of survival. Because metastatic NSCLC is a systemic process, systemic chemotherapy is typically used as the primary treatment modality. Chemotherapy for stage IV NSCLC has been shown to prolong survival and improve quality of life. Several chemotherapy regimens have been proved to provide benefit, and which regimen to use is determined by the histologic and potentially biologic subtypes of NSCLC.

The first-line approach is a two-drug platinum-based combination. Treatment is given for four to six cycles because protracted therapy does not provide additional benefit. A biologic agent such as bevacizumab (a vascular endothelial growth factor inhibitor) or cetuximab (an epidermal growth factor receptor inhibitor) can be added to the two-drug regimen. These agents modestly improve response rates and survival when added to chemotherapy. Second- and third-line therapy may provide palliation and prolong survival because stage IV NSCLC inevitably progresses after, or even during, administration of first-line therapy.

Radiation therapy helps alleviate symptoms of superior vena cava syndrome and obstructive pneumonitis. Brain metastases and spinal cord compression are treated with radiation therapy and occasionally with surgery. Patients with bone metastases may benefit from radiation therapy for pain control and bisphosphonates to control pain and reduce fracture risk. Despite these measures, the median survival of patients with stage IV NSCLC is only 8 to 10 months.

New Therapeutic Approaches

Although approximately 50% of patients with NSCLC have tumors expressing the epidermal growth factor receptor (EGFR), therapeutic agents that target this receptor provide only a modest response in patients with advanced disease. However, patients whose tumors have a mutation in the *EGFR* gene often benefit dramatically from such therapy. When testing a large unscreened patient population, approximately 10% of patients with adenocarcinoma of the lung will be found to have the *EGFR* gene mutation, whereas it is rarely found in patients with squamous cell or large call carcinoma. The typical clinical phenotype of a patient with this mutation is a woman with adenocarcinoma who has never smoked (or has a very limited smoking history) and is often of Asian descent. EGFR tyrosine kinase inhibitors such as erlotinib have a very high response rate in this subset of patients and have the potential for controlling advanced disease for many months. In patients without the *EGFR* gene mutation, these agents have some benefit as second- or third-line therapy but are associated with only very modest response rates and disease control.

KEY POINTS

- Surgery is the primary therapy for patients with stage I and II non–small cell lung cancer.
- Patients with stage III non–small cell lung cancer with N2 lymph node involvement are usually treated with combined radiation therapy and chemotherapy rather than surgery.
- Adding cisplatin-based chemotherapy following attempted curative resection improves 5-year survival rates by approximately 10% in patients with stage II and III non–small cell lung cancer.
- Primary treatment of patients with stage IV non–small cell lung cancer is typically a two-drug platinum-based chemotherapeutic regimen.

Small Cell Lung Cancer

SCLC comprises approximately 15% of all new lung cancer cases diagnosed in the United States and occurs almost exclusively in patients with a history of cigarette smoking. Because most of these tumors are located centrally and often are associated with mediastinal lymph node involvement, signs and symptoms of cough, hemoptysis, chest pain, hoarseness, and dyspnea occur frequently. Because of their rapid growth rate, these tumors are rarely found incidentally. Patients may also present with symptoms related to metastatic disease or to various paraneoplastic syndromes.

Diagnosis and Staging

Because SCLC is often located proximally within the airways, bronchoscopy is generally used for diagnosis. The rare peripheral mass can be approached with CT guidance. Biopsy of metastatic deposits, if present on radiographic studies, establishes the diagnosis.

The TNM classification is not used for SCLC staging. Instead, a simplified two-category classification, defined as limited or extensive stage, is used. Limited-stage SCLC is confined to one hemithorax, including the primary mass plus hilar, mediastinal, and ipsilateral supraclavicular lymph nodes, and suggests that all known disease can be encompassed within a tolerable radiation portal during treatment. Extensive-stage SCLC involves overt spread of disease beyond the hemithorax, including an ipsilateral malignant effusion and metastases to the brain, liver, or bone. Most patients present with advanced-stage disease.

Treatment

SCLC is considered a systemic disease at diagnosis, even if a potentially resectable peripheral lesion is the only finding after diagnostic studies are completed. Surgical resection was formerly the primary treatment, but many patients developed overt metastatic disease during the immediate postoperative period. All patients with SCLC now receive systemic chemotherapy as the mainstay of treatment.

Treatment of Limited-Stage Small Cell Lung Cancer

Patients with limited-stage SCLC are treated with combined chemotherapy and radiation therapy. The chemotherapy regimen is typically cisplatin or carboplatin plus etoposide for four to six cycles. Radiation therapy targeting all disease sites is given concurrently with the first or second chemotherapy cycle, because a combined therapy cycle has been shown to decrease local recurrences and increase overall survival. Although radiation therapy is beneficial, irradiation of the mediastinum has toxic effects, most often radiation esophagitis. Response rates to combinations of chemotherapy and radiation range from 80% to 90%, with about 50% being complete responses. The median survival of patients with limited-stage SCLC is approximately 14 to 18 months.

Although limited-stage SCLC tumors are one of the most chemosensitive types of tumors, there are recurrences in 90% to 95% of patients. To date, attempts to improve outcomes by adding other agents to the standard chemotherapy regimen or by using high-dose chemotherapy with stem cell support have been unsuccessful.

Treatment of Extensive-Stage Small Cell Lung Cancer

Extensive-stage SCLC is generally considered to be incurable. The mainstay of treatment is chemotherapy with cisplatin or carboplatin plus etoposide or irinotecan. Response rates to chemotherapy range from 60% to 80%, with complete responses achieved in 10% to 20% of patients. The average response lasts 4 to 6 months, and the median survival is 8 to 10 months. Salvage chemotherapy may benefit approximately 30% of patients. Radiation therapy is typically reserved for symptom palliation.

Prophylactic Cranial Radiation Therapy

Patients with limited-stage SCLC who complete combination chemotherapy and radiation therapy have a 50% to 80% chance of developing central nervous system (CNS) metastases if they survive for 2 years. In 20% of patients, the CNS is the initial site of systemic disease spread. Prophylactic brain irradiation may reduce the likelihood of symptomatic brain metastases and slightly improve overall survival. Patients with extensive-stage SCLC who have a good response to systemic treatment may also benefit from prophylactic brain irradiation, because this often results in a meaningful reduction in CNS metastases and prevention of neurologic sequelae. Balanced against these benefits are the complications associated with radiation therapy, including a risk of cognitive impairment in many patients who are long-term survivors.

KEY POINTS

- Biopsy of metastatic deposits identified on radiographs establishes the diagnosis of small cell lung cancer.
- Patients with limited-stage small cell lung cancer are treated with combined radiation therapy and chemotherapy, whereas extensive-stage small cell lung cancer is generally considered incurable.
- The mainstay of treatment for patients with extensive-stage small cell lung cancer is chemotherapy.
- Prophylactic brain irradiation reduces the likelihood of symptomatic brain metastases and slightly improves overall survival in patients with small cell lung cancer.

Head and Neck Cancer

Approximately 49,000 cases of head and neck cancer are diagnosed in the United States each year, and about 11,000 cancer-related deaths occur annually. The grouping of head and neck cancer comprises many different cancers that arise from the mucosa lining the upper aerodigestive tract. These tumors are grouped together because of similarities in epidemiology, histology, treatment strategies, and prognosis. However, each primary tumor has unique clinical and biologic features that require management by a team of experienced surgeons and oncologists. Most head and neck cancers are squamous cell carcinomas that develop in the nasal cavity, oral cavity (lips, buccal mucosa, tongue, gingiva, floor of the mouth, and hard palate), pharynx, and larynx. Tumors of the major salivary glands are usually adenocarcinoma or adenoid cystic carcinoma.

Risk Factors

Alcohol and tobacco use are the major risk factors for development of head and neck cancer. All tobacco products, including pipes, cigars, cigarettes, chewing tobacco, and snuff, are associated with an increased risk.

A subset of patients with head and neck cancer has no history of tobacco use. Some of these patients are found to have serologic evidence of Epstein-Barr virus. Similarly, many patients with cancer of the base of tongue or tonsil have evidence of infection with human papillomavirus (HPV), most notably HPV-16. These patients usually present at a younger age than those with head and neck cancer without HPV, have a better prognosis, and do not have a history of tobacco or alcohol use. At issue is whether less intensive treatment is appropriate for these patients to reduce the frequency of treatment-associated complications without affecting the improved prognosis.

Patients with head and neck cancer are also at increased risk for developing other malignancies of the aerodigestive tract. This is known as the field cancerization effect (the concept that different types of tumors may occur within a tissue field that is chronically exposed to carcinogens).

KEY POINTS

- The major risk factors for development of head and neck cancer are alcohol and tobacco use.
- Epstein-Barr virus and human papillomavirus infection may be responsible for development of head and neck cancer in a subset of patients without a history of tobacco use.

Diagnosis and Staging

Presenting signs and symptoms of head and neck cancer depend on the location of the primary tumor. A visible or palpable mass may be found in patients with cancer of the oral cavity, including the lips. Pain in these areas may be caused by local tumor invasion and often suggests an advanced-stage tumor. Referred ear pain, dysphagia, and odynophagia occur in patients with cancer of the oropharynx or hypopharynx. Hoarseness is common in patients with cancer of the larynx. Neck masses due to regional lymph node involvement are also fairly typical findings. Evaluation begins with visual inspection and palpation of the oral cavity and palpation of the cervical lymph node basins. This is followed by fiberoptic endoscopy of the remaining mucosal surfaces with biopsy of any abnormal lesions. Once the mucosal extent of a primary tumor is identified, CT or MRI is performed to detect local invasion and regional lymph node involvement. PET scanning is of additional benefit in identifying the minority of patients with metastatic disease or a second primary tumor.

Patients with cervical lymphadenopathy should be evaluated for evidence of a primary mucosal lesion, including fiberoptic endoscopy performed by a skilled examiner. If none is identified, fine-needle aspiration of a lymph node is performed. Subsequent lymph node biopsy is indicated if the aspirate is nondiagnostic. Biopsy must be performed carefully to avoid compromising possible surgical resection at a later date.

Because head and neck tumors are so diverse, staging varies somewhat by location. However, all tumors are uniformly classified as stage I to stage IV lesions. Stage I and II disease includes smaller tumors without lymph node involvement. Stage III disease is characterized by the presence of small-volume ipsilateral lymph node involvement. Stage IV disease includes larger tumors with local invasion, more extensive lymph node involvement, or distant metastases.

KEY POINTS

- Presenting signs and symptoms of head and neck cancer depend on the location of the primary tumor.
- Patients with cervical lymphadenopathy require expert evaluation of the upper aerodigestive tract to identify a primary lesion; fine-needle aspiration of a palpable lymph node is performed, followed by a lymph node biopsy if the aspirate is nondiagnostic.

H Treatment

Because head and neck cancers tend to recur locally rather than spread systemically, surgical resection and radiation therapy are the primary treatment modalities. Patients with early-stage (stage I and II) disease have no evidence of lymph node involvement either clinically or on CT scans. Early-stage disease is diagnosed in 30% to 40% of patients and is highly curable with surgical resection or radiation therapy of the primary tumor. Patients with primary tumors associated with a moderate risk of microscopic lymph node involvement typically also require irradiation or surgical resection of the involved lymph nodes. Tumors of the larynx and hypopharynx are usually treated with radiation therapy to preserve the voice and swallowing function. Although not superior in outcome compared with surgery, such approaches have benefit in maintaining the voice. Locally advanced stage III or IV tumors are present in approximately 50% of patients at diagnosis. Surgical resection may or may not be an option. Patients with potentially resectable tumors are initially treated with combined radiation therapy and chemotherapy followed by resection of the primary tumor or lymph nodes using modified radical neck dissection. More advanced localized tumors are treated with definitive combined radiation therapy and cisplatin-based chemotherapy. Cure is achieved in 20% to 40% of such patients.

Treatment of head and neck cancer is multidisciplinary. Goals of treatment are to improve survival while preserving organ function and minimizing complications. Because of improved local control rates with use of combined radiation therapy and chemotherapy, organ preservation is possible in some patients with primary tumors of the larynx or base of the tongue. Patients who require laryngectomy are taught alternative methods of speaking.

Complications following surgical resection may include damage to cranial, sensory facial, hypoglossal, and recurrent laryngeal nerves. Patients requiring radiation therapy often develop xerostomia when major salivary glands are located in the treatment field. Other complications of radiation therapy include mucositis, voice changes, altered taste sensation, fibrosis, dental problems, and esophageal strictures. These complications are exacerbated when concurrent chemotherapy is required. Comprehensive treatment therefore requires prophylactic measures to minimize these toxic effects as well as rehabilitative strategies to alleviate complications and include dental extractions, fluoride treatments, feeding tube placement, amifostine for mucositis, and pilocarpine for xerostomia. Chemotherapy is the primary treatment for metastatic disease. H

KEY POINTS

- Goals of treatment of head and neck cancer focus on improving survival while preserving organ function and minimizing complications.
- Early-stage (stage I and II) head and neck cancer is highly curable with surgical resection or radiation therapy.
- Locally advanced stage III and IV head and neck cancer is treated with a combination of surgical resection, radiation therapy, and chemotherapy.
- Complications following treatment of head and neck cancer include damage to cranial and sensory nerves, xerostomia, swallowing dysfunction, voice changes, altered taste sensation, fibrosis, dental problems, and esophageal strictures.

Genitourinary Cancer

Prostate Cancer

Prostate cancer is the second most common malignancy in men worldwide. Approximately 190,000 cases are diagnosed in the United States each year, and about 27,000 cancer-related deaths occur annually.

Epidemiology and Risk Factors

Prostate cancer occurs more often in black men than in white and Hispanic men. Asian Americans are at lowest risk. Other risk factors include increasing age and a history of prostate cancer in a first-degree relative. Some studies suggest that a high-fat, low-fiber diet increases risk. Men with prostatitis are also at slightly increased risk. Contrary to earlier reports, vasectomy is not associated with development of prostate cancer.

Chemoprevention with 5-α-reductase inhibitors has been shown to reduce the incidence of prostate cancer. However, no overall survival benefit has been demonstrated to date, and the side effects of these agents include gynecomastia, decreased libido, and erectile dysfunction. Their use in the primary prevention of prostate cancer is controversial.

KEY POINTS

- Major prostate cancer risk factors include increasing age, black race, and a history of prostate cancer in a first-degree relative.
- 5-α-reductase inhibitors reduce the incidence of prostate cancer but have not demonstrated improved survival to date.

Diagnosis and Staging

Routine screening of asymptomatic men for prostate cancer using prostate-specific antigen (PSA) measurement has become controversial because many of the malignancies discovered in this way may not be clinically significant, and early detection and treatment have not been shown to improve survival and can cause significant harms. Nonetheless, most men with asymptomatic prostate cancer are currently diagnosed following PSA screening. Prostate screening is discussed in MKSAP 16 General Internal Medicine.

The remainder of patients with prostate cancer are diagnosed following an abnormal digital rectal examination (DRE) or based on symptoms. An abnormal DRE may reveal an asymmetric, indurated, or nodular prostate. Diffuse enlargement of the gland is more consistent with benign prostatic hyperplasia than cancer. A normal examination or diffuse enlargement does not preclude the need for biopsy. If the digital rectal examination is abnormal, urologic evaluation is usually warranted, regardless of the serum PSA level.

Obstructive symptoms such as urinary hesitancy, incomplete bladder emptying, and decreased urinary stream or nocturia may occur. Statistically, these symptoms are more likely attributable to benign prostatic hyperplasia than prostate cancer, but biopsy may still be indicated to exclude prostate cancer. New-onset sexual dysfunction may reflect invasion into the neurovascular bundle. Patients with metastatic disease may have bone pain, or occasionally, signs and symptoms of spinal cord compression.

The definitive diagnostic test for prostate cancer is transrectal biopsy with multiple core samples from all parts of the gland. This is a simple office procedure that does not require anesthesia or analgesia. Studies have shown that patients with coronary artery or cerebrovascular disease do not need to stop taking low-dose aspirin before biopsy because the risk of severe bleeding complications is low. Transrectal ultrasonography (TRUS) may help define the anatomy of the prostate and the clinical disease stage and may guide sites for biopsy. However, TRUS is associated with a high false-negative rate, and biopsy is still required in patients with a normal ultrasound. Consequently, this procedure should not be a routine part of the workup. Endorectal MRI is sometimes used for more accurate assessment of the local extent of disease, especially if prostatectomy is being considered.

Clinical staging is the cornerstone of therapeutic decision-making in patients with prostate cancer. The TNM prostate cancer staging system developed by the American Joint Committee on Cancer was updated in 2010 and now incorporates the Gleason score (a histologic grading of prostate cancer that helps determine prognosis) and preoperative PSA values to define prognostic groups more accurately (**Table 41**). T1 cancers are not palpable or visible on imaging studies. T2 cancers are confined within the prostate. T3 lesions extend through the capsule or invade the seminal vesicles, and T4 lesions are fixed or invade adjacent structures. The a, b, and c subsets refer to the magnitude or local extension of tumor within that T subset. The presence of regional lymph node involvement is classified as stage N1 disease. Distant metastases to nonregional lymph nodes, bone, or other organs are classified as stage M1 (metastatic) disease.

KEY POINTS

- An abnormal digital rectal examination or the presence of urologic symptoms should prompt transrectal biopsies to exclude prostate cancer, even in men with normal serum prostate-specific antigen levels.
- The definitive test for diagnosing prostate cancer is transrectal biopsy with multiple core samples from all parts of the gland.

Treatment

Treatment options for patients with newly diagnosed prostate cancer include observation, prostatectomy, radiation therapy, and androgen deprivation therapy (hormonal therapy). Chemotherapy may also be used for patients with metastatic disease. Treatment decisions are based on the estimated risks of extraprostatic disease spread and cancer recurrence. The patient's age, overall health, and life expectancy are critical factors in recommending treatment. Nomograms are available to help guide decision-making.

In general, patients with low-risk disease and a short life expectancy are best managed with observation or watchful waiting. Patients with low-risk disease and long life expectancy are usually offered radical prostatectomy, radiation therapy, or active surveillance. Active surveillance is defined as the postponement of immediate treatment with the intention to provide curative treatment if the disease progresses. The goal of active surveillance is to avoid treatment-related complications for men whose cancer is not likely to progress while maintaining an opportunity for cure in those who show evidence of progression. There are currently no randomized prospective trial data directly comparing this approach to radical prostatectomy and radiation therapy, although two studies are underway as of this writing. Patients with high-risk disease (stage T3 and T4, Gleason score of 8 to 10 or serum PSA level >20 ng/mL) and short life expectancy are usually treated with androgen deprivation therapy or observation. Patients with high-risk disease and long life expectancy have

TABLE 41. AJCC TNM Prostate Cancer Staging System

Anatomic Stage/Prognostic Groups					
Group	**T**	**N**	**M**	**PSA**	**Gleason**
I	T1a-c	N0	M0	PSA <10	Gleason ≤6
	T2a	N0	M0	PSA <10	Gleason≤6
	T1-2A	N0	M0	PSA X	Gleason X
IIA	T1a-c	N0	M0	PSA<20	Gleason 7
	T1a-c	N0	M0	PSA ≥10 <20	Gleason ≤6
	T2a	N0	M0	PSA ≥10 <20	Gleason ≤6
	T2a	N0	M0	PSA<20	Gleason 7
	T2b	N0	M0	PSA<20	Gleason ≤7
	T2b	N0	M0	PSA X	Gleason X
IIB	T2c	N0	M0	Any PSA	Any Gleason
	T1-2	N0	M0	PSA ≥20	Any Gleason
	T1-2	N0	M0	Any PSA	Gleason ≥8
III	T3a-b	N0	M0	Any PSA	Any Gleason
IV	T4	N0	M0	Any PSA	Any Gleason
	Any T	N1	M0	Any PSA	Any Gleason
	Any T	Any N	M1	Any PSA	Any Gleason

Once a diagnosis of prostate cancer is made, patients with high-risk disease (T3, T4, high PSA value, or Gleason score of 8-10) usually have a bone scan. CT should also be considered, especially in patients suspected of having more advanced disease.

AJCC = American Joint Committee on Cancer; PSA = prostate-specific antigen.

Reprinted with permission from the American Joint Committee on Cancer (AJCC), Chicago, IL. The original source for this material is the AJCC Cancer Staging Manual, Seventh Edition (2010) published by Springer Science and Business Media LLC, www.springer.com.

several options, including radiation therapy with combined androgen deprivation or surgery followed by observation, radiation therapy, or androgen deprivation based on pathologic results (**Table 42**).

H

Surgery

Radical prostatectomy performed by an experienced urologic surgeon is generally recommended by urologists for patients with disease confined to the prostate and a life expectancy greater than 10 years. Nerve-sparing surgical techniques reduce the incidence of sexual and urinary dysfunction. Erectile dysfunction is relatively common after radical prostatectomy even after nerve-sparing surgery, with rates ranging from 20% to 60%. Urinary incontinence is less common (15% to 50%) and usually improves with conservative treatment months after surgery. The frequency of these adverse events depends in part on the experience and expertise of the surgeon. New surgical techniques incorporating laparoscopy or robotic assistance reduce postoperative morbidity but have not been shown to improve survival.

Radiation Therapy

External-beam radiation therapy has been a standard technique for treating prostate cancer for many years. Although the potential advantage of surgery compared with radiation therapy is that no cancer cells remain to metastasize postoperatively, many studies report that long-term survival rates are similar for patients receiving either treatment. Radiation therapy avoids the risks of general anesthesia, hospitalization, and perioperative complications such as bleeding and infection. It also results in less urinary incontinence. However, radiation therapy must be given for 6 to 8 weeks and may cause proctitis, cystitis, and long-term erectile dysfunction. Many facilities now use intensity-modulated radiation therapy, which is a more focused radiation technique that has decreased the risk of late toxic effects such as proctitis and cystitis without compromising therapeutic benefit.

Studies involving use of a robotic radiosurgery system with a short course of highly focused intense radiation therapy are ongoing, but this approach is gaining favor in many institutions. Brachytherapy, which places radioactive implants directly into the prostate, is an acceptable alternative to external-beam radiation therapy, although the seeds must be placed very accurately to deliver the optimal radiation dosage. In addition, worldwide experience is much more limited with this technique than with other forms of radiation therapy.

External-beam radiation therapy helps palliate painful bone metastases in patients with metastatic prostate cancer.

TABLE 42. Initial Treatment of Prostate Cancer

Risk	Life Expectancy	Treatment Options
Low	<10 years	Observation
	>10 but <20 years	Observation *or*
		Radiation therapy *or*
		Radical prostatectomy
	≥20 years	Radiation therapy *or*
		Radical prostatectomy
Intermediate	<10 years	Observation *or*
		Radiation therapy *or*
		Radical prostatectomy
	≥10 years	Radiation therapy *or*
		Radical prostatectomy
High	<5 years	Observation with hormonal therapy
	≥5 years	Radiation therapy with hormonal therapy *or*
		Radiation therapy alone *or*
		Radical prostatectomy

Information from NCCN Clinical Practice Guidelines in Oncology: Prostate Cancer. National Comprehensive Cancer Network. www.nccn.org/professionals/physician_gls/PDF/prostate.pdf. Accessed on February 15, 2012.

CONT.

Trials have also shown that pain and bone fracture are reduced in patients with bone metastases who are treated with monthly bisphosphonates (zoledronic acid or pamidronate).

Androgen Deprivation Therapy

Prostate cancer cells usually need testosterone to grow. Surgical or chemical castration is highly effective in reducing serum testosterone levels and suppressing prostate cancer cells. Gonadotropin-releasing hormone (GnRH) agonists/antagonists are used for chemical castration and are administered by intermittent intramuscular or subcutaneous injection for prolonged periods. These agents block the pituitary-testis pathways and reduce serum testosterone levels. Antiandrogens are oral agents that block the androgen receptors on prostate cancer cells and are often added to GnRH agonists/antagonists for combined androgen blockade. Typical side effects of therapy include hot flushes, gynecomastia, impotence, reduced libido, weight gain, osteopenia, and coronary artery disease. Calcium and vitamin D supplements are recommended for men receiving androgen deprivation therapy. Screening for osteopenia is advised, and men with osteopenia should be treated with bisphosphonates.

In patients with high-risk localized or locally advanced prostate cancer, starting GnRH agonists/antagonists before initiation of radiation therapy leads to improved survival compared with radiation therapy alone. The optimal duration of androgen deprivation therapy is unclear, but accumulating data support a longer course of treatment such as 8 months before radiation therapy is initiated.

Chemotherapy

Almost all surviving patients eventually develop hormone-refractory prostate cancer and progressive metastatic disease and may benefit from chemotherapy. Administration of docetaxel plus prednisone is associated with a 3- to 6-month survival advantage compared with mitoxantrone-based chemotherapy, and the mean survival of patients treated with docetaxel approaches 18 months. Recently, cabazitaxel was approved for the treatment of metastatic prostate cancer that progressed after treatment with docetaxel. Survival was modestly prolonged with this agent compared with patients treated with mitoxantrone. Clinical trials are ongoing to determine the effectiveness of newer investigational agents for patients with refractory disease.

Immunotherapy

Sipuleucel-T was recently approved for the treatment of hormone-refractory prostate cancer. This agent is the first autologous cellular immunotherapy. It activates the patient's immune system to target prostate cancer cells.

Prostate Cancer Follow-up and Posttreatment Recurrence

Regularly scheduled digital rectal examinations and serum PSA determinations are recommended for all patients who complete treatment for prostate cancer, especially for patients with higher-risk disease and longer life expectancy. Up to 75% of prostate cancer recurrences occur by the fifth year of follow-up. A rising PSA level without symptoms or radiographic evidence of disease is termed a biochemical recurrence. Such patients are re-staged and offered additional treatment or observation based on the extent of disease, rate of progression, and life expectancy. Recurrent prostate cancer after definitive treatment is incurable. Patients with recurrent disease are usually offered long-term palliation with androgen deprivation therapy and chemotherapy.

KEY POINTS

- Patients with low-risk prostate cancer and a short life expectancy are best managed with observation or watchful waiting.
- Patients with organ-confined prostate cancer and a life expectancy greater than 10 years may be offered radical prostatectomy, radiation therapy, or active surveillance with the intention to cure.
- Patients with high-risk, locally advanced, or metastatic disease are treated with androgen deprivation therapy, and those with hormone-refractory metastatic prostate cancer may benefit from treatment with chemotherapy.
- Regularly scheduled digital rectal examinations and serum prostate-specific antigen determinations are recommended for all patients after prostate cancer treatment.

Testicular Cancer

Testicular cancer is the most common solid tumor in young men. It is also one of the most highly curable of all malignancies. Approximately 8480 cases were estimated to be diagnosed in the United States in 2010, and only 350 cancer-related deaths were expected. The incidence has been slowly increasing.

Germ cell tumors account for 95% of testicular cancers and are classified as either pure seminomas or nonseminomas (nonseminomatous germ cell tumors). Patients with pure seminomas have a better prognosis. Nonseminomas are classified by histologic type as embryonal carcinoma, choriocarcinoma, yolk sac carcinoma, and teratoma or may be of mixed type. The presence of any of these histologic types defines the tumor as a nonseminoma rather than a seminoma.

The primary risk factors for development of testicular cancer are the presence of Klinefelter syndrome, cryptorchidism, and a family history of testicular cancer. In patients with cryptorchidism, surgical correction of an undescended testicle early in life substantially reduces, but does not eliminate, this risk. Testicular cancer can also develop in the normal descended testicle of a patient with cryptorchidism.

KEY POINTS

- Testicular cancer is the most common solid tumor in young men and is one of the most highly curable of all malignancies.
- The primary risk factors for development of testicular cancer are the presence of Klinefelter syndrome, cryptorchidism, and a family history of testicular cancer.

Diagnosis and Staging

Patients with testicular cancer usually present with a unilateral mass or testicular swelling. About 10% of patients have acute pain, which is often attributed to minor trauma; 10% present with signs and symptoms of metastases (for example, back pain, cough, dyspnea, or neurologic abnormalities); and 5% have gynecomastia related to an elevated serum β-human chorionic gonadotropin level.

All patients with a palpable testicular mass should undergo testicular ultrasonography and be referred for urologic evaluation, including radiographic studies and serum tumor marker determinations. A chest radiograph and CT scan of the abdomen and pelvis are done initially. CT of the chest is indicated if the chest radiograph is abnormal or lung metastases are strongly suspected. PET is associated with frequent false-negative results and is therefore not recommended.

Determination of serum tumor markers plays a critical role in the diagnosis, treatment, and follow-up of patients with testicular cancer. Serum α-fetoprotein, β-human chorionic gonadotropin, and lactate dehydrogenase levels are measured at diagnosis. An elevated serum α-fetoprotein level defines the tumor as a nonseminoma. Serum β-human chorionic gonadotropin levels may be elevated in patients with seminomas or nonseminomas. Serum lactate dehydrogenase elevations reflect the rapid turnover of malignant cells.

Staging is performed using the American Joint Committee on Cancer TNM staging system. The primary tumor (T stage) is determined pathologically based on the local extent of cancer found at radical orchiectomy, which is the preferred surgical technique. Involvement of lymph nodes (N stage) and the presence of distant metastases (M stage) are determined by CT scan. Serum tumor marker values are used to develop an S score, which is a unique category used only for classifying testicular cancer. The TNM anatomic stage and S score are combined to determine the final stage, which ranges from stage IA to IIIC. Patients with stage I disease have disease confined to the testicle, those with stage II disease have positive regional lymph nodes, and those with stage III disease have metastases. There is no stage IV for testicular cancer.

KEY POINTS

- Patients with testicular cancer usually present with a unilateral mass or testicular swelling.
- Initial urologic evaluation of a patient with suspected testicular cancer includes a chest radiograph, CT scan of the abdomen and pelvis, and determination of serum tumor marker levels.

Treatment

As noted earlier, all patients with testicular cancer (either seminoma or nonseminoma) require radical orchiectomy.

 Because nonseminomas are associated with a less favorable prognosis, postoperative treatment differs for these two cancer types. H

Seminoma

Stage I seminoma has a very high cure rate after radical orchiectomy. Management options include active surveillance, which requires a compliant patient; radiation therapy to the para-aortic lymph nodes; or single-agent carboplatin chemotherapy. Patients in whom relapse occurs are treated with multiagent chemotherapy, which is associated with a high cure rate. Although radiation therapy is associated with a 95% cure rate in patients with stage I disease, irradiation may impair fertility and occasionally causes second malignancies. One cycle of single-agent carboplatin chemotherapy is well tolerated and is as effective as radiation therapy in treating stage I disease.

Patients with stage IIA or IIB disease are treated with radiation therapy or platinum-based chemotherapy. Bleomycin may be added to the regimen for patients with more advanced tumors. All patients require frequent surveillance after treatment of seminoma. Follow-up includes a history, physical examination, and measurement of serum tumor marker levels every 2 months during the first year. The evaluation is repeated with declining frequency until 10 years after initial treatment. A CT scan of the abdomen and pelvis is obtained at 4 months postoperatively and then as clinically indicated.

Nonseminoma

Patients with nonseminomas have a poorer prognosis than those with seminomas and require more aggressive treatment. Patients with stage IA nonseminoma following radical orchiectomy are treated with either active surveillance or retroperitoneal lymph node dissection (RPLND). Treatment of patients with stage IB disease is RPLND, two cycles of multiagent chemotherapy (platinum, etoposide, and bleomycin), or active surveillance. Active surveillance is associated with a 20% to 30% relapse rate. Patients who develop a relapse are treated with three or four cycles of salvage chemotherapy, which is highly effective.

Patients with a more advanced stage of disease receive RPLND or platinum-based chemotherapy. Treatment decisions may be based on the presence or absence of metastatic disease in resected lymph nodes and the persistence or resolution of elevated tumor marker levels after initial treatment. Patients with residual tumor following initial platinum-based chemotherapy may have surgical resection of the tumor or more chemotherapy using alternative drugs.

All patients who complete treatment for nonseminoma should strictly adhere to recommended follow-up guidelines because of the rapid growth of these tumors and the potential for cure in patients with recurrent disease.

KEY POINTS

- All patients with testicular cancer (either seminoma or nonseminoma) require radical orchiectomy as initial treatment.
- Patients with nonseminoma have a poorer prognosis than those with seminoma and require more aggressive treatment, but even with widespread metastases, may be cured with additional surgery and combination chemotherapy.

Bladder Cancer

Approximately 71,000 cases of bladder cancer are diagnosed in the United States each year, and about 14,000 cancer-related deaths occur annually. About 90% of bladder cancers are of urothelial (transitional cell) origin.

Most bladder cancers occur in men, who are typically older than 60 years of age. The major risk factor is cigarette smoking, and the risk is proportionate to the number of pack-years smoked. Another potential risk is occupational exposure in metal workers, painters, and leather workers, among others. Because the entire urothelial lining may possibly be exposed to a toxin, a field cancerization effect can lead to an increased risk for development of other cancers of the genitourinary system, such as transitional cell cancer of the renal pelvis.

KEY POINTS

- Most bladder cancers occur in men, who are typically over 60 years of age.
- Cigarette smoking is the major risk factor for development of bladder cancer.

Diagnosis and Staging

Patients most often present with painless hematuria. A malignancy is more likely in patients with gross bleeding than in those with microscopic hematuria. Bleeding is typically present throughout micturition. Other symptoms may include urinary frequency, urgency, or pain, although these symptoms are often absent. Pain is more typical of invasive tumors.

All components of the urinary tract must be evaluated in patients with hematuria to identify a potential malignant source (or sources) of bleeding. The initial study is often a CT scan, MRI, or intravenous pyelography of the upper urinary tract followed by cystoscopy to detect areas of mucosal irregularity. Urine specimens are also obtained for cytologic studies. Some urologists prefer voided specimens, whereas others obtain washings at the time of cystoscopy. If a possibly malignant lesion is seen during cystoscopy, examination is performed while the patient is under anesthesia, with cystoscopic mapping of all lesions and complete transurethral resection of the bladder tumor (TURBT), if possible. Biopsy samples of visibly normal areas are also obtained to exclude the field cancerization effect. If malignant cells are found in urine cytology specimens but no visible lesions are detected during cystoscopy, biopsy of all areas is mandatory, including the prostatic urethra, bladder, and ureters by ureteroscopy.

The TNM classification system is used to stage bladder cancer. Approximately 60% of patients present with noninvasive bladder cancer, which includes low-grade papillary tumors (stage Ta) and carcinoma in situ (stage Tis). Ta tumors tend to recur but have a low rate of conversion to a higher-grade lesion and eventual muscle invasion. Tis tumors are dysplastic lesions that have a greater risk for muscle invasion and recurrence. T1 tumors invade the submucosa, and T2 lesions penetrate into the muscular wall of the bladder. Cystoscopy and TURBT with appropriate sampling of the underlying muscle are critical for identifying tumors that invade muscle (stages T2 to T4) because patients with these tumors usually require cystectomy. The anatomic (S) stage is an indicator of prognosis. Noninvasive tumors are classified as stage 0. Stage I includes T1 tumors, stage II indicates muscle invasion without regional lymph node involvement, and stage III includes locally advanced tumors. Stage IV is used to classify patients with lymph node involvement and those with distant metastases.

KEY POINTS

- Patients with bladder cancer most often present with painless hematuria.
- All components of the urinary tract must be evaluated in patients with hematuria to identify a potential malignant source (or sources) of bleeding.
- Approximately 60% of patients with bladder cancer are found to have noninvasive disease at the time of initial TNM staging.

H Treatment

Patients with noninvasive (stage I) bladder cancer are treated with TURBT. The risk for potential recurrence is then determined based on the number of tumors found at surgery, their histologic grade, and whether they invade into the submucosa. Patients with higher-risk tumors are usually treated with intravesicular agents such as bacillus Calmette-Guérin. Intravesicular therapy reduces the risk for recurrence, muscle invasion, and the need for subsequent cystectomy and also improves disease-specific survival. A 6-week induction course is typically given and is followed by maintenance therapy for 1 year. Patients with lower-risk tumors are usually managed with observation or are given a single dose of intravesicular mitomycin or gemcitabine.

After completing treatment, patients with noninvasive disease are followed closely for potential recurrences. Standard recommendations include cystoscopy every 3 months for the first 2 years, every 6 months for the next 2 years, and yearly thereafter. Patients with noninvasive bladder cancer have an excellent prognosis, and cancer-related deaths rarely occur. Patients who develop recurrent disease with favorable tumor characteristics may be retreated with intravesicular therapy but may require cystectomy if higher-risk tumors are found.

Patients with bladder cancer that invades muscle usually require radical cystectomy, including removal of the bladder, adjacent pelvic organs, and regional lymph nodes. Patients undergoing radical cystectomy will require a noncontinent cutaneous urinary diversion with urine collected in a urostomy bag or one of several continent diversions that are now available. Partial cystectomy may be appropriate for some patients with localized tumors. Bladder-sparing treatment, typically using a combination of chemotherapy and radiation therapy, may be an option for some patients. Patients who do not have a complete response to a bladder-sparing procedure are generally advised to undergo cystectomy. Cure rates of 75% to 85% are achieved in patients with stage II disease with muscle invasion following radical cystectomy, and cure rates of 20% to 55% are demonstrated in patients with more locally advanced tumors (T3/T4/N0) following surgery. Patients with lymph node involvement have only a 10% to 20% chance of long-term survival. H

Randomized trials have shown that patients with bladder cancer that invades muscle at initial diagnosis may benefit from preoperative cisplatin-based chemotherapy. A meta-analysis of neoadjuvant chemotherapy trials demonstrated an approximate 5% improvement in overall survival in these patients. If neoadjuvant therapy is not used, adjuvant chemotherapy is given to patients with stage III tumors and those with stage IV disease with lymph node involvement.

Metastatic disease is incurable, and patients have a median survival of 8 to 12 months. Palliative platinum-based chemotherapy is associated with response rates ranging from 30% to 70% in these patients.

KEY POINTS

- Patients with noninvasive bladder cancer are usually treated with transurethral resection of the bladder tumor and have an excellent prognosis.
- Patients with bladder cancer that invades muscle usually require radical cystectomy, including removal of the bladder, adjacent pelvic organs, and regional lymph nodes.
- Metastatic bladder cancer is incurable, and palliative platinum-based chemotherapy is often used in this setting.

Renal Cell Cancer

Approximately 58,000 cases of renal cell cancer are diagnosed in the United States each year, and about 13,000 cancer-related deaths occur annually.

Most renal cell cancers are of the clear cell type, 10% to 15% are papillary tumors, and 10% are chromophobe tumors. A few are oncocytomas, a benign tumor that is usually treated by local excision. Most renal cell cancers originate in the renal cortex. Typically, the small number of tumors occurring in the renal pelvis, which are transitional cell in origin, are also termed renal cancer. Risk factors include cigarette smoking, obesity, occupational exposures (cadmium, asbestos, gasoline), effects of dialysis (acquired cystic kidney disease), and inherited conditions such as the von Hippel–Lindau syndrome.

H Diagnosis and Staging

Most patients are evaluated initially because of a mass found incidentally on a radiographic study performed for other reasons. Although hematuria, pain, and an upper abdominal mass are considered to be the classic triad for diagnosing renal cell cancer, patients rarely present with these findings.

The most important part of the initial evaluation is to determine whether a renal mass is cystic or solid, which is usually done by ultrasonography. Cysts classified as simple are rarely malignant, but complex cysts and solid masses warrant further evaluation. Dedicated renal CT scans can identify extrarenal extension, renal vein invasion, or regional lymphadenopathy. CT-guided biopsies are usually not performed for solid masses measuring more than 3 or 4 cm because of the high likelihood of malignancy. Instead, these masses are resected using partial or radical nephrectomy. Smaller lesions are often biopsied and are treated surgically if malignancy is detected. Observation of lesions less than 1.5 cm is recommended, with subsequent investigation if the lesions begin to grow.

Tumors confined to the kidney are classified as stage I, less than 7cm; or Stage II disease. Stage III disease is defined by extension of the primary tumor into surrounding tissue or vascular structures or by the presence of regional lymph node involvement. Stage IV tumors are metastatic. Cure rates are greater than 90% for stage I tumors, 75% to 90% for stage II tumors, and 60% to 70% for stage III disease. The 5-year survival rate is approximately 10% for patients with metastatic disease. H

KEY POINTS

- Most patients with renal cell cancer present with a mass found incidentally on a radiographic study performed for other reasons.
- Large solid tumors seen on ultrasound imaging are so likely to be renal cell carcinoma that needle biopsy is not needed before definitive surgical resection is planned.

H Treatment

All histologic types of renal cell cancer are treated similarly. However, papillary tumors tend to be early-stage lesions at diagnosis and therefore have a better prognosis. Stage I to III renal cell cancer is treated primarily by partial or radical nephrectomy, depending on tumor size and location. An open procedure or a laparoscopic approach can be used. Partial nephrectomy is appropriate for small tumors measuring less than 4 cm that are not adjacent to the renal pelvis. Such a procedure preserves renal function and has been shown to be as effective as radical nephrectomy for treatment of small tumors. Partial nephrectomy is especially helpful for patients with compromised renal function at baseline or those with a solitary kidney or bilateral tumors. Patients with small tumors and significant comorbid findings, including compromised renal function, can be treated with ablative procedures rather than with nephrectomy.

Important new advances are occurring in the treatment of patients with metastatic renal cell cancer. Nephrectomy may be recommended for patients with metastatic disease despite the therapeutic goal of providing palliative therapy, usually with immunotherapy. This recommendation is based on studies showing that patients who underwent nephrectomy before being treated with interferon alfa immunotherapy had improved survival compared with those who received interferon alfa alone. H

Based on new findings, alternative agents that are more effective than immunotherapy are now available for patients with resected renal cell cancer who develop metastatic disease. Many patients with sporadic clear cell cancer have mutations in the von Hippel–Lindau gene, which leads to overexpression of vascular endothelial growth factor pathways. Therapeutic strategies have focused on inhibiting these pathways by using molecularly targeted agents such as sunitinib, sorafenib, and bevacizumab. Other targeted agents being used include temsirolimus and everolimus, which are inhibitors of the mammalian target of rapamycin (mTOR) pathway. The risk of recurrence in patients with resected renal cell cancer is based on the original disease stage. Most recurrences happen within 5 years of initial diagnosis, and the most common sites of metastases are the lung, bone, liver, brain, and renal fossa. Because surgical resection has been shown to benefit patients with minimal metastatic disease, surveillance protocols have been developed to identify these patients. Recommended follow-up evaluation includes physical examination, laboratory studies, chest radiographs or CT scans of the chest, and CT scans of the abdomen at specified risk-adjusted intervals.

KEY POINTS

- Partial nephrectomy is appropriate for patients with renal cell tumors measuring less than 4 cm that are not adjacent to the renal pelvis.
- Molecularly targeted agents such as sunitinib, sorafenib, bevacizumab, temsirolimus, and everolimus have been shown to be effective in treating patients with resected renal cell cancer who develop metastatic disease.

Lymphadenopathy and Lymphoid Malignancies

Less than 1% of patients presenting with acute lymphadenopathy in the internal medicine setting are found to have a malignancy. Most lymphadenopathy is self-limited or related to a localized or systemic infection, although other nonmalignant causes include adverse drug reactions and autoimmune disease. Lymph node enlargement occurring in younger adults as well as that characterized by short duration and modest size involving cervical or inguinal lymph nodes suggests a benign cause.

Initial assessment requires a detailed history, including recent travel, sexual history, and use of current and recent medications. A comprehensive physical examination focuses on determining the size, number, and consistency (malignant–firm and fixed versus benign–soft and freely movable) of enlarged lymph nodes and the presence of lymphoid organomegaly (such as splenomegaly) and enlarged Waldeyer tonsillar ring nodes

Some patients presenting with lymphadenopathy and benign clinical features need no additional laboratory or imaging studies and should receive reassurance and undergo follow-up evaluation to assess resolution or progression of the lymph node enlargement. Potentially necessary laboratory studies include a complete blood count with differential, peripheral blood smear, erythrocyte sedimentation rate, and serologic studies for HIV and Epstein-Barr virus (EBV) infection. Additional studies for other viral or bacterial causes or connective tissue and autoimmune disease markers may be indicated. A chest radiograph to assess hilar and mediastinal lymphadenopathy, as well as pulmonary parenchymal disease, is usually obtained. Other radiographic studies depend on the duration and extent of lymphadenopathy. If a nonmalignant cause is not identified initially, additional studies such as CT and PET may be appropriate in preparation for obtaining a lymph node biopsy for flow cytometry and histopathologic and genetic studies.

KEY POINTS

- Less than 1% of patients presenting with acute lymphadenopathy in the internal medicine setting are found to have a malignancy, with older patients more likely to have a malignant cause, and adolescents and young adults more likely to have an infectious cause.
- Laboratory studies for patients with clinically worrisome lymphadenopathy include assessments for infectious, autoimmune, and connective tissue diseases.

Epidemiology and Risk Factors of Malignant Lymphomas

Lymphomas (non-Hodgkin lymphoma [NHL] and Hodgkin lymphoma) account for about 5% of all cancers and 3% of all cancer-related deaths in the United States, and they are the fifth most common malignancy. It is estimated that 75,190 men and women will be diagnosed with lymphoma in the United States in 2011, and 20,620 will die of this disease. Most cases are due to NHL. Although the incidence of NHL has more than doubled over the past 30 years, 5-year relative survival rates increased from 48% in 1975 to 67.3% from the period of 2000 to 2007 per most recent Surveillance Epidemiology and End Results statistics.

NHL occurs more often in men than in women. The incidence increases significantly with age. In contrast, most patients with Hodgkin lymphoma are usually between 15 and 45 years of age, and a second increased incidence occurs among patients older than 55 years of age.

The cause of NHL and Hodgkin lymphoma is unknown in most patients. However, patients with diminished immune function are at greater risk as evidenced by the increased incidence of NHL (and to a lesser extent Hodgkin lymphoma) among patients with certain viral infections, including HIV, human T-cell lymphotropic virus type 1 (HTLV-1), hepatitis C virus, and EBV. HIV is associated with anaplastic large cell NHL and Burkitt lymphoma; HTLV-1 with T-cell NHL; hepatitis C virus with low-grade B-cell NHL; and EBV with Burkitt lymphoma, posttransplant lymphoproliferative disorders, and Hodgkin lymphoma. Patients receiving immunosuppressant agents such as cyclosporine or tacrolimus to prevent rejection of solid-organ grafts or development of graft-versus-host disease after allogeneic hematopoietic stem cell transplantation (HSCT) have an increased incidence of high-grade B-cell NHL.

Chronic inflammation due to *Helicobacter pylori* infection predisposes patients to development of gastric mucosa–associated lymphoid tissue lymphoma (MALT lymphoma). Genetic predispositions for lymphoma also exist. Occupational exposures to herbicides, chlorinated organic compounds, and potentially, other pesticides and fertilizers used in farming increase the risk for NHL. Patients who were treated for Hodgkin lymphoma also have a significantly greater risk for NHL.

KEY POINTS

- Non-Hodgkin lymphoma (and to a lesser extent Hodgkin lymphoma) is more common among patients who are immunosuppressed.
- Non-Hodgkin lymphoma is associated with HIV, human T-cell lymphotropic virus type 1, hepatitis C virus, and Epstein-Barr virus infection.
- Patients who were treated for Hodgkin lymphoma have a significantly greater risk of developing non-Hodgkin lymphoma.

Diagnosis of Malignant Lymphomas

Excisional biopsy of an adequate tissue sample that preserves the architecture of the lymph node is required for the diagnosis of lymphoma. Fine-needle aspiration should not be used. Samples are sent for molecular testing (cytogenetics, fluorescence in situ hybridization, and gene expression), immunophenotyping, and histopathologic studies to determine the diagnosis and provide prognostic and therapeutic information. Routine laboratory studies include complete blood count with differential, measurement of serum lactate dehydrogenase and β_2-microglobulin levels, and, when appropriate, screening for viruses, including HIV, EBV, HTLV-1, and hepatitis B and C. PET and CT scans are used to determine the stage and prognosis and to assess the response to therapy. Bone marrow biopsy and aspiration are needed for comprehensive staging. Lumbar puncture is indicated for patients at risk for central nervous system involvement (aggressive NHL involving the sinuses, testes, bone marrow, and ocular sites).

KEY POINTS

- Excisional biopsy, not fine-needle aspiration, should be used in the diagnosis of lymphoma.
- Molecular testing, immunophenotyping, and histopathologic studies are used to determine a diagnosis of lymphoma and provide prognostic and therapeutic information.

Classification, Staging, and Prognosis of Malignant Lymphoma

Most neoplasms in NHL and Hodgkin lymphoma are associated with aberrant somatic mutations of genes in the variable regions of heavy and light chains of germinal and post-germinal center B cells. NHL comprises more than 20 subtypes divided by immunophenotyping into B-cell, T-cell, and natural killer (NK)-cell lymphomas. B-cell lymphomas account for 85% of all NHLs, and T-cell lymphomas constitute 10% to 15%. NK-cell lymphomas are rare. Classifications of NHL and Hodgkin lymphoma are primarily derived from the recently updated World Health Organization Initiative and are based on histology, site of origin, immunophenotype, gene profiling, primary site inflammation/infection, and age of patient at diagnosis (**Table 43**).

When determining prognosis, lymphomas are classified into three groups (indolent, aggressive, and highly aggressive) based on their malignant cell growth rate. Patient age is a new feature of prognostic significance. Pediatric patients with nodal marginal zone lymphomas have less aggressive disease than their adult counterparts. Compared with younger patients, elderly patients with EBV-related diffuse large B-cell lymphoma have more aggressive disease that occurs in extranodal sites. Gene expression profiling (or immunohistochemistry) classifies lymphomas as germinal center B-cell phenotype (favorable prognosis) or activated B-cell phenotype (unfavorable prognosis). Each has a distinct clinical course. Stromal gene signatures are now used to predict responsiveness to standard chemotherapy regimens.

Although indolent NHL is treatable and is associated with prolonged progression-free intervals of 7 to 10 years, it is incurable. Lymphoma-related deaths occur in most patients, except those with isolated (stage I) disease. Aggressive and highly aggressive lymphomas are curable with combination chemotherapy, although resistant tumors have short progressive-free intervals and survival. In patients with B-cell phenotypes, especially those expressing the CD20 antigen, standard therapy is associated with cure rates of 40% to 80%. The wide range of cure rates reflects differences in response to therapy based on extent of disease, presenting symptoms, prognosis, gene expression, patient age, and comorbid conditions. Recent advances in molecular profiling, increased administration of monoclonal antibody agents such as rituximab, use of radioimmunoconjugates such as tositumomab and ibritumomab, and earlier referral for autologous and allogeneic HSCT are changing the expected clinical outcomes in patients with indolent and aggressive B-cell NHL.

The Ann Arbor Staging System remains the standard for determining the extent of disease in patients with NHL and Hodgkin lymphoma (**Figure 25**). The International Prognostic Index (IPI) is a predictive model to determine prognosis in patients with large cell NHL. Prognosis is based on the Ann Arbor stage, patient age, serum lactate dehydrogenase level, performance status, and presence of extranodal involvement. The Follicular Lymphoma International Prognostic Index (FLIPI) uses slightly different criteria (Ann Arbor stage, age of patient, hemoglobin and serum lactate dehydrogenase levels, and number of involved nodal areas) to determine prognosis in patients with follicular lymphoma.

The IPI score is no longer as important for determining prognosis in patients with B-cell NHL because the routine use of rituximab as both initial and maintenance therapy in these patients is associated with improved response rates and duration of responses.

KEY POINTS

- The Ann Arbor Staging System remains the standard for determining the extent of disease in patients with non-Hodgkin lymphoma and Hodgkin lymphoma.
- The International Prognostic Index is no longer as important for determining prognosis in patients with B-cell non-Hodgkin lymphoma because the routine use of rituximab as both initial and maintenance therapy is associated with improved response rates and duration of responses.

TABLE 43. World Health Organization 2008 Classification of Hodgkin and Non-Hodgkin Lymphomas

Mature B Cell	Mature T cell and NK Cell
Chronic lymphocytic leukemia	T-cell prolymphocytic leukemia
B-cell prolymphocytic leukemia	T-cell large granular lymphocytic leukemia
Splenic marginal zone lymphoma	Chronic lymphoproliferative disorder of NK cells[a]
Hairy cell leukemia	Aggressive NK-cell leukemia
Splenic lymphoma/leukemia, unclassifiable	Systemic EBV$^+$ T-cell lymphoproliferative disease of childhood
Lymphoplasmacytic lymphoma (Waldenström)	Hydroa vacciniforme–like lymphoma
Heavy chain diseases (α, γ, μ)	Adult T-cell leukemia/lymphoma
Plasma cell myeloma	Extranodal NK/T-cell lymphoma, nasal type
Solitary plasmacytoma of bone	Enteropathy-associated T-cell lymphoma
Extraosseous plasmacytoma	Hepatosplenic T-cell lymphoma
Extranodal marginal zone B-cell lymphoma of mucosa-associated lymphoid tissue (MALT lymphoma)	Subcutaneous panniculitis-like T-cell lymphoma
Nodal marginal zone B-cell lymphoma	Mycosis fungoides
Follicular lymphoma	Sézary syndrome
Primary cutaneous follicle center lymphoma	Primary cutaneous CD30$^+$ T-cell lymphoproliferative disorder
Mantle cell lymphoma	Primary cutaneous aggressive epidermotropic CD8$^+$ cytotoxic T-cell lymphoma[a]
DLBCL, not otherwise specified	Primary cutaneous $\gamma\delta$ T-cell lymphoma
DLBCL (EBV$^+$) of the elderly	Primary cutaneous small/medium CD4$^+$ T-cell lymphoma
Lymphomatoid granulomatosis	Peripheral T-cell lymphoma, not otherwise specified
Primary mediastinal (thymic) large B-cell lymphoma	Angioimmunoblastic T-cell lymphoma
Intravascular large B-cell lymphoma	Anaplastic large cell lymphoma (ALK$^+$)
Primary cutaneous DLBCL, leg type	Anaplastic large cell lymphoma (ALK$^-$)[a]
ALK$^+$ large B-cell lymphoma	
Plasmablastic lymphoma	
Primary effusion lymphoma	
Large B-cell lymphoma arising in HHV8-associated multicentric Castleman disease	
Burkitt lymphoma	
B-cell lymphoma, unclassifiable with features intermediate between DLBCL and Burkitt lymphoma	
B-cell lymphoma, unclassifiable, with features intermediate between large B-cell lymphoma and classic Hodgkin lymphoma	
Hodgkin lymphoma	
Nodular lymphocyte-predominant Hodgkin lymphoma	
Classic Hodgkin lymphoma	
Nodular sclerosis	
Lymphocyte rich	
Mixed cellularity	
Lymphocyte depleted	

[a]Provisional subtypes and entities.

DLBCL = diffuse large B-cell lymphoma, EBV= Epstein-Barr virus, HHV8 = human herpesvirus 8.

Reprinted with permission from Swerdlow SH, Campo E, Harris NL, et al. (Eds). World Health Organization Classification of Tumours of Haematopoietic and Lymphoid Tissues, IARC Press, Lyon 2008.

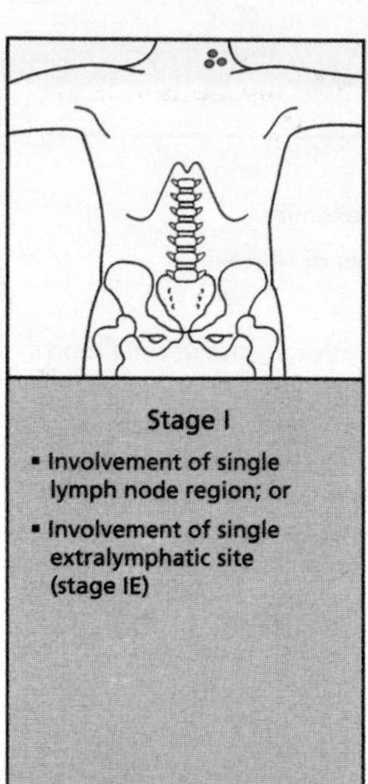
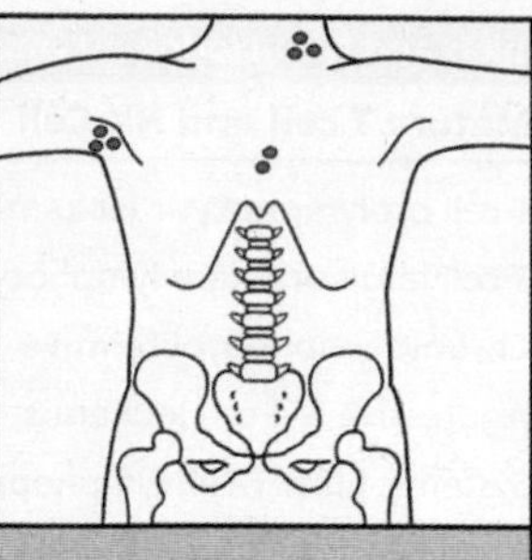
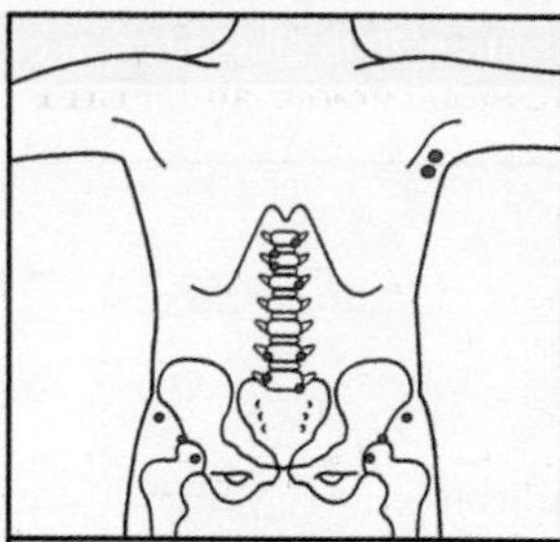
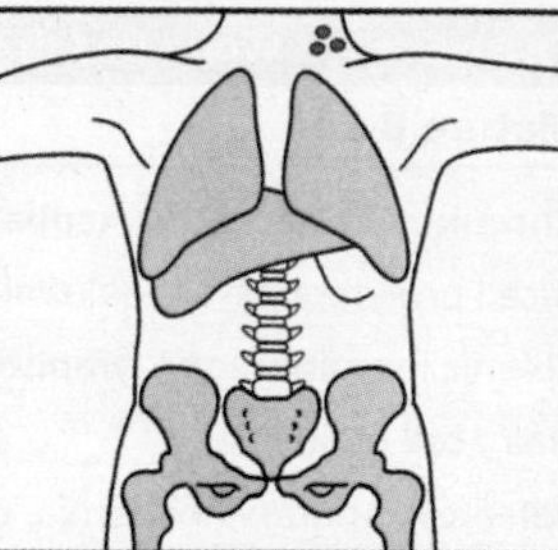

FIGURE 25. Ann Arbor Staging System for Hodgkin and non-Hodgkin lymphoma.

Reprinted with permission from Skarkin, A. The Atlas of Diagnostic Oncology, 3rd Edition. Philadelphia, PA: Mosby. Copyright Elsevier, 2002.

Overview and Treatment of Indolent Lymphomas

Follicular Lymphoma

Follicular lymphoma is the second most common type of NHL in the United States and Europe and accounts for 20% of all NHLs and 70% of indolent NHLs. The incidence increases with age, and the median age at diagnosis is 60 years. Men and women are affected equally.

Most patients present with stage IV disease, and almost all patients have bone marrow involvement. Despite the presence of advanced-stage disease, most patients still experience long-term median survival. Rearrangements of the *bcl-2* oncogene are present in more than 90% of patients, and cytogenetic studies show a t(14;18) defect. The natural history varies according to the grade and FLIPI score. Follicular lymphomas are graded on a scale of 1 to 3 based on the size of the lymphocytes. These grades have prognostic significance. Grade 1 and 2 lymphomas (small cell lymphomas) behave in an indolent manner. Grade 3(b) lymphomas (large cell lymphomas) behave more like diffuse large cell NHLs and require early and aggressive therapy. Despite a high therapeutic response rate, follicular lymphoma is considered incurable in most patients. The median survival is approximately 10 years (**Table 44**).

TABLE 44. IPI (FLIPI) Outcomes for Follicular Lymphoma

Number of Risk Factors[a]	Risk Group	5-Year OS (%)	10-Year OS (%)
0-1	Low	90.6	70.7
2	Intermediate	77.6	50.9
>3	High	52.2	33.5

[a]Risk factors: Age >60 years, Ann Arbor stage III-IV disease, hemoglobin <12.0 g/dL (120 g/L), elevated lactate dehydrogenase level, and involvement of more than four lymph nodes.

FLIPI = Follicular Lymphoma International Prognostic Index; IPI = International Prognostic Index; OS = overall survival.

Treatment varies widely depending on the extent of disease at presentation, rate of progression, grade, and FLIPI score. Early treatment does not improve survival in patients with grade 1 and 2 follicular lymphoma. Delaying treatment until symptoms or organ dysfunction develops (for example, extensive bone marrow involvement or progressive lymphadenopathy) is therefore appropriate. Localized disease is uncommon (5% to 10%) but can be treated effectively with involved-field radiation therapy and single-agent rituximab therapy. Treatment is associated with long-term disease-free survival and possible cure. Several treatment options are available for patients with advanced disease when needed, including single-agent rituximab and rituximab-based combination chemotherapy (rituximab plus cyclophosphamide, vincristine, and prednisone [R-CVP], rituximab plus cyclophosphamide, doxorubicin, vincristine, and prednisone [R-CHOP], and rituximab plus bendamustine). The use of radioimmunoconjugates (tositumomab and ibritumomab) is another treatment option. Both autologous and allogeneic HSCT are appropriate for young patients with relapsed follicular lymphoma who have good performance status. Recent studies have shown improved progression-free and overall survival in patients who receive prolonged (2 years) maintenance treatment with rituximab after standard chemotherapy.

Mucosa-associated Lymphoid Tissue (MALT) Lymphoma

MALT cells line the digestive tract and provide immunologic surveillance and response to foreign antigens. Malignant transformation of these cells results in MALT lymphomas, which are of B-cell origin (CD20-positive). MALT lymphomas account for 50% of all gastric lymphomas. They usually remain localized (stage I and II) and are typically caused by antigens to *Helicobacter pylori*. These lymphomas have a unique clinical presentation (isolated to a single organ) and natural history (having an indolent course). Frequent extranodal presentations of MALT lymphoma involve the orbit, colon, lung, thyroid gland, salivary glands, and bladder. A history of an autoimmune or inflammatory disease, such as Sjögren syndrome or Hashimoto thyroiditis, is common.

Because of their association with *H. pylori* infection, complete and durable remission of gastric MALT lymphomas can often be induced with a combination of antimicrobial agents and proton pump inhibitors (metronidazole, amoxicillin, or clarithromycin plus omeprazole) without the need for additional chemotherapy. Radiation therapy is highly effective for treating localized disease and can be used in combination with rituximab for more advanced disease. Less often, rituximab plus chemotherapy, usually with R-CVP, is required to induce a durable remission. Large cell MALT lymphoma has a course similar to diffuse large B-cell lymphoma and is treated with combination chemotherapy.

MALT lymphoma can primarily involve the spleen. Patients present with splenomegaly without lymphadenopathy and have lymphocytosis and a small monoclonal spike on serum protein electrophoresis. The disease is resistant to chemotherapy but may remit completely after splenectomy.

Chronic Lymphocytic Leukemia

Chronic lymphocytic leukemia (CLL) is the most common form of lymphoid malignancy and accounts for 11% of all hematologic neoplasms. Approximately 100,000 persons in the United States are estimated to be affected. Despite its indolent course, patients with CLL have a shorter median survival than do age-matched healthy individuals.

Most patients are asymptomatic and present with early-stage disease discovered incidentally during routine laboratory testing. Although CLL develops most often in older persons (median age, 70 years), it may occur in younger patients, who tend to have more aggressive disease. No definite environmental, occupational, or infectious risk factors have been associated with the development of CLL. However, the incidence appears to be increased in first-degree relatives. Most patients in Western countries have B-cell CLL, whereas many patients from Asian countries develop T-cell CLL.

Clinical staging of CLL ranges from stage I to stage IV. Most patients present with an asymptomatic increase in circulating lymphocytes (stage 0), and some have lymphadenopathy (stage I) or splenomegaly (stage II). Patients with more advanced disease present with anemia (stage III) or thrombocytopenia (stage IV). Histopathologic studies and immunophenotyping of circulating lymphocytes are diagnostic. Prognosis is based on the clinical stage and rate of disease progression, which is determined by the lymphocyte doubling time and serum β_2-microglobulin level, immunophenotyping, cytogenetic studies, fluorescence in situ hybridization testing, and mutational gene assessment (**Table 45**).

When to initiate therapy in patients with CLL depends on the extent of disease, accompanying symptoms, and rate of progression. As with follicular lymphoma, the disease is incurable, there may be lengthy asymptomatic intervals, and watchful waiting is appropriate. Asymptomatic patients with good-risk prognostic findings should not be treated regardless of the leukocyte count. Patients with symptoms (fever, weight loss, sweating, and pain) or poor prognostic features should be treated initially with purine nucleoside analogue (fludarabine)–based combination chemotherapy. The greatest response rates have been reported using combination chemotherapy and rituximab, with 73% of patients achieving a complete response and a median time to disease progression of greater than 4 years. Molecular profiles suggesting unresponsiveness to purine analogues have been identified, and these patients should receive alternative immunotherapy.

Response to treatment of CLL predicts outcome. Patients who have a complete remission without flow cytometric evidence of minimal residual disease have the longest progression-free and overall survival rates. Autoimmune phenomena, including immune thrombocytopenia and

TABLE 45. Median Survival in Chronic Lymphocytic Leukemia

Prognostic Factor	Good Risk	Median Survival	Poor Risk	Median Survival
Stage	I and II	>100 months[a]	III and IV	58-69 months[a]
Doubling time	>12 months	75 months[b]	<12 months	20 months[b]
β_2-microglobulin	<3.5 mg/L	75 months[b]	>3.5 mg/L	13 months[b]
Heavy gene	Mutated	20 years[a]	Unmutated	8 years[a]
ZAP 70	Negative	10 years[a]	Positive	3 years[a]
del(17p13) (p53)	Absent	>100 months[a]	Present	<3 years[a]

[a]Overall survival.

[b]Progression-free survival.

ZAP 70 = ζ-chain–associated protein 70.

autoimmune hemolytic anemia, are not uncommon complications. Decreasing hemoglobin levels should not be automatically attributed to bleeding, and decreasing platelet counts should not routinely be assumed to be secondary to bone marrow suppression by chemotherapy or replacement by malignant cells. Opportunistic infections also occur in many patients because of immunosuppression caused by the underlying disease and its treatment. The most common opportunistic agents are *Pneumocystis jirovecii*, cytomegalovirus, and herpes simplex virus. Both monoclonal gammopathies and hypogammaglobulinemia may occur. Occasionally, patients require periodic administration of γ-globulin to prevent recurrent sinopulmonary infections caused by low serum IgG levels. Patients with CLL have an increased risk for developing secondary malignancies. Transformation to more aggressive disease, including large cell lymphoma (Richter transformation) and prolymphocytic leukemia, requires treatment with R-CHOP and consideration of HSCT. Allogeneic HSTC is the only curative treatment but is associated with a high risk of morbidity and mortality. Long-term disease-free survival can be achieved after allogeneic transplantation, including for high-risk patients who would otherwise have limited life expectancy.

Hairy Cell Leukemia

Hairy cell leukemia is a rare form of leukemia that is important to recognize because it is highly curable but leads to significant morbidity and mortality when untreated. It occurs most often in older adults and is five times more common in men than in women. Patients present with progressive cytopenia and splenomegaly without lymphadenopathy. Bone marrow aspiration can be difficult because of extensive involvement by lymphoid cells with hair-like cytoplasmic projections (**Figure 26**). Diagnosis is confirmed by immunohistochemistry studies. Treatment with parenteral purine analogues such as cladribine is the standard of care, and durable complete remission is achieved in more than 80% of patients with only one cycle. Patients resistant to cladribine may still achieve significant tumor response to various other agents.

KEY POINTS

- Treatment of follicular lymphoma includes rituximab, either as a single agent or as part of a combined therapeutic regimen.
- Complete and durable remission of gastric mucosa-associated lymphoid tissue lymphomas can often be induced with antimicrobial agents plus proton pump inhibitors without the need for additional chemotherapy.
- Patients with favorable-risk chronic lymphocytic leukemia should not be treated, regardless of the leukocyte count, and symptomatic patients or those with poor prognostic features should be treated with combination chemotherapy and rituximab.
- Hairy cell leukemia is highly curable but leads to significant morbidity and mortality when untreated.

Overview and Treatment of Aggressive Lymphomas

Diffuse Large Cell Lymphoma

Diffuse large cell lymphoma is the most common type of NHL and accounts for approximately 30% of all cases. The

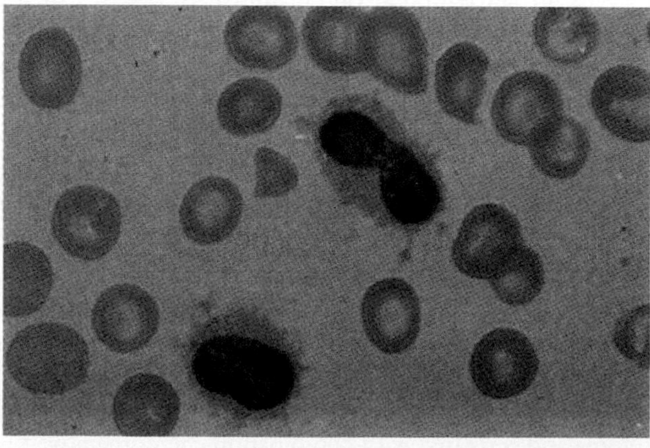

FIGURE 26. Hairy cell leukemia depicted by atypical lymphocytes with thread-like cytoplasmic projections from the cell surface.

lymphomas are of B-cell or T-cell phenotype. B-cell NHL is the most common. Patients usually present with advanced disease (stage III and IV) and both local signs related to lymphadenopathy and "B" systemic symptoms (fever, night sweats, and weight loss). Patients with T-cell NHL have a heterogeneous clinical course based on disease characterization (see Table 43).

Prognosis depends on patient age, performance status, serum lactate dehydrogenase level, and number of extranodal disease sites. Patients with B-cell diffuse NHL require immediate initial therapy with R-CHOP, and possibly, radiation therapy for those with localized and bulky disease. Approximately half of these patients will have sustained disease-free survival, and those who experience relapse should be considered for autologous HSCT. Prospective randomized clinical trials of high-dose chemotherapy and autologous HSCT have demonstrated superior progression-free and overall survival compared with continued standard chemotherapy in patients with chemotherapy-sensitive, recurrent, diffuse large B-cell lymphoma. Allogeneic HSCT remains investigational in this setting. Patients with T-cell NHL are also treated with CHOP but without the addition of rituximab. However, outcomes are inferior to those achieved in patients with diffuse large B-cell lymphoma, and investigation of more effective treatment approaches continues.

Patients with highly aggressive NHL (Burkitt lymphoma and lymphoblastic lymphoma) routinely present with life-threatening metabolic and structural anomalies. Immediate treatment is required with regimens similar to those used for treating acute lymphocytic leukemia. More than 80% of treated patients have high response rates, and therapy is curative in 45% of patients.

Mantle Cell Lymphoma

Patients with mantle cell lymphoma have a varied clinical course depending on the extent of disease at presentation, its morphologic growth pattern, and the aggressiveness of initial therapy. Most patients present with stage IV disease involving extranodal sites that commonly include the small intestine and colon, bone marrow, and peripheral blood. Involvement of the central nervous system occurs less often. The diagnosis of mantle cell lymphoma is established by histopathology, immunophenotyping, immunohistochemistry, and cytogenetic studies. A diagnosis is confirmed by the presence of overexpression of cyclin D1 and a t(11;14) translocation in malignant lymphoid cells.

Most patients treated with rituximab and CHOP have short disease-free periods and a median survival of less than 3 years. Approximately 15% of patients who have localized disease with a low growth rate at diagnosis have a more indolent course with a median survival of greater than 6 years. These patients tend to be younger (<65 years of age), have normal serum lactate dehydrogenase and β_2-microglobulin levels, and do not have B symptoms. Because mantle cell lymphoma has such a variable course, a prognostic score (the Mantle Cell Lymphoma International Prognostic Index, MIPI) has recently been developed to help determine response to therapy. Most patients require aggressive therapy to achieve complete and durable remissions. New aggressive chemotherapeutic regimens with rituximab (R-HYPERCVAD) are now considered standard for patients with mantle cell lymphoma and are associated with a median survival of greater than 3 years. Allogeneic HSCT remains the only curative option for patients with advanced mantle cell lymphoma, especially for those with recurrent disease. Investigational use of autologous HSCT has shown promising preliminary results because some patients experience a median survival of over 4 years and a possible plateau (cure) in the survival curve.

Hodgkin Lymphoma

Hodgkin lymphoma is a highly curable malignancy regardless of stage at presentation. As in patients with NHL, patients with Hodgkin lymphoma usually present with palpable lymphadenopathy or have a mediastinal mass that requires tissue biopsy for diagnosis. The type of therapy is determined by disease stage. Localized disease responds to radiation therapy with or without short-course chemotherapy. More advanced disease requires combination chemotherapy with doxorubicin, bleomycin, vinblastine, and dacarbazine (ABVD) administered over six cycles. In contrast to NHL, in which histology is crucial in determining prognosis and treatment, almost all subtypes of Hodgkin lymphoma are treated the same. The exception is the CD20-positive (lymphocyte-predominant) subtype for which rituximab is added to the treatment regimen.

The goal is to choose therapy aggressive enough to achieve cure without exposing the patient to unnecessary treatment toxicity, including the risk of late secondary malignancies such as leukemia, NHL, and solid tumors that are common in patients with Hodgkin lymphoma. PET findings are predictive of long-term outcomes after two or three cycles of ABVD therapy. At a median follow-up of 2 years, 95% of patients with a complete response after two cycles of ABVD had disease-free PET findings compared with 13% of patients with positive PET findings. Prognostic risk factors are used to help determine therapy. Risk factors include age older than 45 years, male sex, leukocyte count greater than 15,000/µL (15×10^9/L), serum albumin level less than 4 g/dL (40 g/L), and hemoglobin level less than 10.5 g/dL (105 g/L). Regardless of therapy, patients with advanced-stage disease at diagnosis and two or more risk factors have inferior progression-free and overall survival (5-year overall survival rates of 89% in patients without risk factors compared with 56% in patients with five risk factors). Initial use of more intense combination chemotherapy is being evaluated for treatment of high-risk patients. Such alternative chemotherapy is also being evaluated for patients with positive PET scans after completing two cycles of ABVD therapy. Patients with relapsed disease are candidates for autologous HSCT. Allogeneic HSCT can induce durable remission and cure in patients with chemotherapy-refractory disease and in patients who relapse after receiving an autologous transplant.

Cutaneous T-cell Non-Hodgkin Lymphoma

Mycosis fungoides (which affects the skin) and Sézary syndrome (which affects the skin and blood) are the most common forms of cutaneous T-cell NHL. The T cells express CD4 antigen, have a classic histologic appearance with a large "cerebriform" nucleus, and are clonal on T-cell receptor gene rearrangement analysis. Patients usually present with dry, pruritic, erythematous skin patches. In most patients, the disease remains indolent for years but eventually progresses and causes plaques, diffuse erythema, and ulcerated lesions. T-cell infiltration into other organs occurs over time, and a leukemic phase develops. As the disease progresses, it causes increasing cell-mediated immunodeficiency associated with recurrent bacterial infections and septic episodes.

The prognosis for patients with mycosis fungoides depends on the extent of disease. Patients with stage I disease with limited plaque or patch involvement of the skin have a median survival of 20 years or more, whereas those with advanced disease (stage III; diffuse erythrodermal involvement) and stage IV disease (extracutaneous) have a median survival of less than 4 years. Early-stage disease is managed by observation. Topical agents such as corticosteroids and retinoids are used when cutaneous symptoms develop. Psoralen and ultraviolet A light (PUVA) therapy is also highly effective in treating early-stage disease, particularly when combined with interferon alfa. More advanced cutaneous disease may respond to electron-beam radiation therapy or extracorporeal photopheresis. Patients with unresponsive, recurrent, or organ-involving disease may receive systemic therapy, including combination chemotherapy (CHOP). Alemtuzumab is an effective therapy for disease characterized by organ involvement. Allogeneic HSCT may be curative for some younger patients who have matched transplant donors.

KEY POINTS

- Patients with localized Hodgkin lymphoma are treated with extended-field radiation therapy with or without short-course chemotherapy; those with advanced disease receive combination chemotherapy.
- New aggressive chemotherapeutic regimens with rituximab are now considered standard for patients with mantle cell lymphoma and are associated with a median survival of greater than 3 years.
- Patients with early-stage mycosis fungoides are treated with psoralen and ultraviolet A light therapy; those with more advanced disease may respond to electron-beam radiation therapy or extracorporeal photopheresis.

Cancer of Unknown Primary Site

Introduction

Approximately 35,000 patients with cancer of an unknown primary site (CUP) are identified in the United States each year. These patients represent a highly heterogeneous population and one that is changing over time as diagnostic imaging studies continue to improve. A primary site is now readily detected in many patients who would have been diagnosed with CUP 20 or more years ago.

Diagnosis

CUP is a diagnosis of exclusion in a patient who has a pathologically documented solid tumor malignancy without an identifiable primary site after completion of an initial evaluation. This evaluation includes a complete history and physical examination; good-quality CT scans of the chest, abdomen, and pelvis; and other appropriate tests based on symptoms and clinical and radiographic findings. Biopsy samples of tumor from the most accessible location should be obtained for immunohistochemical marker determinations.

Subsequent evaluation also focuses on identifying primary tumors that are suggested by clinical findings and that are most amenable to treatment. The evaluation should not involve an exhaustive search for a primary site because, with a few notable exceptions, finding an asymptomatic and occult primary tumor has not been shown to improve outcome. This is perhaps one of the most important and somewhat paradoxical issues for clinicians to understand and to communicate to patients and family members. Focusing on identifying the primary site only distracts from the most important issue, which is that the patient has a metastatic cancer, and whether the neoplasm is potentially curable needs to be determined. Unfortunately, only about 20% of patients with CUP have a relatively favorable prognosis and can benefit substantially from specific therapeutic interventions.

The presence of tumor markers is rarely diagnostic, and an undirected initial screening for carcinoembryonic antigen, CA-19-9, CA-15-3, CA-125, and other markers is unwarranted. Women require mammography and comprehensive gynecologic evaluation, and men should have an examination of the prostate and testicles and determination of the serum prostate-specific antigen level because a finding of breast, ovary, prostate, or testicular sites of origin may indicate specific, efficacious lines of therapy.

Upper endoscopy and colonoscopy are warranted in patients with gastrointestinal symptoms with or without evidence of gastrointestinal bleeding. Patients who have cervical lymphadenopathy should undergo evaluation for head and neck cancer. PET has not been shown to contribute to the outcome in patients with CUP and is not recommended as part of the standard evaluation.

Companies have begun marketing gene expression profiling analyses in an attempt to identify the site of the unknown primary cancers. At present, such analyses have not been validated in prospective trials, and their use is not recommended. Several favorable prognostic subtypes of CUP have been identified (poorly differentiated carcinoma, isolated regional lymphadenopathy, and peritoneal carcinomatosis in women) and are discussed in detail in the next section. Evaluation should therefore focus on whether a patient with CUP has findings consistent with a treatable primary tumor, as noted above, or one of these treatable subtypes of CUP.

KEY POINTS

- Before more specialized studies are done in patients with cancer of unknown primary site, biopsy samples of tumor from the most accessible location should be obtained for immunohistochemical marker determinations.
- An exhaustive search for a primary tumor should not be done in patients with cancer of unknown primary site because finding an asymptomatic and occult primary tumor has not been shown to improve outcome.
- Evaluation of patients with cancer of unknown primary (CUP) site should focus on whether findings are consistent with a treatable primary tumor or a treatable subtype of CUP.

Favorable Prognostic Subgroups

Poorly Differentiated Carcinoma

Although poorly differentiated histologic findings usually confer an unfavorable prognosis, subgroups of patients with CUP associated with poorly differentiated carcinoma (other than adenocarcinoma) have a better prognosis and may benefit from specific treatment. One such group includes young men with poorly differentiated carcinoma that is predominantly centrally located and relatively symmetric around the midline (bulky retroperitoneal or mediastinal lymphadenopathy). These patients may have an unrecognized germ cell tumor. Studies include careful examination of the testicles, measurement of serum α-fetoprotein and β-human chorionic gonadotropin levels, and, possibly, ultrasonography of the testicles. Treatment involves platinum-based chemotherapy and other germ cell cancer treatment regimens, regardless of whether a primary testicular tumor is identified.

Patients with poorly differentiated neuroendocrine tumors may also benefit from specific aggressive therapy. Such patients typically present with dominant liver metastases that may also frequently involve bone. Treatment with the same platinum-based chemotherapy regimens used to treat small cell lung cancer is associated with high response rates and even a complete clinical response in some patients.

Poorly differentiated carcinoma with a favorable prognosis must be differentiated from poorly differentiated adenocarcinoma. Patients with disseminated adenocarcinoma have an unfavorable prognosis regardless of the degree of differentiation, and aggressive platinum-based chemotherapy regimens are not warranted.

Isolated Regional Lymphadenopathy

Patients with CUP involving a single lymph node or single lymph node region may have potentially treatable disease. Women with isolated axillary lymphadenopathy that is found to be malignant should be assumed to have locoregional breast cancer until proved otherwise. Breast MRI is indicated in this setting. If a primary tumor is identified, the patient no longer has CUP and should receive stage-appropriate breast cancer treatment. If the MRI is normal, the patient should be managed as for stage II breast cancer and should undergo mastectomy and axillary lymph node dissection. Primary breast cancers are identified by pathologic examination in more than 50% of patients after mastectomy. The management and prognosis are similar whether or not a primary breast cancer is identified.

Patients with isolated cervical lymphadenopathy should have a triple endoscopic examination (laryngoscopy, bronchoscopy, and esophagoscopy) to identify a possible head and neck primary tumor. Even if a primary tumor is not identified, treatment with chemotherapy and radiation therapy, based on head and neck cancer treatment protocols, is associated with high response rates. Patients with CUP associated with other types of isolated regional lymphadenopathy also have a better prognosis than patients with disseminated disease. Patients with isolated inguinal lymphadenopathy should have careful anorectal, perineal, and genital examinations. If a primary site is not identified, resection or locoregional radiation therapy is indicated and may result in a favorable outcome and long-term disease-free survival. Patients with isolated enlarged solitary or regional lymph nodes at other sites may be managed similarly.

Peritoneal Carcinomatosis in Women

Women with CUP presenting as abdominal carcinomatosis and ascites should be assumed to have ovarian cancer until proved otherwise. Treatment is the same as for primary ovarian cancer and includes cytoreductive surgery and chemotherapy.

KEY POINTS

- Women with cancer of unknown primary site associated with isolated malignant axillary lymphadenopathy should be assumed to have locoregional breast cancer until proved otherwise.
- Women with cancer of unknown primary site presenting as abdominal carcinomatosis and ascites should be assumed to have ovarian cancer until proved otherwise.

Management of Patients Not in Favorable Prognosis Subgroups

Patients with CUP that is not included in a favorable subgroup generally have a poor prognosis. There are no accepted standard treatment regimens for these patients, and therapy tends to be empiric. Although data regarding efficacy are not available, using gastrointestinal cancer treatment regimens for patients with CUP with a predominantly abdominal distribution and initiating lung cancer treatment regimens for those with a predominantly pulmonary distribution is reasonable. Careful assessment of performance status, as well as liver, kidney, and bone marrow reserve, is critical for developing treatment strategies. Patients who have good performance status (Eastern Oncology Cooperative Group grade 0 or 1) are most likely to tolerate and benefit from aggressive therapy. Supportive therapy alone or hospice care should be considered for patients who are debilitated and have multiple comorbid conditions.

The overwhelming majority of patients with CUP who participate in clinical trials are required to have an excellent performance status before enrollment. Results from these trials regarding safety and efficacy of treatment therefore cannot be extrapolated to patients who have poor performance status.

KEY POINT

- Patients with cancer of unknown primary site that is not included in a favorable subgroup generally have a poor prognosis and typically receive empiric therapy.

Melanoma

Introduction

Approximately 69,000 cases of melanoma are expected to be diagnosed in the United States in 2010, and about 8700 cancer-related deaths are anticipated. The incidence of melanoma is increasing dramatically, perhaps more so than for any other cancer.

Risk Factors and Prognosis

Risk factors for melanoma include sun exposure (especially heavy sun exposure during childhood), a history of multiple sunburns, fair complexion, and the presence of multiple cutaneous nevi. A personal or family history of melanoma or dysplastic nevi also increases the risk. Prognosis is primarily determined by tumor stage, which is based on the thickness of the primary lesion, mitotic index, degree of ulceration, and extent of spread (see MKSAP 16 Dermatology).

The course of melanoma is highly variable. Patients with melanomas that are fully excised, are less than 1 mm thick, and do not have poor prognostic features have an excellent prognosis with a 5-year survival rate of approximately 95%. Patients with tumors greater than 1 mm thick that have not spread to lymph nodes have 5-year survival rates of 50% to 90%. In patients with metastases to regional lymph nodes, 5-year survival rates range from 20% to 70% and are most influenced by the degree of tumor bulk at the time of diagnosis.

KEY POINT

- Risk factors for melanoma include sun exposure, a history of multiple sunburns, fair complexion, the presence of multiple cutaneous nevi, and a personal or family history of melanoma or dysplastic nevi.

Treatment

The primary treatment of local and locoregional melanoma is surgical resection. For early lesions (less than 1 mm thick without ulceration or a high mitotic index), excision alone is believed to be sufficient, and excision margins of 1 cm are generally considered adequate. A 2-cm excision margin is indicated for thicker tumors. Studies evaluating use of excision margins wider than 2 cm have failed to show benefit.

Most trials assessing use of sentinel lymph node biopsy (SLNB) at the time of surgical resection have failed to show that this procedure increases tumor-specific survival. However, SLNB is increasingly being used to provide staging and prognostic information when the primary tumor is greater than 1 mm thick or has poor prognostic features. Patients who have a negative SLNB do not require further surgery. Regional lymph node dissection is recommended for patients with a positive SLNB and for patients with clinically positive regional lymph nodes and no evidence of distant metastatic disease.

The utility of adjuvant therapy for patients with resected melanoma is unclear. Studies of interferon alfa in this setting have not provided consistent data, and most fail to document improvement in overall survival. Observation alone remains an acceptable standard management option. The role of post-treatment surveillance after resection of local or locoregional melanoma is also not resolved. At a minimum, annual lifelong skin examinations are recommended. Physical examination with attention to regional lymph node areas performed one to four times annually for the first 5 years is also recommended. Imaging studies, such as CT, MRI, and PET, have a low yield and fairly high false-positive rates. Therefore, routine surveillance imaging is not universally recommended for asymptomatic patients.

Patients with metastatic disease have a poor prognosis. Resection is indicated for patients with limited metastatic disease that is surgically resectable. There are few treatment options for patients with unresectable metastatic disease. Surgery or stereotactic radiosurgery is often indicated for patients with isolated or limited brain metastases. Until recently, intravenous dacarbazine was the standard systemic therapy. Temozolomide, which is similar to dacarbazine but is administered orally, has essentially the same activity. Paclitaxel plus carboplatin has limited activity and a short duration of benefit. Recently, the immunomodulating agent ipilimumab showed a survival benefit and has received regulatory approval. In addition, the small molecule tyrosine kinase inhibitor vemurafenib has shown activity in the approximately 40% of patients with melanoma whose tumors have a V600E mutation in the *BRAF* gene, and this agent has now received regulatory approval for treatment of these patients.

KEY POINTS

- The primary treatment of local and locoregional melanoma is surgical resection.
- Resection is indicated for patients with limited metastatic melanoma that is surgically resectable.

Primary Central Nervous System Tumors

Approximately 22,000 primary brain tumors are diagnosed in the United States each year, resulting in about 13,000 cancer-related deaths annually. Astrocytomas are the most common primary brain tumor. Most patients present with aggressive grade III (anaplastic astrocytoma) or grade IV tumors (glioblastoma multiforme). See MKSAP 16 Neurology for discussion of the symptoms and differential diagnosis of brain tumors.

Surgery is the initial treatment for both high- and low-grade astrocytomas. When the location precludes resection, stereotactic radiosurgery may be an option. When tumors are inoperable, a stereotactic or open biopsy should be obtained.

Postoperative use of whole-brain radiation therapy is standard in most treatment algorithms. Data are conflicting about the benefits of concurrent chemotherapy. However, carmustine or temozolomide is frequently given concurrent with radiation therapy if patients are well enough to tolerate these agents.

Despite aggressive surgery and radiation therapy, recurrence rates for high-grade tumors are extremely high, and therapeutic options for patients with recurrent disease are limited.

KEY POINTS

- Surgery is the initial treatment for both high- and low-grade astrocytomas (the most common primary brain tumor).
- Postoperative use of whole brain radiation therapy is standard in most treatment algorithms for astrocytoma; data are conflicting regarding the benefits of concurrent chemotherapy.

Oncologic Urgencies and Emergencies

Structural Urgencies and Emergencies

Superior Vena Cava Syndrome

H

Superior vena cava (SVC) syndrome is caused by acute obstruction of blood flow from the head, neck, upper torso, or extremities to the right atrium. Lung cancer accounts for 65% of all cases. Less frequent causes are lymphoblastic and diffuse large B-cell lymphoma, Hodgkin lymphoma, and germ cell tumors.

The onset of SVC syndrome is typically insidious. Most patients develop progressive dyspnea, facial swelling, and cough. Swelling of the upper extremities, chest pain, and dysphagia occur less often. Physical examination findings include distention of the neck and chest veins, facial edema, cyanosis, facial plethora, and upper extremity edema. Approximately 60% of patients present with SVC syndrome as the initial manifestation of a previously undiagnosed malignancy.

The most common radiographic findings include mediastinal widening and pleural effusion; however, 16% of patients have a normal chest radiograph. Mediastinoscopy is routinely used to obtain tissue biopsy samples for histologic diagnosis. The complication rate from this procedure is only 5% in patients with SVC syndrome. Percutaneous transthoracic CT-guided needle biopsy appears to be a safe alternative to mediastinoscopy and has a sensitivity of 75%.

The goal of treatment, which can usually be delayed while a tissue diagnosis is obtained, is to reduce symptoms and treat the underlying malignancy. Primary therapy for the underlying disorder using chemotherapy, radiation therapy, or combined chemotherapy and radiation therapy is usually associated with rapid and complete resolution of symptoms and physical findings of SVC syndrome. Improvement generally occurs within 2 weeks after therapy is begun. When only partial patency is reestablished, anticoagulation is appropriate in some patients. Endovascular stenting, angioplasty, surgery, and thrombolytic therapy have only a limited role when primary treatment is ineffective. H

KEY POINTS

- Superior vena cava syndrome is most often caused by lung cancer; other causes are lymphoblastic and diffuse large B-cell lymphoma, Hodgkin lymphoma, and germ cell tumors.
- Primary therapy for the underlying malignancy is usually associated with rapid and complete resolution of symptoms and physical findings of superior vena cava syndrome.

Brain Metastases Causing Increased Intracranial Pressure

Increased intracranial pressure (ICP) results from mass effect and is common in patients with intracerebral tumors, particularly tumors due to metastatic lung cancer and melanoma. Primary brain tumors and central nervous system lymphomas are also frequently associated with increased ICP. Persistent headache, vomiting, altered mental status, and focal neurologic deficits may occur. If increased ICP is suspected, immediate CT or MRI of the head is required to confirm the diagnosis and prevent later consequences, including brainstem herniation, permanent neurologic dysfunction, and death. Lumbar puncture is contraindicated when increased ICP is due to mass effect because the procedure may precipitate catastrophic brainstem herniation.

Corticosteroids are the initial treatment of choice and can be administered orally or intravenously. Dexamethasone is generally given in moderate doses (8 to 10 mg every 6 hours) because higher doses (100 mg/d) cause more side effects and do not alter outcomes. When primary central nervous system lymphoma is suspected, a tissue biopsy should be performed to establish the diagnosis before initiation of corticosteroid therapy if the patient's condition is stable enough to accommodate such a delay. When the effects of increased ICP are more severe, osmotic diuresis with mannitol may be used in addition to corticosteroids.

Obstructing hydrocephalus usually requires surgical drainage. In patients with an isolated brain metastasis, surgical resection followed by stereotactic or whole-brain radiation therapy is generally appropriate. Patients with multiple brain metastases usually require whole-brain radiation therapy with or without chemotherapy.

KEY POINTS

- Lumbar puncture is contraindicated when increased intracranial pressure is due to mass effect because the procedure may precipitate catastrophic brainstem herniation.
- Corticosteroids such as dexamethasone are initially used to treat patients with increased intracranial pressure.

Spinal Cord Compression

Spinal cord compression develops in 5% to 10% of patients with cancer and is one of the most debilitating complications of this disease. Patients with breast, lung, and prostate cancer are most likely to be affected. Rapid diagnosis, before the patient develops motor deficits, allows treatment that can prevent most, if not all, of the potential consequences. Compression generally results from metastasis to vertebral bodies and growth into the epidural space at an isolated location. Multiple metastatic deposits may also occur along the spinal cord.

Pain is the most frequent initial symptom. A feeling of "heaviness" in the legs and difficulty climbing stairs or rising from a sitting position are also common. Leg weakness and bowel or bladder dysfunction usually develop later in the disease course. Physical examination findings are sometimes nonspecific but may include pain on palpation of the involved vertebral body, hyperreflexia, and decreased muscle strength.

MRI is used most often for rapid diagnosis. The entire spine should be imaged to avoid overlooking asymptomatic lesions. Immediate administration of corticosteroids is required to reverse or prevent ongoing spinal cord injury. Dexamethasone is initially given in a high bolus dose (20 mg intravenously) and is followed by a maintenance dose until definitive therapy is completed. Neurosurgical intervention is appropriate when rapid decompression is required or if the diagnosis is uncertain. Radiation therapy is appropriate for most patients, and concurrent chemotherapy is often used for patients with chemosensitive malignancies such as lymphoma.

KEY POINTS

- Patients with breast, lung, and prostate cancer are most likely to develop spinal cord compression.
- Patients with suspected spinal cord compression require prompt diagnosis (MRI of the spine), usually before any motor deficit is detected, and immediate administration of corticosteroids.

Malignant Pleural and Pericardial Effusions

A malignant pleural effusion may be the initial presentation in patients with previously undiagnosed cancer, although more often, as with malignant pericardial effusions, it reflects advanced malignancy that is incurable. The effusion is most often caused by lung cancer, breast cancer, and lymphoma and less frequently by cancer of unknown primary site.

Patients usually have a history of increasing dyspnea on exertion. Some patients report cough and dull aching or stabbing chest pain. The diagnosis is confirmed by chest radiograph or CT scan of the chest. After radiologic confirmation, a pleural fluid sample is obtained for cell count and cytologic studies, as well as determination of pH, glucose, lactate dehydrogenase, and protein levels. When indicated, pleural fluid microbial studies are also performed.

Thoracentesis is required for immediate palliation, and up to 1500 mL (20 mL/kg body weight) of pleural fluid may be drained. Excessive drainage should be avoided to prevent pulmonary edema following lung re-expansion. Pleural effusions recur in 70% of patients. Chest tube drainage and pleurodesis with antibiotics (tetracycline), cytotoxic agents (bleomycin), or talc are all effective in reducing recurrences. Indwelling pleural catheters provide additional control, and pleurectomy or insertion of a pleuroperitoneal shunt is rarely required.

Patients with pericardial effusion are initially asymptomatic and have an enlarged heart on chest radiographs and

diminished (low-voltage) QRS complexes on electrocardiograms. Progression of the effusion causes early symptoms and signs of cardiac tamponade, including dyspnea, orthopnea, chest pain, and hypotension. Echocardiography is essential to establish the diagnosis before development of cardiac arrest.

Urgent subxiphoid cardiocentesis with drainage alleviates cardiac chamber compression. Partial pericardiectomy or pericardial window placement may provide long-term relief. Radiation therapy or chemotherapy is appropriate for patients with radiosensitive or chemosensitive malignancies.

KEY POINTS

- A malignant pleural effusion is most often caused by lung cancer, breast cancer, and lymphoma, and less frequently by cancer of unknown primary site.
- Thoracentesis is required for immediate palliation of a symptomatic malignant pleural effusion.
- Excessive drainage in patients with malignant pleural effusion should be avoided to prevent pulmonary edema following lung re-expansion.
- Echocardiography is essential to establish the diagnosis of malignant pericardial effusion.

Metabolic Urgencies and Emergencies

Tumor Lysis Syndrome

Tumor lysis syndrome is a life-threatening complication that occurs most often in patients with malignancies associated with rapid cell turnover (leukemia, Burkitt lymphoma) or in patients with bulky disease and high leukocyte counts associated with rapid and significant sensitivity to chemotherapeutic agents (large cell lymphoma, chronic lymphocytic leukemia). Tumor lysis syndrome may be spontaneous or treatment induced. Lysis of tumor cells occurs when rapid cell breakdown causes hyperkalemia, hyperphosphatemia, hyperuricemia, hypocalcemia, disseminated intravascular coagulation, and acute kidney failure.

Prevention and treatment of tumor lysis syndrome require hydration with normal saline and allopurinol to decrease hyperuricemia. However, rasburicase is given when serum uric acid levels are significantly elevated, particularly when chronic kidney disease is present, because its onset of action is much quicker than allopurinol. Treatment, including hemodialysis, may be indicated for hyperphosphatemia, hyperkalemia, fluid overload, and uremia.

KEY POINT

- Prevention and treatment of tumor lysis syndrome require hydration with normal saline as well as allopurinol or rasburicase in high-risk patients to limit the degree of hyperuricemia.

Hypercalcemia

Hypercalcemia occurs in 10% to 20% of patients with a malignancy and is associated with a poor prognosis. Patients with myeloma and breast, kidney, and lung cancer are at greatest risk. Symptoms include nausea and vomiting, constipation, polyuria and polydipsia, weakness, and confusion. Increased serum calcium levels are due to direct bone destruction in 20% of patients and humoral effects caused by parathyroid hormone–related protein released by the malignant cells in 80% of patients.

Treatment requires immediate rehydration with normal saline followed by forced diuresis with furosemide. Corticosteroids may also be used for patients with corticosteroid-responsive malignancies, such as myeloma. Bisphosphonates, including zoledronic acid and pamidronate, may be administered parenterally. Although repeated administration of bisphosphonates may be required to maintain normal serum calcium levels, long-term therapy is associated with cumulative adverse risks, including kidney insufficiency and osteonecrosis of the mandible. See MKSAP 16 Endocrinology and Metabolism for further discussion of hypercalcemia.

KEY POINTS

- Symptoms of hypercalcemia include nausea and vomiting, constipation, polyuria and polydipsia, weakness, and confusion.
- The mainstays of treatment of hypercalcemia are aggressive hydration with normal saline for short-term control and parenteral bisphosphonates for longer-term control.

Effects of Cancer and Cancer Therapy

Acute and chronic adverse events frequently occur following administration of chemotherapy, radiation therapy, and biologic and targeted agents. Common acute toxic effects include temporary suppression of hematopoiesis, life-threatening diarrhea, anaphylactic allergic reactions, mucositis, pneumonitis, and decreased cardiac ejection fraction. Common chronic effects include impaired cardiopulmonary function, cognitive disorders, reproductive disorders, and secondary malignancies.

Hematopoietic Disorders

Neutropenia and Fever

The risk of life-threatening infection significantly increases when the absolute neutrophil count falls below 500/µL (0.5×10^9/L) and as the duration of neutropenia increases. Prospective trials have shown that recombinant granulocyte colony-stimulating factor (G-CSF) and granulocyte-macrophage colony-stimulating factor (GM-CSF) are effective in preventing the development of neutropenia and neutropenic fever and maintaining the dose intensity of

CONT.

chemotherapy. If neutropenia does develop, G-CSF and GM-CSF reduce the duration of the neutropenia and the need for or duration of hospitalization.

Patients with neutropenia who develop fever require rapid administration of broad-spectrum antibiotics, even if no specific site of infection is identified. Monotherapy with an antipseudomonal β-lactam agent (ceftazidime, cefepime, meropenem, imipenem, or piperacillin-tazobactam) or combination therapy directed against both gram-positive and gram-negative organisms may be used. In general, patients are admitted to the hospital for administration of parenteral antibiotics and close observation. Criteria have been developed to identify patients at particularly low risk who may be safely treated with oral antibiotics at home. The feasibility of properly identifying low-risk patients and ensuring adequate outpatient follow up has been problematic; consequently, this approach should probably be reserved for centers with extensive experience and a well-developed infrastructure for follow-up. In most patients, a pathogenic organism is not identified or is identified days after fever first develops. The need for continued broad antibiotic coverage in this setting supersedes the usual recommendations to limit antibiotic use. Prolonged neutropenia with fever following induction chemotherapy for acute myeloid leukemia requires empiric antifungal therapy. H

Myelodysplasia and Leukemia

Development of myelodysplasia and leukemia is a consequence of treatment with alkylating agent–, anthracycline-, and topoisomerase II inhibitor–based chemotherapy and, to a lesser extent, radiation therapy. The adverse consequences of multiagent chemotherapy and radiation can occur many years after completion of therapy. In most patients, the duration and number of chemotherapy agents administered correlate with the risk for developing myelodysplasia.

Disorders of Cardiac Function

Administration of anthracyclines (doxorubicin, idarubicin, epirubicin) requires careful monitoring of the cumulative dose and serial evaluation of left ventricular function because late toxicity is dose dependent and is usually irreversible. The development of liposomal formulations of anthracyclines (liposomal doxorubicin) has reduced the risk of late toxicity. Monoclonal antibodies directed against the *HER2/neu* receptor (trastuzumab) may cause decreased left ventricular function that is not dose dependent. Unlike anthracycline-based heart failure, trastuzumab-induced heart failure is reversible following trastuzumab discontinuation and aggressive medical management. Involved-field radiation therapy, which is commonly used for patients with mediastinal malignancies (lymphoma, thymoma), may cause acute left ventricular dysfunction and late adverse consequences, including premature coronary artery disease and valvular stenosis.

Disorders of Pulmonary Function

Acute and chronic pulmonary toxicity is common following administration of certain classes of chemotherapeutic agents. Bleomycin poses the greatest risk for development of acute pneumonitis and late toxic effects from pulmonary fibrosis. Bleomycin-induced pneumonitis (BIP) must be recognized early so that bleomycin can be discontinued and administration of corticosteroids begun. Limiting the cumulative lifetime dose of bleomycin (<400 IU) and discontinuing bleomycin if serial pulmonary function tests show a greater than 25% decrease in diffusing lung capacity for carbon monoxide have reduced, but not eliminated, the incidence of late pulmonary toxicity.

Radiation therapy to the thorax is associated with the development of pneumonitis, especially in patients who are receiving concurrent chemotherapy or required previous radiation therapy. Pneumonitis is proportionate to the total dose of radiation and volume of lung radiated. Rapid withdrawal of corticosteroids can induce pneumonitis in patients who previously received radiation therapy. Treatment includes resumption of corticosteroids with a slow dose taper.

Disorders of Genitourinary and Renal Function

Chemotherapeutic agents may adversely affect the renal tubules (cisplatin-induced tubular toxicity) and bladder (cyclophosphamide- and ifosfamide-induced hemorrhagic cystitis). Both complications are minimized with proper hydration, diuresis, and concurrent administration of mesna. High-dose methotrexate, which is used to treat lymphoma and sarcomas of bone, may precipitate in the renal tubules and cause tubular injury. Prevention requires careful monitoring of methotrexate dose levels, leucovorin support, and forced hydration with diuresis of alkaline urine. Radiation therapy may cause acute and chronic cystitis and permanent kidney dysfunction.

Sexual Function

Acute and chronic sexual dysfunction is a common complication of cancer therapy. The cause is multifactorial, and structural, hormonal, emotional, and social issues are involved. The use of phosphodiesterase-5 enzyme inhibitors such as sildenafil to treat erectile dysfunction and low-dose topical estrogens to maintain vaginal function are appropriate.

Secondary Malignancies

Both chemotherapy and radiation therapy may cause secondary malignancies. Patients with breast cancer who are treated with combined chemotherapy and radiation therapy have an increased lifetime risk for developing myelodysplasia, leukemia, endometrial cancer, and rarely, soft tissue sarcoma. Female patients with Hodgkin lymphoma who receive mantle field radiation therapy are at increased risk for developing breast cancer, and both male and female patients are at increased risk for developing thyroid, lung, and esophageal cancer.

Other Issues

Long-term administration of aromatase inhibitors in women with breast cancer has significantly increased the incidence of osteopenia and risk for late pathologic fractures. Calcium and vitamin D supplementation and use of bisphosphonates, when appropriate, are indicated based on results of serial bone density scans. Long-term corticosteroid use predisposes patients to aseptic necrosis of the hips, diabetes mellitus, cataracts, and infectious complications of immunosuppression. Other immunosuppressant agents such as alemtuzumab and fludarabine, used to treat chronic lymphocytic leukemia, increase the risk for early and late viral infections. Hypersensitivity reactions, which can be life threatening, are common in patients receiving many chemotherapeutic agents (for example, platinum-containing agents, taxanes, monoclonal antibodies, etoposide, bleomycin).

KEY POINTS

- The risk of life-threatening infection in patients receiving cancer treatment significantly increases with absolute neutrophil counts lower than 500/µL (0.5×10^9/L) and as the duration of neutropenia increases.
- Recombinant granulocyte colony-stimulating factor and granulocyte-macrophage colony-stimulating factor are effective in preventing neutropenia and neutropenic fever and maintaining the dose intensity of chemotherapy.
- Myelodysplasia and leukemia can be caused by chemotherapy and, to a lesser extent, radiation therapy.
- Involved-field radiation therapy may cause acute and chronic cardiac disorders.
- Patients with breast cancer who are treated with combined chemotherapy or radiation have an increased lifetime risk for developing myelodysplasia, leukemia, endometrial cancer, and rarely, soft tissue sarcoma.
- Long-term administration of aromatase inhibitors in women with breast cancer has significantly increased the incidence of osteopenia and risk for late pathologic fractures.

Bibliography

Hematopoietic Stem Cells and Their Disorders

Barbui T, Carobbio A, Rambaldi A, Finazzi G. Perspectives on thrombosis in essential thrombocythemia and polycythemia vera: is leukocytosis a causative factor? Blood. 2009;114(4):759-763. [PMID: 19372254]

Beer PA, Green AR. Pathogenesis and management of essential thrombocythemia. Hematology Am Soc Hematol Educ Program. 2009:621-628. [PMID: 20008247]

Bohlius J, Schmidlin K, Brillant C, et al. Recombinant human erythropoiesis-stimulating agents and mortality in patients with cancer: a meta-analysis of randomised trials [erratum in Lancet. 2009;374(9683):28]. Lancet. 2009;373(9674):1532-1542. [PMID: 19410717]

Druker BJ, Guilhot F, O'Brien SG, et al; IRIS Investigators. Five-year follow-up of patients receiving imatinib for chronic myeloid leukemia. N Engl J Med. 2006;355(23):2408-2417. [PMID: 17151364]

Fenaux P, Mufti GJ, Hellstrom-Lindberg E, et al; International Vidaza High-Risk MDS Survival Study Group. Efficacy of azacitidine compared with that of conventional care regimens in the treatment of higher-risk myelodysplastic syndromes: a randomised, open-label, phase III study. Lancet Oncol. 2009;10(3):223-232. [PMID: 19230772]

List A, Dewald G, Bennett J, et al; Myelodysplastic Syndrome-003 Study Investigators. Lenalidomide in the myelodysplastic syndrome with chromosome 5q deletion. N Engl J Med. 2006;355(14):1456-1465. [PMID: 17021321]

Marsh JC, Ball SE, Cavenagh J, et al; British Committee for Standards in Haematology. Guidelines for the diagnosis and management of aplastic anaemia. Br J Haematol. 2009;147(1):43-70. [PMID: 19673883]

Patnaik MM, Tefferi A. The complete evaluation of erythrocytosis: congenital and acquired. Leukemia. 2009;23(5):834-844. [PMID: 19295544]

Powell BL, Moser B, Stock W, et al. Arsenic trioxide improves event-free and overall survival for adults with acute promyelocytic leukemia: North American Leukemia Intergroup Study C9710. Blood. 2010;116(19):3751-3757. [PMID: 20705755]

Sawada K, Fujishima N, Hirokawa M. Acquired pure red cell aplasia: updated review of treatment. Br J Haematol. 2008;142(4):505-514. [PMID: 18510682]

Shimamura A. Clinial approach to marrow failure. Hematology Am Soc Hematol Educ Program. 2009:329-337. [PMID: 20008218]

Multiple Myeloma and Related Disorders

Dimopoulos MA, Gertz MA, Kastritis E, et al. Update on treatment recommendations from the Fourth International Workshop on Waldensrom's macroglobulinemia. J Clin Oncol. 2009;27(1):120-126. [PMID: 19047284]

Dispenzieri A, Kyle R, Merlini G, et al; International Myeloma Working Group. International Myeloma Working Group guidelines for serum-free light chain analysis in multiple myeloma and related disorders. Leukemia. 2009;23(2):215-224. [PMID: 19020545]

Greipp PR, San Miguel J, Durie BG, et al. International staging system for multiple myeloma [erratum in J Clin Oncol. 2005;23(25):6281]. J Clin Oncol. 2005;23(15):3412-3420. [PMID: 15809451]

Harousseau JL, Attal M, Avet-Loiseau H, et al. Bortezomib plus dexamethasone is superior to vincristine plus doxorubicin plus dexamethasone as induction treatment prior to autologous stem-cell transplantation in newly diagnosed multiple myeloma: results of the IFM 2005-01 phase III trial. J Clin Oncol. 2010;28(30):4621-4629. [PMID: 20823406]

International Myeloma Working Group. Criteria for the classification of monoclonal gammopathies, multiple myeloma and related disorders: a report of the International Myeloma Working Group. Br J Haematol. 2003;121(5):749-757. [PMID: 12780789]

Jaccard A, Moreau P, Leblond V, et al; Myélome Autogreffe (MAG) and Intergroupe Francophone du Myélome (IFM) Intergroup. High-dose melphalan versus melphalan plus dexamethasone for AL amyloidosis. N Engl J Med. 2007;357(11):1083-1093. [PMID: 17855669]

Kyle RA, Durie BG, Rajkumar SV, et al; International Myeloma Working Group. Monoclonal gammopathy of undetermined significance (MGUS) and smoldering (asymptomatic) multiple myeloma: IMWG consensus perspectives risk factors for progression and guidelines for monitoring and management. Leukemia. 2010;24(6):1121-1127. [PMID: 20410922]

Richardson PG, Sonneveld P, Schuster MW, et al; Assessment of Proteasome Inhibition for Extending Remissions (APEX) Investigators. Bortezomib or high-dose dexamethasone for relapsed multiple myeloma. N Engl J Med. 2005;352(24):2487-2498. [PMID: 15958804]

San Miguel JF, Schlag R, Khuageva NK, et al; VISTA Trial Investigators. Bortezomib plus melphalan and prednisone for initial treatment of multiple myeloma. N Engl J Med. 2008;359(9):906-917. [PMID: 18753647]

Weber DM, Chen C, Niesvizky R, et al; Multiple Myeloma (009) Study Investigators. Lenalidomide plus dexamethasone for relapsed multiple myeloma in North America. N Engl J Med. 2007;357(21):2133-2142. [PMID: 18032763]

Approach to Anemia

Andrès E, Fothergill H, Mecili M. Efficacy of oral cobalamin (vitamin B12) therapy. Expert Opin Pharmacother. 2010;11(2):249-256. [PMID: 20088746]

Babitt JL, Lin HY. Molecular mechanisms of hepcidin regulation: implications for the anemia of CKD. Am J Kidney Dis. 2010;55(4):726-741. [PMID: 20189278]

Bacon BR, Adams PC, Kowdley KV, et al; American Association for the Study of Liver Diseases. Diagnosis and management of hemochromatosis: 2011 practice guideline by the American Association for the Study of Liver Diseases. Hepatology. 2011;54(1):328-343. [PMID: 21452290]

Bonham DL, Dover GJ, Brody LC. Screening student athletes for sickle cell trait—a social and clinical experiment. N Engl J Med. 2010;363(11):997-999. [PMID: 20825310]

Brodsky RA. How I treat paroxysmal nocturnal hemoglobinuria. Blood. 2009;113(26):6522-6527. [PMID: 19372253]

Cappellini MD, Fiorelli G. Glucose-6-phosphate dehydrogenase deficiency. Lancet. 2008;371(9606):64-74. [PMID: 18177777]

Cunningham MJ. Update on thalassemia: clinical care and complications. Hematol Oncol Clin North Am. 2010;24(1):215-227. [PMID: 20113904]

Locatelli F, Aljama P, Canaud B, et al; Anaemia Working Group of European Renal Best Practice (ERBP). Target haemoglobin to aim for with erythropoiesis-stimulating agents: a position statement by ERBP following publication of the Trial to Reduce Cardiovascular Events with Aranesp® (TREAT) Study. Nephrol Dial Transplant. 2010;25(9):2846-2850. [PMID: 20591813]

Moake J. Thrombotic thrombocytopenia purpura (TTP) and other thrombotic microangiopathies. Best Pract Res Clin Haematol. 2009;22(4):567-576. [PMID: 19959109]

Nemeth E, Ganz T. The role of hepcidin in iron metabolism. Acta Haematol. 2001;122(2-3):78-86. [PMID: 19907144]

Packman CH. Hemolytic anemia due to warm autoantibodies. Blood Rev. 2008;22(1):17-31. [PMID: 17904259]

Perrotta S, Gallagher PG, Mohandas N. Hereditary spherocytosis. Lancet. 2008;372(9647):1411-1426. [PMID: 18940465]

Petz LD. Cold antibody autoimmune hemolytic anemias. Blood Rev. 2008;22(1):1-15. [PMID: 17904258]

Platt OS. Hydroxyurea for the treatment of sickle cell anemia. N Engl J Med. 2008;358(13):1362-1369. [PMID: 18367739]

Voskaridou E, Christoulas D, Bilalis A, et al. The effect of prolonged administration of hydroxyurea on morbidity and mortality in adult patients with sickle cell syndromes: results of a 17-year, single-center trial (LaSHS). Blood. 2010;115(12):2354-2363. [PMID: 19903897]

Weiss G. Genetic mechanisms and modifying factors in hereditary hemochromatosis. Nat Rev Gastroenterol Hepatol. 2010;7(1):50-58. [PMID: 19918260]

Transfusion

Boucher BA, Hannon TJ. Blood management: a primer for clinicians. Pharmacotherapy. 2007;27(10):1394-1411. [PMID: 17896895]

Hébert PC, Wells G, Blajchman MA, et al. A multicenter, randomized, controlled clinical trial of transfusion requirements in critical care. Transfusion Requirements in Critical Care Investigators, Canadian Critical Care Trials Group [erratum in N Engl J Med. 1999;340(13):1056]. N Engl J Med. 1999;340(6):409-417. [PMID: 9971864]

Hod E, Schwarz J. Platelet transfusion refractoriness. Br J Haematol. 2008;142(3):348-360. [PMID: 18510692]

Marik PE, Corwin HL. Efficacy of red blood cell transfusion in the critically ill: a systematic review of the literature [erratum in Crit Care Med. 2008;36(11):3134]. Crit Care Med. 2008;36(9):2667-2674. [PMID: 18679112]

Roback JD, Caldwell S, Carson J, et al; American Association for the Study of Liver; American Academy of Pediatrics; United States Army; American Society of Anesthesiology; American Society of Hematology. Evidence-based practice guidelines for plasma transfusion. Transfusion. 2010;50(6):1227-1239. [PMID: 20345562]

Silliman CC, Fung YL, Ball JB, Khan SY. Transfusion-related acute lung injury (TRALI): current concepts and misconceptions. Blood Rev. 2009;23(6):245-255. [PMID: 19699017]

Steinbrook R. Erythropoietin, the FDA, and oncology. N Engl J Med. 2007;356:2448-2451. [PMID: 17568025]

Szczepiorkowski ZM, Winters JL, Bandarenko N, et al. Apheresis Applications Committee of the American Society for Apheresis. Guidelines on the use of therapeutic apheresis in clinical practice—evidence-based approach from the Apheresis Applications Committee of the American Society for Apheresis. J Clin Apher. 2010;25(3):83-177. [PMID: 205680980]

Vamvakas EC, Blajchman MA. Transfusion-related mortality: the ongoing risks of allogeneic blood transfusion and the available strategies for their prevention. Blood. 2009;113(15):3406-3417. [PMID: 19188662]

Wang JK, Klein HG. Red blood cell transfusion in the treatment and management of anaemia: the search for the elusive transfusion trigger. Vox Sang. 2010;98(1):2-11. [PMID: 19682346]

Bleeding Disorders

James AH, Manco-Johnson MJ, Yawn BP, Dietrich JE, Nichols WL. Von Willebrand disease: key points from the 2008 National Heart, Lung, and Blood Institute guidelines. Obstet Gynecol. 2009;114(3):674-678. [PMID: 19701049]

Sallah S, Kato G. Evaluation of bleeding disorders. A detailed history and laboratory tests provide clues. Postgrad Med. 1998;103(4):209-210, 215-218. [PMID: 9553596]

Platelets

Favaloro EJ, Lippi G, Franchini M. Contemporary platelet function testing. Clin Chem Lab Med. 2010;48(5):579-598. [PMID: 20148722]

Lo GK, Juhl D, Warkentin TE, Sigouin CS, Eichler P, Greinacher A. Evaluation of pretest clinical score (4 T's) for the diagnosis of heparin-induced thrombocytopenia in two clinical settings. J Thromb Haemost. 2006;4(4):759-765. [PMID: 16634744]

Moake J. Thrombotic thrombocytopenia purpura (TTP) and other thrombotic microangiopathies. Best Pract Res Clin Haematol. 2009;22(4):567-576. [PMID: 19959109]

Provan D, Stasi R, Newland AC, et al. International consensus report on the investigation and management of primary immune thrombocytopenia. Blood. 2010;115(2):168-186. [PMID: 19846889]

Thrombotic Disorders

Bates SM, Jaeschke R, Stevens SM, et al. Diagnosis of DVT: Antithrombotic Therapy and Prevention of Thrombosis, 9th ed: American College of Chest Physicians Evidence-Based Clinical

Practice Guidelines. Chest. 2012;141(2 Suppl):e351S-418S. [PMID: 22315267]

Eikelboom JW, Hirsh J, Spencer FA, et al. Antiplatelet Drugs: Antithrombotic Therapy and Prevention of Thrombosis, 9th ed: American College of Chest Physicians Evidence-Based Clinical Practice Guidelines. Chest. 2012;141(2 Suppl):e89S-e119S. [PMID: 22315278]

Bick RL, Baker WF. Treatment options for patients who have antiphospholipid syndromes. Hematol Oncol Clin North Am. 2008;22(1):145-153. [PMID: 18207072]

Douketis JD, Spyropoulos AC, Spencer FA, et al. Perioperative Management of Antithrombotic Therapy: Antithrombotic Therapy and Prevention of Thrombosis, 9th ed: American College of Chest Physicians Evidence-Based Clinical Practice Guidelines. Chest. 2012;141(2 Suppl):e326S-50S. [PMID: 22315266]

Falck-Ytter Y, Francis CW, Johanson NA, et al. Prevention of VTE in Orthopedic Surgery Patients: Antithrombotic Therapy and Prevention of Thrombosis, 9th ed: American College of Chest Physicians Evidence-Based Clinical Practice Guidelines. Chest. 2012;141(2 Suppl):e278S-325S. [PMID: 22315265]

Gould MK, Garcia DA, Wren SM, et al. Prevention of VTE in Nonorthopedic Surgical Patients: Antithrombotic Therapy and Prevention of Thrombosis, 9th ed: American College of Chest Physicians Evidence-Based Clinical Practice Guidelines. Chest. 2012;141(2 Suppl):e227S-77S. [PMID: 22315263]

Holbrook A, Schulman S, Witt DM, et al. Evidence-Based Management of Anticoagulant Therapy: Antithrombotic Therapy and Prevention of Thrombosis, 9th ed: American College of Chest Physicians Evidence-Based Clinical Practice Guidelines. Chest. 2012;141(2 Suppl):e152S-84S. [PMID: 22315259]

Kahn SR, Lim W, Dunn AS, et al. Prevention of VTE in Nonsurgical Patients: Antithrombotic Therapy and Prevention of Thrombosis, 9th ed: American College of Chest Physicians Evidence-Based Clinical Practice Guidelines. Chest. 2012;141(2 Suppl):e195S-226S. [PMID: 22315261]

Kearon C, Akl EA, Comerota AJ, et al. Antithrombotic Therapy for VTE Disease: Antithrombotic Therapy and Prevention of Thrombosis, 9th ed: American College of Chest Physicians Evidence-Based Clinical Practice Guidelines. Chest. 2012;141(2 Suppl):e419S-94S. [PMID: 22315268]

Khor B, Van Cott EM. Laboratory tests for protein C deficiency. Am J Hematol. 2010;85(6):440-442. [PMID: 20309856]

Kitchens CS. How I treat superficial venous thrombosis. Blood. 2011;117(1):39-44. [PMID: 20980677]

Lijfering WM, Brouwer JL, Veeger NJ, et al. Selective testing for thrombophilia in patients with first venous thrombosis: results from a retrospective family cohort study on absolute thrombotic risk for currently known thrombophilic defects in 2479 relatives. Blood. 2009;113(21):5314-5322. [PMID: 19139080]

Lijfering WM, Rosendaal FR, Cannegieter SC. Risk factors for venous thrombosis—current understanding from an epidemiological point of view. Br J Haematol. 2010;149(6):824-833. [PMID: 20456358]

Mismetti P, Laporte-Simitsidis S, Tardy B, et al. Prevention of venous thromboembolism in internal medicine with unfractionated or low-molecular-weight heparins: a meta-analysis of randomised clinical trials. Thromb Haemost. 2000;83(1):14-19. [PMID: 10669147]

Mismetti P, Laporte S, Darmon JY, Buchmüller A, Decousus H. Meta-analysis of low molecular weight heparin in the prevention of venous thromboembolism in general surgery. Br J Surg. 2001;88(7):913-930. [PMID: 11442521]

Noble S, Pasi J. Epidemiology and pathophysiology of cancer-associated thrombosis. Br J Cancer. 2010;102(suppl 1):S2-S9. [PMID: 20386546]

Patnaik MM, Moll S. Inherited antithrombin deficiency: a review. Haemophilia. 2008;14(6):1229-1239. [PMID: 19141163]

Qaseem A, Chou R, Humphrey LL, Starkey M, Shekelle P; for the Clinical Guidelines Committee of the American College of Physicians. Venous thromboembolism prophylaxis in hospitalized patients: a clinical practice guideline from the American College of Physicians. Ann Intern Med. 2011;155(9):625-632. [PMID: 22041951]

Ray JG. Hyperhomocysteinemia: no longer a consideration in the management of venous thromboembolism. Curr Opin Pulm Med. 2008;14(5):369-373. [PMID: 18664964]

Segal JB, Brotman DJ, Necochea AJ, et al. Predictive value of factor V Leiden and prothrombin G20210A in adults with venous thromboembolism and in family members of those with a mutation: a systematic review. JAMA. 2009;301(23):2472-2485. [PMID: 19531787]

ten Kate MK, van der Meer J. Protein S deficiency: a clinical perspective. Haemophilia. 2008;14(6):1222-1228. [PMID: 18479427]

White RH. The epidemiology of venous thromboembolism. Circulation. 2003;107(23 suppl 1):I4-I8. [PMID: 12814979]

Hematologic Issues in Pregnancy

Bates SM, Jaeschke R, Stevens SM, et al. Diagnosis of DVT: antithrombotic therapy and prevention of thrombosis, 9th ed: American College of Chest Physicians evidence-based clinical practice guidelines. Chest. 2012;141(2)(suppl):e351S-e418S. [PMID: 22315267]

Burrows RF. Platelet disorders in pregnancy. Curr Opin Obstet Gynecol. 2001;13(2):115-119. [PMID: 11315863]

James A; Committee on Practice Bulletins—Obstetrics. Practice bulletin no. 123: thromboembolism in pregnancy. Obstet Gynecol. 2011;118(3):718-729. [PMID: 21860313]

Martí-Carvajal AJ, Peña-Martí GE, Comunián-Carrasco G, Martí-Peña AJ. Interventions for treating painful sickle cell crisis during pregnancy. Cochrane Database Syst Rev. 2009;(1):CD006786. [PMID: 19160301]

Peña-Rosas JP, Viteri FE. Effects and safety of preventive oral iron or iron+folic acid supplementation for women during pregnancy. Cochrane Database Syst Rev. 2009;(4):CD004736. [PMID: 19821332]

Breast Cancer

Burstein HJ, Prestrud A, Seidenfeld J, et al. American Society of Clinical Oncology clinical practice guideline: update on adjuvant endocrine therapy for women with hormone receptor-positive breast cancer. J Clin Oncol. 2010;28(23):3784. [PMID: 20625130]

Chia S, Swain SM, Byrd DR, et al. Locally advanced and inflammatory breast cancer. J Clin Oncol. 2008;26(5):786-790. [PMID: 18258987]

Clarke M, Collins R, Darby S, et al. Effects of radiotherapy and of differences in the extent of surgery for early breast cancer on local recurrence and 15-year survival: an overview of the randomised trials. Lancet. 2005;366(9503):2087. [PMID: 16360786]

Dahabreh IJ, Linardou H, Siannis F, et al. Trastuzumab in the adjuvant treatment of early-stage breast cancer: a systematic review and meta-analysis of randomized controlled trials. Oncologist. 2008;13(6):620-630. [PMID: 18586917]

Early Breast Cancer Trialists' Collaborative Group (EBCTCG). Effects of chemotherapy and hormonal therapy for early breast cancer on recurrence and 15-year survival: an overview of the randomised trials. Lancet. 2005;365(9472):1687. [PMID: 15894097]

Fehm T, Felsenberg D, Krimmel M, et al. Bisphosphonate-associated osteonecrosis of the jaw in breast cancer patients: recommendations for prevention and treatment. Breast. 2009;18(4):213-217. [PMID: 19651512]

Fisher B, Costantino JP, Wickerham DL, et al. Tamoxifen for prevention of breast cancer: report of the National Surgical Adjuvant Breast and Bowel Project P-1 Study. J Natl Cancer Inst. 1998;90(18):1371-1388. [PMID: 9747868]

Higgins MJ, Wolff AC. Therapeutic options in the management of metastatic breast cancer. Oncology. 2008;22(6):614-623. [PMID: 18561551]

Jemal A, Siegel R, Xu J, et al. Cancer statistics, 2010. CA Cancer J Clin. 2010;60(5):277-300. [PMID: 20610543]

Paik S, Tang G, Shak S, et al. Gene expression and benefit of chemotherapy in women with node-negative, estrogen-receptor positive breast cancer. J Clin Oncol. 2006;24(23):3726. [PMID: 16720680]

Smith KL, Isaacs C. Management of women at increased risk for hereditary breast cancer. Breast Dis. 2006-2007;27:51-67. [PMID: 17917140]

Ovarian and Cervical Cancer

Armstrong DK, Bundy B, Wenzel L, et al. Intraperitoneal cisplatin and paclitaxel in ovarian cancer. N Engl J Med. 2006;354(1):34-43. [PMID: 16394300]

Bast RC Jr, Klug TL, St John E, et al. A radioimmunoassay using a monoclonal antibody to monitor the course of epithelial ovarian cancer. N Engl J Med. 1983;309(15):883-887. [PMID: 6310399]

Chemoradiotherapy for Cervical Cancer Meta-Analysis Collaboration. Reducing uncertainties about the effects of chemoradiotherapy for cervical cancer: a systematic review and meta-analysis of individual patient data from 18 randomized trials. J Clin Oncol. 2008;26(35):5802-5812. [PMID: 19001332]

Delgado G, Bundy B, Zaino R, et al. Prospective surgical pathological study of disease- free interval in patients with stage IB Squamous cell cancer of the cervix: a Gynecologic Group Study. Gynecol Oncol. 1990;38:352-357. [PMID: 2227547]

Giede KC, Kieser K, Dodge J, Rosen B. Who should operate on patients with ovarian cancer? An evidence-based review. Gynecol Oncol. 2005;99(2):447-461. [PMID: 16126262]

Jemal A, Siegel R, Ward E, et al. Cancer statistics, 2009. CA Cancer J Clin. 2009;59(4):225-249. [PMID: 19474385]

Parmar MK, Ledermann JA, Colombo N, et al. Paclitaxel plus platinum-based chemotherapy versus conventional platinum-based chemotherapy in women with relapsed ovarian cancer: the ICON4/AGO-OVAR-2.2 trial. Lancet. 2003;361(9375):2099-2106. [PMID: 12826431]

Roman LD, Muderspach LI, Stein SM, et al. Pelvic examination, tumor marker level, and gray-scale and Doppler sonography in the prediction of pelvic cancer. Obstet Gynecol. 1997;89(4):493-500. [PMID: 9083301]

Trimbos JB, Parmar M, Vergote I, et al. International Collaborative Ovarian Neoplasm trial 1 and Adjuvant Chemo Therapy In Ovarian Neoplasm trial: two parallel randomized phase III trials of adjuvant chemotherapy in patients with early-stage ovarian carcinoma. J Natl Cancer Inst. 2003;95(2):105-112. [PMID: 12529343]

Gastrointestinal Malignancies

Andre T, Boni C, Navarro M, et al. Improved overall survival with oxaliplatin, fluorouracil, and leucovorin as adjuvant treatment in stage II or III colon cancer in the MOSAIC trial. J Clin Oncol. 2009;27(19):3109-3116. [PMID: 19451431]

Cunningham D, Allum WH, Stenning SP, et al. Perioperative chemotherapy versus surgery alone for resectable gastroesophageal cancer. N Engl J Med. 2006;355(1):11-20. [PMID: 16822992]

Hidalgo, M. Pancreatic cancer. N Engl J Med. 2010;362(17):1605-1617. [PMID: 20427809]

Hurwitz H, Fehrenbacher L, Novotny W, et al. Bevacizumab plus irinotecan, fluorouracil, and leucovorin for metastatic colorectal cancer. N Engl J Med. 2004;350(23):2335-2342. [PMID: 15175435]

Karapetis CS, Khambata-Ford S, Jonker DJ, et al. K-ras mutations and benefit from cetuximab in advanced colorectal cancer. N Engl J Med. 2008;359(17):1757-1765. [PMID: 18946061]

Kleinberg L, Forastiere AA. Chemoradiation in the management of esophageal cancer. J Clin Oncol. 2007;25(26):4110-4117. [PMID: 17827461]

Macdonald JS, Smalley SR, Benedetti J, et al. Chemoradiotherapy after surgery compared with surgery alone for adenocarcinoma of the stomach or gastroesophageal junction. N Engl J Med. 2001;345(10):725-730. [PMID: 11547741]

Reidy DL, Tang LH, Saltz LB. Treatment of advanced disease in patients with well-differentiated neuroendocrine tumors. Nature Clin Pract Oncol. 2009;6(3):143-152. [PMID: 19190591]

Saltz LB, Clarke S, Díaz-Rubio E, et al. Bevacizumab in combination with oxaliplatin-based chemotherapy as first-line therapy in metastatic colorectal cancer: a randomized phase III study. J Clin Oncol. 2008;26(12):2013-2019. [PMID: 18421054]

Lung Cancer

Subramanian J, Govindan R. Lung cancer in never smokers: a review. J Clin Oncol. 2007;25(5):561-570. [PMID: 17290066]

Humphrey LL, Teutsch S, Johnson M; U.S. Preventive Services Task Force. Lung cancer screening with sputum cytologic examination, chest radiography and computed tomography: an update for the U.S Preventive Services Task Force. Ann Intern Med. 2004;140(9):740-753. [PMID: 15126259]

Peterson RP, Pham D, Burfeind WR, et al. Thoracoscopic lobectomy facilitates the delivery of chemotherapy after resection for lung cancer. Ann Thorac Surg. 2007;83(4):1245-1249; discussion 1250. [PMID: 17383320]

Pignon JP, Tribodet H, Scagliotti GV, et al. Lung adjuvant cisplatin evaluation: a pooled analysis by the LACE Collaborative Group. J Clin Oncol. 2008;26(21):3552-3559. [PMID: 18506026]

Delbaldo C, Michiels S, Syz N, et al. Benefits of adding a drug to a single-agent or a 2-agent chemotherapy regimen in advanced non-small-cell lung cancer: a meta-analysis. JAMA. 2004;292(4):470-484. [PMID: 15280345]

Yang CH, Yu CJ, Shih JY, et al. Specific EGFR mutations predict treatment outcome of stage IIIB/IV patients with chemotherapy naïve non-small-cell lung cancer receiving first-line gefitinib monotherapy. J Clin Oncol. 2008;26(16):2745-2753. [PMID: 18509184]

Hanna N, Bunn PA Jr, Langer C, et al. Randomized phase III trial comparing irinotecan/cisplatin with etoposide/cisplatin in patients with previously untreated extensive-stage disease small-cell lung cancer. J Clin Oncol. 2006;24(13):2038-2043. [PMID: 16648503]

Slotman BJ, Faivre-Finn C, Kramer G, et al. Prophylactic cranial irradiation in extensive small-cell lung cancer. N Engl J Med. 2007;357(7):664-672. [PMID: 17699816]

Head and Neck Cancer

Forastiere AA, Goepfert H, Maor M, et al. Concurrent chemotherapy and radiation therapy for organ preservation in advanced laryngeal cancer. N Engl J Med. 2003;349:2091. [PMID: 14645636]

Pignon JP, le Maitre AL, Maillard E, et al. Meta-analysis of chemotherapy in head and neck cancer (MACH-NC): an update on 93 randomised trials and 17,346 patients. Radiother Oncol. 2009;92:4. [PMID: 19446902]

Ragin CC, Taioli, E. Survival of squamous cell carcinoma of the head and neck in relation to human papilloma virus infection: review and meta-analysis. Int J Cancer. 2007;121:1813. [PMID: 17546592]

Genitourinary Cancer

Blute ML, Bergstralh EJ, Partin AW, et al. Validation of Partin tables for predicting pathological stage of clinically localized prostate cancer. J Urol. 2000;164(5):1591-1595. [PMID: 11025711]

Crook J, Ludgate C, Malone S, et al. Final report of multicenter Canadian Phase III randomized trial of 3 versus 8 months of neoadjuvant androgen deprivation therapy before conventional-dose radiotherapy for clinically localized prostate cancer. Int J Radiat Oncol Biol Phys. 2009;73(2):327-333. [PMID: 18707821]

Davis JW, Sheth SI, Doviak MJ, Schellhammer PT. Superficial bladder carcinoma treated with bacillus Calmette-Guerin: progression-free and disease specific survival with minimum 10-year followup. J Urol. 2002;167(2, pt 1):494-500; discussion 501. [PMID: 11792905]

Flanigan RC, Salmon SE, Blumenstein BA, et al. Nephrectomy followed by interferon alfa-2b compared with interferon alfa-2b alone for metastatic renal-cell cancer. N Engl J Med. 2001;345(23):1655-1659. [PMID: 11759643]

International Germ Cell Consensus Classification: a prognostic factor-based staging system for metastatic germ cell cancer. International Germ Cell Cancer Collaborative Group. J Clin Oncol 1997;15:594-603 [PMID: 9053482]

Jemal A, Siegel R, Ward E, et al. Cancer Statistics, 2009. CA Cancer J Clin. 2009;(4):225-249. [PMID: 19474385]

Jemal A, Siegel R, Xu J, Ward E. Cancer statistics, 2010. CA Cancer J Clin. 2010;60(5):277-300. [PMID: 20610543]

Memorial Sloan-Kettering Cancer Center. Prostate Cancer Prediction Tools. www.mskcc.org/mskcc/html/10088.cfm. Accessed March 1, 2012.

Motzer RJ, Hutson TE, Tomczak P, et al. Sunitinib versus interferon alfa in metastatic renal-cell carcinoma. N Engl J Med. 2007;356(2):115-124. [PMID: 17215529]

Advanced Bladder Cancer Meta-analysis Collaboration. Neoadjuvant chemotherapy in invasive bladder cancer: a systematic review and meta-analysis. Lancet. 2003;361(9373):1927-1934. [PMID: 12801735]

Oliver RT, Mead GM, Fogarty PJ, et al. Radiotherapy versus carboplatin for stage I seminoma: Updated analysis of the MRC/EORTC randomized trial. J Clin Oncol. 2008;26(15s):1006s.

Roach M 3rd, Bae K, Speight J, et al. Short-term neoadjuvant androgen deprivation therapy and external-beam radiotherapy for locally advanced prostate cancer: long-term results of RTOG 8610. J Clin Oncol. 2008;26(4):585-591. [PMID: 18172188]

Roach M 3rd, Lu J, Pilepich MV, et al. Predicting long-term survival, and the need for hormonal therapy: a meta-analysis of RTOG prostate cancer trials. Int J Radiat Oncol Biol Phys. 2000;47(3):617-627. [PMID: 10837944]

Shipley WU, Kaufman DS, Zehr E, et al. Selective bladder preservation by combined modality protocol treatment: long-term outcomes of 190 patients with invasive bladder cancer. Urology. 2002;60(1):62-67;discussion 67-68. [PMID: 12100923]

Smith JA Jr, Labasky RF, Cockett AT, et al. Bladder cancer clinical guidelines panel summary report on the management of nonmuscle invasive bladder cancer (stages Ta, T1 and TIS). The American Urological Association. J Urol. 1999;162(5):1697-1701. [PMID: 10524909]

Stephenson AJ, Chetner MP, Rourke K, et al. Guidelines for the surveillance of localized renal cell carcinoma based on the patterns of relapse after nephrectomy. J Urol. 2004;172(1):58-62. [PMID: 15201737]

Tannock IF, de Wit R, Berry WR, et al; TAX 327 Investigators. Docetaxel plus prednisone or mitoxantrone plus prednisone for advanced prostate cancer. N Engl J Med. 2004;351(15):1502-1512. [PMID: 15470213]

Lymphadenopathy and Lymphoid Malignancies

Buske C, Hasoter E, Dreyling M, et al. The Follicular Lymphoma International Prognostic Index (FLIPI) separates high-risk from intermediate- or low-risk patients with advanced-stage follicular lymphoma treated front-line with rituximab and the combination of cyclophosphamide, doxorubicin, vincristine, and prednisone (R-CHOP) with respect to treatment outcome. Blood. 2006;108(5):1504-1508. [PMID: 16690968]

Else M, Ruchlemer R, Osuji N, et al. Long remissions in hairy cell leukemia with purine analogs: a report of 219 patients with a median follow-up of 12.5 years. Cancer. 2005;104(11):2442-2448. [PMID: 16245328]

Gallimini A, Hutchings M, Rigacci L. Early interim 2-[18F]fluoro-2-deoxy-D-glucose positron emission tomography is prognostically superior to international prognostic score in advanced Hodgkin's Lymphoma: A report from a joint Italian-Danish study. J Clin Oncol. 2007;25(24):3746-3752. [PMID: 17646666]

Hasenclever D, Diehl V. A prognostic score for advanced Hodgkin's disease. International Prognostic Factors Project on Advanced Hodgkin's Disease. N Engl J Med. 1998;339(21):1506-1514. [PMID: 9819449]

Keating M, O'Brian S, Albitar M, et al. Early results of a chemoimmunotherapy regimen of fludarabine, cyclophosphamide, and rituximab as initial therapy for chronic lymphocytic leukemia. J Clin Oncol. 2005;23(18):4079-4088. [PMID: 15767648]

Lenz G, Wright G, Dave SS, et al. Stromal gene signatures in large-B-cell lymphomas. N Engl J Med. 2008; 359:2313-2323. [PMID: 19038878]

Oyama T, Yamamoto K, Asano N, et al. Age-related EBV-associated B-cell lymphoproliferative disorders constitute a distinct clinicopathologic group: a study of 96 patients. Clin Cancer Res. 2007;13(17):5124-5132. [PMID: 17785567]

Rosenwald A, Wright G, Chan WC, et al. The use of molecular profiling to predict survival after chemotherapy for diffuse large-B-cell lymphoma. N Engl J Med. 2002;346(25):1937-1947. [PMID: 12075054]

Swerdlow SH, Campo E, Harris NL, et al. *WHO Classification of Tumours of Haematopoietic and Lymphoid Tissues.* 4th ed. Lyon, France: IARC Press; 2008.

Zucca E, Bertoni F, Roggero E, Cavalli F. The gastric marginal B-cell lymphoma of MALT type. Blood. 2000;96(2):410-419. [PMID: 10887100]

Cancer of Unknown Primary Site

Hainsworth JD, Fizazi K. Treatment for patients with unknown primary cancer and favorable prognostic factors. Semin Oncol. 2009;36(1):44-51. [PMID: 19179187]

Hainsworth JD, Spigel DR, Litchy S, Greco FA. Phase II trial of paclitaxel, carboplatin, and etoposide in advanced poorly differentiated neuroendocrine carcinoma: a Minnie Pearl Cancer Research Network Study. J Clin Oncol. 2006;24(22):3548-3554. [PMID: 16877720]

Muggia FM, Baranda J. Management of peritoneal carcinomatosis of unknown primary tumor site. Semin Oncol. 1993;20(3):268-272. [PMID: 8503022]

Pavlidis N. Cancer of unknown primary: biological and clinical characteristics. Ann Oncol. 2003;14(suppl 3):iii11-18. [PMID: 12821533]

Spigel DR, Hainsworth JD, Greco FA. Neuroendocrine carcinoma of unknown primary site. Semin Oncol. 2009;36(1):52-59. [PMID: 19179188]

Melanoma

Hodi FS, O'Day SJ, McDermott DF, et al. Improved survival with ipilimumab in patients with metastatic melanoma. N Engl J Med. 2010;363(8):711-723. [PMID: 20525992]

Tsao H, Atkins MB, Sober AJ. Management of cutaneous melanoma. N Engl J Med. 2004;351(10):998-1012. [PMID: 15342808]

Primary Central Nervous System Tumors

Glioma Meta-analysis Trialists (GMT) Group. Chemotherapy for high-grade glioma. Cochrane Database Syst Rev. 2002;(4):CD003913. [PMID: 12519620]

Laws Er, Parney IF, Huang W, et al. Survival following surgery and prognostic factors for recently diagnosed malignant glioma: data from the Glioma Outcomes Project. J Neurosurg. 2003;99(3):467-473. [PMID: 12959431]

Stupp R, Hegi ME, Gilbert MR, Chakravarti A. Chemoradiotherapy in malignant glioma: standard of care and future directions. J Clin Oncol. 2007;25(26):4127-4136. [PMID: 17827463]

Oncologic Urgencies and Emergencies

Adams MJ, Lipsitz SR, Colan SD, et al. Cardiovascular status in long-term survivors of Hodgkin's disease treated with chest radiotherapy. J Clin Oncol. 2004;22(15):3139-3148. [PMID: 15284266]

Carver JR, Shapiro L, Ng A, et al; ASCO Cancer Survivorship Expert Panel. American Society of Clinical Oncology clinical evidence review on the ongoing care of adult cancer survivors: cardiac and pulmonary late effects. J Clin Oncol. 2007;25(25):3991-4008. [PMID: 17577017]

Ewer MS, Vooletich MD, Durand JB, et al. Reversibility of trastuzumab-related cardiotoxicity: new insights based on clinical course and response to medical treatment. J Clin Oncol. 2005;23(31):7820-7826. [PMID: 16258084]

Hermelink K, Untch M, Lux MP, et al. Cognitive function during neoadjuvant chemotherapy for breast cancer: results of a prospective, multicenter, longitudinal study. Cancer. 2007;109(9):1905-1913. [PMID: 17351951]

Hillner BE, Ingle JN, Chlebowski RT, et al; American Society of Clinical Oncology. American Society of Clinical Oncology 2003 update on the role of bisphosphonates and bone health issues in women with breast cancer. J Clin Oncol. 2003;21(21):4042-4057. [PMID: 12963702]

Lee SJ, Schover LR, Partridge AH, et al; American Society of Clinical Oncology. American Society of Clinical Oncology Recommendations on fertility preservation in cancer patients. J Clin Oncol. 2006;24(18):2917-2931. [PMID: 16651642]

Sleijfer S. Bleomycin-induced pneumonitis. Chest. 2001;120(2):617-624. [PMID: 11502668]

Hematology and Oncology Self-Assessment Test

This self-assessment test contains one-best-answer multiple-choice questions. Please read these directions carefully before answering the questions. Answers, critiques, and bibliographies immediately follow these multiple-choice questions. The American College of Physicians is accredited by the Accreditation Council for Continuing Medical Education (ACCME) to provide continuing medical education for physicians.

The American College of Physicians designates MKSAP 16 Hematology and Oncology for a maximum of 20 *AMA PRA Category 1 Credits*™. Physicians should claim only the credit commensurate with the extent of their participation in the activity.

Earn "Same-Day" CME Credits Online

For the first time, print subscribers can enter their answers online to earn CME credits in 24 hours or less. You can submit your answers using online answer sheets that are provided at mksap.acponline.org, where a record of your MKSAP 16 credits will be available. To earn CME credits, you need to answer all of the questions in a test and earn a score of at least 50% correct (number of correct answers divided by the total number of questions). Take any of the following approaches:

- ➢ Use the printed answer sheet at the back of this book to record your answers. Go to mksap.acponline.org, access the appropriate online answer sheet, transcribe your answers, and submit your test for same-day CME credits. There is no additional fee for this service.
- ➢ Go to mksap.acponline.org, access the appropriate online answer sheet, directly enter your answers, and submit your test for same-day CME credits. There is no additional fee for this service.
- ➢ Pay a $10 processing fee per answer sheet and submit the printed answer sheet at the back of this book by mail or fax, as instructed on the answer sheet. Make sure you calculate your score and fax the answer sheet to 215-351-2799 or mail the answer sheet to Member and Customer Service, American College of Physicians, 190 N. Independence Mall West, Philadelphia, PA 19106-1572, using the courtesy envelope provided in your MKSAP 16 slipcase. You will need your 10-digit order number and 8-digit ACP ID number, which are printed on your packing slip. Please allow 4 to 6 weeks for your score report to be emailed back to you. Be sure to include your email address for a response.

If you do not have a 10-digit order number and 8-digit ACP ID number or if you need help creating a username and password to access the MKSAP 16 online answer sheets, go to mksap.acponline.org or email custserv@acponline.org.

CME credit is available from the publication date of July 31, 2012, until July 31, 2015. You may submit your answer sheets at any time during this period.

Directions

*Each of the numbered items is followed by lettered answers. Select the **ONE** lettered answer that is **BEST** in each case.*

Hematology Questions

Item 1

A 62-year-old man undergoes a routine examination. He notes increasing fatigue of 8 months' duration but states he can perform his usual daily activities. He has no fever, night sweats, anorexia, or weight loss. The medical history is noncontributory, and he takes no medications.

On physical examination, vital signs are normal. The spleen is palpable three finger breadths below the left midcostal margin. There is no lymphadenopathy or hepatomegaly.

Laboratory studies indicate a hemoglobin level of 12.5 g/dL (125 g/L), a leukocyte count of 14,400/µL (14.4×10^9/L), and a platelet count of 148,000/µL (148×10^9/L).

A peripheral blood smear is shown.

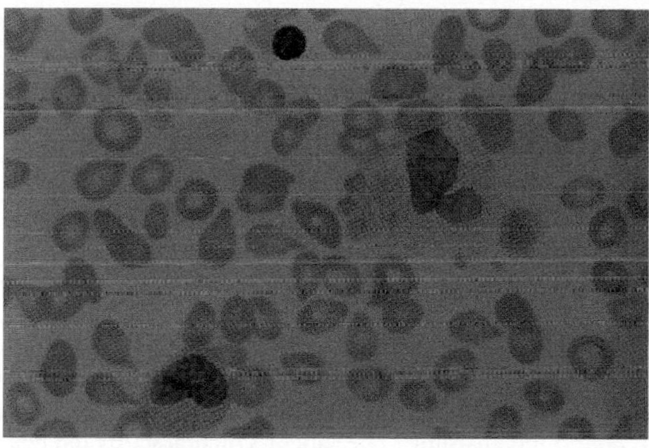

The bone marrow cannot be aspirated, but the bone marrow biopsy reveals a hypercellular marrow with extensive fibrosis and abnormal-appearing megakaryocytes. Results of conventional cytogenetic testing are normal. The *JAK2* mutation assay is positive. Fluorescence in situ hybridization of the bone marrow for the (9;22) translocation is negative.

Which of the following is the most appropriate management of this patient now?

(A) Allogeneic hematopoietic stem cell transplantation
(B) Danazol
(C) Hydroxyurea
(D) Imatinib
(E) Observation

Item 2

A 24-year-old man undergoes follow-up evaluation for treatment of aplastic anemia. Two of his siblings are HLA-identical matches.

Laboratory studies:

Hemoglobin	8.3 g/dL (83 g/L) (following transfusion of 1 unit of irradiated packed erythrocytes last week)
Leukocyte count	500/µL (0.5×10^9/L) with 23% neutrophils, 3% band forms, and 71% lymphocytes
Platelet count	26,000/µL (26×10^9/L)
Reticulocyte count	0.2%

Review of the bone marrow biopsy done 2 weeks ago confirms the diagnosis of aplastic anemia, demonstrating an aplastic bone marrow with normal cytogenetics.

Which of the following is the most appropriate treatment?

(A) Allogeneic hematopoietic stem cell transplantation
(B) Antithymocyte globulin, corticosteroids, and cyclosporine
(C) Autologous hematopoietic stem cell transplantation
(D) Corticosteroids
(E) Granulocyte colony-stimulating factor

Item 3

H

A 32-year-old woman undergoes preoperative evaluation prior to a complex spinal surgery for repair of severe scoliosis. Her expected blood loss is 2.5 liters. She had a severe anaphylactic reaction during a prior erythrocyte transfusion she received for postpartum hemorrhage at age 25 years.

On physical examination, temperature is 36.8 °C (98.4 °F), blood pressure is 132/76 mm Hg, and pulse rate is 78/min.

Laboratory studies indicate a hemoglobin level of 13.6 g/dL (136 g/L), a leukocyte count of 7800/µL (7.8×10^9/L), and a platelet count of 186,000/µL (186×10^9/L). Previous laboratory studies indicate an IgG level of 868 mg/dL (8.68 g/L), an IgA level <5 mg/dL (0.05 g/L), and an IgM level of 64 mg/dL (0.64 g/L). No monoclonal spike is found on serum protein electrophoresis.

Which of the following is the most appropriate erythrocyte product for this patient?

(A) Cytomegalovirus negative
(B) γ-Irradiated
(C) Leukoreduced
(D) Phenotypically matched
(E) Washed

Item 4

H

A 75-year-old man is evaluated in the hospital for community-acquired pneumonia. He is bedbound. He has heart failure and hypertension for which he takes lisinopril and carvedilol.

CONT.

On physical examination, temperature is 38.6 °C (101.4 °F), blood pressure is 110/65 mm Hg, pulse rate is 90/min, and respiration rate is 24/min. BMI is 34. The patient demonstrates right lower lobe bronchial breathing and egophony.

Leukocyte count is 17,000/µL (17×10^9/L).

A chest radiograph shows right lower lobe consolidation.

Which of the following is the most appropriate venous thromboembolism prophylaxis in this patient?

(A) Aspirin, 325 mg/d
(B) Low-dose subcutaneous unfractionated heparin
(C) Pneumatic compression devices
(D) Warfarin, 1 mg/d

H

Item 5

A 48-year-old woman is evaluated in the emergency department for a severe headache that developed about 6 hours ago. She describes the headache as "the worst headache of her life," and her family, who has accompanied her, notes she is now confused, and her speech is slurred. She has a history of myelodysplasia for which she has never required treatment, as well as poorly controlled hypertension. Medications are enalapril and amlodipine.

On physical examination, temperature is 36.4 °C (97.6 °F), blood pressure is 168/84 mm Hg, pulse rate is 66/min, and respiration rate is 18/min. The patient is confused. Her speech is slurred, and she has left-sided weakness. There is no lymphadenopathy or splenomegaly.

Laboratory studies:

Hemoglobin	10.3 g/dL (103 g/L)
Leukocyte count	4500/µL (4.5×10^9/L) with 63% neutrophils and 36% lymphocytes
Mean corpuscular volume	106 fL
Platelet count	32,000/µL (32×10^9/L)

The prothrombin time, activated partial thromboplastin time, and liver chemistry values are normal.

A CT scan of the head shows an intracerebral bleed with extravasation of blood into the ventricular system.

Which of the following is the most appropriate minimum platelet threshold for this patient?

(A) 30,000/µL (30×10^9/L)
(B) 50,000/µL (50×10^9/L)
(C) 100,000/µL (100×10^9/L)
(D) 150,000/µL (150×10^9/L)

Item 6

A 65-year-old man is evaluated for a 1-month history of headaches and blurred vision, early satiety, and itching that occurs after showering. He has a 90-pack-year smoking history. He has no history of cardiopulmonary or sleep disorders, no other medical problems, and he takes no medications.

On physical examination, temperature is normal, blood pressure is 160/90 mm Hg, pulse rate is 90/min, and respiration rate is 18/min. BMI is 35. Oxygen saturation is 97% with the patient breathing ambient air and does not decrease with exertion. His face is erythematous, and engorged retinal veins are noted on funduscopic examination. Cardiopulmonary and neurologic examinations are normal. Abdominal examination shows splenomegaly.

Laboratory studies:

Hemoglobin	19 g/dL (190 g/L)
Leukocyte count	13,500/µL (13.5×10^9/L); normal differential
Platelet count	595,000/µL (595×10^9/L)

The findings on the complete blood count are confirmed. The remaining laboratory studies, including liver chemistry tests, are normal.

Which of the following is the most appropriate next step in diagnosis?

(A) *BCR-ABL* gene analysis
(B) Bone marrow biopsy
(C) *JAK2 V617F* mutational analysis
(D) Polysomnography

Item 7

H

A 27-year-old man is admitted to the emergency department for injuries sustained in a motorcycle accident. There is no head trauma, but he has left lower-quadrant abdominal pain.

On physical examination, temperature is 36.8 °C (98.4 °F), blood pressure is 89/44 mm Hg, pulse rate is 112/min, and respiration rate is 14/min. Abdominal examination reveals left lower-quadrant tenderness, with rebound and guarding. The patient's mental status and neurologic examination findings are normal.

Laboratory studies:

Hemoglobin	8.7 g/dL (87 g/L)
Leukocyte count	11,600/µL (11.6×10^9/L)
Platelet count	188,000/µL (188×10^9/L)
Prothrombin time	12.1 s
Activated partial thromboplastin time	35 s

The patient's blood type is A negative with no alloantibodies.

A CT scan of the abdomen confirms splenic laceration. The blood bank indicates that type A-negative blood is not available.

Which of the following is the most appropriate erythrocyte product for emergency transfusion in this patient?

(A) A positive
(B) AB negative
(C) B positive
(D) O negative

Item 8

A 75-year-old woman is evaluated for a 1-day history of gross hematuria as well as bruising and a nosebleed that have occurred over the past week. She has no personal or family history of abnormal bleeding. The patient has hypertension, hypercholesterolemia, and degenerative joint disease treated with lisinopril, low-dose aspirin, and ibuprofen. She underwent an uncomplicated dental extraction 2 months ago, an uncomplicated cholecystectomy 42 years ago, and a breast biopsy 23 years ago.

On physical examination, temperature is normal, blood pressure is 140/78 mm Hg, pulse rate is 90/min, and respiration rate is 18/min. Dried blood is visible in the nares. Large ecchymoses are present on the torso and upper and lower extremities, and a hematoma is visible on the left flank.

Laboratory studies:

Hemoglobin	8.5 g/dL (85 g/L)
Leukocyte count	Normal
Platelet count	Normal
Prothrombin time	11.5 s
Activated partial thromboplastin time (aPTT)	85 s
aPTT mixing study	48 s

Which of the following is the most likely diagnosis?

(A) Acquired hemophilia
(B) Factor XI deficiency
(C) Lupus inhibitor
(D) Occult liver disease

H Item 9

A 23-year-old woman is admitted to the hospital for plasma exchange. She was recently diagnosed with myasthenia gravis and remains symptomatic despite intravenous immune globulin and pyridostigmine. Medical history is otherwise noncontributory, and she has had no previous reaction to blood products.

Her respiratory function begins to worsen, and therapeutic plasma exchange is begun. Albumin is used as the replacement fluid, and citrate is used as the anticoagulant. One hour into the procedure, the patient becomes lightheaded, vomits, develops extreme anxiety, and experiences perioral numbness and tingling.

On physical examination, temperature is 37.0 °C (98.6 °F), blood pressure is 121/48 mm Hg, pulse rate is 103/min, and respiration rate is 16/min. She has labored breathing, appears agitated, and has lid lag. She also has proximal muscle weakness and muscle twitching. Jugular venous distention and peripheral edema are absent.

Preplasmapheresis exchange laboratory studies:

Complete blood count	Normal
Calcium	9.0 mg/dL (2.25 mmol/L)
Creatinine	0.8 mg/dL (70.7 µmol/L)
Magnesium	2.1 mg/dL (0.87 mmol/L)
Potassium	4.6 meq/L (4.6 mmol/L)
Sodium	144 meq/L (144 mmol/L)

In addition to temporary cessation of plasma exchange, which of the following is the most appropriate treatment?

(A) 0.9% Normal saline
(B) Calcium gluconate
(C) Diphenhydramine
(D) Epinephrine
(E) Heparin

Item 10

A 24-year-old woman undergoes follow-up evaluation for asymptomatic anemia detected on laboratory studies performed during her last visit. She is in the second trimester of an uncomplicated pregnancy and is otherwise healthy, with no history of gastrointestinal bleeding or family history of anemia. She takes only a prenatal vitamin.

On physical examination, temperature is 37.0 °C (98.6 °F), blood pressure is 108/62 mm Hg with no orthostatic changes, pulse rate is 76/min, and respiration rate is 18/min. Conjunctivae are normal. The patient has a gravid uterus. On cardiac examination, a grade 2/6 early systolic murmur associated with physiologic splitting of S_2 is heard at the left upper sternal border.

Laboratory studies indicate a hematocrit of 32%, a hemoglobin level of 10.8 g/dL (108 g/L), and a mean corpuscular volume of 80 fL. The complete blood count is otherwise normal as is the peripheral blood smear.

Which of the following is most likely responsible for this patient's anemia?

(A) Decreased red cell mass
(B) HELLP (*h*emolysis, *e*levated *l*iver enzymes, and *l*ow *p*latelet count) syndrome
(C) Increased plasma volume
(D) Iron deficiency
(E) Low erythropoietin level

Item 11 H

A 34-year-old man is evaluated in the emergency department for severe bleeding following surgical arthroscopy of the right knee 24 hours ago. The patient sustained a penetrating knee injury 1 year ago as a result of a nail gun injury. Over the past year, he has had at least eight recurrent episodes of hemarthroses at the site of the injury, requiring aspiration. As a child, he experienced compartment syndrome in the left forearm after sustaining an injury. He is one of eight siblings, and two of his four brothers have a history of epistaxis and posttraumatic hematomas. His only medication is naproxen.

On physical examination, the temperature is normal, blood pressure is 100/55 mm Hg, pulse rate is 120/min, and respiration rate is 22/min. His wound dressing is saturated, with fresh blood welling from the arthroscopy sites.

Laboratory studies:

Hemoglobin	8.4 g/dL (84 g/L) compared with 15.6 g/dL (156 g/L) preoperatively

CONT.

Platelet count	Normal
Prothrombin time	11.0 s
Activated partial thromboplastin time (aPTT)	60 s
aPTT mixing study	23 s (Normal range: 25-35 s)

Which of the following is the most likely diagnosis?

(A) Acquired factor VIII inhibitor
(B) Factor V deficiency
(C) Factor IX deficiency
(D) Factor XII deficiency

Item 12

A 28-year-old man is evaluated 24 hours after a new diagnosis of a left calf deep venous thrombosis. One week ago, he underwent orthopedic surgery. Two weeks ago, he returned from vacationing in Italy on an 8-hour flight. Current medications are enoxaparin, 80 mg subcutaneously twice daily, and warfarin, 5 mg/d.

On physical examination, temperature is normal, blood pressure is 145/85 mm Hg, pulse rate is 72/min, and respiration rate is 18/min. BMI is 25. His lungs are clear. His left calf is erythematous and edematous.

Duplex ultrasound obtained yesterday confirms a left posterior tibial vein thrombosis. Laboratory results from his emergency department visit reveal factor V Leiden heterozygosity.

The patient asks why he developed this blood clot and how long he will have to take warfarin.

Which of the following is the most appropriate management of this patient's venous thromboembolism?

(A) Low-intensity warfarin (INR, 1.5-2) for at least 3 months
(B) Standard-intensity warfarin (INR, 2-3) for at least 12 months
(C) Standard-intensity warfarin (INR, 2-3) for at least 3 months
(D) Standard-intensity warfarin (INR, 2-3) for life

H

Item 13

A 72-year-old woman is evaluated in the emergency department for the sudden onset of shortness of breath that has progressively worsened over the past 24 hours. She also has a nonproductive cough but no chest pain, fever, chills, or rigors. Medical history is significant for multiple myeloma diagnosed 3 years ago, and chronic myeloma-related kidney insufficiency. Six weeks ago, the patient experienced a myeloma relapse complicated by an impending fracture of the left femur requiring intramedullary nail fixation. Treatment with lenalidomide and high-dose dexamethasone was initiated after surgery. Other medications are oxycodone and enoxaparin, 40 mg subcutaneously once daily.

On physical examination, temperature is 37.3 °C (99.1 °F), blood pressure is 164/92 mm Hg, pulse rate is 124/min, and respiration rate is 20/min. BMI is 36. Oxygen saturation by pulse oximetry with the patient breathing ambient air is 90% at rest and 78% with ambulation. The patient is tachypneic. On cardiopulmonary examination, the lungs are clear to auscultation bilaterally, and there is tachycardia, with a regular rhythm and no murmurs, rubs, or gallops. She has 1+ bilateral lower extremity pitting edema extending just below the knees.

Laboratory studies:

Hemoglobin	9.0 g/dL (90 g/L)
Leukocyte count	5500/µL (5.5×10^9/L)
Platelet count	115,000/µL (115×10^9/L)
Blood urea nitrogen	30 mg/dL (10.7 mmol/L)
Creatinine	1.6 mg/dL (141.4 µmol/L)

A 24-hour urine protein electrophoresis and immunofixation assay performed immediately prior to initiation of lenalidomide and dexamethasone therapy indicates 1810 mg of monoclonal free λ light chains/d. Creatine kinase-MB and troponin T assays are normal.

A posteroanterior/lateral chest radiograph reveals a trace right pleural effusion. An electrocardiogram demonstrates sinus tachycardia with no ST or T-wave changes. Duplex venous ultrasound of the lower extremities reveals no evidence of thrombosis.

Which of the following is the most appropriate next step in the diagnostic evaluation?

(A) CT angiography of the chest
(B) Non-contrast high-resolution CT of the chest
(C) Pulmonary angiography
(D) Ventilation-perfusion scan

Item 14

H

A 48-year-old woman is evaluated in the hospital for shortness of breath, chills, and fever that developed during transfusion of the first unit of packed erythrocytes she received following an uncomplicated left total hip arthroplasty.

On physical examination, temperature is 38.9 °C (102.0 °F), blood pressure is 116/68 mm Hg, pulse rate is 111/min, and respiration rate is 22/min. Oxygen saturation is 86% with the patient breathing oxygen, 2 liters/min by nasal cannula. There is no jugular venous distention or peripheral edema. Cardiopulmonary examination discloses tachycardia with a regular rhythm and no S_3 or murmur.

Laboratory studies indicate a hemoglobin level of 9.3 g/dL (93 g/L), a leukocyte count of 9600/µL (9.6×10^9/L), and a platelet count of 198,000/µL (198×10^9/L).

A preoperative and postoperative type and screen indicate A-positive blood type with a negative antibody screen.

Diffuse bilateral infiltrates are seen on chest radiograph. An electrocardiogram shows sinus tachycardia but no ST changes.

Which of the following is the most likely diagnosis?

(A) Acute hemolytic transfusion reaction
(B) Febrile nonhemolytic transfusion reaction
(C) Transfusion-associated circulatory overload
(D) Transfusion-related acute lung injury

H

Item 15

A 40-year-old man is admitted to the hospital with fever, anemia, and thrombocytopenia. A diagnosis of acute promyelocytic leukemia (APL) is established. Treatment is begun with all-*trans* retinoic acid (ATRA), cytarabine, and idarubicin. The patient has also received numerous blood products since being hospitalized but none in the past 48 hours.

Within the past 24 hours, the patient has had increasing dyspnea, low-grade fever, and lower extremity edema but no chest pain or cough.

On physical examination, temperature is 37.6 °C (99.8 °F), blood pressure is 102/50 mm Hg, pulse rate is 102/min, and respiration rate is 16/min. Weight has increased 5.4 kg (11.9 lb) since admission. Oxygen saturation is 92% with the patient breathing ambient air. There is no jugular venous distension.

Cardiopulmonary examination discloses a regular tachycardia; there are bilateral crackles extending one third of the way up the lung fields. He also has pitting edema extending to the knees.

Laboratory studies:

Hemoglobin	9.6 g/dL (96 g/L)
Leukocyte count	184,000/µL (184 x 10^9/L) compared with 30,000/µL (30 x 10^9/L) on admission
Platelet count	45,000/µL (45 × 10^9/L)
Creatinine	2.1 mg/dL (185.6 µmol/L)

A chest radiograph reveals diffuse interstitial opacities and bilateral pleural effusions.

Which of the following is the most likely diagnosis?

(A) ATRA-induced differentiation syndrome
(B) Heart failure
(C) Pneumonia
(D) Transfusion-related acute lung injury

H

Item 16

A 35-year-old man is evaluated in the emergency department for a progressive, painful episode of superficial venous thrombophlebitis of the right greater saphenous vein. Three weeks ago, he developed an erythematous, painful, nodular swelling in a distal greater saphenous vein. He has had previous episodes treated with ibuprofen with gradual resolution. On this occasion, his superficial venous thrombophlebitis has progressed to involve the greater saphenous vein in the thigh despite ibuprofen therapy. Family history is positive for venous thromboembolism in his father. He smokes 10 cigarettes daily. His only medication is ibuprofen, 400 mg three times daily.

On physical examination, the right greater saphenous vein is erythematous, warm, and tender along its course from the calf up into the mid-upper thigh.

Duplex ultrasound of the right leg reveals extensive thrombosis of the greater saphenous vein up to within 2 cm of the junction with the common femoral vein.

Which of the following is the most appropriate initial management of this patient?

(A) Continue ibuprofen
(B) Place an inferior vena cava filter
(C) Refer for vein ligation
(D) Start therapeutic-dose low-molecular-weight heparin

H

Item 17

A 32-year-old woman is hospitalized with a pulmonary embolism confirmed by CT angiography. She has not had recent surgery, trauma, or travel. The patient has a 2-year history of Raynaud phenomenon and four first-trimester miscarriages. There is no family history of venous thromboembolism.

On physical examination, temperature is normal, blood pressure is 145/85 mm Hg, pulse rate is 92/min, and respiration rate is 20/min; BMI is 35. Oxygen saturation is 95% with the patient breathing oxygen, 2 L/min by nasal cannula. The cardiac rhythm is regular. Heart sounds are normal without murmur or extra sounds. The lungs are clear.

The activated partial thromboplastin time is 56 s.

In addition to beginning heparin, which of the following is the most appropriate diagnostic test?

(A) Antiphospholipid syndrome testing
(B) Antithrombin activity assay
(C) Factor V Leiden DNA testing
(D) Methylene tetrahydrofolate reductase DNA testing

Item 18

A 32-year-old woman is evaluated for the sudden onset of pleuritic chest pain and dyspnea. The patient is pregnant, at 9 weeks' gestation. She is otherwise healthy and other than pregnancy has no risk factors for venous thromboembolic disease. Her only medication is a daily prenatal vitamin.

On physical examination, temperature is 36.2 °C (97.1 °F), blood pressure is 110/65 mm Hg, pulse rate is 100/min, and respiration rate is 26/min. On cardiopulmonary examination, the patient is tachypneic and tachycardic, and the lungs are clear. A Doppler compression ultrasound examination confirms the diagnosis of right-sided deep venous thrombosis in the right popliteal vein.

Which of the following is the most appropriate management?

(A) Place inferior vena cava filter
(B) Start low-molecular-weight heparin (LMWH) and continue for 6 months
(C) Start LMWH and continue until 6 weeks postpartum
(D) Start LMWH and warfarin and continue warfarin until delivery
(E) Start LMWH and continue until delivery

Item 19

A 77-year-old man is evaluated for a 1-year history of extreme fatigue and shortness of breath on exertion and an 8-week history of substernal chest pain with exertion.

On physical examination, temperature is 36.7 °C (98.0 °F), blood pressure is 137/78 mm Hg, pulse rate is 118/min, and respiration rate is 17/min. BMI is 27. The patient has pale conjunctivae. Cardiopulmonary examination reveals a summation gallop, with crackles at the lung bases.

Laboratory studies:

Hemoglobin	5.4 g/dL (54 g/L)
Leukocyte count	6400/µL (6.4×10^9/L)
Mean corpuscular volume	58 fL
Platelet count	154,000/µL (154×10^9/L)
Red cell distribution width	25 (Normal range: 14.6-16.5)

A peripheral blood smear is shown.

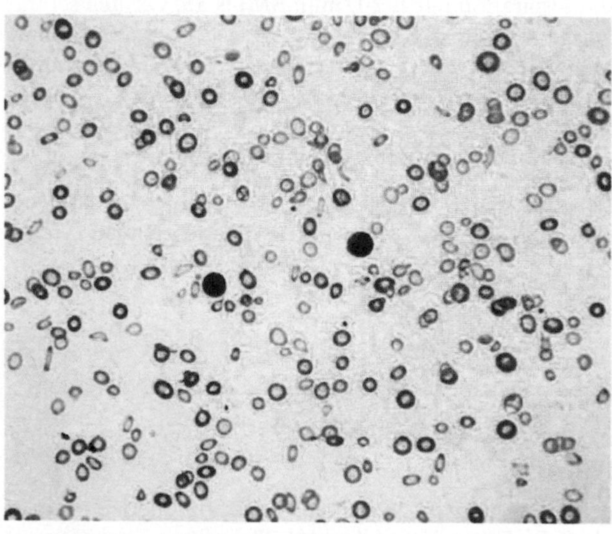

An echocardiogram is normal.

Which of the following is the most likely diagnosis?

(A) Glucose-6-phosphate dehydrogenase deficiency
(B) Iron deficiency
(C) Myelofibrosis
(D) Thrombotic thrombocytopenic purpura

H

Item 20

A 34-year-old man is evaluated following hospitalization for a left main pulmonary artery embolism and a right femoral vein deep venous thrombosis.

He has no personal history of recent surgery, major trauma, hospitalization, or travel. His mother has had multiple episodes of venous thromboses beginning at age 28 years. The patient is currently taking warfarin.

On physical examination, vital signs are normal. There is residual swelling of the right lower extremity. The remainder of the physical examination, including cardiopulmonary examination, is normal.

Which of the following is the most appropriate thrombophilic screening strategy?

(A) Test 2 to 4 weeks after warfarin is discontinued
(B) Test in 1 month
(C) Test now
(D) Test on blood obtained in hospital before warfarin initiation

Item 21

An 18-year-old woman is evaluated for severe menometrorrhagia of 5 years' duration. She has taken multiple varieties of oral contraceptive pills for 4 years to reduce the severity of her bleeding. She also has a history of anemia and takes iron supplementation. Her mother and 16-year-old sister also have menorrhagia, for which her mother had a hysterectomy at age 34 years, and her sister takes oral contraceptive pills.

On physical examination, the blood pressure is 135/88 mm Hg, pulse rate is 90/min, and respiration rate is 18/min. BMI is 22.

Coagulation studies are performed.

Laboratory studies following blood transfusion and estrogen therapy:

Hemoglobin	11 g/dL (110 g/L)
Activated partial thromboplastin time	29 s
von Willebrand factor (vWF) antigen assay	52% (Normal range: 50-150%)
vWF activity assay	58% (Normal range: 55-180%)
Factor VIII activity assay	80% (Normal range: 60-140%)

Which of the following is the most likely cause of her menorrhagia?

(A) Anovulatory cycles
(B) Factor XI deficiency
(C) Hemophilia A
(D) Uterine fibroids
(E) von Willebrand disease

H

Item 22

A 22-year-old woman is evaluated in the hospital for severe vaginal bleeding that developed 24 hours after an uncomplicated, normal spontaneous vaginal delivery. The patient has no personal or family history of a bleeding disorder or menorrhagia. She underwent an uncomplicated tonsillectomy at age 5 years. Her only medication has been a prenatal vitamin.

On physical examination, temperature is normal, blood pressure is 89/55 mm Hg, pulse rate is 120/min, and respiration rate is 24/min. She has bleeding from venipuncture sites. Pelvic examination shows bleeding from the episiotomy suture and brisk cervical bleeding. Dilation and curettage, packing, and re-suturing are unsuccessful in stopping the bleeding.

Laboratory studies:

Hemoglobin	7.2 g/dL (72 g/L)
Leukocyte count	12,000 µL (12×10^9/L) with a normal differential

H CONT.

Platelet count	350,000/μL (350 × 10^9/L)
Prothrombin time	11 s
Activated partial thromboplastin time (aPTT)	75 s
aPTT mixing study	55 s (Normal range: 25-35 s)
Fibrinogen	345 mg/dL (3.5 g/L)
D-dimer	0.5 μg/mL (500 mg/L)

The remaining laboratory studies are normal.

Which of the following is the most appropriate treatment?

(A) Cryoprecipitate
(B) Desmopressin
(C) Fresh frozen plasma
(D) Recombinant activated factor VIIa

Item 23

A 35-year-old woman undergoes evaluation following detection of thrombocytopenia on routine blood studies. The patient has no evidence or history of bruising, nosebleeds, menorrhagia, or upper gastrointestinal or genitourinary bleeding and no family history of bleeding disorders. Medications are oral contraceptive pills and occasional ibuprofen for menstrual discomfort.

On physical examination, vital signs are normal. Examination of the skin discloses no bruising or hematomas. Abdominal examination is normal, with no splenomegaly.

Laboratory studies:

Hematocrit	35%
Hemoglobin	12.9 g/dL (129 g/L)
Leukocyte count	6500/μL (6.5 × 10^9/L)
Mean corpuscular volume	85 fL
Platelet count	55,000/μL (55 × 10^9/L)
Thyroid-stimulating hormone	Normal
HIV serology	Negative
Anti-hepatitis C virus antibody	Negative

The peripheral blood smear shows large platelets, slightly decreased in number.

Which of the following is the most appropriate management?

(A) Initiate corticosteroids
(B) Initiate eltrombopag
(C) Perform antiplatelet antibody assay
(D) Perform bone marrow biopsy
(E) Repeat complete blood count in 1 week

Item 24

A 65-year-old man undergoes follow-up evaluation 2 days after discharge from the hospital for an idiopathic pulmonary embolism that occurred 1 week ago. This was his first thromboembolic event. He was initially treated with low-molecular-weight heparin and was switched to warfarin in the hospital. His INR at the time of hospital discharge was 2.5. He currently takes warfarin, 5 mg/d.

On physical examination, temperature is 36.0 °C (96.8 °F), blood pressure is 130/80 mm Hg, pulse rate is 80/min, and respiration rate is 20/min. BMI is 34.

His INR is 1.2.

In addition to rechecking the INR in 3 to 5 days, which of the following is the most appropriate management?

(A) Increase warfarin to 10 mg/d
(B) Increase warfarin to 7.5 mg/d
(C) Initiate low-molecular-weight heparin and increase warfarin to 7.5 mg/d
(D) Maintain warfarin at the current dose

Item 25

A 65-year-old man is evaluated for a 2-year history of daytime somnolence, snoring, and apneic episodes during the night as witnessed by his wife. He does not have blurred vision, tinnitus, or headache. He has no cardiopulmonary symptoms and does not smoke cigarettes. The patient has hypertension for which he takes lisinopril and atenolol.

On physical examination, temperature is normal, blood pressure is 170/98 mm Hg, pulse rate is 72/min, and respiration rate is 18/min. BMI is 44. Oxygen saturation is 95% with the patient breathing ambient air and does not decrease with modest exertion. The patient's face is erythematous, and his neck is thick. Hepatosplenomegaly is absent.

Laboratory studies:

Hemoglobin	17.5 g/dL (175 g/L)
Leukocyte count	5000/μL (5.0 × 10^9/L)
Platelet count	225,000/μL (225 × 10^9/L)
Erythropoietin	35 mU/mL (35 units/L)

Which of the following is the most appropriate management?

(A) Initiate hydroxyurea
(B) Order sleep study
(C) Perform bone marrow biopsy
(D) Perform phlebotomy

Item 26

A 22-year-old woman undergoes a new patient evaluation. She was recently diagnosed with systemic lupus erythematosus manifesting as painful joints, malar photosensitive rash, oral aphthous ulcers, and a positive antinuclear antibody and anti-Smith antibody titer. Her menstrual pattern is normal, and her medical history is otherwise noncontributory. Her only medications are hydroxychloroquine and a multivitamin.

On physical examination, temperature is 37.2 °C (99.0 °F), blood pressure is 126/78 mm Hg, pulse rate is 88/min, and respiration rate is 17/min. BMI is 20. The patient has a malar rash and thinning hair, but no joint abnormalities, oral lesions, pericardial or pleural rubs, or heart murmurs.

Laboratory studies:

Hemoglobin	8.2 g/dL (82 g/L)
Leukocyte count	3900/µL (3.9 × 10^9/L)
Ferritin	556 ng/mL (556 µg/L)
Iron	18 µg/dL (3.2 µmol/L)
Reticulocyte count	2%
Total iron-binding capacity	180 µg/dL (32 µmol/L)
Transferrin saturation	10%
Creatinine	1.0 mg/dL (88.4 µmol/L)

A peripheral blood smear is shown.

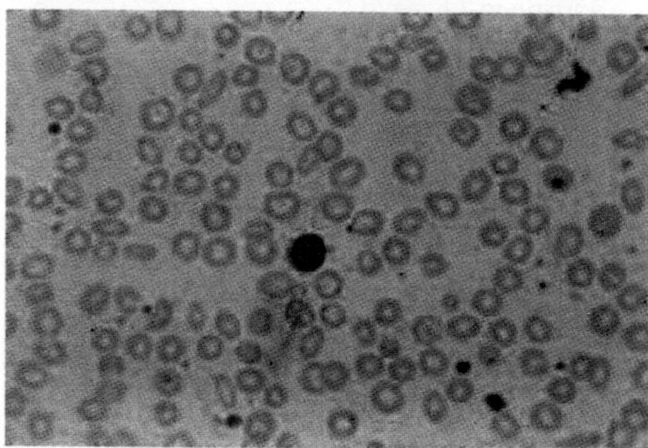

Which of the following is the most likely diagnosis?

(A) Inflammatory anemia
(B) Iron deficiency
(C) Microangiopathic hemolytic anemia
(D) Warm antibody-associated hemolysis

Item 27

A 29-year-old woman undergoes a new patient evaluation. She is a full-time college student, works part time as a waitress, and runs 3 miles twice weekly, but she is mildly fatigued in the evening. Medical history is significant for hereditary spherocytosis diagnosed at age 10 years. Her only medication is folic acid.

On physical examination, temperature is 36.3 °C (97.4 °F), blood pressure is 133/62 mm Hg, pulse rate is 68/min, and respiration rate is 18/min. She has scleral icterus and no lymphadenopathy. Cardiopulmonary examination is normal. On abdominal examination, her spleen is palpable just below the left costal margin.

Laboratory studies:

Hemoglobin	11.2 g/dL (112 g/L) (compared with a value of 11.5 g/dL [115 g/L] 3 years ago)
Leukocyte count	5900/µL (5.9 × 10^9/L)
Mean corpuscular volume	103 fL
Platelet count	172,000/µL (172 × 10^9/L)
Reticulocyte count	3.4%

An abdominal ultrasound shows mild splenomegaly and no gallstones.

Which of the following is the most appropriate treatment?

(A) Cholecystectomy
(B) Corticosteroids
(C) Splenectomy
(D) Supportive care

Item 28

An 87-year-old woman is evaluated for numbness and tingling in her feet of 6 months' duration. She eats a normal diet and does not consume alcohol.

On physical examination, temperature is normal, blood pressure is 127/85 mm Hg, pulse rate is 98/min, and respiration rate is 28/min. BMI is 20. The patient has pale conjunctivae with icterus and decreased vibratory sense in her toes. Her fingernails and toenails are normal.

Laboratory studies:

Hemoglobin	6.9 g/dL (69 g/L)
Leukocyte count	3900/µL (3.9 × 10^9/L) with a normal differential
Platelet count	49,000/µL (49 × 10^9/L)
Total bilirubin	4.9 mg/dL (83.8 µmol/L)
Lactate dehydrogenase	520 units/L
Creatinine	1.1 mg/dL (97.2 µmol/L)
Methylmalonic acid	Elevated
Homocysteine	Elevated
Vitamin B_{12}	224 pg/mL (165.3 pmol/L)

The peripheral blood smear is shown.

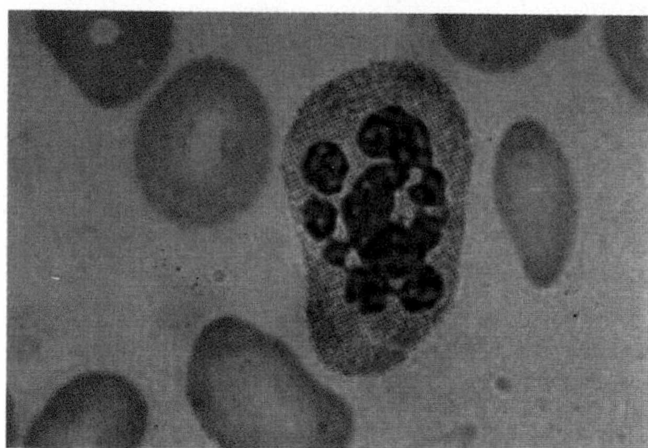

Which of the following is the most appropriate long-term treatment?

(A) Oral cobalamin
(B) Oral folate
(C) Parenteral cobalamin
(D) Parenteral folate

Item 29

H

A 52-year-old man is evaluated in the emergency department for a 5-day history of right leg pain and swelling. He has never had a previous episode of venous thromboembolism.

CONT.

On physical examination, temperature is 36.5 °C (97.7 °F), blood pressure is 120/75 mm Hg, pulse rate is 85/min, and respiration rate is 22/min. BMI is 30. The right lower extremity is swollen. Cardiopulmonary examination discloses clear lungs and tachycardia.

A right popliteal vein deep venous thrombosis is confirmed by venous duplex compression ultrasonography. The patient is given low-molecular-weight heparin (LMWH).

Which of the following is the most appropriate management of this patient's transition to warfarin therapy?

(A) At least 3 days of LMWH plus warfarin with a target INR of 1.5 or higher for 24 hours
(B) At least 3 days of LMWH plus warfarin with a target INR of 2 or higher for 24 hours
(C) At least 5 days of LMWH plus warfarin with a target INR of 2 or higher for 24 hours
(D) At least 5 days of LMWH plus warfarin with a target INR of 1.5 or higher for 24 hours

Item 30

A 35-year-old woman undergoes routine evaluation. She has no current medical problems or history of bleeding symptoms. Her medical history is significant only for iron deficiency 3 years ago that was thought to be diet related. She takes only oral contraceptive pills.

On physical examination, vital signs are normal. Examination of the skin discloses no petechiae or ecchymoses. The remainder of the examination is normal.

Hemoglobin is 13.5 g/dL (135 g/L), the leukocyte count is 8000/µL (8.0×10^9/L) with a normal differential, and the platelet count is 12,000/µL (12×10^9/L). A peripheral blood smear is shown.

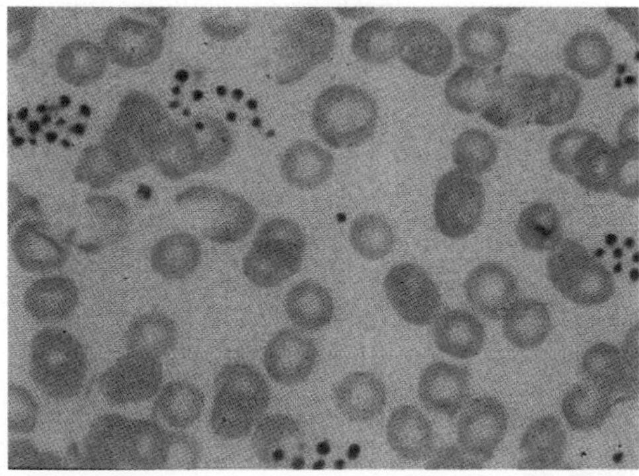

Which of the following is the most appropriate management?

(A) Initiate intravenous immune globulin
(B) Initiate prednisone
(C) Provide platelet transfusion
(D) Repeat complete blood count in a heparin- or citrate-anticoagulated tube

Item 31

A 17-year-old woman undergoes follow-up evaluation for microcytic anemia that was identified on a routine complete blood count 3 weeks ago. She is otherwise healthy. Medical and family histories are noncontributory. Her only medication is an oral contraceptive pill.

On physical examination, temperature is normal, blood pressure is 117/78 mm Hg, pulse rate is 88/min, and respiration rate is 17/min. BMI is 19. She has conjunctival pallor. The remainder of the physical examination is normal.

Laboratory studies:	
Erythrocyte count	5.45×10^6/µL (5.45×10^{12}/L)
Hemoglobin	11.6 g/dL (116 g/L)
Mean corpuscular volume	60 fL
Leukocyte count	5400/µL (5.4×10^9/L)
Platelet count	213,000/µL (213×10^9/L)
Red cell distribution width	15 (Normal range: 14.6-16.5)
Reticulocyte count	2.3%

Which of the following is the most likely diagnosis?

(A) Hereditary spherocytosis
(B) Iron deficiency
(C) Sideroblastic anemia
(D) β-Thalassemia trait

Item 32

A 46-year-old woman is evaluated for a 5-month history of progressive fatigue, night sweats, low-grade fever, early satiety, and a 4.5-kg (10-lb) weight loss.

On physical examination, temperature is 37.9 °C (100.2 °F), blood pressure is 134/82 mm Hg, pulse rate is 84/min, and respiration rate is 14/min. The oropharynx is clear. The cardiopulmonary examination is normal. The spleen is palpable 4 cm below the left midcostal margin. There is no lymphadenopathy or hepatomegaly.

The hemoglobin level is 11.6 g/dL (116 g/L), leukocyte count is 56,000/µL (56×10^9/L), and platelet count is 385,000/µL (385×10^9/L).

A peripheral blood smear is shown.

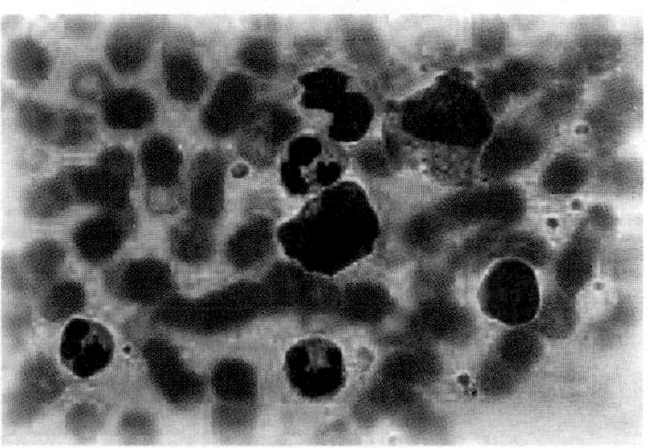

Which of the following is the most appropriate next test to establish the diagnosis?

(A) Flow cytometric analysis of the peripheral blood
(B) Fluorescence in situ hybridization assay for t(9;22)
(C) Heterophile antibody test
(D) *JAK2* mutation analysis

Item 33

A 75-year-old man is evaluated for increasing fatigue of 2 months' duration. He has a 15-year history of type 2 diabetes mellitus and a 5-year history of hypertension. Medications are metformin, glipizide, lisinopril, and aspirin.

On physical examination, temperature is normal, blood pressure is 134/82 mm Hg, pulse rate is 78/min, and respiration rate is 14/min. Funduscopic examination shows early proliferative diabetic retinopathy. The remainder of the examination is noncontributory.

Laboratory studies:

Creatinine	2.5 mg/dL (221 µmol/L) (compared with a value of 1.0 mg/dL [88.4 µmol/L] 6 months ago)
Hemoglobin A_{1c}	8.5%
Serum protein electrophoresis and immunofixation	Trace monoclonal free K light chains
Urinalysis	1+ protein
24-hour urine protein electrophoresis	Monoclonal free K light chains, 340 mg

The complete blood count and serum calcium level are normal. A bone marrow aspirate and biopsy reveals 12% plasma cells that are K light chain–restricted on flow cytometry. Myeloma bone survey and kidney ultrasound are normal.

Which of the following is the most appropriate management?

(A) Abdominal fat pad aspiration
(B) Chemotherapy
(C) Kidney biopsy
(D) Repeat M-protein determination in 12 months

Item 34

A 32-year-old woman is evaluated for a 1-week history of left leg pain and swelling. She is 34 weeks pregnant. The patient has no personal or family history of venous thromboembolism. She takes only a daily prenatal vitamin and has no medication allergies.

On physical examination, temperature is 37.2 °C (98.9 °F), blood pressure is 120/70 mm Hg, pulse rate is 95/min, and respiration rate is 20/min. BMI is 30. There are 2+ pitting edema, erythema, and warmth of the left lower extremity but no signs of skin breakdown.

Duplex ultrasonography confirms the presence of a popliteal vein thrombosis. Prothrombin time and activated partial thromboplastin time are normal.

Which of the following protein S laboratory profiles would be most consistent with this patient's condition?

(A) Increased protein S activity, increased free protein S antigen, increased total protein S AG
(B) Increased protein S activity, increased free protein S antigen, normal total protein S AG
(C) Decreased protein S activity, decreased free protein S antigen, normal total protein S AG
(D) Decreased protein S activity, decreased free protein S antigen, decreased protein S AG

Item 35

H

A 15-year-old boy is evaluated in the emergency department for the subacute onset of fatigue, shortness of breath, and lethargy. He has a 2-week history of fever and arthralgia, which has improved over the past week. Medical history is significant for sickle cell anemia (Hb SS). He has had infrequent pain crises and no history of stroke or acute chest syndrome. He recently had contact with a sick cousin. His immunizations are up to date, and he takes folic acid, 2 mg/d.

On physical examination, temperature is 35.7 °C (96.4 °F), blood pressure is 96/55 mm Hg, pulse rate is 114/min, and respiration rate is 22/min. He has pallor and pale sclerae and appears lethargic. There is no rash. Other than tachycardia, the cardiopulmonary examination is normal. There is no lymphadenopathy or splenomegaly.

Laboratory studies:

Test	**Current value**	**3 months ago**
Hemoglobin	5.2 g/dL (52 g/L)	8.2 g/dL (82 g/L)
Leukocyte count	4900/µL (4.9 ×10^9/L) with a normal differential	7300 (7.3 × 10^9/L) with a normal differential
Platelet count	159,000/µL (159 × 10^9/L)	185,000/µL (185 × 10^9/L)
Reticulocyte count	0.1%	NA

A chest radiograph is normal.

Which of the following is the most likely diagnosis?

(A) Aplastic crisis
(B) Hyperhemolytic crisis
(C) Megaloblastic crisis
(D) Splenic sequestration crisis

Item 36

An 87-year-old man undergoes follow-up evaluation. He has an 8-month history of anemia and is asymptomatic. He also has hypertension and hyperlipidemia for which he takes lisinopril, atorvastatin, and low-dose aspirin.

On physical examination, temperature is 36.7 °C (98.0 °F), blood pressure is 137/78 mm Hg, pulse rate is 88/min, and respiration rate is 17/min. BMI is 19. Cardiac examination reveals an S_4. The remainder of the examination is normal.

Laboratory studies:

Hemoglobin	11.4 g/dL (114 g/L)
Leukocyte count	6200/µL (6.2×10^9/L) with a normal differential
Platelet count	225,000/µL (225×10^9/L)
Mean corpuscular volume	90 fL
Mean corpuscular hemoglobin	34 g/dL (340 g/L)
Reticulocyte count	0.8%
Ferritin	187 ng/mL (187 µg/L)
Iron	78 µg/dL (14 µmol/L)
Total iron-binding capacity	356 µg/dL (64 µmol/L)
Creatinine	1.5 mg/dL (132 µmol/L)

The peripheral blood smear is compatible with a normochromic, normocytic anemia.

Which of the following is the most likely cause of this patient's anemia?

(A) Advanced age
(B) Inflammatory anemia
(C) Iron deficiency
(D) Kidney disease

H Item 37

A 35-year-old woman is evaluated in the emergency department for new-onset peripheral edema, thrombocytopenia, and right upper quadrant pain. She is gravida 1 at 36 weeks' gestation, and her pregnancy has been otherwise uncomplicated. She takes only a prenatal vitamin.

On physical examination, the patient is alert. Temperature is normal, blood pressure is 140/95 mm Hg, pulse rate is 110/min, and respiration rate is 22/min. There is tenderness in the right upper quadrant on abdominal examination. She has a gravid uterus. Deep tendon reflexes are 3+ with no clonus. Pitting edema to the level of the knees is also present.

Laboratory studies:

Hematocrit	35%
Leukocyte count	16,000/µL (16×10^9/L)
Mean corpuscular volume	85 fL
Platelet count	35,000/µL (35×10^9/L)
Fibrinogen	135 mg/dL (1.35 g/L)
Alanine aminotransferase	150 units/L
Aspartate aminotransferase	110 units/L
Total bilirubin	4.5 mg/dL (76.9 µmol/L)
Urinalysis	4+ protein, no cells

A peripheral blood smear is shown (see top of right column).

Which of the following is the most appropriate management?

(A) Corticosteroids
(B) Emergent delivery of fetus
(C) Intravenous immune globulin
(D) Plasma exchange

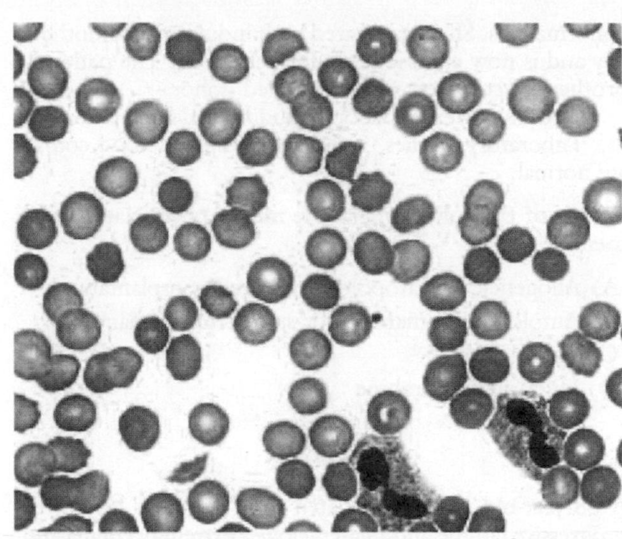

ITEM 37

Item 38

A 55-year-old man is evaluated for intermittent left-sided chest pain of 2 months' duration. The patient also has shortness of breath, diffuse joint pain, blood in his urine, and lower extremity swelling. Medical history is significant for sickle cell trait, hypertension, and high cholesterol levels. He is otherwise healthy and leads an active lifestyle, including lifting weights and jogging three times weekly. His medications include hydrochlorothiazide and simvastatin.

On physical examination, vital signs are normal, and oxygen saturation is 98% with the patient breathing ambient air. Cardiopulmonary examination findings are normal.

Laboratory studies:

Hemoglobin	14.2 g/dL (142 g/L)
Leukocyte count	8600/µL (8.6×10^9/L) with a normal differential
Platelet count	239,000/µL (239×10^9/L)
Mean corpuscular volume	85 fL
Reticulocyte count	1.9%

Hemoglobin electrophoresis shows an Hb A of 59%, Hb S of 39%, and Hb F of 2% (normal adult values: Hb A: 95%-98%; Hb S: 0%; Hb F: 0%-2%).

The peripheral blood smear, electrocardiogram, and chest radiograph are normal.

Which of this patient's symptoms may be due to sickle cell trait?

(A) Blood in the urine
(B) Chest pain
(C) Diffuse joint pain
(D) Lower extremity swelling
(E) Shortness of breath

Item 39

A 40-year-old woman undergoes follow-up evaluation after a 5-week hospital stay. She was recently diagnosed with acute myeloid leukemia, with studies revealing a 5q- chromosomal deletion and five unrelated cytogenetic abnormalities. She was treated with induction chemotherapy and is now experiencing full remission. The patient's brother is a complete HLA-matched donor.

The physical examination, including vital signs, is normal.

Laboratory studies, including complete blood count, are normal.

Which of the following is the most appropriate treatment?

(A) Allogeneic hematopoietic stem cell transplantation
(B) Autologous hematopoietic stem cell transplantation
(C) Azacitidine
(D) High-dose cytarabine

Item 40

A 68-year-old man is evaluated for a 6-month history of progressive fatigue and bilateral lower extremity edema and a 1-month history of dyspnea with exertion and paresthesia and numbness in the soles of the feet.

On physical examination, temperature is normal, blood pressure is 104/60 mm Hg, and pulse rate is 78/min. Oral examination discloses lateral scalloping of the patient's tongue. The liver is enlarged. Lymphadenopathy and splenomegaly are absent.

There is 2+ bilateral lower extremity pitting edema. He has decreased sensation to light touch extending to the ankle level and absent Achilles tendon reflexes.

Laboratory studies:

Hemoglobin	11.0 g/dL (110 g/L)
Leukocyte count	5600/µL (5.6×10^9/L)
Platelet count	180,000/µL (180×10^9/L)
Blood urea nitrogen	32 mg/dL (11 mmol/L)
Creatinine	2.0 mg/dL (177 µmol/L)
Glucose (fasting)	130 mg/dL (7.0 mmol/L)
Alanine aminotransferase	50 units/L
Aspartate aminotransferase	75 units/L
Alkaline phosphatase	130 units/L
Urinalysis	3+ protein with no erythrocytes or erythrocyte casts
Urine protein/creatinine ratio	5.620 mg/mg

Results of serum protein electrophoresis and immunofixation show a monoclonal IgG λ level of 0.3 g/dL. A chest radiograph reveals small bilateral pleural effusions. A bone marrow aspirate and biopsy shows plasma cells that constitute 3% of the total marrow cellularity.

Which of the following is the most appropriate next step in diagnosis?

(A) Abdominal fat pad aspiration
(B) Antineutrophil cytoplasmic antibody assay
(C) Liver biopsy
(D) Serum cryoglobulin measurement

Item 41

A 25-year-old woman is evaluated for recent worsening of lifelong chronic fatigue, an inability to keep up with peers in athletic activities, and occasional yellowing of her eyes. She has a history of mild anemia. Her mother has a history of mild anemia and cholecystectomy due to gallstones. Her only medication is a daily multivitamin.

On physical examination, temperature is 36.8 °C (98.4 °F), blood pressure is 123/65 mm Hg, pulse rate is 98/min, and respiration rate is 16/min. She has mild scleral icterus and no lymphadenopathy. The spleen is palpable 2 cm below the left costal margin.

Laboratory studies:

Hemoglobin	9.2 g/dL (92 g/L)
Leukocyte count	4900/µL (4.9×10^9/L)
Mean corpuscular volume	100 fL (compared with a value of 103 fL 3 years ago)
Mean corpuscular hemoglobin concentration	38 g/dL (380 g/L)
Platelet count	159,000/µL (159×10^9/L)
Reticulocyte count	6.4%
Total bilirubin	2.9 mg/dL (49.6 µmol/L)
Direct bilirubin	0.8 mg/dL (13.7 µmol/L)
Lactate dehydrogenase	420 units/L
Direct Coombs (antiglobulin) test	Negative

A peripheral blood smear is shown.

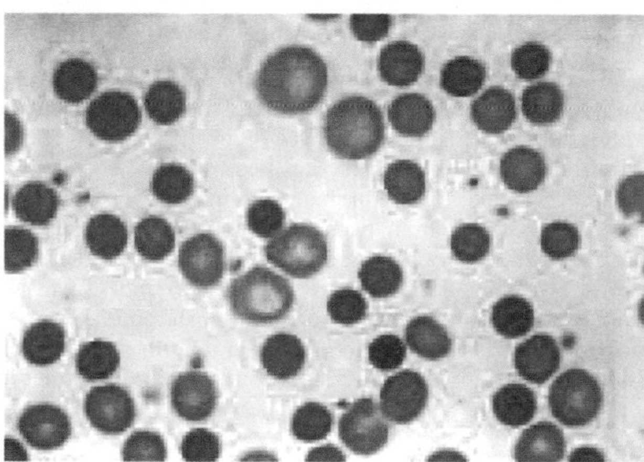

Which of the following is the most likely diagnosis?

(A) α-Thalassemia trait
(B) Glucose-6-phosphate dehydrogenase deficiency
(C) Hereditary spherocytosis
(D) Sickle cell anemia (Hb SS)
(E) Warm autoimmune hemolytic anemia

Item 42

H

A 22-year-old woman is evaluated in the emergency department for a 2-day history of pain in her arms, legs, and back, but she notes no fever, shortness of breath, or chills. The patient has sickle cell anemia and is 29 weeks pregnant. She rarely has more than one to two painful crises per year, and they are often managed at home. Her only medication is folic acid.

CONT.

On physical examination, temperature is 37.0 °C (98.6 °F), blood pressure is 110/63 mm Hg, pulse rate is 96/min, and respiration rate is 16/min. BMI is 22. The patient is in obvious distress from pain and is diffusely tender to touch. She has a gravid uterus. Cardiopulmonary, abdominal, and neurologic examinations are normal.

Laboratory studies indicate a hemoglobin level of 7.4 g/dL (74 g/L) and a leukocyte count of 6800/µL (6.8 × 10^9/L). Urinalysis is normal. The chest radiograph is normal.

Which of the following is the most appropriate treatment?

(A) Hydroxyurea
(B) Ketorolac
(C) Meperidine
(D) Morphine

Item 43

A 35-year-old woman undergoes evaluation after home pregnancy testing indicated that she is pregnant. Her medical history includes a previous idiopathic pulmonary embolism. Her only medication is a daily prenatal vitamin.

On physical examination, temperature is 36.2 °C (97.1 °F), blood pressure is 110/65 mm Hg, pulse rate is 70/min, and respiration rate is 20/min. BMI is 25.

Results of a pregnancy test are positive.

Which of the following is the most appropriate venous thromboembolism prophylaxis for this patient?

(A) Antepartum low-molecular-weight heparin (LMWH) and aspirin
(B) Antepartum and postpartum LMWH
(C) Antepartum and postpartum warfarin
(D) No prophylaxis

Item 44

A 35-year-old woman undergoes follow-up evaluation for recently diagnosed anemia and heavy menstrual flow present since her menarche began at age 13 years. Her menstrual flow is heavy 6 of the 7 days of her period, requiring use of a new pad and tampon every hour. She has a history of bleeding with tooth extractions and experienced postpartum hemorrhage with her two children. She also has a history of iron deficiency. Her sister and mother had hysterectomies in their late 20s for dysfunctional uterine bleeding, and her maternal grandfather died of hemorrhagic stroke in his late 50s. Her only medication is a multivitamin.

On physical examination, blood pressure is 130/85 mm Hg, and pulse rate is 100/min. The complete blood count indicates a hemoglobin level of 7.8 g/dL (78 g/L) and a mean corpuscular volume of 78 fL. The platelet count is normal.

Which of the following tests is most likely to establish the diagnosis?

(A) Activated partial thromboplastin time
(B) Platelet Function Analyzer(PFA-100®)
(C) Prothrombin time
(D) von Willebrand factor antigen and activity assays

Item 45

A 25-year-old woman is evaluated for a 1-day history of epistaxis and a new-onset rash on her shins. Last week, her menses were abnormally heavy.

On physical examination, vital signs are normal. She has bruising over the shins and wrists and a petechial rash over the shins and abdomen. Dried blood is visible in the nares. There is no splenomegaly.

Laboratory studies:

Hemoglobin	11.9 g/dL (119 g/L)
Leukocyte count	6500/µL (6.5 × 10^9/L)
Mean corpuscular volume	85 fL
Platelet count	<18,000/µL (18 × 10^9/L)

Her complete blood count from 1 year ago was normal. The remaining laboratory values, including prothrombin time, activated partial thromboplastin time, and thyroid-stimulating hormone level, are normal, and serologies for HIV and anti-hepatitis C virus antibody are negative. The peripheral blood smear does not demonstrate schistocytes. Blood type is A negative.

Which of the following is the most appropriate treatment?

(A) Corticosteroids and intravenous immune globulin
(B) Eltrombopag
(C) Rituximab
(D) Splenectomy

Item 46

H

A 75-year-old woman is evaluated in the hospital for a 1-day history of right leg swelling. Three days ago, she underwent nephrectomy for renal cell carcinoma. Her only medications are unfractionated heparin, 5000 units subcutaneously twice daily, and lisinopril.

On physical examination, blood pressure is 130/75 mm Hg, pulse rate is 85/min, and respiration rate is 20/min. Weight is 80 kg (176.3 lb). The right lower extremity is swollen, warm, and tender to palpation of the calf. The nephrectomy incision is without erythema or bleeding. The remainder of the examination is normal.

Laboratory studies:

Hematocrit	29%
Platelet count	275,000/µL (275 × 10^9/L)
Creatinine	2.2 mg/dL (194.5 µmol/L)
Estimated glomerular filtration rate	23 mL/min/1.73 m^2

Venous duplex ultrasonography shows a right lower extremity femoral and popliteal vein deep venous thrombosis.

CONT.

A bilateral renal ultrasound indicates no hydronephrosis or surgical site hematoma.

In addition to cessation of subcutaneous unfractionated heparin, which of the following is the most appropriate treatment?

(A) Adjusted-dose, intravenous unfractionated heparin
(B) Enoxaparin, 80 mg twice daily
(C) Fondaparinux, 7.5 mg daily
(D) Warfarin

Item 47

A 35-year-old woman is evaluated for mild fatigue with exertion, which has remained unchanged for years. She is the mother of three children and works full time. Her sister was evaluated for anemia. Her mother is also anemic.

On physical examination, the vital signs and physical examination are normal.

Laboratory studies:

Hemoglobin	11.3 g/dL (113 g/L)
Leukocyte count	5300/μL (5.3 × 10^9/L) with a normal differential
Mean corpuscular volume	74 fL
Platelet count	179,000/μL (179 × 10^9/L)
Reticulocyte count	2.9%
Iron	58 μg/dL (10.3 μmol/L)
Total iron-binding capacity	245 μg/dL (43.6 μmol/L)
Transferrin saturation	24%
Ferritin	58 ng/mL (58 μg/L)

Results of hemoglobin electrophoresis are normal. A peripheral blood smear is shown.

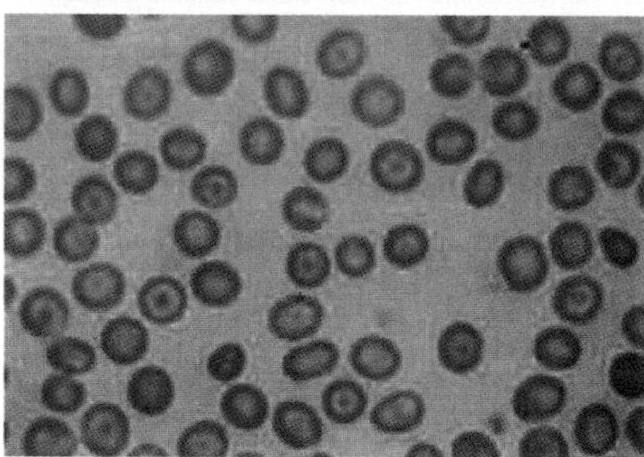

Which of the following is the most likely diagnosis?

(A) α-Thalassemia trait
(B) β-Thalassemia minor
(C) Iron deficiency
(D) Sickle/β^+ thalassemia (Hb Sβ^+)

H Item 48

A 35-year-old woman is evaluated in the emergency department for a 2-week history of abdominal pain, increased abdominal girth, and peripheral edema. Medical history is noncontributory.

On physical examination, temperature is normal, blood pressure is 120/65 mm Hg, pulse rate is 55/min, and respiration rate is 22. Marked scleral and mucosal icterus is present. Cardiopulmonary examination discloses normal heart sounds without murmur and symmetric breath sounds. She has 3+ pitting edema of the lower extremities to the midthigh. Hepatomegaly and ascites are noted on abdominal examination.

Laboratory studies:

Hematocrit	37%
Hemoglobin	12.5 g/dL (125 g/L)
Leukocyte count	10,000/μL (10 × 10^9/L)
Mean corpuscular volume	72 fL
Platelet count	1,095,000/μL (1095 × 10^9/L)
Albumin	1.5 g/dL (15 g/L)
Total bilirubin	6.0 mg/dL (102.6 μmol/L)
Alkaline phosphatase	300 units/L
Alanine aminotransferase	550 units/L
Aspartate aminotransferase	600 units/L
Urinalysis	Normal

Doppler ultrasound of the abdomen shows occlusion of the hepatic veins.

Which of the following is the most appropriate next step in the evaluation of this patient?

(A) Antiphospholipid antibody assay
(B) Antithrombin activity assay
(C) Flow cytometry for paroxysmal nocturnal hemoglobinuria
(D) *JAK2 V617F* mutational analysis
(E) Protein C activity assay

Item 49

A 75-year-old woman is evaluated for progressive fatigue, increasing dyspnea with exertion, and easy bruisability of 4 months' duration. She takes only multivitamins.

On physical examination, temperature is normal, blood pressure is 118/72 mm Hg, pulse rate is 80/min, and respiration rate is 14/min. There are ecchymoses on her arms and petechiae over the shins. Cardiopulmonary examination is normal. There is no lymphadenopathy or hepatosplenomegaly. Position and vibratory sense in the lower extremities are intact.

Laboratory studies:

Hemoglobin	7.2 g/dL (72 g/L)
Haptoglobin	Normal
Leukocyte count	3400/μL (3.4 × 10^9/L)
Absolute neutrophil count	1600/μL (1.6 × 10^9/L)
Mean corpuscular volume	98 fL
Platelet count	26,000/μL (26 × 10^9/L)
Reticulocyte count	1.4%
Lactate dehydrogenase	160 units/L
Vitamin B_{12}	289 pg/mL (213 pmol/L)

A peripheral blood smear shows erythrocytes with basophilic stippling and rare nucleated erythrocytes.

A bone marrow aspirate and biopsy reveals a marrow with 85% cellularity, with erythroid predominance and hypogranular and hypolobated neutrophils. The differential of the aspirate reveals 12% blasts. Conventional cytogenetic studies indicate monosomy 7.

Which of the following is the most appropriate treatment?

(A) Azacitidine
(B) Plasma exchange
(C) Prednisone
(D) Vitamin B_{12}

Item 50

A 34-year-old woman is evaluated for increasing bone pain, dyspnea, and fatigue of 2 days' duration. The patient has sickle cell anemia. She was hospitalized 7 days ago for an elective cholecystectomy for which she received 2 units of AB-negative and C antigen–negative, leukodepleted erythrocytes. The operation was uneventful, and she was discharged to home in 24 hours. Current medications are hydroxyurea and folic acid. A preoperative type and screen indicated the patient was AB-negative with alloantibodies to antigen C.

On physical examination, the patient is in obvious pain. Temperature is 37.4 °C (99.4 °F), blood pressure is 146/85 mm Hg, pulse rate is 116/min, and respiration rate is 12/min. The patient has jaundice. The cardiopulmonary and neurologic examinations are normal.

Laboratory studies:

	Current value	Values at hospital discharge
Hemoglobin	7.4 g/dL (74 g/L)	9.9 g/dL (99 g/L)
Leukocyte count	12,000/µL (12×10^9/L)	8000/µL (8.0×10^9/L)
Platelet count	187,000/µL (187×10^9/L)	207,000/µL (207×10^9/L)
Reticulocyte count	2.3%	5.3% (Normal range: 2% to 3%)
Total bilirubin	4.8 mg/dL (82 µmol/L)	NA
Direct bilirubin	0.6 mg/dL (10.2 µmol/L)	NA

Which of the following laboratory findings would best explain this patient's current clinical presentation?

(A) Antineutrophil antibodies
(B) HLA antibodies
(C) IgA deficiency
(D) New alloantibodies

Item 51

A 28-year-old previously healthy woman is evaluated in the hospital for a 3-week history of progressive fatigue, dyspnea with exertion, and easy bruisability.

On physical examination, temperature is 37.2 °C (98.9 °F), blood pressure is 124/78 mm Hg, pulse rate is 96/min, and respiration rate is 16/min. Oxygen saturation is 97% with the patient breathing ambient air. She has conjunctival pallor. Scattered petechiae are visible over the pretibial area as are ecchymoses on the upper extremities. Lymphadenopathy, consisting of 1.5- to 2.0-cm lymph nodes in the bilateral cervical, axillary, and inguinal lymph node chains, is found. Cardiopulmonary examination is normal. Hepatosplenomegaly is absent.

Laboratory studies:

Hemoglobin	7.4 g/dL (74 g/L)
Leukocyte count	108,400/µL (108.4×10^9/L)
Platelet count	18,000/µL (18×10^9/L)
Absolute neutrophil count	400/µL (0.4×10^9/L)
Direct Coombs (antiglobulin) test	Negative
Blood urea nitrogen	24 mg/dL (8.6 mmol/L)
Creatinine	1.1 mg/dL (97 µmol/L)

The prothrombin time and activated partial thromboplastin time as well as serum calcium, phosphorus, and potassium levels are normal. A peripheral blood smear is shown.

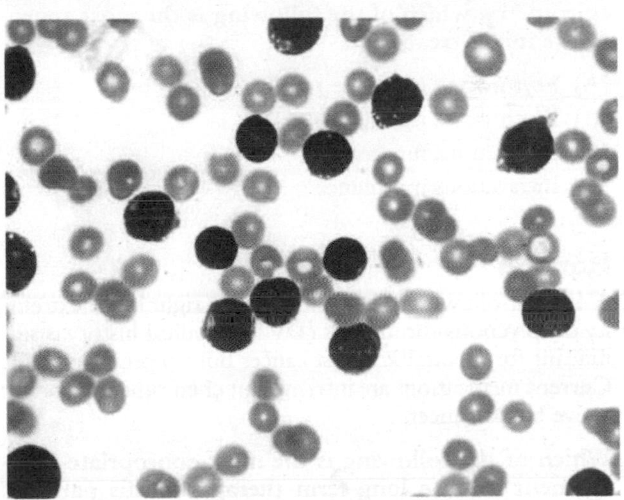

A posteroanterior/lateral chest radiograph is normal.

A bone marrow aspirate and biopsy shows extensive infiltration with cells similar to those found on the peripheral blood smear. The cells are positive for CD34, CD10, CD20, and TdT. Cytogenetics are normal.

In addition to intravenous fluid hydration and allopurinol, which of the following is the most appropriate treatment?

(A) Imatinib
(B) Induction chemotherapy
(C) Leukapheresis
(D) Rituximab

Item 52

A 29-year-old man is evaluated in the emergency department for dyspnea and diffuse severe pain in the arms, legs, back, and chest of 2 days' duration. He has sickle cell anemia and experiences painful episodes one to two times per year. He also has a history of acute chest syndrome and has known

H CONT.

erythrocyte alloantibodies. In addition to increased fluid intake at home, he has been taking oral morphine sulfate, 30 mg twice daily, with no relief. He also takes folic acid.

On physical examination, temperature is 36.8 °C (98.4 °F), blood pressure is 153/65 mm Hg, pulse rate is 108/min, and respiration rate is 20/min. Oxygen saturation is 95% with the patient breathing ambient air. The patient is hunched over in pain, and he is diffusely tender to touch. Cardiopulmonary, abdominal, and neurologic examinations are normal.

Laboratory studies:

Hemoglobin	7.2 g/dL (72 g/L)
Leukocyte count	11,900/µL (11.9×10^9/L) with a normal differential
Platelet count	199,000/µL (199×10^9/L)
Reticulocyte count	5.4%
Lactate dehydrogenase	420 units/L

The patient has alloantibodies to antigens C, E, and K on blood typing and screening.

In addition to intravenous hydration and incentive spirometry, which of the following is the most appropriate initial treatment?

(A) Erythrocyte exchange transfusion
(B) Erythrocyte transfusion
(C) Intravenous meperidine
(D) Intravenous morphine

Item 53

A 49-year-old woman is evaluated for a right lower extremity deep venous thrombosis (DVT). Medical history is significant for metastatic breast cancer but no previous DVT. Current medications are intermittent chemotherapy for her active breast cancer.

Which of the following is the most appropriate management for the long-term therapy of this patient's DVT?

(A) Inferior vena cava filter plus unfractionated heparin and warfarin
(B) Low-molecular-weight heparin
(C) Unfractionated heparin
(D) Warfarin

H

Item 54

A 35-year-old woman is evaluated in the emergency department for the sudden onset of substernal chest pain, dyspnea, and syncope. Medical history is noncontributory.

On physical examination, temperature is normal, blood pressure is 80/45 mm Hg, pulse rate is 55/min, and respiration rate is 22/min. Cardiac examination reveals an S_3. Lungs are clear to auscultation. Splenomegaly is present.

Laboratory studies:

Hematocrit	37%
Hemoglobin	12.5 g/dL (125 g/L)
Leukocyte count	10,000/µL (10×10^9/L) with a normal differential
Mean corpuscular volume	80 fL
Platelet count	1,095,000/µL (1095×10^9/L)
Troponins	Elevated

An electrocardiogram shows an ST elevation in leads II, III, and aVF.

The peripheral blood smear shows increased platelet numbers and circulating megathrombocytes but is otherwise normal.

Which of the following is the most likely cause of this patient's thrombocytosis?

(A) Chronic myeloid leukemia
(B) Essential thrombocythemia
(C) Iron deficiency
(D) Polycythemia vera

Item 55

H

A 65-year-old woman is evaluated in the emergency department for the acute onset of slurred speech and right-sided paralysis. She ate at a church picnic 3 days ago and has been experiencing crampy diarrhea since then. She has no other medical problems and takes no medications.

On physical examination, temperature is 38.9 °C (102.0 °F), blood pressure is 190/110 mm Hg, pulse rate is 110/min, and respiration rate is 22/min. BMI is 34. Funduscopic examination is normal. Carotid upstroke is normal without bruits. The patient has expressive aphasia and dense right-sided hemiplegia. No petechiae or ecchymoses are noted. Cardiopulmonary examination discloses regular rhythm without murmurs or extra sounds and no crackles. The remainder of the physical examination is normal.

Laboratory studies:

Hemoglobin	8.5 g/dL (85 g/L)
Leukocyte count	8000/µL (8.0×10^9/L)
Platelet count	32,000/µL (32×10^9/L)
Creatinine	3.5 mg/dL (309.4 µmol/L)
Lactate dehydrogenase	1200 units/L
Coombs (direct) antiglobulin test	Negative

A CT of the head is negative for bleeding.

Which of the following is the most appropriate next step in the evaluation?

(A) Bone marrow biopsy
(B) *Escherichia coli* O157:H7 titer measurement
(C) MRI of the brain
(D) Peripheral blood smear

Item 56

A 35-year-old woman is evaluated for new-onset thrombocytopenia. She is gravida 1 at 36 weeks' gestation. Her pregnancy has been otherwise uncomplicated. She takes only a prenatal vitamin.

On physical examination, temperature is normal, blood pressure is 110/65 mm Hg, pulse rate is 110/min, and respiration rate is 22/min. There are no ecchymoses or petechiae. Abdominal examination discloses no right upper quadrant pain. She has a gravid uterus. Neurologic examination is normal, and there is no peripheral edema.

Laboratory studies:

Hematocrit	33%
Hemoglobin	11.0 g/dL (110 g/L)
Leukocyte count	9500/µL (9.5×10^9/L)
Mean corpuscular volume	85 fL
Platelet count	95,000/µL (95×10^9/L)
Fibrinogen	350 mg/dL (3.5 g/dL)
Alanine aminotransferase	Normal
Aspartate aminotransferase	Normal
Urinalysis	Normal

No schistocytes or platelet clumping is seen on the peripheral blood smear.

Which of the following is the most appropriate management?

(A) Corticosteroids
(B) Emergent delivery of fetus
(C) Intravenous immune globulin
(D) Plasma exchange
(E) Repeat complete blood count in 1 to 2 weeks

Item 57

A 24-year-old woman is evaluated for mild fatigue of 3 months' duration. She is otherwise asymptomatic. She is a college student and attends all of her classes, works part time, and plays soccer. Her family and personal medical history, including childhood history of infections, is unremarkable. She takes no medication.

On physical examination, the patient is a black woman who appears well. Vital signs and examination findings are normal.

Laboratory studies indicate a hemoglobin level of 12.9 g/dL (129 g/L); a leukocyte count of 3000/µL (3.0×10^9/L) with 40% neutrophils, 52% lymphocytes, and 6% monocytes; and a platelet count of 186,000/µL (186×10^9/L). The calculated absolute neutrophil count is 1200/µL (1.2×10^9/L). The comprehensive metabolic panel is normal. HIV serologic results are negative.

A peripheral blood smear indicates normal erythroid, myeloid, and platelet morphology.

Which of the following is the most appropriate next step in the evaluation?

(A) Antineutrophil antibody assay
(B) Bone marrow aspirate and biopsy
(C) Neutrophil elastase gene analysis
(D) Peripheral blood flow cytometry
(E) Repeat complete blood count in 2 months

Item 58

A 31-year-old man undergoes follow-up evaluation for a recent diagnosis of iron overload. He has no symptoms of heart failure, arthralgia, or diabetes mellitus. Medical history is significant for β-thalassemia major, for which he is transfusion dependent. His only medication is folic acid.

On physical examination, vital signs are normal. Examination of the skin is normal. On cardiopulmonary examination, the lungs are clear, and there is no S_3 or murmur. He has no hepatomegaly.

Laboratory studies indicate a hematocrit of 25%, a serum ferritin level of 2400 ng/mL (2400 µg/L), and a transferrin saturation of 82%. Alanine aminotransferase and aspartate aminotransferase levels are normal.

Which of the following is the most appropriate treatment?

(A) Ascorbic acid
(B) Iron chelation therapy
(C) Monthly phlebotomy
(D) No treatment indicated

Item 59

A 32-year-old man is evaluated for fatigue, dyspnea, lethargy, and yellowing of the eyes of 1 week's duration. Medical history is significant for a recent community-acquired methicillin-resistant *Staphylococcus aureus* skin infection of the right forearm treated with a 14-day course of trimethoprim-sulfamethoxazole. Treatment concluded yesterday, and his infection has resolved.

On physical examination, temperature is 36.8 °C (98.4 °F), blood pressure is 103/53 mm Hg, pulse rate is 112/min, and respiration rate is 16/min. He has scleral icterus. On cardiopulmonary examination, he is tachycardic. The remainder of the physical examination is normal.

Laboratory studies:

Hemoglobin	9.6 g/dL (96 g/L)
Leukocyte count	8900/µL (8.9×10^9/L) with a normal differential
Mean corpuscular volume	104 fL (compared with a value of 85 fL 3 years ago)
Platelet count	259,000/µL (259×10^9/L)
Reticulocyte count	6.4%

Three years ago, the routine complete blood count was normal.

A peripheral blood smear is shown.

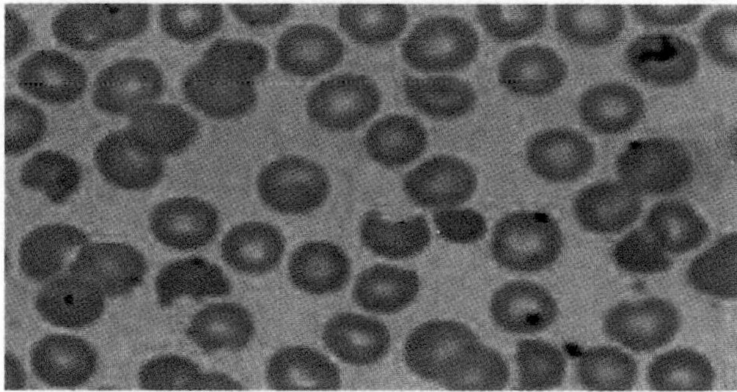

Which of the following is the most likely diagnosis?

(A) Cold agglutinin disease
(B) Glucose-6-phosphate dehydrogenase deficiency

(C) Hereditary spherocytosis
(D) Sickle cell disease
(E) Thalassemia

Item 60

H

A 43-year-old man is evaluated in the hospital for severe abdominal pain of 2 days' duration. He is otherwise healthy except for the recent finding of pancytopenia. Family history is noncontributory. His only medication is a daily multivitamin.

On physical examination, temperature is 36.2 °C (97.2 °F), blood pressure is 143/69 mm Hg, pulse rate is 86/min, and respiration rate is 12/min. The patient appears jaundiced. There is no splenomegaly. The remainder of the examination is normal.

Laboratory studies:

Haptoglobin	Undetectable
Hemoglobin	10.4 g/dL (104 g/L)
Leukocyte count	3400/µL (3.4 × 10^9/L)
Platelet count	89,000/µL (89 × 10^9/L)
Reticulocyte count	7%
Total bilirubin	2.8 mg/dL (48 µmol/L)
Direct bilirubin	0.4 mg/dL (7 µmol/L)
Lactate dehydrogenase	775 units/L

His complete blood count and liver chemistry values from 1 year ago were normal.

A CT scan of the abdomen shows mesenteric vein thrombosis but no lymphadenopathy or splenomegaly.

Which of the following tests is most likely to establish the diagnosis?

(A) Direct Coombs (antiglobulin) test
(B) Factor V Leiden assay
(C) Flow cytometric analysis for CD55 and CD59
(D) Lupus anticoagulant and anticardiolipin antibody assay

Item 61

A 22-year-old woman is evaluated for a 6-month history of decreased exercise tolerance, a lack of a sense of well-being, and headaches. She is otherwise healthy and eats a normal diet. Medical history is unremarkable, and she takes no medications.

On physical examination, temperature is 36.7 °C (98.0 °F), blood pressure is 110/72 mm Hg, pulse rate is 88/min, and respiration rate is 16/min. BMI is 22. The patient has pale conjunctivae. Her lungs are clear, her heart is without murmurs, and the neurologic examination is normal. There is no splenomegaly.

Laboratory studies:

Hemoglobin	7.9 g/dL (79 g/L)
Leukocyte count	5600/µL (5.6 × 10^9/L)
Mean corpuscular volume	62 fL
Platelet count	625,000/µL (625 × 10^9/L)
Red blood cell distribution width	22% (Normal range: 14.6-16.5%)

A peripheral blood smear is shown.

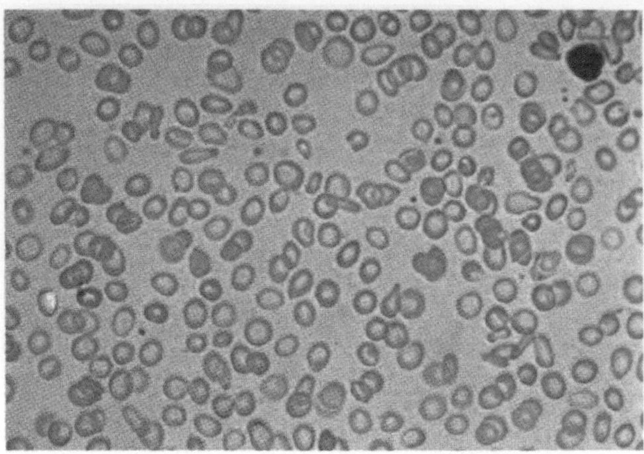

Which of the following is the most effective treatment?

(A) Intramuscular iron dextran
(B) Intravenous iron sucrose
(C) Oral ferrous sulfate
(D) Erythrocyte transfusion

Item 62

H

A 21-year-old woman is admitted to the hospital with a sickle cell pain crisis. Over the next 48 hours, she develops worsening dyspnea, chest pain, and fever. She takes daily folic acid supplementation and morphine delivered by a patient-controlled analgesia device with bolus and demand infusions.

On physical examination, temperature is 38.0 °C (100.4 °F), blood pressure is 123/65 mm Hg, pulse rate is 118/min, and respiration rate is 22/min and labored. There is no jugular venous distention. Cardiopulmonary examination discloses decreased bilateral breath sounds at the lung bases, but no crackles or S_3. There is no peripheral edema.

Laboratory studies:

Hemoglobin	6.2 g/dL (62 g/L)
Leukocyte count	6900/µL (6.9 × 10^9/L) with a normal differential
Mean corpuscular volume	84 fL
Platelet count	179,000/µL (179 × 10^9/L)
Reticulocyte count	4.4%

Oxygen saturation is 86% with the patient breathing oxygen, 3 L/min by nasal cannula.

Chest radiograph shows multilobar infiltrates not present on admission chest radiograph. An electrocardiogram demonstrates sinus tachycardia with no ST changes.

Broad-spectrum antibiotics are begun, incentive spirometry is initiated, and morphine is continued.

Which of the following is the most appropriate additional treatment?

(A) Erythrocyte transfusion
(B) Fluid bolus
(C) Furosemide
(D) Hydroxyurea

H

Item 63

A 78-year-old man is evaluated in the emergency department for dizziness, fatigue, dyspnea, and blurred vision of 3 weeks' duration and increasing somnolence of 3 days' duration. He has also had intermittent epistaxis controlled with pressure. The patient has hypertension. Medications are hydrochlorothiazide and lisinopril.

On physical examination, temperature is 37.2 °C (98.9 °F), blood pressure is 172/88 mm Hg, pulse rate is 68/min, and respiration rate is 16/min. The oxygen saturation by pulse oximetry is 96% with the patient breathing ambient air. Funduscopic examination reveals dilated, segmented, and tortuous retinal veins. Cardiopulmonary examination discloses scant bibasilar crackles but no murmurs or gallops. The spleen is palpable below the mid left costal margin. There is no hepatomegaly or lymphadenopathy.

Laboratory studies:

Hemoglobin	8.2 g/dL (82 g/L)
Leukocyte count	8400/µL (8.4 × 10^9/L)
Platelet count	108,000/µL (108 × 10^9/L)
Blood urea nitrogen	22 mg/dL (7.9 mmol/L)
Calcium	9.8 mg/dL (2.5 mmol/L)
Creatinine	1.3 mg/dL (115 µmol/L)
Total protein	12.2 g/dL (122 g/L)
Sodium	133 meq/L (133 mmol/L)
Urinalysis	8 leukocytes/hpf with no leukocyte esterase, nitrite, or erythrocytes

A serum protein electrophoresis and immunofixation assay reveals an IgM K M-protein level of 4.8 g/dL.

A peripheral blood smear is shown.

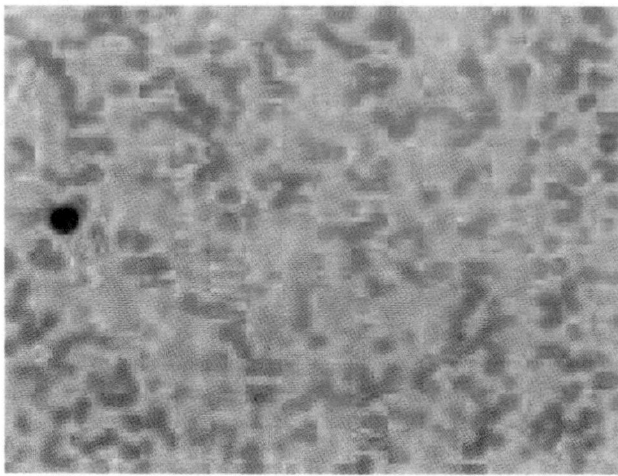

A posteroanterior/lateral chest radiograph is normal. An electrocardiogram shows no acute changes.

Which of the following is the most appropriate treatment?

(A) Ciprofloxacin
(B) Erythrocyte transfusion
(C) Furosemide and labetalol
(D) Plasmapheresis

Item 64

A 57-year-old woman is evaluated for a 2-week history of decreased exercise tolerance and substernal chest pain on exertion. She also has an 8-month history of macrocytic anemia.

On physical examination, temperature is 36.7 °C (98.0 °F), blood pressure is 137/78 mm Hg, pulse rate is 104/min, and respiration rate is 17/min. BMI is 25. The patient has pale conjunctivae. Cardiopulmonary and neurologic examination findings are normal.

Initial laboratory studies indicate a hemoglobin level of 7.4 g/dL (74 g/L), a mean corpuscular volume of 104 fL, a serum vitamin B_{12} level in the low-normal range, and a normal red cell folate level. Subsequent testing indicates elevated serum homocysteine and methylmalonic acid levels.

An electrocardiogram is normal.

Which of the following is the most likely diagnosis?

(A) Cobalamin deficiency
(B) Combined folate and cobalamin deficiency
(C) Folate deficiency
(D) Transcobalamin II deficiency

Item 65

A 36-year-old man is evaluated for a 1-month history of progressive fatigue, dyspnea, and cola-colored urine. He underwent mechanical mitral valve replacement at age 26 years for which he now takes warfarin. Family history is noncontributory.

On physical examination, temperature is 36.7 °C (98.2 °F), blood pressure is 123/69 mm Hg, pulse rate is 106/min, and respiration rate is 18/min. Cardiopulmonary examination discloses a distinct metallic S_1 and a new grade 2/6 holosystolic murmur heard best at the left cardiac apex.

Laboratory studies:

Haptoglobin	<9 mg/dL (90 mg/L)
Hemoglobin	8.2 g/dL (82 g/L)
Leukocyte count	9900/µL (9.9 × 10^9/L) with a normal differential
Platelet count	199,000/µL (199 × 10^9/L)
Reticulocyte count	7.4%
Total bilirubin	4.9 mg/dL (83.8 µmol/L)
Direct bilirubin	1.1 mg/dL (18.9 µmol/L)
Lactate dehydrogenase	1420 units/L

Complete blood count 1 year ago was normal. A peripheral blood smear is shown (see next page).

Which of the following is the most appropriate next step in the evaluation?

(A) ADAMTS-13 assay
(B) Blood cultures
(C) Direct Coombs (antiglobulin) test
(D) Echocardiography
(E) Osmotic fragility test

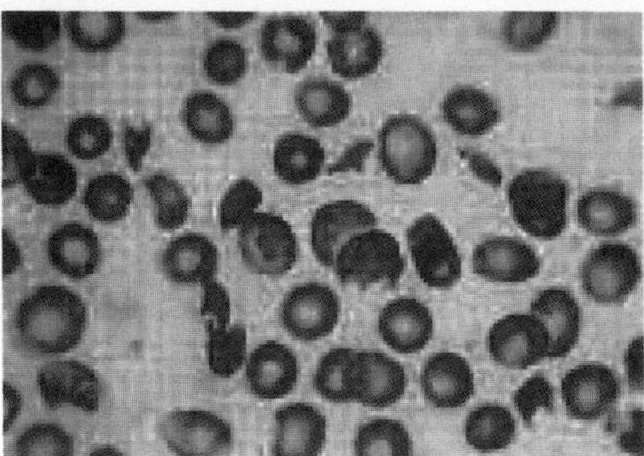

ITEM 65

Item 66

A 19-year-old man is evaluated in the hospital for a 3-week history of nose bleeds, malaise, and fever. He recently had a viral syndrome, which resolved about 6 weeks ago. He takes no medications and has no allergies.

On physical examination, temperature is 38.6 °C (101.6 °F), blood pressure is 102/54 mm Hg, pulse rate is 114/min, and respiration rate is 12/min. Examination of the skin discloses petechiae and bruising of the lower extremities. There is no lymphadenopathy or splenomegaly.

Laboratory studies:

Hemoglobin	7.8 g/dL (78 g/L)
Leukocyte count	1000/µL (1.0×10^9/L) with 20% neutrophils and 80% lymphocytes
Platelet count	28,000/µL (28×10^9/L)
Reticulocyte count	0.2%

Findings from a bone marrow biopsy are shown.

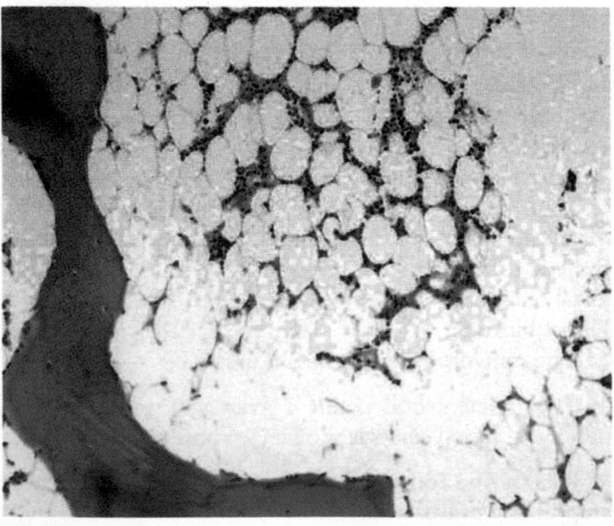

Which of the following is the most likely diagnosis?

(A) Acute myeloid leukemia
(B) Aplastic anemia
(C) Chronic lymphocytic leukemia
(D) Myelodysplasia

Item 67

A 16-year-old boy undergoes preoperative consultation prior to a planned elective cholecystectomy for symptomatic gallstones. The patient has sickle cell disease and experiences two to three painful episodes per year. He has no history of stroke, acute chest syndrome, or prior transfusion. He takes daily folic acid supplementation.

On physical examination, temperature is 36.7 °C (98.2 °F), blood pressure is 113/59 mm Hg, pulse rate is 78/min, and respiration rate is 16/min. The patient has scleral icterus. Abdominal examination is normal.

Laboratory studies:

Hemoglobin	8.0 g/dL (80 g/L)
Leukocyte count	9900/µL (9.9×10^9/L) with a normal differential
Platelet count	209,000/µL (209×10^9/L)
Reticulocyte count	3.4%

Blood typing and screening reveal blood type O positive, with a negative antibody screen. The erythrocyte phenotype is available on file.

Which of the following blood products will best minimize the risk for erythrocyte alloimmunization in this patient?

(A) Hb S negative
(B) Irradiated
(C) Phenotypically matched
(D) Washed

Item 68

A 67-year-old man with chronic kidney insufficiency is evaluated in the hospital for thrombocytopenia. Five days ago, he was hospitalized with severe pain and swelling of the left lower extremity. He was diagnosed with an occlusive proximal deep venous thrombosis with compartment syndrome, and he underwent percutaneous catheter thrombectomy followed by an intravenous infusion of unfractionated heparin. Today his platelet count is 45,000/µL (45×10^9/L) compared with a baseline value of 450,000/µL (450×10^9/L).

On physical examination, temperature is normal, blood pressure is 155/95 mm Hg, pulse rate is 105/min, and respiration rate is 18/min. The left leg appears normal without edema. There are no ecchymoses or petechiae and no evidence of bleeding.

Results of the platelet factor-4 enzyme-linked immunosorbent assay are pending.

In addition to discontinuing heparin and monitoring the platelet count every 2 or 3 days, which of the following is the most appropriate treatment?

(A) Argatroban
(B) Enoxaparin
(C) Fondaparinux
(D) Lepirudin
(E) No further treatment is needed

H

Item 69

A 64-year-old woman is evaluated in the hospital for fatigue and shortness of breath of 2 months' duration, prior to which she was well and took no medications.

On physical examination, temperature is 37.3 °C (99.1 °F), blood pressure is 144/68 mm Hg, and pulse rate is 106/min. She has pallor. Cardiopulmonary examination is normal. There is no lymphadenopathy. The spleen is palpable 3 cm below the left costal margin. Hepatomegaly is absent. The remainder of the physical examination is normal.

Laboratory studies:

Hemoglobin	4.3 g/dL (43 g/L)
Leukocyte count	7500/µL (7.5×10^9/L) with 35% neutrophils and 65% lymphocytes
Platelet count	156,000/µL (156×10^9/L)
Reticulocyte count	0.1%

Liver chemistry values and comprehensive metabolic panel are normal. HIV serologic testing is negative.

A representative leukocyte from a peripheral blood smear is shown.

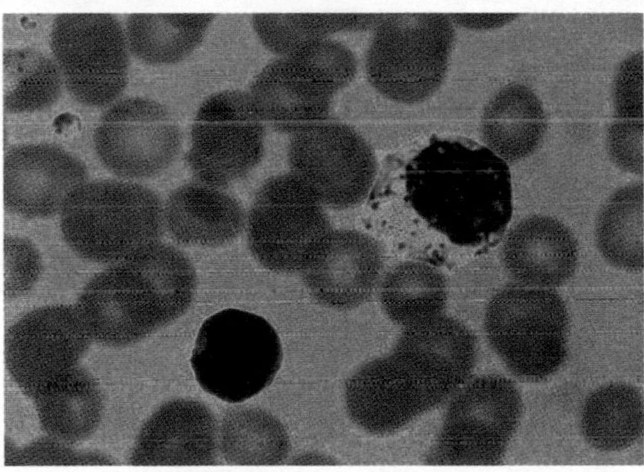

A chest radiograph shows no infiltrates, and CT scans of the head, neck, chest, abdomen, and pelvis are normal. A bone marrow biopsy shows an absence of erythroid precursors but is otherwise unremarkable. Results of flow cytometry, cytogenetics, and viral stains are pending.

Which of the following is the most likely diagnosis?

(A) Large granular lymphocytosis
(B) Myelodysplasia
(C) Parvovirus B19 infection
(D) Thymoma

Item 70

A 62-year-old man is evaluated for fatigue. The patient was diagnosed with symptomatic free λ light-chain multiple myeloma 2 months ago and has recently begun his third cycle of chemotherapy and is being considered for autologous stem cell transplantation. Medications are bortezomib, dexamethasone, pamidronate, and over-the-counter ibuprofen.

On physical examination, temperature is 36.8 °C (98.2 °F), blood pressure is 144/88 mm Hg while supine and 122/72 mm Hg while standing, pulse rate is 84/min while supine and 102/min while standing, and respiration rate is 16/min.

Laboratory studies:

Blood urea nitrogen	24 mg/dL (8.6 mmol/L)
Calcium	10.0 mg/dL (2.5 mmol/L)
Creatinine	3.2 mg/dL (283 µmol/L) (compared with a value of 1.7 mg/dL [150 µmol/L] at diagnosis)
Urinalysis	Negative for protein

His current serum free λ light chain concentration is 12.4 mg/dL compared with a value of 64.0 mg/dL at diagnosis. His current 24-hour urine protein electrophoresis shows 200 mg of monoclonal λ light chains compared with 1420 mg at diagnosis.

Which of the following is the most likely diagnosis?

(A) Cast nephropathy
(B) NSAID-induced nephrotoxicity
(C) Pamidronate-induced nephrotoxicity
(D) Renal amyloidosis

H

Item 71

A 56-year-old man is admitted to the hospital with exertional chest pain. Medical history is significant for hypertension and type 2 diabetes mellitus. Medications are lisinopril, atorvastatin, and metformin.

On physical examination, temperature is 37.1 °C (98.8 °F), blood pressure is 126/67 mm Hg, pulse rate is 106/min, and respiration rate is 18/min. BMI is 27. The patient has pale conjunctivae and icteric sclerae. Cardiopulmonary examination reveals clear lungs and an S_4. His abdomen is soft and nontender, with no organomegaly.

Laboratory studies:

Hemoglobin	7.6 g/dL (76 g/L)
Leukocyte count	3900/µL (3.9×10^9/L)
Platelet count	56,000/µL (56×10^9/L)
Reticulocyte count	0.5%
Alanine aminotransferase	29 units/L
Aspartate aminotransferase	27 units/L
Total bilirubin	4.9 mg/dL (84 µmol/L)
Direct bilirubin	1.0 mg/dL (17 µmol/L)
Lactate dehydrogenase	427 units/L

Results of the direct Coombs (antiglobulin) test are negative.

A peripheral blood smear is shown (see next page).

An electrocardiogram is normal.

Which of the following is the most likely diagnosis?

(A) Cobalamin deficiency
(B) Hereditary spherocytosis
(C) Paroxysmal cold hemoglobinuria
(D) Warm autoimmune hemolytic anemia

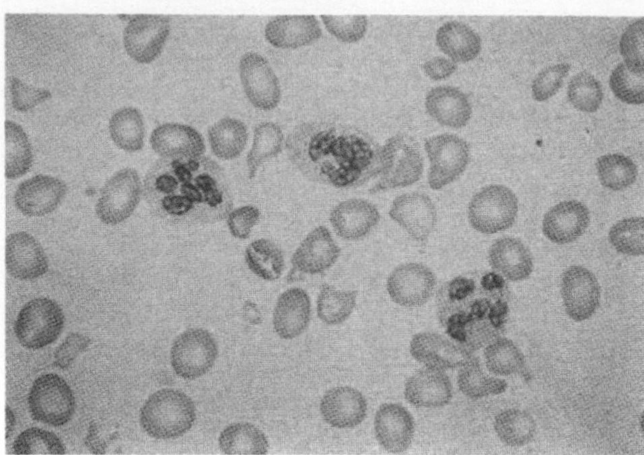

ITEM 71

Item 72

A 19-year-old man is admitted to the hospital with an acute pain crisis. He has sickle cell anemia and has developed macrocytic red cell indices over the past 6 months. He experiences pain crises two times per year. Medications are hydroxyurea and folic acid both started 9 months ago.

On physical examination, temperature is 36.7 °C (98.0 °F), blood pressure is 127/68 mm Hg, pulse rate is 108/min, and respiration rate is 17/min. BMI is 25. The patient has moderate pain in his upper and lower extremities. The remainder of the physical examination is normal.

Laboratory studies indicate a hematocrit of 21%, a hemoglobin level of 7.4 g/dL (74 g/L), and a mean corpuscular volume of 106 fL. A peripheral blood smear shows sickled erythrocytes and rare nucleated erythrocytes and macrocytes but is otherwise normal. A chest radiograph is normal.

Which of the following is the most likely cause of this patient's macrocytosis?

(A) Cobalamin deficiency
(B) Hydroxyurea
(C) Myelodysplasia
(D) Sickle cell anemia

Item 73

A 56-year-old man is evaluated in the emergency department for a 4-week history of progressive fatigue, increased sleepiness, dyspnea on exertion, and chest pain with moderate activity. He also notes an inability to perform all his duties as a construction worker. Family and medical history are noncontributory, and he takes no medications.

On physical examination, temperature is 36.7 °C (98.2 °F), blood pressure is 123/69 mm Hg, pulse rate is 98/min, and respiration rate is 16/min. The patient has scleral icterus and no lymphadenopathy. Abdominal examination discloses splenomegaly.

Laboratory studies:

Hemoglobin	8.1 g/dL (81 g/L)
Leukocyte count	4900/μL (4.9×10^9/L) with a normal differential
Platelet count	159,000/μL (159×10^9/L)
Reticulocyte count	5.4%
Direct Coombs (antiglobulin) test	IgG, strongly positive; C3, weakly positive

The complete blood count from 1 year ago was normal. The peripheral blood smear is shown.

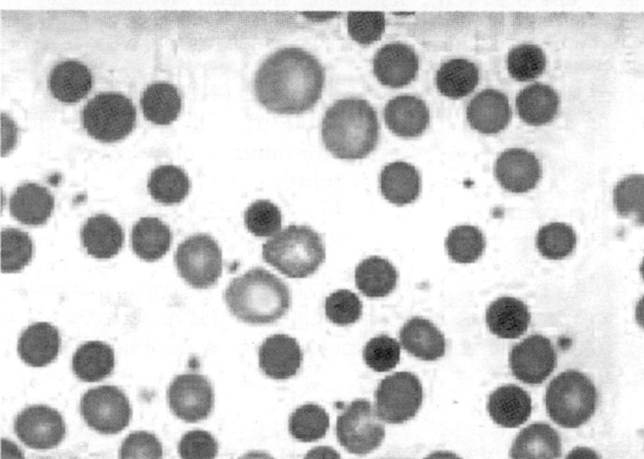

Which of the following is the most likely diagnosis?

(A) Cold agglutinin disease
(B) Glucose-6-phosphate dehydrogenase deficiency
(C) Hereditary spherocytosis
(D) Thrombotic thrombocytopenic purpura
(E) Warm autoimmune hemolytic anemia

Item 74

A 72-year-old man is evaluated in the emergency department for a severe headache, nausea, vomiting, and change in consciousness of 1 hour's duration that developed after he fell earlier today. He has atrial fibrillation for which he takes warfarin and metoprolol.

On physical examination, temperature is normal, blood pressure is 160/90 mm Hg, pulse rate is 50/min, and respiration rate is 26/min. The patient is obtunded but responds to verbal commands and is able to follow simple instructions and swallow. No focal neurologic findings are present.

The INR is 12.

A CT scan of the head shows a subdural hematoma with a mass effect.

Which of the following is the most appropriate treatment?

(A) Fresh frozen plasma
(B) Intravenous vitamin K
(C) Intravenous vitamin K and prothrombin complex concentrate
(D) Oral vitamin K
(E) No additional treatment

Oncology Questions

H Item 75

A 72-year-old man is evaluated in the hospital following a diagnosis of grade III follicular lymphoma.

On physical examination, temperature is 38.0 °C (100.4 °F), blood pressure is 140/70 mm Hg, pulse rate is 110/min, and respiration rate is 28/min. He has bilateral axillary and inguinal lymphadenopathy. Abdominal examination discloses a distended and tender abdomen and a palpable spleen 4 cm below the left costal margin.

Laboratory studies:

Hemoglobin	9.5 g/dL (95 g/L)
Leukocyte count	6000/µL (6.0×10^9/L) with 48% neutrophils and 52% lymphocytes
Platelet count	90,000/µL (90×10^9/L)

A CT scan of the chest reveals mediastinal lymphadenopathy. A CT scan of the abdomen and pelvis shows massive retroperitoneal and iliac lymphadenopathy with splenomegaly causing displacement of the bowel. No bowel obstruction or perforation is evident.

Which of the following is the most appropriate treatment?

(A) Hematopoietic stem cell transplantation
(B) Radioimmunoconjugate therapy
(C) Rituximab, combination chemotherapy, and prednisone followed by rituximab maintenance therapy
(D) Watchful waiting

Item 76

A 72-year-old man is evaluated for hoarseness and a mild sore throat of several weeks' duration. He has had no fever or chills, recent cough, shortness of breath, or hemoptysis. He has been smoking since he was a teenager and has more than a 100-pack-year smoking history.

On physical examination, vital signs, including temperature, are normal. There is no evident erythema of the oropharynx or palpable lymphadenopathy. The remainder of the physical examination is normal.

Fiberoptic endoscopy reveals a fixed mass in the right larynx. Biopsy indicates squamous cell carcinoma. CT scan of the neck confirms the presence of the laryngeal mass and several right-sided cervical lymph nodes measuring 1 to 2 cm. A PET/CT scan shows radiographic uptake in the primary tumor and regional lymph nodes and a 2-cm right lung mass.

Which of the following is the most appropriate next step in the management of this patient?

(A) Chemotherapy and radiation to the laryngeal mass
(B) CT-guided lung biopsy
(C) Fine-needle aspiration of the cervical lymph nodes
(D) Partial laryngectomy with postoperative radiation

Item 77

A 58-year-old woman is evaluated for enlarging, but asymptomatic, bilateral cervical, axillary, and inguinal lymphadenopathy that has intermittently decreased and increased in size over a 2-year period. She reports no fever, night sweats, weight loss, or discomfort. The remainder of the medical history is noncontributory.

On physical examination, temperature is 37.0 °C (98.6 °F), blood pressure is 120/60 mm Hg, and pulse rate is 70/min and regular. She has diffuse, firm, and nontender lymphadenopathy. The remainder of the physical examination is unremarkable.

Laboratory studies:

Hemoglobin	13.5 g/dL (135 g/L)
Leukocyte count	4000/µL (4.0×10^9/L) with 68% neutrophils and 32% lymphocytes
Platelet count	260,000/µL (260×10^9/L)

A peripheral blood smear is unremarkable. A lymph node biopsy reveals a CD20-positive grade II follicular lymphoma, and a bone marrow biopsy shows infiltration with small CD20-positive lymphocytes representing 20% of the cellular elements. A chest radiograph is unremarkable.

Which of the following is the most appropriate management?

(A) Prednisone
(B) Rituximab
(C) Rituximab, combination chemotherapy, and prednisone
(D) Total lymph node irradiation
(E) Watchful waiting

Item 78

A 77-year-old man is evaluated during a 3-month follow-up examination for stage IIA prostate cancer (Gleason score of 7) treated with external-beam radiation therapy. He reports feeling well except for mild fatigue. Urine function is normal.

On physical examination, blood pressure is 142/70 mm Hg, pulse rate is 72/min, and respiration rate is 14/min. No lymphadenopathy is noted. The cardiopulmonary examination is normal. Bowel sounds are normal and active. The prostate is firm but without nodules.

Laboratory studies, including a complete blood count and serum chemistries, are normal. Prostate-specific antigen (PSA) level is 0.1 ng/mL (0.1 µg/L).

Which of the following is the most appropriate management?

(A) Adjuvant androgen deprivation therapy
(B) Adjuvant chemotherapy
(C) Annual CT and bone scans for 5 years
(D) PSA measurement and digital rectal examination every 6 to 12 months

Item 79

A 62-year-old woman is evaluated for a 6-month history of intermittent pain and occasional small amounts of bright red blood on defecation. She is otherwise well with no significant medical or family history.

On physical examination, temperature is 36.8 °C (98.2 °F), blood pressure is 125/85 mm Hg, pulse rate is 80/min, and respiration rate is 14/min. The abdomen is soft with no distention or organomegaly, and bowel sounds are normal. The remainder of the examination is normal.

Colonoscopy is performed, and a 3-cm mass is identified starting 7 cm from the anal verge. A biopsy of the mass reveals invasive adenocarcinoma. An endorectal ultrasound shows involvement of the mucosa and submucosa. The mass penetrates into, but not fully through, the rectal wall with no lymph node metastases (T2N0). A high-resolution, contrast-enhanced CT scan of the chest, abdomen, and pelvis demonstrates only rectal wall thickening and no evidence of metastatic disease.

Which of the following is the most appropriate treatment?

(A) Chemotherapy
(B) Concurrent chemotherapy and radiation therapy, followed by surgery, and then further chemotherapy
(C) Radiation therapy
(D) Radiofrequency ablation
(E) Surgery

Item 80

A 48-year-old man is evaluated for chronic dyspepsia and intermittent midabdominal pain of 6 months' duration. He has had no fatigue, vomiting, weight loss, fever, or night sweats. He has otherwise been well and takes no medications.

On physical examination, vital signs are normal. The abdominal examination reveals midepigastric tenderness to palpation but no evidence of masses or peritoneal signs. The remainder of the physical examination is normal.

Laboratory studies:

Hemoglobin	13.5 g/dL (135 g/L)
Leukocyte count	5000/µL (5.0×10^9/L) with 65% neutrophils and 45% lymphocytes
Platelet count	290,000/µL (290×10^9/L)
Lactate dehydrogenase	60 units/L

Upper endoscopy shows a small gastric ulcer. Small clonal mucosa-associated B cells expressing CD20 antigen are identified on biopsy along with *Helicobacter pylori* organisms. CT scans of the chest, abdomen, and pelvis are unremarkable.

Which of the following is the most appropriate management?

(A) Cyclophosphamide, vincristine, and prednisone
(B) Involved-field radiation therapy
(C) Metronidazole, amoxicillin, and omeprazole
(D) Single-agent rituximab
(E) Observation with repeat endoscopy in 3 to 6 months

Item 81

A 57-year-old woman is evaluated in the emergency department for shortness of breath associated with wheezing and pain with inspiration. The patient has a 25-pack-year history of cigarette smoking. She takes no medications.

On physical examination, temperature is normal, blood pressure is 138/82 mm Hg, and respiration rate is 18/min. Wheezing is heard on pulmonary examination. The remainder of the examination is normal.

Laboratory studies are unremarkable. A chest radiograph is normal, and a spiral CT scan reveals multiple pulmonary emboli in addition to several bilateral pulmonary nodules, each measuring 2 to 4 mm.

The patient is admitted to the hospital, and heparin and warfarin therapy are begun.

Which of the following is the most appropriate next diagnostic step in the evaluation of the patient's pulmonary nodules?

(A) Bronchoscopy with cytologic analysis
(B) CT-guided biopsy of the largest nodule after withdrawal of anticoagulation
(C) Follow-up CT in 12 months
(D) PET/CT now

Item 82

A 41-year-old woman undergoes follow-up evaluation for stage II invasive squamous cell cervical cancer.

She recently underwent total abdominal hysterectomy and bilateral salpingo-oophorectomy with pelvic lymph node sampling. Pathologic examination reveals a 3.3-cm tumor with multiple high-risk features.

Which of the following is the most appropriate next step in management?

(A) Human papillomavirus testing
(B) Pelvic radiation therapy
(C) Pelvic radiation therapy and concurrent chemotherapy
(D) Observation with serial CT scans and pelvic examinations every 4 months

Item 83

A 31-year-old woman is evaluated for a palpable left breast mass that has been present for 6 months. She is nulliparous and is of Ashkenazi Jewish descent. Her medical history is unremarkable. Her mother was adopted; her father is 72 years old and has a history of prostate cancer. Her paternal aunt was diagnosed with ovarian cancer at age 48 years. Another paternal aunt was diagnosed with breast cancer at age 49 years. Her paternal grandmother died of complications from breast cancer at age 60 years.

On physical examination, there is a 4-cm mass in the left breast affixed to the chest wall and a 1-cm, freely movable left axillary lymph node. She undergoes core needle biopsy of the breast mass and lymph node. Pathologic examination of the node and mass reveals moderately differentiated estrogen receptor–positive and progesterone receptor–positive, *HER2*-negative invasive ductal carcinoma. CT and bone scan do not show metastatic disease. Echocardiogram shows a normal ejection fraction.

She will receive preoperative chemotherapy followed by surgery. She undergoes counseling for fertility preservation.

Which of the following will be most helpful in determining the best surgical approach?

(A) Counseling and genetic testing
(B) Genomic profile assay
(C) PET scan
(D) Tumor marker testing

Item 84

An 80-year-old man undergoes an annual physical examination. He has had mild stable nocturia for many years. He reports no bone pain, weight loss, fever, chest pain, or shortness of breath. Medical history is notable for hypertension and type 2 diabetes mellitus for which he takes antihypertensive and diabetic medications.

On physical examination, blood pressure is 148/84 mm Hg, pulse rate is 60/min, and respiration rate is 15/min. No lymphadenopathy is noted. The lungs are clear to auscultation, and the abdomen is soft, with normal bowel sounds. Rectal examination reveals an enlarged prostate gland with a nodule on the right side.

Prostate-specific antigen level is 6.4 ng/mL (6.4 µg/L).

Prostate biopsy reveals several small foci of adenocarcinoma in 2 of 12 cores on the right side, with a Gleason score of 6.

Which of the following is the most appropriate management?

(A) Androgen deprivation therapy
(B) Radiation with androgen deprivation therapy
(C) Radical prostatectomy
(D) Observation

Item 85

A 65-year-old man is evaluated for a 3-week history of hemoptysis and a recent 4.5-kg (10-lb) weight loss. He has a 90-pack-year smoking history.

On physical examination, vital signs are normal. The pulmonary examination reveals occasional crackles at the posterior right midlung field. The remainder of the physical examination is normal.

A chest radiograph demonstrates a large right hilar mass. A CT scan of the chest shows a 5-cm right hilar mass with bulky mediastinal lymphadenopathy. Bronchoscopic examination reveals small cell lung cancer. Results of staging studies with an MRI of the brain and a bone scan are negative.

The patient receives six cycles of cisplatin and etoposide chemotherapy with radiation to the lung mass and regional disease concurrent with the first cycle of chemotherapy. A follow-up CT scan of the chest shows a residual 1.5-cm right hilar abnormality.

Which of the following is the most appropriate next step in this patient's management?

(A) Biopsy of the residual mass
(B) Three additional cycles of chemotherapy
(C) Whole-brain radiation
(D) Observation

Item 86

A 45-year-old woman undergoes evaluation after a recent diagnosis of stage II hormone receptor–positive, *HER2*-negative breast cancer. She is premenopausal. She was treated with modified radical mastectomy and just completed adjuvant chemotherapy. She had a deep venous thrombosis associated with oral contraceptive pill use 20 years ago. Her family history is negative for venous thromboembolism. She is a nonsmoker and is very physically active.

On physical examination, temperature is 37.0 °C (98.6 °F), blood pressure is 100/60 mm Hg, pulse rate is 72/min, and respiration rate is 14/min. No jugular venous distention is present. The lungs are clear to percussion and auscultation.

Laboratory studies show a hemoglobin level of 12.8 g/dL (128 g/L) and a leukocyte count of 5600/µL (5.6×10^9/L).

Which of the following is the most appropriate next step in management?

(A) Adjuvant aromatase inhibitor therapy
(B) Adjuvant trastuzumab therapy
(C) Baseline imaging with whole-body CT scan or PET scan
(D) Ovarian ablation

Item 87

A 64-year-old woman undergoes follow-up evaluation for stage II sigmoid cancer diagnosed 3 years ago. She was treated with primary resection but no adjuvant chemotherapy. Two months ago, she was found to have recurrent disease with multiple liver metastases. She began palliative chemotherapy with 5-flourouracil, oxaliplatin, and bevacizumab. Ten days later, severe abdominal pain, nausea and vomiting develop.

Free air is noted on an abdominal radiograph on presentation to the emergency department.

Which of the following is most likely responsible for this patient's findings?

(A) Bevacizumab
(B) 5-Fluorouracil
(C) Oxaliplatin
(D) Typhlitis

Item 88

A 48-year-old woman is evaluated for a sore throat and fatigue of 3 weeks' duration and an enlarging cervical lymph node. She has had no fever, night sweats, or weight loss.

On physical examination, temperature is normal, blood pressure is 110/60 mm Hg, and pulse rate is 95/min. She has bilateral axillary lymphadenopathy, an enlarged left tonsil, and an enlarged left anterior cervical lymph node. The spleen is palpable 2 cm below the left costal margin. The remainder of the physical examination is unremarkable.

Laboratory studies:

Hemoglobin	10.5 g/dL (105 g/L)
Leukocyte count	9000/µL (9.0×10^9/L) with 40% neutrophils and 60% lymphocytes
Platelet count	160,000/µL (160×10^9/L)

Epstein-Barr virus serology is negative.

The peripheral blood smear demonstrates atypical lymphoid cells. CT of the chest and abdomen show extensive lymphadenopathy above and below the diaphragm as well as splenomegaly. Bone marrow biopsy reveals diffuse infiltration with small monoclonal lymphoid cells. Immunohistochemistry discloses overexpression of cyclin D1, and cytogenetic analysis shows a t(11;14) translocation. A subsequent colonoscopy is performed, and biopsy indicates mucosal infiltration with lymphoid cells expressing B-cell markers.

Which of the following is the most likely diagnosis?

(A) Diffuse large B-cell lymphoma
(B) Follicular lymphoma
(C) Mantle cell lymphoma
(D) Mycosis fungoides

Item 89

A 69-year-old woman is evaluated for a lump under her arm found on self-examination. She is otherwise healthy and has no other symptoms. Medical and family histories are unremarkable, and she takes no medications.

On physical examination, temperature is 37.4 °C (99.3 °F), blood pressure is 110/70 mm Hg, pulse rate is 72/min, and respiration rate is 14/min. The patient has a hard, fixed, 2-cm mass palpable in the right axilla. The remainder of the examination, including breast examination, is normal.

Complete blood count and serum creatinine, total bilirubin, and alkaline phosphatase levels are normal.

A needle aspirate of the right axillary mass reveals adenocarcinoma. Bilateral mammography and breast MRI are normal. CT scan of the chest, abdomen, and pelvis demonstrates the enlarged axillary lymph node and no other abnormalities.

Which of the following is the most appropriate initial treatment?

(A) Breast cancer chemotherapy regimen
(B) Excision of the axillary lymph node
(C) Mastectomy with axillary lymph dissection
(D) Radiation therapy to the right axilla

Item 90

A 55-year-old man is evaluated for a 2-month history of increasing dysphagia. He has a history of gastroesophageal reflux with "heartburn." He has no difficulty drinking liquids, but some solid foods give him a "sticking" sensation. His weight has been stable. He takes over-the-counter omeprazole and antacids regularly for heartburn symptoms.

On physical examination, temperature is 36.9 °C (98.4 °F), blood pressure is 130/85 mm Hg, pulse rate is 78/min, and respiration rate is 12/min. The physical examination is unremarkable. The abdomen is soft with no distention or organomegaly, and bowel sounds are normal. No supraclavicular lymph nodes are palpable.

An upper endoscopy reveals a mass at the gastroesophageal junction. Biopsy of the mass shows adenocarcinoma, and biopsy of the surrounding mucosa reveals Barrett esophagus. Endoscopic ultrasound indicates a stage III (T3N1) tumor with involvement of one lymph node. A contrast-enhanced CT scan of the chest and abdomen shows a thickening of the gastroesophageal junction with no evidence of metastatic disease.

Which of the following is the most appropriate treatment?

(A) Chemotherapy
(B) Endoscopic placement of an esophageal stent, followed by radiation therapy
(C) Radiation therapy
(D) Surgical resection
(E) Surgical resection with perioperative chemotherapy

Item 91

A 56-year-old woman is evaluated for a persistent cough of 2.5 months' duration. She also notes a 4.5-kg (10-lb) weight loss. The patient has no history of pulmonary disease and has never smoked cigarettes.

On physical examination, vital signs are normal. There is no peripheral lymphadenopathy, and pulmonary and neurologic findings are normal.

A chest radiograph reveals a large peripheral right lung mass. Right hilar and subcarinal lymphadenopathy, as well as several hepatic hypodensities consistent with metastatic disease, are identified on CT scans of the chest and abdomen. MRI of the brain is normal. A radionuclide bone scan notes uptake in several ribs. A CT-guided lung biopsy demonstrates adenocarcinoma.

Which of the following is the most appropriate next step in the evaluation of this patient?

(A) CT-guided biopsy of the liver
(B) Epidermal growth factor receptor mutation tumor analysis
(C) Mediastinoscopy with biopsy
(D) Serum chromogranin measurement

Item 92

A 66-year-old man is evaluated for vague abdominal pain of several months' duration and a 10-kg (22-lb) weight loss. He drinks alcohol socially but does not smoke. The patient is otherwise well, has good performance status, and takes no medications.

On physical examination, vital signs are normal. No lymphadenopathy is noted. Cardiopulmonary examination is normal. He has a slightly distended abdomen with vague left-sided upper abdominal fullness but without tenderness, rebound, or guarding. The rectal examination is normal, and the fecal occult blood test is guaiac-negative.

Laboratory studies indicate a hemoglobin level of 11.4 g/dL (114 g/L) and a mean corpuscular volume of 81 fL. Urinalysis reveals microscopic hematuria.

A CT scan of the abdomen demonstrates a 15-cm left upper kidney mass with 3-cm perirenal lymph node enlargement and multiple 1-cm pulmonary nodules on the lowest cuts of the chest portion of the scan. A thoracic CT confirms pulmonary nodules consistent with metastatic disease. A bone scan is negative.

Which of the following is the most appropriate initial management of this patient?

(A) CT-guided lung biopsy
(B) CT-guided kidney biopsy
(C) Cytotoxic chemotherapy
(D) Left nephrectomy

Item 93

A 73-year-old man is evaluated for a 6-month history of progressive nocturia.

On physical examination, vital signs are normal. Rectal examination reveals a hard, irregular, and markedly enlarged prostate gland. The remainder of the physical examination is normal.

Prostate-specific antigen level is 22.5 ng/mL (22.5 µg/L). All other laboratory studies are normal. Bone scan is negative. CT scan reveals a markedly enlarged prostate gland and extension into the seminal vesicles. No lymphadenopathy or evidence of metastatic disease is present. Prostate biopsy reveals adenocarcinoma in all 12 cores with a Gleason score of 8. He has high-risk T3 stage III prostate cancer.

Which of the following is the most appropriate treatment?

(A) Androgen deprivation therapy (ADT)
(B) ADT and radiation therapy
(C) Brachytherapy
(D) Radiation therapy
(E) Radical prostatectomy

Item 94

A 58-year-old man is evaluated for a sore throat and neck pain of 5 weeks' duration. He has a 50-pack-year smoking history.

On physical examination, vital signs are normal. A firm mass at the base of the tongue and a 3-cm firm mass at the angle of the jaw on the right are noted. The remainder of the physical examination is normal.

Fiberoptic examination reveals a biopsy-proven squamous cell carcinoma of the tongue base. An MRI suggests invasion into adjacent cortical bone. PET/CT demonstrates several enlarged lymph nodes in the right neck, the largest measuring 3.3 cm.

Which of the following is the most appropriate treatment?

(A) Chemotherapy
(B) Chemotherapy and radiation therapy
(C) Radiation
(D) Surgical resection

Item 95

A 48-year-old man is evaluated during a routine physical examination. He feels well with no symptoms. Medical and family histories are unremarkable, and he takes no medications.

On physical examination, vital signs are normal. A nontender liver edge is palpable 4 cm below the right costal margin. The remainder of the examination is normal.

Laboratory studies indicate a hemoglobin level of 14.9 g/dL (149 g/L), a serum alkaline phosphatase level of 121 units/L, and a serum total bilirubin level of 0.7 mg/dL (12.0 µmol/L). Serum alanine and aspartate aminotransferase levels are normal.

A right upper quadrant abdominal ultrasound reveals multiple hypodense lesions in the liver. A follow-up CT scan of the abdomen confirms approximately 15 hypodense lesions ranging in size from 0.5 to 2 cm scattered throughout all lobes of the liver. No pancreatic lesions are seen. A needle biopsy of the most accessible liver lesion reveals low-grade, well-differentiated neuroendocrine carcinoma consistent with carcinoid tumor. A subsequent serotonin level is normal.

Which of the following is the most appropriate management?

(A) Hepatic arterial embolization
(B) Radiofrequency ablation
(C) Repeat CT scan in 3 to 4 months
(D) Streptozocin plus 5-fluorouracil

Item 96

A 52-year-old man is evaluated for a 5-week history of hemoptysis and a 6-month history of cough occasionally productive of sputum for which he did not seek medical attention. He also had a 4.5-kg (10-lb) weight loss during this period. He has a 62-pack-year smoking history.

On physical examination, vital signs are normal. There is an expiratory wheeze localized to the left upper pulmonary lobe. The remainder of the physical examination is normal.

A chest radiograph demonstrates a large left upper lobe pulmonary mass. A CT scan of the thorax and abdomen reveals a 7-cm pulmonary mass in the left upper lobe and small mediastinal lymph node enlargement. A CT-guided biopsy of a lung lesion shows squamous cell carcinoma. A PET/CT scan indicates extensive uptake in the mass but a low level of uptake in the mediastinal lymph nodes. An MRI of the brain is normal. Mediastinoscopy and lymph node sampling reveal no evidence of cancer. Stage II disease is confirmed.

Which of the following is the most appropriate treatment of this patient?

(A) Combination radiation and chemotherapy
(B) Surgical resection
(C) Surgical resection followed by chemotherapy
(D) Systemic chemotherapy

Item 97

A 57-year-old man is evaluated prior to initiating adjuvant chemotherapy following a recent diagnosis of stage III colon cancer. Three weeks ago, he underwent a hemicolectomy with removal of all evidence of tumor. His postoperative recovery has been uneventful. He has no symptoms.

On physical examination, vital signs are normal. Abdominal examination reveals a well-healing surgical scar and is otherwise unremarkable.

A regimen of chemotherapy with oxaliplatin and infusional 5-fluorouracil is recommended.

Which of the following is the most appropriate goal of this patient's recommended adjuvant chemotherapy?

(A) Improved clinical benefit rate
(B) Improved disease-free survival
(C) Improved disease-specific survival
(D) Prevention of a second gastrointestinal malignancy

Item 98

A 31-year-old man is evaluated for a 1- to 2-week history of fatigue, loss of appetite, and abdominal pain. He also reports night sweats and low-grade fever without chills or rigors. Medical and family histories are unremarkable, and he takes no medications.

On physical examination, temperature is 37.9 °C (100.2 °F), blood pressure is 110/70 mm Hg, pulse rate is 92/min, and respiration rate is 18/min. BMI is 19. Oral membranes are dry. Chest examination is unremarkable. The abdomen is distended with normal bowel sounds. Testicular examination is normal without masses or tenderness. Rectal examination is normal. Fecal occult blood test results are negative.

Laboratory studies reveal a blood urea nitrogen level of 30 mg/dL (10.7 mmol/L) and a creatinine level of 1.3 mg/dL (115 µmol/L). Complete blood count, serum total bilirubin level, and alkaline phosphatase levels are normal.

Contrast-enhanced CT scan of the chest, abdomen, and pelvis demonstrates diffusely enlarged mediastinal and retroperitoneal lymphadenopathy, with masses ranging up to 7 cm in diameter. The lungs, liver, and pancreas appear normal. A needle biopsy of a large retroperitoneal node is obtained and reveals poorly differentiated carcinoma.

Which of the following is the most appropriate initial empiric treatment?

(A) Bevacizumab therapy
(B) Cisplatin-based chemotherapy
(C) Retroperitoneal and mediastinal lymph node dissection
(D) Radiation therapy to the retroperitoneum and mediastinum

Item 99

A 68-year-old woman is evaluated for dry, pruritic, erythematous skin patches of 12 years' duration for which she has never sought care and that recently have begun to raise and ulcerate. In the past year, she has experienced recurrent sinus and pulmonary infections requiring repeated courses of antimicrobial agents, as well as anorexia and weight loss. The remainder of the medical history is noncontributory. Her only medication is an over-the-counter antihistamine for pruritus.

On physical examination, temperature is 37.0 °C (98.6 °F), blood pressure is 110/60 mm Hg, and pulse rate is 75/min. She has bilateral cervical lymphadenopathy and a diffuse erythematous rash with multiple raised plaques, many of which are ulcerated. There is no evidence of generalized lymphadenopathy. Abdominal examination discloses hepatosplenomegaly.

Laboratory studies:	
Hemoglobin	10 g/dL (100 g/L)
Leukocyte count	10,000/µL (10×10^9/L) with 70% neutrophils and 30% lymphocytes
Platelet count	90,000/µL (90×10^9/L)
Erythrocyte sedimentation rate	20 mm/h
Lactate dehydrogenase	300 units/L
β_2-Microglobulin	4.1 mg/L (high)

The peripheral blood smear and flow cytometry demonstrate large, atypical lymphoid CD4-positive cells. CT scans show extensive lymphadenopathy above and below the diaphragm as well as hepatomegaly and splenomegaly. Bone marrow biopsy reveals diffuse infiltration with large, atypical CD4-positive lymphoid cells with cerebriform nuclei.

Which of the following is the most appropriate next step in management?

(A) Alemtuzumab
(B) Topical corticosteroids
(C) Total body irradiation
(D) Continued observation

Item 100

A 59-year-old woman is evaluated for the recent onset of persistent lower abdominal pressure. She notes no other pelvic symptoms or problems with bowel function. Her appetite is decreased, but she has not lost weight. She reports no fever, shortness of breath, or chest pain. She has never been pregnant and is a former cigarette smoker with a 25-pack-year history. Breast cancer developed in her maternal grandmother at the age of 75 years.

On physical examination, vital signs are normal. No lymphadenopathy is noted. The chest is clear to auscultation. The abdomen is soft with a positive fluid wave and shifting dullness. Pelvic examination discloses nontender fullness in the right adnexa with a normal-appearing cervix. The remainder of the examination is unremarkable.

Abdominal ultrasound reveals a right adnexal mass and moderate ascites.

Which of the following is the most appropriate next step in establishing a diagnosis?

(A) *BRCA1* and *BRCA2* genetic testing
(B) Laparotomy and biopsy
(C) Pap smear
(D) Paracentesis with cytologic analysis
(E) Serum CA-125 measurement

Item 101

A 65-year-old man is evaluated for a 6-week history of weakness on climbing stairs, difficulty raising his arms above his head, and the need to push off the arms of a chair to rise from a seated position. The patient also has dry eyes and mouth and new-onset erectile dysfunction. Medical history is significant for limited-stage small cell lung cancer for which he completed treatment with cisplatin-etoposide and mediastinal radiation therapy, followed by prophylactic cranial irradiation, 3 months ago.

On physical examination, temperature is normal, and blood pressure is 136/74 mm Hg. There is no lymphadenopathy. The cardiopulmonary and abdominal examinations are unremarkable. He scores 30/30 on the Mini–Mental State Examination. Neurologic evaluation reveals no evidence of muscle atrophy. There is bilateral ptosis and 4/5 proximal weakness of the upper and lower extremities, mild weakness of the distal musculature, and absent reflexes. After a brief isometric exercise involving the upper extremities, the triceps tendon reflex returns to normal, and proximal arm strength returns to normal.

Laboratory studies are unremarkable.

Which of the following is the most likely diagnosis?

(A) Brain metastases
(B) Lambert-Eaton syndrome
(C) Radiation toxicity
(D) Spinal cord compression

Item 102

A 52-year-old man is evaluated for a changing mole. Medical and family histories are not significant, and he takes no medications.

On physical examination, vital signs are normal. The patient has a macular lesion measuring approximately 0.5 cm in longest diameter with an irregular border on the dorsal aspect of the right forearm.

The lesion is excised with a margin more than 1 cm. Pathologic evaluation reveals a melanoma with a maximal tumor thickness of 0.6 mm. The tumor has no specific poor prognostic features.

Which of the following is the most appropriate management?

(A) Axillary lymph node dissection
(B) Radiation therapy
(C) Treatment with alfa interferon
(D) No further intervention

Item 103

A 38-year-old man is evaluated for hoarseness and a sore throat of several weeks' duration. He has no other symptoms. His medical and family histories are unremarkable. He does not smoke, and he drinks alcohol only socially.

On physical examination, vital signs are normal. A 3-cm firm lymph node is palpable beneath the angle of the jaw on the right. Visual inspection of the oral cavity is normal. Abdominal examination discloses no palpable organomegaly.

Which of the following is the most appropriate next step in evaluation?

(A) Endoscopic evaluation of the oropharynx
(B) Excisional biopsy of the lymph node
(C) MRI of the neck
(D) Whole-body PET/CT scan

Item 104

A 63-year-old woman is evaluated for abdominal pain and fever of 2 days' duration. She has mild diarrhea, nausea, and occasional vomiting. The remainder of the medical history is noncontributory.

On physical examination, the patient appears uncomfortable. She has a temperature of 37.9 °C (100.2 °F), blood pressure of 148/88 mm Hg, pulse rate of 102/min, and respiration rate of 16/min. Abdominal examination discloses left lower quadrant tenderness with mild guarding without rebound.

A CT scan indicates diverticulitis and a 4-cm left kidney hypodensity but no liver abnormalities. She is hospitalized for intravenous antibiotics, hydration, and bowel rest.

Which of the following is the most appropriate next step in evaluation?

(A) CT-guided kidney biopsy
(B) Follow-up CT scan in 6 months
(C) Kidney ultrasonography
(D) MRI of the abdomen

H Item 105

A 63-year-old man is evaluated in the emergency department for facial swelling, cough, and progressive dyspnea. He reports no headache, change in vision, or chest pain. He has a 40-pack-year history of tobacco use.

On physical examination, temperature is 37.0 °C (98.6 °F), blood pressure is 160/95 mm Hg, pulse rate is 110/min, and respiration rate is 24/min. Oxygen saturation is 90% with the patient breathing ambient air. He has facial plethora and cyanosis as well as bilateral jugular venous distention. Wheezing is noted in the left upper lung field, but the lungs are otherwise clear. Cardiac examination is normal without extra sounds or murmurs. There is no peripheral edema and no cervical, supraclavicular, or axillary lymphadenopathy.

Chest radiograph reveals a widened mediastinum and a left upper lobe infiltrate. CT scan of the chest demonstrates a left upper lobe mass with impingement on the superior vena cava and mediastinal lymphadenopathy.

Which of the following is the most appropriate next step in management?

(A) Chemotherapy
(B) Combination chemotherapy and radiation therapy
(C) Corticosteroids
(D) Mediastinoscopy and biopsy
(E) Radiation therapy

Item 106

A 54-year-old woman is evaluated for shortness of breath of 3 months' duration and a 4.5-kg (10-lb) weight loss over the preceding 2 months. She has a 35-pack-year smoking history.

On physical examination, temperature is 36.9 °C (98.4 °F), blood pressure is 145/82 mm Hg, and pulse rate is 108/min. Oxygen saturation is 92% with the patient breathing ambient air. No palpable lymphadenopathy is noted. The patient has clubbing of the fingertips. The lung fields are clear on the left, with diminished breath sounds and dullness to percussion over the lower half of the right lung. The remainder of the examination is normal.

A chest radiograph reveals a large right pleural effusion. A thoracentesis demonstrates an exudate, with cytologic analysis indicating adenocarcinoma. A chest tube is placed, and talc pleurodesis is performed. A CT scan reveals a 4-cm right peripheral lung mass with no obvious lymphadenopathy. A bone scan and a brain MRI are normal.

Which of the following is the most appropriate treatment?

(A) Combination chemotherapy and radiation
(B) Radiation
(C) Surgical resection of the lung mass
(D) Systemic chemotherapy

Item 107

A 56-year-old woman undergoes follow-up evaluation for stage IIIC ovarian carcinoma with intermediate histologic grade, which was treated with a course of six cycles of intraperitoneal and intravenous chemotherapy. During chemotherapy, she experienced moderately severe neuropathy in her hands and feet, lost 13.6 kg (30 lb), and experienced severe weakness.

Her CA-125 level is normal at the completion of chemotherapy. Follow-up abdominal and pelvic CT scans are negative.

Which of the following is the most appropriate management?

(A) CT scans of the abdomen and pelvis every 4 months during the first year
(B) History, physical examination, pelvic examination, and CA-125 measurement every 4 months
(C) History, physical examination, pelvic examination, and CA-125 measurement yearly
(D) Maintenance chemotherapy with paclitaxel for 1 year

Item 108

A 37-year-old woman undergoes follow-up evaluation for recently diagnosed invasive squamous cell cervical cancer. She feels well and has had no weight loss, abdominal or pelvic pain, or vaginal bleeding. She has three children and plans no further pregnancies.

The physical examination, including vital signs, is normal. Pelvic examination demonstrates a 1.5-cm palpable irregular mass on the right side of the cervix. Appropriate diagnostic imaging confirms stage IB disease.

Which of the following is the most appropriate next step in management?

(A) Adjuvant cisplatin chemotherapy
(B) Conization and close observation
(C) Pelvic radiation therapy and concurrent cisplatin chemotherapy
(D) Radical hysterectomy

Item 109

A 46-year-old woman is evaluated for the recent onset of headaches that are most intense on waking in the morning and are not relieved by analgesics. She has no nausea or vomiting but notes some difficulty with fine motor skills when using her right hand. The patient has a 2-year history of stage II breast cancer last treated with chemotherapy 2 years ago.

On physical examination, temperature is 37.0 °C (98.6 °F), blood pressure is 140/95 mm Hg, pulse rate is 90/min, and respiration rate is 12/min. Funduscopic examination reveals papilledema. She has reduced strength (4/5+) in her right hand. The reminder of the examination is unremarkable.

A CT scan of the head reveals two separate masses, both involving the left temporal lobe, with associated edema, as well as blastic lesions involving the skull.

Which of the following is the most appropriate management?

(A) Chemotherapy
(B) Intravenous dexamethasone and radiation therapy
(C) Lumbar puncture
(D) Resection of the masses

Item 110

A 61-year-old man is evaluated for increased fatigue, anorexia, and a 6.8-kg (15-lb) weight loss over the past 6 months. He reports dull right upper quadrant abdominal pain. His energy is greatly diminished, and he is spending much of the day limited to bed or a chair. Medical history is unremarkable, and he has no allergies. His only medication is ibuprofen for abdominal pain.

On physical examination, temperature is 37.7 °C (99.9 °F), blood pressure is 110/70 mm Hg, pulse rate is 86/min, and respiration rate is 18/min. The patient has icteric sclerae. Neck examination is notable for bilateral 2- to 3-cm supraclavicular lymphadenopathy. Cardiopulmonary examination is normal. Ascites is present. The liver edge is palpable 8 cm below the right costal margin. Rectal examination is normal, and stool is guaiac-negative.

Laboratory studies:

Hemoglobin	13.1 g/dL (131 g/L)
Leukocyte count	10,100/µL (10.1×10^9/L)
Platelet count	329,000/µL (329×10^9/L)
Albumin	2.7 g/dL (27 g/L)
Alkaline phosphatase	287 units/L
Total bilirubin	4.2 mg/dL (71.8 µmol/L)
Prostate-specific antigen	2.0 ng/mL (2.0 µg/L)

CT scan of the chest, abdomen, and pelvis demonstrates multiple hypodense lesions consistent with metastases replacing greater than 50% of the liver, and ascites. No other abnormalities are seen. A needle biopsy from one of the liver lesions demonstrates moderately differentiated adenocarcinoma. Upper endoscopy and colonoscopy are normal.

Empiric chemotherapy for which of the following cancer types is most appropriate?

(A) Gastrointestinal
(B) Lung
(C) Neuroendocrine
(D) Prostate
(E) Testicular

Item 111

A 70-year-old man is evaluated for an 8-day history of painless blood in the urine that is present throughout micturition. He has no other voiding symptoms. He also has atrial fibrillation for which he takes atenolol and warfarin. He has a 55-pack-year smoking history.

On physical examination, blood pressure is 144/68 mm Hg, and heart rate is 84/min and irregularly irregular. There is no flank or abdominal tenderness. Rectal examination reveals an enlarged prostate without tenderness or nodularity.

Laboratory studies are unremarkable. The INR is in the therapeutic range. Urinalysis is positive for more than 100 erythrocytes/hpf but no leukocytes or casts or dysmorphic erythrocytes.

Which of the following is the most appropriate next step in the evaluation of this patient?

(A) Cystoscopy
(B) Prostate-specific antigen testing
(C) Urine culture
(D) Urine cytology

Item 112

A 65-year-old woman is evaluated for a 2-cm right breast mass discovered on routine mammography.

Vital signs and general physical examination are unremarkable, and there is no palpable breast mass or lymphadenopathy.

Ultrasound-guided needle biopsy reveals a well-differentiated, estrogen receptor–positive and progesterone receptor–positive, *HER2*-negative invasive ductal carcinoma.

Which of the following is the most appropriate next step in management?

(A) Right breast lumpectomy
(B) Right breast lumpectomy, sentinel lymph node biopsy, and radiation
(C) Right breast mastectomy
(D) Right breast mastectomy, sentinel lymph node biopsy, and radiation

Item 113

A 72-year-old man is evaluated for progressive fatigue and abdominal distention of 3 months' duration. He has had no fever, chest or abdominal pain, nausea, or vomiting.

On physical examination, temperature is 37.0 °C (98.6 °F), blood pressure is 140/70 mm Hg, pulse rate is 100/min, and respiration rate is 14/min. He has pallor. The spleen is palpable 7 cm below the left costal margin. The remainder of the physical examination is unremarkable.

Laboratory studies:

Hemoglobin	9.5 g/dL (95 g/L)
Leukocyte count	2000/µL (2.0×10^9/L) with 35% neutrophils and 65% lymphocytes
Platelet count	90,000/µL (90×10^9/L)

A bone marrow aspirate is attempted but is unsuccessful ("dry tap"), and a biopsy shows diffuse infiltration with small lymphocytes with hair-like projections expressing CD20 but not CD5. Megakaryocytes and neutrophils are reduced. Results of peripheral blood flow cytometry are pending. A diagnosis of hairy cell leukemia is established.

Which of the following is the most appropriate management?

(A) Cladribine
(B) CT of the chest, abdomen, and pelvis
(C) PET scan
(D) Observation

Item 114

A 37-year-old man undergoes follow-up evaluation after receiving two planned cycles of chemotherapy with doxorubicin, bleomycin, vinblastine, and dacarbazine for stage IVB nodular sclerosing Hodgkin lymphoma.

On physical examination, temperature is 37.0 °C (98.6 °F), blood pressure is 110/60 mm Hg, and pulse rate is 75/min. Near complete resolution of all pretreatment palpable lymphadenopathy is noted. The remainder of the physical examination is unremarkable.

Laboratory studies:

Hemoglobin	12.5 g/dL (125 g/L)
Leukocyte count	6000/μL (6.0×10^9/L) with 58% neutrophils and 42% lymphocytes
Platelet count	180,000/μL (180×10^9/L)
Erythrocyte sedimentation rate	20 mm/h
Lactate dehydrogenase	200 units/L
β_2-Microglobulin	Normal

A PET scan that had previously shown diffuse activity in mediastinal and iliac lymph nodes and bone sites is now negative.

Which of the following is the most appropriate next step in management?

(A) Biopsy the residual enlarged lymph nodes
(B) Finish remaining cycles of current chemotherapy
(C) Initiate high-dose chemotherapy and autologous hematopoietic stem cell transplantation
(D) Initiate total lymph node irradiation

Item 115

A 51-year-old man is evaluated for a 6-month history of increased fatigue and decreased exercise tolerance. He is otherwise well with no significant medical history.

On physical examination, temperature is 37.3 °C (99.1 °F), blood pressure is 115/75 mm Hg, pulse rate is 76/min, and respiration rate is 14/min. The abdomen is soft with no distention or organomegaly, and bowel sounds are normal. The remainder of the physical examination is normal.

Fecal occult blood testing results disclose brown, guaiac-positive stool.

Laboratory studies indicate a hemoglobin level of 8.4 g/dL (84 g/L) and a mean corpuscular volume of 80 fL.

Colonoscopy is performed, and a 5-cm mass is identified in the cecum. A biopsy of the mass reveals moderately differentiated adenocarcinoma. A contrast-enhanced CT scan of the chest, abdomen, and pelvis demonstrates the cecal mass and no evidence of metastatic disease. The patient undergoes a right hemicolectomy from which he recovers uneventfully. Final pathology reveals a tumor penetrating into the pericolonic fat, with 3 of 28 lymph nodes positive for cancer (T3N1M0; stage III). All margins of resection are clear of tumor.

Which of the following is the most appropriate management?

(A) 5-Fluorouracil and leucovorin
(B) 5-Fluorouracil, leucovorin, and oxaliplatin (FOLFOX)
(C) Radiation therapy
(D) Radiation therapy plus 5-fluorouracil followed by FOLFOX

Item 116

A 59-year-old man is evaluated for a 4-month history of anal and rectal pain and bleeding on defecation. He is HIV positive. Medications are antiretroviral medications and ibuprofen for rectal pain.

On physical examination, temperature is 37.4 °C (99.3 °F), blood pressure is 120/75 mm Hg, pulse rate is 68/min, and respiration rate is 12/min. The physical examination is notable for a firm, tender mass approximately 3 cm in diameter, palpable in the anal canal. The abdomen is soft with no distention or organomegaly, and bowel sounds are normal. The remainder of the physical examination is normal.

A colonoscopy is performed, and no additional masses are seen. A biopsy of the anal mass reveals invasive squamous cell carcinoma. An endorectal ultrasound confirms a 3.2-cm mass in the anal canal, with no perirectal lymph node involvement. A contrast-enhanced CT scan of the chest, abdomen, and pelvis confirms the anal mass and shows no enlarged lymph nodes and no indication of metastatic disease.

Which of the following is the most appropriate treatment?

(A) Radiation therapy
(B) Radiation therapy followed by surgery
(C) Radiation therapy with concurrent chemotherapy
(D) Radiation therapy with concurrent chemotherapy followed by surgery
(E) Surgery

Item 117

A 26-year-old man is evaluated for pain, swelling, and a tender lump in his left testicle. He is otherwise healthy. His weight is stable and he has had no fever or other symptoms. He takes no medications.

On physical examination, temperature is normal, blood pressure is 103/70 mm Hg, and pulse rate is 52/min. No lymphadenopathy is noted. The lungs are clear to auscultation. The abdomen is soft and nontender without masses. Testicular examination reveals a firm 3-cm nodule in the upper pole of the left testicle, which is tender. There is no other area of testicular tenderness.

Laboratory studies reveal a leukocyte count of 4600/µL (4.6×10^9/L), a lactate dehydrogenase level of 300 units/L, an α-fetoprotein level of 39 ng/mL (39 µg/L), and a β-human chorionic gonadotropin level of 853 milliunits/mL (853 units/L) (normal <5 milliunits/mL [5 units/L]). Urinalysis is normal.

Which of the following is the most likely diagnosis?

(A) Epididymitis
(B) Hematoma
(C) Nonseminoma germ cell tumor
(D) Seminoma
(E) Torsion of the testicle

Item 118

A 45-year-old man is evaluated for gradually worsening fatigue and pallor of 7 months' duration, as well as fever, weight loss, night sweats, and pain.

On physical examination, temperature is 38.0 °C (100.4 °F), blood pressure is 140/70 mm Hg, pulse rate is 110/min, and respiration rate is 28/min. He has bilateral cervical and axillary lymphadenopathy. Abdominal examination discloses a palpable spleen 4 cm below the left costal margin.

Laboratory studies:

Hemoglobin	6.5 g/dL (65 g/L)
Leukocyte count	165,000/µl (165×10^9/L) with 30% neutrophils and 70% lymphocytes
Platelet count	90,000/µL (90×10^9/L)
β_2-Microglobulin	12.4 mg/L (elevated)

The peripheral blood smear shows excessive small lymphoid cells and multiple smudge forms.

Flow cytometry of the peripheral blood reveals monoclonal B cells expressing CD20, CD52, CD10, CD5, and ζ-chain–associated protein 70. Cytogenetic analysis reveals a deletion of 17p, and the heavy-gene mutational status is unmutated.

Which of the following is the most appropriate treatment of this patient?

(A) Allogeneic hematopoietic stem cell transplantation
(B) Cyclophosphamide, vincristine, and prednisone
(C) Fludarabine
(D) Rituximab

Item 119

A 52-year-old man is evaluated for recurrent, biopsy-proven lymphoma involving the mediastinum. He was diagnosed with stage III diffuse large B-cell lymphoma 3 years ago for which he received combination chemotherapy and rituximab and sustained a complete response.

The patient receives two cycles of salvage multiagent chemotherapy with rituximab.

Physical examination following two cycles of therapy is unremarkable, and vital signs are normal.

Laboratory studies:

Hemoglobin	13.5 g/dL (135 g/L)
Leukocyte count	6000/µL (6.0×10^9/L) with 70% neutrophils and 30% lymphocytes
Platelet count	360,000/µL (360×10^9/L)

The enlarged mediastinal mass is reduced in size by 90% on CT of the chest. A PET scan is negative.

Bone marrow biopsy reveals normal cellularity and no evidence of lymphoma.

Which of the following is the most appropriate treatment?

(A) Involved-field radiation
(B) Continuation of rituximab
(C) Autologous hematopoietic stem cell transplantation
(D) No additional therapy

Item 120

A 45-year-old woman is evaluated for severe hot flushes that significantly limit her quality of life as well as vaginal dryness that is controlled with local lubricants. She has a history of stage II, estrogen receptor–positive, progesterone receptor–positive, *HER2*-negative, invasive left breast cancer that was diagnosed 1 year ago for which she underwent lumpectomy and received chemotherapy and radiation therapy. She has not had a menstrual cycle since her fourth cycle of chemotherapy. She began taking tamoxifen 3 months ago after completing radiation therapy. She has tried nonpharmacologic interventions for hot flushes without any improvement.

Physical examination is normal other than evidence of surgery on the left breast and radiation changes on her skin.

Which of the following is the most appropriate therapy for this patient?

(A) Fluoxetine
(B) Low-dose estrogen-progesterone
(C) Red clover
(D) Venlafaxine

Item 121

A 62-year-old woman is evaluated for a 3-month history of progressive, right-sided pelvic pressure. She reports no weight loss, fever, nausea, vomiting, or change in bowel habits. Her family history is unremarkable.

On physical examination, she is afebrile. Blood pressure is 140/74 mm Hg, pulse rate is 80/min, and respiration rate is 14/min. There is no lymphadenopathy. The lungs are clear to auscultation. The abdomen is soft and nontender. Pelvic examination reveals a right adnexal mass.

Pelvic ultrasound reveals a complex cystic structure in the right adnexa measuring 5 cm. No ascites is noted. CT scan of the abdomen and pelvis confirms the ultrasound findings and is negative for ascites or other sites of disease.

The patient undergoes total abdominal hysterectomy and bilateral salpingo-oophorectomy. Pelvic washings are negative for malignant cells. The final pathologic diagnosis is stage IA epithelial ovarian carcinoma confined to one ovary and with low histologic grade.

Which of the following is the most appropriate next step in management?

(A) Adjuvant chemotherapy
(B) Adjuvant chemotherapy followed by second-look surgery
(C) Intraperitoneal and adjuvant chemotherapy
(D) Observation

Item 122

A 29-year-old woman is evaluated during a routine examination. She performs monthly breast self-examinations and has not noticed any nipple discharge, skin changes, or masses. She is nulliparous. Her medical history is significant for Hodgkin lymphoma, which was diagnosed 10 years ago and required chemotherapy and mantle radiation. There is no family history of breast or ovarian cancer. She takes levothyroxine for hypothyroidism.

On physical examination, there is no lymphadenopathy. Breast examination discloses no lumps, redness, or edema. The remainder of the physical examination is normal.

Which of the following is the most appropriate recommendation regarding breast cancer screening at this time?

(A) Bilateral breast ultrasonography yearly
(B) Bilateral mammography and breast MRI yearly
(C) CA-27.29 blood testing yearly
(D) No screening at this time

Item 123

A 65-year-old woman is evaluated during a routine examination. She is asymptomatic. She has a history of stage I, hormone receptor–negative, *HER2*-negative left breast cancer that was diagnosed 3 years ago. She was treated with modified radical mastectomy followed by chemotherapy with docetaxel and cyclophosphamide.

On physical examination, vital signs are normal. The left chest wall is well healed with no nodularity. No right breast masses, axillary lymphadenopathy, or supraclavicular lymphadenopathy is present. The remainder of the examination is unremarkable.

The patient will undergo periodic mammography and routine health maintenance.

Which of the following would be the most appropriate additional evaluation in this patient?

(A) Bone scan yearly
(B) CT scan yearly
(C) PET scan yearly
(D) Tumor marker measurement, complete blood count, and comprehensive metabolic panel yearly
(E) No additional studies

Item 124

A 24-year-old man is evaluated in the hospital for new-onset high fever, chills, and rigors. He reports no other symptoms. The patient was recently diagnosed with diffuse large B-cell lymphoma for which he received his first cycle of multiagent chemotherapy 10 days ago. He does not have an indwelling venous catheter.

On physical examination, temperature is 39.0 °C (102.2 °F), blood pressure is 90/40 mm Hg, pulse rate 130/min, and respiration rate is 24/min. There is no evidence of rash or mucositis. The chest is clear to auscultation. Other than tachycardia and hypotension, cardiac examination is normal. The abdomen has normal bowel sounds and is nontender. There is no evidence of a perianal abscess.

Laboratory studies:

Hemoglobin	11.5 g/dL (115 g/L)
Leukocyte count	800/µL (0.8×10^9/L) with 10% neutrophils and 90% lymphocytes
Platelet count	100,000/µL (100×10^9/L)

Chest radiograph is normal. Blood and urine cultures are pending.

Which of the following is the most appropriate immediate next step in treatment?

(A) Begin empiric piperacillin-tazobactam
(B) Begin targeted antimicrobial therapy once culture results are available
(C) Begin vancomycin
(D) Begin vancomycin, amphotericin, and acyclovir

Item 125

A 50-year-old woman undergoes follow-up evaluation after a recent diagnosis of breast cancer. She was diagnosed with poorly differentiated, *HER2*-positive, estrogen receptor–negative, progesterone receptor–negative invasive ductal carcinoma for which she underwent simple mastectomy with sentinel lymph node evaluation. Pathology revealed a 2.4-cm invasive ductal carcinoma; the sentinel lymph node was negative for tumor. She is perimenopausal and has no comorbidities.

Physical examination reveals a healing mastectomy scar with an expander in place and a healing sentinel lymph node biopsy scar. The remainder of the physical examination is normal.

Postoperative radiation therapy and trastuzumab-based chemotherapy are planned.

Which of the following studies is necessary before initiating postoperative breast cancer therapy?

(A) Assessment of left ventricular function
(B) Chest CT angiography
(C) Exercise stress test
(D) Vaginal ultrasonography

Item 126

A 59-year-old man is evaluated for new-onset seizures. Medical history is significant for a melanoma resected 2 years ago. He takes no medications and has no known allergies.

On physical examination, temperature is 37.2 °C (99.0 °F), blood pressure is 128/82 mm Hg, pulse rate is 72/min, and respiration rate is 14/min. There is no palpable lymphadenopathy. The physical examination, including the neurologic examination, is normal.

CT scan of the chest reveals numerous 1-cm nodules in both lungs. An abdominal CT scan reveals several nodules in the liver. A gadolinium MRI of the brain demonstrates a 2-cm mass consistent with metastasis in the right frontal lobe.

Which of the following is the most appropriate treatment?

(A) Chemotherapy
(B) Palliative care
(C) Surgical resection of cerebral metastasis
(D) Whole-brain radiation therapy

Item 127

A 69-year-old man is evaluated for hematuria of 3 weeks' duration. He has no pain or fever. The remainder of the medical history is noncontributory.

The physical examination, including vital signs, is normal.

Urinalysis reveals many erythrocytes but no erythrocyte casts or leukocytes.

Cystoscopic analysis demonstrates multiple bladder lesions, with biopsy revealing papillary transitional cell carcinoma with invasion limited to the submucosa.

The patient undergoes surgery, and all visible disease is resected.

Which of the following is the most appropriate next step in management?

(A) Intravesicular bacillus Calmette-Guérin
(B) Radiation
(C) Radical cystectomy
(D) Observation

Item 128

A 26-year-old man is evaluated for a 2-week history of rapidly enlarging cervical and axillary lymphadenopathy and abdominal distention as well as a 1-week history of fever.

On physical examination, temperature is 39.0 °C (102.4 °F), blood pressure is 90/60 mm Hg, pulse rate is 115/min, and respiration rate is 24/min. He has massive cervical and axillary lymphadenopathy. On abdominal examination, a palpable spleen 8 cm below the left costal margin and a firm intraabdominal mass are noted.

Laboratory studies:

Hemoglobin	10.5 g/dL (105 g/L)
Leukocyte count	65,000/µL (65×10^9/L) with 35% neutrophils and 65% atypical lymphocytes
Platelet count	90,000/µL (90×10^9/L)
Creatinine	3.8 mg/dL (336 µmol/L)
Lactate dehydrogenase	12,000 units/L
Phosphorus	9.9 mg/dL (3.20 mmol/L)
Potassium	6.6 meq/L (6.6 mmol/L)
Uric acid	18.6 mg/dL (1.10 mmol/L)

A biopsy of a cervical lymph node confirms Burkitt lymphoma.

Which of the following is the most appropriate immediate next step in treatment?

(A) Combination chemotherapy
(B) Corticosteroid therapy
(C) Hemodialysis, intravenous normal saline, and rasburicase
(D) Radiation therapy

Item 129

A 28-year-old woman is evaluated for fatigue of 5 weeks' duration. She reports no fever, night sweats, weight loss, or pruritus. She has previously been well and takes no medications.

On physical examination, temperature is 37.0 °C (98.6 °F), blood pressure is 110/60 mm Hg, and pulse rate is 75/min. She has rubbery, nontender bilateral cervical lymphadenopathy; one node on the right measures 3 × 2 cm and one node on the left measures 3 × 3 cm. The remainder of the physical examination is unremarkable.

Laboratory studies:

Hemoglobin	13.5 g/dL (135 g/L)
Leukocyte count	4000/µL (4.0×10^9/L) with 58% neutrophils and 42% lymphocytes
Platelet count	390,000/µL (390×10^9/L)
Erythrocyte sedimentation rate	8 mm/h
Lactate dehydrogenase	Low
β_2-Microglobulin	Low

Cervical lymph node excisional biopsy reveals nodular sclerosing Hodgkin lymphoma. CT/PET of the chest, abdomen, and pelvis shows only PET scan–positive bilateral cervical and subcarinal lymphadenopathy.

A bone marrow biopsy is unremarkable.

Which of the following is the most appropriate management?

(A) Chemotherapy and radiation therapy
(B) Radiation therapy
(C) Rituximab
(D) Watchful waiting

Item 130

A 27-year-old man is evaluated for a 4-week history of fatigue, intermittent fever, sore throat, and left upper quadrant abdominal discomfort. He has no night sweats, weight loss, cough, dysuria, or diarrhea.

On physical examination, temperature is 38.0 °C (100.4 °F), blood pressure is 105/60 mm Hg, and pulse rate is 105/min. He has bilateral soft, freely movable but tender cervical lymphadenopathy. The spleen is palpable 3 cm below the left costal margin and tender to touch. The remainder of the physical examination is unremarkable.

Laboratory studies:

Hemoglobin	11.5 g/dL (115 g/L)
Leukocyte count	9000/µL (9.0×10^9/L) with 32% neutrophils and 68% lymphocytes
Platelet count	160,000/µL (160×10^9/L)

A peripheral blood smear shows large atypical lymphocytes representing 10% of the lymphoid cells.

Which of the following is the most appropriate next step in the diagnostic evaluation?

(A) Anti–Epstein-Barr virus antibody assay
(B) Bone marrow biopsy and PET/CT
(C) Lymph node biopsy
(D) Peripheral blood flow cytometry

Item 131

A 70-year-old man is evaluated for a 1-year history of progressive fatigue and easy bruising. Medical history is significant for Hodgkin lymphoma diagnosed and treated 20 years ago with combination chemotherapy plus radiation therapy. He has no other symptoms and takes no medications.

On physical examination, temperature is 37.0 °C (98.6 °F), blood pressure is 110/60 mm Hg, and pulse rate is 75/min. He has conjunctival pallor. The remainder of the examination is unremarkable.

Laboratory studies:

Hemoglobin	7.0 g/dL (70 g/L)
Leukocyte count	1100/µL (1.1×10^9/L) with 28% neutrophils, 69% lymphocytes, and 3% myeloid blasts
Platelet count	40,000/µL (40×10^9/L)

A bone marrow biopsy reveals enlarged and atypical erythroid precursors with ringed sideroblasts, reduced mononuclear megakaryocytes, and 6% CD34-positive myeloblasts. Bone marrow cytogenetics demonstrate multiple chromosomal translocations and deletions.

Which of the following is the most likely cause of this patient's findings?

(A) Acute lymphoblastic leukemia
(B) Chemotherapy- and radiation therapy–related myelodysplastic syndrome
(C) Parvovirus B19 infection
(D) Recurrent Hodgkin lymphoma

Item 132

A 70-year-old woman undergoes a routine examination. She is asymptomatic and is not taking any medications.

On physical examination, the vital signs are normal. The patient has palpable, small, nontender cervical, axillary, and inguinal lymphadenopathy that was not present on her previous examination 3 years ago. The remainder of the physical examination is unremarkable.

Laboratory studies:

Hemoglobin	12.5 g/dL (125 g/L)
Leukocyte count	65,000/µl (65×10^9/L), with 30% neutrophils and 70% lymphocytes
Platelet count	190,000/µL (190×10^9/L)

Review of the peripheral blood smear reveals numerous small lymphoid cells. Flow cytometry of the peripheral blood shows monoclonal B cells expressing CD20, CD10, and CD5.

Which of the following will provide the most prognostic information in the diagnostic evaluation?

(A) Bone marrow biopsy and aspirate
(B) β_2-Microglobuin measurement and molecular testing
(C) CT of the chest, abdomen, and pelvis
(D) PET scan

Item 133

A 26-year-old man is evaluated for a 3-week history of dry cough and chest pain but no fever. He also reports right testicular pain and swelling, as well as dyspnea on exertion and recent-onset mid-back pain that is not associated with movement. He has lost 3.6 kg (8.0 lb) in 1 month. He takes no medications.

On physical examination, temperature is 37.4 °C (99.3 °F), blood pressure is 108/76 mm Hg, and pulse rate is 62/min. No lymphadenopathy is noted. Lung examination reveals dullness and decreased breath sounds at the left base. The abdomen is soft and nontender without masses. No spinal tenderness is present. Testicular examination reveals a firm 5-cm nodule in the mid pole of the right testicle. Results of the neurologic examination are nonfocal.

Laboratory studies reveal an α-fetoprotein level of 1289 ng/mL (1289 µg/L) and a β-human chorionic gonadotropin level of 1455 milliunits/mL (1455 units/L) (normal, <5 milliunits/mL [5 units/L]). Testicular ultrasound confirms a 6-cm solid right testicular mass. CT scan reveals a 4-cm left midlung mass associated with a left pleural effusion. Mediastinal and retroperitoneal lymphadenopathy is noted.

Which of the following is the most appropriate next step in treatment?

(A) Chemotherapy
(B) Inguinal orchiectomy and biopsy of lung lesion
(C) Inguinal orchiectomy followed by chemotherapy
(D) Left lung lobectomy followed by chemotherapy

Item 134

A 55-year-old woman is evaluated for a cough, weakness, and fatigue of 4 weeks' duration. She has a 40-pack-year history of cigarette smoking.

On physical examination, temperature is normal, blood pressure is 136/78 mm Hg, and pulse rate is 68/min. No palpable lymphadenopathy is noted. The cardiopulmonary and neurologic examinations are normal.

A chest radiograph demonstrates a 5-cm left upper lobe pulmonary mass. A subsequent CT scan shows the mass but no evident mediastinal lymphadenopathy. A PET scan displays radiographic uptake in the mass but no disease elsewhere. A CT-guided biopsy demonstrates squamous cell carcinoma.

Which of the following is the most appropriate treatment?

(A) Combination chemotherapy and radiation
(B) Radiation
(C) Surgery and adjuvant chemotherapy
(D) Systemic chemotherapy

Item 135

A 68-year-old woman underwent a right hemicolectomy 2 years ago for stage III colon cancer. She received 6 months of chemotherapy with 5-fluorouracil, leucovorin, and oxaliplatin (FOLFOX) after surgery. On a recent routine follow-up visit, a serum carcinoembryonic antigen level was found to be elevated to 43 ng/mL (upper limit of normal, 5 ng/mL). She has no known medical comorbidities and takes no medications. She works full time and recently returned from a ski vacation.

On physical examination, temperature is 37.1 °C (98.8 °F), blood pressure is 125/85 mm Hg, pulse rate is 80/min, and respiration rate is 14/min. The physical examination is notable for a palpable liver edge just below the right costal margin. The abdomen is soft with no distention or masses, and bowel sounds are normal. No supraclavicular lymph nodes are palpable.

Laboratory studies indicate a hemoglobin level of 13.5 g/dL (135 g/L), a leukocyte count of 9000/µL (9.0×10^9/L), and a platelet count of 288,000/µL (288×10^9/L).

Contrast-enhanced CT scan of the chest, abdomen, and pelvis demonstrates three hypodense lesions on the right lobe of the liver ranging in diameter from 1.5 to 4.0 cm. No other abnormalities are seen on the scan.

Which of the following is the most appropriate management?

(A) CT-guided fine-needle aspiration of liver lesion
(B) Hepatic arterial embolization
(C) Palliative systemic chemotherapy
(D) Radiation therapy to the liver
(E) Right hepatectomy

Item 136

A 42-year-old woman is evaluated following a partial mastectomy and postoperative radiation therapy for intermediate-grade ductal carcinoma in situ that was estrogen receptor–positive and progesterone receptor–positive. The patient is premenopausal. Before surgery, she had been taking an oral contraceptive that has since been discontinued.

On physical examination, vital signs are normal. The breast shows a well-healing surgical scar and cutaneous signs of radiation treatment. The remainder of her physical examination is normal.

Which of the following is the most appropriate additional therapy?

(A) Anastrazole
(B) Chemotherapy
(C) Raloxifene
(D) Tamoxifen

Item 137

A 60-year-old woman is evaluated for a 6-week history of worsening left hip and right arm pain. She has a history of stage III, hormone receptor–positive, *HER2*-negative right breast cancer that was diagnosed 5 years ago. She underwent modified radical mastectomy, chemotherapy, and postmastectomy radiation. The patient declined adjuvant hormonal therapy.

Physical examination reveals tenderness over the left sacroiliac joint and the right humerus. The remainder of the examination is otherwise noncontributory.

Bone scan reveals increased uptake in the bilateral femurs, lumbar spine, and right humerus consistent with metastases. CT shows no abnormalities in the lungs or liver, but bony lesions are evident and are consistent with the bone scan findings. No pathologic fractures are present.

Which of the following is the most appropriate intervention?

(A) Aromatase inhibitor
(B) Bone biopsy
(C) Chemotherapy
(D) Radiation therapy
(E) Trastuzumab therapy

Item 138

A 38-year-old woman undergoes follow-up evaluation after recent genetic testing indicated that she is positive for the *BRCA* gene mutation. She was tested for the mutation after her sister was diagnosed with breast cancer at 32 years of age and was found to be *BRCA* positive. She is healthy and has no medical problems. She has four children aged 4 to 10 years and has no plans to have more children. Her medical history is unremarkable. She does not know of any other family members who have had cancer. She has been taking oral contraceptive pills for the past 4 years.

On physical examination, vital signs are normal. The remainder of the examination is normal.

Which of the following recommendations is associated with the greatest reduction of cancer risk?

(A) Bilateral salpingo-oophorectomy
(B) Bilateral salpingo-oophorectomy and bilateral mastectomy
(C) CA-125 monitoring and pelvic examination every 6 months
(D) Continuation of oral contraceptive pills
(E) Pelvic ultrasound every 6 months

Item 139

A 63-year-old man is evaluated for fatigue and a persistent cough of 7 weeks' duration. He has a 60-pack-year smoking history.

On physical examination, vital signs and physical examination are normal.

A chest radiograph reveals a right hilar mass. A CT scan of the thorax confirms the presence of a right perihilar mass and enlarged hilar and mediastinal lymph nodes.

An endobronchial mass is identified by bronchoscopy; brushings and biopsy reveal small cell lung cancer. A CT scan of the chest and abdomen is negative. A bone scan and MRI of the brain are negative.

Which of the following is the most appropriate next step in the management of this patient?

(A) Chemotherapy with adjunctive radiation therapy
(B) Mediastinoscopy
(C) Radiation therapy
(D) Resection for cure

H Item 140

A 40-year-old woman is evaluated for a 36-hour history of fever and central abdominal pain localized to the right lower quadrant followed by nausea and vomiting. Medical history is unremarkable, and she takes no medications.

On physical examination, temperature is 39.1 °C (102.4 °F), blood pressure is 110/75 mm Hg, pulse rate is 92/min, and respiration rate is 16/min. No skin lesions are present. The patient has right lower quadrant abdominal pain with tenderness, guarding, and rebound. The chest is clear to auscultation and percussion. There are no heart murmurs, and no palpable lymphadenopathy is noted.

Contrast-enhanced CT scan of the abdomen and pelvis is consistent with acute appendicitis. No other abnormalities are seen. The patient undergoes a laparoscopic appendectomy without incident. Pathologic examination shows acute appendicitis with the finding of a well-differentiated carcinoid tumor, 0.8 cm in maximal diameter. The patient has fully recovered from her surgery and is back to full activities.

Which of the following is the most appropriate management?

(A) Indium-111 pentetreotide scan
(B) Octreotide
(C) Right hemicolectomy
(D) Streptozocin plus 5-fluorouracil
(E) No further intervention

Item 141

A 54-year-old woman is evaluated for a several-month history of increasing abdominal girth accompanied by bloating and decreased appetite. Medical and family histories are not significant, and she takes no medications.

On physical examination, temperature is 37.5 °C (99.5 °F), blood pressure is 115/75 mm Hg, pulse rate is 72/min, and respiration rate is 18/min. The patient appears fatigued. Breath sounds are dull at the lung bases bilaterally. The abdomen is nontender and distended with ascites, and bowel sounds are normal. Rectal examination is normal

Laboratory studies are normal.

Contrast-enhanced CT scan of the chest, abdomen, and pelvis demonstrates ascites with omental thickening and scattered masses consistent with peritoneal carcinomatosis. Ovaries appear normal without masses. Transvaginal ultrasound confirms normal-appearing ovaries bilaterally. A needle biopsy of a large omental nodule is obtained and reveals adenocarcinoma.

Which of the following is the most appropriate initial management?

(A) Chemotherapy
(B) Palliative care
(C) Paracentesis followed by chemotherapy
(D) Radiation therapy
(E) Surgical debulking followed by chemotherapy

Item 142

A 53-year-old woman undergoes follow-up evaluation for recently diagnosed, well-differentiated, estrogen receptor–positive/progesterone receptor–positive, *HER2*-negative breast cancer. The patient is postmenopausal. She underwent lumpectomy and sentinel lymph node evaluation, which revealed a 2.3-cm invasive ductal carcinoma with no lymph node involvement, followed by radiation therapy.

On physical examination, vital signs are normal. Other than postsurgical and radiation findings, her general physical examination is normal.

Her most recent chest radiograph was negative. Her last screening colonoscopy was performed 3 years ago and was normal. Her last pelvic examination and Pap smear were performed 6 months ago and were normal.

Which of the following is the most appropriate treatment?

(A) Anastrazole for 5 years
(B) Anastrazole for 5 years followed by tamoxifen for 5 years
(C) Trastuzumab for 1 year
(D) No further therapy

Item 143

A 57-year-old woman is seen during follow-up evaluation 8 months after undergoing left hemicolectomy for a nonobstructing stage III adenocarcinoma of the descending colon, followed by 6 months of adjuvant chemotherapy. The patient has recovered fully and has resumed full activities, including regular exercise. Medical history is otherwise noncontributory. Her only medication is a multivitamin with iron.

On physical examination, temperature is 36.7 °C (98.1 °F), blood pressure is 135/85 mm Hg, pulse rate is 82/min, and respiration rate is 14/min. Well-healed surgical scars are visible. The abdomen is soft, with no tenderness, distention, or organomegaly, and bowel sounds are normal. The remainder of the examination is normal.

Laboratory studies:

Hemoglobin	13.1 g/dL (131 g/L)
Leukocyte count	6000/µL (6.0×10^9/L)
Platelet count	329,000/µL (329×10^9/L)
Total bilirubin	0.7 mg/dL (12.0 µmol/L)
Carcinoembryonic antigen (CEA)	2.1 ng/mL (2.1 µg/L) (upper limit of normal 5.0 ng/mL [5.0 µg/L])

Alanine and aspartate aminotransferase levels are normal.

CEA monitoring every 3 to 6 months and colonoscopy 1 year after resection, with follow-up colonoscopy repeated at 3- to 5-year intervals, are scheduled.

Which of the following is the most appropriate additional follow-up management?

(A) CT scan annually for 3 years
(B) CT scan annually for 10 years
(C) CT scan every 3 months for 3 years
(D) PET scan annually for 5 years
(E) No additional evaluation

Item 144

A 64-year-old man is evaluated for a 3-month history of progressive midback pain and a 2-week history of lower extremity weakness. He reports no history of trauma or cardiopulmonary disease.

On physical examination, temperature is 37.0 °C (98.6 °F), blood pressure is 110/60 mm Hg, pulse rate is 110/min, and respiration rate is 18/min. He has point tenderness over the T10 and T11 vertebral bodies, decreased lower extremity muscle strength ($3^+/5^+$), increased reflexes isolated to both lower extremities, and bilateral extensor plantar reflexes. The remainder of the physical examination is unremarkable.

Laboratory studies:

Hemoglobin	6.5 g/dL (65 g/L)
Leukocyte count	8500/µL (8.5×10^9/L)
Calcium	12 mg/dL (3 mmol/L)
Total protein	13 g/dL (130 g/L)

A chest radiograph is unremarkable. MRI of the thoracic and lumbar spine shows a vertebral body mass with extension into the epidural space (T12) and compression of the spinal cord. Bone marrow biopsy reveals sheets of atypical plasma cells with eccentric immature nuclei representing 80% of the cellular elements.

Which of the following is the most appropriate next step in management?

(A) Biopsy of the epidural mass
(B) Corticosteroids followed by radiation therapy
(C) Lenalidomide
(D) Radiation therapy

Answers and Critiques

Hematology Answers

Item 1 Answer: E

Educational Objective: Manage a patient with low-risk primary myelofibrosis.

The most appropriate management of this patient now is observation. This patient has primary myelofibrosis, which is a chronic myeloproliferative disorder characterized by overproduction of megakaryocytes and bone marrow stromal cell-mediated collagen deposition. The peripheral blood smear shows marked leukoerythroblastic findings with tear drop–shaped erythrocytes and megathrombocytes. The bone marrow aspirate is often "dry" (unsuccessful aspirate), and bone marrow biopsy shows marked fibrosis. This patient has low-risk primary myelofibrosis (PMF) given the absence of high-risk features such as age older than 65 years; fever, night sweats, and a weight loss of 10% or more; a hemoglobin concentration of less than 10 g/dL (100 g/L); a leukocyte count greater than 25,000/µL (25×10^9/L); and circulating blasts of 1% or more. As such, his median overall survival is 135 months or approximately 11 years. Given his favorable prognosis, he requires only observation for now.

Allogeneic hematopoietic stem cell transplantation is potentially curative in patients with PMF but is associated with significant morbidity and mortality and would not be a good choice for a patient with low-risk disease, but it could be considered if the disease progresses. Transplantation is the preferred treatment for younger patients with two or more adverse prognostic features.

Danazol is used to treat PMF-related anemia and leads to responses in 37% of patients with transfusion-dependent anemia or a hemoglobin level less than 10 g/dL (100 g/L). This treatment is not indicated in this patient considering his hemoglobin level of 12.5 g/dL (125 g/L).

Hydroxyurea would be a reasonable therapy if the patient had constitutional symptoms such as fever, weight loss, night sweats, symptomatic splenomegaly, or problematic thrombocytosis; however, this treatment is not required now.

Imatinib is appropriate therapy in patients with chronic myeloid leukemia, but it is not effective in treating PMF.

KEY POINT

- **Close observation, with palliative care as needed, is appropriate for patients with low-risk primary myelofibrosis.**

Bibliography

Cervantes F, Dupriez B, Pereira A, et al. New prognostic scoring system for primary myelofibrosis based on a study of the International Working Group for Myelofibrosis Research and Treatment. Blood. 2009;113(13):2895-2901. [PMID: 18988864]

Item 2 Answer: A

Educational Objective: Treat aplastic anemia in a young patient.

The most appropriate treatment is allogeneic hematopoietic stem cell transplantation (HSCT). Aplastic anemia is classified by the severity of the neutropenia. Moderate aplastic anemia is diagnosed when the absolute neutrophil count (ANC) is 500 to 1000/µL ($0.5\text{-}1.0 \times 10^9$/L). Severe aplastic anemia occurs when two or more of the following are present: ANC 200 to 500/µL ($0.2\text{-}0.5 \times 10^9$/L), platelet count less than 20,000/µL (20×10^9/L), and reticulocyte count less than 0.2%. Very severe aplastic anemia is diagnosed when the ANC is less than 200/µL (0.2×10^9/L). ANC is calculated as leukocyte count × percentage of polymorphonuclear cells + band forms. This patient has very severe aplastic anemia. Patients with severe aplastic anemia who have an HLA-identical sibling and are younger than 40 years should be offered allogeneic HSCT as initial therapy. Because of the high mortality rate associated with this procedure, HSCT is generally not recommended as initial therapy for patients older than 40 years or those who are not medically fit to undergo transplantation or who have no HLA-identical sibling; these patients are typically treated with antithymocyte globulin and cyclosporine as initial therapy. Because this patient is young, healthy, and has two siblings who are an HLA-identical match, he should be offered allogeneic transplantation as initial therapy.

In some clinical trials of patients who are not transplant candidates, intravenous antithymocyte globulin plus corticosteroids and cyclosporine can result in partial and complete responses in 60% to 80% of patients. Many of these patients become transfusion independent, although response is often delayed for 3 to 6 months, and relapses can occur when the cyclosporine is tapered.

Autologous HSCT would not be an appropriate treatment choice because this patient has an essentially acellular bone marrow.

Prednisone as a single agent produces a very low response rate in patients with aplastic anemia.

Growth factors such as granulocyte colony-stimulating factor should not be given as primary therapy for aplastic anemia, and the use of growth factors as concomitant therapy is controversial. These agents are expensive, and some reports suggest a lower response rate to immunosuppressive therapy and a higher relapse rate when granulocyte colony-stimulating factor is used.

KEY POINT

- **Patients with severe aplastic anemia who have an HLA-identical sibling and are younger than 40 years should be offered allogeneic hematopoietic stem cell transplantation as initial therapy.**

Bibliography

Marsh JC, Ball SE, Cavaenagh J, et al. Guidelines for the diagnosis and management of aplastic anaemia. Br J Haematol. 2009;147(1):43-70. [PMID: 19673883]

H

Item 3 Answer: E

Educational Objective: Manage a patient with a history of transfusion-associated anaphylaxis.

Of the choices listed, the most appropriate erythrocyte product to minimize the risk of an anaphylactic transfusion reaction is washed erythrocytes. The diagnosis of severe IgA deficiency should be considered in any patient with a history of anaphylaxis during a blood transfusion. Most patients with IgA deficiency are asymptomatic although they are also prone to gastrointestinal infections (particularly *Giardia lamblia*) and have an increased risk for autoimmune disorders including rheumatoid arthritis and systemic lupus erythematosus. Some patients with severe IgA deficiency develop anti-IgA antibodies, which may lead to an anaphylactic reaction when blood products containing IgA are used in transfusion. Although fresh frozen plasma (FFP) is the main blood component containing anti-IgA antibodies, erythrocytes and platelet products also contain small amounts of plasma; consequently, anaphylaxis may occur with FFP, platelets, and erythrocytes. Washing erythrocytes and platelets can remove plasma proteins and greatly decrease the incidence of anaphylaxis. Transfusion of blood products from an IgA-deficient donor would be another viable option to minimize transfusion-associated risk of anaphylaxis.

Cytomegalovirus-negative blood would not be indicated in this patient who has normal T-cell function and is not at risk for cytomegalovirus infection.

γ-irradiation of erythrocytes minimizes the incidence of graft-versus-host disease by eradicating lymphocytes but would not decrease the risk for anaphylaxis and would not be indicated in this immunocompetent patient.

Leukoreduction of erythrocytes decreases the incidence of febrile nonhemolytic transfusion reactions, cytomegalovirus transmission, and alloimmunization but not anaphylaxis.

Phenotypically matched erythrocytes are indicated in patients in whom there is a high risk for alloimmunization and subsequent delayed hemolytic transfusion reaction such as those with sickle cell disease; however, phenotypically matched (matched for ABO, Rh, and Kell antigens) erythrocytes would not decrease the risk for anaphylaxis.

KEY POINT

- **Using washed erythrocytes and platelets minimizes the risk for transfusion-associated anaphylaxis.**

Bibliography

Sandler SG. How I manage patients suspected of having had an IgA anaphylactic transfusion reaction. Transfusion. 2006;46(1):10-13. [PMID: 16398725]

Item 4 Answer: B

H

Educational Objective: Manage a medical inpatient with venous thromboembolism risk factors.

The most appropriate treatment is low-dose subcutaneous unfractionated heparin. This patient is immobilized and has at least two major risk factors for venous thromboembolism (VTE): age 75 years and community-acquired pneumonia. Therefore, he should receive pharmacologic VTE prophylaxis with low-dose unfractionated heparin for at least the duration of his hospitalization.

Aspirin, 325 mg/d, is not appropriate VTE prophylaxis for this medically ill patient who is at high risk for VTE. Aspirin, which is effective for prevention of stroke and myocardial infarction, has not been shown to be efficacious as VTE prophylaxis. Appropriate options for this patient would include low-dose subcutaneous unfractionated heparin, low-molecular-weight heparin, or fondaparinux.

Use of pneumatic compression devices would not be the optimal approach to VTE prophylaxis in this patient. Intermittent pneumatic compression devices have been demonstrated to be an effective form of VTE prophylaxis, but the data supporting their efficacy are almost exclusively limited to surgical patients, and these devices have not been demonstrated to significantly reduce the incidence of pulmonary embolism. Furthermore, there are serious deficiencies regarding compliance with mechanical prophylaxis in routine care settings. Therefore, in patients without contraindications to its use, pharmacologic treatment should be used for VTE prophylaxis.

Warfarin, 1 mg/d, is not the appropriate VTE prophylaxis for this medical inpatient. Although an initial study of low-dose warfarin demonstrated efficacy in DVT in patients with central venous catheters, subsequent studies have not replicated these promising results. Low-intensity, fixed-dose warfarin has never been demonstrated to be useful in VTE prophylaxis. In patients with total hip arthroplasty and knee arthroplasty, adjusted-dose warfarin (INR 2-3) has been shown to be efficacious in preventing VTE, but studies of this regimen have never been conducted in medical inpatients.

KEY POINT

- **Medical inpatients with two major risk factors for venous thromboembolism (VTE) should receive pharmacologic VTE prophylaxis for at least the duration of their hospitalization.**

Bibliography

Kahn SR, Lim W, Dunn AS, et al. Prevention of VTE in nonsurgical patients: Antithrombotic Therapy and Prevention of Thrombosis, 9th ed: American College of Chest Physicians Evidence-Based Clinical Practice Guidelines. Chest. 2012;141(2 Suppl):e195S-226S. [PMID: 22315261]

H

Item 5 Answer: C

Educational Objective: Manage the transfusion requirements in a patient with thrombocytopenia and intracranial hemorrhaging.

The most appropriate transfusion strategy is to maintain the platelet count at a level of 100,000/µL (100×10^9/L). This patient has life-threatening intracranial bleeding. The bleeding source is most likely due to hypertensive vasculopathy, and the patient is at risk for continued intracerebral bleeding because of her myelodysplasia-associated thrombocytopenia. Although no randomized trials exist, expert opinion and guidelines generally recommend maintaining the platelet count at a level greater than 100,000/µL (100×10^9/L) for the first few days after central nervous system bleeding or immediately prior to and after planned central nervous system surgery.

A platelet count of 30,000/µL (30×10^9/L) would not be high enough in this patient with intracranial bleeding.

A platelet count of 50,000/µL (50×10^9/L) is generally recommended for nonneurosurgical procedures or non–central nervous system bleeding, but transfusion to achieve a higher platelet count is recommended in this patient with intracranial hemorrhaging.

Guidelines do not suggest any additional benefit to maintaining a minimum platelet count greater than 100,000/µL (100×10^9/L).

KEY POINT

- **Platelet transfusion to maintain the platelet count at 100,000/µL (100×10^9/L) for the first few days after central nervous system bleeding or immediately prior to and after a planned central nervous system surgery is recommended.**

Bibliography

Slichter SJ. Evidence-Based Platelet Transfusion Guidelines. Hematology Am Soc Hematol Educ Program. 2007:172-178. Review. [PMID: 18024626]

Item 6 Answer: C

Educational Objective: Diagnose polycythemia vera.

The most appropriate next step in the management of this patient is to obtain a *JAK2 V617F* analysis. Polycythemia vera (PV) should be suspected in patients with an increased hemoglobin level or hematocrit and an oxygen saturation greater than 92%. The suspicion for PV is increased in patients with other manifestations of the disease, including erythromelalgia (a burning sensation in the palms and soles, possibly caused by platelet activation), plethora, warm water–induced pruritus, and thrombotic and bleeding symptoms. Previously, diagnosis of PV relied on detection of an increased red blood cell mass in the absence of other causes of secondary erythrocytosis. Assessment of red cell mass is no longer available at most laboratories. However, an elevated red cell mass can be identified indirectly by the presence of a hemoglobin level greater than 18.5 g/dL (185 g/L) in men or greater than 16.5 g/dL (165 g/L) in women. Concomitant leukocytosis (often with basophilia) and thrombocytosis further support the diagnosis. The diagnosis of PV can be confirmed with a *JAK2 V617F* analysis in patients with elevated hemoglobin or hematocrit levels and no evidence of conditions that may cause secondary erythrocytosis. This mutation is found in more than 97% of patients with PV.

The *BCR-ABL* (Philadelphia chromosome) is associated with chronic myeloid leukemia (CML). The diagnosis of CML requires the identification of this oncogene in a patient who has a leukoerythroblastic peripheral blood smear (increased granulocytes with a marked left shift plus early erythrocyte precursors) and hypercellular bone marrow with marked myeloid proliferation. These findings are not present in this patient.

Bone marrow biopsy is usually reserved for patients in whom a myeloproliferative disorder is suspected but in whom *JAK2* mutation testing results are negative. Bone marrow findings usually show a hypercellular marrow with clusters of abnormal megakaryocytes. Increased reticulin fibrosis may also be seen. These findings are nonspecific but can be used to confirm the suspicion of a myeloproliferative neoplasm.

Polysomnography (a sleep study) can be performed in patients in whom nocturnal oxygen desaturation secondary to obstructive sleep apnea is suspected as a cause of secondary erythrocytosis; however, obstructive sleep apnea is not associated with postbathing pruritus, splenomegaly, leukocytosis, or thrombocythemia, all of which are present in this patient.

KEY POINT

- **Identification of the *JAK2 V617F* mutation in patients with a hemoglobin level greater than 18.5 g/dL (185 g/L) in men or greater than 16.5 g/dL (165 g/L) in women, with concomitant leukocytosis, thrombocytosis, and hepatosplenomegaly, is diagnostic of polycythemia vera.**

Bibliography

Tefferi A, Skoda R, Vardiman JW. Myeloproliferative neoplasms: contemporary diagnosis using histology and genetics. Nat Rev Clin Oncol. 2009;6(11):627-637. [PMID: 19806146]

Item 7 Answer: D

Educational Objective: Manage ABO and Rh compatibility issues in a patient who requires emergent erythrocyte transfusion.

This patient should undergo transfusion with O-negative erythrocyte products. Whenever possible, erythrocytes should be ABO and Rh compatible between the recipient and the donor. When an exact ABO and Rh match is not available or when there is not time for blood typing and screening to be done for patients who require emergent transfusion, the least incompatible blood products should be transfused. Humans develop antibodies against ABO and Rh antigens not present on their erythrocytes. Therefore, this patient will have developed antibodies against blood group B but not blood group A. He will also have developed antibodies against Rh(D) because his blood type is Rh negative. Consequently, the most compatible blood of the choices listed is O negative. Because type O-negative blood lacks both A and B antigens as well as the Rh(D) antigen, it is considered the universal erythrocyte donor product and should be given when emergent transfusion is indicated and the recipient blood type is unknown or when an exact ABO and Rh match is not available.

The use of A-positive erythrocytes is not the best option because of Rh incompatibility, which could lead to an acute or delayed hemolytic transfusion reaction. However, this approach could be considered in emergency situations if A-negative and O-negative blood were not available.

AB-negative erythrocytes would be incompatible because of anti-B antibodies present in the patient's plasma, which would react against donor erythrocytes and could lead to an acute hemolytic transfusion reaction.

B-positive erythrocytes would also be both ABO and Rh incompatible and are therefore not an appropriate transfusion product for this patient.

KEY POINT

- **Type O-negative erythrocytes are considered the universal erythrocyte donor product and should be given when emergent transfusion is indicated and the recipient's blood type is unknown or when an exact ABO and Rh match is not available.**

Bibliography

Goodell PP, Uhl L, Mohammed M, Powers AA. Risk of hemolytic transfusion reactions following emergency-release RBC transfusion. Am J Clin Pathol. 2010;134(2):202-206. [PMID: 20660321]

Item 8 Answer: A

Educational Objective: Diagnose acquired hemophilia.

The most likely diagnosis is acquired hemophilia. This patient has no family or personal history of bleeding, but she now has bleeding and anemia. Her prothrombin time (PT) is normal, but her activated partial thromboplastin time (aPTT) is prolonged, and the aPTT fails to completely and fully correct on 1:1 mixing with normal plasma, findings that suggest acquired hemophilia or an acquired inhibitor to factor VIII. The factor VIII autoantibody inhibits the function of factor VIII, leading to prolongation of the aPTT. The presence of an acquired factor VIII inhibitor is a rare, life-threatening autoimmune condition, typically occurring in elderly patients, although some younger patients with other autoimmune conditions or those in the postpartum state can also be affected. Unlike congenital hemophilia, bleeding in acquired hemophilia tends to be mucocutaneous and multifocal, and hemarthroses are rare.

Liver disease causes bleeding through several mechanisms. First, liver failure results in a defect in the synthesis of all clotting factors. Levels of all clotting factors except factor VIII are diminished, with levels of factor VII the most affected because of factor VII's very short half-life of 3 to 4 hours. Conversely, factor VIII levels are increased for reasons that are not fully understood but may be because of synthesis in other endothelial cells and decreased clearance. Second, platelets are decreased in number and diminished in function. Lastly, there is increased fibrinolysis. Liver disease results in a prolonged PT. The aPTT and thrombin clotting time may also be prolonged. The mixing study for the aPTT will correct completely.

Factor XI deficiency alone would not lead to a prolonged mixing study. This condition can be heterogeneous in its bleeding manifestations and occurs most commonly in patients of Ashkenazi Jewish descent.

Lupus inhibitors can sometimes interfere with the coagulation cascade as measured by the aPTT or the PT, causing a prolongation that is not corrected by a mixing study. Although they prolong in vitro coagulation tests, they are associated with an increased risk for venous and arterial thromboembolism, not a bleeding tendency.

KEY POINT

- **Mucocutaneous and multifocal bleeding in the absence of a personal or family bleeding history, a normal prothrombin time, and a prolonged activated partial thromboplastin time that does not correct on mixing studies suggest the presence of acquired hemophilia, due to an acquired autoantibody to factor VIII.**

Bibliography

Barnett B, Kruse-Jarres R, Leissinger CA. Current management of acquired factor VIII inhibitors. Curr Opin Hematol. 2008;15(5):451-455. [PMID: 18695367]

Item 9 Answer: B

Educational Objective: Treat a patient with plasma exchange–associated hypocalcemia.

The most appropriate treatment is intravenous calcium gluconate. This patient's anxiety, vomiting, neurologic instability, and perioral numbness and tingling during plasma exchange are the classic symptoms of hypocalcemia, and, if left untreated, could lead to more severe neurologic and cardiac instability. Citrate, the anticoagulant used in most plasma exchange procedures, can lead to chelation of calcium and subsequent hypocalcemia. Given her symptoms, immediate infusion of intravenous calcium gluconate is warranted.

Intravenous fluids such as 0.9% normal saline would not correct this patient's hypocalcemia-related symptoms but would be helpful if there were associated hypotension.

Diphenhydramine, an antihistamine, would be useful if the patient had developed hives or other allergic symptoms but would not be indicated for her current symptoms.

Epinephrine would be indicated in the setting of anaphylaxis or more severe symptoms of cardiovascular instability but would not be the best option now because it will not reverse the patient's hypocalcemia.

Heparin would be warranted if a pulmonary embolism were suspected, but pulmonary embolism cannot explain her muscle twitching.

KEY POINT

- **Anxiety, vomiting, neurologic instability, and perioral numbness and tingling during plasma exchange are the classic symptoms of hypocalcemia, which requires immediate treatment with calcium gluconate.**

Bibliography

Okafor C, Ward D, Mokrzycki MH, et al. Introduction and overview of therapeutic apheresis. J Clin Apher. 2010;25(5):240-249. [PMID: 20806281]

Item 10 Answer: C

Educational Objective: Diagnose gestational anemia.

Increased plasma volume is most likely responsible for this patient's anemia. Pregnancy is associated with a physiologic anemia. Although red cell mass increases in pregnancy in response to increased levels of erythropoietin, the plasma volume expands to a greater extent, leading to a mild anemia. The resulting increase in red cell mass, with a correspondingly higher increase in plasma volume, leads to the delivery of low-viscosity blood providing oxygen to the developing fetus.

The HELLP (*h*emolysis, *e*levated *l*iver enzymes, and *l*ow *p*latelet count) syndrome is characterized by right upper-quadrant pain; elevated liver enzymes; and preeclampsia, including hypertension, peripheral edema, and proteinuria, most commonly in the third trimester of pregnancy. Patients with the HELLP syndrome have an abnormal peripheral blood smear showing thrombocytopenia and fragmented erythrocytes (schistocytes). This patient does not have hemolysis or other signs or symptoms consistent with the HELLP syndrome.

As in nonpregnant patients, pregnant patients with iron deficiency have a microcytic, hypochromic anemia with low serum iron and ferritin levels and an elevated total iron-binding capacity. Symptoms may include fatigue, lack of sense of well-being, irritability, decreased exercise tolerance, and headaches. Although pregnancy can be associated with iron deficiency, this patient has no signs or symptoms of iron deficiency, with a normal mean corpuscular volume and a normal peripheral smear.

Erythropoietin production does not decrease, but rather increases, during pregnancy. Therefore, a low erythropoietin level would not be responsible for this pregnant patient's anemia in the absence of conditions known to suppress erythropoietin, such as chronic kidney disease.

KEY POINT

- **Anemia in pregnancy predominantly results from a dramatic increase in plasma volume that is proportionally larger than the increase in erythrocyte production.**

Bibliography

Milman N. Prepartum anaemia: prevention and treatment. Ann Hematol. 2008;87(12):949-959. [PMID: 18641987]

Item 11 Answer: C

Educational Objective: Diagnose factor IX deficiency (hemophilia).

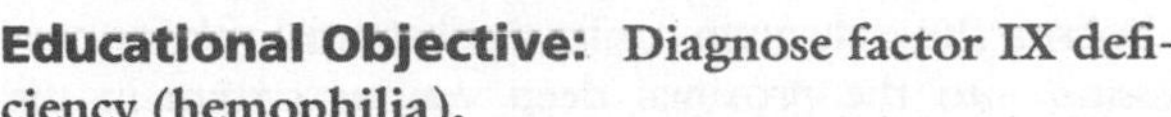

This patient most likely has a factor IX deficiency (hemophilia B). His bleeding history is suggestive of a congenital X-linked bleeding disorder, most likely hemophilia B because of the presentation in adulthood; however, it could be hemophilia A or B because the laboratory studies for the two conditions are indistinguishable. Also suggestive of this disorder are the patient's normal prothrombin time (PT) and prolonged activated partial thromboplastin time (aPTT) that fully corrects on mixing with a 1:1 ratio of normal plasma. Milder cases of hemophilia B may remain undiagnosed until adulthood, but postoperative and traumatic bleeding may be severe. This patient's history of compartment syndrome is a manifestation of a bleeding diathesis. Hemophilia A (factor VIII deficiency) and hemophilia B are X-linked hemorrhagic disorders, with most bleeding episodes occurring in the articular spaces. Soft tissue bleeding is also common. Replacement of the deficient factor is the treatment of choice. Severe hemophilia A and B are characterized by recurrent hemarthroses that result in chronic, crippling degenerative joint disease unless treated prophylactically with factor replacement. Central nervous system hemorrhage is especially hazardous, remaining one of the leading causes of death. Aspirin and NSAIDs are contraindicated in patients with hemophilia.

Patients with an acquired factor VIII inhibitor have a normal PT and a prolonged aPTT, but the mixing study fails to completely correct.

CONT.

Factor V deficiency would be expected to produce prolongation of both the PT and the aPTT, not just the aPTT.

Factor XII deficiency also produces a normal PT and prolonged aPTT but is not associated with bleeding manifestations.

KEY POINT

- **Factor IX deficiency (hemophilia B) is an X-linked hemorrhagic disorder characterized by a normal prothrombin time and prolonged activated partial thromboplastin time that fully corrects with the mixing study.**

Bibliography

Stine KC, Becton DL. Bleeding disorders: when is normal bleeding not normal? J Ark Med Soc. 2009;106(2):40-42. [PMID: 19715248]

Item 12 Answer: C

Educational Objective: Evaluate a patient for venous thromboembolism risk factors.

Standard-intensity warfarin (INR, 2 to 3) for at least 3 months is the most appropriate management of this patient with a triggered episode of venous thromboembolism (VTE). Although distal (calf vein) deep venous thrombosis (DVT) is associated with a low risk for pulmonary embolism, these thrombi confer a substantial risk for progression into the proximal deep venous system in the absence of anticoagulation. In one randomized study, 29% of patients treated with a 5-day course of unfractionated heparin alone developed recurrent VTE compared with none in the group receiving warfarin for 3 months.

This patient has several identifiable risk factors for VTE: recent major orthopedic surgery, recent travel, and factor V Leiden heterozygosity. Major inpatient surgery is associated with a 70-fold increased risk for VTE; ambulatory surgery is associated with a 10-fold increased risk. The risk associated with surgery is greatest in the first few weeks after surgery and declines thereafter, reaching baseline as long as 12 months later. Therefore, this patient's recent orthopedic surgery played a major role in the pathogenesis of his calf vein DVT. In comparison, travel is associated with a modest twofold increased risk for VTE, and factor V Leiden is associated with a fivefold increased risk of VTE. Although factor V Leiden is associated with a significant risk for initial VTE, it is not associated with a significant risk for recurrent VTE (1.5-fold). Consequently, the presence of factor V Leiden in this patient does not mandate prolonged therapy.

Low-intensity warfarin (INR, 1.5-2) for 3 months would not be the optimal choice for this patient's triggered episode of calf vein DVT. Low-intensity warfarin therapy was found to be inferior to standard-intensity warfarin therapy (INR, 2-3) for treatment of patients with idiopathic VTE. Low-intensity therapy was initiated after at least 3 months of standard-intensity therapy (INR, 2-3). Low-intensity warfarin therapy has never been tested for the initial 3 months of VTE treatment.

Life-long warfarin (INR, 2-3) is not the best management approach for this patient with a triggered episode of VTE. The bleeding risks of long-term warfarin (at least 1% to 2% per year) outweigh the risk of recurrence (0.7% per year).

KEY POINT

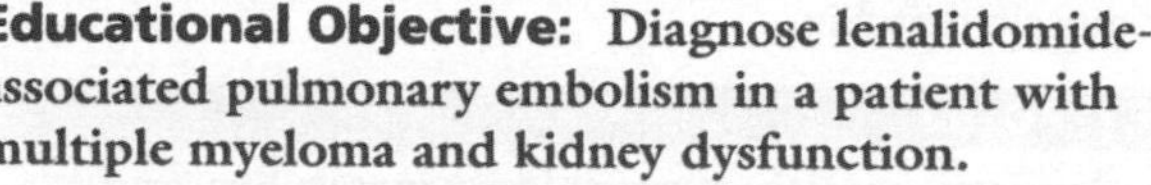

- **Standard intensity warfarin for at least 3 months is the most appropriate management for patients with risk factors for venous thromboembolism.**

Bibliography

Kearon C. Long-term anticoagulation for venous thromboembolism: duration of treatment and management of warfarin therapy. Clin Chest Med. 2010;31(4):719-730. [PMID: 21047578]

Item 13 Answer: D

H

Educational Objective: Diagnose lenalidomide-associated pulmonary embolism in a patient with multiple myeloma and kidney dysfunction.

The most appropriate next step in the diagnostic evaluation is a ventilation-perfusion scan. The patient has a high pretest probability for a pulmonary embolism. Lenalidomide and high-dose dexamethasone treatment in patients with relapsed multiple myeloma is associated with an 8% to 16% risk for venous thromboembolism; the risk is even higher in newly diagnosed patients. Considering this patient's baseline kidney insufficiency, a ventilation-perfusion scan would be the preferred imaging modality.

The risk of thalidomide- or lenalidomide-associated thrombosis is increased when these agents are combined with corticosteroids at high doses, anthracyclines, or multiagent cytotoxic chemotherapy. Other factors that increase the risk for venous thromboembolism in these patients include a previous history of venous thrombosis, hyperviscosity from paraproteinemia, the presence of a central venous catheter, recent surgery, and immobilization. Although the use of prophylactic-dose, low-molecular-weight heparin is appropriate under these circumstances, it does not eliminate the risk for venous thromboembolism. Phase 3 studies evaluating optimal prevention of venous thromboembolism in these patients are lacking.

Patients with multiple myeloma are particularly vulnerable to nephrotoxic agents. The intravenous contrast dye associated with CT angiography of the chest and pulmonary angiography would confer an excessive risk for worsening kidney failure, particularly given the patient's baseline kidney insufficiency and high burden of free λ light chains. High-resolution CT of the chest without contrast would eliminate the risk associated with intravenous contrast dye; however, it would not detect a pulmonary embolism. Furthermore, given the sudden onset of symptoms, the lack of fever, and the absence of crackles on auscultation, pneumonia is a less likely diagnosis.

KEY POINT

- **Lenalidomide in combination with high-dose dexamethasone is associated with an increased risk for venous thromboembolism in patients with multiple myeloma.**

Bibliography

Palumbo A, Rajkumar SV, Dimopoulos MA, et al. Prevention of thalidomide- and lenalidomide-associated thrombosis in myeloma. Leukemia. 2008;22(2):414-423. [PMID: 18094721]

H

Item 14 Answer: D

Educational Objective: Diagnose transfusion-related acute lung injury.

The most likely diagnosis is transfusion-related acute lung injury (TRALI). This patient developed a fever, dyspnea, diffuse pulmonary infiltrates, and hypoxia during a blood transfusion. This presentation is very consistent with TRALI, a reaction caused by antileukocyte antibodies in the donor blood product directed against recipient leukocytes, which then sequester in the lungs, usually during or within 6 hours of a transfusion. TRALI can occur with any blood product, even erythrocytes and platelets, which may have small amounts of plasma. Treatment of TRALI is primarily supportive, and most patients fully recover within days or 1 week.

An acute hemolytic transfusion reaction (AHTR) is most commonly caused by a clerical error leading to ABO incompatibility. Very early in the transfusion, affected patients develop hypotension and disseminated intravascular coagulation, but this patient presented primarily with hypoxia and is therefore unlikely to be experiencing an AHTR.

Febrile nonhemolytic transfusion reactions occur commonly during transfusion and are also characterized by fever. However, a febrile nonhemolytic transfusion reaction would not lead to hypoxia and pulmonary infiltrates.

TRALI can be difficult to distinguish from transfusion-associated circulatory overload. However, transfusion-associated circulatory overload is less likely than TRALI in this patient because she had only received a single unit of packed erythrocytes, had no underlying cardiac disease, and had no jugular venous distention, S_3, or peripheral edema.

KEY POINT

- **Transfusion-related acute lung injury is characterized by hypoxia, and dyspnea, as well as fever and hypotension, occurring during or within hours of a transfusion and resembles noncardiac pulmonary edema.**

Bibliography

Silliman CC, Fung YL, Ball JB, Khan SY. Transfusion-related acute lung injury (TRALI): current concepts and misconceptions. Blood Rev. 2009;23(6):245-255. [PMID: 19699017]

H

Item 15 Answer: A

Educational Objective: Diagnose all-*trans*-retinoic acid–induced differentiation syndrome.

The most likely diagnosis is all-*trans*-retinoic acid (ATRA)–induced differentiation syndrome (retinoic acid syndrome). ATRA is a differentiating agent that interferes with PML/RARα protein function, and, when included as part of induction therapy, has induced sustained remissions and cures in 80% to 90% of patients. The ATRA-induced differentiation syndrome occurs in 25% of patients with acute promyelocytic leukemia (APL) who receive ATRA or arsenic trioxide therapy. The mechanism of action likely results from the release of cytokines or other factors from differentiating promyelocytes, which leads to a capillary leak syndrome. Symptom onset occurs in a bimodal fashion, with 47% of patients presenting within the first week and 25% within the third week of treatment. Patients may have dyspnea, peripheral edema, weight gain, fever, hypotension, and acute kidney injury. Pulmonary infiltrates or pleural or pericardial effusions may also occur. Prompt recognition is crucial because dexamethasone therapy leads to improvement of clinical manifestations.

Heart failure would not explain the patient's fever, acute kidney injury, and absent jugular venous distention and S_3 gallop.

In patients with ATRA-induced differentiation syndrome, pneumonia can be difficult to exclude, and treatment for both entities is often necessary. Because there is physical and radiographic evidence of capillary leak (edema, weight gain, and positive chest radiograph findings), a diagnosis of ATRA-induced differentiation syndrome is favored.

Transfusion-related acute lung injury is associated with fever, dyspnea, and pulmonary infiltrates, but peripheral edema, weight gain, and acute kidney injury would not be expected. Furthermore, the patient has not received blood products within the last 48 hours.

KEY POINT

- **Symptoms and findings of all-*trans*-retinoic acid–induced differentiation syndrome may include dyspnea, peripheral edema, weight gain, fever, hypotension, acute kidney injury, and pleural and pericardial effusions, with onset generally in the first to third week of treatment.**

Bibliography

Montesinos P, Bergua JM, Vellenga E, et al. Differentiation syndrome in patients with acute promyelocytic leukemia treated with all-trans retinoic acid and anthracycline chemotherapy: characteristics, outcome, and prognostic factors. Blood. 2009;113(4):775-783. [PMID: 18945964]

H

Item 16 Answer: D

Educational Objective: Manage a patient with superficial venous thrombophlebitis.

The most appropriate management is to initiate low-molecular-weight heparin and transition the patient to

CONT.

warfarin (INR, 2-3). Superficial venous thrombophlebitis is traditionally managed with NSAIDs or compression stockings. However, recent studies indicate that superficial venous thrombophlebitis shares many similarities with deep venous thrombosis (DVT), including recurrence risk factors (intravenous catheters, thrombophilia, cancer) and the potential to progress and cause DVT and pulmonary embolism. Therefore, serious consideration of conventional anticoagulation therapy should be given to patients with progressive or extensive superficial venous thrombophlebitis. This patient's superficial venous thrombophlebitis has progressed to involve most of the greater saphenous vein and is close to entering the common femoral vein. Therefore, he is at high risk for DVT and pulmonary embolism and requires therapeutic anticoagulation.

Continuation of ibuprofen therapy would not be appropriate because it would be unlikely to prevent progressive thrombosis and possible thromboembolism.

An inferior vena cava filter is not necessary in this patient because he does not have a contraindication to anticoagulation.

Vein ligation may be useful in preventing symptomatic recurrent episodes in a particular target vessel but should not be used for treatment in the setting of progressive superficial venous thrombophlebitis with near involvement of the deep venous system.

KEY POINT

- **Patients with progressive or extensive superficial venous thrombophlebitis may require conventional anticoagulation therapy to avoid involvement of the deep venous system.**

Bibliography

Kitchens CS. How I treat superficial venous thrombosis. Blood. 2011;117(1):39-44. [PMID: 20980677]

H

Item 17 Answer: A

Educational Objective: Diagnose antiphospholipid syndrome.

The most appropriate next diagnostic test is evaluation for the antiphospholipid syndrome. This patient's history of four previous miscarriages and newly diagnosed pulmonary embolism are suggestive of antiphospholipid syndrome (APS). Diagnosis of APS requires the occurrence of objectively documented venous or arterial thromboembolism or pregnancy morbidity (three or more first-trimester miscarriages or one fetal death) and positive laboratory results (dilute Russell viper venom time [dRVVT], anticardiolipin antibody assay, β_2 glycoprotein I antibody assay) on at least two occasions at least 12 weeks apart. The dRVVT is a highly phospholipid-dependent test that is sensitive and specific for detecting antiphospholipid antibodies. Because of the possibility of false-negative and false-positive results, multiple diagnostic tests for APS are necessary. This patient should also receive the anticardiolipin antibody and β_2 glycoprotein I antibody assays as well as the dRVVT. In addition, her prolonged activated partial thromboplastin time (aPTT) should be further evaluated with mixing studies with normal pooled plasma. Abnormal tests should be repeated to confirm the diagnosis in 12 weeks.

Antithrombin deficiency is a potent thrombophilic disorder associated with up to a 20-fold increased risk for VTE with onset early in life and an increased risk for pregnancy morbidity. However, this patient does not have a positive family history for VTE, has had early first-trimester losses, and has a prolonged aPTT, findings compatible with APS but not typical of antithrombin deficiency.

Although factor V Leiden heterozygosity is associated with a fivefold increased risk for venous thromboembolism (VTE) and has been associated with an increased incidence of pregnancy morbidity, it is not associated with first-trimester miscarriages. Additionally, factor V Leiden would not result in an abnormal aPTT.

Methylene tetrahydrofolate reductase (MTHFR) mutations are associated with mild to moderate hyperhomocysteinemia. MTHFR mutations are associated with a modestly increased risk of VTE (1.5 fold) but not with excess pregnancy losses. The patient's personal history is much more compatible with APS than MTHFR mutations.

KEY POINT

- **Diagnosis of the antiphospholipid syndrome requires the occurrence of objectively documented venous or arterial thromboembolism or pregnancy morbidity (three or more first-trimester miscarriages or one fetal death) and positive laboratory results (dilute Russell viper venom time, anticardiolipin antibody assay, β_2 glycoprotein I antibody assay) on at least two occasions at least 12 weeks apart.**

Bibliography

Baker WF Jr, Bick RL. The clinical spectrum of antiphospholipid syndrome. Hematol Oncol Clin North Am. 2008;22(1):33-52. [PMID: 18207064]

Item 18 Answer: C

Educational Objective: Treat a pregnant patient with a pulmonary embolism.

The next step in management of this pregnant patient with a deep venous thrombosis (DVT) and presumed pulmonary embolism is initiation of low-molecular-weight heparin (LMWH), with continuation of anticoagulation until 6 weeks postpartum.

Approximately 50% of patients with a pulmonary embolism have a DVT on imaging studies. If the duplex ultrasound is positive, performing a CT angiography would not be needed, thus avoiding exposure of the patient and her fetus to unnecessary radiation because the treatment of DVT and PE are the same.

The patient will remain at risk for recurrent venous thromboembolism (VTE) until 6 weeks postpartum. Therefore, anticoagulation therapy should not continue only for 6 months, which would result in anticoagulation cessation during the patient's third trimester, or simply to the end of pregnancy.

Pregnancy does not constitute a contraindication to anticoagulation with heparin. Therefore, placement of an inferior vena cava filter is not necessary.

Pregnancy is a contraindication to warfarin therapy because warfarin is teratogenic.

KEY POINT

- **The duration of anticoagulation for venous thromboembolism in a pregnant patient is at least 6 months and should extend 6 weeks beyond parturition.**

Bibliography

Chunilal SD, Bates SM. Venous thromboembolism in pregnancy: diagnosis, management and prevention. Thromb Haemost. 2009;101(3):428-438. [PMID: 19277402]

Item 19 Answer: B

Educational Objective: Diagnose iron deficiency in a patient with anisopoikilocytosis.

The most likely diagnosis is iron deficiency. This patient's peripheral smear is remarkable for variations in erythrocyte size and shape (anisopoikilocytosis) and increased central pallor. Patients with mild iron deficiency may report fatigue, irritability, decreased exercise tolerance, and headaches before they become anemic. This patient's clinical manifestations, including extreme fatigue, dyspnea on exertion, and chest pain, are symptoms of decreased oxygen-carrying capacity of the blood. The peripheral blood smear findings and complete blood count showing extreme anisopoikilocytosis and microcytosis are consistent with iron deficiency. Thrombocytosis is noted frequently in patients with iron deficiency.

In patients with glucose-6-phosphate dehydrogenase (G6PD) deficiency, blister (or "bite") cells, which are characterized by eccentrically located hemoglobin confined to one side of the cell, are present on the peripheral blood smear. In contrast to iron deficiency, the mean corpuscular volume is often normal or slightly increased in G6PD deficiency because of the reticulocytosis occurring in patients with G6PD-mediated hemolysis.

Patients with myelofibrosis typically have signs and symptoms of anemia plus night sweats and weight loss and exhibit a leukoerythroblastic picture, including nucleated erythrocytes and a left shift in the leukocyte lineage. Additionally, myelofibrosis is typically associated with teardrop cells and megathrombocytes, which are not present on this patient's peripheral blood smear.

Patients with thrombotic thrombocytopenic purpura (TTP) have fragmented erythrocytes (schistocytes) and low platelet counts, two features not found in this patient. In addition, patients with TTP typically have one or two additional findings, including acute kidney injury, mental status changes, and ecchymosis.

KEY POINT

- **Symptoms and signs demonstrating decreased oxygen-carrying capacity of the blood as well as laboratory findings showing anisopoikilocytosis and microcytosis are consistent with iron deficiency.**

Bibliography

Jain S, Kamat D. Evaluation of microcytic anemia. Clin Pediatr. 2009;48:7-13. [PMID: 18832550]

Item 20 Answer: A

Educational Objective: Perform thrombophilic screening in a patient with idiopathic venous thromboembolism.

Testing this patient for a thrombophilic disorder should take place 2 to 4 weeks after completion of warfarin therapy. Laboratory testing for thrombophilia is fraught with great confusion and misunderstanding concerning the use of assays. Expert opinion is divided regarding the benefit of screening for thrombophilic disorders. Those in favor of screening suggest that tests should be performed only in patients with unusual or idiopathic events or in those whose events occurred at a young age. If testing is performed, it should not be done in the setting of an acute thrombotic event but rather weeks or months after the event has occurred and when anticoagulant therapy has been discontinued because active thrombosis may alter the level of some proteins. Therefore, testing on blood obtained in the hospital prior to the initiation of warfarin will not be helpful if those levels are low.

Warfarin reduces protein C and protein S activity with a lesser decline in immunologic levels. Warfarin can rarely increase antithrombin levels in patients with antithrombin deficiency into the normal range. Therefore, testing for thrombophilic disorders should not be performed when the patient is taking warfarin.

Advocates for thrombophilic screening base their recommendations on whether patients are determined to be strongly or weakly thrombophilic; screening is appropriate in the former group, whereas it may not be cost-effective in the latter group. Patients who are considered strongly thrombophilic will often have had their first idiopathic venous thrombosis before 50 years of age, may have a history of recurrent thrombotic episodes, and may have first-degree relatives in whom a documented thromboembolism has occurred before the age of 50 years. Weakly thrombophilic patients with a venous thromboembolism (VTE) have none, or perhaps one, of these characteristics. This patient had an idiopathic VTE at a young age and has a first-degree relative

CONT.

who had a VTE at a young age; some experts would screen this patient for a thrombophilic disorder.

In patients who undergo screening for thrombophilic disorders, testing typically includes assays for activated protein C resistance, factor V Leiden, the prothrombin gene mutation, antiphospholipid antibodies, a lupus inhibitor, antithrombin deficiency, protein C deficiency, and protein S deficiency.

KEY POINT

- **If screening for thrombophilic disorders is undertaken, it should be performed after an acute thrombotic event and several weeks following discontinuation of warfarin.**

Bibliography

Favaloro EJ, McDonald D, Lippi G. Laboratory investigation of thrombophilia: the good, the bad, and the ugly. Semin Thromb Hemost. 2009;35(7):695-710. [PMID: 20013536]

Item 21 Answer: E

Educational Objective: **Diagnose probable von Willebrand disease.**

This patient's personal and family history of mucocutaneous bleeding is suggestive of von Willebrand disease (vWD). Although the patient's von Willebrand factor (vWF) levels are technically in the normal range, a diagnosis of vWD cannot be excluded because she is taking estrogen-containing oral contraceptive pills (OCPs). Levels of vWF fluctuate, increasing in response to estrogens, stress, exercise, inflammation, and bleeding, and diagnosis is often difficult to establish, particularly in patients with mild disease. A patient such as this one, with a personal and family history of mucocutaneous bleeding who has borderline levels of vWF while taking OCPs, can be considered to have "possible vWD." Making a definitive diagnosis of vWD may require testing of affected family members or requesting the patient discontinue OCPs and remeasuring vWF levels 4 to 6 weeks later.

Anovulatory cycles are a common cause of menorrhagia in girls just past menarche but would not be associated with borderline-low levels of vWF, nor would they be found in the patient's mother.

Factor XI deficiency can be associated with a personal and family history of mucocutaneous bleeding, but the activated partial thromboplastin time (aPTT) would be expected to be prolonged.

Hemophilia A is an X-linked disorder. Women can be affected under rare circumstances (for example, in homozygotes, usually in cases of consanguineous parents; in women with Turner syndrome; and in lyonized carriers of factor VIII deficiency). However, in these cases, the factor VIII level would be expected to be low and the aPTT prolonged.

Uterine fibroid tumors are rare in this age group and would be even less likely to affect the patient's 16-year-old sister.

KEY POINT

- **Patients with a personal and family history of mucocutaneous bleeding who have borderline-low levels of von Willebrand factor while taking oral contraceptive pills have possible von Willebrand disease.**

Bibliography

Abildgaard CF, Suzuki Z, Harrison J, Jefcoat K, Zimmerman TS. Serial studies in von Willebrand's disease: variability versus "variants". Blood. 1980;56(4):712-716. [PMID: 6774790]

Item 22 Answer: D

Educational Objective: **Manage acquired hemophilia.**

This patient requires recombinant activated factor VIIa (rVIIa). She had an uncomplicated vaginal delivery 24 hours ago and has no bleeding history and a prolonged activated partial thromboplastin time (aPTT) that failed to fully correct on 1:1 mixing with normal plasma. This suggests the presence of an acquired inhibitor, most likely to factor VIII, which can develop in the postpartum setting. rVIIa is approved for treating bleeding episodes in patients with acquired factor VIII inhibitors. rVIIa acts to bypass the need for factor VIII by binding to the surface of activated platelets, where it can generate factor Xa, leading to the production of a burst of thrombin and the formation of fibrin.

Disseminated intravascular coagulation (DIC) is characterized by a microangiopathic hemolytic anemia, low platelet levels, a prolonged prothrombin time, a low or decreasing fibrinogen level, and an elevated D-dimer level. This patient's normal prothrombin time, platelet count, and fibrinogen level make DIC less likely. Consequently, fresh frozen plasma and cryoprecipitate are not indicated.

Desmopressin is indicated in patients with von Willebrand disease (vWD), which can cause postpartum hemorrhage. However, this patient's lack of history of menorrhagia and absence of bleeding with tonsillectomy make vWD less likely; therefore, desmopressin is unlikely to be of benefit. Additionally, although desmopressin may be helpful in patients with acquired hemophilia who have low-titer inhibitor levels and mild mucocutaneous bleeding, it would be unlikely to provide significant benefit in patients with this degree of hemorrhage and aPTT prolongation.

KEY POINT

- **Recombinant activated factor VIIa is approved for treating bleeding episodes in patients with acquired factor VIII inhibitors.**

Bibliography

Barnett B, Kruse-Jarres R, Leissinger CA. Current management of acquired factor VIII inhibitors. Curr Opin Hematol. 2008;15(5):451-455. [PMID: 18695367]

Item 23 Answer: E

Educational Objective: **Manage a patient with immune thrombocytopenic purpura.**

This patient should have a repeat complete blood count in 1 week. She has new-onset thrombocytopenia with an otherwise normal complete blood count. The lack of clinical manifestations or systemic symptoms, normal physical examination including absence of splenomegaly, and the normal peripheral blood smear provide no clues to an underlying disorder. She is not taking any medication known to cause thrombocytopenia. She most likely has immune thrombocytopenic purpura (ITP). ITP is a diagnosis of exclusion and is often discovered incidentally, but patients may have clinical signs or symptoms of mild to severe bleeding or hemorrhage in the setting of an otherwise normal blood count and the absence of organ dysfunction. ITP can be drug induced or part of a broader illness with abnormal immune regulation. Asymptomatic patients without evidence of bleeding and platelet counts above 30,000 to 40,000/µL (30-40 × 10^9/L) have less than a 15% chance of developing more severe thrombocytopenia requiring treatment. The most appropriate course of action is to counsel the patient on potential bleeding symptoms and repeat the complete blood count at a designated interval such as 1 week.

In adult patients with ITP, therapy may be required for those with platelet counts lower than 30,000 to 40,000/µL (30-40 × 10^9/L) or with bleeding. Given her lack of bleeding symptoms and platelet count of greater than 50,000/µL (50 × 10^9/L), she does not require corticosteroid or thrombopoietin-mimetic agent therapy.

Antibody testing in patients with suspected ITP commonly results in false-negative and false-positive results. Consequently, antiplatelet antibody testing is found to have little predictive value in the diagnosis of ITP and is not recommended.

The patient's complete blood count is normal except for thrombocytopenia, which makes bone marrow dysfunction less likely; therefore, bone marrow biopsy is not indicated.

KEY POINT

- **Asymptomatic patients with immune thrombocytopenic purpura without evidence of bleeding and platelet counts above 30,000 to 40,000/µL (30-40 × 10^9/L) have a very low incidence of developing more severe thrombocytopenia requiring treatment.**

Bibliography

Provan D, Stasi R, Newland AC, et al. International consensus report on the investigation and management of primary immune thrombocytopenia. Blood. 2010;115(2):168-186. [PMID: 19846889]

Item 24 Answer: C

Educational Objective: **Manage a patient with a history of idiopathic venous thromboembolism after hospital discharge.**

The most appropriate management is administration of low-molecular-weight heparin (LMWH) and an increased warfarin dosage. In addition, the INR should be rechecked in 3 to 5 days. In the first month after an episode of venous thromboembolism (VTE), the recurrence risk in the absence of anticoagulation is 40%. Therefore, patients who have subtherapeutic INR values during this period are at increased risk for recurrent VTE and should be treated with LMWH and increased dosages of warfarin until the INR returns to the therapeutic range. Ideally, this should be confirmed by two INR determinations at least 24 hours apart. With an INR of 1.2, a warfarin dose increase of 10% to 20% would be appropriate. It takes at least 3 days for the dose increase to begin to take effect, whereas the complete impact of a dose change can take as long as 7 to 10 days. Rechecking the INR in 3 to 5 days allows enough time for the patient to respond to the change in dose and to determine whether additional dose increases may be necessary.

Management of INR values that are out-of-range differs for patients treated chronically with warfarin who have had stable therapeutic levels. If a single INR is less than or equal to 0.5 below the desired therapeutic level, it is recommended that the current dose be continued and that the INR be rechecked in 1-2 weeks without bridging LMWH. This would not be appropriate in this patient whose initial therapeutic dose has not been established following his acute thromboembolic event.

Increasing the warfarin dosage to 7.5 mg/d or to 10 mg/d would represent a dose increase of 50% and 100%, respectively, which is excessive and would likely result in a supratherapeutic INR. Furthermore, without concomitant coverage with LMWH, the patient would be at increased risk for recurrent thrombosis.

KEY POINT

- **In the first month following a thromboembolic episode, patients who have subtherapeutic INR values should be treated with low-molecular-weight heparin and a warfarin dose adjustment until the INR returns to the therapeutic range.**

Bibliography

Douketis JD, Spyropoulos AC, Spencer FA, et al; American College of Chest Physicians. Perioperative management of antithrombotic therapy: Antithrombotic Therapy and Prevention of Thrombosis, 9th ed: American College of Chest Physicians Evidence-Based Clinical Practice Guidelines. Chest. 2012;141(2 Suppl):e326S-330S. [PMID: 22315266]

Item 25 Answer: B

Educational Objective: **Manage secondary erythrocytosis.**

This patient requires a sleep study to diagnose obstructive sleep apnea and nocturnal oxygen desaturation as a cause of secondary erythrocytosis. The diagnosis of secondary erythrocytosis is suggested by the elevated hemoglobin concentration and elevated erythropoietin level. In patients with polycythemia vera (PV), the erythropoietin level is suppressed. The most common cause of secondary erythrocytosis is hypoxic pulmonary disease. However, this patient's oxygen saturation is normal at rest and following modest exertion. Nocturnal oxygen desaturation due to obstructive sleep apnea is also a cause of secondary erythrocytosis, and this diagnosis is suggested by his snoring, obesity, and increased neck size, as well as his witnessed apneic episodes. If obstructive sleep apnea is confirmed by polysomnography, the patient's management would include continuous positive airway pressure.

PV is characterized by nonspecific symptoms including tinnitus, blurred vision, headache, and more specific symptoms including generalized pruritus that often worsens after bathing, erythromelalgia (a burning sensation in the palms and soles possibly caused by platelet activation), and splenomegaly, none of which are present in this patient. In addition, his leukocyte and platelet counts are not elevated as they often are in PV, and his elevated erythropoietin level essentially excludes PV. Treatment of PV is directed toward reducing the red blood cell mass and preventing thrombosis. Therapeutic phlebotomy and low-dose aspirin is the primary therapy for most patients. Hydroxyurea is often used in older symptomatic patients whose disorder cannot be controlled with phlebotomy and aspirin alone. Because this patient does not have PV, phlebotomy, low-dose aspirin, and hydroxyurea are not indicated.

An increased number of megakaryocytes and a hypercellular bone marrow are characteristic of PV, but bone marrow findings are not part of the Polycythemia Vera Study Group diagnostic criteria. Furthermore, although a hypercellular bone marrow is likely in a patient with secondary erythrocytosis, this finding does not establish the cause of the condition.

KEY POINT

- **In patients with confirmed erythrocytosis, an elevated serum erythropoietin level helps exclude polycythemia vera and suggests the presence of secondary erythrocytosis.**

Bibliography

Patnaik MM, Tefferi A. The complete evaluation of erythrocytosis: congenital and acquired. Leukemia. 2009;23(5):834-844. [PMID: 19295544]

Item 26 Answer: A

Educational Objective: Diagnose inflammatory anemia in a patient with systemic lupus erythematosus.

The patient has inflammatory anemia. Inflammatory anemia typically results in mild to moderate anemia, with a hemoglobin level usually greater than 8 g/dL (80 g/L). This type of anemia is initially normocytic and normochromic but can become hypochromic and microcytic over time. The reticulocyte count is typically low in inflammatory anemia. Inflammatory anemia is the result of elevated hepcidin levels that develop in response to inflammatory cytokines, including interleukin-1, interleukin-6, and interferon. Hepcidin decreases iron absorption from the gut and the release of iron from macrophages by causing internalization and proteolysis of the membrane iron pore, ferroportin. Patients with inflammatory anemia typically have normal or low serum iron levels. The peripheral blood smear may be normal or may show microcytic hypochromic erythrocytes as in iron deficiency; however, compared with patients with iron deficiency, patients with inflammatory anemia have a low total iron-binding capacity and elevated serum ferritin level. Inflammatory anemia usually does not require specific therapy. Importantly, iron replacement is not necessary in inflammatory anemia and will not lead to improvement in erythropoiesis. Treating the underlying inflammatory disorder in patients with inflammatory anemia can improve the anemia itself. Chronic infections such as tuberculosis or osteomyelitis, malignancies, and collagen vascular diseases are associated with inflammatory anemia. This patient has systemic lupus erythematosus (SLE). Although microangiopathic hemolytic anemia and warm antibody-mediated hemolysis can occur in the setting of SLE, the peripheral blood smear in these conditions would show schistocytes and microspherocytes, respectively.

KEY POINT

- **Patients with inflammatory anemia typically have normal or low serum iron levels, a low total iron-binding capacity and elevated serum ferritin level, and normal findings or microcytic hypochromic erythrocytes on the peripheral blood smear.**

Bibliography

Cheng PP, Jiao XY, Wang XH, Lin JH, Cai YM. Hepcidin expression in anemia of chronic disease and concomitant iron-deficiency anemia. Clin Exp Med. 2011;11(1)33-42. [PMID: 20499129]

Item 27 Answer: D

Educational Objective: Treat a patient with mildly symptomatic hereditary spherocytosis.

The most appropriate treatment for this patient is supportive care. The clinical course of patients with hereditary spherocytosis varies widely from severe symptomatic anemia to mild asymptomatic disease. Affected patients often have a family history of anemia (most cases transmitted as an autosomal dominant disorder), splenomegaly, may develop leg ulcers and pigmented gallstones secondary to chronic hemolysis, and have spherocytes on the peripheral blood smear. Although this patient presents with fatigue, she is able to attend college full time, work part time, and run twice weekly. In addition, she has very mild anemia, which has been relatively stable over the past 3 years. Supportive care is indicated and should include close clinical follow-up, maintenance of immunizations, and continued folic acid supplementation.

The role of prophylactic cholecystectomy in patients with hereditary spherocytosis is controversial in patients with gallstones but is not indicated in patients without cholelithiasis. In patients with known gallstones who are undergoing splenectomy, prophylactic cholecystectomy should be considered.

Prednisone may be effective in treating autoimmune hemolytic anemia but would provide no benefit in patients with hereditary spherocytosis.

Patients with more severe disease leading to symptomatic anemia, growth retardation, skeletal changes, painful splenomegaly, or extramedullary hematopoietic tumors respond very well to splenectomy, with improvement in anemia, but it is not indicated in this patient.

KEY POINT

- **Patients with hereditary spherocytosis with mild asymptomatic disease should receive supportive care consisting of close clinical follow-up, maintenance of immunizations, and continued folic acid supplementation.**

Bibliography

Schilling RF. Risks and benefits of splenectomy versus no splenectomy for hereditary spherocytosis—a personal view. Br J Haematol. 2009;145(6):728-732. [PMID: 19388926]

Item 28 Answer: A

Educational Objective: Treat an older patient with cobalamin deficiency.

The most appropriate treatment in this patient is oral cobalamin. This patient has cobalamin deficiency as evidenced by elevations in homocysteine and cobalamin, with a typical peripheral blood smear. Peripheral blood smear findings in cobalamin deficiency typically show oval macrocytes, and, sometimes, basophilic stippling; hypersegmented neutrophils with more than five lobes may also be found and are highly specific for megaloblastic anemia. Because cobalamin deficiency leads to ineffective hematopoiesis, elevations in serum lactate dehydrogenase and total bilirubin levels can occur. Early neurologic complications include lack of vibratory sense and paresthesias and may progress to loss of position sense, weakness, spasticity, paraplegia, and bladder incontinence. The most common cause of cobalamin deficiency is malabsorption, especially in older patients. Sometimes, patients can have serum cobalamin levels in the low-normal range but can have true cobalamin deficiency that is detected by elevations in homocysteine and methylmalonic acid levels. Management of cobalamin deficiency is best accomplished by high-dose oral supplementation (1000 to 2000 micrograms daily), which is less expensive and easier to administer than parenteral replacement and just as effective.

Folate deficiency is characterized by a peripheral blood smear identical to that of cobalamin deficiency; however, in patients with folate deficiency, only the serum homocysteine level is elevated. Additionally, folate deficiency is not associated with neurologic findings. Folate replacement in patients with cobalamin deficiency can improve anemia but does not suspend or reverse the neurologic complications. Folate is typically replaced orally when replacement is needed.

KEY POINT

- **Oral cobalamin replacement is the appropriate treatment of cobalamin deficiency.**

Bibliography

Andrès E, Vogel T, Federici L, Zimmer J, Kaltenbach G. Update on oral cyanocobalamin (vitamin B12) treatment in elderly patients. Drugs Aging. 2008;25(11):927-932. [PMID: 18947260]

Item 29 Answer: C

Educational Objective: Treat a patient with acute venous thromboembolism.

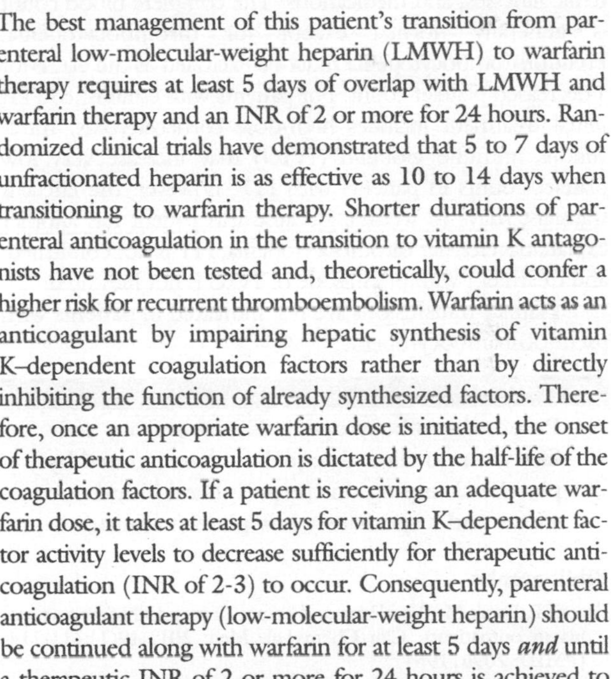

The best management of this patient's transition from parenteral low-molecular-weight heparin (LMWH) to warfarin therapy requires at least 5 days of overlap with LMWH and warfarin therapy and an INR of 2 or more for 24 hours. Randomized clinical trials have demonstrated that 5 to 7 days of unfractionated heparin is as effective as 10 to 14 days when transitioning to warfarin therapy. Shorter durations of parenteral anticoagulation in the transition to vitamin K antagonists have not been tested and, theoretically, could confer a higher risk for recurrent thromboembolism. Warfarin acts as an anticoagulant by impairing hepatic synthesis of vitamin K–dependent coagulation factors rather than by directly inhibiting the function of already synthesized factors. Therefore, once an appropriate warfarin dose is initiated, the onset of therapeutic anticoagulation is dictated by the half-life of the coagulation factors. If a patient is receiving an adequate warfarin dose, it takes at least 5 days for vitamin K–dependent factor activity levels to decrease sufficiently for therapeutic anticoagulation (INR of 2-3) to occur. Consequently, parenteral anticoagulant therapy (low-molecular-weight heparin) should be continued along with warfarin for at least 5 days *and* until a therapeutic INR of 2 or more for 24 hours is achieved to avoid an increased risk for recurrent thromboembolism.

KEY POINT

- **In patients with acute venous thromboembolism, parenteral anticoagulation should be administered concomitantly with warfarin for at least 5 days and until an INR of 2 or more has been achieved for 24 hours.**

Bibliography

Kearon C, Akl EA, Comerota AJ, Prandoni P, et al. Antithrombotic therapy for VTE disease: Antithrombotic Therapy and Prevention of Thrombosis, 9th ed: American College of Chest Physicians

Evidence-Based Clinical Practice Guidelines. Chest. 2012;141(2 Suppl):e419S-494S. [PMID: 22315268]

Item 30 Answer: D

Educational Objective: Manage a patient with pseudothrombocytopenia.

The patient's peripheral blood smear shows platelet clumping, which suggests pseudothrombocytopenia. Pseudothrombocytopenia is a laboratory artifact in which platelets drawn into an ethylenediaminetetraacetic acid (EDTA)-anticoagulated test tube clump and fail to be counted accurately by the automated counter, resulting in a spuriously low platelet count. This patient's thrombocytopenia is therefore a laboratory artifact and requires no therapy. Pseudothrombocytopenia can be confirmed when the platelet count normalizes after the count is repeated in a tube containing citrate or heparin as the anticoagulant.

Immune thrombocytopenic purpura (ITP) is a relatively common cause of thrombocytopenia. The diagnosis is based on excluding other causes of thrombocytopenia, other systemic illnesses, and medications. The complete blood count is generally normal except for thrombocytopenia. Pseudothrombocytopenia must be excluded as the cause for a decreased platelet count. For patients with established ITP, initial treatment includes high-dose corticosteroids. Intravenous immune globulin (IVIG) may increase very low platelet counts in patients with ITP; however, the effect is transient (days to weeks). Because this patient has another explanation for her thrombocytopenia, ITP is not confirmed, and treatment with prednisone or IVIG is not indicated.

Platelet transfusions are not indicated in patients with pseudothrombocytopenia.

KEY POINT

- **Pseudothrombocytopenia is a laboratory artifact with no clinical sequelae, characterized by platelet clumping on the peripheral blood smear and a spuriously low platelet count.**

Bibliography

Froom P, Barak M. Prevalence and course of pseudothrombocytopenia in outpatients. Clin Chem Lab Med. 2011;49(1):111-114. [PMID: 20961195]

Item 31 Answer: D

Educational Objective: Diagnose β-thalassemia trait using erythrocyte count.

The most likely diagnosis is β-thalassemia trait. β-Thalassemia is caused by various abnormalities in the β-gene complex. Decreased β-chain synthesis leads to impaired production of hemoglobin A ($\alpha_2\beta 2$) and resultant increased synthesis of hemoglobin A^2 ($\alpha_2\delta 2$) or hemoglobin F ($\alpha_2\gamma 2$). Patients with mildly decreased expression of a single β gene have β-thalassemia trait (β+) and present with mild anemia, microcytosis, hypochromia, and target cells. Microcytic anemia associated with a normal or slightly increased erythrocyte count is characteristic of β-thalassemia. The Mentzer index is a ratio of the mean corpuscular volume (MCV) in fluid liters divided by the erythrocyte count. Values less than 13 are associated with β-thalassemia.

Hereditary spherocytosis is characterized by a normal to increased MCV depending on the degree of erythrocytosis and erythrocytes on peripheral blood smear that lack the normal central pallor.

Patients with iron deficiency may note fatigue, lack of sense of well-being, irritability, decreased exercise tolerance, and headaches, which may appear before symptoms of overt anemia occur. They also typically have reduced erythrocyte counts and microcytic cells, leading to an index greater than 13. These findings are not consistent with those in this patient.

Sideroblastic anemia is characterized by a decreased erythrocyte count caused by ineffective erythropoiesis and hypochromic normocytic or macrocytic erythrocytes with basophilic stippling that stain positive for iron. This is not consistent with this patient's normal (or increased) erythrocyte count.

KEY POINT

- **Microcytic anemia associated with an abnormal or slightly increased erythrocyte count is characteristic of β-thalassemia.**

Bibliography

Mentzer WC Jr. Differentiation of iron deficiency from thalassaemia trait. Lancet. 1973;1(7808):882. [PMID: 4123424]

Item 32 Answer: B

Educational Objective: Diagnose chronic myeloid leukemia.

The most appropriate next test to establish the diagnosis of chronic myeloid leukemia (CML) is the fluorescence in situ hybridization (FISH) assay for t(9;22). This patient's hematologic findings are strongly suggestive of a myeloproliferative disorder versus a leukemoid reaction. Given her symptoms, including fatigue, night sweats, weight loss, and early satiety, and basophilia on the peripheral blood smear, CML is likely. FISH testing of the peripheral blood will detect CML in virtually all patients, including those harboring cryptic, or silent, (9;22) translocations that might be missed by conventional cytogenetic testing.

Flow cytometry of the peripheral blood would be useful if a hematologic malignancy characterized by a homogeneous population of cells (acute lymphoblastic leukemia, chronic lymphocytic leukemia, non-Hodgkin lymphoma, or acute myeloid leukemia) were suspected; however, the cells in the peripheral blood of patients with CML are at various stages of myelopoiesis and do not express aberrant cell surface markers, rendering flow cytometry of limited utility.

A heterophile antibody test would be indicated in the diagnosis of infectious mononucleosis, which can be associated with fever, fatigue, and splenomegaly. However, the leukocytosis associated with mononucleosis is caused by an increase in atypical reactive lymphocytes. In addition, other clinical features of mononucleosis, such as pharyngitis and lymphadenopathy, would be present.

The *JAK2* mutation is found in 95% of patients with polycythemia vera and 50% to 60% of patients with essential thrombocythemia and primary myelofibrosis. However, this patient's absence of erythrocytosis and thrombocytosis argues against a diagnosis of polycythemia vera or essential thrombocythemia. In addition, primary myelofibrosis would typically be associated with a leukoerythroblastic peripheral blood smear characterized by nucleated and tear drop-shaped erythrocytes.

KEY POINT

- **Establishing the diagnosis of chronic myeloid leukemia in patients with compatible symptoms and findings can be done by fluorescence in situ hybridization assay for t(9;22).**

Bibliography

Le Gouill S, Talmant P, Milpied N, et al. Fluorescence in situ hybridization on peripheral-blood specimens is a reliable method to evaluate cytogenetic response in chronic myeloid leukemia. J Clin Oncol. 2000;18(7):1533-1538. [PMID: 10735902]

Item 33 Answer: C

Educational Objective: Diagnose symptomatic multiple myeloma.

The most appropriate management is kidney biopsy. This patient has multiple myeloma by definition because he has 10% or more clonal plasma cells on bone marrow biopsy. However, a diagnosis of symptomatic myeloma requires evidence of end-organ damage (defined by the presence of hypercalcemia, kidney dysfunction, anemia, and/or bone disease) ***related to the underlying myeloma***. The distinction between an asymptomatic and symptomatic myeloma is critical because close observation would be appropriate in the former case versus prompt initiation of chemotherapy in the latter. This patient has two potential explanations for worsening kidney function: diabetic nephropathy and myeloma-related kidney disease (myeloma cast nephropathy). A kidney biopsy will allow distinction between these two possibilities and help guide appropriate therapy.

An abdominal fat pad aspirate would be a noninvasive way to evaluate for AL amyloidosis, but this patient does not have nephrotic-range proteinuria or other manifestations of this disease, which could include a peripheral sensorimotor neuropathy, autonomic neuropathy, carpal tunnel syndrome, periorbital purpura, diarrhea and malabsorption, macroglossia, and heart failure.

Chemotherapy would not be appropriate until kidney biopsy results determine whether the patient's myeloma is symptomatic.

A follow-up determination of the M-protein level in 12 months would be appropriate for a patient with established monoclonal gammopathy of unknown significance, which is defined as less than 10% clonal plasma cells on a bone marrow aspirate and biopsy, an M protein level of less than 3 g/dL, and no evidence of end-organ damage related to the underlying plasma cell dyscrasia. However, this patient may have symptomatic myeloma and requires further evaluation.

KEY POINT

- **To establish a diagnosis of symptomatic multiple myeloma, evidence of myeloma-related end-organ damage (defined by the presence of hypercalcemia, kidney dysfunction, anemia, and/or bone disease) is required.**

Bibliography

International Myeloma Working Group. Criteria for the classification of monoclonal gammopathies, multiple myeloma and related disorders: a report of the International Myeloma Working Group. Br J Haematol. 2003;121(5):749-757. [PMID: 12780789]

Item 34 Answer: C

Educational Objective: Predict the laboratory evaluation for a patient with venous thromboembolism associated with pregnancy and acquired protein S deficiency.

The most likely laboratory findings in this pregnant patient with no family or personal history of thrombophlebitis are decreased protein S activity, decreased free protein S antigen, and normal total protein S antigen. Pregnancy is associated with a dramatic increase in factor VIII activity, von Willebrand factor, and C4b binding protein. Protein S exists in the plasma in two forms, an unbound free form that is more functionally active and a bound and less functionally active protein that circulates in a complex with C4b binding protein. During pregnancy, the concentration of C4b binding protein rises, peaking in the third trimester. This rise drives the equilibrium between bound and free protein S toward an increasing proportion of the bound form of protein S, resulting in a reduction in protein S activity. This temporal reduction in protein S activity contributes to the hypercoagulable state of pregnancy. Congenital protein S deficiency is most commonly caused by mutations in the protein S gene or regulatory elements that reduce protein S synthesis, producing equivalent reductions in protein S antigen and activity. Although not all patients with inherited thrombophilia have a positive family history, congenital protein S deficiency is relatively rare.

This patient is pregnant and is therefore more likely to have an acquired, rather than a congenital, protein S deficiency. Other conditions that may result in a temporary decline in protein S activity include acute thrombosis, warfarin therapy, vitamin K deficiency, and estrogen therapy. In practice, screening for protein S deficiency is not routinely performed because results are unlikely to alter treatment recommendations and patient outcomes. If it is clinically important to screen for thrombophilic disorders, for example, in patients with a strong family and personal history of thrombosis, protein S activity and antigen levels should be measured 4 to 6 weeks after delivery or 4 weeks following cessation of warfarin therapy in nonpregnant patients.

KEY POINT

- **Acute thrombosis, warfarin therapy, and pregnancy can cause transient declines in functional protein S levels.**

Bibliography

ten Kate MK, van der Meer J. Protein S deficiency: a clinical perspective. Haemophilia. 2008;14(6):1222-1228. [PMID: 18479427]

H

Item 35 Answer: A

Educational Objective: Diagnose aplastic crisis in a patient with sickle cell anemia.

The most likely diagnosis is aplastic crisis. This patient with sickle cell anemia has an acute worsening of his chronic anemia. His recent viral syndrome, which presented with fever and arthralgia, is consistent with parvovirus B19 infection. Aplastic crisis can occur when patients with chronic hemolytic anemia and shortened erythrocyte survival are infected with parvovirus B19, which leads to suppression of erythrocyte production. His recent contact with a sick cousin and the very low reticulocyte count are also highly suggestive of parvovirus B19 infection. Confirmation may be obtained by demonstrating IgM antibodies against parvovirus B19 or polymerase chain reaction studies detecting parvovirus B19 DNA.

Hyperhemolytic crisis is characterized by a sudden worsening of sickle cell anemia with reticulocytosis. This complication is rare, and its cause is unknown.

Megaloblastic crisis refers to an acquired anemia occurring in patients with increased folate demands such as those with chronic hemolysis, and rarely, pregnant patients, children with accelerated growth, or the elderly. Although a low reticulocyte count may be consistent with a megaloblastic crisis, this condition would be unlikely to occur so acutely after a viral illness and would be very unlikely in a patient who takes chronic folic acid replacement.

Splenic sequestration crisis is the result of splenic vasoocclusion and splenic pooling of erythrocytes, causing a rapid drop in hemoglobin concentration, reticulocytosis, and a rapidly enlarging spleen. Splenic sequestration is also often accompanied by left upper-quadrant pain and splenomegaly and would not be characterized by a very low reticulocyte count.

KEY POINT

- **Aplastic crisis can occur when patients with chronic hemolytic anemia and shortened erythrocyte survival are infected with parvovirus B19, which leads to suppression of erythrocyte production.**

Bibliography

Servey JT, Reamy BV, Hodge J. Clinical presentations of parvovirus B19 infection. Am Fam Physician. 2007;75(3):373-376. [PMID: 17304869]

Item 36 Answer: D

Educational Objective: Diagnose anemia of kidney disease in an older patient.

This patient most likely has anemia secondary to kidney disease. Because erythropoietin is produced in the kidney, kidney disease is associated with an underproduction anemia caused by renal cortical loss. The anemia of kidney disease is usually normochromic and normocytic with a low reticulocyte count. Patients with minor increases in serum creatinine levels may have reduced erythropoietin levels. Measurement of the serum erythropoietin level may be useful in confirming a diagnosis of underproduction anemia in patients with minimally elevated creatinine levels in whom the origin of anemia is uncertain. The peripheral blood smear in patients with uremia frequently shows "burr cells" or echinocytes. Although the patient's creatinine level is 1.5 mg/dL (132 µmol/L), his estimated creatinine clearance using the abbreviated MDRD Study equation, based on age, creatinine level, and sex, is 55.3. Patients with symptomatic anemia secondary to kidney disease typically respond to a supplemental erythropoietin-stimulating agent; however, this treatment would not be necessary in this patient. Before attributing anemia to chronic kidney disease, other potential causes of anemia should be eliminated. The typical evaluation includes complete blood count with erythrocyte indices, absolute reticulocyte count, serum iron, total iron-binding capacity (TIBC), percent transferrin saturation, serum ferritin, and exclusion of gastrointestinal bleeding with appropriate testing.

Although the prevalence of anemia does increase with age, most patients have an associated disease process, such as chronic kidney disease, iron deficiency, or an inflammatory state. Ascribing anemia to advanced age, per se, would be inappropriate in the presence of a known cause of anemia. Inflammatory anemia is associated with normal or low serum iron levels, low TIBC, and an elevated serum ferritin level. Iron deficiency is associated with an elevated TIBC and a reduced ferritin level. This patient has a normal iron level, TIBC, and ferritin level.

KEY POINT

- **Measurement of the serum erythropoietin level may be useful in confirming a diagnosis of underproduction anemia in patients with minimally elevated serum creatinine levels in whom the origin of anemia is uncertain.**

Bibliography

Fishbane S, Nissenson AR. Anemia management in chronic kidney disease. Kidney Int Suppl. 2010;(117):S3-S9. [PMID: 20671741]

H

Item 37 Answer: B

Educational Objective: Treat a patient with the HELLP (*h*emolysis, *e*levated *l*iver enzymes, and *l*ow *p*latelets) syndrome and preeclampsia.

The appropriate management is emergent delivery of the fetus. About 10% of patients with preeclampsia develop the HELLP (*h*emolysis, *e*levated *l*iver enzymes, and *l*ow *p*latelets) syndrome. The HELLP syndrome is characterized by right upper-quadrant pain and elevated liver enzymes. Preeclampsia typically presents with hypertension, peripheral edema, and proteinuria, most commonly in the third trimester of pregnancy. The cause of the HELLP syndrome is unknown but probably represents endothelial injury, platelet activation, and subsequent platelet destruction. The HELLP syndrome is associated with a wide range of systemic symptoms, and abnormal laboratory findings may be difficult to differentiate from those caused by thrombotic thrombocytopenic purpura, hemolytic uremic syndrome, and, occasionally, disseminated intravascular coagulation. Suggested criteria for diagnosis include microangiopathic hemolytic anemia, a platelet count less than 100,000/µL (100×10^9/L), a serum total bilirubin level greater than 1.2 mg/dL (20.52 µmol), a serum aspartate aminotransferase level greater than 70 units/L, and a serum lactate dehydrogenase level greater than 600 units/L. This patient has new-onset hypertension, proteinuria, elevated liver chemistry test results, hemolytic anemia, and thrombocytopenia. The optimal treatment of HELLP syndrome is emergent delivery of the fetus.

Corticosteroids may be necessary to mature the lungs of the immature fetus but, alone, are not the therapy of choice and would not be instituted prior to emergent delivery of the fetus.

Intravenous immune globulin is not indicated in the treatment of the HELLP syndrome or preeclampsia.

Plasma exchange would be appropriate if this patient's symptoms were to persist after delivery, but it is not indicated now.

KEY POINT

- **About 10% of patients with preeclampsia develop the HELLP (*h*emolysis, *e*levated *l*iver enzymes, *l*ow *p*latelets) syndrome for which urgent delivery of the fetus is the optimal treatment.**

Bibliography

D'Angelo A, Fattorini A, Crippa L. Thrombotic microangiopathy in pregnancy. Thromb Res. 2009;123 Suppl 2:S56-62. [PMID: 19217478]

Item 38 Answer: A

Educational Objective: Understand the clinical manifestations of sickle cell trait.

Of the choices listed, only hematuria occurs with increased incidence in patients with sickle cell trait, which was previously diagnosed in this patient and is confirmed by his normal complete blood count and hemoglobin electrophoresis results. Sickle cell trait is generally considered a benign condition, although hematuria, renal medullary carcinoma, risk of splenic rupture at high altitudes, venous thromboembolism, and sudden death during extreme conditions have been reported. Hematuria is by far the most common complication of sickle cell trait, and up to half of cases are due to renal papillary necrosis. Although the exact mechanism of papillary necrosis is not entirely understood, several factors contributing to this process have been described. Renal papillary necrosis results from local microinfarctions in the renal medulla. The hypoxemia, hypertonicity, acidosis, and hyperthermia of arterial blood passing through the long vasa recta of the renal medulla, a consequence of the countercurrent exchange in the renal medulla, promote polymerization of deoxyhemoglobin S. Renal papillary necrosis often presents with painless gross hematuria. Although the risk for sudden death in patients with sickle cell death remains quite low, screening is performed prior to participation in collegiate athletic activities; however, there is significant controversy surrounding this issue, and some medical organizations have voiced opposition to this recommendation. It is uniformly recommended that individuals with sickle cell trait should remain well hydrated during strenuous activity.

Although hematuria may be due to renal papillary necrosis in patients with sickle cell trait (and sickle cell disease), alternative causes of hematuria, such as stones and lower urinary tract neoplasms, should always be considered in these patients, and the diagnostic workup should not be different from that performed in patients with normal hemoglobin.

Chest pain, shortness of breath, diffuse joint pain, and lower extremity swelling do not occur with increased frequency in patients with sickle cell trait, and alternative explanations should be sought for these symptoms. Patients with sickle cell trait also do not experience pain crises; therefore, bone and joint pain should not be ascribed to sickle cell trait.

KEY POINT

- **The diagnostic workup of most medical conditions should not differ between patients with sickle cell trait and those with normal hemoglobin.**

Bibliography

Tsaras G, Owusu-Ansah A, Boateng FO, Amoateng-Adjepong Y. Complications associated with sickle cell trait: a brief narrative review. Am J Med. 2009;122(6):507-512. [PMID: 19393983]

Item 39 Answer: A

Educational Objective: **Treat a younger patient with high-risk acute myeloid leukemia.**

The most appropriate treatment is allogeneic hematopoietic stem cell transplantation (HSCT). This patient has high-risk acute myeloid leukemia (AML) as demonstrated by her complex karyotype and the presence of a 5q- deletion. Phase III studies in which patients underwent transplantation or received chemotherapy have consistently demonstrated an improvement in disease-free survival with allogeneic HSCT. The overall survival benefit has been less consistent because of higher treatment-related mortality associated with allogeneic stem cell transplantation. However, a recent meta-analysis demonstrated an improvement in relapse-free survival and overall survival with the use of allogeneic stem cell transplantation in first complete remission in patients with intermediate- and high-risk cytogenetics.

Numerous phase III studies have evaluated the use of autologous HSCT as a consolidation strategy in AML and have shown inconsistent effects on relapse-free survival and no improvement in overall survival compared with standard chemotherapy.

Azacitidine is approved for use in patients with higher-risk myelodysplastic syndrome but remains unproven in AML.

The likelihood of cure with standard consolidation chemotherapy including high-dose cytarabine in a patient with AML and high-risk cytogenetics is remote and would not be considered appropriate for a patient with a suitable HLA-matched donor. Younger patients with favorable-risk cytogenetics (t(8;21), inv(16)) should receive high-dose cytarabine as consolidation therapy.

KEY POINT

- **Allogeneic hematopoietic stem cell transplantation results in an improvement in disease-free and overall survival in younger patients with high-risk acute myeloid leukemia compared with chemotherapy.**

Bibliography

Koreth J, Schlenk R, Kopecky KJ, et al. Allogeneic stem cell transplantation for acute myeloid leukemia in first complete remission: systematic review and meta-analysis of prospective clinical trials. JAMA. 2009;301(22):2349-2361. [PMID: 19509382]

Item 40 Answer: A

Educational Objective: **Diagnose AL amyloidosis.**

The most appropriate next step in diagnosis is abdominal fat pad aspiration. This patient has classic features of AL amyloidosis, including macroglossia, hepatomegaly, nephrotic syndrome, peripheral neuropathy, and the presence of an IgG lambda M-protein. A diagnosis of AL amyloidosis requires characteristic findings on tissue biopsy, the presence of a monoclonal plasma cell disorder, and evidence of clonal light chains within the amyloid deposits. When done properly, an abdominal fat pad aspiration has a sensitivity of approximately 80%, with a high specificity approaching 100%. If AL amyloidosis is suspected and the bone marrow and fat pad testing results are negative, biopsy of a clinically involved organ is required (for example, a kidney or liver biopsy). However, performing bone marrow and abdominal fat pad biopsy is the first choice because these tests are less dangerous to the patient, yet the combination of the two is highly sensitive (90% in some series).

Antineutrophil cytoplasmic antibody–related vasculitis is unlikely because it does not cause neuropathy or macroglossia, and it typically produces an active urine sedimentation.

Cryoglobulinemia can cause nephrotic-range proteinuria and neuropathy but does not typically produce macroglossia. Also, cryoglobulinemia is associated with lower extremity purpura, which is inconsistent with this patient's findings.

KEY POINT

- **In patients with suspected AL amyloidosis, the combination of bone marrow biopsy and abdominal fat pad aspiration has a sensitivity of approximately 90%.**

Bibliography

van Gameren II, Hazenberg BP, Bijzet J, Rijswijk MH. Diagnostic accuracy of subcutaneous abdominal fat tissue aspiration for detecting systemic amyloidosis and its utility in clinical practice. Arthritis Rheum. 2006;54(6):2015-2021. [PMID: 16732553]

Item 41 Answer: C

Educational Objective: **Diagnose hereditary spherocytosis.**

The most likely diagnosis is hereditary spherocytosis. The clinical spectrum in patients with hereditary spherocytosis varies widely, ranging from the presence of no symptoms to significant hemolysis. Affected patients often have a family history of anemia (most cases transmitted as an autosomal dominant disorder), splenomegaly, and may develop leg ulcers and pigmented gallstones secondary to chronic hemolysis. Spherocytes may be seen on the peripheral blood smear. This patient's exercise intolerance and inability to keep up with her peers is a common presentation of mild to moderate hereditary spherocytosis. Some patients may experience episodes of severe anemia caused by parvovirus B19 infection leading to a transient aplastic crisis. The usual reticulocyte count ranges from 5% to 20%, and elevations of serum bilirubin and lactate dehydrogenase levels may reflect chronic hemolysis. A positive osmotic fragility test would help to establish the diagnosis.

α-Thalassemia trait (–α/–α or ––/αα) is associated with mild anemia, microcytosis, hypochromia, target cells on the peripheral blood smear, and, in adults, normal hemoglobin electrophoresis results.

Glucose-6-phosphate dehydrogenase (G6PD) deficiency is the most common erythrocyte enzyme defect, occurring most frequently in men, often of African American descent. It is characterized by a peripheral blood smear that may be normal between crises but would reveal bite cells during an acute hemolytic episode. G6PD deficiency is not associated with spherocytosis. Consequently, hereditary spherocytosis is a more likely diagnosis than G6PD deficiency.

Sickle cell anemia (Hb SS) is associated with moderate to severe anemia and frequent pain crises. It is not characterized by splenomegaly, is usually normocytic, and is notable for sickle cells on the peripheral blood smear.

This patient's negative direct Coombs (antiglobulin) test and positive family history of anemia and cholecystectomy are helpful in differentiating hereditary spherocytosis from warm autoimmune hemolytic anemia, although spherocytes would be present on the blood smear in both conditions.

KEY POINT

- **Hereditary spherocytosis is characterized by splenomegaly, a personal and family history of anemia, leg ulcers, gallstones, and spherocytes on the peripheral blood smear.**

Bibliography

Perrotta S, Gallagher PG, Mohandas N. Hereditary spherocytosis. Lancet. 2008;372(9647):1411-1426. [PMID: 18940465]

H

Item 42 Answer: D

Educational Objective: Treat a pregnant patient with sickle cell anemia and a typical painful crisis.

The most appropriate treatment is morphine. The pregnancy-related mortality rate in women with sickle cell anemia is between 0.5% and 2%. Because of the associated increased fetal morbidity and maternal mortality, pregnancy in women with sickle cell disease should be managed by a team of medical personnel, including an obstetrician, internist, and hematologist. The incidence of pain crises in patients with sickle cell anemia is increased in pregnancy. Patients with painful crises present with severe pain in the arms, legs, chest, abdomen, and back and are managed with hydration, supplemental oxygen in the setting of hypoxia, and opiate analgesics such as morphine, which is not known to be teratogenic.

Hydroxyurea is contraindicated in pregnancy because of teratogenic effects when used in the first trimester. It should be stopped at least 3 months before conception whenever possible. Although case reports of successful pregnancies in women taking hydroxyurea have been published, there are currently no guidelines concerning the management of patients who become pregnant while taking this drug; therefore, discontinuation of this agent seems advisable.

NSAIDs are typically not used in pregnancy, and ketorolac is a pregnancy class C drug that is potentially teratogenic, based on animal studies.

Meperidine is contraindicated in the treatment of pain because of its tendency to induce seizures owing to the accumulation of normeperidine.

KEY POINT

- **Morphine is the therapy of choice for the long-term treatment of pain in all patients, including pregnant women, with sickle cell anemia and painful crises.**

Bibliography

Rogers DT, Molokie R. Sickle cell disease in pregnancy. Obstet Gynecol Clin North Am. 2010;37:223-237. [PMID: 20685550]

Item 43 Answer: B

Educational Objective: Prevent venous thromboembolism (VTE) in a pregnant patient with a history of idiopathic VTE.

This patient should receive antepartum and postpartum heparin. Patients such as this one with a previous history of idiopathic venous thromboembolism (VTE) are at a fourfold increased risk for recurrent VTE compared with patients with a history of triggered VTE. Although outcomes data are limited, it is currently recommended that pregnant women at moderate to high risk of recurrent VTE (as in this patient with a single unprovoked pulmonary embolism) receive prophylactic-dose or intermediate-dose low-molecular-weight heparin (LMWH) during pregnancy and for 6 weeks postpartum.

Prophylaxis with both low-dose aspirin and low- or moderate-dose unfractionated heparin or LMWH is indicated for women with recurrent fetal loss and the antiphospholipid syndrome. This patient does not have the antiphospholipid syndrome or previous fetal loss, and combined aspirin and heparin treatment is not indicated.

Warfarin is contraindicated during the first trimester because of the potential for warfarin-induced embryopathy. In addition, warfarin is rarely used in the United States during the second and third trimesters, generally because of the fear of liability in the event of any fetal adverse events, whether or not they are warfarin related.

Administering no prophylaxis to this patient with a high risk for recurrent VTE would not be prudent.

KEY POINT

- **Pregnant women with a history of idiopathic venous thromboembolism should receive antepartum and postpartum prophylactic anticoagulation.**

Bibliography

Bates SM, Jaeschke R, Stevens SM, et al. Diagnosis of DVT: antithrombotic therapy and prevention of thrombosis, 9th ed: American College of Chest Physicians evidence-based clinical practice guidelines. Chest. 2012;141(2)(suppl):e351S-e418S. [PMID: 22315267]

Item 44 Answer: D

Educational Objective: Evaluate a patient with von Willebrand disease.

The next step in the diagnostic evaluation is von Willebrand factor (vWF) antigen and activity assays. This patient has a personal and family history of mucocutaneous bleeding with a pattern that appears to be autosomal dominant. The most common inherited bleeding disorder is von Willebrand disease (vWD). Patients with vWD typically have low levels of vWF antigen and activity. Because levels of vWF fluctuate in response to estrogens, stress, exercise, inflammation, and bleeding, repeated assays may be required to establish the diagnosis.

Factor VIII levels in vWD may be low enough to prolong the activated partial thromboplastin time (aPTT), but a prolonged aPTT is not diagnostic of vWD, and prothrombin time (PT) and aPTT prolongations are more often found in patients with deficiencies of humoral clotting factors who typically have joint or muscle bleeding rather than mucocutaneous bleeding. The exception is factor XI deficiency, which can produce mucocutaneous bleeding and a prolonged aPTT, found most commonly in persons of Ashkenazi Jewish descent. The most common causes of a prolonged PT include warfarin use, vitamin K deficiency, and chronic liver disease. Rare causes include acquired or inherited factor VII deficiency. As with other coagulation factor deficiencies, patients with factor VII deficiency are most likely to present with mucosal, joint, and muscle bleeding. None of these conditions is compatible with this patient's long history of bleeding, the nature of her bleeding, and family history. Consequently, neither the PT nor aPTT is the appropriate next diagnostic test.

Results of the Platelet Function Analyzer-100 (PFA-100®) are expected to be prolonged in patients with hemoglobin values below 10 g/dL (100 g/L); therefore, this test would provide no additional information and is not indicated.

KEY POINT

- **Patients with suspected von Willebrand disease should undergo von Willebrand factor and activity assays to confirm the diagnosis.**

Bibliography

Castaman G, Montgomery RR, Meschengieser SS, et al. von Willebrand's disease diagnosis and laboratory issues. Haemophilia. 2010;16 Suppl 5:67-73. [PMID: 20590859]

Item 45 Answer: A

Educational Objective: Treat a patient with immune thrombocytopenic purpura.

The appropriate treatment is corticosteroids and intravenous immune globulin. This patient has new-onset thrombocytopenia as well as wet purpura and other hemorrhagic symptoms; she most likely has immune (also termed "idiopathic") thrombocytopenic purpura (ITP) and requires immediate therapy. ITP is a diagnosis of exclusion but can include mild to severe bleeding or hemorrhage in the setting of an otherwise normal blood count and the absence of organ dysfunction. ITP can be drug induced or associated with abnormal immune regulation. Therapy may be required in patients with platelet counts lower than 30,000 to 40,000/µL (30-40 × 10^9/L) or with bleeding. Adjunctive therapy, including intravenous immune globulin or anti-D immune globulin, with corticosteroids, is appropriate for the initial therapy of patients in whom a rapid rise in platelets is desirable because of bleeding or in those with a platelet count lower than 10,000/µL (10 × 10^9/L). Intravenous immune globulin may increase very low platelet counts in patients with ITP. It can be used as an option to quickly elevate the platelet count while corticosteroids are taking effect. Intravenous anti-D immune globulin is an alternative therapy that may sometimes be effective in patients with an intact spleen and Rh-positive blood. In these patients, anti-D binds to the erythrocyte D antigen, and immune-mediated clearance of the anti-D-associated erythrocytes occupies the Fc-γ receptors in the spleen, minimizing removal of the ITP-antibody–coated platelets.

Eltrombopag is a thrombopoietin receptor mimetic that can significantly increase platelet counts in patients with ITP. Eltrombopag is not approved for first-line use in patients with ITP; patients must demonstrate no response to corticosteroids before eltrombopag can be used. In addition, its use is currently restricted to physicians enrolled in a special prescribing and distribution program.

Rituximab is not FDA approved for the treatment of ITP and would take longer than 2 weeks to produce a response.

Splenectomy is reserved for patients with refractory ITP and is not indicated as first-line therapy.

KEY POINT

- **Adjunctive therapy, including intravenous immune globulin or anti-D immune globulin, plus corticosteroids, is appropriate for the initial therapy of patients with immune thrombocytopenic purpura in whom a rapid rise in platelets is desirable because of bleeding or a platelet count lower than 10,000/µL (10 × 10^9/L).**

Bibliography

Provan D, Stasi R, Newland AC, et al. International consensus report on the investigation and management of primary immune thrombocytopenia. Blood. 2010;115(2):168-186. [PMID: 19846889]

Item 46 Answer: A

H

Educational Objective: Treat a patient with kidney insufficiency and acute venous thromboembolism in the postoperative period.

Intravenous unfractionated heparin (UFH) adjusted to achieve a therapeutic activated partial thromboplastin

H CONT.

time (aPTT) is the most appropriate treatment for this patient who recently underwent a major surgical procedure and has chronic kidney disease. UFH is primarily cleared by the reticuloendothelial system rather than the kidneys; therefore, it is preferable to the other choices for acute therapy for deep venous thrombosis (DVT). UFH also has a short-half life and is completely reversible with protamine.

Enoxaparin, 1 mg/kg subcutaneously every 12 hours, is the standard dosing regimen for patients with an estimated glomerular filtration rate (GFR) greater than 30 mL/min/1.73 m^2. This patient's GFR is estimated to be less than 30 mL/min/1.73 m^2. Therefore, the suggested dose is too high and would unnecessarily increase the risks of bleeding in this postoperative patient. In addition to the potential for drug accumulation, enoxaparin has a longer half-life than UFH and is only 60% reversible with protamine. Therefore, any bleeding complications that arise with enoxaparin would be more difficult to treat. Consequently, UFH is a safer choice than enoxaparin for venous thromboembolism (VTE) therapy in this postoperative patient with renal insufficiency.

Fondaparinux has a long half-life (17-21 hours in patients with normal kidney function), and it is exclusively cleared by the kidneys. Therefore, it is contraindicated in this postoperative patient with poor renal function (estimated GFR <30 mL/min/1.73 m^2). In addition, fondaparinux is not reversible with protamine; consequently, any potential bleeding will be much more difficult to treat. Although the anticoagulant effects of fondaparinux can be treated with recombinant human factor VIIa, this factor concentrate has been associated with an increased thromboembolic risk, an important limitation in a patient with recent VTE.

Warfarin is metabolized by the liver and will therefore not accumulate in the presence of worsening kidney function; however, warfarin's anticoagulant activity is delayed in onset by at least 5 to 7 days and is initially associated with transient hypercoagulability. Therefore, initial anticoagulation with warfarin in patients with acute thromboembolism is always done concomitantly with a parenteral agent such as UFH.

KEY POINT

- **Intravenous unfractionated heparin is the most appropriate treatment for deep venous thrombosis in patients who have undergone recent surgery and have chronic kidney disease.**

Bibliography

Hirsh J, Bauer KA, Donati MB, Gould M, Samama MM, Weitz JI; American College of Chest Physicians. Parenteral anticoagulants: American College of Chest Physicians Evidence-Based Clinical Practice Guidelines (8th Edition). [Erratum in: Chest. 2008;134(2):473]. Chest. 2008;133(6 Suppl):141S-159S. [PMID: 18574264]

Item 47 Answer: A

Educational Objective: Diagnose α-thalassemia trait.

The most likely diagnosis is α-thalassemia trait. Decreased or absent synthesis of normal α or β chains resulting from genetic defects is the hallmark of the thalassemic syndromes. The result is ineffective erythropoiesis, intravascular hemolysis caused by precipitation of the excess insoluble globin chain, and decreased hemoglobin production. α-Thalassemia trait (–α/–α or – –/αα) is associated with mild anemia, microcytosis, hypochromia, target cells on the peripheral smear, and, in adults, normal hemoglobin electrophoresis results. The (–α/–α) variant is found in 2% to 3% of blacks and is often mistaken for iron deficiency. This patient's peripheral blood smear demonstrating target cells makes a thalassemic syndrome the most likely diagnosis, and the normal hemoglobin electrophoresis results are suggestive of α-thalassemia trait. α-Thalassemia can be more definitively diagnosed by globin gene synthesis studies but is more often suggested by chronic microcytic anemia, target cells, normal iron studies, and normal hemoglobin electrophoresis results. No treatment is necessary for α-thalassemia trait.

The clinical presentation and peripheral blood smear findings of β-thalassemia minor may be similar to those of α-thalassemia trait, but the hemoglobin electrophoresis results usually show an elevated Hb A_2 ($\alpha_2\delta2$) band.

The peripheral blood smear in patients with iron deficiency is remarkable for microcytic, hypochromic erythrocytes, with marked anisopoikilocytosis (that is, abnormalities in erythrocyte size and shape). The serum iron concentration is usually low in patients with iron deficiency; the total iron-binding capacity (TIBC) is high; the percentage of transferrin saturation (iron/TIBC) is low; and the serum ferritin concentration is low. This patient's iron studies are not consistent with iron deficiency.

Patients with sickle/β^+ thalassemia (Hb Sβ^+) usually have symptoms typical for sickle cell disease and abnormal hemoglobin electrophoresis results showing Hb S, Hb A, and an elevated Hb A_2 band.

KEY POINT

- **α-Thalassemia trait is characterized by microcytosis, normal iron studies, target cells on the peripheral blood smear, and normal hemoglobin electrophoresis results.**

Bibliography

Cunningham MJ. Update on thalassemia: clinical care and complications. Hematol Oncol Clin North Am. 2010;24(1):215-227. [PMID: 20113904]

Item 48 Answer: D

H

Educational Objective: Evaluate a patient with essential thrombocythemia.

JAK2 V617F mutational analysis is the most appropriate next step in the evaluation of this patient. She has

CONT.

Budd-Chiari syndrome, which is characterized by thrombosis of the hepatic veins, upper-quadrant pain, and hepatomegaly, with rapid development of jaundice and ascites. Liver chemistry tests are abnormal, and serum aminotransferases can range from 100 to 200 units/L to more than 600 units/L. An estimated 60% of patients with this syndrome have or eventually will be diagnosed with a myeloproliferative disorder, particularly polycythemia vera (PV) and essential thrombocytosis. The *JAK2 V617F* gene mutation is present in 97% of patients with PV and in 50% of those with essential thrombocythemia and should be measured in all patients with Budd-Chiari syndrome. Positive findings indicate a myeloproliferative disorder and suggest the need for cytoreductive therapy.

The antiphospholipid syndrome is associated with an increased risk for venous and arterial thromboembolism. Common sites of thrombosis include the calf but may also include the renal and hepatic veins. There is also a strong correlation between this syndrome and pregnancy loss. The antiphospholipid syndrome is not associated with thrombocytosis.

Flow cytometric analysis for GPI-anchored proteins on the surface of erythrocytes or leukocytes is the best choice for diagnosis of paroxysmal nocturnal hemoglobinuria (PNH), which is also associated with Budd-Chiari syndrome but not thrombocytosis. PNH is associated with complement-mediated hemolytic anemia or with the development of aplastic anemia.

Antithrombin deficiency is an autosomal dominant disorder, and protein C deficiency is inherited as an autosomal recessive trait. Deficiencies of protein C and antithrombin lead to an increased risk for venous thromboembolism, usually of the calf, and are not associated with thrombocytosis.

KEY POINT

- **Fifty to 60% of patients with Budd-Chiari syndrome have or eventually will be diagnosed with a myeloproliferative disorder, particularly polycythemia vera and essential thrombocytosis.**

Bibliography

Smira G, Gheorghe L, Iacob S, Coriu D, Gheorghe C. Budd Chiari syndrome and V617F/JAK 2 mutation linked with the myeloproliferative disorders. J Gastrointestin Liver Dis. 2010;19(1):108-109. [PMID: 20361090]

Item 49 Answer: A

Educational Objective: Treat high-risk myelodysplastic syndrome in an older patient.

The most appropriate treatment is azacitidine. The patient has a newly diagnosed myelodysplastic syndrome (MDS). She meets the World Health Organization criteria for refractory anemia with excess blasts-2 (10% to 19% blasts and unilineage or multilineage dysplasia). The patient has an International Prognosis Scoring System score of 2, placing her in a higher-risk category (1.5 points for 10% to 19% blasts, 0.5 points for two or three types of cytopenia). A phase III study was conducted in higher-risk patients with MDS, comparing azacitidine with best conventional care, which could consist of supportive care alone, low-dose cytarabine, or intensive chemotherapy. Azacitidine resulted in a prolonged median overall survival (24.5 vs. 15 months), improved 2-year overall survival (51% vs. 26%), and less toxicity than the standard-care arm. Azacitidine is therefore the standard of care for patients with higher-risk MDS.

Plasma exchange and prednisone would be appropriate therapy for thrombotic thrombocytopenic purpura (TTP). The pentad of findings in TTP includes thrombocytopenia, microangiopathic hemolytic anemia, neurologic deficits, kidney impairment, and fever; in addition, schistocytes are present on the peripheral blood smear. This patient's clinical manifestations and normal haptoglobin and LDH, lack of schistocytes, and bone marrow findings do not support this diagnosis.

Vitamin B_{12} deficiency can lead to cytopenia, hemolysis, and elevated lactate dehydrogenase levels from ineffective erythropoiesis. Additionally, the bone marrow morphology can be highly abnormal and difficult to distinguish from that associated with MDS. Although the serum vitamin B_{12} level in this patient is low-normal, vitamin B_{12} deficiency is not associated with abnormal cytogenetics; consequently, this diagnosis is unlikely.

KEY POINT

- **Azacitidine results in prolonged survival and less toxicity than conventional care (supportive care alone, low-dose cytarabine, or intensive chemotherapy) in patients with higher-risk myelodysplastic syndromes.**

Bibliography

Fenaux P, Mufti GJ, Hellstrom-Lindberg E, et al. Efficacy of azacitidine compared with that of conventional care regimens in the treatment of higher-risk myelodysplastic syndromes: a randomised, open-label, phase III study. Lancet Oncol. 2009;10(3):223-232. [PMID: 19230772]

Item 50 Answer: D

Educational Objective: Evaluate a patient with a delayed hemolytic transfusion reaction.

The presence of new alloantibodies would best explain this patient's current clinical presentation. She has sickle cell anemia and has received a blood transfusion in the past week. This patient's severe pain crisis occurring 5 to 10 days after a receiving a transfusion is classic for a delayed hemolytic transfusion reaction (DHTR). Her clinical course, including jaundice, an elevated indirect bilirubin level, and a hemoglobin level lower than her recent value, combined with a type and screen demonstrating the presence of a new alloantibody, would be most characteristic of a DHTR. Because this patient has a known alloantibody against the C antigen, she is at risk for further alloantibody formation and subsequent delayed hemolytic transfusion reaction, which occurs commonly in patients with sickle cell anemia.

The presence of antibodies against recipient neutrophils present in donor plasma is known to cause transfusion-related acute lung injury (TRALI), which may mimic noncardiogenic pulmonary edema, including radiographic evidence of pulmonary edema and pulmonary infiltrates. Patients may also have fever and hypotension. This constellation of symptoms and findings is not consistent with this patient's presentation, which is most characteristic of a pain crisis. In addition, TRALI occurs during or soon after a transfusion, and this patient's symptoms were delayed several days after the transfusion.

Platelet refractoriness is an inappropriately low increment in the platelet count following a transfusion, generally defined as an increment of less than 10,000/µL (10×10^9/L). HLA alloimmunization can cause platelet refractoriness, but this patient did not receive platelets, and HLA alloimmunization would not explain her current symptoms.

Anaphylaxis during blood transfusion can rarely occur in patients with a severe IgA deficiency, but this patient did not experience anaphylaxis.

KEY POINT

- **Clinical symptoms of delayed hemolytic transfusion reaction typically develop approximately 5 to 10 days after erythrocyte transfusion and include anemia, jaundice, and fever and a worsening pain crisis in patients with sickle cell disease.**

Bibliography

Scheunemann LP, Ataga KI. Delayed hemolytic transfusion reaction in sickle cell disease. Am J Med Sci. 2010;339(3):266-269. [PMID: 20051821]

H

Item 51 Answer: B

Educational Objective: Treat newly diagnosed acute lymphoblastic leukemia.

The most appropriate treatment is induction chemotherapy consisting of daunorubicin, vincristine, L-asparaginase, and prednisone. This patient meets the diagnostic criteria for B-cell acute lymphoblastic leukemia (ALL) with 25% lymphoblasts or more on bone marrow examination. The blasts can be identified as lymphoid because they are TdT-positive and because CD10 and CD20 are B-cell markers. Standard induction therapies vary, but an anthracycline agent plus vincristine, a corticosteroid, and L-asparaginase constitute the core for most regimens used today. Although complete remission rates with induction therapy are very high (>90%), relapse remains a problem. Higher-risk patients with a suitable donor are often considered for allogeneic stem cell transplantation during first remission.

Imatinib is a *BCR-ABL* inhibitor used for the treatment of chronic myeloid leukemia. It is used to treat Philadelphia chromosome–positive ALL, most commonly in combination with cytotoxic chemotherapy. However, because this patient's cytogenetics are normal, imatinib would not be appropriate.

Leukapheresis is not indicated. Although this patient has a high circulating blast count, she has no symptoms or signs of hyperleukocytosis, which is characterized by respiratory abnormalities, including dyspnea and diffuse interstitial and/or alveolar infiltrates on chest imaging, and neurologic symptoms consisting of dizziness, mental status changes, visual changes, headaches, and tinnitus. Furthermore, symptomatic hyperleukocytosis is more common in acute myeloid leukemia (AML) and rarely occurs in ALL. Lastly, the benefits of leukapheresis in the setting of symptomatic hyperleukocytosis remain unclear.

Although this patient's lymphoblasts are CD20-positive, the role of rituximab in the treatment of CD20-positive B-cell ALL is unproven.

KEY POINT

- **Induction therapy consisting of combination chemotherapy constitutes the basis for most regimens used today to treat B-cell acute lymphoblastic leukemia.**

Bibliography

Pui CH, Evans WE. Treatment of acute lymphoblastic leukemia. N Engl J Med. 2006;354(2):166-178. [PMID: 16407512]

Item 52 Answer: D

H

Educational Objective: Treat a typical painful episode in a patient with sickle cell disease.

The most appropriate initial treatment is intravenous morphine. This patient has sickle cell anemia and presents with a severe painful episode. No reliable physical or laboratory findings are useful surrogate markers for excluding vasoocclusion; therefore, treatment is based on reported symptoms. Consensus guidelines and expert opinion guide the management of acute painful episodes in sickle cell disease. Management of an uncomplicated painful episode generally includes hydration, nonopioid and opioid analgesia, and incentive spirometry. Morphine and hydromorphone are the opioid analgesics of choice.

Erythrocyte transfusion and exchange transfusion are not indicated for uncomplicated painful episodes but would be indicated in the acute management of stroke and acute chest syndrome. Unless transfusion is absolutely indicated, it should be avoided given the presence of this patient's multiple alloantibodies, which could increase the risk for a delayed hemolytic transfusion reaction. If transfusion were necessary, phenotypically matched erythrocytes would be indicated to minimize this risk.

Meperidine use is avoided in most patients, including those with sickle cell disease, because of its short half-life

CONT.

and low seizure threshold and no benefit over morphine or hydromorphone.

KEY POINT

- **Management of an uncomplicated painful episode in a patient with sickle cell disease generally includes hydration, nonopioid and opioid analgesia such as morphine and hydromorphone, and incentive spirometry.**

Bibliography

Field JJ, Knight-Perry JE, Debaun MR. Acute pain in children and adults with sickle cell disease: management in the absence of evidence-based guidelines. Curr Opin Hematol. 2009;16(3): 173-178. [PMID: 19295432]

Item 53 Answer: B

Educational Objective: Treat a patient with a deep venous thrombosis and cancer.

Cancer-associated venous thromboembolism (VTE) confers a high risk for recurrence. Heparin therapy (unfractionated or low-molecular-weight heparin [LMWH]) is currently recommended for initial therapy for VTE in patients with cancer. In patients with an active malignancy, extended treatment (greater than 3 months and continuing while the malignancy is active) with LMWH is indicated instead of vitamin K antagonist therapy, which is frequently used in individuals without cancer requiring long-term treatment. Although there may ultimately be viable alternatives to LMWH in patients with active malignancy, the role of newer oral anticoagulant medications, such as dabigatran or rivaroxaban, remains to be established.

The traditional indications for an inferior vena cava (IVC) filter are the inability to use an anticoagulant (usually because the risk of bleeding is too high) or the failure of an anticoagulant. Neither of these situations exists in this patient; therefore, the use of an IVC filter is unnecessary.

Although UFH is commonly used for acute therapy for VTE, it is infrequently used for chronic therapy because of the requirement for laboratory monitoring of intravenous UFH and the large injection volumes required for subcutaneous administration. A randomized controlled trial demonstrated that unmonitored subcutaneous UFH was equivalent to subcutaneous LMWH for acute therapy, but no study of chronic therapy has been conducted. Long-term UFH has been associated with an increased risk of osteoporosis compared with LMWH; consequently, it is not a particularly attractive agent for chronic VTE treatment.

KEY POINT

- **Cancer-associated deep venous thrombosis confers a high risk for recurrence, and extended treatment with low-molecular-weight heparin while the malignancy remains active is recommended.**

Bibliography

Guyatt GH, Akl EA, Crowther M, Schünemann HJ, Gutterman DD, Zelman Lewis S. Introduction to the Ninth Edition: Antithrombotic Therapy and Prevention of Thrombosis, 9th ed: American College of Chest Physicians Evidence-Based Clinical Practice Guidelines. Chest. 2012;141(2 Suppl):48S-52S. [PMID: 22315255]

Item 54 Answer: B

Educational Objective: Diagnose essential thrombocythemia.

The most likely cause of this patient's thrombocytosis is essential thrombocythemia. Essential thrombocythemia is a myeloproliferative disorder characterized by an elevated platelet count in the absence of conditions known to cause secondary thrombocytosis. Other blood counts are typically normal. Twenty percent of those affected are younger than 40 years, and complications including arterial or venous thrombosis can occur in 20% to 30% of patients. Extreme thrombocytosis involving platelet counts greater than 1 million/µL (1000×10^9/L), as demonstrated in this patient strongly suggests essential thrombocythemia. When the platelet count increases to more than 1.5 million/µL (1500×10^9/L), patients can develop a qualitative functional defect analogous to type 2 von Willebrand disease. The peripheral blood smear typically shows circulating megathrombocytes, and a mild leukocytosis may be present. Approximately 40% to 50% of patients have splenomegaly, and about 20% have hepatomegaly. Patients may also have basophilia. The diagnosis of essential thrombocythemia is one of exclusion. A reactive thrombocytosis (such as iron deficiency, an underlying inflammatory disorder, or cancer) must be excluded. To establish the diagnosis, the platelet count must be greater than 600,000/µL (600×10^9/L) on two different occasions separated by at least 1 month, and bone marrow examination must show hypercellular marrow and morphologically abnormal megakaryocytic hyperplasia with the megakaryocytes in clusters. Approximately 50% of patients have the *JAK2* mutation, which may be present in all of the myeloproliferative disorders.

In patients with chronic myeloid leukemia, the median leukocyte count is approximately 100,000/µL (100×10^9/L), and the differential includes cells in various stages of maturation from myeloblasts to mature neutrophils. This patient has none of these findings.

Iron deficiency is unlikely in this patient with a normal hemoglobin level and mean corpuscular volume.

Polycythemia vera is excluded if the hematocrit is normal as it is in this patient.

KEY POINT

- **Extreme thrombocytosis involving platelet counts greater than 1 million/µL (1000×10^9/L) strongly suggests essential thrombocythemia.**

Bibliography

Beer PA, Green AR. Pathogenesis and management of essential thrombocythemia. Hematology Am Soc Hematol Educ Program. 2009:621-628. [PMID: 20008247]

H

Item 55 Answer: D

Educational Objective: Evaluate a patient with suspected thrombotic thrombocytopenic purpura.

The next step in evaluation is a peripheral blood smear. This patient has findings suggestive of thrombotic thrombocytopenic purpura (TTP). TTP is primarily a disorder of the systemic circulation caused by microvascular aggregation of platelets in the brain and other organs. The pentad of findings in TTP includes thrombocytopenia, microangiopathic hemolytic anemia, neurologic deficits, kidney impairment, and fever. All five findings do not need to be present for the diagnosis to be established, but TTP should always be considered in all patients with both thrombocytopenia and microangiopathic hemolytic anemia. A peripheral blood smear is essential to determine whether the anemia is caused by a microangiopathic hemolytic process as indicated by the presence of schistocytes. TTP is treated with plasma exchange, which should be instituted emergently at diagnosis because 10% of patients die of this disease despite therapy, usually within the first 24 hours.

Patients with thrombocytopenia need bone marrow biopsies if they are considered to have a primary marrow failure or malignancy of the bone marrow, typically indicated by pancytopenia or the finding of abnormal leukocytes on the peripheral blood smear.

The finding of *Escherichia coli* O157:H7 in a patient with apparent infectious diarrhea and suspected TTP may suggest the overlap syndrome of TTP-hemolytic uremic syndrome; however, making this distinction would not change the decision to commence therapy with plasma exchange.

An MRI of the brain might confirm the presence of an ischemic stroke but would not alter the decision to initiate plasma exchange in this patient.

KEY POINT

- **Thrombotic thrombocytopenic purpura should be suspected in patients with the presence of (1) microangiopathic hemolytic anemia, characterized by schistocytes on the peripheral smear and increased lactate dehydrogenase, and (2) thrombocytopenia.**

Bibliography

Moake J. Thrombotic microangiopathies: multimers, metalloprotease, and beyond. Clin Transl Sci. 2009;2(5):366-373. [PMID: 20443921]

Item 56 Answer: E

Educational Objective: Manage gestational thrombocytopenia.

Repeating the complete blood count in 1 to 2 weeks is appropriate. This patient has new-onset asymptomatic thrombocytopenia developing in the last trimester of pregnancy that is characterized by a platelet count higher than 50,000/µL (50×10^9/L), which suggests gestational thrombocytopenia. Gestational thrombocytopenia is the most common cause of pregnancy-associated thrombocytopenia. The cause of gestational thrombocytopenia is unknown, although it is not believed to have an immune basis. Gestational thrombocytopenia occurs in approximately 5% of pregnancies. Conversely, thrombocytopenia developing in the first two trimesters of pregnancy that is characterized by platelet counts lower than 50,000/µL (50×10^9/L) suggests immune (also termed "idiopathic") thrombocytopenic purpura.

Several studies have confirmed that maternal and fetal outcomes are excellent in patients with platelet counts higher than 50,000/µL (50×10^9/L), and no resulting maternal or fetal complications, such as fetal thrombocytopenia, should occur. Consequently, no therapeutic interventions, including intravenous immune globulin, plasma exchange, or corticosteroids, are required in this patient, and the fetus does not need to be emergently delivered.

KEY POINT

- **Gestational (mild) thrombocytopenia is the most common cause of pregnancy-associated thrombocytopenia and has a benign course.**

Bibliography

Schwartz KA. Gestational thrombocytopenia and immune thrombocytopenias in pregnancy. Hematol Oncol Clin North Am. 2000;14(5):1101-1116. [PMID: 11005036]

Item 57 Answer: E

Educational Objective: Diagnose mild congenital asymptomatic neutropenia.

The most appropriate next step in the evaluation is to repeat the complete blood count in 2 months (or review previous blood counts). This patient's mild fatigue is unlikely related to her neutropenia, and she is still able to fully participate in her daily activities. She has mild congenital asymptomatic neutropenia (absolute neutrophil count [ANC] of 1200/µL [1.2×10^9/L]) with no history of recent infections or frequent childhood infections. Mild congenital asymptomatic neutropenia is characterized by ANCs between 1000/µL and 1500/µL ($1.0\text{-}1.5 \times 10^9$/L) and is common in certain ethnic populations, including blacks, Yemenite Jews, and Jordanian Arabs. This condition is not associated with increased infections and requires no therapy. If prior or repeat leukocyte counts are similar to today's value, no further evaluation is necessary.

An antineutrophil antibody assay would be appropriate in the evaluation of autoimmune neutropenia if the patient's neutropenia were to worsen, especially in the setting of other autoimmune disorders. However, in the absence of findings suggesting other autoimmune disorders, this test is not necessary.

A bone marrow aspirate and biopsy would be indicated if the patient's neutropenia were to worsen or if she were to develop concomitant thrombocytopenia or anemia. At this point, however, no signs or symptoms suggest a more serious bone marrow disorder.

The neutrophil elastase gene is mutated in patients with severe congenital neutropenia, which is characterized by onset early in life and life-threatening infections. This diagnosis is unlikely in this patient given her very mild neutropenia and lack of any serious childhood infections.

Flow cytometric analysis might be warranted if a lymphoproliferative disorder were suspected. However, other than fatigue, the patient is asymptomatic and has no lymphadenopathy, and, besides leukopenia, has no increased levels of circulating lymphocytes in the blood count or peripheral blood smear. Consequently, a lymphoproliferative disorder is unlikely.

KEY POINT

- **Mild congenital asymptomatic neutropenia is characterized by absolute neutrophil counts of 1000/µL to 1500/µL ($1.0\text{-}1.5 \times 10^9$/L); is common among blacks, Yemenite Jews, and Jordanian Arabs; is not associated with increased infections; and requires no therapy.**

Bibliography

Dale DC, Link DC. The many causes of severe congenital neutropenia. N Engl J Med. 2009;360(1):3-5. [PMID: 19118300]

Item 58 Answer: B

Educational Objective: Treat a patient with secondary iron overload from β-thalassemia major.

The most appropriate treatment for this patient is iron chelation therapy such as deferasirox. Patients with β-thalassemia major develop iron overload because of inappropriately increased iron absorption caused by ineffective erythropoiesis and from multiple transfusions. An elevated serum ferritin level and an increased transferrin saturation are indications for treatment, even in the absence of signs and symptoms of iron overload. Patients with secondary iron overload from thalassemia are best managed with iron chelators. The oral iron chelator, deferasirox, is often used because of its ease of administration and efficacy. Deferasirox is generally well tolerated, but it can cause rare, serious side effects, including agranulocytosis and kidney failure.

Ascorbic acid is a potential iron chelator and rapidly mobilizes iron into the plasma. However, the release of iron into plasma may occur too quickly, causing acute iron toxicity; consequently, ascorbic acid is not first-line treatment as a single agent for iron overload.

Phlebotomy would be contraindicated in a patient with an underlying hemolytic anemia, such as this one. Phlebotomy is most useful in patients with iron overload who are not transfusion dependent, such as patients with hereditary hemochromatosis.

Patients with secondary iron overload can develop the same complications as those with hemochromatosis, including heart failure, liver failure, arthralgia, and pituitary and islet cell dysfunction. These complications are delayed or prevented entirely with institution of iron chelation therapy. Consequently, providing no therapy would not be appropriate.

KEY POINT

- **Patients with secondary iron overload from thalassemia are best managed with iron chelators such as oral deferasirox.**

Bibliography

Hershko C. Pathogenesis and management of iron toxicity in thalassemia. Ann N Y Acad Sci. 2010;1202:1-9. [PMID: 20712765]

Item 59 Answer: B

Educational Objective: Diagnose glucose-6-phosphate dehydrogenase deficiency.

The most likely diagnosis is glucose-6-phosphate dehydrogenase (G6PD) deficiency. Erythrocyte morphology in conjunction with clinical history is often useful in identifying the cause of a type of hemolytic anemia. A clinical history characterized by an acquired hemolytic episode after exposure to an oxidant drug such as trimethoprim-sulfamethoxazole is classic for G6PD deficiency, which occurs most commonly in black males. The peripheral blood smear findings in this disorder include bite cells, which have the appearance of a "bite" having been removed from the surface membrane. Dapsone and primaquine are other fairly common drugs that can lead to hemolysis in G6PD-deficient patients.

Cold agglutinin disease is characterized by agglutination of erythrocytes on the peripheral blood smear and a spuriously high mean corpuscular volume.

Hereditary spherocytosis is characterized by spherocytes on the peripheral blood smear. Spherocytes are recognized as erythrocytes that have a spherical shape and lack central pallor.

Sickle cell disease is less likely given this patient's prior normal complete blood count and previously benign clinical course. Sickle cells are thin, elongated, irregularly shaped erythrocytes.

Target cells are found in the peripheral blood smears of patients with thalassemic syndromes. The acquired nature of this patient's anemia and previously normal mean corpuscular volume make this choice less likely than G6PD deficiency.

KEY POINT

- **A clinical history characterized by an acquired hemolytic episode after exposure to an oxidant drug such as trimethoprim-sulfamethoxazole, along with bite cells on the peripheral blood smear, are classic for glucose-6-phosphate dehydrogenase deficiency.**

Bibliography

Cappellini MD, Fiorelli G. Glucose-6-phosphate dehydrogenase deficiency. Lancet. 2008;371(9606):64-74. [PMID: 18177777]

Item 60 Answer: C

Educational Objective: Diagnose paroxysmal nocturnal hemoglobinuria.

The most appropriate test to establish a diagnosis is flow cytometric analysis for CD55 and CD59 on leukocytes or erythrocytes. This patient most likely has paroxysmal nocturnal hemoglobinuria (PNH), which is a primary acquired stem cell disorder characterized by a wide spectrum of clinical and laboratory findings, such as unprovoked venous thrombosis at an unusual location, hemolytic anemia, and mild to moderate pancytopenia. The diagnosis of PNH is made by flow cytometry, which can identify a subpopulation of erythrocytes or leukocytes lacking specific glycosylphosphatidylinositol-anchored surface proteins, such as CD55 or CD59.

The direct Coombs (antiglobulin) test is useful in the evaluation of autoimmune hemolysis. Autoimmune hemolytic anemia may be characterized by splenomegaly, spherocytic-shaped erythrocytes, reticulocytosis, elevated levels of unconjugated bilirubin and lactate dehydrogenase, and depressed levels of haptoglobin. Although this patient has some of these findings, he has no splenomegaly, and autoimmune hemolysis would not explain his pancytopenia or thrombosis.

Factor V Leiden is the most common inherited thrombophilic disorder and accounts for approximately half of the inherited thrombophilias in patients with venous thromboembolism. Although it may increase the risk for deep venous thrombosis, factor V Leiden would not explain this patient's pancytopenia or hemolysis.

The antiphospholipid syndrome is associated with an increased risk for venous and arterial thromboembolism. Common sites of thrombosis include the lower extremities but may also include the visceral veins. There is also a strong correlation between this syndrome and pregnancy loss. Antiphospholipid syndrome could explain the patient's unprovoked thrombosis but would not account for his pancytopenia or hemolysis.

KEY POINT

- **The diagnosis of paroxysmal nocturnal hemoglobinuria is established by flow cytometric analysis of CD55 and CD59 on leukocytes and erythrocytes.**

Bibliography

Brodsky RA. How I treat paroxysmal nocturnal hemoglobinuria. Blood. 2009;113(26):6522-6527. [PMID: 19372253]

Item 61 Answer: C

Educational Objective: Treat iron deficiency in a menstruating woman.

The most appropriate treatment is oral ferrous sulfate. Iron deficiency can result from blood loss or malabsorption in addition to increased iron use. Women of reproductive age may lose enough iron through normal menstrual blood loss to become iron deficient in the absence of uterine or gastrointestinal disease. Patients with mild iron deficiency may note fatigue, lack of sense of well-being, irritability, decreased exercise tolerance, and headaches before symptoms of overt anemia occur. This patient has signs and symptoms of iron deficiency, likely secondary to menstrual blood loss. The peripheral blood smear in patients with iron deficiency is remarkable for microcytic, hypochromic erythrocytes, with marked anisopoikilocytosis (that is, abnormalities in erythrocyte size and shape). The variation in the size of erythrocytes is quantified in the red blood cell distribution width (RDW) measurement. An increased RDW is most often associated with a nutrient deficiency such as iron, folate, or vitamin B_{12}. Patients with iron deficiency anemia caused by blood loss can have a mild thrombocytosis, which resolves with treatment of iron deficiency and does not require the use of cytoreductive agents such as hydroxyurea. For simple iron deficiency, oral ferrous sulfate is the least expensive and simplest treatment option, and, therefore, the most appropriate.

Parenteral iron is reserved for patients receiving dialysis or for patients who cannot absorb or tolerate oral iron replacement.

Erythrocyte transfusion would be reserved for patients with severe symptomatic anemia in whom rapid correction is necessary to prevent cardiovascular complications, including heart failure and infarction.

KEY POINT

- **For patients with simple iron deficiency, oral ferrous sulfate is the least expensive and simplest treatment option.**

Bibliography

Killip S, Bennett JM, Chambers MD. Iron deficiency anemia. Am Fam Physician. 2007;75(5):671-678. [PMID: 1737551]

Item 62 Answer: A

Educational Objective: Treat acute chest syndrome in a patient with sickle cell disease.

The most appropriate treatment is erythrocyte transfusion. An uncomplicated painful episode is often the initial presenting symptom for patients with sickle cell disease who

CONT.

subsequently develop more severe complications, such as acute chest syndrome or multiorgan failure. This patient meets the criteria for the acute chest syndrome, which includes identification of a new infiltrate on chest radiograph that includes at least one segment and one or more of the following: chest pain; temperature less than 38.5 °C (101.3 °F); tachypnea, wheezing or cough or labored breathing; and hypoxia relative to baseline. Management includes empiric broad-spectrum antibiotics, supplemental oxygen, pain medication to diminish chest splinting, and avoidance of overhydration. Bronchodilators may be helpful in patients with concomitant reactive airways disease. Erythrocyte transfusion is indicated if hypoxia persists despite supplemental oxygen as in this patient. Erythrocyte exchange transfusion may be preferred if the hypoxia continues to progress.

A fluid bolus is not indicated in this patient because she is not hypovolemic or hypotensive, although maintenance fluid should be continued.

Furosemide may be helpful in those patients who are hypovolemic, but there is no clinical evidence to support this diagnosis in this patient. Furosemide-induced hypovolemia should be avoided because it can lead to increased sickling.

Hydroxyurea is effective in decreasing the incidence of acute chest syndrome but is not indicated for treatment in the acute setting.

KEY POINT

- **Management of acute chest syndrome in patients with sickle cell disease includes empiric broad-spectrum antibiotics, supplemental oxygen, pain medication, avoidance of overhydration, bronchodilators as needed, and erythrocyte transfusion for persistent hypoxia despite supplemental oxygen.**

Bibliography

Gladwin MT, Vichinsky E. Pulmonary complications of sickle cell disease. N Engl J Med. 2008;359(21):2254-2265. [PMID: 19020327]

H

Item 63 Answer: D

Educational Objective: **Treat hyperviscosity syndrome in a patient with Waldenström macroglobulinemia.**

The most appropriate treatment is plasmapheresis. This patient has Waldenström macroglobulinemia. Waldenström macroglobulinemia is a lymphoplasmacytic lymphoma characterized by production of monoclonal IgM antibodies. Constitutional symptoms, lymphadenopathy, and hepatosplenomegaly may be present. In addition, clinical manifestations of hyperviscosity syndrome, such as those in this patient, may occur, including dizziness, blurred vision, and characteristic dilated, tortuous, segmented retinal veins on funduscopic examination. This patient's epistaxis is the result of qualitative platelet dysfunction attributable to the M-protein. Hyperviscosity from Waldenström macroglobulinemia constitutes a medical emergency requiring the prompt initiation of plasmapheresis.

Although this patient's urinalysis demonstrates leukocytes, it is negative for leukocyte esterase and nitrite, and he is afebrile and hemodynamically stable; consequently, a urinary tract infection and sepsis is unlikely, and ciprofloxacin is not indicated.

Erythrocyte transfusion or diuresis may exacerbate symptoms of hyperviscosity syndrome and should be avoided until after the patient's serum viscosity is controlled with plasmapheresis.

Hypertensive encephalopathy presents with changes in the level of consciousness, focal neurologic deficits, and visual field defects. Retinal hemorrhages, exudates, or papilledema may also be present on examination. This patient's retinal findings and laboratory evaluation strongly favor a diagnosis of hyperviscosity syndrome rather than hypertensive crisis. Therefore, labetalol and furosemide are not indicated.

KEY POINT

- **Waldenström macroglobulinemia–related hyperviscosity syndrome constitutes a medical emergency and requires prompt initiation of plasmapheresis.**

Bibliography

Treon, SP. How I treat Waldenstrom macroglobulinemia. Blood. 2009;114(12):2375-2385. [PMID: 19617573]

Item 64 Answer: A

Educational Objective: **Diagnose cobalamin deficiency.**

The most likely diagnosis is cobalamin (vitamin B_{12}) deficiency. Patients with vitamin B_{12} deficiency have elevated homocysteine and methylmalonic acid levels, whereas patients with folate deficiency have only an elevated homocysteine level. In addition, an elevated methylmalonic acid level is more sensitive and specific for diagnosing vitamin B_{12} deficiency than a low serum vitamin B_{12} level because serum vitamin B_{12} levels do not adequately assess tissue vitamin B_{12} stores, especially in patients with vitamin B_{12} levels in the low-normal range. Consequently, homocysteine and methylmalonic acid should be measured in patients with suspected vitamin B_{12} deficiency. Similarly, red blood cell folate can be low in patients with folate or vitamin B_{12} deficiency. Because folate supplementation can correct the anemia of vitamin B_{12} deficiency but not the progression of neurologic defects, vitamin B_{12} deficiency must be excluded before supplemental folate is administered to a patient with macrocytic anemia and a low red cell folate level.

Patients with vitamin B_{12} deficiency have elevated homocysteine and methylmalonic acid levels, whereas patients with folate deficiency have only an elevated homocysteine level. Therefore, this patient does not have folate or combined folate-cobalamin deficiency.

Patients with transcobalamin II deficiency have normal serum vitamin B_{12} levels because transcobalamin II is the primary transporter protein for vitamin B_{12} entry into cells. Deficiency of transcobalamin II is quite rare and typically presents in childhood as a megaloblastic anemia with normal vitamin B_{12} and red cell folate levels.

KEY POINT

- **An elevated serum methylmalonic acid level is more sensitive and specific for diagnosing cobalamin (vitamin B_{12}) deficiency than a low serum vitamin B_{12} level.**

Bibliography

Galloway M, Hamilton M. Macrocytosis: pitfalls in testing and summary of guidance. BMJ. 2007;335(7625):884-886. [PMID: 17962289]

Item 65 Answer: D

Educational Objective: Evaluate a patient with mechanical heart valve–related microangiopathic hemolytic anemia.

The most appropriate test to perform next is echocardiography. This patient has acquired hemolytic anemia with evidence of intravascular hemolysis based on low serum haptoglobin and high lactate dehydrogenase levels. In addition, his peripheral blood smear shows schistocytes, a finding diagnostic for microangiopathic hemolytic anemia. This patient's history of a mechanical heart valve that is more than 10 years old, together with a murmur over the mitral area, makes hemolysis due to a dysfunctional mechanical heart valve most likely. An echocardiogram to identify a regurgitant jet or paravalvular leak should be performed.

An ADAMTS-13 assay can be helpful in estimating the prognosis of thrombotic thrombocytopenic purpura (TTP). Patients with TTP have microangiopathic hemolytic anemia, increased lactate dehydrogenase levels, and thrombocytopenia. Although the diagnosis of TTP must be considered, the normal platelet count and chronicity of the patient's symptoms make this diagnosis less likely. An ADAMTS-13 assay could be performed for further evaluation of TTP but only after other diagnoses are excluded.

Blood cultures are used to diagnose septicemia. Septicemia could lead to disseminated intravascular coagulation and microangiopathic hemolytic anemia, but this patient is afebrile and has stable vital signs, making this diagnosis unlikely.

Although the direct Coombs (antiglobulin) test is often one of the initial tests used in the evaluation of hemolytic anemia, the presence of schistocytes on the blood smear makes warm or cold autoimmune hemolytic anemia unlikely.

The osmotic fragility test is used to evaluate hereditary spherocytosis. Hereditary spherocytosis is characterized by a personal or family history of anemia, jaundice, splenomegaly, or gallstones; spherocytes on the peripheral blood smear; and a negative direct Coombs test. This diagnosis is unlikely in this patient given his recent normal complete blood count, schistocytes on the peripheral blood smear, and a negative personal and family medical history for anemia.

KEY POINT

- **Hemolysis in patients with mechanical heart valves should prompt echocardiographic evaluation to identify a regurgitant jet or paravalvular leak.**

Bibliography

Shapira Y, Vaturi M, Sagie A. Hemolysis associated with prosthetic heart valves: a review. Cardiol Rev. 2009;17(3):121-124. [PMID: 19384085]

Item 66 Answer: B

Educational Objective: Diagnose aplastic anemia.

The most likely diagnosis is aplastic anemia. Aplastic anemia refers to a condition in which the bone marrow fails to produce blood cells, resulting in a hypocellular bone marrow and pancytopenia. This patient's nosebleeds (thrombocytopenia), malaise and fatigue (anemia), and fever (neutropenia) are the classic symptoms associated with pancytopenia. He also had a viral syndrome approximately 6 weeks ago, which may be significant because certain viral illnesses such as Epstein-Barr virus and cytomegalovirus infection can cause aplastic anemia. This patient has a very low reticulocyte count and a bone marrow biopsy that is essentially devoid of cellular elements, which are consistent with aplastic anemia.

AML is a malignancy of myeloid progenitor cells characterized by a median age at diagnosis of 67 years. The presentation of AML is similar to that of aplastic anemia. However, the bone marrow biopsy in AML would show an abundance of myeloid blasts, which are not present in this patient's bone marrow findings.

Chronic lymphocytic leukemia (CLL) is the most common form of lymphoid malignancy, with a median age at diagnosis of 70 years. Symptoms vary greatly, and many patients are asymptomatic at diagnosis. Development of CLL would be quite unusual in a younger patient such as this one. In addition, the leukocyte count in CLL is typically elevated, not depressed, at presentation, and the bone marrow biopsy would show a preponderance of lymphocytes.

The myelodysplastic syndromes (MDS) are a group of clonal hematopoietic stem cell disorders characterized by ineffective hematopoiesis and a variable rate of transformation to acute myeloid leukemia (AML). The incidence of MDS increases with age. In this patient, myelodysplasia is

CONT.

unlikely because of the acute onset of his symptoms and his young age. In addition, the bone marrow findings in myelodysplasia are typically hypercellular, although, less commonly, hypocellular variants exist.

KEY POINT

- **Aplastic anemia is characterized by hypocellular bone marrow and symptoms associated with pancytopenia, such as bleeding, fever, and fatigue.**

Bibliography

Marsh JC, Ball SE, Cavaenagh J, et al. Guidelines for the diagnosis and management of aplastic anaemia. Br J Haematol. 2009;147(1):43-70. [PMID: 19673883]

Item 67 Answer: C

Educational Objective: Perform a preoperative evaluation in a patient with sickle cell disease requiring erythrocyte transfusion.

This patient requires phenotypically matched blood products. Preoperative transfusion to achieve a hemoglobin level of 10 g/dL (100 g/L) is typically performed to minimize the risk for acute chest syndrome and other major complications in patients with sickle cell disease (SCD). Transfusion in patients with SCD is associated with a high risk for erythrocyte alloimmunization compared with transfusion in patients without SCD. One possible explanation is differing frequencies of various erythrocyte antigens of the primarily white donor pool compared with the typical black patient with SCD. Erythrocyte alloimmunization can lead to an increased risk for a delayed hemolytic transfusion reaction. To minimize this risk, patients with SCD should receive erythrocytes phenotypically matched for the C, E, and K antigens whenever possible, as well as for any antigens to which they have already developed an alloantibody.

Using Hb S-negative units is appropriate to decrease the risk for vasoocclusive complications but would not affect the rate at which alloimmunization occurs.

Irradiation of erythrocytes minimizes the risk for transfusion-associated graft-versus-host disease in immunocompromised patients, but it is not indicated in patients with SCD.

Washing of erythrocytes decreases the risk for allergic reactions but does not affect the incidence of erythrocyte alloimmunization.

KEY POINT

- **Patients with sickle cell disease who require transfusion should receive erythrocytes phenotypically matched for the C, E, and K antigens whenever possible, as well as for any antigens to which they have already developed an alloantibody, to avoid the risk for alloimmunization and subsequent delayed hemolytic transfusion reaction.**

Bibliography

Wahl S, Quirolo KC. Current issues in blood transfusion for sickle cell disease. Curr Opin Pediatr. 2009;21(1):15-21. [PMID: 19242238]

Item 68 Answer: A

Educational Objective: Treat a patient with heparin-induced thrombocytopenia.

This patient requires initiation of argatroban. He most likely has heparin-induced thrombocytopenia (HIT), which develops 5 to 7 days after exposure to heparin, with a decrease in platelet counts of 50% or more, and, in some patients, paradoxical arterial or venous thrombotic events despite the presence of thrombocytopenia. Additional criteria include exclusion of other causes of thrombocytopenia, reversal of thrombocytopenia on cessation of heparin, and positive laboratory test results. The diagnosis is often made on clinical grounds with confirmation by a specific antibody assay such as the enzyme-linked immunosorbent assay (ELISA) or the serotonin-release assay, the results of which generally take several days to become available. Simply discontinuing the heparin would be insufficient because 30% to 50% of patients experience thromboses at 30 days after withdrawal when treated with heparin cessation alone; therefore, an alternative anticoagulant must be initiated. Anticoagulants approved for the treatment of HIT include the direct thrombin inhibitors lepirudin, argatroban, and danaparoid. Because lepirudin is cleared through the kidneys, it is contraindicated in patients with kidney insufficiency. Argatroban, which is cleared through the liver, requires dose adjustments in patients with elevated liver chemistry test values.

Enoxaparin is a low-molecular-weight heparin and may potentiate the devastating mechanisms underlying HIT and worsen this patient's thrombocytopenia and thrombotic risk. Additionally, it is contraindicated in patients with severe kidney insufficiency.

Fondaparinux has a theoretical role in treatment of HIT in lieu of a direct thrombin inhibitor, but there is a dearth of high-quality evidence supporting this role. Current guidelines prefer lepirudin or argatroban over fondaparinux in patients with HIT, and fondaparinux is not approved by the FDA for this indication. Fondaparinux is renally cleared and cannot be used in patients with kidney insufficiency.

Providing no further treatment in this patient with HIT and the risk for thrombosis would be inappropriate.

KEY POINT

- **Patients with heparin-induced thrombocytopenia require immediate heparin cessation and anticoagulation with lepirudin or argatroban to avoid thrombosis.**

Bibliography

Hong MS, Amanullah AM. Heparin-induced thrombocytopenia: a practical review. Rev Cardiovasc Med. 2010;11(1):13-25. [PMID: 20495512]

H

Item 69 Answer: A

Educational Objective: Diagnose large granular lymphocytosis as a cause of pure red cell aplasia.

The most likely diagnosis is large granular lymphocytosis (LGL). This patient has an acquired severe hypoproliferative anemia. The findings on the bone marrow examination are diagnostic of pure red cell aplasia (PRCA). PRCA is characterized by severe anemia, lack of reticulocytosis, and an absence of erythroid precursors in the bone marrow. In contrast to aplastic anemia, leukocyte and platelet production are not affected in PRCA. PRCA may be idiopathic or develop secondary to other diagnoses. Although parvovirus B19 infection, thymoma, and myelodysplasia are potential causes, the peripheral blood smear in this patient reveals a classic-appearing large granular lymphocyte with abundant cytoplasm and azurophilic granules, which is most suggestive of LGL. Flow cytometry revealing CD57+ T cells and clonality on T-cell receptor gene rearrangement studies are diagnostic.

The myelodysplastic syndromes are clonal stem cell disorders characterized by ineffective hematopoiesis and various peripheral cytopenias and bone marrow findings showing a hypercellular marrow with dyserythropoiesis. This patient's bone marrow biopsy did not show myelodysplastic changes.

Parvovirus B19 infection is a viral syndrome characterized by malaise, fever, and arthralgia; 25% of patients are asymptomatic. Splenomegaly is not consistent with parvovirus B19 infection. Moreover, the bone marrow biopsy of patients with parvovirus B19 infection would typically show giant pronormoblasts, and the peripheral blood smear would not show large granular lymphocytes.

Thymoma is associated with various paraneoplastic effects, the most common being myasthenia gravis. Other paraneoplastic syndromes associated with thymoma include PRCA and hypogammaglobulinemia. Teratomas may be evident on plain chest radiograph or CT scan. The presence of splenomegaly, the patient's blood smear morphology, and CT findings are not consistent with thymoma (although normal CT findings do not entirely exclude thymoma).

KEY POINT

- **Large granular lymphocytosis is a cause of pure red cell aplasia.**

Bibliography

Sawada K, Hirokawa M, Fujishima N. Diagnosis and management of acquired pure red cell aplasia. Hematol Oncol Clin North Am. 2009;23(2):249-259. [PMID: 19327582]

Item 70 Answer: B

Educational Objective: Diagnose NSAID-induced toxicity in a patient with multiple myeloma.

This patient has NSAID-induced nephrotoxicity. Acute kidney injury is common in patients with myeloma, occurring in 43% of patients at diagnosis, and it is associated with worse overall survival. Patients with multiple myeloma are particularly vulnerable to nephrotoxic medications, including NSAIDs and intravenous contrast dye. NSAID toxicity is more likely to occur in those who are intravascularly volume depleted or have baseline chronic kidney disease or hypercalcemia.

Cast nephropathy, in which filtered free light chains cause obstruction from intratubular precipitation, is the most common cause of kidney dysfunction. Prompt institution of chemotherapy is used to reduce the light-chain burden in affected patients. Although this patient likely had a component of cast nephropathy at initial diagnosis, he has responded well to therapy, with a substantial reduction in the burden of free monoclonal light chains on serologic and 24-hour urine testing. Consequently, cast nephropathy does not adequately explain his recent deterioration in kidney function.

The incidence of pamidronate-associated kidney dysfunction in patients with multiple myeloma is approximately 5% to 10%. Risk factors include long-term therapy, doses higher than those indicated by the FDA, and rapid infusion times (<2 hours). The type of kidney injury most commonly associated with pamidronate is focal segmental glomerulosclerosis with notable proteinuria, which is not consistent with this patient's findings.

Renal amyloidosis is highly unlikely because this condition typically produces significant nonselective proteinuria/albuminuria, which this patient does not have.

KEY POINT

- **Patients with multiple myeloma are vulnerable to nephrotoxic medications, including NSAIDs and intravenous contrast dye; patients with intravascular volume depletion, baseline chronic kidney disease, or hypercalcemia are particularly vulnerable.**

Bibliography

Dimopoulos MA, Terpos E, Chanan-Khan A, et al. Renal impairment in patients with multiple myeloma: a consensus statement on behalf of the International Myeloma Working Group. J Clin Oncol. 2010;28(33):4976-4984. [PMID: 20956629]

Item 71 Answer: A

H

Educational Objective: Diagnose cobalamin deficiency.

The most likely diagnosis is cobalamin deficiency. This patient's peripheral blood smear shows macroovalocytes and hypersegmented polymorphonuclear cells consistent with cobalamin deficiency. Because cobalamin is necessary for erythrocyte maturation, cobalamin deficiency results in ineffective erythropoiesis that can present as hemolysis. Some patients with cobalamin deficiency may have glossitis, weight loss, and pale yellow skin caused by the combination of anemia and hemolysis, as well as

possible neurologic manifestations, including loss of position or vibratory sense that can progress to spastic ataxia.

Warm autoimmune hemolytic anemia is characterized by insidious symptoms and findings of anemia or jaundice and a peripheral blood smear showing spherocytes, which are erythrocytes that have lost their central pallor. In addition, the direct Coombs (antiglobulin) test is frequently strongly positive for IgG and negative or weakly positive for complement.

Paroxysmal cold hemoglobinuria is a rare cause of hemolysis in adults and is caused by IgG antibodies that bind to the P-antigen on erythrocytes in the cold, resulting in complement fixation and hemolysis upon warming. Macrocytosis and hypersegmented polymorphonuclear cells are not seen in paroxysmal cold hemoglobinuria, which may be associated with microspherocytes.

Hereditary spherocytosis is an inherited disorder of the red cell membrane characterized by spherocytes on the peripheral blood smear and an increased likelihood of calcium bilirubinate gallstones. Splenomegaly is common in patients with this disorder.

KEY POINT

- **Patients with cobalamin deficiency can have macroovalocytes and hypersegmented polymorphonuclear cells on the peripheral blood smear and hemolysis.**

Bibliography

Acharya U, Gau JT, Horvath W, Ventura P, Hsueh CT, Carlsen W. Hemolysis and hyperhomocysteinemia caused by cobalamin deficiency: three case reports and review of the literature. J Hematol Oncol. 2008;18:1-26. [PMID: 20003131]

Item 72 Answer: B

Educational Objective: Recognize hydroxyurea as a cause of macrocytic anemia.

Hydroxyurea has been shown to decrease the incidence of painful crises in patients with sickle cell anemia. Hydroxyurea is an RNA-reductase inhibitor that causes macrocytosis because of its effect on DNA synthesis. In fact, adherence to hydroxyurea therapy can be confirmed by identification of an increased mean corpuscular volume (MCV). Patients with sickle cell anemia who are not treated with hydroxyurea typically have a normal MCV, and the hemoglobin abnormality does not in and of itself lead to increased cell volumes.

Clinical manifestations and findings of cobalamin deficiency include glossitis, weight loss, macroovalocytes and hypersegmented polymorphonuclear cells on the peripheral blood smear, and hemolysis; neurologic findings may also occur. This patient's presentation is not suggestive of cobalamin deficiency. In addition, although cobalamin deficiency is associated with macrocytosis, cobalamin deficiency typically takes years to manifest, and this patient's MCV increased over several months.

The myelodysplastic syndromes (MDS) are a group of clonal hematopoietic stem cell disorders characterized by ineffective hematopoiesis and a variable rate of transformation to acute myeloid leukemia. The incidence of MDS increases with age. Patients have signs and symptoms referable to a specific cytopenia (most often megaloblastic anemia) and bone marrow findings showing a hypercellular marrow with dyserythropoiesis. Alcohol abuse and nutritional deficiencies, especially vitamin B_{12} and folate deficiencies, may be associated with similar findings, and, therefore, must be excluded. This patient has no signs or symptoms of myelodysplasia, such as leukopenia, thrombocytopenia, or other abnormalities on the peripheral blood smear, and myelodysplasia would be uncommon in a young patient.

KEY POINT

- **Hydroxyurea, an RNA-reductase inhibitor used to decrease the incidence of painful crises in sickle cell disease, causes macrocytosis because of its effect on DNA synthesis.**

Bibliography

Burns ER, Reed LJ, Wenz B. Volumetric erythrocyte macrocytosis induced by hydroxyurea. Am J Clin Pathol. 1986;85:337-341. [PMID: 3790210]

Item 73 Answer: E

Educational Objective: Diagnose warm autoimmune hemolytic anemia.

The most likely diagnosis is warm autoimmune hemolytic anemia. Warm autoimmune hemolytic anemia is characterized by insidious symptoms of anemia, jaundice, splenomegaly, and a peripheral blood smear showing spherocytes, which are erythrocytes that have lost their central pallor. In addition, the direct Coombs (antiglobulin) test is frequently strongly positive for IgG and negative or weakly positive for complement.

In cold agglutinin disease, the direct Coombs test is negative for IgG and positive for complement, reflecting the properties of the pathogenic IgM antibody.

Although patients with glucose-6-phosphate dehydrogenase (G6PD) deficiency may have episodic hemolysis, the peripheral blood smear is more likely to show "bite cells," which are characterized by eccentrically located hemoglobin confined to one side of the cell, rather than spherocytes. A positive direct Coombs test is not consistent with G6PD deficiency.

Hereditary spherocytosis is characterized by a personal or family history of anemia, jaundice, splenomegaly, or gallstones; spherocytes on the peripheral blood smear; and negative direct Coombs test. The positive direct Coombs test, noncontributory personal and family medical history, and the patient's prior normal complete blood count help to differentiate warm autoimmune hemolytic anemia from hereditary spherocytosis, although the peripheral blood smear may be similar in both conditions.

CONT.

Patients with thrombotic thrombocytopenic purpura (TTP) have microangiopathic hemolytic anemia (schistocytes on the peripheral smear and an increased lactate dehydrogenase level) and thrombocytopenia. TTP is unlikely in this patient given the normal platelet count, positive direct Coombs test, and lack of schistocytes on the peripheral blood smear.

KEY POINT

- **Warm autoimmune hemolytic anemia is characterized by insidious symptoms of anemia, jaundice, splenomegaly, spherocytes on the peripheral blood smear, and direct Coombs (antiglobulin) test results that are strongly positive for IgG and negative or weakly positive for complement.**

Bibliography

Packman CH. Hemolytic anemia due to warm autoantibodies. Blood Rev. 2008;22(1):17-31. [PMID: 17904259]

H

Item 74 Answer: C

Educational Objective: Treat a patient with life-threatening bleeding who takes warfarin.

This patient with life-threatening bleeding requires warfarin reversal with vitamin K, 10 mg intravenously over 1 hour, plus prothrombin complex concentrate (PCC). PCCs are lyophilized plasma products that contain each of the vitamin K–dependent coagulation factors. PCCs can be reconstituted in minutes and therefore represent the ideal product for rapid reversal of warfarin. It is also important to administer vitamin K to patients in this setting to ensure sustained reversal of warfarin therapy. Recombinant human factor VIIa (rhFVIIa) has also been used for warfarin reversal. However, it does not contain factors IX, X, and II, so, theoretically, it would be expected to be a less optimal warfarin-reversal product than a PCC. Randomized trials of PCC and rhFVIIa have not been conducted.

FFP has been the traditional plasma product used to reverse warfarin therapy. However, preparation and administration of plasma often requires several hours. Therefore, it is not the optimal plasma product for warfarin reversal in a patient with life-threatening bleeding. Furthermore, when plasma is administered, it should always be administered in conjunction with vitamin K to ensure sustained warfarin reversal because some of the coagulation factors in FFP have a short half-life. Intravenous vitamin K is an ideal warfarin-reversal agent because it allows the liver to begin synthesizing new vitamin K–dependent coagulation factors. However, vitamin K, even when administered intravenously, requires hours to reverse the effects of warfarin, which is too long for a patient with life-threatening bleeding. Nonetheless, intravenous vitamin K should always be a part of the treatment regimen for warfarin reversal, but it should be used in conjunction with PCCs in patients with life-threatening bleeding.

Oral vitamin K results in slower reversal of warfarin (24 hours) than intravenous vitamin K and therefore should not be used in patients with life-threatening bleeding.

No additional treatment would be inappropriate for a patient with life-threatening bleeding. Withholding warfarin would result in an INR reversal over 5 to 7 days, which is appropriate for an asymptomatic patient with an elevated INR but not a patient with life-threatening bleeding.

KEY POINT

- **Intravenous vitamin K and prothrombin complex concentrate constitute the warfarin-reversal therapy in patients with life-threatening bleeding.**

Bibliography

Holbrook A, Schulman S, Witt DM, et al. Evidence-based management of anticoagulant therapy: Antithrombotic Therapy and Prevention of Thrombosis, 9th ed: American College of Chest Physicians Evidence-Based Clinical Practice Guidelines. Chest. 2012;141(2 Suppl):e152S-84S. [PMID: 22315259]

Oncology Answers

H

Item 75 Answer: C

Educational Objective: Treat a patient with advanced symptomatic follicular lymphoma.

The most appropriate treatment is rituximab; combination chemotherapy with cyclophosphamide, vincristine, doxorubicin; prednisone; and 2 years of rituximab maintenance therapy. This patient has advanced symptomatic follicular lymphoma requiring immediate therapy and not watchful waiting. The addition of anthracyclines (doxorubicin) to cyclophosphamide, vincristine, and prednisone has been shown to increase responses and improve progression-free survival outcomes. However, with three risk factors (age >60 years, hemoglobin <12 g/dL [120 g/L], and more than four areas of lymph node involvement), this patient has a high follicular lymphoma International Prognostic Index score, and, despite standard chemotherapy, has a 5-year projected overall survival of only 52%. Recent data suggest the addition of rituximab to initial chemotherapy followed by a 2-year regimen of maintenance rituximab results in greater overall survival.

Hematopoietic stem cell transplantation may be appropriate for patients with relapsed follicular lymphoma after they have not responded to primary treatment but is not used as initial therapy.

Radioimmunoconjugates are appropriate therapy for follicular lymphoma but not in the acute setting in which immediate treatment is required because this form of treatment is associated with delays resulting from administration of therapy and time to response.

KEY POINT

- In patients with advanced symptomatic follicular lymphoma, the addition of rituximab to initial chemotherapy followed by a 2-year regimen of maintenance rituximab results in greater overall survival.

Bibliography

Hainsworth JD, Litchy S, Burris HA III, et al. Rituximab as front-line and maintenance therapy for patients with indolent non-Hodgkin's lymphoma. J Clin Oncol. 2002;20(20):4261-4267. [PMID: 12377971]

Item 76 Answer: B

Educational Objective: Manage a patient with laryngeal cancer and a field cancerization effect.

The most appropriate next step in management is CT-guided lung biopsy. In addition to laryngeal cancer, this patient's staging studies reveal modestly enlarged regional lymph nodes suggestive of a more advanced disease process as well as a small lung mass. It is important to determine whether the lung mass represents metastatic disease, which is an unlikely presentation for head and neck cancer, or a second primary tumor. Most head and neck cancers are local or regional squamous cell carcinomas; distant, metastatic cancer occurs in only about 10% of patients at diagnosis. In addition, there is a high frequency of secondary head and neck and lung cancers, suggesting that the entire respiratory mucosa (including the upper gastrointestinal tract) may be predisposed to malignancy, the so-called field cancerization effect. A biopsy of the lung mass must be performed to exclude the presence of a concurrent early-stage lung cancer or to allow both tumors to potentially be treated with curative intent.

Chemotherapy with radiation would be appropriate therapy to preserve the voice but only after determination of whether the lung lesion represents metastatic laryngeal cancer or a new primary tumor. If this lesion is found to be a metastasis, although unlikely, chemotherapy for stage IV disease would be most appropriate.

Even if no lung lesion were present, fine-needle aspiration of the cervical lymph nodes would not be recommended because the findings would not alter management. A tissue diagnosis was made at the primary site, and all regional lymph nodes (normal or abnormal appearing) require treatment to eradicate any possible microscopic involvement. Finally, evidence of lymph node enlargement on CT and PET imaging makes malignant involvement highly likely but still does not alter the treatment approach.

Laryngectomy with postoperative radiation would be a treatment option for laryngeal cancer but is not as desirable as voice-sparing therapy consisting of chemotherapy and radiation. In addition, treatment of this patient's laryngeal cancer would only be appropriate after CT-guided biopsy of the lung lesion.

KEY POINT

- Patients with head and neck cancer are subject to a field cancerization effect, which confers a risk for development of another primary malignancy within the aerodigestive system.

Bibliography

Chu EA, Kim YJ. Laryngeal cancer: diagnosis and preoperative work-up. Otolaryngol Clin North Am. 2008;41(4):673-695. [PMID: 18570953]

Item 77 Answer: E

Educational Objective: Manage a patient with advanced asymptomatic follicular lymphoma.

The most appropriate management of this patient is watchful waiting. Follicular lymphoma is the second most common type of non-Hodgkin lymphoma in the United States and Europe. Incidence increases with age, and the median age at diagnosis is 60 years. Follicular lymphoma has a varied course, and regardless of the stage at presentation, patients can be safely observed for years without initiation of therapy until symptoms develop. Most patients present with stage IV disease, and almost all patients have bone marrow involvement as does this patient; however, this patient is otherwise asymptomatic and has normal blood counts. Immediate intervention would not change the natural history of the disease process or change her prognosis but would subject her to unnecessary treatment-related morbidity.

Prednisone as single-agent therapy would only be appropriate for symptomatic relief of painful lymphadenopathy or to treat associated autoimmune phenomena, such as lymphoma-related idiopathic thrombocytopenia. However, in the absence of these indications, this patient should not receive prednisone.

Single-agent rituximab may become an appropriate initial treatment option for asymptomatic patients with follicular lymphoma pending clinical trial results; however, currently, it should be reserved for symptomatic management in patients requiring therapy.

Rituximab, combination chemotherapy, and prednisone would be appropriate management if symptoms developed or blood counts began to decrease, but it would not be appropriate for this patient now.

Total lymph node irradiation for follicular lymphoma is not appropriate management under any circumstance because follicular lymphocytes circulate and would re-establish disease upon completion of radiation. Moreover, the extent of radiation delivered with total lymph node irradiation would limit marrow reserve and potentially adversely affect later treatments because of cytopenias.

KEY POINT

- **Regardless of the stage at presentation, patients with asymptomatic follicular lymphoma can be followed without therapeutic intervention until they experience symptoms.**

Bibliography

Czuczman M, Straus D, Gribben J, et al. Management options, survivorship, and emerging treatment strategies for follicular and Hodgkin lymphomas. Leuk Lymphoma. 2010;51 Suppl 1:41-49. [PMID: 20658953]

Item 78 Answer: D

Educational Objective: Manage prostate cancer follow-up.

The most appropriate management is prostate-specific antigen (PSA) measurement and digital rectal examination every 6 to 12 months. This patient has average-risk prostate cancer based on his clinical stage of IIA and good response to radiation therapy. After initial treatment, patients should be followed with serial digital rectal examinations and serum PSA measurement. As many as 75% of recurrences are discovered by the fifth year of follow-up. A rising PSA level indicates biochemical recurrence, and estimates of survival can be made from the time of completion of treatment to the rise in the PSA, the rate of that rise, and the initial Gleason score. Although recurrent disease after definitive therapy of early-stage prostate cancer is incurable, significant palliation can be achieved with hormone deprivation therapy and chemotherapy.

Androgen deprivation (hormonal) therapy is recommended for patients with high-risk localized disease or patients with locally advanced disease. It is usually initiated before radiation and continues for months after completing radiation. The optimal duration of adjuvant androgen deprivation therapy is unclear, but longer courses are gaining acceptance. This patient has average-risk disease (low Gleason score and clinical stage), and, therefore, did not receive hormonal therapy with his radiation.

Chemotherapy with docetaxel is an established treatment for patients with hormone-refractory metastatic prostate cancer. However, there is no evidence of benefit from chemotherapy in patients without metastatic prostate cancer.

Serial radiographic examinations are not recommended in the adjuvant setting for monitoring patients with prostate cancer.

KEY POINT

- **Patients with average-risk prostate cancer who achieve remission after radiation therapy should receive follow-up with serial digital rectal examinations and serum prostate-specific antigen measurement every 6 to 12 months.**

Bibliography

Mohler J, Bahnson RR, Boston B, et al. NCCN clinical practice guidelines in oncology: prostate cancer. J Natl Compr Canc Netw. 2010;8(2):162-200. [PMID: 20141676]

Item 79 Answer: E

Educational Objective: Treat stage I rectal cancer.

This patient has cancer of the midrectum that penetrates into, but not fully through, the rectal wall with no lymph node metastases (T2N0M0 stage I), and surgery alone is the treatment of choice for stage I disease. The appropriate management is a low anterior resection using the total mesorectal excision technique to assure full removal of the rectum and the mesorectum. The mesorectum is a fatty sheath surrounding the rectum that contains the locoregional lymph nodes. Careful pathologic evaluation of these nodes will be necessary to confirm the stage of disease. If the tumor is found on pathologic inspection to be a higher T stage than expected (T3 or T4) or if any of the locoregional lymph nodes are found to be positive for cancer (N1 or N2), then postoperative chemoradiation and chemotherapy would be indicated; however, if pathology confirms stage I disease, no further treatment is indicated.

Chemotherapy, radiation therapy, nor combined therapy has been demonstrated to improve outcome in stage I disease. Radiofrequency ablation is a technique that can be used to ablate some focal sites of metastatic disease that are not amenable to resection; however, it does not currently have a role in the treatment of colorectal primary tumors.

KEY POINT

- **Primary surgical resection is the standard treatment for patients with stage I rectal cancer.**

Bibliography

Garcia-Aguilar J, Holt A. Optimal management of small rectal cancers: TAE, TEM, or TME? Surg Oncol Clin North Am. 2010;19(4):743-760. [PMID: 20883951]

Item 80 Answer: C

Educational Objective: Manage a patient with *Helicobacter pylori*–associated gastric lymphoma.

The most appropriate treatment of this patient is a 14-day course of metronidazole, amoxicillin, and omeprazole. Mucosa-associated lymphoid tissue (MALT) lines the digestive tract and provides immune surveillance. Malignant transformation of small MALT B cells is a consequence of chronic antigen stimulation, particularly from *Helicobacter pylori* infection in the context of gastric ulcers. Removal of the antigenic stimulus can result in complete remission of MALT lymphomas. A 14-day course of antimicrobial agents with acid suppression has resulted in a high rate of complete and durable remission in patients with *H. pylori*–associated gastric MALT lymphomas.

Involved-field radiation therapy would only be appropriate for large cell gastric lymphoma or MALT lymphomas unresponsive to antimicrobial therapy. Similarly, rituximab or chemotherapy would only be appropriate if the antimicrobial therapy were to fail.

Observation would not be appropriate. This patient requires treatment of his ulcer. In addition, he requires treatment of the gastric MALT lymphoma, which can progress and disseminate if left untreated, ultimately requiring more aggressive, and, potentially toxic, therapy compared with proton pump inhibitor and antimicrobial therapy.

KEY POINT

- **Gastric mucosa-associated lymphoid tissue lymphoma, when associated with *Helicobacter pylori* infection, can be effectively treated with antimicrobial agents and acid suppression.**

Bibliography

Stathis A, Bertoni F, Zucca E. Treatment of gastric marginal zone lymphoma of MALT type. Expert Opin Pharmacother. 2010;11(13):2141-2152. [PMID: 20586708]

H

Item 81 Answer: C

Educational Objective: Evaluate a patient with small, asymptomatic pulmonary nodules.

The most appropriate next diagnostic step in the evaluation of this patient's pulmonary nodules is follow-up CT in 12 months. This patient has pulmonary emboli confirmed by spiral CT scan. The pulmonary nodules identified were likely asymptomatic because of their size, and, as such, were incidentally found. Evaluation of a pulmonary nodule must balance the need to detect and treat a malignancy quickly and the desire to avoid invasive procedures for a benign nodule. A solitary pulmonary nodule is defined as a nodular opacity that is up to 3 cm in diameter and surrounded by normal lung and not associated with lymphadenopathy. Lesions larger than 3 cm are considered lung masses. CT screening studies have shown that when a cancer is detected, other smaller benign nodules are usually present. When one predominant 1-cm or larger nodule and one or more tiny nodules are present, the larger nodule should be considered separately. The Fleischner Society for Thoracic Imaging and Diagnosis has published recommendations for the need and frequency of follow-up for incidentally discovered nodules of various sizes. In low-risk individuals (never smokers, no history of a first-degree relative with lung cancer, or significant radon or asbestos exposure), follow-up imaging is not required in patients with nodules less than or equal to 4 mm. For high-risk individuals (smoking history, environmental exposure), nodules less than 4 mm require follow-up imaging in 12 months.

Bronchoscopy with cytologic assessment is reasonable for larger, central lesions in which an endobronchial component can be identified but would not be appropriate for evaluation of this patient's nodules with low malignant potential.

Performing a biopsy of lesions as small as those in this patient is not recommended because of the low risk for malignancy and increased risk for biopsy-related complications.

A PET/CT scan would not be likely to provide additional information because it would be unlikely to detect small nodules less than 1 cm in size.

KEY POINT

- **For individuals at higher risk for lung cancer (smoking history, environmental exposure), incidentally discovered nodules less than 4 mm require follow-up imaging in 12 months.**

Bibliography

MacMahon H, Austin JH, Gamsu G, et al; Fleischner Society. Guidelines for management of small pulmonary nodules detected on CT scans: a statement from the Fleischner Society. Radiology. 2005;237(2):395-400. [PMID: 16244247]

Item 82 Answer: C

Educational Objective: Manage a patient with locally advanced, high-risk cervical cancer.

The most appropriate management is pelvic radiation therapy and cisplatin chemotherapy. Patients diagnosed with early-stage cervical cancer should undergo clinical staging with pelvic examination and radiographic imaging. Surgical resection often follows, and a surgical stage is established that often differs from the preoperative clinical stage. Patients with high-risk features identified at surgery (large primary tumor, deep stromal invasion, lymphovascular invasion, or positive lymph nodes), such as this patient, should receive adjuvant treatment with a combination of chemotherapy and radiation. Large randomized clinical trials have confirmed a survival advantage with this approach.

Human papillomavirus (HPV) infection is an important risk factor for the development of cervical cancer. However, knowledge of HPV status after diagnosis does not help with current management.

Pelvic radiation alone would help reduce the risk of local recurrence, but studies have shown that adding chemotherapy to radiation therapy improves survival.

Close observation after treatment is important to monitor for recurrence. Patients who have completed therapy should have a pelvic examination and Pap smear every 3 to 6 months for 2 years, then every 6 months for the next 3 years, and then annually. Patients with advanced disease may require periodic chest radiographs, CT scans of the abdomen and pelvis, or both. However, the best treatment recommendation after surgical resection is to maximize the chance of cure with chemotherapy and radiation treatment.

KEY POINT

- **Patients with cervical cancer who have high-risk features identified at surgery (large primary tumor, deep stromal invasion, lymphovascular invasion, or positive lymph nodes) should receive adjuvant treatment with a combination of chemotherapy and radiation.**

Bibliography

Chemoradiotherapy for Cervical Cancer Meta-Analysis Collaboration. Reducing uncertainties about the effects of chemoradiotherapy for cervical cancer: a systematic review and meta-analysis of individual patient data from 18 randomized trials. J Clin Oncol. 2008:26(35):5802-5812. [PMID: 19001332]

Item 83 Answer: A

Educational Objective: Manage a patient with newly diagnosed breast cancer who meets criteria for genetic testing.

Counseling and genetic testing will be most helpful in guiding this patient's treatment. Because of her young age at diagnosis, her significant paternal family history for breast and ovarian cancer, and Ashkenazi Jewish heritage, she should undergo genetic counseling and testing during preoperative chemotherapy. *BRCA1* or *BRCA2* mutations are the most common genetic mutations found in women with breast cancer. If this patient is a carrier of a deleterious mutation, she is at increased risk for a second primary breast cancer and ovarian cancer. This may inform her decision on two basic surgical strategies: (1) breast-conserving surgical resection of the tumor with intensive surveillance for a second breast primary and ovarian cancer, or (2) prophylactic bilateral mastectomy and salpingo-oophorectomy with no cancer surveillance needed. If she opts for breast conservation, she will need regular breast MRI examinations as an adjunct to mammography. Although no randomized controlled trials show benefit, she may opt for CA-125 and vaginal ultrasound monitoring for ovarian cancer. Prophylactic mastectomies would reduce her risk for developing a new primary breast cancer by more than 90%. Prophylactic bilateral salpingo-oophorectomy would also reduce her risk for breast cancer by 50% and ovarian cancer by more than 90%. Her choice of local surgery will not affect her risk of systemic recurrence from her current malignancy.

Genomic profile assays are useful in patients who have lymph node–negative and hormone receptor–positive disease to determine the risk for recurrence and potential benefit from adjuvant chemotherapy. This assay would not help guide this patient's surgical decision.

PET scanning and measurement of tumor markers are useful in evaluating women with metastatic breast cancer to determine benefit from systemic treatment.

KEY POINT

- **For women who have breast cancer and are at high risk for *BRCA1* or *BRCA2* mutations, genetic testing and counseling may inform surgical options.**

Bibliography

Tirona MT, Sehgal R, Ballester O. Prevention of breast cancer (Part II): risk reduction strategies. Cancer Invest. 2010;28(10):1070-1077. [PMID: 20932221]

Item 84 Answer: D

Educational Objective: Manage low-risk prostate cancer in an elderly patient.

The most appropriate management is observation. This elderly patient has low-risk, stage I prostate cancer based on his clinical stage, low prostate-specific antigen (PSA) level, and low Gleason score. Patients with newly diagnosed prostate cancer have several options for treatment. Urologists tailor their recommendations to patients based on the patient's estimated risk of progression or recurrence. The patient's age and overall health also play an important role in clinical decision making. This patient with low-risk disease and short life expectancy would be best managed with observation.

Androgen deprivation therapy is generally reserved for patients with newly diagnosed high-risk disease who receive radiation therapy or patients with metastatic, hormone-sensitive cancer.

Radiation therapy alone is appropriate treatment for patients at low or average risk. These patients (T1 or T2 cancer with Gleason score <8 and PSA <20 ng/mL [20 µg/L]) have good outcomes with radiation therapy alone. Although radiation alone would be a reasonable choice in this setting, the addition of androgen deprivation therapy is usually only recommended for high-risk patients.

Radical prostatectomy is recommended for younger patients with organ-confined disease and a life expectancy greater than 10 years. This patient's age and underlying medical problems make him a poor candidate for aggressive surgical intervention.

KEY POINT

- **Patients with low-risk prostate cancer and a short life expectancy are optimally managed with observation.**

Bibliography

Mohler J, Bahnson RR, Boston B, et al. NCCN clinical practice guidelines in oncology: prostate cancer. J Natl Compr Canc Netw. 2010;8(2):162-200. [PMID: 20141676]

Item 85 Answer: C

Educational Objective: Prevent central nervous system metastases in a patient with limited-stage small cell lung cancer.

The most appropriate management of this patient is prophylactic brain irradiation. This patient has limited-stage small cell lung cancer (SCLC). The definition of limited-stage disease consists of disease limited to one hemithorax, with hilar and mediastinal lymphadenopathy that can be encompassed within one tolerable radiotherapy portal. Combination chemotherapy is the cornerstone of treatment for both limited-stage and extensive-stage SCLC.

Response rates to combination chemotherapy and mediastinal radiation in patients with limited-stage SCLC range from 80% to 90%, with about 50% experiencing complete responses. However, patients who complete this therapeutic regimen have a 50% to 80% chance of developing central nervous system metastases if they survive for 2 years. Prophylactic brain irradiation may decrease central nervous system relapses and prolong median survival and is therefore recommended for patients who respond positively to treatment. Patients who undergo prophylactic cranial irradiation sometimes report a decline in neuropsychologic function; the degree to which prophylactic cranial irradiation contributes to this decline is controversial.

Cures are rare in SCLC, with viable cancer remaining in most patients. Performing a biopsy of the residual mass would not therefore be recommended because finding residual cancer would not change this patient's management.

Although the duration of chemotherapy for SCLC is not well defined, typical recommendations range from four to six cycles. Additional chemotherapy beyond six cycles has not been shown to be beneficial in patients with SCLC, but it does increase morbidity.

Observation without prophylactic brain irradiation will deprive this patient of additional benefits, including a reduced likelihood for symptomatic brain metastases and subsequent neurologic sequelae as well as slightly improved overall survival.

KEY POINT

- **Patients with limited-stage small cell lung cancer who respond to chemotherapy and radiation should receive prophylactic brain irradiation to decrease central nervous system relapses and prolong median survival.**

Bibliography

Samson DJ, Seidenfeld J, Simon GR, et al; American College of Chest Physicians. Evidence for management of small cell lung cancer: ACCP evidence-based clinical practice guidelines (2nd edition). Chest. 2007;132(3 Suppl):314S-323S. [PMID: 17873177]

Item 86 Answer: D

Educational Objective: Manage a patient with breast cancer and a history of venous thromboembolism.

The most appropriate next step in the management of this patient is ovarian ablation. This premenopausal patient has hormone receptor–positive, moderate-risk, stage II breast cancer. Endocrine therapy following completion of surgery and chemotherapy is recommended. However, because of her history of deep venous thrombosis, tamoxifen is contraindicated because this agent is associated with an increased risk for venous thromboembolism. In this setting, ovarian ablation would be the treatment of choice.

Aromatase inhibitors are only indicated in postmenopausal patients because they cause ovarian stimulation.

This patient has *HER2*-negative breast cancer; therefore, adjuvant therapy with trastuzumab is not indicated.

Routine radiographic imaging following completion of adjuvant chemotherapy is not indicated according to American Society of Clinical Oncology guideline recommendations because it has not been shown to improve survival.

KEY POINT

- **Tamoxifen can increase the risk for thromboembolic complications.**

Bibliography

Early Breast Cancer Trialists' Collaborative Group (EBCTCG). Effects of chemotherapy and hormonal therapy for early breast cancer on recurrence and 15-year survival: an overview of the randomised trials. Lancet. 2005;365(9472):1687-1717. [PMID: 15894097]

Item 87 Answer: A

Educational Objective: Diagnose bevacizumab-induced vascular perforation.

This patient with stage IV colon cancer has a bevacizumab-induced intestinal perforation. Bevacizumab is an agent that targets the vascular endothelial growth factor receptor, with hypertension as its most common toxicity. However, bevacizumab can also disrupt normal vasculature, resulting in poor wound healing and vascular catastrophes, including bleeding or thromboses. Perforations of previously asymptomatic peptic ulcers or diverticula can result in an acute abdomen such as that in this patient. In addition, dehiscence of prior surgical wounds can also been seen with this drug, but not typically 3 years after the original surgery.

Toxicities of 5-fluorouracil are typically diarrhea and mucositis. This agent can sometimes cause significant intestinal mucosal damage but does not cause perforations.

Oxaliplatin can cause neurotoxicity, typically related to cold, as well as a distal sensory neuropathy; however, oxaliplatin nerve toxicity does not manifest as a bowel perforation.

Typhlitis, also called neutropenic enterocolitis, can result as a complication of myelosuppressive chemotherapy and presents with fever and abdominal pain in profoundly neutropenic patients. Perforation would not be common. In addition, the chemotherapy given for colon cancer does not usually cause significant neutropenia.

KEY POINT

- **Bevacizumab can cause hypertension, poor wound healing, and vascular catastrophes, including bleeding or thromboses.**

Bibliography

Keefe D, Bowen J, Gibson R, Tan T, Okera M, Stringer A. Noncardiac vascular toxicities of vascular endothelial growth factor inhibitors in advanced cancer: a review. Oncologist. 2011;16(4):432-444. [PMID: 21441297]

Item 88 Answer: C

Educational Objective: Diagnose mantle cell lymphoma.

The patient has mantle cell lymphoma. Most patients with mantle cell lymphoma present with advanced-stage disease involving extranodal sites, including the bowel, peripheral blood, and bone marrow. Mantle cell lymphoma is characterized by the worst features of indolent and aggressive lymphomas. This disease is considered incurable (as are disseminated indolent lymphomas) but has a shorter median survival than disseminated indolent lymphomas of approximately 3 years. A diagnosis is confirmed by the presence of overexpression of cyclin D1 and a t(11;14) translocation in the malignant lymphoid cells.

Diffuse large B-cell lymphoma can also involve multiple organs, including the bowel; however, the cells in diffuse large B-cell lymphoma are large and do not over express cyclin D1.

Similarly, follicular lymphoma does not usually involve the bowel and is not characterized by overexpression of cyclin D1 or CD5.

CD4-positive T-cell leukemia characterized by major skin involvement is known as mycosis fungoides. When the leukemic phase is also prominent, it is referred to as Sézary syndrome. The cells in mycosis fungoides have a folded or cerebriform nucleus morphology. Skin involvement in patients with mycosis fungoides ranges from patchy areas to diffuse erythroderma. Infection of skin lesions is common, and infection leading to sepsis is the leading cause of death. Usually, there is no bowel involvement. The constellation of symptoms and findings found in mycosis fungoides is not consistent with that of this patient.

KEY POINT

- **Mantle cell lymphoma commonly involves multiple extranodal sites, including the bowel and bone marrow; overexpression of cyclin D1 and a t(11:14) translocation are diagnostic.**

Bibliography

Kurtin PJ. Indolent lymphomas of mature B lymphocytes. Hematol Oncol Clin North Am. 2009;23(4):769-790. [PMID: 19577169]

Item 89 Answer: C

Educational Objective: Treat cancer of unknown primary site.

Mastectomy and axillary lymph dissection should be performed, and the patient should be treated for breast cancer. A patient is considered to have cancer of unknown primary (CUP) site when a tumor is detected at one or more metastatic sites and routine evaluation fails to define a primary site. The initial workup of patients presenting with presumed CUP should not be exhaustive but should focus on evaluation of likely primary sites. Women who present with axillary lymphadenopathy without other findings should be treated for stage II breast cancer. An occult primary tumor is identified on mastectomy in 50% to 60% of these patients, even when the physical examination and mammogram are normal. MRI of the breast can often identify a primary site even if mammography is normal and can often lead to breast conservation and is a recommended part of the evaluation. Patients who have CUP with axillary lymphadenopathy only and who are found to have breast cancer have the same survival rate as patients with stage II disease.

This patient has potentially curable disease, and neither chemotherapy alone nor radiation therapy alone, which is palliative, is adequate. Excision of the lymph node alone would also be insufficient because the breast is the presumed source of the primary tumor, and there may be tumor involvement in additional lymph nodes.

KEY POINT

- **Cancer of unknown primary site presenting as axillary lymphadenopathy in women should be managed as stage II breast cancer.**

Bibliography

Hainsworth JD, Fizazi K. Treatment for patients with unknown primary cancer and favorable prognostic factors. Semin Oncol. 2009;36(1):44-51. [PMID: 19179187]

Item 90 Answer: E

Educational Objective: Treat locally advanced gastroesophageal junction adenocarcinoma.

This patient requires surgery plus perioperative chemotherapy for locally advanced (stage III) adenocarcinoma of the gastroesophageal junction. Risk factors for esophageal adenocarcinoma include male sex, Barrett esophagus, and gastroesophageal reflux disease. Barrett esophagus, a metaplastic condition in which columnar or glandular epithelium replaces normal squamous epithelium in the distal esophagus, is a major risk factor, conferring a substantially increased risk for esophageal adenocarcinoma compared with the unaffected population. The patient is a prime candidate for curative therapy. He has no known comorbidities that would be contraindications to surgery or chemotherapy. A large randomized trial (the MAGIC trial) compared surgery alone with surgery plus a chemotherapy regimen of epirubicin, cisplatin, and 5-fluorouracil (the ECF regimen) for 3 months before and 3 months after surgery. The group that received surgery plus perioperative chemotherapy had a 36% 5-year survival rate versus a 23% 5-year survival rate in the surgery-only arm. Thus, surgery plus perioperative chemotherapy is preferred to surgery alone.

Radiation therapy or chemotherapy alone could be used for palliative treatment; however, this patient, although he would be at high risk for recurrence, can be offered potentially curative therapy with surgical resection of the tumor and the surrounding lymph nodes in addition to perioperative chemotherapy.

KEY POINT

- Gastroesophageal cancers are treated with surgical resection and perioperative chemotherapy.

Bibliography

Cunningham D, Allum WH, Stenning SP, et al; MAGIC Trial Participants. Perioperative chemotherapy versus surgery alone for resectable gastroesophageal cancer. N Engl J Med. 2006;355(1):11-20. [PMID: 16822992]

Item 91 Answer: B

Educational Objective: Evaluate a patient with metastatic non–small cell lung cancer.

This patient with metastatic adenocarcinoma and no smoking history should undergo epidermal growth factor receptor (EGFR) mutation tumor analysis because it is possible the patient's tumor harbors an EGFR mutation. Patients whose tumors have a mutation in the EGFR gene often benefit dramatically from therapy that targets this receptor. These mutations most commonly occur in women with adenocarcinoma who are never smokers or have a very limited smoking history and in women of East Asian descent. Although patients with EGFR mutations typically present with advanced-stage disease, they tend to have an improved survival compared with patients with adenocarcinoma without the mutation. Chemotherapy is the most common treatment recommended in the typical patient with metastatic disease. Medications that target the EGFR, such as erlotinib and gefitinib, produce an approximately 70% response rate, with a median survival longer than the usual 8 to 10 months associated with advanced non–small cell lung cancer treated with standard chemotherapeutic agents.

Biopsy of the liver would not typically be recommended given the likelihood of multiple sites of metastatic disease as demonstrated by the results of this patient's staging scans. However, a solitary focus of disease outside the lung would be considered for biopsy because the result would change the stage of disease, and, consequently, prognosis and treatment.

Mediastinoscopy is usually performed in patients with potentially resectable non–small cell lung cancer to determine whether mediastinal lymph nodes are involved. However, this patient's CT and radionuclide bone scans suggest advanced disease, which would preclude surgery as a therapeutic option.

Serum chromogranin levels may be elevated in patients with neuroendocrine tumors such as carcinoid and in those with small cell lung cancer; however, chromogranin elevations are not associated with adenocarcinomas.

KEY POINT

- Patients with epidermal growth factor receptor (EGFR) gene tumor mutations—most commonly women with adenocarcinoma who are never smokers or have a very limited smoking history and women of East Asian descent—often benefit dramatically from therapy targeting this receptor.

Bibliography

Gridelli C, De Marinis F, Di Maio M, Cortinovis D, Cappuzzo F, Mok T. Gefitinib as first-line treatment for patients with advanced non-small-cell lung cancer with activating epidermal growth factor receptor mutation: Review of the evidence. Lung Cancer. 2011;71(3):249-257. [PMID: 21216486]

Item 92 Answer: D

Educational Objective: Manage a patient with advanced kidney cancer.

The most appropriate management of this patient is left nephrectomy. This patient has advanced kidney disease as manifested by the classic triad of pain, a mass, and hematuria, and chest imaging is consistent with metastatic disease. Studies in patients presenting with advanced disease and treated with interferon alfa demonstrated that survival was improved by resection of the primary tumor. This is the only malignancy in which removing the primary tumor in the setting of metastatic disease can improve overall outcome rather than just reduce local symptoms. It is necessary to carefully select patients for nephrectomy; only those patients eligible for immunotherapy should be offered cancer resection.

CT-guided lung biopsy would be a reasonable method for documenting metastatic disease but only after the primary tumor has been resected.

A biopsy of the kidney mass is not recommended because biopsy results, positive or negative, would not change the need to perform a nephrectomy. In this patient with perirenal lymphadenopathy and pulmonary nodules suggestive of metastatic disease, a negative biopsy would be viewed as a false-negative result and would require follow-up surgical removal.

Systemic treatments, including vascular endothelial growth factor tyrosine kinase inhibitors such as sunitinib or sorafenib, may be helpful in patients with advanced-stage or metastatic renal cell cancer; however, cytotoxic chemotherapy has little effect in this setting.

KEY POINT

- Kidney cancer is the only malignancy in which removing the primary tumor in the setting of metastatic disease can improve overall outcome rather than just reduce local symptoms.

Bibliography

Chen DY, Uzzo RG. Evaluation and management of the renal mass. Med Clin North Am. 2011;95(1):179-189. [PMID: 21095421]

Item 93 Answer: B

Educational Objective: Treat high-risk, locally advanced prostate cancer.

The most appropriate management is androgen deprivation therapy (ADT) and radiation therapy. Patients with high-risk disease (T3, T4, Gleason score 8 to 10 or prostate-specific antigen [PSA] level >20 ng/mL [20 µg/L]) may benefit from short-term (4 to 6 months) ADT (hormonal therapy) using a gonadotropin-releasing hormone (GnRH) agonist. Androgen-blocking agents given before, during, and after radiation therapy have been shown to improve survival in patients with high-risk localized or locally advanced disease. ADT is also used as first-line treatment for patients with a rising serum PSA level after initial definitive therapy for prostate cancer or for those with metastatic disease.

Brachytherapy (radioactive seed implants) is a therapeutic option for patients at low or average risk (T1 or T2 cancer with Gleason score <8 and PSA level <20 ng/mL [20 µg/L]). However, it is not appropriate in this high-risk patient.

Radiation therapy alone is appropriate treatment for patients with low- or average-risk prostate cancer. These patients have good outcomes with radiation therapy alone.

Radical prostatectomy is recommended for patients with organ-confined disease and a life expectancy greater than 10 years. Patients with extension beyond the prostate gland, a high PSA level (>20 ng/mL [20 µg/L]), or a high Gleason score (8 to 10) have a high risk for disease spread beyond the prostate and are not usually candidates for surgery.

KEY POINT

- **Patients with high-risk prostate cancer are optimally managed with a combination of androgen deprivation therapy and radiation.**

Bibliography

Crook J, Ludgate C, Malone S, et al. Final report of multicenter Canadian Phase III randomized trial of 3 versus 8 months of neoadjuvant androgen deprivation therapy before conventional-dose radiotherapy for clinically localized prostate cancer. Int J Radiat Oncol Biol Phys. 2009;73(2):327-333. [PMID: 18707821]

Item 94 Answer: B

Educational Objective: Treat a patient with advanced-stage head and neck cancer.

The most appropriate treatment is chemotherapy and radiation therapy. Treatment for head and neck cancer is highly complex, not only because of the variety of tumor subsites involved in this disease, but also because of the anatomic constraints of the head and neck region and the importance of maintaining organ function during and after treatment. The treatment of patients with locoregionally advanced head and neck cancer (stages III and IVA and IVB disease without distant metastases) generally involves a combination of multiple treatment modalities, including radiation, chemotherapy, and surgery. Selection of therapy for this group of patients depends on careful assessment of prognosis as well as preservation of organ function. Integration of multiple modalities of treatment into the therapeutic regimen of patients with head and neck cancer has led to improvements in cure and local control rates, but multimodality therapy–associated toxicity is substantially increased compared with single-modality treatment. This patient has advanced (stage IV) cancer of the tongue base as evidenced by an extensive primary tumor and several enlarged lymph nodes (T4,N2). The risk of local recurrence is high in patients with advanced-stage head and neck cancer despite optimal therapy. Radiation can encompass the entire primary tumor, even with bone invasion, as well as the regional lymph nodes. The chances of long-term control in a patient with such extensive local disease with a single modality are low. Consequently, chemotherapy, usually cisplatin, is offered with the radiation. Because of improved local control rates with combined radiation therapy and chemotherapy, organ preservation is possible in some patients with primary tumors of the larynx or base of the tongue.

Because head and neck cancers tend to recur locally rather than spread systemically, surgical resection and radiation therapy are the primary treatment modalities. Chemotherapy alone is not used as definitive therapy in patients with head and neck cancer; however, it is used as the primary treatment of patients with metastatic disease.

Patients with early-stage (stages I and II) head and neck cancer receive surgery or radiation with curative intent. Because both modalities result in similar rates of local control and survival, the therapeutic choice is usually based on an assessment of competing modalities, functional outcomes, and accessibility. However, neither surgery nor radiation would be used as the sole treatment of a tumor as extensive as that in this patient because it would be ineffective in achieving disease control.

KEY POINT

- **The treatment of patients with locoregionally advanced head and neck cancer (stages III and IVA and IVB disease without distant metastases) generally involves a combination of multiple modalities, including radiation, chemotherapy, and surgery.**

Bibliography

Casasola RJ. Head and neck cancer. J R Coll Physicians Edinb. 2010;40(4):343-345; quiz 345. [PMID: 2113214]

Item 95 Answer: C

Educational Objective: Manage a patient with metastatic carcinoid tumor.

An observational interval of 3 to 4 months, with repeat CT scans to assess for changes, would be appropriate management of this patient's disease. The patient has an incidental finding of small-volume, asymptomatic, metastatic, low-grade, well-differentiated neuroendocrine tumor (NET), and because of the lack of symptoms and near-normal liver chemistry test results, it is very likely this cancer has been present for many years, and intervention will not be required at this point. The pattern of disease, with numerous small lesions scattered throughout the liver, is clearly unresectable and incurable. It is also asymptomatic and causing no substantial impact on liver chemistry studies. As is true for up to 75% of carcinoid tumors, this tumor appears to be hormonally nonfunctional, as demonstrated by a normal blood serotonin level and no clinical evidence of carcinoid syndrome (which can include diarrhea, flushing, and wheezing). If serial scans show little or no growth, then continued observation will permit the patient to delay the risks and toxicity associated with interventions. If substantial tumor growth occurs under observation or tumor-related symptoms develop, then treatment should be considered.

Hepatic arterial embolization may be an appropriate consideration in growing or symptomatic liver metastases of NET but would not be appropriate at this early, asymptomatic stage.

Although radiofrequency ablation can be used to treat a limited number of liver metastases, it does not have a role in treating a patient with numerous small, asymptomatic lesions.

Although chemotherapy has some modest activity in pancreatic NETs, CT scan shows a normal pancreas. Therefore, streptozocin-based therapy, which can be modestly active in pancreatic NETs, would not be appropriate in this patient. Furthermore, given this patient's asymptomatic small-volume disease, the risks of cytotoxic chemotherapy would not be warranted at this time, even if he had a pancreatic NET.

KEY POINT

- **Asymptomatic patients with indolent, well-differentiated metastatic carcinoid tumors can often be managed with expectant observation and serial imaging studies.**

Bibliography

Reidy DL, Tang LH, Saltz LB. Treatment of advanced disease in patients with well-differentiated neuroendocrine tumors. Nature Clin Pract Oncol. 2009;6(3):143-152. [PMID: 19190591]

Item 96 Answer: C

Educational Objective: **Treat a patient with stage II non–small cell lung cancer.**

The most appropriate management of this patient is surgical resection followed by chemotherapy. The primary goals of staging are to identify patients who can receive treatment with curative intent as quickly and efficiently as possible, to minimize expensive and invasive testing, and to identify patients with incurable disease to diminish the risks associated with surgery or combined-modality approaches. This patient has non–small cell lung cancer (NSCLC), classified as stage II disease because of the size of the tumor and absence of mediastinal lymph node involvement or distant disease. This early-stage cancer is potentially curable with surgical resection, but the risk for recurrence with surgery alone is approximately 40% to 50%. The use of adjuvant chemotherapy has been shown to consistently improve survival in patients with early-stage NSCLC (stage IB-III) treated with surgical resection. Conversely, the use of adjuvant radiation therapy in patients with early-stage NSCLC has not been associated with a survival benefit and may actually be deleterious to overall survival. Adjuvant chemotherapy with a cisplatin-based regimen would be recommended postoperatively to reduce the risk for recurrence.

Combination treatment with chemotherapy and radiation is typically recommended for patients with localized disease that is not considered surgically resectable (that is, stage III disease), but it would not be recommended for this patient with stage II resectable disease.

Systemic chemotherapy would not be recommended as primary treatment for this patient's localized disease because it is not as effective as surgery and adjuvant chemotherapy. Metastatic stage IV disease should be treated with chemotherapy only. In these patients, selective use of radiation therapy can palliate lung cancer symptoms by decreasing bronchial compression, reducing hemoptysis, improving superior vena cava syndrome, and treating bony metastases.

KEY POINT

- **Stage II non–small cell lung cancer is potentially curable with surgical resection and adjuvant postoperative chemotherapy to reduce the recurrence risk.**

Bibliography

Sangha R, Price J, Butts CA. Adjuvant therapy in non-small cell lung cancer: current and future directions. Oncologist. 2010;15(8):862-872. [PMID: 20682608]

Item 97 Answer: B

Educational Objective: **Treat a patient with stage III colon cancer.**

The most appropriate goal of this patient's recommended adjuvant chemotherapy is to improve overall survival, which can be considered equivalent to cure. Because clinical trials are limited in duration and follow-up, the term "cure" is not often used. Prolonging the disease-free interval means that, at a minimum, patients are living longer without a recurrence. This may mean the recurrence has either been delayed, or optimally, prevented from ever developing. Studies have shown that improved disease-free survival is a valid end point of adjuvant colon cancer studies because it translates into an overall survival benefit with longer follow-up. This patient has stage III colon cancer (tumor involving regional lymph nodes) with an approximate 30% to 60% chance of cure with surgical resection alone. Adjuvant chemotherapy for colon cancer reduces recurrence rates and increases the likelihood for cure by an additional 7% to 15%.

Clinical benefit rate is a term used to describe an outcome of cancer therapies given palliatively rather than curatively. In metastatic disease, treatment may only stabilize the disease rather than result in significant tumor shrinkage. The sum of measurable complete and partial responses as well as those with disease stability is termed the clinical benefit rate.

Disease-specific survival is a term describing the percentage of patients alive without having a recurrence of the particular disease. Although this would seem to define the appropriate goal of adjuvant therapy, this term excludes deaths from treatment itself, as well death from other causes, whether related or not. The goal of adjuvant therapy is survival and not just prevention of cancer recurrence and death.

Adjuvant chemotherapy has not been shown to decrease the risk for second colon cancers or other gastrointestinal malignancies.

KEY POINT

- **Adjuvant chemotherapy for colon cancer reduces recurrence rates and increases the likelihood for disease-free survival.**

Bibliography

Sargent DJ, Patiyil S, Yothers G, et al; ACCENT Group. End points for colon cancer adjuvant trials: observations and recommendations based on individual patient data from 20,898 patients enrolled onto 18 randomized trials from the ACCENT Group. J Clin Oncol. 2007;25(29):4569-4574. [PMID: 178760008]

Item 98 Answer: B

Educational Objective: **Manage cancer of unknown primary site.**

The patient has a cancer of unknown primary (CUP) site that is relatively symmetrical around the midline, and cisplatin-based therapy would have the potential for a favorable and durable response. Patients with poorly differentiated carcinoma are a heterogeneous group that includes a few with highly responsive neoplasms and therefore require special attention in the initial clinical and pathologic evaluation. Young men with a predominant tumor location in the mediastinum and retroperitoneum may have the extragonadal germ cell cancer syndrome. Serum levels of human chorionic gonadotropin and α-fetoprotein should be measured, and these patients should be treated as though they had poor-prognosis testicular cancer, with chemotherapy administration and surgical resection of residual radiographic abnormalities.

Bevacizumab is a monoclonal antibody against vascular endothelial growth factor. It has modest activity in some solid tumors but is not part of CUP treatment algorithms because of lack of efficacy in this setting.

The patient's tumor is far too diffuse for surgical or radiation therapy management.

KEY POINT

- **Young men with cancer of unknown primary site and a predominant tumor location in the mediastinum and retroperitoneum may have the extragonadal germ cell cancer syndrome.**

Bibliography

Hainsworth JD, Fizazi K. Treatment for patients with unknown primary cancer and favorable prognostic factors. Semin Oncol. 2009;36(1):44-51. [PMID: 19179187]

Item 99 Answer: A

Educational Objective: **Manage a patient with progressing mycosis fungoides/Sézary syndrome.**

The most appropriate management of this patient is alemtuzumab monoclonal antibody therapy directed against CD52. Mycosis fungoides (which affects the skin) and Sézary syndrome (which affects the skin and blood) are the most common forms of cutaneous T-cell non-Hodgkin lymphoma. Mycosis fungoides commonly presents with indolent localized disease manifesting as dry, pruritic, erythematous patches that can be observed or treated with topical corticosteroids. As the disease progresses, T cells infiltrate multiple organs, lymph nodes, and skin, causing organomegaly and organ dysfunction. When CD4-positive cells with cerebriform nuclei are observed in the peripheral blood as in this patient, the disease is characterized as Sézary syndrome. As the disease advances, patients experience progressive immunodeficiency, and, commonly, recurrent infections. Disease with extracutaneous involvement (stage IV) requires systemic therapy. Alemtuzumab is an effective therapy for disease characterized by organ involvement.

Although topical corticosteroids would be appropriate for treating the skin manifestations of localized disease, they would not be appropriate in this patient who now has progressing disease with organ involvement.

Total body irradiation would not be indicated unless it was administered as part of allogeneic hematopoietic stem cell transplantation.

Observation would not be appropriate in this patient who has advanced disease characterized by organ involvement and immunodeficiency.

KEY POINT

- **Mycosis fungoides can remain indolent for many years but eventually progresses and requires systemic therapy.**

Bibliography

Galper SL, Smith BD, Wilson LD. Diagnosis and management of mycosis fungoides. Oncology (Williston Park). 2010;24(6):491-501. [PMID: 2056859]

Item 100 Answer: D

Educational Objective: Evaluate a postmenopausal woman for suspected ovarian cancer.

The most appropriate next step is paracentesis with cytologic analysis. Patients with ovarian cancer have vague symptoms that often are not apparent until late in the disease owing to the free-floating position of the ovaries within the peritoneal cavity; consequently, more than 70% of women with ovarian cancer have metastatic disease beyond the pelvis at presentation. On physical examination of patients with ovarian cancer, abdominal distention and a fluid wave may be detected. Because the normal postmenopausal ovary is not palpable, any palpable adnexal mass found during the pelvic examination of postmenopausal women should be considered suspicious for ovarian cancer. The finding of a pelvic or adnexal mass and ascites in a postmenopausal woman is suspicious for advanced ovarian cancer. This patient's history of nulliparity and smoking increases the likelihood of ovarian cancer.

BRCA testing is useful for evaluating the risk for development of breast or ovarian cancer, but it would not help to establish the diagnosis in this setting. This patient's family history is positive for cancer in only a second-degree relative, which makes a genetic disorder very unlikely.

The diagnostic yield from paracentesis with cytologic analysis would be high from this procedure, and it is much less invasive than laparotomy and biopsy. Laparotomy would confirm the diagnosis, but it is usually reserved for definitive staging and treatment rather than as an initial diagnostic strategy.

Given the patient's age, the advanced disease discovered on ultrasound, and the normal-appearing cervix on pelvic examination, cervical cancer is much less likely. Consequently, a Pap smear, although reasonable to do, is not likely to establish a diagnosis.

Serum CA-125 measurement is neither sensitive nor specific enough to establish a diagnosis of ovarian cancer but would be useful for monitoring treatment after the diagnosis is established. CA-125 can be elevated in other malignancies and several benign settings, including endometriosis, pelvic inflammatory disease, and peritonitis.

KEY POINT

- **Paracentesis with cytologic analysis is recommended as the most appropriate diagnostic strategy for a postmenopausal woman who presents with ascites and a pelvic mass.**

Bibliography

Roman LD, Muderspach LI, Stein SM, Laifer-Narin S, Groshen S, Morrow CP. Pelvic examination, tumor marker level, and gray-scale and Doppler sonography in the prediction of pelvic cancer. Obstet Gynecol. 1997;89(4):493-500. [PMID: 9083301]

Item 101 Answer: B

Educational Objective: Diagnose Lambert-Eaton syndrome in a patient with lung cancer.

The most likely diagnosis is Lambert-Eaton syndrome. Lambert-Eaton myasthenic syndrome is a rare neuromuscular junction transmission disorder caused by antibodies directed against presynaptic voltage-gated P/Q-type calcium channels. This syndrome occurs in 5% of patients who have small cell lung cancer and also in patients with other cancers. Patients typically report progressive proximal limb weakness, and most have symptoms of dysautonomia, such as dry eyes, dry mouth, constipation, and erectile dysfunction. Lambert-Eaton myasthenic syndrome should be considered in any patient with findings of proximal limb weakness and absent deep tendon reflexes on neurologic examination. Facilitation (improvement of deep tendon reflexes and muscle strength after brief isometric exercise) may also be noted on neurologic examination and is a cardinal bedside confirmatory test. Electromyographic testing and positive assays for P/Q-type calcium channel antibodies establish the diagnosis. The development of this paraneoplastic syndrome does not necessarily suggest lung cancer activity or recurrence.

Brain metastases may be asymptomatic or, more often, characterized by focal neurologic findings (such as aphasia, unilateral motor or sensory changes) and headache. Brain metastases would not cause generalized weakness or decreased reflexes.

Central nervous system radiation can result in neurologic toxicities, most notably cognitive difficulties; however, this patient has demonstrated no problems in cognitive function and therefore is unlikely to be experiencing radiation toxicity.

Spinal cord compression can occur in patients with small cell lung cancer, but it is typically associated with back pain. Weakness of the extremities below the spinal cord lesion may also occur but is usually associated with hyperreflexia, proximal and distal motor weakness, and, often, incontinence. Dry mouth and dry eyes are not characteristic of spinal cord compression

Central nervous system irradiation, spinal cord compression, and brain metastases are not associated with improved muscle strength or facilitation of reflexes with exercise, which is very specific for Lambert-Eaton syndrome.

KEY POINT

- **Lambert-Eaton syndrome is a myasthenic illness most often associated with small cell lung cancer and other cancers and is characterized by proximal weakness and absent deep tendon reflexes that typically improve with activity, as well as signs of autonomic insufficiency.**

Bibliography

Petty R. Lambert Eaton myasthenic syndrome. Pract Neurol. 2007;7(4):265-267. [PMID: 17636143]

Item 102 Answer: D

Educational Objective: Manage early-stage melanoma.

This patient requires no further intervention. He has an early melanoma less than 0.75 mm in thickness, with no poor prognostic features, such as a thickness greater than 0.75 mm, a positive deep margin, or lymphovascular invasion, and simple excision with a 1-cm margin is acceptable therapy. Surgery is the mainstay of therapy for patients with melanoma. Because melanoma tumor cells can extend beyond the visible borders of the melanoma, wide excision is necessary to ensure that all melanoma is removed. The extent of surgery depends on the thickness of the primary melanoma and is best performed by a specialist. Complete excision of thin (less than 1 mm in depth), nonulcerated melanomas is associated with good outcomes, with survival rates greater than 95%.

Sentinel lymph node biopsy is generally recommended for patients with tumors greater than 1 mm thick; however, it has not consistently been shown to benefit long-term survival. Tumors thicker than 1 mm require a 2-cm margin of resection, and tumors with clinically positive nodes require lymph node dissection.

Radiation therapy after surgery does not play a role in the management of melanoma.

Adjuvant interferon alfa is of questionable benefit, even in more advanced tumors, but would not be a consideration in lesions less than 1 mm in thickness.

KEY POINT

- **For early melanoma, excision alone, with 1-cm surgical margins, is sufficient.**

Bibliography

Tsao H, Atkins MB, Sober AJ. Management of cutaneous melanoma [erratum in N Engl J Med. 2004;351(23):2461]. N Engl J Med. 2004;351(10):998-1012. [PMID: 15342808]

Item 103 Answer: A

Educational Objective: Evaluate a patient for head and neck cancer.

The most appropriate next step in the evaluation of this patient is endoscopic evaluation of the oropharynx. This patient, with a sore throat and a palpable lymph node in the jugulodigastric chain, is unlikely to have an infection in the absence of visible pharyngeal erythema or exudate. In addition, the location and isolated nature of this enlarged lymph node in the high neck and the presence of a sore throat are unusual for lymphoma. Consequently, he should undergo evaluation to exclude oropharyngeal cancer because squamous cell cancers of the head and neck can occur in patients without risk factors, presumably owing to infection with Epstein-Barr virus or human papillomavirus (HPV). In fact, the presence of HPV antibodies in patients with squamous cell cancer of the oral cavity or pharynx confers a better prognosis than the absence of such antibodies in patients with this type of cancer. Common symptoms and signs of head and neck cancer include the presence of a painless mass; mucosal ulcer; localized (often referred) pain of the mouth, teeth, throat, or ear; odynophagia or dysphagia; proptosis; diplopia or loss of vision; hearing loss; persistent unilateral sinusitis; and unilateral tonsillar enlargement in adults. The optimal sequence of steps in diagnosis begins with fiberoptic inspection of all mucosal surfaces, followed by a biopsy of any abnormal areas. This examination is not only useful for documenting the presence, site, and extent of tumors in the upper aerodigestive tract, but it can also identify other primary tumors. In the absence of lesions, a fine-needle aspirate (FNA) of the palpable lymph node is recommended to establish the diagnosis.

Excisional biopsy should be avoided in patients with suspected head and neck cancer because it could compromise the potential surgical approach by disrupting tissue planes in the neck. If an FNA is performed and is nondiagnostic, a surgeon skilled in malignancies of the head and neck should perform the lymph node biopsy, anticipating potential resection later.

An MRI is an appropriate test to order in the staging of a patient with a head and neck malignancy but is not the first test to order in the evaluation of a palpable lymph node.

PET/CT may be ordered as part of a staging evaluation but would not be warranted before a tissue diagnosis is established.

KEY POINT

- **Fiberoptic endoscopy of all mucosal surfaces, followed by a biopsy of any abnormal areas, are the appropriate initial diagnostic steps in patients with suspected head and neck cancer.**

Bibliography

Casasola RJ. Head and neck cancer. J R Coll Physicians Edinb. 2010;40(4):343-345; quiz 345. [PMID: 21132146]

Item 104 Answer: C

Educational Objective: Evaluate a patient with an incidentally found kidney mass.

The most appropriate next step in the evaluation is kidney ultrasonography. This patient's otherwise asymptomatic kidney mass was found incidentally during evaluation for diverticulitis. Many kidney cancers are found incidentally. Although hematuria, pain, and an upper abdominal mass are considered to be the classic triad for diagnosing renal cell cancer, patients rarely present with these findings. The most appropriate next step in the evaluation of a kidney mass is ultrasonography to determine whether the mass is cystic or solid. A simple cyst is extremely unlikely to represent a malignancy, and further evaluation would not be necessary. If the mass does not fulfill the ultrasound criteria for a simple cyst, then additional imaging is required, most often a contrast-enhanced CT scan. In addition, CT scans are used to identify the presence of extension into surrounding tissues, involvement of the renal vein, or the presence of regional lymphadenopathy.

Ordering a biopsy of kidney masses greater than 3 cm is not typically recommended because it is highly likely such masses are malignant and will require resection by a urologist. Smaller lesions of uncertain cause can be biopsied, and lesions that are less than 1.5 cm are followed for evidence of growth.

Solid masses measuring more than 3 to 4 cm are highly suspicious for malignancy; therefore, it would not be prudent to perform a follow-up CT in this patient in 6 months. In this case, she would require immediate evaluation for surgical resection.

MRI of the abdomen to exclude metastatic liver disease would not be recommended now before ultrasonographic assessment to determine whether the mass is a simple cyst, complex cyst, or solid mass.

KEY POINT

- **After the initial identification of a kidney mass on radiographic imaging, kidney ultrasonography is appropriate to determine whether the mass is cystic or solid.**

Bibliography

Chen DY, Uzzo RG. Evaluation and management of the renal mass. Med Clin North Am. 2011;95(1):179-189. [PMID: 2109542]

H

Item 105 Answer: D

Educational Objective: Manage a patient with superior vena cava syndrome.

The most appropriate management of this patient is mediastinoscopy and biopsy. Superior vena cava (SVC) syndrome is most commonly caused by lung cancer but can also be caused by lymphoma, including Hodgkin lymphoma, and mediastinal germ cell tumors. SVC syndrome is the initial manifestation in approximately 60% of patients with previously undiagnosed malignancy, and its onset is insidious. Common symptoms and findings include progressive dyspnea, facial swelling, cough, distention of the neck and chest veins, facial edema, cyanosis, facial plethora, and upper extremity edema. Common radiographic findings include mediastinal widening and pleural effusion.

The appropriate immediate management of patients with SVC syndrome depends on the histopathology; therefore, it is necessary to first obtain a tissue diagnosis. In the absence of more accessible sites such as peripheral lymphadenopathy, mediastinoscopy and biopsy has a high likelihood of providing adequate tissue for a diagnosis and is associated with a low incidence of complications (5%). The goal of treatment, which can usually be delayed while a tissue diagnosis is obtained, is to reduce symptoms and treat the underlying malignancy.

Oral corticosteroids might be effective for treating lymphoma or Hodgkin lymphoma but would not be appropriate for lung cancer.

Although radiation therapy alone would be appropriate for treating non–small cell lung cancer, and chemotherapy alone would be appropriate for small cell lung cancer, a histologic diagnosis must first be established before a treatment regimen can be selected. Similarly, combination chemotherapy and radiation may be appropriate in some cases; however, whether combination therapy is appropriate cannot be determined until a tissue diagnosis is made.

KEY POINT

- **A tissue diagnosis should be obtained before a therapeutic intervention is initiated in patients with superior vena cava syndrome.**

Bibliography

Wan JF, Bezjak A. Superior vena cava syndrome. Hematol Oncol Clin North Am. 2010;24(3):501-513. [PMID: 20488350]

Item 106 Answer: D

Educational Objective: Treat a patient with advanced-stage non–small cell lung cancer.

The most appropriate treatment is systemic chemotherapy. This patient has stage IV non–small cell lung cancer (NSCLC) as evidenced by a malignant pleural effusion. The 7th edition of the TNM staging system has reclassified malignant pleural effusion as a distant metastasis, automatically placing such patients into stage IV disease status. In patients with stage IV disease, the most appropriate treatment is chemotherapy. Because metastatic NSCLC is a systemic process, systemic chemotherapy is typically used as the primary treatment modality. Goals of therapy are symptom palliation and possible prolongation of survival.

Combination chemotherapy and radiation is offered to patients with unresectable stage III disease in which the tumor and regional lymph nodes can be encompassed in a radiation field but would not be appropriate for this patient.

Although radiation therapy can be used palliatively in the setting of superior vena cava syndrome and obstructive pneumonitis, brain metastases and spinal cord compression, and bone metastases, it is not recommended as first-line therapy for this patient with advanced-stage disease.

Surgery would not be recommended in this patient because the presence of a malignant pleural effusion confirms that this patient's disease is not curable. Surgery will add to her morbidity without improving her survival.

KEY POINT

- **Patients with non–small cell lung cancer and a malignant pleural effusion have, by definition, metastatic disease, and the most appropriate therapy is palliative systemic chemotherapy.**

Bibliography

Tsim S, O'Dowd CA, Milroy R, Davidson S. Staging of non-small cell lung cancer (NSCLC): a review. Respir Med. 2010;104(12):1767-1774. [PMID: 20833010]

Item 107 Answer: B

Educational Objective: Manage a patient with advanced-stage ovarian cancer in complete remission after initial adjuvant chemotherapy.

The most appropriate management is a history, physical examination, pelvic examination, and CA-125 measurement every 4 months. This patient had advanced stage IIIC ovarian cancer, so adjuvant chemotherapy was administered. Studies have shown that adjuvant platinum-based chemotherapy improves survival in patients with advanced-stage disease (IC or higher) or in patients with high-grade cancer. After completion of adjuvant chemotherapy, patients in complete remission should be monitored closely for relapse with history, physical examination, and CA-125 measurement every 3 to 4 months for the first 2 years, then less frequently thereafter. Second-line chemotherapy is highly effective at prolonging survival, so close monitoring for relapse is important. Delay in diagnosing relapse can result in bowel complications, such as obstruction.

Serial CT scans have not been associated with increased survival; therefore, National Comprehensive Cancer Network guidelines recommend their use only as clinically indicated.

Ovarian cancer relapse rates are high (>70%) in patients with stage III and IV disease, and treatment for relapse can prolong survival; therefore, once-yearly follow-up is not frequent enough.

Maintenance chemotherapy has an unclear role in the management of ovarian cancer. In addition, this patient's clinical condition after completing her intraperitoneal chemotherapy regimen is suboptimal for receiving additional chemotherapy now.

KEY POINT

- **Patients with advanced-stage ovarian cancer that is in remission require close monitoring for relapse, but routine CT scans have not been shown to improve survival.**

Bibliography

Morgan RJ Jr, Alvarez RD, Armstrong DK, et al; National Comprehensive Cancer Network. Ovarian cancer. Clinical practice guidelines in oncology. J Natl Compr Canc Netw. 2008;6(8):766-794. [PMID: 18926089]

Item 108 Answer: D

Educational Objective: Manage a patient with early-stage cervical cancer.

The most appropriate management is radical hysterectomy. Patients diagnosed with early-stage cervical cancer should undergo clinical staging with pelvic examination and radiographic imaging. Most patients with stage I and II average-risk disease (small primary tumors) are offered surgery with radical hysterectomy or more limited procedures. They may also be offered radiation therapy alone without chemotherapy. Prognosis is excellent for this subgroup.

Adjuvant cisplatin chemotherapy alone has activity in cervical cancer but is not as effective as combined radiation and chemotherapy in patients with advanced disease. No data suggest an advantage for treatment with cisplatin alone in patients with early-stage disease, such as this patient.

Stage IA1 (microscopic) cancers have a small chance of recurrence and lymph node metastasis; therefore, younger women desiring fertility may be treated with the loop electrical excision procedure (LEEP) or conization and close observation to preserve childbearing instead of hysterectomy. This patient has a macroscopic tumor, is a surgical candidate, and does not plan on having more children; consequently, simple conization surgery and observation would be inappropriate.

Pelvic radiation with concurrent cisplatin chemotherapy is recommended for patients with high-risk disease, characterized by bulky primary tumors or advanced disease (large primary tumor, deep stromal invasion, lymphovascular invasion, positive lymph nodes, or positive surgical margins).

KEY POINT

- **Patients with early-stage, average-risk (small primary tumors) cervical cancer should be managed with surgery alone or radiation therapy alone.**

Bibliography

Delgado G, Bundy B, Zaino R, Sevin BU, Creasman WT, Major F. Prospective surgical-pathological study of disease-free interval in patients with stage IB squamous cell carcinoma of the cervix: a Gynecologic Oncology Group study. Gynecol Oncol. 1990;38(3):352-357. [PMID: 2227547]

Item 109 Answer: B

Educational Objective: Manage brain metastasis and increased intracranial pressure in a patient with breast cancer.

The most appropriate management of this patient is corticosteroids and radiation therapy. Increased intracranial pressure (ICP) results from mass effect and is common in patients with intracerebral tumors, particularly tumors due to metastatic breast cancer, lung cancer, and melanoma. Headache is the most common symptom of increased ICP and is often severe and persistent despite analgesia and is of maximum intensity in the morning on awakening. Although a severe morning headache may occur as a sign of increased ICP, nonspecific headaches, cognitive changes, focal neurologic findings, and seizures may all be manifestations. Funduscopic examination may reveal papilledema. Brain metastasis associated with increased intracranial pressure is a medical emergency that requires immediate administration of parenteral corticosteroids and surgical resection or radiation therapy to avoid progressive neurologic deficits. In this case, the patient's breast cancer has recurred as evidenced by the multiple blastic bone lesions seen on CT.

Combination chemotherapy may eventually be appropriate management; however, such therapy is not appropriate initially because of the need for immediate treatment with corticosteroids and radiation therapy to prevent later consequences from increased ICP and brain metastases, including brainstem herniation, permanent neurologic dysfunction, and death. In addition, chemotherapeutic agents have limited efficacy in treating brain metastases.

ICP due to mass effect is an absolute contraindication for lumbar puncture because the procedure may precipitate catastrophic brain stem herniation.

Surgery to remove the lesions is less desirable because more than one mass is present, and the patient has evidence of systemic breast cancer, which eventually will require systemic treatment with chemotherapy.

KEY POINT

- **Immediate corticosteroid administration and early initiation of radiation therapy are indicated to treat brain metastasis and increased intracranial pressure.**

Bibliography

Khasraw M, Posner JB. Neurological complications of systemic cancer. Lancet Neurol. 2010;9(12):1214-1227. [PMID: 21087743]

Item 110 Answer: A

Educational Objective: Manage cancer of unknown primary site.

This patient, who has a moderately differentiated adenocarcinoma of unknown primary site, is somewhat debilitated by his disease, and empiric chemotherapy with a regimen for a gastrointestinal malignancy is the most reasonable treatment option. Further evaluation is unlikely to yield clinically useful information, and an empiric trial of therapy is reasonable. When adenocarcinoma of unknown primary site presents in a pattern predominantly below the diaphragm, treatment for a gastrointestinal malignancy is appropriate. When the distribution is largely above the diaphragm, treatment following a lung cancer paradigm is often used.

Platinum-based regimens such as carboplatin plus paclitaxel or cisplatin plus etoposide would be reasonable considerations for either a poorly differentiated cancer of unknown primary site or a poorly differentiated neuroendocrine cancer of unknown primary site.

A poorly differentiated tumor in a central distribution may be an unrecognized germ cell tumor and can be treated with a platinum-based regimen; however, if the differentiation is such that it can be identified as an adenocarcinoma, then it is not a germ cell tumor and, therefore, should not be treated as such. The patient's biopsy result does not support empiric treatment for either of these cancers.

Antiandrogen therapy, an approach with potential activity against prostate cancer, might be considered in a male patient with extensive bony metastases and an elevated prostate-specific antigen level, neither of which is present in this patient.

KEY POINT

- **Gastrointestinal cancer treatment regimens are appropriate for patients with cancer of unknown primary site with a predominantly abdominal distribution.**

Bibliography

Pavlidis N, Pentheroudakis G. Cancer of unknown primary site: 20 questions to be answered. Ann Oncol. 2010;21 Suppl 7:vii303-vii307. [PMID: 20943633]

Item 111 Answer: A

Educational Objective: Evaluate an older patient with suspected bladder cancer.

The most appropriate next step in the evaluation of this patient is cystoscopy. In an older person with a history of cigarette smoking and painless gross hematuria, a malignancy must be excluded. Bladder cancer commonly presents with bleeding, typically throughout micturition. Less commonly, kidney cancer can present with gross bleeding. Bladder cancer is usually diagnosed by cystoscopy and biopsy. Urine cytology is often used in combination with cystoscopy to assess for the presence of carcinoma in situ that may not have a lesion visible on cystoscopy and to evaluate for the presence of upper tract lesions that would not be visible on cystoscopy. Isolated genitourinary bleeding would be unusual in a patient with a hemostasis disorder such as that induced by warfarin therapy. Therefore, this patient should be evaluated for genitourinary cancer, regardless of the INR, to rule out bladder neoplasia.

Patients with prostate cancer may experience obstructive symptoms such as urinary hesitancy, incomplete bladder emptying, decreased urinary stream, or nocturia, as well as new-onset sexual dysfunction, but they rarely have bleeding. This patient's constellation of symptoms and findings is not consistent with prostate cancer; therefore, measuring the prostate-specific antigen level is not indicated.

A urine culture is not necessary because a urinary tract infection is unlikely in the absence of discomfort and elevated leukocytes.

Urine cytology is intended to identify abnormal genitourinary cells and may be useful in the evaluation of patients with a suspected lower genitourinary tract malignancy. Unfortunately, despite having a high specificity for bladder malignancies, it is relatively insensitive, particularly for low-grade tumors. It has the highest yield when used in conjunction with other diagnostic modalities and may be combined with other interventions, such as cystoscopy, particularly if an obvious source of bleeding is not identified. However, it would not be an appropriate next singular study in a patient with ongoing gross hematuria.

KEY POINT

- **Bladder cancer must be excluded in an older person with a history of cigarette smoking and painless gross hematuria that typically occurs throughout micturition.**

Bibliography

Morgan TM, Keegan KA, Clark PE. Bladder cancer. Curr Opin Oncol. 2011;23(3)275-282. [PMID: 21311329]

Item 112 Answer: B

Educational Objective: Manage a patient with early-stage invasive ductal carcinoma with breast conservation therapy.

The most appropriate management is right breast lumpectomy, sentinel lymph node biopsy, and radiation. With a small mass and no palpable lymphadenopathy, this patient is an ideal candidate for breast conservation therapy. Breast conservation therapy involves primary tumor excision and radiation to the remaining ipsilateral breast tissue. Lymph node evaluation is also important for prognostic and treatment purposes. Overall survival of patients who receive lumpectomy and radiation is equivalent to modified radical mastectomy but is associated with improved cosmetic results and less morbidity. Sentinel lymph node evaluation is now the standard of care instead of axillary node dissection. The first draining (or sentinel) lymph node is identified by injecting blue dye and radioactive colloid into the tumor site. If the sentinel lymph node does not contain metastases, it is unlikely that more distal axillary lymph nodes will contain metastases; consequently, no further surgery is indicated in this setting, and the toxicity from a full axillary lymph node dissection is avoided. However, if the sentinel lymph node shows metastatic involvement, then axillary lymph node dissection is performed to determine the number of involved lymph nodes (which has prognostic value) and possibly, to reduce the odds for recurrence.

Approximately 25% of women with breast cancer are not appropriate candidates for breast conservation surgery. Mastectomy is indicated for patients who are not eligible for breast conservation (those in whom complete excision is not technically possible with lumpectomy alone or those in whom radiation is contraindicated). Patients with scleroderma or previous chest wall irradiation should generally undergo mastectomy. The risk of systemic tumor recurrence does not change whether breast conservation or mastectomy is the surgical treatment.

Lumpectomy or simple mastectomy alone does not provide information on the axillary lymph node status needed to make important decisions regarding adjuvant chemotherapy.

Most patients undergoing mastectomy do not require radiation to complete local therapy. However, radiation therapy to the chest wall and surrounding lymph nodes may be indicated after mastectomy, particularly for patients with large tumors (greater than 5 cm) or with four or more positive axillary lymph nodes.

KEY POINT

- **Breast conservation therapy, which consists of excision of the primary tumor and radiation therapy, is equivalent to mastectomy in long-term survival.**

Bibliography

McCready D, Holloway C, Shelley W, et al; Breast Cancer Disease Site Group of Cancer Care; Ontario's Program in Evidence-Based Care. Surgical management of early stage invasive breast cancer: a practice guideline. Can J Surg. 2005;48(3):185-194. [PMID: 10613621]

Item 113 Answer: A

Educational Objective: Manage a patient with hairy cell leukemia.

The most appropriate management of this patient is cladribine. Hairy cell leukemia is a rare form of leukemia that is highly curable but leads to significant morbidity and mortality when untreated. Older patients, particularly men who have pancytopenia and an enlarged spleen without lymphadenopathy, should be evaluated for hairy cell leukemia. The presence of a dry aspirate on bone marrow sampling and finding of lymphoid cells with hair-like projections are diagnostic. A single cycle of parenteral cladribine, a purine analog, is curative in more than 80% of patients.

Further imaging evaluation, including CT of the chest, abdomen, and pelvis, or PET scanning, is unnecessary because it will not alter the prognosis or treatment.

Hairy cell leukemia is a chronic and progressive illness leading to pancytopenia and immune deficiency if not treated; therefore, observation would not be appropriate.

KEY POINT

- **A single cycle of parenteral cladribine is curative in more than 80% of patients with hairy cell leukemia.**

Bibliography

Allsup DJ, Cawley JC. The diagnosis and treatment of hairy cell leukemia. Blood Rev. 2002;16(4):255-262. [PMID: 12350368]

Item 114 Answer: C

Educational Objective: Manage a patient with advanced Hodgkin lymphoma and negative findings on PET scan following therapy.

The most appropriate management of this patient is completion of the recommended six cycles of therapy with doxorubicin, bleomycin, vinblastine, and dacarbazine (ABVD). Patients with stage IV Hodgkin lymphoma can have a poor outcome regardless of initial therapy. This has resulted in a management approach that is adaptive to patients' response to chemotherapy. Regardless of stage at presentation, patients with Hodgkin lymphoma who achieve a negative PET scan result after two to three cycles of ABVD can expect a high likelihood (>90%) of achieving a complete and durable remission with completion of ABVD chemotherapy.

In patients with advanced disease who have continued evidence of activity on PET scans after two to three cycles of ABVD, expected disease-free survival at 2 years is less than 15%. In this group, intensification with bleomycin, etoposide, doxorubicin, cyclophosphamide, vincristine, and procarbazine, as well as prednisone therapy and consideration of early high-dose chemotherapy and autologous stem cell support, are warranted.

It is unnecessary to perform a biopsy on residual lymphadenopathy not visible on a PET scan because the results are unlikely to show residual viable malignant cells.

Total lymph node irradiation has no role in the treatment of stage IV Hodgkin lymphoma, particularly in patients with bone involvement, because it is not effective in achieving a complete and durable remission and can limit additional therapy owing to marrow suppression.

KEY POINT

- **Patients with Hodgkin lymphoma and a negative PET scan after two to three cycles of doxorubicin, bleomycin, vinblastine, and dacarbazine chemotherapy, regardless of the disease stage at presentation, have a high likelihood of cure with completion of standard therapy.**

Bibliography

Kostakoglu L, Coleman M, Leonard JP, Kuji I, Zoe H, Goldsmith SJ. PET predicts prognosis after 1 cycle of chemotherapy in aggressive lymphoma and Hodgkin's disease. J Nucl Med. 2002;43(8):1018-1027. [PMID: 12163626]

Item 115 Answer: B

Educational Objective: Manage stage III colon cancer.

This patient has stage III colon cancer with the tumor invading the pericolonic fat and three lymph nodes involved (T3N1M0), and the preferred treatment is a chemotherapy regimen of 5-fluorouracil (5-FU), leucovorin, and oxaliplatin (FOLFOX). Stage III colon cancer is potentially curable, and the rate of cure is statistically significantly increased by the use of adjuvant chemotherapy. 5-FU plus leucovorin was established as an appropriate standard adjuvant treatment for stage III colon cancer in the mid-1990s; however, in 2004, a large, randomized trial comparing adjuvant 5-FU plus leucovorin versus the FOLFOX regimen showed that the FOLFOX regimen led to a greater disease-free survival at both 3 and 5 years after surgery. Thus, the FOLFOX regimen, or some modification of it, is the current accepted standard for postoperative management of stage III colon cancer.

Because local recurrence is not a common event with colon cancer, and because it can be difficult to isolate the small bowel from the radiation field, radiation therapy, alone or in combination with chemotherapy, does not have a role in the routine management of stage III colon cancer (radiation to the small bowel can cause substantial toxicity). However, in the rectum, local recurrence is a greater problem, and it is far easier to isolate the small bowel out of the radiation field; therefore, the combination of radiation and chemotherapy, usually preoperatively, is routinely used in stage II and III rectal cancer.

KEY POINT

- **An adjuvant chemotherapy regimen of 5-fluorouracil, leucovorin, and oxaliplatin (FOLFOX) has been shown to improve disease-free survival in patients with stage III colon cancer.**

Bibliography

André T, Boni C, Navarro M, et al. Improved overall survival with oxaliplatin, fluorouracil, and leucovorin as adjuvant treatment in stage II or III colon cancer in the MOSAIC trial. J Clin Oncol. 2009;27(19):3109-3116. [PMID: 19451431]

Item 116 Answer: C

Educational Objective: Treat locally advanced anal cancer.

The most appropriate treatment is radiation therapy with concurrent chemotherapy. The patient has a locally invasive anal cancer, with a T2N0M0 (stage II) staging based on a tumor between 2 and 5 cm and no lymph node metastases. The preferred treatment is radiation therapy with concurrent chemotherapy using 5-fluorouracil and mitomycin. Randomized data have shown that outcomes are more favorable with radiation plus chemotherapy versus radiation alone and that the combination of 5-fluorouracil plus mitomycin is superior to 5-fluorouracil alone, although toxicity is higher.

The only cancer surgery that would provide adequate margins of resection would be an abdominal perineal resection, which would remove the sphincter muscles and result in a permanent colostomy. Until the 1960s, this operation was the standard treatment for this disease. Subsequently, it has been shown that stages I, II, and III anal cancer can be potentially cured with radiation therapy plus chemotherapy, without the need for a disfiguring operation. Surgery therefore is reserved as an alternative for patients in whom the tumor recurs or progresses locally after treatment with radiation plus chemotherapy. This is in marked contrast to rectal cancer, which is an adenocarcinoma and requires surgical tumor resection.

KEY POINT

- **Mitomycin plus 5-fluorouracil used in conjunction with radiation therapy is the preferred treatment of anal cancer.**

Bibliography

Meyer J, Willett C, Czito B. Current and emerging treatment strategies for anal cancer. Curr Oncol Rep. 2010;12(3):168-174. [PMID: 20425076]

Item 117 Answer: C

Educational Objective: **Diagnose testicular cancer.**

The most likely diagnosis is a nonseminoma germ cell tumor. Patients typically present with a painless solid testicular mass or a testicular mass associated with mild discomfort or swelling. It is important to check serum α-fetoprotein (AFP) and β-human chorionic gonadotropin (β-hCG) levels in all patients presenting with a testicular mass. This patient has a unilateral testicular mass and elevated testicular tumor markers. An elevated serum AFP level always indicates that the tumor has a nonseminomatous component because this marker is produced by embryonal or yolk sac tumor cells, whereas elevated β-hCG may be present in seminomatous or nonseminomatous tumors. Any testicular cancer that has a nonseminomatous component based on histologic examination or the presence of an elevated serum AFP level is considered a nonseminoma and is treated as such.

Epididymitis is a possible diagnosis in a patient with a tender testicular mass and low-grade fever. However, this patient's normal leukocyte count, normal urinalysis, pain limited to the nodule, and elevated tumor markers make a diagnosis of testicular cancer much more likely.

Hematoma is possible after testicular trauma, but it would not cause an elevation of serum cancer markers.

Patients with a seminoma usually have an elevated β-hCG level; however, the presence of an elevated AFP level rules out seminoma as a possible diagnosis.

Patients with torsion may be in severe pain (more so than with epididymitis) and may have nausea and vomiting. Absence of the cremasteric reflex on the affected side is nearly 99% sensitive for torsion. In torsion, the testis is usually high within the scrotum and may lie transversely, with the epididymis lying anteriorly, medially, or laterally, depending on the number of twists. Finally, torsion is not associated with a tender nodule and an elevated AFP level.

KEY POINT

- **An elevated serum α-fetoprotein level always indicates that a testicular tumor has a nonseminomatous component, whereas elevated β-human chorionic gonadotropin may be present in seminomatous or nonseminomatous testicular tumors.**

Bibliography

Motzer RJ, Bolger GB, Boston B, et al; National Comprehensive Cancer Network. Testicular cancer. Clinical practice guidelines in oncology. J Natl Compr Canc Netw. 2006;4(10):1038-1058. [PMID: 17112452]

Item 118 Answer: A

Educational Objective: **Treat a younger patient with advanced-stage chronic lymphocytic leukemia and poor prognostic risk factors.**

The most appropriate treatment for this patient is alemtuzumab-based chemotherapy and consideration of allogeneic hematopoietic stem cell transplantation (HSCT) upon identification of an appropriate donor. This patient has newly diagnosed advanced-stage (stage IV) chronic lymphocytic leukemia (CLL) as demonstrated by the presence of lymphadenopathy, splenomegaly, anemia, and thrombocytopenia. He also has multiple poor prognostic risk factors, such as an elevated β_2-microglobulin level, an unmutated heavy gene, ζ-chain–associated protein 70 expression, and a 17p deletion. His median overall survival would be less than 3 years without treatment. Criteria for initiating treatment in patients with CLL include B symptoms (fever, weight loss, and night sweats), symptoms due to lymph node enlargement, hepatosplenomegaly, or worsening cytopenia. No treatment short of allogeneic HSCT has curative potential in affected patients. HSCT is applicable only to a few patients because the median age of patients with CLL is 70 years. The risk of graft-versus-host disease and other toxicities increases with age and often precludes its use. In this younger patient with advanced disease and multiple poor risk features, early use of allogeneic HSCT upon identification of an adequate donor would be appropriate.

Cyclophosphamide, vincristine, prednisone, single-agent fludarabine, or rituximab would not be optimal management for advanced disease associated with multiple poor prognostic features.

KEY POINT

- **In younger patients with advanced-stage chronic lymphocytic leukemia and multiple poor risk features, early use of allogeneic hematopoietic stem cell transplantation upon identification of an adequate donor is appropriate.**

Bibliography

Dreger P, Montserrat E. Autologous and allogeneic stem cell transplantation for chronic lymphocytic leukemia. Leukemia. 2002;16(6):985-992. [PMID: 12040430]

Item 119 Answer: C

Educational Objective: Treat a patient with recurrent, chemotherapy-sensitive diffuse large cell B-cell lymphoma.

The most appropriate treatment of this patient is high-dose chemotherapy and autologous hematopoietic stem cell transplantation (HSCT) after sufficient stem cell collection. Diffuse large B-cell lymphoma is the most common of the aggressive lymphomas. The primary therapy for this malignancy is rituximab plus cyclophosphamide, doxorubicin, vincristine, and prednisone (R-CHOP) for six cycles; approximately 50% of patients will have sustained disease-free survival, and 50% will experience relapse. Prospective randomized clinical trials of high-dose chemotherapy and autologous HSCT have demonstrated superior progression-free and overall survival compared with continued standard chemotherapy in patients with chemotherapy-sensitive, recurrent diffuse large B-cell lymphoma. The risk for developing late toxicities from high-dose chemotherapy with stem cell rescue, including acute myeloid leukemia and myelodysplastic syndrome, needs to be balanced against any potential benefits of treatment.

Radiation therapy for stage III large B-cell lymphoma would not be appropriate because lymphoma cells circulate, and, in this setting, would limit the ability to collect stem cells in the future owing to radiation-induced stem cell damage.

Sustaining a response with maintenance rituximab therapy would also be insufficient after administration of only two cycles of salvage therapy. Relapsed large cell lymphoma is partially resistant to standard-dose therapy, whereas high-dose therapy can achieve complete and durable remissions.

Providing no additional therapy to a patient with recurrent, aggressive, chemosensitive lymphoma who has the potential to sustain a complete and durable remission with high-dose chemotherapy and autologous HSCT would not be appropriate.

KEY POINT

- **High-dose chemotherapy and autologous hematopoietic stem cell transplantation offer the greatest likelihood of complete and durable remission in patients with chemotherapy-sensitive, recurrent diffuse large B-cell lymphoma.**

Bibliography

Philip T, Guglielmi C, Hagenbeek A, et al. Autologous bone marrow transplantation as compared with salvage chemotherapy in relapsed chemotherapy-sensitive non-Hodgkin's lymphoma. N Engl J Med. 1995;333(23):1540-1545. [PMID: 7477169]

Item 120 Answer: D

Educational Objective: Manage a patient with menopausal symptoms caused by tamoxifen therapy.

The most appropriate pharmacologic intervention is venlafaxine. Many women experience amenorrhea with chemotherapy, and this sudden change is often associated with disabling menopausal symptoms. Tamoxifen also causes hot flushes. Tamoxifen must be converted to its active metabolite, endoxifen, through CYP2D6 metabolism. For women in whom estrogen-progesterone replacement therapy is contraindicated, there are modest data suggesting some benefit from antidepressants (SSRIs, the serotonin-norepinephrine reuptake inhibitor venlafaxine) and gabapentin. Some antidepressants such as paroxetine and fluoxetine are moderate to strong inhibitors of CYP2D6. The effect of these drugs in combination with tamoxifen on breast cancer recurrence or survival is unknown. Therefore, patients receiving tamoxifen should be treated with drugs such as venlafaxine or gabapentin that are least likely to inhibit tamoxifen.

Hormone replacement therapy with estrogen-progesterone is worth considering in nonsmokers without other significant cardiovascular risks, a history of thromboembolic disease, a personal history of breast cancer, or a first-degree relative with breast cancer. Hormone replacement therapy is contraindicated in women with hormone receptor–positive breast cancer. Additionally, this patient's risk for venous thromboembolism would be even higher with concomitant tamoxifen and hormone replacement therapy.

Insufficient evidence currently exists demonstrating the effectiveness of physical exercise or herbal remedies, such as soy proteins, black cohosh, red clover, dong quai, evening primrose, or ginseng, in relieving menopausal symptoms.

KEY POINT

- **Selective serotonin reuptake inhibitors that are potent CYP2D6 inhibitors (such as fluoxetine and paroxetine) should be avoided in patients with menopausal symptoms caused by tamoxifen.**

Bibliography

Burstein HJ, Prestrud AA, Seidenfeld J, et al; American Society of Clinical Oncology. American Society of Clinical Oncology clinical practice guideline: update on adjuvant endocrine therapy for women with hormone receptor-positive breast cancer. J Clin Oncol. 2010;28(23):3784-3796. [PMID: 20625130]

Item 121 Answer: D

Educational Objective: Manage a patient with low-risk ovarian cancer.

The most appropriate management is observation. Patients who undergo surgical cytoreduction for ovarian cancer should be evaluated for possible adjuvant chemotherapy. Proper surgical staging includes total abdominal hysterectomy and bilateral salpingo-oophorectomy, omentectomy, and lymph node sampling in addition to pelvic washings for cytology. The final pathologic evaluation includes analysis of all the sampled tissues and assignment of histologic grade, which also has prognostic significance. This patient has an early-stage (IA), low-grade cancer, so adjuvant chemotherapy is not required. Studies have shown no survival advantage with the use of adjuvant chemotherapy for patients at low risk. Observation is recommended in such patients.

Adjuvant chemotherapy with paclitaxel and carboplatin has been shown to improve survival in patients with advanced-stage (IC or higher) disease or high-grade cancer. It would not be appropriate in this patient with early-stage, low-grade cancer.

Second-look surgery is no longer recommended in the management of ovarian cancer because it has not been shown to improve survival.

Intraperitoneal and intravenous chemotherapy have been shown to improve survival compared with intravenous chemotherapy alone in patients with stages II and III ovarian cancer; however, this approach is not indicated in early-stage disease.

KEY POINT

- **Low-risk ovarian cancer is best managed with surgical resection alone; adjuvant chemotherapy for such patients does not improve survival.**

Bibliography

Trimbos JB, Parmar M, Vergote I, et al; International Collaborative Ovarian Neoplasm 1; European Organisation for Research and Treatment of Cancer Collaborators–Adjuvant ChemoTherapy in Ovarian Neoplasm. International Collaborative Ovarian Neoplasm trial 1 and Adjuvant ChemoTherapy In Ovarian Neoplasm trial: two parallel randomized phase III trials of adjuvant chemotherapy in patients with early-stage ovarian carcinoma. J Natl Cancer Inst. 2003;95(2):105-112. [PMID: 12529343]

Item 122 Answer: B

Educational Objective: Manage a patient who is at high risk of developing breast cancer.

The most appropriate recommendation is bilateral mammography and breast MRI yearly. Patients at high risk for breast cancer should undergo screening earlier than the general population. This patient has a history of mantle radiation, which increases her lifetime risk of breast cancer to more than 25%. She is nulliparous, which also increases her risk for breast cancer. Although no data currently exist supporting early-onset radiographic screening in high-risk subgroups, an expert panel convened by the American Cancer Society recommended that patients who received mantle radiation, as well as those who are carriers of the *BRCA1* or *BRCA2* mutation, should undergo yearly mammography and breast MRI. MRI is more sensitive than mammography in detecting breast cancer but results in more false-positive test results. Despite the increased MRI test sensitivity, there are as of yet no data supporting decreased mortality from breast cancer using this screening modality.

Breast ultrasonography is not sensitive enough to detect breast cancer, especially in high-risk groups.

A number of blood tests have been suggested as potential early signals for recurrent breast cancer, including CA 15-3, carcinoembryonic antigen (CEA), and CA 27.29. However, none of these tests are recommended for routine surveillance because their use has not resulted in increased survival among patients with breast cancer. Similarly, blood tests such as CA-27.29 have not been shown to be useful for breast cancer detection.

Performing no screening is not appropriate because this patient is at increased risk for breast cancer owing to her history of mantle radiation therapy.

KEY POINT

- **Screening for breast cancer in high-risk populations consists of yearly breast MRI and bilateral mammography.**

Bibliography

Saslow D, Boetes C, Burke W, et al; American Cancer Society Breast Cancer Advisory Group. American Cancer Society guidelines for breast screening with MRI as an adjunct to mammography [erratum in CA Cancer J Clin. 2007;57(3):185]. CA Cancer J Clin. 2007;57(2):75-89. [PMID: 17392385]

Item 123 Answer: E

Educational Objective: Manage routine follow-up in a breast cancer survivor.

The most appropriate management is routine health maintenance. In the absence of suspicious symptoms, intensive laboratory and radiologic follow-up testing to detect metastases in patients with early-stage breast cancer after systemic therapy has not demonstrated a survival or quality-of-life benefit. Therefore, the standard post-therapy follow-up monitoring of these patients should address long-term complications of therapy, quality-of-life issues, and routine medical care. The American Society of Clinical Oncology states that appropriate breast cancer follow-up consists of a regular history, physical examination, and mammography. The appropriate timing of examinations for the first 3 years is every 3 to 6 months. For years 4 and 5, examination should be performed every 6 to 12 months. After 5 years, examinations should be performed annually. In patients who have received breast-conserving surgery, mammography should be performed 1 year after the initial mammogram and at least 6 months after completion of radiation therapy. Yearly mammography should be performed subsequently. Genetic counseling is appropriate for patients at high risk for familial breast cancer syndromes. Other testing (such as a complete blood count, chemistry panels, tumor markers, bone scanning, CT, and PET) are not indicated as part of routine follow-up for breast cancer in otherwise asymptomatic patients.

KEY POINT

- **The use of screening blood tests (including tumor markers) and imaging is not recommended for routine breast cancer follow-up in an otherwise asymptomatic patient with no specific findings on clinical examination.**

Bibliography

Tolaney SM, Winer EP. Follow-up care of patients with breast cancer. Breast. 2007;16 (suppl 2):S45-S50. [PMID: 17697780]

H

Item 124 Answer: A

Educational Objective: Treat a patient with febrile neutropenia.

The most appropriate treatment of this patient is to begin immediate empiric therapy with piperacillin-tazobactam. Neutropenia occurring 10 to 14 days after chemotherapy for diffuse large B-cell lymphoma is common. Febrile neutropenia is a medical emergency that can lead to septic shock and death within hours of presentation without immediate initiation of broad-spectrum antimicrobial agents. Initiation of a broad-spectrum antimicrobial such as piperacillin-tazobactam, a penicillin/β-lactamase inhibitor, and cefepime, a third-generation cephalosporin covering gram-positive and gram-negative organisms, is essential immediately after blood and urine cultures are obtained.

Delaying broad-spectrum antibiotic therapy pending the results of the patient's blood and urine cultures places him at risk for sepsis and death. Rapid recognition and empiric treatment of febrile neutropenia are keys to improved outcome. Additionally, only 30% of patients with febrile neutropenia have a positive urine or blood culture.

Mucositis occurs throughout the alimentary system in patients receiving chemotherapy, and endogenous flora from the gastrointestinal tract are probably responsible for most cases of febrile neutropenia. Initiating only vancomycin would therefore not offer sufficiently broad antimicrobial coverage to effectively treat this patient.

Empiric antifungal therapy is generally initiated in patients with neutropenia who remain febrile without an identified source of infection following 4 to 7 days of broad-spectrum antimicrobial therapy.

Viral infection is not a typical cause of infection in patients with febrile neutropenia, and empiric therapy with an antiviral such as acyclovir is not indicated.

KEY POINT

- **Febrile neutropenia requires immediate empiric treatment with a broad-spectrum antibiotic such as piperacillin-tazobactam.**

Bibliography

Paul M, Yahav D, Bivas A, Fraser A, Leibovici L. Anti-pseudomonal beta-lactams for the initial, empirical, treatment of febrile neutropenia: comparison of beta-lactams. Cochrane Database Syst Rev. 2010;(11):CD005197. [PMID: 21069685]

Item 125 Answer: A

Educational Objective: Manage potential cardiac toxicity in a patient with breast cancer requiring trastuzumab therapy.

Assessment of left ventricular function is necessary before initiating adjuvant chemotherapy with trastuzumab. *HER2* is a member of the epidermal growth factor receptor family of tyrosine kinases and is amplified or overexpressed in 20% to 30% of breast cancers. Trastuzumab is a humanized monoclonal antibody to the *HER2* receptor. Several large, randomized trials have demonstrated that 52 weeks of adjuvant trastuzumab therapy reduces the risk for breast cancer recurrence by approximately 50% and may even reduce mortality by as much as 30%. Trastuzumab has been associated with induction of heart failure, particularly when used concurrently with an anthracycline. Additional risk factors include hypertension and age older than 50 years. Patients should undergo monitoring of left ventricular function before trastuzumab treatment; left ventricular function should also be assessed frequently during and after trastuzumab treatment. Trastuzumab-induced cardiotoxicity is not dose-related and is usually at least partially reversible when this agent is discontinued. Therefore, measurement of the baseline left ventricular ejection fraction and intermittent monitoring of ejection fraction are strongly recommended in the adjuvant setting.

Tamoxifen is an agent that is used in the treatment of selected patients with estrogen receptor–positive breast cancer. Tamoxifen is associated with an increased risk for thromboembolic disease and endometrial cancer. This patient will not receive tamoxifen because she has an estrogen receptor– and progesterone receptor–negative cancer. Even if this patient were to receive tamoxifen, there is no role for pretherapy screening for endometrial cancer or thromboembolic disease with transvaginal ultrasonography or CT angiography.

Radiation therapy to the mediastinum (as in the treatment of Hodgkin lymphoma) may result in progressive cardiac sequelae, including inflammation and fibrosis of all structures in the heart, which can lead to abnormalities in left ventricular function and mass, valvular dysfunction, and premature coronary artery disease. The typical patient receiving breast cancer radiation does not have significant radiation to the heart or mediastinal structures. In the absence of cardiac symptoms, exercise stress testing is not indicated prior to the initiation of radiation therapy for either breast cancer or Hodgkin lymphoma.

KEY POINT

- **Trastuzumab is associated with cardiac toxicity; patients who will receive adjuvant trastuzumab for 1 year require evaluation of the left ventricular ejection fraction before and during treatment.**

Bibliography

Bird BR, Swain SM. Cardiac toxicity in breast cancer survivors: review of potential cardiac problems. Clin Cancer Res. 2008;14(1):14-24. [PMID: 18172247]

Item 126 Answer: C

Educational Objective: Treat metastatic melanoma.

This patient has metastatic melanoma with a symptomatic brain metastasis, and surgical resection offers the best palliation of his symptoms. Stereotactic radiosurgery is another acceptable option but is not available at all centers. He has incurable small-volume lung and liver disease; however, these are not causing substantial symptoms. The brain metastasis is his major clinical issue.

Chemotherapy is only marginally active against melanoma and might be tried for tumor control after definitive management of the brain metastasis, but it would be inadequate, either alone or with radiation therapy, for control of a symptomatic brain metastasis.

Because surgery can offer excellent palliation, and this otherwise medically fit person has not had any treatment for his metastatic melanoma, comfort and hospice care alone would be premature at this point.

Whole-brain radiation therapy is unlikely to provide long-term control, and melanoma is relatively radioresistant.

KEY POINT

- Surgery or stereotactic radiosurgery is often indicated for symptomatic relief of patients with isolated or limited brain metastases and incurable cancer.

Bibliography

Eigentler TK, Figl A, Krex D, et al; Dermatologic Cooperative Oncology Group and the National Interdisciplinary Working Group on Melanoma. Number of metastases, serum lactate dehydrogenase level, and type of treatment are prognostic factors in patients with brain metastases of malignant melanoma. Cancer. 2011;117(8):1697-1703. [PMID: 21472716]

Item 127 Answer: A

Educational Objective: Manage a patient with high-risk, early-stage bladder cancer.

The most appropriate next step in management is intravesicular bacillus Calmette-Guérin (BCG) immunotherapy. This patient has stage I bladder cancer with tumor invading the submucosa. Early-stage bladder cancer, in situ and minimally invasive, confers a risk for local recurrence, with potential invasion into the muscular layer. High-risk, early-stage lesions are treated with intravesicular medication, typically BCG immunotherapy. Such therapies reduce local recurrence, muscle invasion, and the need for potential cystectomy. Because of the high likelihood of bladder cancer recurrence, patients are typically followed with repeat cystoscopy and urine cytologic studies every 3 months.

Radiation is only used to treat disease that invades the muscle in an attempt to spare the bladder, usually concurrent with chemotherapy. This therapy would not be recommended for patients with early-stage bladder cancer that does not invade the bladder.

Radical cystectomy is recommended for patients who have a tumor that invades muscle, unlike this patient. Cystectomy is recommended for treating patients with bladder carcinoma in situ that recurs following BCG therapy or for patients who have early-stage disease with incomplete resection.

Observation would not be appropriate for this patient who has bladder cancer as confirmed by biopsy results.

KEY POINT

- High-risk, early-stage bladder cancer is treated with intravesicular medication, typically bacillus Calmette-Guérin immunotherapy.

Bibliography

Morgan TM, Keegan KA, Clark PE. Bladder cancer. Curr Opin Oncol. 2011;23(3)275-282. [PMID: 21311329]

Item 128 Answer: C

Educational Objective: Treat a patient with tumor lysis syndrome.

This patient has tumor lysis syndrome and requires immediate treatment with hemodialysis, aggressive hydration with normal saline, and rasburicase. Tumor lysis syndrome is a life-threatening complication that occurs most often in patients with malignancies associated with rapid cell turnover (leukemia, Burkitt lymphoma) or in patients with bulky disease and high leukocyte counts associated with rapid and significant sensitivity to chemotherapeutic agents (large cell lymphoma, chronic lymphocytic leukemia). The manifestations of tumor lysis syndrome include hyperkalemia, hyperuricemia, hyperphosphatemia, hypocalcemia, acute kidney injury, and disseminated intravascular coagulation. In this case, any further acceleration of tumor cell turnover resulting from institution of immediate chemotherapy occurring before the patient's current metabolic condition is addressed would be potentially life threatening. In patients at risk for tumor lysis syndrome, prophylactic treatment with aggressive hydration with diuresis and use of allopurinol and rasburicase are indicated. In this patient, hemodialysis and administration of rasburicase would be appropriate treatment for his hyperkalemia and hyperuricemia. Once the patient's life-threatening metabolic condition is stabilized, therapy for his malignancy can be instituted.

Besides hemodialysis, aggressive hydration with normal saline, and rasburicase, any form of therapy, including corticosteroids, would accelerate this patient's tumor lysis syndrome; consequently, immediate antineoplastic therapy and corticosteroids are contraindicated.

Radiation therapy has no role in the treatment of Burkitt lymphoma, and, in any event, treatment of the patient's tumor lysis syndrome takes precedence.

KEY POINT

- **Prophylactic treatment of tumor lysis syndrome consists of aggressive hydration with diuresis and use of allopurinol and rasburicase, and when necessary, hemodialysis, before initiation of antineoplastic therapy.**

Bibliography

Abu-Alfa AK, Younes A. Tumor lysis syndrome and acute kidney injury: evaluation, prevention, and management. Am J Kidney Dis. 2010;55(5 Suppl 3):S1-13; quiz S14-9. [PMID: 20420966]

Item 129 Answer: A

Educational Objective: Manage a patient with early-stage Hodgkin lymphoma.

The most appropriate management is two to three cycles of doxorubicin, bleomycin, vinblastine, and dacarbazine (ABVD) and radiation therapy. Common findings in patients with Hodgkin lymphoma include palpable lymphadenopathy or a mediastinal mass. Treatment selection is based on disease stage. Regardless of the stage at presentation, Hodgkin lymphoma is highly curable. The emphasis of current therapy is the administration of less toxic therapies without compromising efficacy. The most concerning of these toxicities is the development of secondary malignancies. Radiation therapy with or without short-course chemotherapy is used for localized disease such as that in this patient, and ABVD administered over six cycles is appropriate for patients with more advanced disease. This patient has stage IIA Hodgkin lymphoma limited to above the abdomen. Limited chemotherapy (two to three cycles of ABVD) and radiation therapy offer the greatest likelihood of prolonged remission with the least long-term toxicity risk.

Data show that combination chemotherapy followed by involved-field radiation therapy results in high cure rates for favorable stage I to II Hodgkin lymphoma and is superior to treatment with radiation therapy alone, although chemotherapy alone is sufficient for many favorable-risk patients in whom radiation therapy can safely be omitted. Radiation therapy alone would not be sufficient treatment for this patient.

Single-agent rituximab has a role only in lymphocyte-predominant, CD20-positive Hodgkin lymphoma, which is not the case in this patient.

Because Hodgkin lymphoma is a highly curable malignancy at all disease stages, watchful waiting would not be appropriate, regardless of disease stage.

KEY POINT

- **Patients with stages I and II in Hodgkin lymphoma are effectively treated with limited (two to three cycles) chemotherapy and radiation therapy.**

Bibliography

Fermé C, Eghbali H, Meerwaldt JH, et al; EORTC-GELA H8 Trial. Chemotherapy plus involved-field radiation in early-stage Hodgkin's disease. N Engl J Med. 2007;357(19):1916-1927. [PMID: 17989384]

Item 130 Answer: A

Educational Objective: Evaluate a patient with benign lymphadenopathy.

The most appropriate next step in the diagnostic evaluation is anti–Epstein-Barr virus (EBV) antibody assay. The history and physical examination are critical in determining which patients need further evaluation for lymphadenopathy. The patient's age is one of the most helpful pieces of information; age older than 40 years is associated with a 20-fold higher risk for malignancy or granulomatous disease compared with younger patients. The setting in which the lymphadenopathy occurs is also important; acute onset following an infection suggests an infectious or reactive lymphadenopathy, whereas subacute onset in a cigarette smoker suggests malignancy. Timing is another helpful clue because most benign immunologic reactions resolve in 2 to 4 weeks, whereas more serious conditions are associated with persistent or progressive lymphadenopathy. Finally, the presence of systemic symptoms suggests a more serious underlying illness. B symptoms (fever, night sweats, and weight loss), for example, are sometimes present in Hodgkin lymphoma, whereas a rash is often associated with specific infectious or inflammatory diseases (secondary syphilis, drug hypersensitivity reaction, systemic lupus erythematosus). A 1-month history of fatigue and intermittent fever with tender, but soft and freely moveable lymphadenopathy, and splenomegaly associated with atypical lymphocytosis in a young male patient are most consistent with infectious mononucleosis caused by EBV infection.

A bone marrow biopsy and PET/CT scan to identify evidence of malignancy or leukemia would be unnecessary before the presence of mononucleosis is confirmed. Similarly, a lymph node biopsy would not be necessary until mononucleosis is confirmed or excluded.

Peripheral blood flow cytometry would not add useful information because this patient's illness would result in a polyclonal increase in lymphocytes. Flow cytometry is best used to help establish a diagnosis when evaluating for a malignancy that would reveal a monoclonal population of cells with a specific phenotype.

KEY POINT

- **Cervical lymphadenopathy that is soft, tender to the touch, and freely movable in association with fever is usually not of malignant origin.**

Bibliography

Pangalis GA, Vassilakopoulos TP, Boussiotis VA, Fessas P. Clinical approach to lymphadenopathy. Semin Oncol. 1993;20(6):570-582. [PMID: 8296196]

Item 131 Answer: B

Educational Objective: Diagnose chemotherapy-related myelodysplastic syndrome.

The most likely cause of this patient's findings is chemotherapy- and radiation therapy–related myelodysplastic syndrome. The adverse consequences of multiagent chemotherapy and radiation can occur many years after completion of therapy. The myelodysplastic syndromes are stem cell clonal disorders characterized by ineffective hematopoiesis and various peripheral cytopenias. Patients have signs and symptoms referable to a specific cytopenia (most often, megaloblastic anemia) and bone marrow findings showing a hypercellular marrow with dyserythropoiesis. Many chromosomal abnormalities are associated with myelodysplastic syndromes, including abnormal numbers of chromosomes, translocations, and structural abnormalities. This patient's absence of lymphadenopathy and hepatosplenomegaly and presence of multiple chromosomal abnormalities on cytogenetic examination of the bone marrow make this diagnosis likely; the multiple chromosomal translocations and deletions present in the bone marrow confirm the diagnosis.

Acute lymphoblastic leukemia (ALL) is a disorder of committed stem cells characterized by a proliferation of immature lymphoblasts. ALL constitutes less than 20% of acute leukemias in adult patients, with the highest incidence occurring in the seventh decade of life. Patients present with lymphocytosis, neutropenia, anemia, and thrombocytopenia, as well as lymphadenopathy and hepatosplenomegaly.

Parvovirus B19 infection can lead to abnormal-appearing erythroid precursors but would not be associated with the multiple abnormal cytogenetic changes or excess blasts demonstrated in this patient.

Disease in almost all patients with recurrent Hodgkin lymphoma is detected within 12 years of initial therapy, most within 2 years. Relapsed Hodgkin lymphoma is characterized by the finding of a palpable mass on physical examination or the presence of lymphoma symptoms, such as fever, anorexia, weight loss, and pruritus. Finally, recurrent Hodgkin lymphoma would not account for this patient's peripheral blood findings or bone marrow chromosomal abnormalities.

KEY POINT

- **Myelodysplastic syndrome can be a late adverse consequence of combination chemotherapy and radiation therapy.**

Bibliography

Borthakur G, Estey AE. Therapy-related acute myelogenous leukemia and myelodysplastic syndrome. Curr Oncol Rep. 2007;9(5):373-377. [PMID: 17706165]

Item 132 Answer: B

Educational Objective: Evaluate a patient with newly diagnosed chronic lymphocytic leukemia.

The most appropriate next step in the evaluation of this patient is β_2-microglobuin measurement and peripheral blood cytogenetic analysis, ζ-chain–associated protein 70 assay, and heavy-chain mutational status. Chronic lymphocytic leukemia (CLL) is the most common form of lymphoid malignancy of all the hematologic neoplasms, and its incidence increases with age. Most patients are asymptomatic and present with early-stage disease discovered incidentally during routine laboratory testing. The natural history of CLL is highly variable. Patients are stratified into risk groups based on presenting features. This risk stratification constitutes the staging criteria, which include the presence of lymphadenopathy, hepatosplenomegaly, anemia, or thrombocytopenia (excluding immune thrombocytopenic purpura). This patient has stage I disease (lymphocytosis and lymphadenopathy without splenomegaly or other organomegaly). Further prognostic information is required to determine her risk for progression and need for treatment. The β_2-microglobuin level, heavy gene mutational status, and cytogenetics all provide independent prognostic information that guides the decision on the frequency of follow-up and when to initiate treatment.

Bone marrow biopsy and aspiration are not required because all relevant prognostic tests may be done using the peripheral blood.

CT scans would not provide additional prognostic information that will help guide therapy in an asymptomatic patient with CLL.

PET scanning has a limited role in CLL and should be reserved for patients in whom a transformation to aggressive lymphoma is suspected. In patients with suspected transformed lymphoma, the detection of foci of intense uptake on PET scanning supports the diagnosis.

KEY POINT

- **In patients with chronic lymphocytic leukemia, the β_2-microglobuin level, heavy gene mutational status, and cytogenetics provide independent prognostic information on appropriate follow-up monitoring and time to initiate treatment.**

Bibliography

Gribben JG, O'Brien S. Update on therapy of chronic lymphocytic leukemia. J Clin Oncol. 2011;29(5):544-550. [PMID: 21220603]

Item 133 Answer: C

Educational Objective: Treat a patient with suspected advanced-stage testicular cancer.

The most appropriate next step in treatment is inguinal orchiectomy followed by platinum, etoposide, and bleomycin (PEB) chemotherapy. The presence of a lung mass and pleural effusion in a young patient who presents with a testicular mass and elevated testicular tumor markers strongly suggests advanced-stage nonseminoma germ cell cancer. Radical orchiectomy is the preferred initial diagnostic strategy to confirm the histologic diagnosis even in the presence of metastatic disease. Following orchiectomy to confirm the diagnosis and tissue type, four cycles of PEB chemotherapy should be administered. Cure is often achieved even in patients with advanced-stage disease.

All patients with suspected testicular cancer should undergo a complete staging evaluation, including orchiectomy with pathology review. Chemotherapy alone without confirmation of a tissue diagnosis is not recommended.

Resection of metastatic lesions that persist after initial chemotherapy for advanced-stage testicular cancer is a common strategy. These persistent lesions may harbor residual cancer or teratoma that must be removed surgically. Because this malignancy is extremely sensitive to platinum-based chemotherapy, initial resection of metastatic lesions is not recommended. Furthermore, surgical resection of the testicle and lung mass without chemotherapy is inappropriate in this patient with an advanced-stage, chemotherapy-sensitive malignancy.

KEY POINT

- **Patients with advanced-stage testicular cancer should undergo orchiectomy followed by platinum-based chemotherapy.**

Bibliography

Motzer RJ, Bolger GB, Boston B, et al; National Comprehensive Cancer Network. Testicular cancer. Clinical practice guidelines in oncology. J Natl Compr Canc Netw. 2006;4(10):1038-1058. [PMID: 17112452]

Item 134 Answer: C

Educational Objective: Treat a patient with early-stage non–small cell lung cancer.

The most appropriate treatment for this patient is surgery and adjuvant chemotherapy. This patient with a 5-cm lung mass and no apparent spread of disease has early-stage non–small cell lung cancer (NSCLC). A solitary tumor without regional (peribronchial or hilar) or mediastinal lymph node involvement is classified as stage I. For patients with early-stage (stages I and II) disease, the most appropriate treatment is surgery. Patients with stage I NSCLC have the most favorable prognosis, but only 60% of these patients are cured following surgery. Stage I is subdivided into stage IA, comprising tumors less than 3 cm in greatest diameter, and stage IB, including all larger tumors. Currently, the benefits of adjuvant chemotherapy have not been demonstrated for patients with better-prognosis, stage IA disease. However, in patients with stage IB NSCLC, which this patient has, improvements in overall survival have been seen, and adjuvant chemotherapy should be considered after surgical resection.

Chemotherapy plus radiation is indicated for locally advanced tumors (that is, stage III disease characterized by mediastinal lymph node involvement) and is not appropriate therapy for patients with earlier-stage disease such as this patient.

Radiation therapy is rarely used as the sole treatment for lung cancer. In patients with early-stage disease, it may add to morbidity without improving chances of cure. In patients with advanced disease, radiation therapy alone is not as effective as chemotherapy in prolonging survival and disease-free remission.

Chemotherapy is used as palliative therapy in advanced-stage disease, not in those with early-stage disease. Chemotherapy alone in patients with early disease does not offer the best chance of cure compared with surgery and adjuvant chemotherapy.

KEY POINT

- **For patients with early-stage (Stage I and II) non–small cell lung cancer (NSCLC), the most appropriate treatment is surgery; adjuvant chemotherapy is appropriate for patients with stage IB NSCLC.**

Bibliography

Gewanter RM, Rosenzweig KE, Chang JY, et al. ACR Appropriateness Criteria: nonsurgical treatment for non-small-cell lung cancer: good performance status/definitive intent. Curr Probl Cancer. 2010;34(3):228-249. [PMID: 20541060]

Item 135 Answer: E

Educational Objective: Manage oligometastatic colorectal cancer.

This patient has a potential for curative resection and should undergo a right hepatectomy if no other sites of disease are identified during exploratory surgery. She has a limited number of metastatic foci of cancer confined to one organ, or oligometastatic disease.

A fine-needle aspiration is not indicated because the results of this invasive procedure will not change management. The clinical presentation is suggestive enough of metastatic disease in the liver that a negative needle aspiration will not sufficiently exclude the presence of cancer, and a definitive resection will still be required. Thus, in the setting of what appears to be resectable disease, a needle aspiration or biopsy should not be done.

Hepatic arterial embolization is a procedure used in the palliation of hepatocellular or neuroendocrine tumors; however, the procedure is not indicated in colorectal cancer, and because it is not curative, it would not be an appropriate consideration in a patient whose disease might be curable with surgery.

Radiation therapy is rarely used for treatment of liver metastases and does not have the potential to be curative. Because this patient may have curable disease, noncurative treatment such as palliative chemotherapy is not appropriate.

KEY POINT

- **Surgical resection of a few isolated metastatic lesions may be curative for patients with colorectal cancer.**

Bibliography

House MG, Ito H, Gönen M, et al. Survival after hepatic resection for metastatic colorectal cancer: trends in outcomes for 1,600 patients during two decades at a single institution. J Am Coll Surg. 2010;210(5):744-755. [PMID: 20421043]

Item 136 Answer: D

Educational Objective: Treat a patient with ductal carcinoma in situ with tamoxifen.

The most appropriate treatment is tamoxifen. Tamoxifen, like raloxifene, is a selective estrogen receptor modulator. Tamoxifen is used as adjuvant endocrine therapy in selected women with breast cancer. Adjuvant endocrine therapy is beneficial only in patients with estrogen receptor (ER)–positive or progesterone receptor (PR)–positive tumors. In premenopausal women with ER-positive and PR-positive tumors, 5 years of tamoxifen is the standard endocrine adjuvant therapeutic regimen; treatment longer than 5 years with this drug is not recommended. The NSABP P-1 trial showed that women who took tamoxifen had an approximately 50% reduction in new primary invasive breast cancer compared with placebo. Side effects of tamoxifen include endometrial cancer, venous thromboembolism, hot flushes, and cataracts.

Several large, prospective, randomized trials have shown that the aromatase inhibitors, such as anastrozole, letrozole, or exemestane, appear to be more effective in reducing risk for recurrence than tamoxifen in postmenopausal women with ER-positive breast cancer. Aromatase inhibitors are not indicated in premenopausal women because of concerns that reduced feedback of estrogen to the hypothalamus and pituitary will stimulate gonadotropin secretion, leading to an increase in ovarian androgen substrate and aromatase production and thus stimulating the growth of hormonally responsive cancers.

Ductal carcinoma in situ (DCIS) is a noninvasive breast cancer and by definition is confined to the ductal system of the breast. Because DCIS is not a systemic disease, chemotherapy provides no benefit for this condition.

Raloxifene is specifically approved for the treatment of osteoporosis and the prevention of invasive breast cancer in patients at increased risk; however, there are no data regarding its efficacy as adjuvant therapy for breast cancer; therefore, it should not be substituted for tamoxifen in this setting.

KEY POINT

- **For premenopausal women with hormone receptor–positive ductal carcinoma in situ or invasive breast cancer, the standard of care is tamoxifen for 5 years to reduce both the risk of recurrence and the development of a new primary tumor in the ipsilateral or contralateral breast.**

Bibliography

Fisher B, Dignam J, Wolmark N, et al. Tamoxifen in treatment of intraductal breast cancer: National Surgical Adjuvant Breast and Bowel Project B-24 randomised controlled trial. Lancet. 1999;353(9169):1993-2000. [PMID: 10376613]

Item 137 Answer: B

Educational Objective: Manage a patient with recurrent breast cancer.

This patient most likely has recurrent breast cancer with bony metastases and should undergo bone biopsy to confirm metastatic disease and assess estrogen-progesterone and *HER2* status of the new lesions. A small, but significant, number of patients have new lesions with a different receptor status than their primary tumor. Intravenous bisphosphonate therapy with pamidronate or zoledronic acid is indicated to decrease the chance of skeletal complications and new metastases. The goal of therapy in metastatic breast cancer is to maintain quality of life while antineoplastic therapy is being administered. In general, the standard of care is hormonal therapy such as tamoxifen or an aromatase inhibitor. However, the hormone-receptor status of the metastatic tumor should be determined prior to prescribing hormonal therapy.

Similarly, the *HER2* status of the tumor must be determined to make recommendations regarding treatment with trastuzumab therapy.

Women with rapidly progressive metastatic disease, particularly with involvement of visceral organs and organ dysfunction, may respond better to chemotherapy than to hormonal therapy. This patient does not have visceral disease or evidence of severe organ dysfunction, so there is no reason to start chemotherapy.

If the bone biopsy confirms metastatic breast cancer, radiation can be used for an impending fracture or to alleviate significant pain. However, it is not appropriate until the diagnosis is confirmed with bone biopsy.

KEY POINT

- **A lesion due to a first recurrence of breast cancer should be biopsied to confirm malignancy and hormone receptor and *HER2* status, which then guides treatment.**

Bibliography

Beslija S, Bonneterre J, Burstein HJ, et al; Central European Cooperative Oncology Group (CECOG). Third consensus on medical treatment of metastatic breast cancer. Ann Oncol. 2009;20(11):1771-1785. [PMID: 19608616]

Item 138 Answer: B

Educational Objective: Manage a patient with the *BRCA* gene mutation who is at increased risk for developing ovarian cancer.

The strategy associated with the greatest reduction in cancer risk is bilateral salpingo-oophorectomy and bilateral mastectomy. Ovarian cancer is predominantly a disease of postmenopausal women, but patients with *BRCA* gene mutations have a markedly increased lifetime risk for ovarian cancer, including early onset of disease. Although multiparity and history of oral contraceptive use provide some protection from ovarian cancer, the lifetime risk of developing cancer is so high in patients with this mutation that guideline recommendations call for prophylactic bilateral salpingo-oophorectomy after childbearing is complete, and, ideally, before age 40 years. This procedure reduces the risk of developing ovarian cancer by 95%. The two most effective breast cancer risk-reduction strategies are surgical removal of breast tissue (prophylactic mastectomy) and endocrinologic manipulation using selective estrogen receptor modulators (SERMs). Among *BRCA* carriers, the largest risk reduction results from prophylactic mastectomy. Bilateral salpingo-oophorectomy also reduces risk for breast cancer but not to the degree achieved by bilateral mastectomy.

Serial monitoring of serum CA-125 levels and frequent pelvic examinations are appropriate for patients who decline oophorectomy, but they do not prevent cancer development in patients at very high risk.

Oral contraceptive pills decrease the risk of developing ovarian cancer in patients who carry *BRCA* gene mutations, but their use in this prophylactic setting is controversial because of the increased risk of developing breast cancer.

Screening with pelvic ultrasonography can potentially detect early-stage ovarian cancer in high-risk patients and is appropriate for patients who decline the preferred recommendation for bilateral salingo-oophorectomy before age 40 years.

KEY POINT

- **Patients who are positive for *BRCA* gene mutations have the greatest reduction in cancer risk by bilateral salpingo-oophorectomy and bilateral mastectomy.**

Bibliography

Rebbeck TR, Lynch HT, Neuhausen SL, et al; Prevention and Observation of Surgical End Points Study Group. Prophylactic oophorectomy in carriers of *BRCA1* and *BRCA2* mutations. N Engl J Med. 2002;346(21):1616-1622. [PMID: 12023993]

Item 139 Answer: A

Educational Objective: Manage a patient with limited-stage small cell lung cancer.

The most appropriate management of this patient with small cell lung cancer (SCLC) is radiation and chemotherapy. Patients with SCLC rarely present with disease that is sufficiently localized to allow for surgical resection, so the TNM system is generally not used in these patients. Instead, the Veterans Administration Lung Study Group staging system is typically used, which classifies disease as limited or extensive. The definition of limited-stage disease consists of disease limited to one hemithorax, with hilar and mediastinal lymphadenopathy that can be encompassed within one tolerable radiotherapy portal. Extensive-stage disease consists of any disease that exceeds those boundaries. If disease is confined to the chest (that is, limited stage) as in this patient, then chemotherapy is initiated with the addition of radiation to the chest concurrent with the first or second cycle of chemotherapy. In this setting, radiation decreases rates of a local recurrence and increases median survival. Routine use of chest radiotherapy in extensive-stage disease does not prolong survival. Also, if a significant response is evident, prophylactic brain radiation is administered after the chemotherapy is complete. If advanced-stage disease is identified, chemotherapy alone is recommended.

Mediastinoscopy is indicated in patients with non–small cell lung cancer if there is mediastinal lymph node involvement (stage III disease) to assess for the presence or absence of cancer and the patient's suitability for surgical cure. It is not typically used in patients with SCLC.

Radiation is used only as an adjunct to systemic chemotherapy and is not appropriate as single-modality therapy.

SCLC is an aggressive form of lung cancer that tends to disseminate early in the vast majority of patients. Patients rarely have disease that is localized enough to allow for surgical resection; therefore, surgical referral for cure in patients with SCLC is not typically recommended. SCLC is not treated by surgical resection unless it is found incidentally.

KEY POINT

- **Patients with limited-stage small cell lung cancer are treated with combination chemotherapy and radiation therapy.**

Bibliography

Stinchcombe TE, Gore EM. Limited-stage small cell lung cancer: current chemoradiotherapy treatment paradigms. Oncologist. 2010;15(2):187-195. [PMID: 20145192]

Item 140 Answer: E

Educational Objective: Manage early-stage carcinoid tumor.

No further treatment or follow-up is required for this patient. She has a small, incidentally found, well-differentiated

carcinoid tumor of the appendix, and appendectomy is curative in virtually all such cases.

An indium-111 pentetreotide scan, which identifies somatostatin-receptor–expressing tumors, can be useful in identifying a primary tumor but is inappropriate in the setting of a negative CT scan and small appendiceal primary tumor. The likelihood of a false-positive finding is relatively high, whereas the likelihood of a true-positive finding is very small.

Octreotide is a somatostatin analogue useful in the management of the hormonal symptoms of neuroendocrine tumors when they are present (not the case in this patient) and may slow progression of metastatic carcinoid tumors; however, although it has these established uses in metastatic disease, octreotide has no role in the postresection, or adjuvant, treatment of localized and resected neuroendocrine tumors.

For large carcinoid tumors (≥2 cm) of the appendix or for tumors of the appendix of any size that have a more aggressive histology such as high-grade neuroendocrine tumors or adenocarcinomas, a right hemicolectomy would be indicated. The lymph node drainage of the appendix is to the nodes of the right mesocolon, and clearing and sampling of those nodes would be necessary in such cases.

Streptozocin plus 5-fluorouracil is a regimen with some antitumor activity in pancreatic neuroendocrine tumors, but it has no activity in carcinoid tumors.

KEY POINT

- **Treatment of well-differentiated, early-stage carcinoid tumors of the appendix is simple appendectomy.**

Bibliography

Moertel CG, Weiland LH, Nagorney DM, Dockerty MB. Carcinoid tumor of the appendix: treatment and prognosis. N Engl J Med. 1987;317(27):1699-1701. [PMID: 3696178]

Item 141 Answer: E

Educational Objective: Manage cancer of unknown primary site.

The patient should be treated as if she had ovarian cancer. In women presenting with a combination of peritoneal carcinomatosis and malignant ascites, ovarian cancer should be strongly considered. If no extraovarian site is determined, these patients should be treated as though they had stage III ovarian cancer, with initial cytoreductive surgery followed by chemotherapy. In these patients, measurement of serum CA-125 levels can be useful in monitoring the response to therapy. Approximately 15% to 20% of patients survive 5 years.

This patient was well before the development of this malignancy and has a reasonable chance of substantial benefit from treatment; therefore, palliative care would not be appropriate at this time.

Drainage of ascites without tumor debulking would be insufficient as would chemotherapy without tumor debulking therapy.

Radiation therapy to the entire abdomen could result in significant morbidity because the small bowel toxicity would be substantial, and such an approach is not recommended.

KEY POINT

- **Women with carcinoma of unknown primary site presenting as abdominal carcinomatosis and ascites should be treated for stage III ovarian cancer.**

Bibliography

Hainsworth JD, Fizazi K. Treatment for patients with unknown primary cancer and favorable prognostic factors. Semin Oncol. 2009;36(1):44-51. [PMID: 19179187]

Item 142 Answer: A

Educational Objective: Treat a postmenopausal patient with newly diagnosed breast cancer with an aromatase inhibitor.

The most appropriate treatment is anastrazole for 5 years. This patient has stage II hormone receptor–positive, *HER2*-negative breast cancer treated with local therapy. She has at least a 20% risk of systemic recurrence with no further therapy. Five years of adjuvant hormonal therapy should be offered to reduce her risk of recurrence and mortality. Postmenopausal women with hormone receptor–positive breast cancer should take an aromatase inhibitor as primary therapy for 5 years, after 2 to 3 years of initial tamoxifen therapy, or for 5 additional years after completion of 5 years of adjuvant tamoxifen. Side effects include arthralgia, hot flushes, and osteopenia/osteoporosis. Aromatase inhibitors are associated with superior disease-free survival compared with tamoxifen in the adjuvant setting. Aromatase inhibitors can cause osteopenia but are not thrombogenic like tamoxifen. Tamoxifen also increases the risk for endometrial carcinoma.

Trastuzumab is indicated for tumors that overexpress *HER2*, and this patient's tumor is *HER2*-negative; therefore, trastuzumab is not indicated.

KEY POINT

- **Adjuvant hormonal therapy is indicated in patients with newly diagnosed breast tumors that over express estrogen or progesterone receptors; aromatase inhibitors are the standard of care for postmenopausal women with these tumors.**

Bibliography

Burstein HJ, Prestrud AA, Seidenfeld J, et al; American Society of Clinical Oncology. American Society of Clinical Oncology clinical practice guideline: update on adjuvant endocrine therapy for women with hormone receptor-positive breast cancer. J Clin Oncol. 2010;28(23):3784-3796. [PMID: 20625130]

Item 143 Answer: A

Educational Objective: **Manage long-term follow-up of stage III colon cancer.**

This patient has completed therapy for stage III colon cancer, and postoperative surveillance should include physical examination and carcinoembryonic antigen monitoring every 3 to 6 months and CT scanning of the chest, abdomen, and pelvis annually for 3 to 5 years; a colonoscopy should be performed 1 year after resection and then repeated at 3- to 5-year intervals. The reason for surveillance is to identify patients with relapse whose disease is potentially surgically curable. The risks of radiation exposure versus benefits also must be considered. For these reasons, annual CT scanning of the chest, abdomen, and pelvis is thought to be reasonable.

Routine CT scanning annually for 10 years after resection is not warranted.

Routine CT scans four times per year in the absence of specific abnormalities would be excessive.

PET scans may be useful adjuncts to evaluate equivocal abnormalities seen on CT scans; however, they are not recommended for routine surveillance following resection of colorectal cancer.

Some degree of cancer-specific follow-up is indicated, so scheduling no additional follow-up evaluations would not be appropriate.

KEY POINT

- **Postoperative surveillance for stage III colon cancer includes physical examination and carcinoembryonic antigen monitoring every 3 to 6 months; chest/abdomen/pelvic CT scanning annually for 3 to 5 years; and colonoscopy 1 year after resection and then repeated at 3- to 5-year intervals.**

Bibliography

Desch CE, Benson AB III, Somerfield MR, et al; American Society of Clinical Oncology. Colorectal cancer surveillance: 2005 update of an American Society of Clinical Oncology practice guideline [erratum in J Clin Oncol. 2006;24(7):1221]. J Clin Oncol. 2005;23(33):8512-8519. [PMID: 16260687]

Item 144 Answer: B

Educational Objective: **Manage spinal cord compression.**

The most appropriate management of this patient is corticosteroids followed by radiation therapy. This patient has MRI-confirmed spinal cord compression characterized by midback pain and physical findings of lower extremity hyperreflexia and weakness. Spinal cord compression occurs in 5% to 10% of patients with cancer and is one of this disease's most debilitating complications. To avoid progressive neurologic deterioration and reverse the lower extremity weakness, immediate corticosteroid therapy followed by radiation therapy is indicated. The presence of excess atypical immature plasma cells on bone marrow biopsy with corresponding hypercalcemia, anemia, and an elevated serum total protein level confirm a diagnosis of plasma cell myeloma. Corticosteroid therapy in this case has the added benefit of directly treating the hypercalcemia and plasma cell myeloma.

Biopsy of the epidural mass is not necessary because of the finding of malignant plasma cells on bone marrow biopsy and could delay initiation of corticosteroids and radiation therapy.

Plasma cell myeloma causes suppression of hematopoiesis, manifesting as anemia and thrombocytopenia. Treatment with an immunomodulatory derivative chemotherapeutic agent such as lenalidomide is appropriate but would not have the required immediate effect of corticosteroids and radiation therapy in preventing progressive neurologic damage.

Radiation therapy alone would not address the swelling associated with spinal cord compression nor the hypercalcemia or underlying systemic plasma cell myeloma.

KEY POINT

- **Spinal cord compression is a medical emergency requiring immediate treatment to reduce swelling and avoid progression or permanent spinal cord injury.**

Bibliography

Taylor JW, Schiff D. Metastatic epidural spinal cord compression. Semin Neurol. 2010;30(3):245-253. [PMID: 20577931]

Index

Note: Page numbers followed by f and t denote figures and tables, respectively. Test questions are indicated by Q.

Index

A **NAME AND ADDRESS (Please complete.)**

Last Name | First Name | Middle Initial

Address

Address cont.

City | State | ZIP Code

Country

Email address

B **Order Number**

(Use the Order Number on your MKSAP materials packing slip.)

C **ACP ID Number**

(Refer to packing slip in your MKSAP materials for your ACP ID Number.)

ACP American College of Physicians INTERNAL MEDICINE | Doctors for Adults

Medical Knowledge Self-Assessment Program® 16

TO EARN *AMA PRA CATEGORY 1 CREDITS*™ YOU MUST:

1. Answer all questions.
2. Score a minimum of 50% correct.

TO EARN *FREE* SAME-DAY *AMA PRA CATEGORY 1 CREDITS*™ ONLINE:

1. Answer all of your questions.
2. Go to **mksap.acponline.org** and access the appropriate answer sheet.
3. Transcribe your answers and submit for CME credits.
4. You can also enter your answers directly at **mksap.acponline.org** without first using this answer sheet.

To Submit Your Answer Sheet by Mail or FAX for a $10 Administrative Fee per Answer Sheet:

1. Answer all of your questions and calculate your score.
2. Complete boxes A–F.
3. Complete payment information.
4. Send the answer sheet and payment information to ACP, using the FAX number/address listed below.

COMPLETE FORM BELOW ONLY IF YOU SUBMIT BY MAIL OR FAX

Last Name | First Name | MI

Payment Information. Must remit in US funds, drawn on a US bank.

The processing fee for each paper answer sheet is $10.

☐ Check, made payable to ACP, enclosed

Charge to ☐ VISA ☐ MasterCard ☐ AMERICAN EXPRESS ☐ DISCOVER

Card Number ____________________

Expiration Date ______ / ______ (MM / YY)

Security code (3 or 4 digit #s) ____________________

Signature ____________________

Fax to: 215-351-2799

Mail to:
Member and Customer Service
American College of Physicians
190 N. Independence Mall West
Philadelphia, PA 19106-1572

Questions?
Go to **mskap.acponline.org** or email **custserv@acponline.org**

D

TEST TYPE	Maximum Number of CME Credits
◯ Cardiovascular Medicine	18
◯ Dermatology	10
◯ Gastroenterology and Hepatology	14
◯ Hematology and Oncology	20
◯ Neurology	14
◯ Rheumatology	14
◯ Endocrinology and Metabolism	12
◯ General Internal Medicine	24
◯ Infectious Disease	16
◯ Nephrology	16
◯ Pulmonary and Critical Care Medicine	16

E

CREDITS CLAIMED ON SECTION (1 hour = 1 credit)

Enter the number of credits earned on the test to the nearest quarter hour. Physicians should claim only the credit commensurate with the extent of their participation in the activity.

☐☐.☐☐

F

Enter your score here.

Instructions for calculating your own score are found in front of the self-assessment test in each book.

You must receive a minimum score of 50% correct.

__________ %

Credit Submission Date: __________

1 (A) (B) (C) (D) (E)
2 (A) (B) (C) (D) (E)
3 (A) (B) (C) (D) (E)
4 (A) (B) (C) (D) (E)
5 (A) (B) (C) (D) (E)

6 (A) (B) (C) (D) (E)
7 (A) (B) (C) (D) (E)
8 (A) (B) (C) (D) (E)
9 (A) (B) (C) (D) (E)
10 (A) (B) (C) (D) (E)

11 (A) (B) (C) (D) (E)
12 (A) (B) (C) (D) (E)
13 (A) (B) (C) (D) (E)
14 (A) (B) (C) (D) (E)
15 (A) (B) (C) (D) (E)

16 (A) (B) (C) (D) (E)
17 (A) (B) (C) (D) (E)
18 (A) (B) (C) (D) (E)
19 (A) (B) (C) (D) (E)
20 (A) (B) (C) (D) (E)

21 (A) (B) (C) (D) (E)
22 (A) (B) (C) (D) (E)
23 (A) (B) (C) (D) (E)
24 (A) (B) (C) (D) (E)
25 (A) (B) (C) (D) (E)

26 (A) (B) (C) (D) (E)
27 (A) (B) (C) (D) (E)
28 (A) (B) (C) (D) (E)
29 (A) (B) (C) (D) (E)
30 (A) (B) (C) (D) (E)

31 (A) (B) (C) (D) (E)
32 (A) (B) (C) (D) (E)
33 (A) (B) (C) (D) (E)
34 (A) (B) (C) (D) (E)
35 (A) (B) (C) (D) (E)

36 (A) (B) (C) (D) (E)
37 (A) (B) (C) (D) (E)
38 (A) (B) (C) (D) (E)
39 (A) (B) (C) (D) (E)
40 (A) (B) (C) (D) (E)

41 (A) (B) (C) (D) (E)
42 (A) (B) (C) (D) (E)
43 (A) (B) (C) (D) (E)
44 (A) (B) (C) (D) (E)
45 (A) (B) (C) (D) (E)

46 (A) (B) (C) (D) (E)
47 (A) (B) (C) (D) (E)
48 (A) (B) (C) (D) (E)
49 (A) (B) (C) (D) (E)
50 (A) (B) (C) (D) (E)

51 (A) (B) (C) (D) (E)
52 (A) (B) (C) (D) (E)
53 (A) (B) (C) (D) (E)
54 (A) (B) (C) (D) (E)
55 (A) (B) (C) (D) (E)

56 (A) (B) (C) (D) (E)
57 (A) (B) (C) (D) (E)
58 (A) (B) (C) (D) (E)
59 (A) (B) (C) (D) (E)
60 (A) (B) (C) (D) (E)

61 (A) (B) (C) (D) (E)
62 (A) (B) (C) (D) (E)
63 (A) (B) (C) (D) (E)
64 (A) (B) (C) (D) (E)
65 (A) (B) (C) (D) (E)

66 (A) (B) (C) (D) (E)
67 (A) (B) (C) (D) (E)
68 (A) (B) (C) (D) (E)
69 (A) (B) (C) (D) (E)
70 (A) (B) (C) (D) (E)

71 (A) (B) (C) (D) (E)
72 (A) (B) (C) (D) (E)
73 (A) (B) (C) (D) (E)
74 (A) (B) (C) (D) (E)
75 (A) (B) (C) (D) (E)

76 (A) (B) (C) (D) (E)
77 (A) (B) (C) (D) (E)
78 (A) (B) (C) (D) (E)
79 (A) (B) (C) (D) (E)
80 (A) (B) (C) (D) (E)

81 (A) (B) (C) (D) (E)
82 (A) (B) (C) (D) (E)
83 (A) (B) (C) (D) (E)
84 (A) (B) (C) (D) (E)
85 (A) (B) (C) (D) (E)

86 (A) (B) (C) (D) (E)
87 (A) (B) (C) (D) (E)
88 (A) (B) (C) (D) (E)
89 (A) (B) (C) (D) (E)
90 (A) (B) (C) (D) (E)

91 (A) (B) (C) (D) (E)
92 (A) (B) (C) (D) (E)
93 (A) (B) (C) (D) (E)
94 (A) (B) (C) (D) (E)
95 (A) (B) (C) (D) (E)

96 (A) (B) (C) (D) (E)
97 (A) (B) (C) (D) (E)
98 (A) (B) (C) (D) (E)
99 (A) (B) (C) (D) (E)
100 (A) (B) (C) (D) (E)

101 (A) (B) (C) (D) (E)
102 (A) (B) (C) (D) (E)
103 (A) (B) (C) (D) (E)
104 (A) (B) (C) (D) (E)
105 (A) (B) (C) (D) (E)

106 (A) (B) (C) (D) (E)
107 (A) (B) (C) (D) (E)
108 (A) (B) (C) (D) (E)
109 (A) (B) (C) (D) (E)
110 (A) (B) (C) (D) (E)

111 (A) (B) (C) (D) (E)
112 (A) (B) (C) (D) (E)
113 (A) (B) (C) (D) (E)
114 (A) (B) (C) (D) (E)
115 (A) (B) (C) (D) (E)

116 (A) (B) (C) (D) (E)
117 (A) (B) (C) (D) (E)
118 (A) (B) (C) (D) (E)
119 (A) (B) (C) (D) (E)
120 (A) (B) (C) (D) (E)

121 (A) (B) (C) (D) (E)
122 (A) (B) (C) (D) (E)
123 (A) (B) (C) (D) (E)
124 (A) (B) (C) (D) (E)
125 (A) (B) (C) (D) (E)

126 (A) (B) (C) (D) (E)
127 (A) (B) (C) (D) (E)
128 (A) (B) (C) (D) (E)
129 (A) (B) (C) (D) (E)
130 (A) (B) (C) (D) (E)

131 (A) (B) (C) (D) (E)
132 (A) (B) (C) (D) (E)
133 (A) (B) (C) (D) (E)
134 (A) (B) (C) (D) (E)
135 (A) (B) (C) (D) (E)

136 (A) (B) (C) (D) (E)
137 (A) (B) (C) (D) (E)
138 (A) (B) (C) (D) (E)
139 (A) (B) (C) (D) (E)
140 (A) (B) (C) (D) (E)

141 (A) (B) (C) (D) (E)
142 (A) (B) (C) (D) (E)
143 (A) (B) (C) (D) (E)
144 (A) (B) (C) (D) (E)
145 (A) (B) (C) (D) (E)

146 (A) (B) (C) (D) (E)
147 (A) (B) (C) (D) (E)
148 (A) (B) (C) (D) (E)
149 (A) (B) (C) (D) (E)
150 (A) (B) (C) (D) (E)

151 (A) (B) (C) (D) (E)
152 (A) (B) (C) (D) (E)
153 (A) (B) (C) (D) (E)
154 (A) (B) (C) (D) (E)
155 (A) (B) (C) (D) (E)

156 (A) (B) (C) (D) (E)
157 (A) (B) (C) (D) (E)
158 (A) (B) (C) (D) (E)
159 (A) (B) (C) (D) (E)
160 (A) (B) (C) (D) (E)

161 (A) (B) (C) (D) (E)
162 (A) (B) (C) (D) (E)
163 (A) (B) (C) (D) (E)
164 (A) (B) (C) (D) (E)
165 (A) (B) (C) (D) (E)

166 (A) (B) (C) (D) (E)
167 (A) (B) (C) (D) (E)
168 (A) (B) (C) (D) (E)
169 (A) (B) (C) (D) (E)
170 (A) (B) (C) (D) (E)

171 (A) (B) (C) (D) (E)
172 (A) (B) (C) (D) (E)
173 (A) (B) (C) (D) (E)
174 (A) (B) (C) (D) (E)
175 (A) (B) (C) (D) (E)

176 (A) (B) (C) (D) (E)
177 (A) (B) (C) (D) (E)
178 (A) (B) (C) (D) (E)
179 (A) (B) (C) (D) (E)
180 (A) (B) (C) (D) (E)